Samuel Sharpe

The Hebrew Scriptures

Being a revision of the Authorized English Old Testament. Vol. 3

Samuel Sharpe

The Hebrew Scriptures
Being a revision of the Authorized English Old Testament. Vol. 3

ISBN/EAN: 9783337318048

Printed in Europe, USA, Canada, Australia, Japan

Cover: Foto ©Lupo / pixelio.de

More available books at **www.hansebooks.com**

THE
HEBREW SCRIPTURES,

TRANSLATED BY

SAMUEL SHARPE,

BEING

A REVISION OF THE AUTHORIZED ENGLISH
OLD TESTAMENT.

IN THREE VOLUMES.

VOL. III.

PROVERBS,	EZEKIEL,	MICAH,
ECCLESIASTES,	DANIEL,	NAHUM,
THE SONG OF	HOSEA,	HABAKKUK,
SOLOMON,	JOEL,	ZEPHANIAH,
ISAIAH,	AMOS,	HAGGAI,
JEREMIAH,	OBADIAH,	ZECHARIAH,
LAMENTATIONS,	JONAH,	MALACHI.

Second Edition.

LONDON:
J. RUSSELL SMITH, 36, SOHO SQUARE.
1871.

THE PROVERBS.

1 THE PROVERBS OF SOLOMON the son of David, king of Israel;
2 To know wisdom and instruction;
To understand the words of understanding;
3 To receive the instruction of wisdom,
Righteousness, and judgment, and equity;
4 To give prudence to the simple,
To the young man knowledge and discretion.
5 A wise man will hear, and will increase learning;
And a man of understanding will gain wise counsels;
6 To understand a proverb, and a hidden meaning,
The words of the wise, and their dark sayings.
7   The fear of Jehovah is the beginning of knowledge;
But fools despise wisdom and instruction.
8 My son, hear the instruction of thy father,
And forsake not the law of thy mother.
9 For they will be a wreath of grace to thy head,
And a necklace about thy neck.
10   My son, if sinners entice thee, consent thou not.
11 If they say, 'Come with us, let us lay wait for blood,
'Let us lurk privily without cause for the innocent;
12 'Let us swallow them up alive as the grave,
'And whole, as those that go down into the pit;
13 'We shall find all precious wealth,
'We shall fill our houses with spoil;
14 'Cast in thy lot among us; let us all have one purse;'
15 My son, walk not thou in the way with them;
Refrain thy foot from their path;
16 For their feet run to evil, and hasten to shed blood.
17 But in the sight of any bird the net is spread in vain.
18 And they lay wait for their own blood;
They lurk privily for their own lives.
19 So are the ways of every one greedy of gain;
It taketh away the life of its owners.
20   Wisdom crieth aloud in the street;
She uttereth her voice in the broad places;

She crieth in the chief place of concourse ; 21
In the openings of the gates, in the city.
She uttereth her words, [saying,]
' How long, ye simple ones, will ye love simplicity ? 22
' And the scorners delight in their scorning ?
' And fools hate knowledge ?
' Turn you at my reproof ; 23
' Behold, I will pour out my spirit upon you,
' I will make known my words unto you.
   ' Because I called, and ye refused ; 24
' I stretched out my hand, and no man regarded ;
' And ye have set at nought all my counsel, 25
' And would have none of my reproof ;
' I also will laugh at your calamity ; 26
' I will mock when your fear cometh.
   ' When your fear cometh as a tempest, 27
' And your calamity cometh on as a whirlwind ;
' When distress and anguish come upon you ;
' Then will they call on me, but I will not answer ; 28
' They will seek me early, but they shall not find me ;
' Because they hated knowledge, 29
' And did not choose the fear of Jehovah.
   ' They would have none of my counsel ; 30
' They despised all my reproof ;
' And they shall eat of the fruit of their own ways, 31
' And be filled with their own devices.
' For the backsliding of the simple shall slay them, 32
' And the prosperity of fools shall destroy them.
' But whoso hearkeneth unto me shall dwell safely, 33
' And shall be quiet from fear of evil.'

My son, if thou wilt receive my words, 1
And lay up my commandments with thee ;
So that thou give thine ear unto wisdom, 2
And incline thy heart to understanding ;
Yea, if thou criest after knowledge, 3
And liftest up thy voice for understanding ;
If thou seekest for her as silver, 4
And searchest for her as for hidden treasures ;
Then shalt thou understand the fear of Jehovah, 5
And thou shalt find the knowledge of God.
For Jehovah giveth wisdom ; 6
From his mouth come knowledge and understanding.

7 He layeth up safe counsel for the righteous;
    He is a shield to them that walk in honesty,
8 To guard the paths of judgment;
    And he preserveth the way of his godly ones.
9 Then shalt thou understand righteousness,
    And judgment, and equity, with every good path.
10   When wisdom entereth into thy heart,
    And knowledge is pleasant to thy soul;
11 Discretion shall watch over thee,
    Understanding shall guard thee;
12 To deliver thee from the way of the evil man,
    From the man that speaketh froward things;
13 Who leaveth the paths of uprightness,
    To walk in the ways of darkness;
14 Who rejoice to do evil,
    And delight in the frowardness of the wicked;
15 Whose ways are crooked, and they go aside in their paths;
16   To deliver thee from the strange woman,
    From the foreigner who flattereth with her words;
17 Who forsaketh the guide of her youth,
    And forgetteth the covenant of her God,
18 For her house inclineth unto death,
    And her paths unto the evil spirits;
19 None that go unto her return again,
    Neither attain they to the paths of life.
20   So that thou mayest walk in the way of good men,
    And keep the paths of the righteous.
21 For the upright shall dwell in the land,
    And the honest shall be allowed to remain in it.
22 But the wicked shall be cut off from the land,
—And transgressors shall be rooted out of it.
1   My son, forget not my law;
    But let thy heart keep my commands;
2 For length of days, and years of life,
    And peace, shall they add to thee.
3 Let not kindness and truth forsake thee;
    Bind them about thy neck;
    Write them upon the table of thy heart;
4 So shalt thou find favour and good success
    In the sight of God and man.
5   Trust in Jehovah with all thy heart;
    And lean not upon thine own understanding.

In all thy ways acknowledge him, 6
And he will direct thy paths.
    Be not wise in thine own eyes; 7
Fear Jehovah, and depart from evil.
It will be health to thy muscles, and marrow to thy bones. 8
    Honour Jehovah with thy riches, 9
And with the firstfruits of all thine increase;
So shall thy barns be filled with plenty, 10
And thy presses shall burst out with grape juice.
    My son, despise not the chastening of Jehovah; 11
Neither be weary of his correction.
For whom Jehovah loveth he correcteth; 12
Even as a father the son in whom he delighteth.
    Happy is the man that findeth Wisdom, 13
And the man that getteth understanding.
For the trade of it is better than the trade of silver, 14
And the gain thereof than fine gold.
She is more precious than pearls; 15
And all thou canst desire is not to be compared to her.
Length of days is in her right hand; 16
And in her left hand riches and honour.
Her ways are ways of pleasantness, 17
And all her paths are peace.
She is a tree of life to them that lay hold of her; 18
And happy is every one that keepeth her fast.
    By wisdom Jehovah founded the earth; 19
By understanding he established the heavens.
By his knowledge the deep springs do burst forth, 20
And the skies drop down the dew.
    My son, let not these things depart from thine eyes; 21
Keep safe counsel and discretion.
So shall they be life to thy soul, and grace to thy neck. 22
Then shalt thou walk in thy way safely, 23
And thy foot shall not stumble.
When thou liest down, thou shalt not be afraid; 24
Yea, thou shalt lie down, and thy sleep shall be sweet.
Be not afraid of sudden fear, 25
Nor of desolation by wicked men, when it cometh.
For Jehovah will be thy confidence, 26
And he will keep thy foot from being caught.
    Withhold not good from them to whom it is due, 27
When it is in the power of thy hand to do it.

²⁸ Say not to thy neighbour, 'Go, and come again,
  'And to-morrow I will give;' when thou hast it by thee.
²⁹ Devise not evil against thy neighbour,
  Seeing he dwelleth trustfully by thee.
³⁰ Strive not with a man without cause,
  If he have done thee no harm.
³¹   Envy thou not the man of violence,
  And choose none of his ways.
³² For the froward man is an abomination to Jehovah;
  But His friendship is with the righteous.
³³ The curse of Jehovah is on the house of the wicked;
  But he blesseth the habitation of the just.
³⁴ Surely he scorneth the scorners;
  But he giveth grace to the lowly.
³⁵ The wise will inherit glory;
—But disgrace raiseth up the fools.
¹   Hear, ye children, the instruction of a father,
  And attend to know understanding.
² For I give you good doctrine, forsake ye not my law.
³ For I was a son tender to my father,
  And only-beloved in the sight of my mother.
⁴ He taught me also, and said to me,
  'Let thy heart retain my words;
  'Keep my commandments, and live.'
⁵   Get Wisdom, get understanding; forget it not;
  Neither decline from the words of my mouth.
⁶ Forsake her not, and she will preserve thee;
  Love her, and she will keep thee.
⁷ Wisdom is the chief thing; get wisdom;
  And with all thy getting get understanding.
⁸ Exalt her, and she will raise thee;
  She will bring thee to honour, if thou embracest her.
⁹ She will give to thy head a wreath of grace;
  A crown of beauty will she deliver to thee.
¹⁰   Hear, O my son, and receive my sayings;
  And the years of thy life will be many.
¹¹ I have taught thee in the way of wisdom;
  I have guided thee in right roads.
¹² When thou walkest, thy steps will not be hindered;
  And when thou runnest, thou shalt not stumble.
¹³ Take fast hold of instruction; let her not go;
  Keep her; for she is thy life.

Enter not into the path of the wicked, 14
And be not led into the way of evil men.
Avoid it, pass not along it, turn from it, and pass on. 15
For they sleep not, unless they have done evil; 16
And their sleep is spoiled, unless they cause ruin.
For they eat the bread of wickedness, 17
And drink the wine of violence.
But the path of the righteous is as the clear light, 18
That shineth more and more unto the perfect day.
The way of the wicked is as darkness; 19
They know not at what they stumble.
  My son, attend to my words; 20
Incline thine ear unto my sayings.
Let them not depart from thine eyes; 21
Keep them in the midst of thy heart.
For they are life unto those that find them, 22
And medicine to all their flesh.
  Keep thy heart with all diligence; 23
For out of it are the issues of life.
Put away from thee frowardness of mouth, 24
And perverseness of lips put far from thee.
Let thine eyes look right on, 25
And let thine eyelids be set straight before thee.
Consider well the path of thy feet, 26
And let all thy ways be ordered aright.
Turn not to the right hand nor to the left; 27
Remove thy foot from evil.
  My son, attend unto my wisdom, 1
Bow thine ear to my reasons;
That thou mayest regard discretion, 2
And that thy lips may keep knowledge.
Though the lips of a strange woman drop honey, 3
And her mouth is smoother than oil;
Yet her end is bitter as wormwood, 4
Sharp as a two-edged sword.
Her feet go down to death; her steps take hold on hell. 5
Lest thou shouldest consider well the path of life, 6
Her ways are moveable, thou canst not know them.
Hear me now therefore, O ye sons, 7
And depart not from the words of my mouth.
Remove thy way far from her, 8
And come not nigh the doorway of her house;

9 Lest thou give thine honour unto others,
  And thy years unto the cruel one;
10 Lest strangers be filled with thy wealth;
  And thy labours be in the house of a foreigner;
11 And thou groan in grief at the last,
  When thy flesh and thy body are consumed;
12 And thou say, 'How I hated instruction,
  'And my heart despised reproof;
13 'And I obeyed not the voice of my teachers,
  'Nor inclined mine ear to mine instructors!
14 'I was in almost all evil
  'In the midst of the assembly and congregation.'
15   Drink waters from thine own cistern,
  And running waters out of thine own well;
16 So shall thy fountains be dispersed abroad,
  As streams of waters in the broad places.
17 Let them be thine only, and not strangers' with thee.
18 So shall thy fountain be blessed,
  And rejoice thou with the wife of thy youth.
19 As a loving hind or a pleasant roe,
  Let her breasts refresh thee at all times;
  And be thou ravished always with her love.
20 And why, my son, be ravished with a strange woman,
  And embrace the bosom of a foreigner?
21 For the ways of a man are before the eyes of Jehovah,
  And he considereth well all his goings.
22 His own iniquities will catch the wicked man;
  And he will be held with the cords of his sin.
23 That man will die without instruction;
—And in the greatness of his folly he goeth astray.
1   My son, if thou hast given bond to thy neighbour,
  Or hast struck thy hands [in promise] with a stranger,
2 Thou art snared with the words of thy mouth,
  Thou art caught with the words of thy mouth.
3 Do this now, my son, and deliver thyself,
  Because thou art come into the grasp of thy neighbour;
  Go, humble thyself, and let thy neighbour be proud.
4 Give not sleep to thine eyes, nor slumber to thine eyelids.
5 Deliver thyself as a roe from a man's hand,
  And as a bird from the hand of the fowler.
6   Go to the ant, thou sluggard;
  Consider her ways, and be wise;

Who having no guide, overseer, or ruler, 7
Provideth her bread in the summer, 8
And gathereth her food in the harvest.
How long wilt thou lie in bed, O sluggard? 9
When wilt thou arise out of thy sleep?
Yet a little sleep, a little slumber, 10
A little folding of the hands for lying down;
And thy poverty will come as one that travelleth, 11
And thy want as an armed man.
    A man of sin, an evil one, walketh with froward mouth. 12
He winketh with his eyes, he speaketh with his feet, 13
He teacheth with his fingers;
Fraud is in his heart, he deviseth mischief; 14
He is at all times casting abroad discord.
Therefore shall his calamity come on a sudden; 15
Suddenly shall he be broken without remedy.
    These six things doth Jehovah hate; 16
Yea, seven are an abomination to his soul;
Haughty eyes, a lying tongue, 17
And hands that shed innocent blood,
A heart that deviseth wicked imaginations, 18
Feet that are swift in running to mischief,
A false witness that breatheth lies, 19
And he that soweth discord among brethren.
    My son, keep thy father's command, 20
And forsake not the law of thy mother;
Bind them continually upon thy heart, 21
Tie them about thy neck.
When thou goest about, it will lead thee; 22
When thou liest down, it will watch over thee;
And when thou awakest, it will be thy meditation.
For a command is a lamp; and a law is a light; 23
And reproofs of the teacher are the way of life;
To keep thee from the evil woman, 24
From the flattery of the tongue of a foreign woman.
    Lust not after her beauty in thy heart; 25
Neither let her take thee with her eyelids.
For by a harlot man is brought to a piece of bread; 26
And the adulteress hunteth for the precious soul.
Can a man take fire in his bosom, 27
And his clothes not be burned?
Or can a man walk on hot coals, 28

And his feet not be scorched?
29 So is he that goeth in to his neighbour's wife;
Whosoever toucheth her will not be guiltless.
30   Men do not despise a thief,
If he steal to satisfy his soul when he is starving;
31 But if he be found out, he shall restore sevenfold;
He shall give all the wealth of his house.
32   The adulterer lacketh understanding;
He that doeth it destroyeth his own soul.
33 Wounds and dishonour shall he get;
And his reproach shall not be wiped away.
34 For jealousy is the rage of a husband;
And he will not spare in the day of vengeance.
35 He will not regard any ransom;
—Nor be content, though thou givest many bribes.
1   My son, keep my words,
And lay up my commands with thee.
2 Keep my commands, and live,
And my law as the apple of thine eye.
3 Bind them upon thy fingers,
Write them upon the table of thy heart.
4 Say unto Wisdom, 'Thou art my sister;'
And call Understanding thy kinswoman;
5 That they may keep thee from the strange woman,
From the foreigner who flattereth with her words.
6   When at the window of my house
I looked through my casement,
7 And I beheld among the simple ones,
I observed among the youths,
A young man void of understanding,
8 Passing through the street near the corner;
And he went the way to her house,
9 In the twilight, in the evening of the day,
In the very middle of the night, or in the dark;
10 And, behold, there met him a woman
With the attire of a harlot, and subtil of heart.
11 (She is loud and bold; her feet abide not at home;
12 Now is she without, now in the streets,
And she lieth in wait near to every corner.)
13 So she caught him, and kissed him,
She hardened her face and said to him,
14 'I have sacrifices of peace offerings with me;

' This day have I payed my vows.
' Therefore came I forth to meet thee, 15
' Diligently to seek thy face ; and I have found thee.
' I have decked my bedstead with coverings of tapestry, 16
' With embroidered fine linen of Egypt.
' I have sprinkled my bed with myrrh, aloes, and cinnamon. 17
' Come, let us take our fill of love till the morning ; 18
' Let us delight ourselves with loves.
' For my husband is not at home, he is gone a long journey ; 19
' He hath taken a bag of money in his hand ; 20
' He will come home on the day of the full moon.'
With her many arts she led him aside ; 21
With the flattering of her lips she forced him.
He goeth after her at once, as an ox to the slaughter, 22
He cometh even as one in fetters to a fool's punishment ;
Till a dart strike though his liver ; 23
As a bird hasteneth to the snare,
And knoweth not that it is for his life.
 Now therefore, hearken unto me, O ye children, 24
And attend to the words of my mouth.
Let not thy heart turn aside to her ways, 25
Go not astray in her paths.
For she hath cast down many wounded ; 26
Yea, strong men have all been slain by her.
Her house is the way to hell, 27
Going down to the chambers of death.

 Doth not Wisdom cry ? 1
And understanding put forth her voice ?
On the top of high places, by the way, 2
She placeth her house by the paths.
By the side of the gates, at the entrance of the city, 3
Coming in at the doorways, she crieth aloud ; [saying,]
 ' To you, O men, I call ; 4
' And my voice is to the sons of Adam.
' O ye simple, understand prudence ; 5
' And, ye fools, be ye of an understanding heart.
' Hear ; for I will speak of excellent things ; 6
' And the opening of my lips shall be right things.
' For my mouth shall speak truth ; 7
' And wickedness is an abomination to my lips.
' All the words of my mouth are in righteousness ; 8
' There is nothing crooked or perverse in them.

9 'They are all plain to him that understandeth,
'And right to them that have found knowledge.
10 'Receive my instruction, and not silver;
'And knowledge is to be chosen rather than gold.
11 'For wisdom is better than pearls;
'And all that may be desired cannot be compared to it.
12 'I Wisdom dwell with prudence,
'And I find out the knowledge of counsels.
13 'The fear of Jehovah is to hate evil;
'Pride, and arrogance, and the evil way,
'And the froward mouth, do I hate.
14 'Advice is mine, and safe counsel;
'I am understanding; I have strength.
15 'By me kings reign, and princes decree justice.
16 'By me rulers rule, and nobles, all the judges of the earth.
17 'I love them that love me;
'And those that seek me early shall find me.
18 'Wealth and honour are with me;
'Yea, durable riches and righteousness.
19 'My fruit is better than gold, yea, than fine gold;
'And my revenue is to be chosen rather than silver.
20 'I walk in the way of righteousness,
'In the midst of the paths of judgment;
21 'To cause those that love me to inherit wealth;
'And I fill their storehouses.
22 'Jehovah possessed me in the beginning of his way,
'Before he began his works, from of old.
23 'I was poured out [or begotten] from everlasting,
'From the beginning, before the earth was.
24 'When there were no waters below, I was brought forth,
'When there were no fountains abounding with water.
25 'Ere yet the mountains were settled,
'Before the hills was I brought forth;
26 'While yet he had not made the earth, nor the plains,
'Nor the highest part of the dust of the world.
27 'When he prepared the heavens, I was there;
'When he fixed the arch upon the face of the deep;
28 'When he made firm the skies above;
'When he stopped up the fountains of the deep;
29 'When he gave to the sea his decree,
'That the waters should not pass its shore;
'When he fixed the foundations of the earth;

'Then I was by him as a nursling; 30
'And I have been a daily delight, sporting ever before him;
'Sporting in the habitable part of his earth; 31
'And my delights are with the sons of Adam.
   'Now therefore hearken unto me, O ye children; 32
'For blessed are they that keep my ways.
'Hear instruction, and be wise, and refuse it not. 33
'Blessed is the man that heareth me, 34
'Watching daily at my doors, waiting at my doorposts.
'For whoso findeth me findeth life, 35
'And he will obtain favour from Jehovah.
'But sinners wrong their own souls; 36
'All they that hate me love death.'

   Wisdom hath builded her house, 1
She hath hewn out her seven pillars;
She hath killed her meat; she hath mingled her wine; 2
She hath also furnished her table.
She hath sent forth her maidens; 3
She crieth on the high battlements of the city, [saying,]
'Whoso is simple, let him turn in hither.' 4
To him that wanteth understanding she saith,
'Come ye, eat of my bread, 5
'And drink of the wine which I have mingled.
'Forsake the simple ones, and live; 6
'And go in the way of understanding.'
   Whoso teacheth a scorner getteth to himself shame; 7
And he that reproveth a wicked man, his own blot.
Reprove not a scorner, lest he hate thee; 8
Reprove a wise man, and he will love thee.
Instruct a wise man, and he will be yet wiser; 9
Teach a righteous man, and he will learn more.
The fear of Jehovah is the beginning of wisdom; 10
And the knowledge of holy things is understanding.
For by me thy days shall be multiplied, 11
And the years of thy life shall be increased.
If thou be wise, thou wilt be wise for thyself; 12
And if thou scornest, thou alone wilt bear it.
   A foolish woman is clamorous; 13
She is simple, and knoweth nothing whatever.
For she sitteth at the doorway of her house, 14
On a seat in the high places of the city,
To call to those who are passing on their way, 15

Who are going right on their road; [saying,]
16 'Whoso is simple, let him turn in hither.'
And to him that wanteth understanding she saith,
17 'Stolen waters are sweet,
'And the bread of secrecy is pleasant.'
18 But he knoweth not that evil spirits are there;
And that her guests are in the depths of hell.

1   THE PROVERBS OF SOLOMON.
A wise son gladdeneth his father;
But a foolish son is the grief of his mother.
2   The treasures of wickedness profit nothing;
But righteousness delivereth from death.
3   Jehovah will not let the soul of the righteous famish;
But he driveth away the desires of the wicked.
4   He will be poor that worketh with an idle hand;
But the hand of the diligent maketh rich.
5   He that gathereth in summer is a wise son;
He that sleepeth in harvest is a son that causeth shame.
6   Blessings are on the head of the righteous man;
But the mouth of the wicked concealeth violence.
7   The memory of the righteous man is blessed;
But the name of the wicked shall rot.
8   The wise in heart will receive commands;
But a prating fool will fall headlong.
9   Whoso walketh in honesty walketh without fear;
But he that maketh his ways crooked will be known.
10 He that winketh with the eye causeth sorrow;
And a prating fool will fall headlong.
11 The mouth of a righteous man is a wellspring of life;
But the mouth of the wicked concealeth violence.
12 Hatred stirreth up strifes;
But love covereth over all transgressions.
13 In the lips of a prudent man wisdom is found;
But a rod is for the back of him that is void of sense.
14 Wise men treasure up knowledge;
But the mouth of the fool is near unto ruin.
15 The rich man's wealth is his strong city;
Their poverty is the ruin of the poor.
16 The labour of the righteous tendeth to life;
The fruit of the wicked unto sin.

He that keepeth instruction is in the way of life ;	17
But he that refuseth reproof will go wrong.	
He that hideth hatred hath lying lips,	18
And he that uttereth a slander is a fool.	
In the multitude of words there wanteth not sin ;	19
But he that refraineth his lips is wise.	
The tongue of the just is as choice silver ;	20
The heart of the wicked is little worth.	
The lips of the righteous feed many ;	21
But fools die for want of sense.	
The blessing of Jehovah, it maketh rich,	22
And he addeth no more labour with it.	
To make mischief is as sport to a fool ;	23
So is wisdom to a man of understanding.	
The fear of the wicked man, it shall come upon him ;	24
But the desire of the righteous will be granted.	
As the whirlwind passeth, so the wicked is no more ;	25
But the righteous hath an everlasting foundation.	
As vinegar to the teeth, and as smoke to the eyes,	26
So is the sluggard to them that send him.	
The fear of Jehovah prolongeth days ;	27
But the years of the wicked will be shortened.	
The hope of the righteous will be gladness ;	28
But the expectation of the wicked perisheth.	
The way of Jehovah is strength to the honest ;	29
But a terror to the workers of iniquity.	
The righteous man will never be removed ;	30
But the wicked shall not inhabit the land.	
The mouth of the just bringeth forth wisdom ;	31
But the froward tongue shall be cut out.	
The lips of the righteous know what is acceptable ;	32
But the mouth of the wicked speaketh frowardness.	—
False balances are an abomination to Jehovah ;	1
But a just weight is his delight.	
When boasting cometh, then cometh shame ;	2
But with the lowly is wisdom.	
The honesty of the upright will guide them ;	3
But the perverseness of deceivers destroyeth them.	
Riches will not profit in the day of wrath ;	4
But righteousness will deliver from death.	
The righteousness of the honest man directeth his way ;	5
But the wicked will fall by his own wickedness.	

6   The righteousness of the upright will deliver them;
But deceivers will be taken in their own desires.
7   When a wicked man dieth, his hope perisheth;
And the expectation of unjust men perisheth.
8   The righteous man is delivered out of trouble,
And the wicked cometh into it in his stead.
9   The ungodly man with his mouth destroyeth his friend;
But by knowledge are the righteous delivered.
10   In the welfare of the righteous the city rejoiceth;
And when the wicked perish, there is joyful shouting.
11   By the blessing of the upright the city is exalted;
But it is overthrown by the mouth of the wicked.
12   Whoso despiseth his neighbour is void of sense;
But a man of understanding holdeth his peace.
13   A talebearer goeth about revealing secrets;
But he that is of a faithful spirit concealeth a matter.
14   Where there is no guidance, the people fall;
But in the multitude of counsellors there is safety.
15   He that is surety for a stranger shall sorely smart;
And he that hateth giving bond is sure.
16   A gracious woman obtaineth honour;
And violent men obtain riches.
17   The man of kindness getteth good to his soul;
But he that is cruel troubleth his own flesh.
18   The wicked man worketh for deceitful wages;
But he that soweth righteousness hath a sure reward.
19   As righteousness leadeth to life;
So he that pursueth evil goeth to his own death.
20   Men of froward heart are abomination to Jehovah;
But such as are honest in their way are his delight.
21   As hand fitteth hand, crime will not be unpunished;
But the seed of the righteous will be delivered.
22   As a ring of gold in a swine's snout,
So is a fair woman who departeth from discretion.
23   The desire of the righteous is only for good;
But the expectation of the wicked is wrath.
24   There is that scattereth, and yet increaseth;
But withholding what is meet leadeth only to poverty.
25   The soul that blesseth will be made fat;
And he that watereth will be watered also himself.
26   Him that withholdeth corn, the people will curse;
But blessing will be on the head of him that selleth.

He that seeketh good early searcheth for favour; 27
But he that seeketh mischief, it will come on him.
He that trusteth in his riches will fall; 28
But the righteous will flourish as a leaf.
Whoso troubleth his own house will inherit the wind; 29
And the fool will be servant to the wise of heart.
The fruit of the righteous is a tree of life; 30
And he that winneth souls is wise.
Behold, the righteous man is recompensed on earth; 31
Much more are the wicked and the sinner.
Whoso loveth instruction loveth knowledge; 1
But he that hateth reproof is brutish.
A good man obtaineth favour from Jehovah; 2
But a man of wicked devices will he condemn.
A man shall not be established by wickedness; 3
But the root of the righteous shall not be moved.
A virtuous woman is a crown to her husband; 4
But the shameful is as rottenness in his bones.
The thoughts of the righteous are as just laws; 5
But the counsels of the wicked are deceit.
The words of the wicked lie in wait for blood; 6
But the mouth of the upright shall deliver them.
The wicked are overthrown, and are not; 7
But the house of the righteous shall stand.
A man shall be praised according to his wisdom; 8
But he that is of a perverse heart will be despised.
Better is he that is slighted, and hath a servant, 9
Than he that honoureth himself, and lacketh bread.
A righteous man careth for the life of his beast; 10
But the bowels of the wicked are cruel.
He that tilleth his land will be filled with bread; 11
But he that followeth vanities is void of sense.
The wicked man coveteth the booty of evil men; 12
But the root of the righteous yieldeth fruit.
The wicked man is ensnared by the trespass of his lips; 13
But the righteous will come out of trouble.
A man is filled with good by the fruit of his mouth; 14
And the reward of a man's hands will be repaid to him.
The way of a fool is right in his own eyes; 15
But he that hearkeneth unto counsel is wise.
A fool maketh known his wrath on the same day; 16
But a prudent man covereth his dishonour.

17 He that uttereth truth sheweth righteousness;
But a false witness sheweth forth deceit.
18 There are those that speak like the stabs of a sword;
But the tongue of the wise bringeth health.
19 The lip of truth shall be established for ever;
But the lying tongue is but for a moment.
20 Deceit is in the heart of them that contrive evil;
But unto the counsellors of peace is joy.
21 No misfortune happeneth to the righteous;
But the wicked will be filled with evil.
22 Lying lips are an abomination to Jehovah;
But they that deal truly are his delight.
23 A prudent man concealeth what he knoweth;
But the heart of fools proclaimeth foolishness.
24 The hand of the diligent will bear rule;
But the slothful will be under tribute.
25 Care in the heart of man maketh it stoop;
But a good word maketh it glad.
26 The righteous man searcheth the way for his friend;
But the way of the wicked leadeth them astray.
27 The slothful man roasteth not what he took in hunting;
But the wealth of a rich man is his industry.
28 In the way of righteousness is life;
—But the trodden way leadeth to death.
1 A wise son heareth his father's instruction;
But a scorner heareth not rebuke.
2 A man shall eat good by the fruit of his mouth;
But the soul of the transgressors shall eat violence.
3 He that guardeth his mouth keepeth his life;
He that openeth wide his lips will have destruction.
4 The sluggard desireth, and his soul hath nothing;
But the soul of the diligent will be made fat.
5 A righteous man hateth words of falsehood;
But wickedness polluteth and bringeth to shame.
6 Righteousness guardeth the honest man in his way
But wickedness overthroweth the sinner.
7 One man sheweth himself rich, yet hath nothing;
Another sheweth himself poor, yet hath great riches.
8 The ransom of a man's life are his riches;
But the poor man heareth not rebuke.
9 The light of the righteous rejoiceth;
But the lamp of the wicked shall be put out.

A vain man by boasting causeth strife ;	10
But with the well-advised is wisdom.	
Wealth gotten by vanity will be lessened ;	11
But that gathered by the hand's labour will increase.	
Hope deferred maketh the heart sick ;	12
But when the desire cometh, it is a tree of life.	
Whoso despiseth the word will be punished ;	13
But he that feareth the command will be rewarded.	
The law of the wise is a wellspring of life,	14
To turn aside from the snares of death.	
Good understanding giveth favour ;	15
But the way of transgressors is hard.	
Every prudent man worketh with knowledge ;	16
But a fool spreadeth abroad his folly.	
A wicked messenger falleth into mischief ;	17
But a faithful ambassador bringeth health.	
Want and shame are for him that refuseth advice ;	18.
But he that regardeth reproof will be honoured.	
Desire accomplished is sweet to the soul ;	19
But it is hateful to fools to depart from evil.	
He that walketh with wise men will become wise ;	20
But a companion of fools will suffer evil.	
Evil pursueth sinners ;	21
But to the righteous good will be repayed.	
A good man leaveth an inheritance to his sons' sons ;	22
And the wealth of the sinner is laid up for the just.	
Much food cometh of the tillage of the poor ;	23
But wealth is wasted by want of judgment.	
He that spareth his rod hateth his son ;	24
But he that loveth him is quick to chasten him.	
The righteous man eateth till his soul is satisfied ;	25
But the belly of the wicked will want.	
Every wise woman buildeth up her house ;	1
But the foolish plucketh it down with her own hands.	
Whoso walketh in his uprightness feareth Jehovah ;	2
But he that is perverse in his ways despiseth him.	
In the mouth of the foolish is a rod for pride ;	3
But the lips of wise men will preserve them.	
Where no oxen are, the crib is clean ;	4
But much increase is by the strength of the ox.	
A faithful witness will not lie ;	5
But a false witness breatheth lies.	

6 A scorner seeketh wisdom, and findeth it not;
But knowledge is easy to a man of understanding.
7 Go from the presence of a man who is foolish,
Or in whom thou perceivest not lips of knowledge.
8 The wisdom of the prudent teacheth his way;
But the folly of fools is deceit.
9 Guilt joineth fools in fellowship;
But between the righteous there is favour.
10 The heart knoweth its own bitterness;
And a stranger doth not partake of its joy.
11 The house of the wicked will be overthrown;
But the tent of the upright will flourish.
12 There is a way which seemeth right to a man;
But at the end thereof are the ways of death.
13 Even in laughter the heart is sorrowful;
And the end of mirth is sadness.
14 The backslider in heart is full of his own ways;
And a good man will be satisfied with himself.
15 The simple believeth every word;
But the prudent man looketh well to his going.
16 A wise man feareth, and departeth from evil;
But the fool rusheth on, and is confident.
17 He that is soon angry acteth foolishly;
And a man of wicked devices is hated.
18 The simple inherit folly;
But the prudent are crowned with knowledge.
19 Evil men bow down before the good;
And the wicked are at the gates of the righteous.
20 The poor man is hated even by his own neighbour;
But the rich man hath many friends.
21 He that despiseth his neighbour sinneth;
But he that sheweth favour to the poor, happy is he.
22 Do not they err that work evil?
But kindness and truth are workers of good.
23 In all labour there is profit;
But the talk of the lips tendeth only to want.
24 The crown of the wise is their riches;
But the foolishness of fools is folly.
25 A true witness delivereth souls;
But deceit uttereth lies.
26 In the fear of Jehovah is strong confidence;
And his children have a place of refuge.

The fear of Jehovah is a wellspring of life,   27
To turn aside from the snares of death.
   In the multitude of people is the king's honour;   28
And in the want of people is the prince's ruin.
   Slowness to anger is great discretion;   29
But a hasty spirit setteth up folly.
   A sound heart is the life of the flesh;   30
But envy is the rottenness of the bones.
   Whoso oppresseth the poor defieth his Maker;   31
But he honoureth Him that sheweth favour to the needy.
   The wicked man is driven away by his wickedness;   32
But the righteous man hath hope in his death.
   Wisdom resteth quiet in the understanding heart;   33
But that which is within fools is made known.
   Righteousness exalteth a nation;   34
But sin is a reproach to any people.
   The king's favour is toward a wise servant;   35
But his wrath is against him that causeth shame.

   A soft answer turneth away wrath;   1
But vexing words stir up anger.
   The tongue of the wise maketh knowledge pleasant;   2
But the mouth of fools poureth out foolishness.
   The eyes of Jehovah are in every place,   3
Beholding the evil and the good.
   A healing tongue is a tree of life;   4
But perverseness therein is a breach of the spirit.
   A fool despiseth his father's instruction;   5
But he that regardeth reproof is prudent.
   In the house of the righteous is much treasure;   6
But in the revenues of the wicked is trouble.
   The lips of the wise scatter knowledge;   7
But the heart of the foolish doeth not so.
   The sacrifice of the wicked is abomination to Jehovah;   8
But the prayer of the upright is his delight.
   The way of the wicked is abomination to Jehovah;   9
But he loveth him that followeth after righteousness.
   Advice is grievous to him that forsaketh the way;   10
He that hateth reproof shall die.
   Hell and the pit of destruction are open to Jehovah;   11
Much more then are the hearts of the children of Adam.
   A scorner loveth not one that reproveth him;   12
Neither will he go unto the wise.

13   A merry heart maketh a cheerful face;
But by sorrow of heart the spirit is broken.
14   The understanding heart seeketh knowledge;
But the mouth of fools feedeth on foolishness.
*15   All the days of the afflicted are evil;
But a man of a merry heart hath a continual feast.
16   Better is little with the fear of Jehovah,
Than great treasure and trouble therewith.
17   Better is a dinner of herbs where love is,
Than a stalled ox and hatred therewith.
18   A wrathful man stirreth up strife;
But he that is slow to anger quieteth contention.
19   The way of the slothful is as a thicket of thorns;
But the path of the righteous is a paved road.
20   A wise son maketh his father glad;
But a foolish man despiseth his mother.
21   Folly is joy to him that is void of sense;
But a man of understanding walketh uprightly.
22   Without counsel purposes are defeated;
But they are established in the multitude of counsellors.
23   A man hath joy by the answer of his mouth;
And a word in due season, how good is it!
24   The way of life to the wise is upward,
So that he may depart from hell below.
25   Jehovah will destroy the house of the proud;
But he will set up the landmark of the widow.
26   The thoughts of the wicked man are hateful to Jehovah;
But the words of the pure are pleasant to him.
27   He that is greedy of gain troubleth his own house;
But he that hateth gifts maketh it live.
28   The heart of the righteous man studieth how to answer;
But the mouth of the wicked poureth out evil.
29   Jehovah is far from the wicked;
But he hearkeneth to the prayer of the righteous.
30   The light of the eyes rejoiceth the heart;
Hearing what is good maketh the bones fat.
31   The ear that heareth the reproof of life
Will dwell among the wise.
32   Whoso refuseth instruction despiseth his soul;
But he that heareth reproof getteth sense.
33   The fear of Jehovah is what wisdom teacheth;
—And before honour is humility.

1 The devices of the heart are of man;
But the answer of the tongue is from Jehovah.
2 All the ways of a man are clean in his own eyes;
But Jehovah weigheth the spirits.
3 Commit thy works unto Jehovah,
And thy purposes shall be established.
4 Every work of Jehovah hath its own purpose;
Yea, even the wicked man is for the day of evil.
5 All pride of heart is an abomination to Jehovah;
As hand fitteth hand, it shall not be unpunished.
6 By kindness and truth iniquity is purged;
And by the fear of Jehovah men depart from evil.
7 When a man's ways please Jehovah,
He maketh even his enemies to be at peace with him.
8 Better is a little with righteousness,
Than great revenues without justice.
9 A man's heart deviseth his way;
But Jehovah directeth his steps.
10 Divination belongeth to the lips of the king;
His mouth transgresseth not in judgment.
11 A just balance and scales are of Jehovah;
All the weights of the bag are his work.
12 It is an abomination for kings to commit wickedness;
For the throne is established by righteousness.
13 Righteous lips are the delight of kings;
And he loveth the words of the upright.
14 The wrath of a king is as messengers of death;
And a wise man will pacify it.
15 In the light of the king's countenance is life;
And his favour is as the clouds of the latter rain.
16 How much better is it to get wisdom than gold!
And to get understanding is to be chosen before silver.
17 The highway of the upright leadeth away from evil;
He that keepeth his way preserveth his soul.
18 Pride goeth before destruction,
And a haughty spirit before a fall.
19 Better it is to be of a meek spirit with the lowly,
Than to divide the spoil with the proud.
20 He that handleth a matter wisely findeth good;
And whoso trusteth in Jehovah, happy is he.
21 The wise in heart shall be called prudent;
And sweetness of the lips increaseth learning.

22 Prudence is a wellspring of life to him that hath it;
But the advice of fools is folly.
23 The heart of the wise man teacheth his mouth;
And addeth learning to his lips.
24 Pleasant words are a honeycomb of sweets;
Sweet to the soul, and healthful to the bones.
25 There is a way that seemeth right to a man,
But at the end thereof are the ways of death.
26 The appetite of a labourer maketh him to labour;
For his mouth hath laid a burden on him.
27 An ungodly man diggeth up evil;
And in his lips there is as a burning fire.
28 A froward man casteth abroad strife;
And a talebearer separateth chief friends.
29 An injurious man enticeth his neighbour,
And leadeth him into the way that is not good;
30 He shutteth his eyes to devise fraud;
Slightly moving his lips he bringeth evil to pass.
31 The hoary head is a crown of glory,
It is found in the way of righteousness.
32 He that is slow to anger is better than the mighty;
And he that ruleth his spirit than he that taketh a city.
33 The lot is cast into the lap;
—But its whole deciding is from Jehovah.
1 Better is a dry morsel, and quietness therewith,
Than a house full of sacrifices with strife.
2 A wise servant ruleth over a son that causeth shame,
And he hath part of the inheritance among the brethren.
3 The fining pot is for silver, and the furnace for gold;
But Jehovah trieth the hearts.
4 A wicked man giveth heed to evil lips;
And a liar giveth ear to a wicked tongue.
5 Whoso mocketh the poor defieth his Maker;
He that is glad at calamities is not guiltless.
6 Children's children are the crown of old men;
And the glory of children are their fathers.
7 Excellent speech becometh not a fool;
Much less do lying lips a prince.
8 A gift is a precious stone in the eyes of its owner;
Whithersoever it turneth, it maketh him prosper.
9 He that covereth a transgression seeketh love;
But he that repeateth a matter parteth friends.

A reproof entereth deeper into a wise man, 10
Than a hundred stripes upon a fool.
An evil man seeketh only rebellion; 11
And a cruel messenger should be sent against him.
Let a bear robbed of her cubs come upon a man, 12
Rather than a fool in his folly.
Whoso repayeth evil in return for good, 13
Evil shall not depart from his house.
The beginning of a quarrel is a letting out of water; 14
But before it is made bitter, strife may be left off.
Acquitting the wicked, and condemning the just, 15
Even both these are an abomination to Jehovah.
Wherefore is there purchase money in the hand of a fool 16
To buy wisdom, seeing he hath no sense?
A friend loveth at all times, 17
And a brother is born for adversity.
A man void of sense striketh hands [in promise], 18
And becometh surety in the presence of his friend.
He loveth transgression that loveth strife; 19
And he that exalteth his doorway seeketh destruction.
He that hath a perverse heart findeth no good; 20
And he that hath a double tongue falleth into evil.
He that begetteth a fool doeth it to his sorrow; 21
And the father of a fool hath no joy.
A merry heart doeth good like a medicine; 22
But a broken spirit drieth the bones.
A wicked man taketh a bribe out of his bosom 23
To turn aside the ways of judgment.
Wisdom is in front of him that hath understanding; 24
But the eyes of a fool are at the ends of the earth.
A foolish son is a grief to his father, 25
And bitterness to her that bare him.
Also to punish the righteous is not good, 26
Nor to strike princes for being just.
He that hath knowledge spareth his words; 27
A man of understanding is of a quiet spirit.
Even a fool, when silent, is counted wise; 28
And he that shutteth his lips, a man of understanding.
The unsociable man seeketh his own desire; 1
And he quarrelleth with all safe counsel.
A fool hath no delight in understanding, 2
But rather that his heart may shew itself.

3 When wickedness cometh, then cometh contempt,
  And with ignominy is reproach.
4 The words of a man's mouth are deep waters,
  And the wellspring of wisdom is a flowing brook.
5 It is not good to respect the person of the wicked man,
  So as to overthrow the righteous in judgment.
6 A fool's lips enter into contention,
  And his mouth calleth for blows.
7 A fool's mouth is his destruction,
  And his lips are the snare of his soul.
8 The words of a talebearer are as dainty morsels,
  And they go down into the chambers of the belly.
9 He also that is slothful in his work
  Is brother to him that hath a habit of wasting.
10 The name of Jehovah is a tower of strength;
   The righteous man runneth unto it, and is set aloft.
11 The rich man's wealth is his strong city,
   And is as a high wall, in his own conceit.
12 Before destruction the heart of man is haughty;
   But before honour is humility.
13 He that returneth an answer before he heareth,
   It is folly and shame unto him.
14 The spirit of a man will sustain his weakness;
   But a wounded spirit who can bear?
15 The heart of the prudent getteth knowledge;
   And the ear of the wise seeketh knowledge.
16 A man's gift maketh room for him,
   And bringeth him into the presence of great men.
17 He that is first in his pleadings seemeth just;
   But his neighbour cometh and cross-examineth him.
18 Casting of lots causeth contentions to cease,
   And parteth between the mighty.
19 A brother offended is stronger than a strong city;
   And their contentions are like the bars of a castle.
20 A man's belly is filled with the fruit of his mouth;
   And with the produce of his lips shall he be filled.
21 Death and life are in the power of the tongue;
   And they that love it will eat the fruit thereof.
22 Whoso findeth a wife findeth a good thing,
   And obtaineth favour from Jehovah.
23 The poor man uttereth entreaties;
   But the rich man answereth roughly.

A man of many companions is nigh to ruin; 24
But there is a friend that sticketh closer than a brother. —
Better is the poor man that walketh in his honesty, 1
Than he that is perverse in his lips, and is a fool.
Also, without knowledge a soul is not good; 2
And he that hasteneth with his feet sinneth.
The foolishness of man perverteth his way; 3
And then his heart fretteth against Jehovah.
Wealth addeth many companions; 4
But the poor man is separated from his neighbour.
A false witness will not be held guiltless, 5
And he that uttereth lies shall not escape.
Many entreat the countenance of the prince; 6
And every man is a friend to him that giveth gifts.
All the brethren of the poor man do hate him; 7
How much more do his friends go far from him!
He pursueth words, but they are nothing.
He that getteth sense loveth his own soul; 8
He that keepeth understanding shall find good.
A false witness will not be held guiltless, 9
And he that uttereth lies will perish.
Delicate living is not seemly for a fool; 10
Much less for a servant to have rule over princes.
The discretion of a man delayeth his anger; 11
And it is his glory to pass over a transgression.
The king's wrath roareth like a lion; 12
But his favour is as dew upon the grass.
A foolish son is the calamity of his father; 13
And the brawls of a wife are a continual dropping.
House and riches are the inheritance from fathers; 14
But a prudent wife is from Jehovah.
Slothfulness casteth into a deep sleep; 15
And an idle soul shall suffer hunger.
He that keepeth a command keepeth his soul; 16
But he that despiseth its ways shall die.
He that hath pity on the poor lendeth to Jehovah; 17
And that which he hath given will He pay him again.
Chasten thy son while there is hope; 18
Yet desire not to have him put to death.
A man of great wrath will suffer punishment; 19
For if thou deliver him, thou must even do it again.
Hear counsel and receive instruction, 20

So that thou mayest be wise in thy latter days.
21 There are many devices in a man's heart;
But the counsel of Jehovah, that shall stand.
22 What is desired of a man is his kindness;
And a poor man is better than a liar.
23 The fear of Jehovah leadeth to life;
And those filled with it abide unvisited by evil.
24 A slothful man hideth his hand in the dish,
And will not even bring it up to his mouth again.
25 Smite a scorner, and the simple will beware;
But who adviseth the wise teacheth knowledge.
26 Who robbeth his father, and chaseth away his mother,
Is a son that causeth shame, and bringeth reproach.
27 Cease, my son, to hearken to one that adviseth
To stray from the words of knowledge.
28 An ungodly witness scorneth judgment;
And the mouth of the wicked devoureth iniquity.
29 Judgments are prepared for scorners,
—And stripes for the back of fools.
1 Wine is a mocker, strong drink is raging;
And whosoever is led astray thereby is not wise.
2 The king's terribleness roareth like a lion;
Whoso maketh him angry sinneth against his own life.
3 It is an honour for a man to cease from strife;
But every fool maketh himself angry.
4 The sluggard will not plow by reason of winter;
He will beg in harvest time, and have nothing.
5 Counsel in the heart of man is like deep water;
And a man of understanding will draw it out.
6 Many men proclaim each his own kindness;
But a faithful man who can find?
7 The righteous man walketh in his honesty;
His children are blessed after him.
8 A king that sitteth on a throne of judgment
Scattereth away all evil with his eyes.
9 Who can say, 'I have made my heart clean,
'I am pure from my sin?'
10 Divers weights, and divers measures,
Both of them are alike an abomination to Jehovah.
11 Even a child maketh himself known by his doings,
Whether his work be pure, and whether it be right.
12 The hearing ear, and the seeing eye,

Jehovah hath made even both of them.

13 Love not sleep, lest thou come to poverty;
Open thine eyes, thou shalt be filled with bread.

14 'It is bad, it is bad,' saith the buyer;
But when he is gone his way, then he boasteth.

15 There may be gold, and a multitude of pearls;
But the lips of knowledge are a precious jewel.

16 Take his garment that is surety for a stranger;
And if for foreigners take a pledge of him.

17 Bread of deceit is sweet to a man;
But after it his mouth shall be filled with gravel.

18 Every purpose is established by counsel;
And with good advice make war.

19 Whoso walketh as a talebearer revealeth secrets;
And meddle not with him that enticeth with his lips.

20 Whoso curseth his father or his mother,
His lamp shall be put out in darkest darkness.

21 An inheritance may be gotten greedily at first;
But its end shall not be blessed.

22 Say not thou, 'I will recompense evil;'
But wait for Jehovah, and he will save thee.

23 Divers weights are an abomination to Jehovah;
And deceiving balances are not good.

24 Man's goings are from Jehovah;
How can a man then understand his own way?

25 It is a snare if a man rashly declare a thing holy,
And after vowing make inquiry.

26 A wise king winnoweth out the wicked,
And bringeth the threshing-wheel over them.

27 The spirit of man is the lamp of Jehovah,
Searching all the chambers of the belly.

28 Kindness and truth guard the king;
And his throne is upheld by kindness.

29 The glory of young men is their strength;
And the ornament of old men is grey hair.

30 The bruises of a wound are a remedy against evil;
So are stripes for the chambers of the belly.

1 The king's heart is a water pipe in the hand of Jehovah;
He turneth it whithersoever he will.

2 Every way of a man is right in his own eyes;
But Jehovah weigheth the hearts.

3 To do righteousness and justice

Is more acceptable to Jehovah than sacrifice.
4   A high look, and a proud heart,
Which are the lamp of the wicked, are sin.
5   The purposes of the diligent lead only to plenty;
But those of every hasty man only to want.
6   The getting of treasures by a lying tongue
Is a fleeting vanity of them that seek death.
7   The violence of the wicked hurrieth them away,
Because they refuse to do justice.
8   The way of a guilty man is very crooked;
But as for the pure his work is right.
9   It is better to dwell in a corner of the housetop,
Than to share the house with a brawling woman.
10   The soul of the wicked man desireth evil;
His neighbour findeth no favour in his eyes.
11   When a scorner is punished, the simple is made wise;
And when the wise is taught, he receiveth knowledge.
12   The righteous man considereth the house of the wicked,
And overthroweth the wicked for their wickedness.
13   Whoso stoppeth his ears at the cry of the poor,
He also shall cry himself, and not be answered.
14   A gift in secret pacifieth anger;
And a reward in the bosom, strong wrath.
15   To do justice bringeth joy to the righteous;
But destruction to the workers of iniquity.
16   The man that wandereth out of the way of wisdom
Will rest in the assembly of the departed spirits.
17   He that loveth pleasure will be a poor man;
He that loveth wine and oil will not be rich.
18   The wicked man will be a ransom for the righteous;
And the transgressor in the place of the upright.
19   It is better to dwell in the land of the desert,
Than with a contentious and an angry woman.
20   Coveted treasure and oil are in the wise man's home;
But a foolish man swalloweth it up.
21   He that followeth righteousness and kindness
Findeth life, righteousness, and honour.
22   A wise man scaleth the city of warriors,
And casteth down the strength of its confidence.
23   Whoso keepeth his mouth and his tongue
Keepeth his soul from troubles.

    Proud and haughty scorner is his name,   24
Who dealeth in proud wrath.
    The desire of the slothful man killeth him;   25
For his hands refuse to labour.
    Covetousness coveteth all the day long;   26
But the righteous man giveth and withholdeth not.
    The sacrifice of the wicked is an abomination;   27
Much more if he bringeth it with a wicked purpose.
    A false witness shall perish;   28
And the man that heareth should speak truthfully.
    A wicked man hardeneth his face;   29
But as for the upright, he directeth his way.
    There is no wisdom nor understanding   30
Nor counsel against Jehovah.
    The horse is prepared for the day of battle;   31
But safety is from Jehovah.

    A name is rather to be chosen than great riches,   1
And favour is better than silver and gold.
    The rich and poor will meet together;   2
Jehovah is the Maker of them all.
    A prudent man foreseeth evil and hideth himself;   3
But the simple pass on, and are punished.
    The reward of humility and of the fear of Jehovah   4
Are riches, and honour, and life.
    Thorns and snares are in the way of the froward;   5
He that keepeth his soul will be far from them.
    Train up a child in the way he should go;   6
And when he is old he will not depart from it.
    The rich man ruleth over the poor;   7
And the borrower is servant to the lender.
    He that soweth iniquity will reap vanity;   8
And the rod of His wrath will consume him.
    He that hath a bountiful eye will be blessed;   9
For he giveth some of his bread to the poor.
    Cast out the scorner, and contention will go;   10
Yea, strife and reproach will cease.
    He that loveth pureness of heart   11
Hath grace on his lips; the king will be his friend.
    The eyes of Jehovah guard knowledge,   12
And he overthroweth the words of the transgressor.
    The slothful saith, 'There is a lion in the street,   13
'I shall be slain in the broad places.'

14   The mouth of a strange woman is a deep pitfall;
     He that falleth therein is abhorred by Jehovah.
15   Foolishness is bound into the heart of a youth;
     The rod of correction shall drive it far from him.
16   Whoso oppresseth the poor to increase himself,
     Giveth to a rich man, and he will surely come to want.

---

17   Turn thine ear, and hear the WORDS OF THE WISE,
     And apply thy heart unto my knowledge.
18   For it is pleasant if thou keep them in thy breast;
     They will be fitted and joined to thy lips.
19   That thy trust may be in Jehovah,
     I make them known to thee this day, yea, to thee.
20   Have not I written to thee heretofore
     With counsels and knowledge,
21   To teach thee for certain the words of truth,
     To answer the words of truth to them that sent thee?
22   Rob not the poor man, because he is poor;
     Neither oppress the afflicted at the city gate;
23   For Jehovah will plead their cause,
     And will steal the soul of those that steal from them.
24   Make no friendship with an angry man;
     And with a furious man thou shalt not go;
25   Lest thou learn his ways, and get a snare to thy soul.
26   Be not one of them that strike hands [in promise],
     Or of them that are sureties for debts.
27   If thou hast nothing to pay,
     Why should he take away thy bed from under thee?
28   Remove not the ancient landmark,
     Which thy fathers have set up.
29   Seest thou a man diligent in his business?
     He shall stand in the presence of kings;
     —He shall not stand in the presence of mean men.
1   When thou sittest to eat with a ruler,
     Consider diligently what is before thee;
2   And put a knife to thy throat, if thou be greedy.
3   Be not desirous of his better dainties;
     For they are food offered in falsehood.
4   Toil not to be rich; cease from thine own wisdom.
5   Wilt thou set thine eyes to fly after what is not?
     For it certainly maketh itself wings;
     It flieth away as an eagle towards the heavens.

    Eat not the bread of him that hath an evil eye,   6
Neither desire thou his better dainties.
For as he thinketh in his heart, so is he;   7
'Eat and drink,' saith he to thee;
But his heart is not with thee.
The morsel thou hast eaten wilt thou vomit up,   8
And thou wilt lose thy words of pleasantness.
    Speak not in the ears of a fool;   9
For he will despise the wisdom of thy sayings.
    Remove not the ancient landmark;   10
And enter not into the fields of the fatherless;
For their Avenger is mighty;   11
He will plead their cause with thee.
    Apply thy heart unto instruction,   12
And thine ears to the words of knowledge.
    Withhold not correction from the youth;   13
But if thou beat him with the rod, let it not be to death.
Thou shalt beat him with the rod,   14
And shalt deliver his soul from hell.
    My son, when thy heart is wise,   15
My heart rejoiceth; yea, I myself
And my reins rejoice, when thy lips speak aright.   16
Let not thy heart envy sinners;   17
But be in the fear of Jehovah all the day long;
For surely there will be an hereafter;   18
And thine expectation will not be cut off.
    Hear thou, my son, and be wise,   19
And guide thy heart in the way.
Be not thou among winebibbers;   20
Among those who are wasteful of their own flesh;
For the drunkard and the riotous liver come to poverty;   21
And drowsiness clotheth a man with rags.
Hearken unto thy father who begat thee,   22
And despise not thy mother when she is old.
Buy the truth, and sell it not;   23
Also wisdom, and instruction, and understanding.
The father of the righteous will greatly rejoice;   24
And he that begetteth a wise son will have joy in him.
Thy father and thy mother will be glad,   25
And she that bare thee will rejoice.
    My son give me thy heart,   26
And let thine eyes delight in my ways.

27 For a harlot is a deep pit-fall;
And a foreign woman is a narrow well.
28 She also lieth in wait as a robber,
And increaseth the transgressors among men.
29 Who hath woe? who hath misery?
Who hath contentions? who complaining?
Who hath wounds without cause? who dulness of eyes?
30 They that tarry long at the wine;
They that go to seek mixed wine.
31 Look not thou upon the wine when it is red,
When it sparkleth in the cup, and danceth aright.
32 At last it biteth like a serpent,
And stingeth like an adder.
33 Thine eyes will look after strange women,
And thy heart will utter perverse things.
34 Yea, thou wilt be as if lying in the midst of the sea,
Or as if lying upon the top of a mast, [saying,]
35 'They have knocked me down, and I am not sore;
'They have beaten me, though I knew it not;
—'When I awake I will seek it yet again.'
1 Be not thou envious against evil men,
Neither desire to be with them,
2 For their heart studieth destruction,
And their lips talk of mischief.
3 By wisdom is a house builded;
And by understanding it is established;
4 And by knowledge are the chambers filled
With all precious and pleasant riches.
5 A wise man is powerful in strength;
Yea, a man of knowledge more than one of great might.
6 For by wise counsel thou shalt make thy war;
And in multitude of counsellors there is safety.
7 Wisdom is too high for a fool;
He openeth not his mouth at the city gate.
8 He that deviseth to do evil
Shall be called a mischievous person.
9 The device of foolishness is sin;
And the scorner is an abomination to men.
10 If thou faint in a day of trouble, thy strength is small.
11 Deliver thou them that are drawn unto death,
And those that are hurried away to be slain.
12 If thou forbear and say, 'Behold, we know him not;'

Will not He that weigheth the heart consider it?
And He that keepeth thy soul, he knoweth;
And he rendereth to man according to his works.

 My son, eat thou honey, because it is good;   13
And the honeycomb, which is sweet to thy palate;
So is knowledge of wisdom to thy soul;   14
If thou find it, then there will be an hereafter,
And thine expectation will not be cut off.

 Lie not in wait, O wicked man,   15
Against the dwelling of the righteous;
Plunder not his resting place;
For the righteous may fall seven times, and yet rise;   16
But the wicked will fall headlong into evil.

 Rejoice not when thine enemy falleth,   17
And let not thy heart be glad when he stumbleth;
Lest Jehovah see it, and it displease him,   18
And he turn away his wrath from him.

 Fret not thyself because of evil men,   19
Neither be thou envious of the wicked;
For there will be no hereafter to the evil man;   20
The lamp of the wicked will be put out.

 My son, fear thou Jehovah and the king;   21
And meddle not with them that are given to change.
For their calamity will rise suddenly;   22
And who knoweth the ruin of them both?

 These also are [sayings] of THE WISE MEN,   23
It is not good to respect persons in judgment.
He that saith to the wicked, 'Thou art righteous;'   24
Him peoples will curse, and nations abhor;
And in them that rebuke him will men delight,   25
And a good blessing will come upon them.
Men kiss his lips that giveth a right answer.   26

 Prepare thy work without, and make it fit in the field; 27
Go afterwards and build thy house.

 Be not a witness against thy neighbour without cause, 28
Nor deceive him with thy lips. Say not,   29
'I will do so to him as he hath done to me;
'I will render to the man according to his work.'

 I went by the field of the slothful man,   30
And by the vineyard of the man void of sense;
And, lo, it was all grown over with thistles.   31

Nettles had covered the face thereof;
And the stone wall thereof was broken down.
³² Then I saw, and considered it in my heart;
I looked upon it, and received instruction.
³³ Yet a little sleep, a little slumber,
A little folding of the hands for lying down;
³⁴ And thy poverty will come as one that journeyeth,
—And thy want as an armed man.

1 These also are PROVERBS OF SOLOMON, which the men of Hezekiah king of Judah copied out.
² It is the glory of God to conceal a matter;
But the glory of kings is to search out a matter.
³ The heavens for height, and the earth for depth,
But the heart of kings is unsearchable.
⁴ Take away the dross from the silver,
And there will come forth a vessel for the finer.
⁵ Take away wickedness from before the king,
And let his throne be established in righteousness.
⁶ Honour not thyself in the presence of the king,
And stand not up in the place of great men;
⁷ for better it is that it be said to thee, 'Come up hither;'
than 'Go lower,' in the presence of the prince whom thine eyes have looked upon.
⁸ Go not forth hastily to strive,
Consider what thou shalt do in the end thereof,
When thy neighbour hath put thee to shame.
⁹ Debate thy cause with thy neighbour himself;
And discover not the secret to another;
¹⁰ Lest he that heareth it put thee to shame,
And thine infamy turn not away.
¹¹ As apples of gold on figured work of silver,
So is a word spoken in a fit season.
¹² As an earring of gold, and an ornament of fine gold,
So is a wise reprover upon an obedient ear.
¹³ As the cold of snow in the time of harvest,
So is a faithful messenger to them that send him;
For he refresheth the soul of his masters.
¹⁴ As are light clouds and wind when there is no rain,
So is he that boasteth himself of a deceiving gift.
¹⁵ By slowness of anger is a prince persuaded,
And a soft tongue breaketh the bone.

Hast thou found honey? eat what is enough for thee, 16
Lest thou be filled therewith, and vomit it.
Let thy foot be seldom in thy neighbour's house; 17
Lest he be weary of thee, and so hate thee.
As a mallet, and a sword, and a sharp arrow; 18
Is he that beareth false witness against his neighbour.
As a broken tooth, or an unsteady foot; 19
So is trust in a faithless man in a day of trouble.
As splendour of raiment on a frosty day, 20
Or as vinegar upon nitre;
So is he that singeth songs to a heavy heart.
If thine enemy be hungry, give him bread to eat; 21
And if he be thirsty, give him water to drink;
For thou wilt heap coals of fire upon his head, 22
And Jehovah will reward thee.
The north wind bringeth forth rain; 23
So doth a backbiting tongue angry looks.
It is better to dwell in the corner of the housetop, 24
Than to share the house with a brawling woman.
As cold waters to a thirsty soul, 25
So is good news from a far country.
As a muddy well, or a corrupt spring, 26
So is a righteous man bowing down before the wicked.
It is not good to eat too much honey; 27
Nor is it glorious for men to search for their own glory.
As a city that is broken down, and without walls; 28
So is he that restraineth not his own spirit.

As snow in summer, and as rain in harvest, 1
So honour is not seemly for a fool.
As a sparrow is for wandering, as a swallow for flying, 2
So the causeless curse shall not come to pass.
A whip for the horse, a bridle for the ass, 3
And a rod for the back of fools.
Answer not a fool according to his folly, 4
Lest thou also become like unto him.
Answer a fool according to his folly, 5
Lest he be wise in his own eyes.
He cutteth off his feet, and drinketh damage, 6
Who sendeth a message by the hand of a fool.
The legs of the lame hang useless; 7
So is a proverb in the mouth of fools.
As he that bindeth up the stone in the sling, 8

So is he that giveth honour to a fool.
9 As a thorn goeth up into the hand of a drunkard,
So is a proverb in the mouth of fools.
10 The quarrelsome man overturneth all things;
He both hireth the fool, and hireth the passers by.
11 As a dog returneth to his vomit,
So a fool repeateth his folly.
12 Seest thou a man wise in his own eyes?
There is more hope of a fool than of him.
13 The slothful saith, 'A roaring lion is in the pathway;
'A lion is in the broad places.'
14 As the door turneth upon its hinges,
So doth the slothful man upon his bed.
15 The slothful man hideth his hand in the dish;
It wearieth him to bring it again to his mouth.
16 The slothful man is wiser in his own eyes
Than seven men that can render a reason.
17 Like one that taketh a passing dog by the ears,
Is he that meddleth with strife belonging not to him.
18 As a madman who casteth darts, arrows, and death,
19 So is the man that deceiveth his neighbour,
And saith, 'Am I not in sport?'
20 When there is no wood, the fire goeth out;
So where there is no talebearer, the strife ceaseth.
21 As coals are to burning embers, and wood to the fire,
So is a contentious man to kindle strife.
22 The words of a talebearer are as dainty morsels,
And they go down into the chambers of the belly.
23 Warm lips and a wicked heart
Are like silver dross spread over a potsherd.
24 He that hateth dissembleth with his lips,
And layeth up deceit within him;
25 If he maketh his voice gracious, believe him not;
For there are seven abominations in his heart.
26 Though his hatred is covered by deceit,
His wickedness will be laid bare in the Assembly.
27 Whoso diggeth a pit will fall therein;
And he that rolleth a stone, it will return on him
28 A lying tongue hateth those that it woundeth;
—And a flattering mouth worketh ruin.
1 Boast not thyself of to-morrow;
For thou knowest not what a day may bring forth.

Let another praise thee, and not thine own mouth; 2
A stranger, and not thine own lips.
 A stone is heavy and the sand weighty; 3
But a fool's wrath is heavier than them both.
 Wrath is cruel, and anger is outrageous; 4
But who is able to stand before jealousy?
 Better is rebuke that sheweth than love that hideth; 5
Faithful are the wounds of a friend; 6
But earnest are the kisses of an enemy.
 The satisfied soul trampleth on the honeycomb; 7
But to the hungry soul every bitter thing is sweet.
 As a bird that wandereth from her nest, 8
So is a man that wandereth from his place.
 Ointment and perfume rejoice the heart; 9
And sweeter is a man's friend than scented wood.
 Thine own friend and thy father's friend, forsake not; 10
But go not to thy brother's house in the day of thy ruin;
Better is a near neighbour than a brother far off.
 My son, be wise, and make my heart glad, 11
That I may answer him that reproacheth me.
 A prudent man seeth evil, and hideth himself; 12
But the simple pass on and are punished.
 Take his garment that is surety for a stranger, 13
And if for foreigners take a pledge of him.
 He that blesseth his friend with a loud voice, 14
Rising early in the morning,
It shall be counted a curse to him.
 A continual dropping in a very rainy day, 15
And a contentious woman are alike.
Whoso would shut her in, would shut in the wind, 16
And he would ask for oil in his right hand.
 Iron sharpeneth iron; 17
So a man sharpeneth the countenance of his friend.
 Whoso keepeth the fig tree shall eat its fruit; 18
So he that waiteth on his master shall be honoured.
 As water showeth the face to the face, 19
So doth the heart, the man to the man.
 Hell and the pit of destruction are never full; 20
So the eyes of man are never satisfied.
 The fining pot is for silver, and the furnace for gold; 21
So let a man be to the mouth of him that praiseth him.

22 If thou bruise a fool in a mortar among corn with a pestle,
Yet will not his foolishness depart from him.
23 Be thou diligent to know the face of thy flocks,
And give good heed to thy herds.
24 For possessions are not for ever;
Nor doth the crown endure to all generations.
25 When the hay shall be gone, and the tender grass sheweth itself,
And the herbs of the mountains are gathered;
26 Thou wilt have the lambs for thy clothing,
And the goats for the price of thy field,
27 And goats' milk enough for thy food,
—For thy house's food, and to nourish thy maidens.
1 The wicked flee when no man pursueth;
But the righteous are bold as a lion.
2 During the rebellion of a land many are its princes;
But by men of understanding and knowledge
Its state will be prolonged.
3 A strong poor man, and he that oppresseth the needy,
Are like a sweeping rain which leaveth no food.
4 They that forsake the law praise the wicked;
But such as keep the law contend against them.
5 Evil men understand not judgment;
But they that seek Jehovah understand all things.
6 Better is the poor man that walketh in his honesty,
Than a man perverse in his ways, though he be rich.
7 Whoso keepeth the law is a wise son;
But the companion of riotous livers shameth his father.
8 Whoso by usury and increase increaseth his wealth,
Is gathering it for him that will pity the poor.
9 Whoso turneth away his ear from hearing the law,
Even his prayer will be an abomination.
10 Whoso causeth the upright to stray in a bad road,
He will fall himself into his own pit;
But the honest will inherit what is good.
11 The rich man is wise in his own eyes;
But a poor man of understanding searcheth him out.
12 When righteous men rejoice, there is great glory;
But when the wicked rise, men hide themselves.
13 He that covereth his transgressions will not prosper;
But whoso confesseth and quitteth them will find mercy.

Happy is the man that feareth always;	14
But he that hardeneth his heart will fall into evil.	
As a roaring lion, and a bear running loose;	15
So is a wicked ruler over a poor people.	
A ruler void of sense also addeth exactions;	16
He that hateth unjust gain will prolong his days.	
A man that is oppressed by the guilt of bloodshed	17
Is fleeing to the Pit; let no man stay him.	
Whoso walketh in honesty will be saved;	18
But he that is perverse in his ways will fall at once.	
He that tilleth his land will have plenty of bread;	19
But whoso followeth vanities will have want enough.	
A faithful man will abound with blessings;	20
But he that hasteneth to be rich will not be guiltless.	
To have respect to persons is not good;	21
And for a piece of bread will that man transgress.	
He that hasteneth after wealth hath an evil eye,	22
And knoweth not that poverty will come upon him.	
Whoso rebuketh men will afterwards find favour,	23
Rather than he that flattereth with the tongue.	
Whoso robbeth his father or his mother,	24
And saith, 'It is no transgression;'	
The same is the companion of a destroyer.	
He that is of a proud soul stirreth up strife;	25
But he that trusteth in Jehovah will be made fat.	
He that trusteth in his own heart is a fool;	26
But whoso walketh wisely, he will be delivered.	
He that giveth unto the poor will not lack;	27
But he that hideth his eyes will have many curses.	
When the wicked rise, men hide themselves;	28
But when they perish, the righteous increase.	
He that when reproved hardeneth his neck,	1
Will be destroyed suddenly, and without remedy.	
When the righteous increase, the people rejoice;	2
But when a wicked man beareth rule, the people mourn.	
Whoso loveth wisdom rejoiceth his father;	3
But the companion of harlots spendeth his wealth.	
The king by judgment establisheth the land;	4
But he that receiveth gifts overthroweth it.	
A man that flattereth his neighbour	5
Spreadeth a net for his footsteps.	
In the transgression of an evil man there is a snare;	6

But the righteous man doth sing and rejoice.
7 The righteous man considereth the cause of the poor;
But the wicked regardeth it not to know it.
8 Scornful men raise a flame in a city;
But wise men turn away wrath.
9 If a wise man reasoneth with a foolish man,
Whether he rage, or laugh, there is no rest.
10 The bloodthirsty hate an honest man;
But the righteous men seek his soul.
11 A fool uttereth all his mind;
But a wise man keepeth it in till afterwards.
12 If a ruler hearken to lying words,
All his servants become wicked.
13 When the poor man and the plunderer meet together,
Jehovah giveth light to the eyes of both.
14 The king that faithfully judgeth the poor,
His throne will be established for ever.
15 The rod and reproof give wisdom;
But a neglected child bringeth his mother to shame.
16 When the wicked increase, transgression increaseth;
But the righteous will see their fall.
17 Correct thy son, and he shall give thee quiet;
Yea, he shall give delight unto thy soul.
18 When there is no divine vision, the people are unruly;
But he that keepeth the law, happy is he.
19 A servant will not be corrected by words;
For though he understand he will not answer.
20 Seest thou a man that is hasty in his words?
There is more hope of a fool than of him.
21 He that indulgeth his servant from a child,
Will have him afterwards become his son.
22 An angry man stirreth up strife,
And a wrathful man aboundeth in transgression.
23 A man's pride will make him stumble;
But the humble in spirit will obtain honour.
24 Whoso is partner with a thief hateth his own soul;
He heareth cursing, and maketh it not known.
25 The being afraid of man bringeth a snare;
But whoso trusteth in Jehovah will be set on high.
26 Many seek the countenance of the ruler;
But judgment for a man cometh from Jehovah.

An unjust man is abomination to the righteous;
And the upright in his way is abomination to the wicked.—

THE WORDS OF AGUR the son of Jakeh, even the Burden, the inspired word of the man unto Ithiel, even unto Ithiel and Ucal.
Surely I am more brutish than a man, and have not the understanding of men. I have neither learned wisdom, nor have I the knowledge of holy things.
Who hath gone up to heaven, and come down again? who hath gathered the wind in his two hands? who hath wrapt up the waters in a garment? who hath established all the ends of the earth? what is his name, and what his son's name, if thou knowest?
Every word of God is pure, he is a shield to them that trust in him. Add thou not unto his words, lest he reprove thee, and thou be found a liar.
Two things do I ask of thee; deny me not before I die; remove far from me vanity and lies; give me neither poverty nor riches; help me to get the food convenient for me; lest I be full, and deny thee, and say, 'Who is ' Jehovah?' or lest I be poor, and steal, and profane the name of my God.
Slander not a servant unto his master, lest he curse thee, and thou be found guilty.
There is a generation that curseth its father, and doth not bless its mother; a generation that is pure in its own eyes, and yet is not washed from its filthiness; a generation, O how lofty are its eyes! and its eyelids are lifted up; a generation, whose teeth are swords, and its cheek-teeth are knives, to devour the poor from off the earth, and the needy from among men.
The horseleach hath two daughters, [crying,] 'Give, ' give.' There are three things that are never satisfied, yea, four say not, 'It is enough;' the grave; and the barren womb; the earth that is not filled with water; and the fire also saith not, 'It is enough.'
The eye that mocketh at its father, and despiseth to obey its mother, the ravens of the valley shall pick it out, and the young eagles shall eat it.
There are three things too wonderful for me, yea, four

19 which I understand not; the way of an eagle in the air; the way of a serpent upon a rock; the way of a ship in the midst of the sea; and the way of a man with a maiden.

20 Such is the way of an adulterous woman; she eateth, and wipeth her mouth, and saith, 'I have done no wickedness.'

21 For three things the earth is disquieted, and for four
22 which it cannot bear; for a servant when he reigneth; and
23 a fool when he is filled with food; for a hateful woman when she is married; and a handmaid that dispossesseth her mistress.

24 There are four things which are little upon the earth,
25 but they are wiser than the wise men. The ants are a people not strong, yet they prepare their food in the
26 summer; the conies are a people not powerful, yet make
27 they their houses in the rocks; the locusts have no king,
28 yet go they forth all of them by bands; the lizard taketh hold with its hands, and is in kings' palaces.

29 There are three things which do well in walking, yea,
30 four are comely in going; a lion which is strongest among
31 beasts, and turneth not away for any; a war-horse and perhaps a he-goat; and a king against whom there is no rising up.

32 If thou hast foolishly lifted up thyself, or if thou hast
33 thought evil, lay thy hand on thy mouth. Surely the pressing of milk bringeth forth curds, and the pressing of the nose bringeth forth blood; so the pressing against —wrath bringeth forth strife.

---

1 THE WORDS OF KING LEMUEL, the Burden that his mother taught him.

2 What, my son? And what, the son of my womb? And what, the son of my vows?

3 Give not thy strength unto women, Nor thy ways to that which destroyeth kings.

4 It is not for kings, Lemuel, not for kings to drink wine; Nor for princes [to ask] 'Where is strong drink;'

5 Lest they drink, and forget the law, And pervert the cause of any son of affliction.

6 Give strong drink to him that is ready to perish, And wine to those that be of bitter spirit.

7 Let him drink, and forget his poverty,

And remember his trouble no more.
Open thy mouth for the dumb 8
In the cause of all fatherless children.
Open thy mouth, judge righteously, 9
And plead the cause of the poor and needy.

א Who can find a VIRTUOUS WOMAN? 10
   For her price is far above pearls.
ב The heart of her husband doth trust her, 11
   So that he will have no need of plunder.
ג She will do him good and not evil 12
   All the days of her life.
ד She seeketh wool, and flax, 13
   And worketh willingly with her hands.
ה She is like the merchants' ships; 14
   She bringeth her food from afar.
ו She riseth also while it is yet night, 15
   And giveth meat to her house, and a task to her maids.
ז She considereth a field, and buyeth it; 16
   With the fruit of her hands she planteth a vineyard.
ח She girdeth her loins with strength, 17
   And strengtheneth her arms.
ט She trieth her merchandise that it is good; 18
   Her lamp goeth not out by night.
י She layeth her hands to the spindle, 19
   And her hands hold the distaff.
כ She stretcheth out her open hand to the poor; 20
   Yea, she reacheth forth her hands to the needy.
ל She feareth not the snow for her household; 21
   For all her household are doubly clothed.
מ She maketh for herself bed-coverings; 22
   Her clothing is silk and purple.
נ Her husband is known at the city gates, 23
   When he sitteth among the elders of the land.
ס She maketh linen garments, and selleth them; 24
   And delivereth girdles unto the merchant.
ע Strength and honour are her clothing; 25
   And she will rejoice in the time to come.
פ She openeth her mouth with wisdom; 26
   And on her tongue is the law of kindness.
צ She looketh well to the ways of her household; 27
   And eateth not the bread of idleness.

²⁸ ק Her children rise up, and call her blessed;
Her husband also, and he praiseth her, [saying,]
²⁹ ר 'Many daughters have done virtuously,
'But thou excellest them all.'
³⁰ ש Favour is deceitful, and beauty is vain;
A woman that feareth Jehovah, she will be praised.
³¹ ת Give to her some of the fruit of her hands;
And let her own works praise her at the city gates.

ECCLESIASTES; OR, THE PREACHER.

¹ THE WORDS OF THE PREACHER, the son of David, king
² of Jerusalem. Vanity of vanities, saith the Preacher,
³ vanity of vanities; all is vanity. What profit hath a man of all his labour in which he laboureth under the sun?
⁴ A generation passeth away, and a generation cometh;
But the earth abideth for ever.
⁵ The sun also ariseth, and the sun goeth down,
And hasteneth to its place where it arose.
⁶ Going to the south, and turning about to the north,
The wind goeth turning about and turning about;
And the wind cometh back again in its many turnings.
⁷ All the rivers run into the sea; yet the sea is not full;
To the place from whence the rivers flow,
Thither they return to flow again.
⁸ All things are full of labour; man cannot utter it;
The eye is not satisfied with seeing,
Nor the ear filled with hearing.
⁹ The thing that hath been is what will be;
And what hath been done is that which will be done;
And there is no new thing under the sun.
¹⁰ Is there a thing whereof it is said, 'See, this is new?'
It hath been already in the old time, which was before us.
¹¹ There is no memory of former things;
Nor will there be memory of future things
With those that shall come hereafter.
¹² I the Preacher was king over Israel in Jerusalem. And
¹³ I gave my heart to seek and search out by wisdom concerning all things that are done under heaven. This sore labour hath God given to the sons of Adam to afflict them
¹⁴ therewith. I have seen all the works that are done under the sun; and, behold, all is vanity and vexation of spirit.

What is crooked cannot be made straight; ¹⁵
And what is wanting cannot be numbered.

I spake with mine own heart, saying, 'Lo, I am come ¹⁶ 'to great estate, and have got more wisdom than all they 'that have been before me in Jerusalem.' Yea, my heart hath seen abundance of wisdom and knowledge. And I ¹⁷ gave my heart to know wisdom, and to know madness and folly; I perceived that this also is vexation of spirit.
For in much wisdom is much grief; ¹⁸
And he that increaseth knowledge increaseth sorrow. —

I said in my heart, 'Go to now, I will prove thee with ¹ 'mirth, therefore look on what is good.' And, behold, this also was vanity. I said of laughter, 'It is mad;' and of ² mirth, 'What doeth it?' I sought in my heart to indulge ³ my flesh with wine, yet acquainting my heart with wisdom; and to lay hold on folly, till I might see what was that good thing for the sons of Adam, which they should do under the heavens all the days of their life. I made me ⁴ great works; I builded me houses; I planted me vineyards. I made me gardens and orchards, and I planted trees in ⁵ them of all kind of fruits. I made me pools of water, to ⁶ water therewith the forest that bringeth forth trees. I ⁷ bought me servants and maidens, and had servants born in my house; also I had great possessions of herds and flocks above all that were in Jerusalem before me. I ga- ⁸ thered me also silver and gold, and the peculiar treasure of kings and of the provinces. I got me men singers and women singers, and the delights of the sons of Adam, a wife and wives. So I was great, and increased more than ⁹ all that were before me in Jerusalem; also my wisdom remained with me. And whatsoever mine eyes desired I ¹⁰ kept not from them, I withheld not my heart from any joy; for my heart rejoiced in all my labour. And this was my portion of all my labour; that I turned to all the works ¹¹ that my hands had wrought, and to the labour that I had laboured to do; and, behold, all was vanity and vexation of spirit, and there was no profit under the sun.

And I turned myself to behold wisdom, and madness, ¹² and folly; for what can the man do that cometh after the king? even that which hath been already done. Then I ¹³ saw that wisdom excelleth folly, as far as light excelleth darkness. The wise man's eyes are in his head; but the ¹⁴

fool walketh in darkness; and I myself perceived also that
¹⁵ one event happeneth to them all. Then said I in my heart,
'As it happeneth to the fool, so it will happen even to
'me; and why was I then more wise?' Then I said in
¹⁶ my heart, that this also is vanity. For there is no remembrance of the wise man more than of the fool for ever;
seeing that what hath already been shall in the days to
come all be forgotten. And how dieth the wise man? as
¹⁷ the fool. Therefore I hated life; because the work that is
wrought under the sun is grievous to me; for all is vanity
and vexation of spirit.
¹⁸ Yea, I hated all my labour wherein I had laboured under
the sun; because I should leave it to a man that will be
¹⁹ after me. And who knoweth whether he will be a wise
man or a fool? Yet will he have rule over all my labour
wherein I have laboured, and wherein I have shewed myself wise under the sun. This also is vanity.
²⁰ Therefore I went about to cause my heart to despair of
²¹ all the labour wherein I had laboured under the sun. For
there may be a man whose labour is in wisdom, and in
knowledge, and in equity; yet to a man that hath not
laboured therein shall he leave it for his portion. This
²² also is vanity and a great evil. For what will a man have
of all his labour, and of the vexation of his heart, wherein
²³ he hath laboured under the sun? For all his days are sorrows, and his travail grief; yea, his heart taketh not rest
in the night. This also is vanity.
²⁴ There is nothing better for a man, than that he should
eat and drink, and that he should make his soul look for
good in his labour. This also I saw, that it was from the
²⁵ hand of God. For who can eat, or who else can enjoy
²⁶ pleasure, more than I? For to a man that is good in his
sight [God] giveth wisdom, and knowledge, and joy; but
to the sinner he giveth travail, to gather and to heap up
what he must give to him that is good before God. This
—also is vanity and vexation of spirit.
¹ To every thing there is a season,
And a time to every purpose under the heavens.
² A time to be born, and a time to die;
A time to plant, and a time to root up what is planted;
³ A time to kill, and a time to heal;
A time to break down, and a time to build up;

A time to weep, and a time to laugh; 4
A time to mourn, and a time to dance;
A time to cast stones, and a time to gather stones; 5
A time to embrace, and a time to avoid embracing;
A time to seek, and a time to lose; 6
A time to keep, and a time to cast away;
A time to rend, and a time to sew; 7
A time to keep silence, and a time to speak;
A time to love, and a time to hate; 8
A time of war, and a time of peace.

What profit hath he that worketh in that wherein he 9 laboureth? I have seen the travail, which God hath given 10 to the sons of Adam to afflict them in it. He hath made 11 everything beautiful in its time; also he hath set eternity in their heart, so that no man can find out the work that God hath made from the beginning to the end. I know 12 that there is no good in them, but for a man to rejoice, and to do good in his life. And also that every man should 13 eat and drink, and look on the good of all his labour; it is the gift of God. I know that, whatsoever God doeth, 14 it shall be for ever; nothing can be added to it, nor anything taken from it; and God doeth it, that men should fear before him. That which hath already been is now; 15 and that which is to be hath already been; and God requireth back that which is past before.

And moreover I saw under the sun the place of judg- 16 ment, that wickedness was there; and the place of righteousness, that wickedness was there. I said in my heart, 17 'God will judge the righteous and the wicked; for there will be then a time for every purpose and for every work.' I said in my heart concerning the estate of the sons of 18 Adam, that God was setting them apart, and making them see that they themselves are like the beasts. For that 19 which befalleth the sons of Adam befalleth beasts; even one thing befalleth them; as the one dieth, so dieth the other; yea, they have all one breath; so that a man hath no pre-eminence above a beast; for all is vanity. All go 20 to one place; all are from the dust, and all turn to dust again.

Who knoweth the spirit of the sons of Adam that it 21 goeth upward, and the spirit of the beast that it goeth downward to the earth? Therefore I perceive that there 22 is nothing better, than that a man should rejoice in his own works; for that is his portion; for who shall bring him to see what shall be after him?

1 So I returned, and considered all the oppressions that are done under the sun; and behold the tears of the oppressed, and they had no comforter; and on the side of their oppressors there was power; and they had no com-
2 forter. Therefore I praised the dead who are already
3 dead more than the living who are yet alive. Yea, better than both they is he that hath not yet been, who hath not
4 seen the evil work that is done under the sun. And I saw all labour, and every success in work, that for this a man is envied by his neighbour. This also is vanity and vexation of spirit.
5 The fool foldeth his hands and eateth his own flesh.
6 Better is a handful with quietness,
Than both hands full with toil and vexation of spirit.
7 Then I returned, and I saw a vanity under the sun.
8 There may be one alone, and without a second; yea, he may have neither child nor brother; yet is there no end to all his labour; neither is his eye satisfied with riches. And for whom do I labour, and bereave my soul of good? This also is vanity, yea, it is a sore trouble.
9 Two are better than one;
Because they have a good reward for their labour.
10 For if they fall, the one will lift up his fellow;
But woe to him that falleth when he is alone,
And hath not another to lift him up.
11 Again, if two lie together, then they have heat;
But how can one be warm alone?
12 And if one attack him, two can withstand him;
And a threefold cord is not quickly broken.
13 Better is a poor and a wise child
Than a king old and foolish, who can no more be taught.
14 For out of a prison the one may come to reign;
Even though in the other's kingdom he was born poor.
15 I considered all the living who walk about under the sun, with the child, the second that shall stand up in his
16 stead. There is no end of all the people, even of all that have been before them; they also that come after shall not rejoice in him. Surely this also is vanity and vexation of spirit.

¹ Keep thy foot when thou goest to the House of God, and be more ready to hear, than to give the sacrifice of fools; for they consider not that they do evil. ² Be not rash with thy mouth, and let not thy heart be hasty to utter any thing before God; for God is in heaven, and thou upon earth; therefore let thy words be few. ³ For a dream cometh with much business; and a fool's voice with a multitude of words. ⁴ When thou vowest a vow to God, delay not to pay it; for He hath no pleasure in fools; pay that which thou hast vowed. ⁵ Better is it that thou shouldest not vow, than that thou shouldest vow and not pay. ⁶ Suffer not thy mouth to cause thy flesh to sin; neither say thou before the preacher that it was a sin of ignorance. Wherefore should God be angry at thy voice, and destroy the work of thy hands? ⁷ For in the multitude of dreams are also vanities and words many; but do thou fear God.

⁸ If thou seest the oppression of the poor, and a violent perverting of judgment and justice in the province, marvel not at the matter; for He that is higher than the highest regardeth; and there are higher than they. ⁹ Moreover the profit of the land is for all; the king himself is served by the field. ¹⁰ He that longeth for silver will not be satisfied with silver; and he that longeth for abundance hath no increase. This also is vanity.

¹¹ When goods increase, they increase that eat them;
And what gain is there to the owners thereof,
Save the beholding of them with their eyes?
¹² The sleep of a labouring man is sweet,
Whether he eat little or much;
But the fulness of the rich suffereth him not to sleep.

¹³ There is a sore evil which I have seen under the sun, namely, riches kept for the owners thereof to their own hurt. ¹⁴ But those riches perish by evil doings; and he begetteth a son, and there is nothing whatever in his hand. ¹⁵ As he came forth naked from his mother's womb, he will return to go as he came, and he will take nothing whatever by his labour, to carry away in his hand.

¹⁶ And this also is a sore evil, that in all points as he came, so will he go; and what profit hath he that hath laboured for the wind? ¹⁷ All his days also he eateth in darkness, and he hath much sorrow and sickness to himself and anger.

18 Behold that which I have considered good, that it is comely for one to eat and to drink, and to look upon the good of all his labour that he hath taken under the sun all the days of his life, which God giveth him; for that
19 is his portion. Every man also to whom God hath given riches and wealth, and hath given him power to eat thereof, and to take his portion, and to rejoice in his labour;
20 this is the gift of God. For he will not much remember the days of his life; because while his heart rejoiceth God —afflicteth him.
1 There is an evil which I have seen under the sun, and
2 it is common among men; a man to whom God hath given riches, and wealth, and honour, so that he wanteth nothing for his soul of all that he desireth, yet God giveth him not power to eat thereof, but a foreigner eateth it. This is vanity, and it is an evil disease.
3 If a man beget a hundred children, and live many years, so that the days of his years be many, and his soul be not satisfied with good, and also that he have no burial; I say,
4 that one born dead is better than he. For he came in with vanity, and will depart in darkness, and his name shall be
5 covered with darkness. Moreover he that hath not seen nor known the sun, he hath more rest than the other.
6 Yea, though he live a thousand years twice told, yet hath he seen no good. Do not all go to one place?
7 All the labour of man is for his mouth,
And yet the appetite is not filled.
8 For what hath the wise more than the fool?
What hath the poor, that knoweth to walk before the living?
9 Better is what is seen by the eyes
Than the wandering of the desire.
This also is vanity and vexation of spirit.
10 What is he whose name hath been long celebrated,
And of whom it is known what man he was?
Yet he cannot contend with one mightier than he.
11 Seeing there be many things that increase vanity, what
12 is man the better? For who knoweth what is good for man in life? All the days of his vain life he even spendeth as a shadow; for who can tell a man what shall be after —him under the sun?
1 Better is a good name than precious ointment;
And the day of death than the day of one's birth.

Better is it to go to the house of mourning,   2
Than to go to the house of drinking-feasts;
For that is the end of all men;
And the living will lay it to his heart.
Better is sorrow than laughter;   3
For by sadness of face the heart is made better.
The heart of the wise is in the house of mourning;   4
But the heart of fools is in the house of mirth.
Better is it to hear the rebuke of a wise man,   5
Than for a man to hear the song of fools.
For as the crackling of thorns under a pot,   6
So is the laughter of the fool. This also is vanity.
   Surely oppression maketh a wise man foolish;   7
And a bribe destroyeth the heart.
Better is the end of a thing than its beginning;   8
Better is the patient in spirit than the proud in spirit.
Be not hasty in thy spirit to be angry;   9
For anger resteth in the bosom of fools.
Say not, 'Why were the former days better than these?'   10
For thou dost not inquire wisely concerning this.
   Wisdom is as good as an inheritance,   11
And is a profit to them that see the sun.
For wisdom is a shelter, as money is a shelter;   12
But the excellence of the knowledge of wisdom,
Is that it giveth life to its owners.
   Consider the work of God;   13
For who can straighten what He maketh crooked?
In the day of happiness be happy,   14
But in the day of evil consider;
God also hath set the one against the other,
To the end that man should find nothing after him.
   All these have I seen in the days of my vanity;   15
Here the righteous is perishing in his righteousness,
And there the wicked is living long in his wickedness.
Be not over-righteous; neither be too wise;   16
Why shouldest thou wear thyself out?
Be not over-wicked, neither be thou foolish;   17
Why shouldest thou die before thy time?
It is good that thou shouldest take hold of this;   18
Yea, also from this withdraw not thy hand;
For he that feareth God will come forth from them all.
   Wisdom strengtheneth the wise   19

More than ten mighty men that are in the city.
20 For there is not a righteous man upon earth,
That doeth good, and sinneth not.
21 Also take not heed to all words that are spoken,
Lest thou hear thy servant curse thee;
22 For oftentimes also thine own heart knoweth
That thou thyself likewise hast cursed others.
23 All this have I proved by wisdom; I said, 'I will be
24 'wise;' but it was far from me. That which is far off, and
25 exceeding deep, who can find it out? I applied my heart to know, and to search, and to seek out wisdom, and reason, and to know that wickedness is folly, and folly is
26 madness; and I find more bitter than death the woman whose heart is snares and nets, and her hands as fetters; whoso is good in the sight of God will escape from her;
27 but the sinner will be taken by her. Behold, this have I found, saith the preacher, weighing one by one, to find
28 out the reason, which yet my soul seeketh, but I find not; one man among a thousand have I found, but a woman among all those have I not found. Lo, this only
29 have I found, that God hath made men upright; but —they have sought out many devices.

1 Who is as the wise man?
And who knoweth the interpretation of a thing?
A man's wisdom maketh his face to shine,
And the strength of his face will be changed.
2 I counsel thee to keep the king's command,
And that in regard of the oath before God.
3 Be not hasty to go out of his sight;
Continue not in evil, for he doeth all that he wisheth.
4 Where the word of a king is, there is power;
And who may say unto him, 'What doest thou?'
5 Whoso keepeth a command will know no evil;
And a wise heart knoweth both time and a judgment.
6 For to every purpose there is time and judgment,
Although the misery of man is great upon him.
7 For he knoweth not that which will be;
For who can tell him when it will be?
8 No man hath power over the wind, to stay the wind;
Nor power [over his breath] in the day of death;
And there is no discharge in that warfare;
Neither will wickedness deliver its followers.

All this have I seen, and I applied my heart to every ⁹ work that hath been done under the sun. There is a time wherein one man ruleth over another to his own hurt. And so I saw the wicked receive burial, who had come ¹⁰ and gone from the Holy Place, and they were forgotten in the city where they had so done. This also is vanity.

Because sentence against an evil work is not executed ¹¹ speedily, therefore the heart of the sons of Adam is fully set in them to do evil. Though a sinner do evil a hundred ¹² times, and his days be prolonged, yet surely I know that it will be well with them that fear God, who fear in his presence; but it will not be well with the wicked, neither ¹³ will his days be lengthened as the shadow; because he feareth not before God. There is a vanity which is done ¹⁴ upon the earth; that there are righteous men, unto whom it happeneth according to the work of the wicked; again, there are wicked men, to whom it happeneth according to the work of the righteous; I said that this also is vanity. Then I commended mirth, because a man hath no better ¹⁵ thing under the sun, than to eat, and to drink, and to be merry; for that will abide with him in his labour during the days of his life, which God giveth him under the sun.

When I applied my heart to know wisdom, and to see ¹⁶ the business that is done upon the earth; (for also there may be one that neither day nor night seeth sleep with his eyes;) then I beheld all the work of God, that a man ¹⁷ cannot find out the work that is done under the sun; because though a man labour to seek it out, yet he shall not find it; yea farther; though a wise man think to know it, yet shall he not be able to find it. —

For all this I considered in my heart even to make all ¹ this clear, that the righteous, and the wise, and their deeds, are in the hand of God. No man knoweth either love or hatred. All things are before them; all things, because unto ² all there is one event; to the righteous, and to the wicked; to the good, and to the clean, and to the unclean; to him that sacrificeth, and to him that sacrificeth not; as is the good, so is the sinner; and he that sweareth, as he that feareth an oath. This is an evil among all things that are ³ done under the sun, that there is one event unto all; yea, also the heart of the sons of Adam is full of evil, and madness is in their heart while they live, and after that they

⁴ go to the dead. For who is excepted? Unto all the living there is hope; for a living dog is better than a dead ⁵ lion. For the living know that they shall die; but the dead know not any thing, neither have they any more a ⁶ reward; for the memory of them is forgotten. Also their love, and their hatred, and their envy, is now perished; neither have they any more a portion for ever in any thing that is done under the sun.

⁷ Go thy way, eat thy bread with joy, and drink thy wine with a merry heart; for God already hath pleasure in thy ⁸ works. Let thy garments be always white; and let thy ⁹ head lack no ointment. Enjoy life with the wife whom thou lovest all the days of the life of thy vanity, which he giveth thee under the sun, all the days of thy vanity; for that is thy portion in life, and in thy labour which thou ¹⁰ takest under the sun. Whatsoever thy hand findeth to do, do it with thy might; for there is no work, nor device, nor knowledge, nor wisdom, in the grave, whither thou goest.

¹¹ I returned, and saw under the sun, that the race is not to the swift, nor the battle to the strong, neither yet bread to the wise, nor yet riches to men of understanding, nor yet favour to men of skill; but time and chance happeneth ¹² to them all. For man also knoweth not his time; as the fishes that are taken in an evil net, and as the birds that are caught in the snare; so are the sons of Adam snared in an evil time, when it falleth suddenly upon them.

¹³ This wisdom have I seen also under the sun, and it ¹⁴ seemed great to me; there was a little city, and few men within it; and there came a great king against it, and en- ¹⁵ compassed it, and built great bulwarks against it; now there was found in it a poor wise man, yet he by his wisdom delivered the city; yet no man remembered that ¹⁶ same poor man. Then said I, 'Wisdom is better than 'strength; nevertheless the poor man's wisdom is despised, 'and his words are not heard.'

¹⁷ The words of wise men are heard in quiet,
More than the cry of him that ruleth among fools.
¹⁸ Wisdom is better than weapons of war;
—But one sinner destroyeth much good.
¹ Dead flies corrupt the scent of the ointment of the apothecary; so doth a little folly him that is in reputation for wisdom and honour.

A wise man's heart is at his right hand; but a fool's ² heart at his left. Yea, also, when he that is a fool walketh ³ along the way, his sense faileth, and he telleth to every one that he is a fool.

If the spirit of the ruler rise up against thee, quit not ⁴ thy place; for yielding pacifieth great offences.

There is an evil which I have seen under the sun, as an ⁵ error which proceedeth from the ruler; folly is set in great ⁶ dignity, and the rich sit in low place. I have seen servants ⁷ upon horses, and princes walking as servants upon the ground.

He that diggeth a pit will fall into it; ⁸
And whoso breaketh a hedge a serpent will bite him.
Whoso moveth a boundary-stone will be hurt by it; ⁹
He that cleaveth trees will be endangered thereby.
If the iron be blunt, and he sharpen not the edge, ¹⁰
Then must he add more strength;
But wisdom is profitable to direct.
If the serpent bite because not whispered to, ¹¹
Then there is no gain in having a tongue.
The words of a wise man's mouth are gracious; ¹²
But the lips of a fool swallow himself up.
The beginning of the words of his mouth is folly; ¹³
And the end of his talk is mischievous madness.

A fool also multiplieth words. A man knoweth not ¹⁴ what will be; and what will be after him, who can tell him? The labour of the foolish wearieth him, because he ¹⁵ knoweth not how to go to the city.

Alas for thee, O land, when thy king is a child, and thy ¹⁶ princes eat in the morning! Blessed art thou, O land, ¹⁷ whose king is the son of nobles, and thy princes eat in due season, for strength, and not for drinking's sake!

By much sloth the building decayeth, ¹⁸
And by idleness of hands the house leaketh.
A feast is made for laughter, and wine cheereth life; ¹⁹
But money answereth for all things.
Curse not the king, no, not in thy thought; ²⁰
And curse not the rich in thy bedchamber;
For a bird of the air will carry the voice,
And that which hath wings will tell the matter.

Cast thy bread seed upon the face of the waters; ¹
For thou wilt find it after many days.

2 Give a portion to seven, and also to eight;
For thou knowest not what evil will be on the earth.
3 If clouds be full of rain, they pour out on the earth;
And if a tree fall to the south, or to the north,
In the place where the tree falleth, there let it be.
4 He that observeth the wind will never sow;
And he that regardeth the clouds will never reap.
5 As thou knowest not what is the way of the wind,
How the bones grow in the child-bearing womb,
So thou knowest not the works of God who maketh all.
6 In the morning sow thy seed,
And in the evening withhold not thy hand;
For thou knowest not if this will prosper, or that,
Or whether they both will be alike good.
7 Truly the light is sweet, and pleasant it is for the eyes
8 to behold the sun. But if a man live many years, and rejoice in them all; yet let him remember the days of darkness; for they will be many. All that cometh is vanity.
9 Rejoice, O young man, in thy childhood; and let thy heart cheer thee in the days of thy youth, and walk in the ways of thy heart, and in the sight of thine eyes; but know thou, that for all these things God will bring thee
10 into judgment. Therefore remove anger from thy heart, —and put away wickedness from thy flesh; for childhood
1 and the dawn of day are vanity. Remember now thy Creator in the days of thy youth, while the evil days come not, nor the years draw nigh, when thou shalt say,
2 'I have no pleasure in them;' while yet the sun, or the light, or the moon, or the stars, be not darkened, nor the
3 clouds return after the rain; in the day when the keepers of the house shall tremble, and the strong men shall bow themselves, and the grinding women cease because they
4 are few, and those that look out of the windows be darkened, and the doors shall be shut in the streets, when the sound of the grinding is low, and a man shall be roused at the voice of the bird, and all the daughters of music
5 shall be brought low; also when they shall be afraid of that which is high, and terrors shall be in the way, and the almond blossom shall be despised, and the grasshopper shall lie heavy, and the caper-berries [or stimulants] shall fail; because man goeth to his long home, and
6 the mourners go about the streets; before the silver cord

be loosed, or the golden lamp-bowl broken, or the pitcher cracked at the fountain, or the wheel broken at the well; then will the dust return to the earth as it was; and the ⁷ spirit will return unto God who gave it.

Vanity of vanities, saith the preacher; all is vanity. ⁸ And moreover, because the preacher was wise, he still ⁹ taught the people knowledge; yea, he gave good heed, and sought out, and set in order many proverbs. The preacher ¹⁰ sought to find out acceptable words, and what had been written aright, even words of truth.

The words of the wise are as goads, and as stakes fas- ¹¹ tened by the owners of the flocks, when they are given up by a shepherd. And further, by these, my son, be admo- ¹² nished; of making many books there is no end; and much study is a weariness of the flesh.

Let us hear the conclusion of the whole matter; fear ¹³ God, and keep his commandments; for this is the whole duty of man. For God shall bring every work into judg- ¹⁴ ment, with every secret thing, whether it be good, or whether it be evil.

THE SONG OF SOLOMON.

THE SONG OF SONGS, which is Solomon's. 1
[Bride.] Let him kiss me with the kisses of his mouth; 2
[Women.] For thy love is better than wine.
Because of the savour of thy good ointments 3
Thy name is as ointment poured forth.
Therefore do the damsels love thee.
[B.] Lead me on. 4
[W.]   We will run after thee.
[B.] The king hath brought me into his chambers.
[W.] We will be glad and rejoice in thee;
We will celebrate thy love more than wine;
The upright love thee.
[B]. I am dark,— 5
[W.]   —but comely,—
[B.]   —O ye daughters of Jerusalem,
As the tents of Kedar,—
[W.]   —as the curtains of Solomon.

⁶ [B.] Look not upon me, because I am brown,
Because the sun hath burnt me.
My mother's sons were angry with me;
They made me cultivator of the vineyards;
But mine own vineyard have I not cultivated.
⁷ Tell me, O beloved of my soul, where feedest thou,
Where restest thou [thy flock] at noon,
For why should I be as one veiled by the flocks of thy
    companions?
⁸ [W.] If thou know not, O fairest of women,
Go thy way forth in the footsteps of the flock,
And feed thy kids beside the shepherds' tents.

---

⁹ [Solomon.] To the steeds of my Pharaoh-chariot,
I have compared thee, O my Love,
¹⁰ Thy cheeks are comely with rows of pearls,
Thy neck with chains of precious stones.
¹¹ [Youths.] We will make for thee strings of gold,
With studs of silver.
¹² [B.] While the king is on his supper-couch,
My spikenard shall send forth its smell.
¹³ A bunch of myrrh is my Beloved to me;
He shall lie all night betwixt my breasts.
¹⁴ A branch of cypress is my beloved to me,
In the vineyards of Ain-gedi.
¹⁵ [S.] Behold, thou art fair, my Love;
Behold, thou art fair; thou hast doves' eyes.
¹⁶ [B.] Behold, thou art fair, my Beloved,
Yea, pleasant; also our couch is green.
¹⁷ [S.] The beams of our house are of cedar, our rafters of
    fir.
¹ [B.] I am a crocus of Sharon, a lily of the valleys.
² [S.] As the lily among thorns,
So is my Love among the daughters.
³ [B.] As an apple tree among the trees of the forest,
So is my Beloved among the sons.
    I delighted in its shade and sat down;
And its fruit was sweet to my palate.
⁴ Let him bring me to the banqueting house,
And let his banner over me be love.

Do ye support me with dried grapes,   5
Do ye comfort me with apples; for I am sick for love.
His left hand shall be under my head,   6
And his right hand shall embrace me.
[S.] I charge you, O ye daughters of Jerusalem,   7
By the roes, and by the hinds of the field,
That ye stir not, nor awaken my Love, till she please.

[B.] The voice of my Beloved! behold, he cometh   8
Leaping on the mountains, skipping on the hills.
My Beloved is like a roe or a fawn of the deer.   9
    Behold, he standeth behind our wall,
He looketh through the window,
Quickly glancing through the lattice.
    My Beloved spake, and said unto me,   10
'Rise up, my Love, my fair one, and come away.
'For, lo, the winter is past, the rain is over and gone;   11
'The flowers appear on the earth;   12
'The time of singing is come,
'And the voice of the turtle-dove is heard in our land;
'The fig tree ripeneth its green figs,   13
'And the vines in flower give their smell.
    'Rise up, my Love, my fair one, and come away.
'O my dove, in the clefts of the rock,   14
'In the secret places of the steep roads,
'Let me see thy countenance, let me hear thy voice;
'For sweet is thy voice, and thy countenance comely.
'Seize for us the foxes, the little foxes,   15
'That rob the vines, when our vines are in flower.'
    My Beloved is mine, and I am his;   16
He feedeth his flocks among the lilies,
Till the day become cool, and the shadows flee away.   17
Turn, and be thou, my Beloved, like a roe
Or a fawn of the deer on the hills of the Rugged Country.—

[B.] By night on my bed I sought my soul's beloved;   1
I sought him, but I found him not.
I will rise now, and go about the city in the streets,   2
And in the broad ways I will seek my soul's beloved;
I sought him, but I found him not.
The guards that go about the city found me.   3

'Have ye seen' [I said] 'my soul's beloved?'
4 It was but a little that I passed from them,
When I found my soul's beloved.
I held him, and I would not let him go,
Until I had brought him into my mother's house,
And into the chamber of her that conceived me.
5 [S.] I charge you, O daughters of Jerusalem,
By the roes, and by the hinds of the field,
That ye stir not, nor awaken my Love, till she please.

---

6 [B.] Who is this that cometh up out of the desert,
As a pillar of smoke, scattering scent of myrrh,
And incense of all the powders of the merchant?
7 [W.] Behold his bed, it is Solomon's;
Sixty warriors are about it, of the warriors of Israel.
8 They all hold swords, being expert in war;
The sword of each is on his thigh for fear in the night.
9   King Solomon hath made a litter-bed
Of the wood of Lebanon.
10 He made its pillars of silver, its bottom of gold;
Its cushion is of purple, its middle is paved
With love, for the daughters of Jerusalem.
11 [B.] Go, ye daughters of Zion, and see king Solomon,
With the crown wherewith his mother crowned him
—On his wedding day, and on the day of his heart's joy.
1 [S.] Lo, thou art fair, my Love; lo, thou art fair;
Thou hast doves' eyes behind thy veil.
Thy hair is as a flock of goats lying on mount Gilead;
2 Thy teeth as a shorn flock brought up from washing,
All of which bear twins, and not one of them is barren.
3   Thy lips are like a thread of scarlet,
And thy speech is comely;
Thy cheeks like pieces of a pomegranate behind thy veil.
4 Thy neck is like David's tower built for an armoury;
On it hang a thousand bucklers, all shields of warriors.
5   Thy two breasts are like two young fawns,
Twins of the roe which feed among the lilies.
6 Till the day become cool, and the shadows flee away,
I will get me to the mountain of myrrh,
And to the hill of frankincense.

Thou art all fair, my Love; there is no spot in thee.

[S.] With me from Lebanon, my bride,
Come with me from Lebanon;
Look about from the top of Amana,
From the top of Senir and Hermon,
From the lions' dens, from the hills of the leopards.
    Thou hast ravished my heart, my sister, my bride;
Thou hast ravished my heart with one of thine eyes,
With one chain of thy necklace.
How fair is thy love, my sister, my bride!
How much better is thy love than wine!
And the smell of thine ointments than all spices!
Thy lips, O my bride, drop as the honeycomb;
Honey and milk are under thy tongue;
And the smell of thy garments is as the smell of Leb-
    anon.
A garden locked up is my sister, my bride;
A well locked up, a fountain sealed.
Thy plants are an orchard of pomegranates,
With precious fruits; camphire, with spikenard,
Spikenard and saffron; sweet cane and cinnamon,
With all trees of frankincense;
Myrrh and aloes, with all the chief spices;
A garden fountain, a well of living waters,
And streams from Lebanon.
[B.] Awake, O north wind; and come, thou south wind;
Blow on my garden, that its spices may flow out.
Let my Beloved come into his garden,
And eat its precious fruits.
[S.] I am come into my garden, my sister, my bride.
I have gathered my myrrh with my spice;
I have eaten my honeycomb with my honey;
I have drunk my wine with my milk.
Eat, O friends, drink; yea, drink freely, beloved ones.

[B.] I am asleep, but my heart waketh.
It is the voice of my Beloved, who knocketh, [saying,]
' Open to me, my sister, my Love, my dove, my undefiled;
' For my head is filled with dew,
' And my locks with the drops of the night.'
I have put off my under coat; how shall I clothe myself?

I have washed my feet; how shall I defile them?
4 My Beloved put in his hand by the opening,
   And my bowels were moved for him.
5   I rose up to open to my Beloved;
   And my hands dropped myrrh,
   And my fingers liquid myrrh, on the handles of the lock.
6 I opened to my Beloved; but my Beloved was gone;
   He had passed by; my soul failed when he spake.
.. I sought him, but I could not find him;
   I called to him, but he gave me no answer.
7 The guards that went about the city found me,
   They smote me, they wounded me;
   The keepers of the walls took my veil from me.
8 I charge you, O daughters of Jerusalem,
   If ye find my Beloved, that ye tell him, that I am sick for love.
9 [W.] What is thy Beloved more than another beloved,
   O fairest of women?
   What is thy Beloved more than another beloved,
   That thou so chargest us?
10 [B.] My Beloved is white and ruddy,
   A standard bearer among ten thousand.
11 His head is as the most fine gold,
   His locks are flowing, and black as a raven.
12 His eyes are as doves by the rivers of waters,
   Washed with milk, and fixed in their settings;
13 His cheeks as beds of spices, as mounds of scented herbs;
   His lips like lilies, dropping liquid myrrh;
14 His hands are as gold rings set with chrysolite;
   His body as wrought ivory overlaid with sapphires;
15 His legs as pillars of marble set on bases of gold.
   His countenance is as Lebanon, excellent as cedars;
16 His mouth is most sweet; yea, he is all lovely.
   This is my Beloved, and this is my friend,
-- O daughters of Jerusalem.
1 [W.] Where went thy Beloved, O fairest of women?
   Where turned thy Beloved, that we seek him with thee?
2 [B.] My Beloved is gone to his garden, to the spice beds,
   To feed his flock in the gardens, and to gather lilies.
3   I am my Beloved's, and my Beloved is mine;
   He feedeth his flock among the lilies.

[S.] Thou art beautiful, O my Love, as Tirzah, 4
Comely as Jerusalem, terrible as a host with banners.
Turn away thine eyes from me, for they excite me. 5
Thy hair is as a flock of goats lying upon Gilead;
Thy teeth are as a flock of sheep brought up from washing, 6
All of which bear twins, and none of them are barren.
As pieces of pomegranate are thy cheeks behind thy veil. 7
There are sixty queens, and eighty concubines, 8
And damsels without number.
But my dove, my undefiled is but one; 9
She is the only one of her mother,
She is the chosen one of her that bare her.
The daughters see her, and they call her blessed;
The queens and concubines, and they praise her, [Saying,]
'Who is she that looketh forth as the dawn, 10
'Fair as the moon, clear as the sunshine,
'And terrible as a host with banners?'
I went down into the nut-garden 11
To see the fruits of the valley,
To see the vine flourish, and the pomegranates bud.
I know not how, but my soul set me 12
Among the chariots of my people's nobles.
[Y.] Return, return, O Shulamite; 13
Return, return, that we may look upon thee.
[W.] What will ye see in the Shulamite?
[Y.] As it were the dance of two companies. —

[W.] How fair are thy feet in shoes, O prince's daughter! 1
The joints of thy thighs are like jewels,
The work of an artist's hands.
Thy navel is a round goblet, that wanteth not spiced wine; 2
Thy belly is a heap of wheat set about with lilies;
Thy two breasts are like two fawns, twins of the roe. 3
   Thy neck is as a tower of ivory; 4
Thine eyes like the pools in Heshbon,
By the Beth-rabbim gate;
Thy nose is as the tower of Lebanon
Which looketh toward Damascus.
Thy head upon thee is like Carmel, 5
And the locks of thy head like purple thread;
The king is bound in the curls.
[S.] How fair and how pleasant art thou, O Love, for delights! 6

7 This thy stature is like to a palm tree,
  And thy breasts to bunches of dates.
8 I said, 'I will go up to the palm tree,
  'I will take hold of its boughs.'
  Now also thy breasts shall be as clusters of the vine,
  And the smell of thy nose like apples;
9 And the roof of thy mouth like the best wine.
  [B.] Let it flow down for my Beloved smoothly,
  Gliding through the lips of those that are sleepy.
10 I am my Beloved's, and his desire is toward me.
11 Come, my Beloved, let us go forth into the field;
  Let us lodge in the villages.
12 Let us get up early to the vineyards;
  Let us see if the vine flourish,
  If the vine blossoms open, and the pomegranates bud.
  There will I give thee my loves.
13 The mandrakes give a smell at our doors;
—All the best, new and old, I lay up for thee, my Beloved.
1 O that thou wert as my brother,
  Who sucked the breasts of my mother!
  When I found thee without, I would kiss thee;
  Yet I should not be despised.
2 I would lead thee, and bring thee to my mother's house;
  She would teach me to make thee to drink wine,
  Spiced with the juice of my pomegranate.
3 His left hand should be under my head,
  And his right hand should embrace me.
4 [S.] I charge you, O daughters of Jerusalem,
  That ye stir not, nor awaken my Love, until she please.

5 [W.] Who is this that cometh up from the desert,
  Leaning upon her Beloved?
  [S.] I waked thee up under the apple tree;
  There thy mother gave thee in pledge;
  There she that bare thee gave thee in pledge.
6 [B.] Set me as a seal on thy heart, as a seal on thine arm;
  For love is strong as death, jealousy cruel as hell;
  Its flames are flames of fire, as the lightning of Jah.
7 [S.] Many waters cannot quench love,
  Neither can the floods drown it.
  If a man would give all the wealth of his house,
  In the matter of love, it would be utterly despised.

[Brother.] We have a little sister, and she hath no breasts; 8
What shall we do for our sister
In the day when she shall be spoken for?
[Br.] If she be a wall, we will build on her a tower of silver; 9
And if a door, we will close her with a board of cedar.
[B.] I am a wall, and my breasts like towers; 10
Then was I in his eyes as one that found favour.
[Brother.] Solomon hath a vineyard at Baal-hamon; 11
He hath let out the vineyard unto cultivators;
Each for its fruit bringeth a thousand pieces of silver.
[B.] My vineyard, which is mine, is before me; 12
Thou, O Solomon, shalt have the thousand,
And those that cultivate its fruit two hundred.
[S.] O thou that dwellest in the gardens, 13
Companions are listening to thy voice; let me hear it.
[B.] Hasten, my Beloved, and be thou like a roe 14
Or a fawn of the deer on the mountains of spices.

ISAIAH.

THE VISION OF ISAIAH the son of Amoz, which he saw 1 concerning Judah and Jerusalem, in the days of Uzziah, Jotham, Ahaz, and Hezekiah, kings of Judah. Hear, O heavens, and give ear, O earth; for Jehovah 2 speaketh. I have nourished and brought up children, and they have rebelled against me. The ox knoweth his owner, 3 and the ass his master's crib; but Israel doth not know, my people doth not consider. Ah sinful nation, a people 4 laden with iniquity, a seed of evil doers, children that are corrupters; they have forsaken Jehovah; they have despised the Holy One of Israel, they have gone away backward.

Why should ye be stricken any more? Ye revolt more 5 and more; the whole head is sick, and the whole heart faint. From the sole of the foot even unto the head there 6 is no soundness in it; but wounds, and bruises, and fresh sores; they have not been closed, nor bound up, nor softened with oil. Your country is desolate, your cities 7 are burned with fire; your land, strangers devour it in your presence, and it is desolate, as overthrown by strangers. And the daughter of Zion is left as a booth in a 8

vineyard, as a lodge in a cucumber-garden, as a besieged
9 city. Unless Jehovah of hosts had left to us a small remnant, we should have been as Sodom, and we should have been like unto Gomorrah.

10 Hear the word of Jehovah, ye rulers of Sodom; give ear
11 to the law of our God, ye people of Gomorrah. For what is the multitude of your sacrifices unto me? saith Jehovah. I am full of burnt offerings of rams, and the fat of fed beasts; and I delight not in the blood of bullocks, or lambs,
12 or he-goats. When ye come to appear before me, who hath required this at your hand, to tread down my courts?
13 Bring no more vain meal offerings; incense is an abomination to me; the new moon days and sabbaths, the calling of convocations, I cannot endure; it is iniquity, even the
14 day of restraint [from work]. Your new moon days and your appointed feasts my soul hateth; they are a trouble to
15 me; I am weary to bear them. And when ye spread forth your hands, I will hide mine eyes from you; yea, when ye make many prayers, I will not hear; your hands are full of
16 blood. Wash yourselves, make you clean; put away the evil of your doings from before mine eyes; cease to do
17 evil, learn to do well; seek justice, relieve the oppressed, do justice to the fatherless, plead for the widow.

18 Come now, and let us reason together, saith Jehovah; though your sins be as scarlet, they shall be as white as snow; though they be red like crimson, they shall be as
19 wool. If ye be willing and obedient, ye shall eat the good
20 of the land; but if ye refuse and rebel, ye shall be eaten by the sword; for the mouth of Jehovah hath spoken it.
21 How is the faithful city become a harlot! It was full of justice; righteousness lodged in it; but now mur-
22 derers. Thy silver is become dross, thy wine mixed with
23 water. Thy princes are rebellious, and companions of thieves; every one loveth bribes, and followeth after rewards, they do not do justice to the fatherless, neither doth
24 the cause of the widow come unto them. Therefore the Lord Jehovah of hosts, the Mighty One of Israel, hath said it, Ah, I will ease myself of mine adversaries, and take
25 vengeance on mine enemies; and I will turn my hand upon thee, and purely purge away thy dross, and take away
26 all thy mixed metal; and I will bring back thy judges as at first, and thy counsellors as at the beginning; afterward

thou shalt be called, The city of righteousness, the faithful city. Zion shall be redeemed by justice, and those that ²⁷ are brought back to her by righteousness. But destruction ²⁸ shall be on the transgressors and the sinners together, and they that forsake Jehovah shall be consumed. For they ²⁹ shall be ashamed of the trees which ye have desired, and ye shall blush for the gardens that ye have chosen. For ye shall be as a tree whose leaf fadeth, and as a ³⁰ garden that hath no water. And the strong man shall ³¹ be as tow, and his work as a spark, and they shall both burn together, and none shall quench them.

(The word that Isaiah the son of Amoz saw concerning 1 Judah and Jerusalem. And it shall come to pass in the 2 last days, that the mountain of the House of Jehovah shall be established on the top of the mountains, and shall be exalted above the hills; and all the nations shall flow unto it. And many peoples shall go, and say, 'Come ye, and 3 'let us go up to the mountain of Jehovah, to the House 'of the God of Jacob; and he will teach us his ways, and 'we will walk in his paths; for out of Zion shall go forth 'the Law, and the word of Jehovah from Jerusalem.' And he will judge among the nations, and will rebuke 4 many peoples; and they shall beat their swords into plowshares, and their spears into pruning-hooks; nation shall not lift up sword against nation, neither shall they learn war any more.)

O house of Jacob, come ye, and let us walk in the light 5 of Jehovah.

For thou hast forsaken thy people the house of Jacob, 6 because they are full of the East, and are observers of clouds like the Philistines, and they join hands with the children of foreigners. Their land is also full of silver 7 and gold, neither is there any end of their treasures; and their land is full of horses, neither is there any end of their chariots. Their land is also full of idols; they worship the 8 work of their own hands, that which their own fingers have made. And the sons of Adam will bow down, and 9 man be humbled; but thou wilt not forgive them.

Enter into the rock, and hide thee in the dust, from 10 before the terror of Jehovah, and from the glory of his majesty. The lofty looks of the sons of Adam shall be 11 humbled, and the haughtiness of men shall be bowed down, and Jehovah alone will be exalted in that day.

12 For Jehovah of hosts will have a day upon every one that is proud and lofty, and upon every one that is lifted
13 up; and he shall be humbled; and upon all the cedars of Lebanon, that are high and lifted up, and upon all the
14 oaks of Bashan, and upon all the high mountains, and upon
15 all the hills that are lifted up, and upon every high tower,
16 and upon every fenced wall, and upon all ships of Tarshish,
17 and upon all things pleasant to sight. And the loftiness of the sons of Adam shall be bowed down, and the haughtiness of men shall be humbled; and Jehovah alone will be exalted in that day.
18 And the idols he will utterly abolish. And men shall
19 go into the holes of the rocks, and into the caves in the dust, from before the terror of Jehovah, and from the glory
20 of his majesty, when he ariseth to terrify the earth. In that day men shall cast their idols of silver, and their idols of gold, which they made each for himself to worship, to
21 the moles and to the bats; to go into the clefts of the rocks, and into the cracks in the cliffs, from before the terror of Jehovah, and from the glory of his majesty, when he ariseth to terrify the earth.
22 Cease ye from [trusting in] man, whose breath is in his nostrils; for wherein is such a one to be esteemed?

1 For, behold, the Lord, Jehovah of hosts, doth take away from Jerusalem and from Judah the stay and the staff, the
2 whole stay of bread, and the whole stay of water, the warrior, and the man of war, the judge, and the prophet, and the
3 diviner, and the elder, the captain of fifty, and the man of high station, and the counsellor, and the skilful workman,
4 and him that understandeth enchantments. And I will give children to be their princes, and babes shall rule over
5 them. And the people shall be oppressed, every one by the other, and every one by his neighbour; the young man will be proud against the elder, and the base against the
6 honourable. When a man shall take hold of his brother in the house of his father, [saying,] 'Thou hast clothing, 'be thou our ruler, and let this ruin be under thy hand;'
7 in that day shall he swear, saying, 'I will not be a healer; 'for in my house is neither bread nor clothing; make me
8 'not a ruler of the people.' For Jerusalem is ruined, and Judah is fallen; because their tongue and their doings are against Jehovah, in rebellion against the eyes of his glory.

The strangeness of their countenance doth witness against ⁹ them; and they declare their sin as Sodom, they hide it not. Woe unto their soul! for they have earned evil to themselves. Say ye to the righteous man, that it shall be well ¹⁰ with him; for they shall eat the fruit of their doings. Woe unto the wicked! it shall be ill with him; for the ¹¹ reward of his hands shall be given him.

As for my people, babes are their oppressors, and women ¹² rule over them. O my people, they that guide thee cause thee to err, and destroy the way of thy paths. Jehovah ¹³ standeth up to plead, and standeth to judge the peoples. Jehovah will enter into judgment with the elders of his ¹⁴ people, and the princes thereof; for ye have wasted the vineyard; the plunder of the poor is in your houses. What mean ye that ye crush my people, and grind the ¹⁵ faces of the poor? the Lord Jehovah of hosts hath said it.

Moreover Jehovah saith, Because the daughters of Zion ¹⁶ are haughty, and walk with stretched-forth necks and wanton eyes, walking and mincing as they go, and wearing ankle-rings at their feet; therefore the Lord will smite with ¹⁷ a scab the crown of the head of the daughters of Zion, and Jehovah will uncover their nakedness. In that day the ¹⁸ Lord will take away the bravery of their ankle-rings, and their little suns, and their little moons, the ear-drops, and ¹⁹ the bracelets, and the veils, the head-dresses, and the ankle- ²⁰ chains, and the girdles, and the scent-boxes, and the amulets, the rings, and nose jewels, the holiday clothes, and the ²¹ mantles, and the handkerchiefs, and the purses, the mirrors, ²² and the linen garments, and the turbans, and the shawls. ²³ And it shall come to pass, that instead of a sweet smell ²⁴ there shall be rottenness; and instead of a girdle a rope; and instead of well-set hair baldness; and instead of a stomacher a girding of sackcloth; and a branded mark instead of beauty. Thy men [O Zion] shall fall by the sword, ²⁵ and thy warriors in the war. And her doorways shall sigh ²⁶ and mourn; and she shall sit desolate upon the ground.

And in that day seven women shall take hold of one ¹ man, saying, 'We will eat our own bread, and wear our 'own apparel; only let us be called by thy name, to take 'away our reproach.'

(In that day shall the Branch of Jehovah be beautiful and ² glorious, and the fruit of the earth shall be excellent and

3 comely for them that are escaped of Israel. And it shall come to pass, that he that was left in Zion, and he that remained in Jerusalem, shall be called holy, even every 4 one that is written among the living in Jerusalem; when the Lord shall have washed away the filth of the daughters of Zion, and shall have cleansed the bloodshed of Jerusalem from the midst thereof by the spirit of judgment, 5 and by the spirit of burning. Then Jehovah will create upon every dwelling-place of mount Zion, and upon her convocations, a cloud by day, and smoke and the shining of a flaming fire by night; for the Glory shall be a cover- 6 ing upon all. And there shall be a Tabernacle for shade 7 in the daytime from the heat, and for a place of refuge, —and for a covert from storm and from rain.)

1 Now LET ME SING to my beloved a song of love touching his vineyard. My beloved hath a vineyard on a very 2 fruitful hill. And he raked it, and gathered out its stones, and planted it with the choicest vines, and built a tower in the midst of it, and also hollowed out a winepress therein. And he looked that it should bring forth grapes, and it 3 brought forth wild berries. And now, O inhabitants of Jerusalem, and men of Judah, judge, I pray you, betwixt 4 me and my vineyard. What could have been done more to my vineyard, that I have not done in it? wherefore, when I looked that it should bring forth grapes, brought it forth 5 wild berries? And now let me tell you what I will do to my vineyard. I will take away its hedge, and it shall be wasted; I will break down its wall, and it shall be trodden 6 down. And I will make it a waste; and it shall not be pruned, nor digged; but there shall come up briars and thorns; I will also command the clouds that they rain no 7 rain upon it. For the vineyard of Jehovah of hosts is the house of Israel, and the men of Judah the plant of his delight; and he looked for justice, but behold bloodshed; for righteousness, but behold a cry.

8 Woe unto them that join house to house, that lay field to field, till there be no place, and ye dwell alone in the 9 midst of the land! Jehovah of hosts [hath said] in mine ears, Of a truth many houses shall be desolate, even those 10 that are great and fair, without inhabitant. Yea, ten acres of vineyard shall yield only a Bath [or seven gallons],

and the seed of a Homer shall yield only an Ephah [or a tenth part].

Woe unto them that rise up early in the morning, that [11] they may follow strong drink; that continue until twilight, till wine inflame them; and the harp, and the psaltery, [12] the timbrel, and the pipe, and wine, are in their drinking feasts; but they regard not the work of Jehovah, neither consider the doings of his hands.

Therefore my people are gone into captivity, because [13] they have no knowledge; and their honourable men are famished, and their multitude dried up with thirst. Therefore [14] Hell hath enlarged herself, and hath opened her mouth without measure; and their glory, and their multitude, and their tumult, shall go down and rejoice in her. And the sons of Adam shall be brought down, and man [15] shall be humbled, and the eyes of the lofty shall be humbled; but Jehovah of hosts shall be exalted in justice, [16] and God that is holy shall be sanctified in righteousness. Then shall the lambs feed as in their own pasture, and in [17] the deserted places of the fat ones shall strangers eat.

Woe unto them that draw iniquity with cords of vanity, [18] and sin as it were with a cart rope; that say, 'Let Him [19] 'make speed, and hasten his work, so that we may see 'it. And let the counsel of the Holy One of Israel draw 'nigh and come, that we may know it!'

Woe unto them that call evil good, and good evil; that [20] put darkness for light, and light for darkness; that put bitter for sweet, and sweet for bitter! Woe unto them [21] that are wise in their own eyes, and prudent in their own sight! Woe unto them that are mighty to drink wine, [22] and men of valour to mingle strong drink; who acquit the [23] wicked for the sake of a bribe, and take away the righteousness of the righteous from him! Therefore as the [24] tongue of the fire devoureth the stubble, and the flame consumeth the dry grass, so their root shall be as rottenness, and their blossom shall go up as dust; because they have cast away the Law of Jehovah of hosts, and have despised the word of the Holy One of Israel. Therefore [25] is the anger of Jehovah kindled against his people, and he hath stretched forth his hand against them, and hath smitten them. And the mountains tremble, and their carcases are as dung in the midst of the streets.

Because of all this his anger is not turned away, but his hand is stretched out still.

26 And he will lift up an ensign to the nations from far, and will whistle for them from the end of the earth; and, 27 behold, they will come with speed swiftly. None shall be weary nor stumble among them; none shall slumber nor sleep; neither shall the girdle of their loins be loosed, nor 28 the latchet of their shoes be broken. Their arrows are sharp, and all their bows bent; their horses' hoofs are accounted like flint, and their chariot wheels like a whirl- 29 wind. Their roaring will be like a lioness, they will roar like young lions; yea, they will rage, and lay hold of the prey, and will carry it away safe, and none shall deliver 30 it. And in that day they shall rage against them like the raging of the sea; and if one look unto the land, behold darkness of distress, and the light is darkened in the —heavy clouds thereof.

6 1 IN THE YEAR that king Uzziah died [B.C. 750], then I saw the Lord sitting upon a throne, high and lifted up, 2 and the train of his garments filled the temple. Above it stood the Seraphs [or fiery serpents]. Each one had six wings; with twain he covered his face, and with twain he 3 covered his feet, and with twain he did fly. And one cried to the other, and said,

'Holy, holy, holy, is Jehovah of hosts;
'The whole earth is full of his glory.'

4 And the foundations of the threshold were moved at the voice of him that cried, and the House was filled with 5 smoke. Then said I, 'Woe is me! for I am undone; be-
'cause I am a man of unclean lips, and I dwell in the
'midst of a people of unclean lips, for mine eyes have seen
6 'the King, Jehovah of hosts.' Then one of the Seraphs flew to me, having a live coal in his hand, which he had 7 taken with the tongs from off the altar. And he made it touch my mouth, and said, 'Lo, this hath touched thy 'lips; and thine iniquity is taken away, and thy sin for-
8 'given.' Also I heard the voice of the Lord, saying, 'Whom shall I send, and who will go for us?' Then said 9 I, 'Here am I; send me.' And he said, 'Go, and tell this 'people, Ye hear indeed, but understand not; and ye see 10 'indeed, but perceive not. Make the heart of this people 'fat, and make their ears heavy, and close up their eyes;

'lest they see with their eyes, and hear with their ears, and understand with their heart, and be turned, and be healed.' Then said I, 'Lord, how long?' And he answered, 'Until the cities be wasted without inhabitant, and the houses without man, and the land be wasted with desolation, and Jehovah have removed the men far away, and there be a great forsaking in the midst of the land. But there shall yet be in it a tenth, and it shall return, and shall be for a kindling. As a teil tree, or as an oak, which when they cast their leaves, have an abiding stock [the misletoe] on them; so the holy seed shall be its abiding stock.'

AND IT CAME to pass in the days of Ahaz the son of Jotham, the son of Uzziah, king of Judah, that Rezin the king of Syria, and Pekah the son of Remaliah, king of Israel, went up toward Jerusalem to war against it, but could not prevail against it. And it was told to the house of David, saying, 'Syria is encamped with Ephraim.' And his heart was shaken, and the heart of his people, as the trees of the forest are shaken before the wind.

Then said Jehovah to Isaiah, 'Go forth now to meet Ahaz, thou, and Shearjashub thy son, at the end of the conduit of the Upper Pool in the highway of the fuller's field; and say to him, Take heed, and be quiet; fear not, neither be fainthearted because of the two tails of these smoking firebrands, at the fierce anger of Rezin and Syria, and of the son of Remaliah. Because Syria hath taken evil counsel against thee with Ephraim, and the son of Remaliah, saying, 'Let us go up against Judah, and vex it, and let us make a breach therein for us, and set a king in the midst of it, even the son of Tabeal;' thus said the Lord Jehovah, It shall not stand, neither shall it come to pass. For as the head of Syria is Damascus, and as the head of Damascus is Rezin; so within sixty and five years shall Ephraim be broken, that it be not a people. But as the head of Ephraim is Samaria, and as the head of Samaria is Remaliah's son; so if ye will not believe, surely ye shall not be established.

Moreover Jehovah spake again to Ahaz, saying, 'Ask unto thee a sign from Jehovah thy God; ask it either in the depth, or in the height above.' But Ahaz said, 'I will not ask, neither will I try Jehovah.' And he said,

Hear ye now, O house of David; is it a small thing for you
14 to weary men, but will ye weary my God also? Therefore the Lord himself shall give you a sign; Behold, the young woman shall conceive, and bear a son, and shall
15 call his name Immanuel [or God is with us]. Curds and honey shall he eat, that he may know to refuse the evil,
16 and choose the good. For before the child shall know to refuse the evil, and to choose the good, the land by whose two kings thou art vexed shall be made desolate.
17 Jehovah will bring upon thee, and upon thy people, and upon thy father's house, days that have not come, from the day that Ephraim departed from Judah; even
18 the king of Assyria. And it shall come to pass in that day, that Jehovah will whistle for the fly that is in the uttermost part of the rivers of Egypt, and for the bee that
19 is in the land of Assyria. And they shall come, and shall rest all of them in the desolate valleys, and in the holes of the rocks, and upon all thorn bushes, and upon all pas-
20 tures. In the same day shall the Lord shave with a razor that is hired, namely, by them beyond the River [Euphrates], by the king of Assyria, the head, and the hair of
21 the feet; and it shall also cut off the beard. And it shall come to pass in that day, that a man shall nourish a young
22 cow, and two sheep; and it shall come to pass, from the abundance of milk that they shall give that he shall eat curds; for curds and honey shall every one eat that is left
23 in the land. And it shall come to pass in that day, that every place shall be, where there were a thousand vines worth a thousand pieces of silver, shall even be for briers
24 and thorns. With arrows and with bows shall men come thither; because all the land shall be briers and thorns.
25 But on all hills that shall be digged with the spade, there shall not come thither the fear of briers and thorns; but it shall be for the sending forth of oxen, and for a sheep
2 and goat walk.
1 Moreover Jehovah said to me, 'Take to thee a great 'tablet, and write on it with a man's pen concerning
2 'Maher-shalal Hash-baz.' And I took to me faithful witnesses to record, Uriah the priest, and Zechariah the son of
3 Jeberechiah. And I went in unto the prophetess; and she conceived, and bare a son. Then said Jehovah to me, 'Call his name Maher-shalal Hash-baz [or Spoil hasteneth,

'Prey speedeth]. For before the child shall have know- 4
'ledge to cry, "My father, and my mother," the riches of
'Damascus and the spoil of Samaria shall be taken away
'in the face of the king of Assyria.'

And Jehovah spake to me again, saying, Forasmuch as 5
this people refuseth the waters of the Siloah that go softly, 6
and rejoiceth in Rezin and in Remaliah's son; now there- 7
fore, behold, the Lord bringeth up upon them the waters
of the River [Euphrates], strong and many, even the king
of Assyria, and all his glory. And it shall come up over
all its channels, and go over all its banks. And it shall 8
pass through Judah; it shall overflow and go over, it shall
reach even to the neck; and the stretching out of its wings
shall fill the breadth of thy land, O Immanuel [or God is
with us].

Do your worst, O ye peoples, but ye shall be broken in 9
pieces. And give ear, all ye of far countries; gird yourselves, but ye shall be broken in pieces; gird yourselves,
but ye shall be broken in pieces. Take counsel together, 10
but it shall come to nought; speak the word, but it shall
not stand; for—God is with us.

For Jehovah spake thus to me with a strong hand, and 11
instructed me that I should not walk in the way of this
people, saying, Say ye not, 'There is a confederacy.' Of 12
all them of whom this people shall say, 'There is a con-
'federacy;' neither fear ye their fear, nor be in dread.
Sanctify Jehovah of hosts himself; and let him be your 13
fear, and let him be your dread; and he shall be for a 14
Sanctuary. But he shall be for a stone to strike against,
and for a stumbling-block to both the houses of Israel, for
a trap and for a snare to the inhabitants of Jerusalem.
And many among them shall stumble, and fall, and be 15
broken, and be ensnared, and be taken.

Bind up the testimony, set a seal upon the law among 16
my disciples. And I will wait upon Jehovah, who hideth 17
his face from the house of Jacob, and I will look for him.
Behold, I and the children whom Jehovah hath given me, 18
are for signs and for wonders in Israel from Jehovah of
hosts, who dwelleth on mount Zion. And when they shall 19
say to you, 'Seek to them that have speaking bottles [or
'the ventriloquists], and to wizards that chirp, and that
'mutter;' should not a people seek unto their God on be-

20 half of the living ? [Should they seek] unto the dead for the law and for the testimony ? If they speak not according
21 to this word, it is because light dawneth not on them. And they shall pass through it, distressed and hungry. And it shall come to pass, that when they shall be hungry, they shall fret themselves, and curse their king and their God,
22 and look upward. And they shall look to the earth ; and behold trouble and darkness, dimness of anguish ; and
1 they shall be driven into darkness. Nevertheless the dimness shall not be such as was her vexation, when at the first He lightly afflicted the land of Zebulun and the land of Naphtali, and afterward did more grievously afflict the land by the way of the Sea, and that beyond the Jordan, and Galilee [or the Circle] of the Nations.
2 The people that walked in darkness have seen a great light ; they that dwell in the land of the shadow of death,
3 upon them hath the light shined. Thou hast multiplied the nation, and increased its joy. They joy before thee according to the joy in harvest, and as men rejoice when
4 they divide the spoil. For thou hast broken the yoke of its burden, and the staff on its shoulder, the rod of its
5 oppressor, as in the day of Midian. For every soldier's shoe is muddied in the confusion, and his garments are rolled in blood ; and this shall be with burning and fuel
6 of fire. For unto us a child is born, unto us a son hath been given [probably Hezekiah's son]; and the government shall be upon his shoulder ; and his name shall be called Wonderful, Counsellor, Mighty God, Everlasting Father, Prince of
7 Peace. To the greatness of his government and to peace there shall be no end, upon the throne of David, and upon his kingdom, to order it, and to establish it with justice, and with righteousness from henceforth, even for ever. The jealousy of Jehovah of hosts will perform this.
8 THE LORD SENT A WORD unto Jacob, and it hath fallen
9 upon Israel. And all the people shall know, even Ephraim and the inhabitant of Samaria, for their pride and stout-
10 ness of heart in saying, 'The bricks are fallen down, but 'we will build with hewn stones ; the sycamores are cut
11 'down, but we will change them for cedars.' But Jehovah will set up the enmity of Rezin against him, and will arm
12 his enemies, the Syrians before, and the Philistines behind ; and they shall devour Israel with open mouth.

Because of all this his anger is not turned away, but his hand is stretched out still.

For the people turneth not to him that smiteth them, ¹³ neither do they seek Jehovah of hosts. Therefore Jehovah ¹⁴ will cut off from Israel head and tail, palm-branch and bulrush, in one day. The elder and the man of high station, ¹⁵ he is the head; and the prophet that teacheth lies, he is the tail. For the guides of this people cause them to err; ¹⁶ and they that are guided by them are destroyed. There- ¹⁷ fore the Lord will have no joy in their young men, neither will have pity on their fatherless and widows; for every one is ungodly and an evil-doer, and every mouth speaketh folly.

Because of all this his anger is not turned away, but his hand is stretched out still.

For wickedness burneth as the fire; it shall devour ¹⁸ the briers and thorns, and shall kindle in the thickets of the forest, and the rising of the smoke shall curl upwards. Through the wrath of Jehovah of hosts is the land ¹⁹ scorched, and the people shall be as the fuel of the fire; no man shall spare his brother. And he shall snatch on ²⁰ the right hand, and be hungry; and he shall eat on the left hand, and they shall not be satisfied; they shall eat every man the flesh of his own arm; Manasseh that of ²¹ Ephraim; and Ephraim that of Manasseh; and both together shall be against Judah.

Because of all this his anger is not turned away, but his hand is stretched out still. | 10

Woe unto them that decree unrighteous decrees, and ¹ that write misery by what they write; to turn aside judg- ² ment from the needy, and to take away justice from the poor of my people, that widows may be their prey, and that they may rob the fatherless! And what will ye do in the ³ day of visitation, and in the desolation which shall come from far? To whom will ye flee for help? and where will ye leave your wealth? Without me they shall bow down ⁴ among the prisoners, and they shall fall among the slain.

Because of all this his anger is not turned away, but his hand is stretched out still.

WOE UNTO THE ASSYRIAN, the rod of mine anger; and ⁵ the staff in their hand is mine indignation. I will send ⁶ him against an ungodly nation, and over the people of

my wrath will I give him a charge, to take the spoil, and to take the prey, and to tread them down like the mire of
⁷ the streets. Howbeit he meaneth not so, neither doth his heart so purpose; but it is in his heart to destroy and to
⁸ cut off nations not a few. For he saith, 'Are not my
⁹ 'princes altogether kings? Is not Calno as Carchemish? is 'not Hamath as Arpad? is not Samaria as Damascus?
¹⁰ 'Since my hand hath had to do with the kingdoms of idols, 'and of graven images worse than those of Jerusalem and
¹¹ 'Samaria; shall I not, as I have done to Samaria and her 'idols, so do to Jerusalem and her images?'
¹² Therefore it shall come to pass, that when the Lord hath performed his whole work on mount Zion and on Jerusalem, I will punish the fruit of the stout heart of the
¹³ king of Assyria, and the glory of his high looks. For he said, 'By the strength of my hand I have done it, and by 'my wisdom; for I am prudent. And I have removed the 'boundaries of the peoples, and have robbed their treasures, 'and I have put down the inhabitants like a valiant man.
¹⁴ 'And my hand hath found as a nest the riches of the 'peoples. And as one gathereth eggs that are left, have I 'gathered all the earth; and there was none that moved 'the wing, or opened the mouth or chirped.'
¹⁵ Shall the axe boast itself against him that heweth therewith? or shall the saw magnify itself against him that moveth it? as if the rod could move itself against them that lift it up, or as if the staff could be lifted up if it were not
¹⁶ wood. Therefore will the Lord, the Lord of hosts, send among his fat ones leanness; and for his glory he will
¹⁷ kindle a burning like the burning of a fire. And the Light of Israel shall be for a fire, and his Holy One for a flame; and it shall burn and devour his thorns and his briers in
¹⁸ one day; and the glory of his forest, and of his fruitful field, both soul and body shall it consume; and they shall be as
¹⁹ when a sick man fainteth. And the rest of the trees of his forest shall be few, that a child may take account of them.
²⁰ And it shall come to pass in that day, that the remnant of Israel, and such as are escaped of the house of Jacob, shall no more again lean upon him that smiteth them; but shall lean upon Jehovah, the Holy One of Israel, in truth.
²¹ A remnant shall return, even a remnant of Jacob, unto the
²² mighty God. For though thy people, O Israel, be as the

sand of the sea, yet only a remnant of them shall return; the consumption that is decreed shall overflow with righteousness. For the consumption and decree of the Lord Jehovah of hosts will he make in the midst of all the land.

Therefore thus said the Lord Jehovah of hosts, O my people that dwellest in Zion, be not afraid of the Assyrian; he will smite thee with a rod, and will lift up his staff against thee, on the way to Egypt. For yet a very little while, and indignation shall be accomplished, and then mine anger shall be for their destruction. And then Jehovah of hosts will stir up a scourge for him according to the slaughter of Midian at the rock of Oreb; and his rod shall be upon the sea, and he will lift it up on the way to Egypt. And it shall come to pass in that day, that his burden shall be taken away from off thy shoulder, and his yoke from off thy neck, and the yoke shall be destroyed because of the fatness.

He is come to Aiath; he is passed over [the Jordan] to Migron; at Michmash he hath laid up his baggage; they are passed through the passage; they have taken up their lodging at Geba; Ramah is afraid; Gibeah of Saul is fled. Shout with thy voice, O daughter of Gallim; hearken, O Laish, O poor Anathoth. Madmenah is removed; the inhabitants of Gebim flee away. As yet he will remain the day at Nob; he shaketh his hand against the mount of the daughter of Zion, the hill of Jerusalem. Behold, the Lord Jehovah of hosts will lop the bough with terrible violence; and the high ones of stature shall be hewn down, and the haughty shall be humbled. And he will cut down the thickets of the forest with iron, and Lebanon shall fall by a mighty one.

And a rod shall come forth from the stem of Jesse,
And an off-shoot shall grow out of his roots;
And the spirit of Jehovah shall rest on him;
The spirit of wisdom and understanding,
The spirit of counsel and might,
The spirit of knowledge and of the fear of Jehovah.
And he will take delight in the fear of Jehovah;
And he will not judge after the sight of his eyes,
Neither reprove after the hearing of his ears.
But with righteousness will he judge the poor,
And reprove with equity for the meek of the earth.

And he shall smite the earth with the rod of his mouth,
And with the breath of his lips shall he slay the wicked.
5 And righteousness shall be the girdle of his loins,
And faithfulness the girdle of his reins.
6 Then the wolf shall dwell with the lamb,
And the leopard shall lie down with the kid;
And the calf, and the young lion, and the fatling together;
And a little child shall lead them.
7 And the cow and the bear shall feed,
Their young ones shall lie down together.
And the lion shall eat straw like the ox.
8 Then the sucking child shall play on the asp's hole,
And the weaned child put his hand on the viper's den.
9 They shall not hurt nor destroy in all my holy mountain;
For the earth shall be full of the knowledge of Jehovah,
As the waters cover the sea.
10 And in that day there shall be a root of Jesse, who shall stand for an ensign of the peoples; to it shall the
11 Nations seek. And his resting place shall be glorious. And it shall come to pass in that day, that the Lord will set his hand again a second time to redeem the remnant of his people, which shall be left, from Assyria, and from Lower Egypt, and from Pathros [or Upper Egypt], and from Ethiopia, and from Elam [or Western Persia], and from Shinar [or Babylonia], and from Hamath [or Syria], and
12 from the islands of the sea. And he will set up an ensign for the nations, and will assemble the outcasts of Israel, and gather together the dispersed of Judah from the four
13 corners of the earth. The envy also of Ephraim shall depart, and the adversaries of Judah shall be cut off; Ephraim shall not envy Judah, and Judah shall not vex
14 Ephraim. But they shall fly against the borders of the Philistines toward the west; at the same time they shall plunder the Children of the East. Edom and Moab shall stretch forth their hands; and the Children of Ammon shall
15 obey them. And Jehovah will utterly destroy the tongue [or Bay] of the Egyptian sea; and with his mighty wind he will wave his hand over the River, and will smite it into
16 seven streams, and make men go over dryshod. And there shall be a highway for the remnant of his people who shall be left from Assyria, like as it was for Israel in the day —that he came up out of the land of Lower Egypt.

And in that day thou shalt say, 1
' Jehovah, I praise thee, though thou wast angry with me;
' May thine anger turn away, and do thou comfort me.
' Lo, God is my salvation; I will trust, and not be afraid; 2
' For Jah-Jehovah is my strength and my song;
' He also is become my salvation.'
Therefore with joy shall ye draw water out of the wells 3
of salvation. And in that day shall ye say, 4
  ' Praise ye Jehovah, call upon his name,
' Declare his doings among the peoples,
' Make mention that his name is exalted.
' Sing to Jehovah; for he hath done excellent things; 5
' Let this be known in all the earth.
' Cry out and shout, thou inhabitant of Zion; 6
' For great is the Holy One of Israel in the midst of thee.'—

THE BURDEN OF BABYLON, which Isaiah the son of 1
   Amoz did see as a vision.
Lift ye up a banner upon the bare mountain, exalt the 2
voice to them [the Medes], wave the hand that they may
go into the doorways of the tyrants. I have commanded 3
those consecrated for my purpose; yea, I have called
warriors for mine anger, even them that rejoice in mine
excellence.

There is the noise of a rabble on the mountains, the 4
likeness of a great people; a tumultuous noise of the kingdoms of nations gathered together. Jehovah of hosts mus-
tereth the host of the battle. They come from a far country, 5
from the end of the heavens, even Jehovah, and the weapons of his indignation, to destroy the whole land.

Howl ye; for the day of Jehovah is at hand; it shall 6
come as a destruction from the Almighty. Therefore shall 7
all hands be faint, and every man's heart shall melt. And 8
they shall be afraid; pangs and sorrows shall take hold of
them; they shall be in pain as a woman that travaileth.
They shall be amazed one at another; their faces shall
be as the faces of flames.

Behold, the day of Jehovah cometh, cruel both with 9
wrath and fierce anger, to lay the land desolate; and he
will destroy the sinners thereof out of it. For the stars 10
of the heavens and the constellations thereof shall not
give their light; the sun shall be darkened in his going

forth, and the moon shall not cause her light to shine.
¹¹ And I will punish the world for their evil, and the wicked for their iniquity; and I will cause the arrogance of the proud to cease, and will lay low the haughtiness of the
¹² terrible. I will make a man more precious than fine gold,
¹³ and a son of Adam than the gold of Ophir. Therefore I will shake the heavens; and the earth shall tremble out of its place, in the wrath of Jehovah of hosts, and in the day of his fierce anger.
¹⁴ And it [Babylon] shall be as the chased roe, and as sheep that no man gathereth together. They shall every man turn to his own people, and flee every one into his own
¹⁵ land. Every one that is found shall be thrust through; and every one that would hide himself shall fall by the
¹⁶ sword. Their babes also shall be dashed to pieces before their eyes; their houses shall be plundered, and their
¹⁷ wives ravished. 'Behold, I will stir up the Medes against them, who regard not silver; and as for gold, they have
¹⁸ no delight in it. Their bows also shall dash the young men to pieces; and they shall have no mercy on the fruit of the womb; their eye shall have no pity for
¹⁹ children. And Babylon, the glory of kingdoms, the beauty of the Chaldees' excellence, shall be as when God overthrew
²⁰ Sodom and Gomorrah. It shall not be inhabited for the future, neither shall it be dwelt in for generations and generations. Neither shall the Arabian pitch his tent there; neither shall the shepherds make their fold there.
²¹ But wild beasts of the desert shall lie there; and their houses shall be full of yelling creatures; and ostriches
²² shall dwell there, and satyrs shall skip about there. And the howling beasts shall cry in their palaces, and jackals in their pleasant halls; and her time is near to come, and her days shall not be prolonged.'
¹ For Jehovah will have mercy on Jacob, and' will yet choose Israel, and set them at rest in their own land. And strangers shall be joined with them, and shall cleave to the
² house of Jacob. And the peoples shall take them, and bring them to their place; and the house of Israel shall possess them in the land of Jehovah for servants and for handmaids. And they shall take for captives those whose captives they were; and they shall rule over their oppressors.
³ And it shall come to pass in the day that Jehovah shall

give thee rest from thy labour, and from thy fear, and from the hard bondage wherein thou wast made to serve, that thou shalt take up this proverb against the king of Babylon, [Belshazzar,] and say, 'How hath the oppressor 'ceased! the gold-exacting city ceased! Jehovah hath 'broken the staff of the wicked, the sceptre of the rulers, 'which smote the peoples in wrath with an unceasing stroke, 'which ruled the nations in anger, which persecuted, and 'none hindered. The whole earth is at rest, and is quiet; 'they break forth into singing. Yea, the fir trees rejoice 'at thee, and the cedars of Lebanon, [saying,] Since thou 'art laid down, no woodcutter is come up against us. Hell 'from beneath is moved for thee to meet thy coming. It stir- 'reth up the departed spirits for thee, even all the leader- 'goats of the earth ; it hath raised up from their thrones 'all the kings of the nations. All they shall speak and say 'to thee, Art thou also become weak as we? art thou be- 'come like to us? Thy pomp is brought down to hell, and 'the noise of thy psalteries. The maggot is spread under 'thee, and the worms cover thee. How art thou fallen 'from the heavens, O Day-star, son of the morning! how 'art thou cut down to the ground, thou who didst crush 'the nations! For thou hast said in thy heart, I will ascend 'into heaven, I will exalt my throne above the stars of 'God; I will sit also upon the mountain of the assembly '[of gods], in the recesses of the north. I will ascend above 'the heights of the clouds; I will be like the Most High. 'Yet thou shalt be brought down to hell, to the recesses 'of the pit. They that see thee shall gaze upon thee, and 'consider of thee, Is this the man that made the earth to 'tremble, that did shake kingdoms ; that made the world 'as a desert, and laid waste the cities thereof; that released 'not his prisoners to their home? All the kings of the 'nations, even all of them, lie in glory, every one in his 'own house. But thou art cast out of thy grave like a vile 'off-shoot, as the raiment of those that are slain, that are 'thrust through with a sword, that go down to the stones 'of the pit. Thou art as a carcase trodden under feet. 'Thou shalt not be joined with them in burial, because 'thou hast destroyed thy land, and slain thy people. The 'seed of evil doers will never be renowned.'

Prepare slaughter for his children because of the iniquity ²¹

4
5
6
7
8
9
10
11
12
13
14
15
16
17
18
19
20
21

of their fathers; that they do not rise, nor possess the land,
²² nor fill the face of the world with cities. For I will rise up against them, Jehovah of hosts hath said it; and I will cut off from Babylon the name, and the remnant, both
²³ the sons, and the sons' sons, Jehovah hath said it. I will also make it a possession for the hedgehog, and stagnant pools of water; and I will sweep it with the besom of destruction; Jehovah of hosts hath said it.

²⁴ JEHOVAH OF HOSTS hath sworn, saying, Surely as I had in mind, so shall it come to pass; and as I have purposed,
²⁵ so shall it stand, that I will break the Assyrian in my land, and upon my mountains I will tread him under foot. Then shall his yoke depart from off them, and his burden depart
²⁶ from off their shoulders. This is the purpose that is purposed upon the whole earth; and this is the hand that is
²⁷ stretched out upon all the nations. For Jehovah of hosts hath purposed, and who shall annul it? and his hand is stretched out, and who shall turn it back?

²⁸ IN THE YEAR that king Ahaz died [B.C. 726] was this burden.
²⁹ Rejoice not, all thou Land of the Philistines, because the rod of him that smote thee is broken; for out of the serpent's root shall come forth a viper, and its fruit shall
³⁰ be a fiery flying serpent. And the firstborn of the poor shall be fed, and the needy shall lie down in safety; and I will kill thy root with famine, and the remnant of thee
³¹ shall be slain. Howl, O city gate; cry, O city; thou, Land of the Philistines, art dissolved all of thee. For there shall come from the North a smoke, and not a straggler shall
³² be among his appointed ones. What then shall one answer to the messengers of the nation? 'That Jehovah hath 'founded Zion, and the poor of his people shall flee for —'safety there.'

¹ THE BURDEN OF MOAB, when in the night Ar of Moab was laid waste, and brought to silence; when in the night Kir of Moab was laid waste, and brought to silence.
² He is gone up to the House, even to Dibon, to weep on the High Places. Moab howleth over Nebo, and over Medeba. On all their heads is baldness, and every beard
³ is cut off. In their streets they gird themselves with

sackcloth; on the tops of their houses, and in their broad places, every one howleth, going down while weeping. And Heshbon crieth, and Elealeh; their voice is heard even unto Jahaz. Therefore the armed soldiers of Moab make a noise; his life is become grievous to him. My heart crieth out for Moab; its fugitives flee to Zoar, as a heifer of three years old. For by the hill road of Luhith with weeping they go up; for in the way of Horonaim they raise up a cry of destruction. For the waters of Nimrim are desolate; for the hay withereth away, the grass faileth, there is no green thing. Therefore the remnant they have gotten, and what they have laid up, they carry away to the Valley of Willows. For the cry is gone round about the boundaries of Moab; the howling thereof to Eglaim, and the howling thereof to Beer-elim. For the waters of Dimon [or Dibon in Gad] shall be full of blood. For I will bring yet more upon Dimon, lions upon him of Moab that escapeth, and upon the remnant of the land.

Send ye the lamb [tribute] of the ruler of the land from Sela [or Petra] in the desert, to the Mountain of the daughter of Zion. For it shall be, that, as a wandering bird cast out of the nest, so the daughters of Moab shall be at the fords of the Arnon, [saying,] 'Give ye counsel, do what is just; 'make thy shade in the midst of the noonday as the night; 'hide the outcasts; betray not him that fleeth. Let the 'outcasts of Moab dwell with thee; be thou a covert to them 'from the face of the spoiler. For the extortioner is at an 'end, the spoiler ceaseth, the oppressors are consumed out 'of the land. And in kindness shall the throne be established. 'And one shall sit upon it in truth in the tent of David, 'judging, and seeking justice, and hastening righteousness.'

We have heard of the pride of Moab; he is very haughty; even of his haughtiness, and his pride, and his wrath; but his vain boasting shall not stand. Therefore shall Moab howl over Moab, every one shall howl. Over the ruins of Kir-hareseth shall ye sigh; surely they are stricken. For the fields of Heshbon languish, and the vine of Sibmah. The lords of the Nations have trampled down the best vines thereof; they are come even to Jazer, they wander through the desert; her branches are cast forth, they are gone over the sea. Therefore I will weep with the weeping of Jazer for the vine of Sibmah. I will water thee with

my tears, O Heshbon, and Elealeh; because the joyous shout over thy summer fruits and over thy harvest hath
10 ceased. And gladness is taken away, and joy out of the plentiful field; and in the vineyards there shall be no singing, neither shall there be shouting. The traders shall tread out no wine in their presses; I have made the joyous
11 shout to cease. Therefore my bowels shall moan like a harp for Moab, and mine inward parts for Kir-haresh.
12 And it shall come to pass, when it is seen that Moab is weary of the High Place [or altar], that it shall come to His Sanctuary to pray, but shall not prevail.
13 (This is the word that Jehovah hath hitherto spoken
14 concerning Moab. But now Jehovah hath spoken, saying, Within three years, as the years of a hireling, and the glory of Moab shall be brought to shame, with all that great rabble; and the remnant shall be less than small, — and not strong.)

1 THE BURDEN OF DAMASCUS.
Behold, Damascus is taken away from being a city, and
2 it shall be a ruinous heap. The cities of Aroer are forsaken; they shall be for flocks, which shall lie down, and
3 none shall make them afraid. The fortress also shall cease from Ephraim, and the kingdom from Damascus and the remnant of Syria; they shall be as the glory of the children of Israel, Jehovah of hosts hath said it.
4 And in that day it shall come to pass, that the glory of Jacob shall be made thin, and the fatness of his flesh shall
5 grow lean. And it shall be as when the reaper with his arm gathereth the standing corn, and reapeth the ears; and it shall be as when one picketh up ears of corn in the
6 Valley of Giants. And only gleanings shall be left on it, as the shaking of an olive tree, two or three berries on the top of the uppermost bough, four or five on the outmost fruit-bearers thereof; Jehovah the God of Israel hath said it.
7 In that day shall a man look to his Maker, and his eyes
8 shall have regard to the Holy One of Israel. And he shall not look to the altars, the work of his hands, neither shall regard that which his fingers have made, either the groves of Ashera, or the Sun-images.
9 In that day shall his strong cities be as a forsaken bough of the forest, and as an uppermost branch, which they left because of the children of Israel. And there shall be de-

solation. Because thou hast forgotten the God of thy sal- 10
vation, and hast not been mindful of the Rock of thy
strength, therefore shalt thou plant pleasant plants, and
shalt set it with strange slips; in the day of thy planting 11
thou shalt make a hedge, and in the morning thou shalt
make thy seed to flourish; but the harvest shall flee away in
the day of possession, and there shall be desperate sorrow.

WOE TO THE RABBLE OF MANY PEOPLES, who make a 12
noise like the noise of the ocean; and to the rushing of
nations, that make a rushing like the rushing of mighty
waters! The nations shall rush like the rushing of many 13
waters. But [God] will rebuke them, and they shall flee far
off, and shall be chased as the chaff of the mountains before
the wind, and like thistledown before the whirlwind. And 14
behold at eveningtide there are death-terrors; and before
the morning he is not. This is the portion of them that
plunder us, and the lot of them that rob us. —

WOE TO [Abyssinia] THE LAND OF THE WINGED TSALTSAL 1
[or Spear-fly], which is beyond the rivers of Ethiopia; that 2
sendeth ambassadors by the sea, even in vessels of paper-
reeds upon the face of the waters, [saying,] 'Go, ye swift
' messengers, to a nation [Israel] scattered and made bare,
' to a people terrible from their beginning and hitherto; a
' nation measured out and trodden down, whose land the
' Rivers [Tigris and Euphrates] have plundered!'

All ye inhabitants of the world, and dwellers on the 3
earth, see ye, when he lifteth up an ensign on the mountains; and when he bloweth a trumpet, hear ye. For thus 4
Jehovah said to me, 'I will take my rest, and I will con-
' sider in my dwelling-place as in the bright heat of the
' noon's height, and as when there is a cloud of dew in the
' heat of harvest.' For afore the harvest, when the bud is 5
perfect, and the sour grape is ripening on the flower, he
will both cut off the sprigs with pruning knives, and will
take away the branches that are cut down. They shall be 6
left together for the ravenous birds of the mountains, and
for the beasts of the earth; and the ravenous birds shall
pass the summer upon them, and all the beasts of the earth
shall winter upon them.

At that time shall presents be brought to Jehovah of 7
hosts from a people scattered and made bare, and who are
some of the people terrible from the beginning and hither-

to, the nation measured out and trodden down, whose land
the Rivers have plundered, to the Place of the name of
—Jehovah of hosts, the mount Zion.

1 THE BURDEN OF EGYPT.
Behold, Jehovah rideth upon a swift cloud, and will
come into Egypt; and the idols of Egypt shall be moved
at his presence, and the heart of Egypt shall melt in the
2 midst of it. And I will arm the Egyptians against the
Egyptians; and they shall fight every one against his brother, and every one against his neighbour; city against city,
3 and kingdom against kingdom. And the spirit of Egypt
shall fail in the midst of it; and I will destroy its counsel.
And they shall seek to the idols, and to the whisperers
[or serpent-charmers], and to the speaking bottles [or
4 ventriloquists], and to the wizards. And the Egyptians
will I give over into the hand of a cruel lord; and a fierce
king shall rule over them; the Lord, Jehovah of hosts,
hath said it.
5 And the waters shall fail from the sea, and the river shall
6 be wasted and dried up. And the rivers shall become
putrid; and the streams of Lower Egypt shall be emptied
7 and dried up; the reeds and flags shall wither. The
meadows by the river [Nile], by the mouth of the river,
and everything sown by the river, shall wither, be driven
8 away, and be no more. The fishers also shall mourn, and all
they that cast a hook into the river shall lament, and they
that spread nets upon the face of the waters shall languish.
9 Moreover they that work in combed flax, and they that
10 weave white cloths, shall be confounded. And her pillars
[or princes] shall be broken, all that work for hire shall
be sad in soul.
11 Surely the princes of Zoan [or Tanis] are fools, the
counsel of the wise counsellors of Pharaoh is become brutish. How say ye to Pharaoh, 'I am the son of the wise,
12 'the son of ancient kings'? Where are now thy wise
men? And let them tell thee now, and let them make
known what Jehovah of hosts hath purposed upon Egypt.
13 The princes of Zoan are become fools, the princes of Noph
[or Memphis] are deceived; they have also seduced Egypt,
14 even the corner-turrets of its tribes. Jehovah hath mingled a spirit of perverseness in the midst thereof; and
they have caused Egypt to err in all its work, as a drunken

man staggereth in his vomit. Neither shall there be any 15 work for Egypt, which the head or tail, palm-branch or bulrush, may do.

In that day shall Egypt be like women; and it shall 16 be afraid and in fear because of the shaking of the hand of Jehovah of hosts, which he shaketh against it. And 17 the land of Judah shall be a terror to Egypt, every one that maketh mention thereof to himself shall be afraid, because of the counsel of Jehovah of hosts which he hath determined against it.

In that day there shall be five cities in the land of Egypt 18 which speak the language of Canaan, and swear by Jehovah of hosts; one shall be called, The city of destruction.

In that day shall there be an altar to Jehovah in the 19 midst of the land of Egypt, and at its boundary a pillar to Jehovah. And it shall be for a sign and for a witness 20 unto Jehovah of hosts in the land of Egypt. For they shall cry to Jehovah because of the oppressors, and he will send them a saviour, and he shall defend, and shall deliver them. And Jehovah shall be known to Egypt, and 21 the Egyptians shall know Jehovah in that day, and shall bring sacrifice and meal offerings; yea, they shall vow a vow to Jehovah, and shall perform it. And Jehovah 22 will smite Egypt; he will smite it and heal it. And they shall return even to Jehovah, and he will be entreated by them, and will heal them.

In that day shall there be a highway out of Egypt to 23 Assyria, and the Assyrians shall come into Egypt, and the Egyptians into Assyria, and the Egyptians shall serve the Assyrians. In that day shall Israel be the third with 24 Egypt and with Assyria, even a blessing in the midst of the land; whom Jehovah of hosts will bless, saying, 25 'Blessed be Egypt my people, and Assyria the work of 'my hands, and Israel mine inheritance.' —

IN THE YEAR that Tartan came to Ashdod [or Azotus], 1 (when Sargon the king of Assyria sent him), and fought against Ashdod, and took it; at the same time spake Je- 2 hovah by the hand of Isaiah the son of Amoz, saying, 'Go and loose the sackcloth from off thy loins, and put 'off thy shoe from thy foot.' And he did so, walking naked and barefoot. And Jehovah said, Like as my ser- 3 vant Isaiah hath walked naked and barefoot three years

for a sign and wonder upon Egypt and upon Ethiopia;
4 so shall the king of Assyria lead away the Egyptians
prisoners,' and the Ethiopians captives, young and old,
naked and barefoot, even with their buttocks uncovered,
5 to the shame of Egypt. And [Israel] shall be afraid and
ashamed of Ethiopia their expectation, and of Egypt their
6 glory. And the inhabitant of this coast shall say in that
day, 'Behold, such is our expectation, when we flee there
'for help to be delivered from the king of Assyria; and
—'how shall we escape?'

1 THE BURDEN OF THE DESERT BY THE SEA.
As a whirlwind in the South Country when passing
through, cometh from the desert, from a terrible land;
2 so a grievous vision is declared to me; the cheater cheateth, and the spoiler spoileth. Go up, O Elam [or Persia];
besiege, O Media; all the sighing about it have I made
3 to cease. Whereas my loins were filled with pain; pangs
had taken hold upon me, as the pangs of a woman that
travaileth; I was bowed down, and I could not hear it;
4 I was dismayed, and I could not see it. My heart panted,
terrors affrighted me; the night of my pleasures was
turned into fear unto me.
5 The table is prepared, the watch is in the watch-tower,
they eat and drink. Arise, ye princes, and anoint the
6 shield. For thus hath the lord said to me, 'Go, set a
7 'watchman, let him declare what he seeth.' And he saw
a chariot with a couple of men riding, one riding on an
ass, and one riding on a camel; and he hearkened diligently with much heed.
8 gently with much heed. And he cried out like a lion;
'My lord [Belshazzar], I stand continually upon the
'watch-tower in the daytime, and I am set in my ward
9 'every night. And, behold, here cometh a man in a
'chariot with a couple of horsemen.' And he answered
and said, 'Babylon is fallen, is fallen; and all the graven
10 'images of her gods are broken to the ground.' O my
crushed one, and child of my threshing floor; that which
I have heard from Jehovah of hosts, the God of Israel, I
have declared to you.
11 THE BURDEN OF DUMAH.
One calleth to me out of Seir, 'Watchman, what of the
12 'night? Watchman, what of the night?' The watchman

said, 'The morning cometh, and also the night. If ye will 'inquire, inquire ye; return and come again.'

THE BURDEN UPON ARABIA.

13 In the forest in Arabia shall ye lodge, O ye travelling companies of Dedanites. 14 The inhabitants of the land of Tema brought water to meet him that was thirsty, they hastened with their bread to him that fled. 15 For they fled from the swords, from the drawn sword, and from the bent bow, and from the grievousness of war.

16 For thus hath the Lord said to me, Within a year, according to the years of a hireling, and all the glory of Kedar shall fail. 17 And the residue of the number of archers, the warriors of the children of Kedar, shall be diminished; for Jehovah the God of Israel hath spoken it.

THE BURDEN OF THE VALLEY OF VISIONS.

1 What aileth thee now [O Jerusalem], that thou art all of thee gone up to the housetops? 2 Thou that wast full of noises, a tumultuous town, a joyous city; thy slain men are not slain with the sword, nor dead in battle. 3 All thy rulers are fled together, they are taken captive by the archers. All of thee that are found are taken captive together, who fled afar off.

4 Therefore I said, Look away from me; I will weep bitterly, labour not to comfort me, because of the spoiling of the daughter of my people. 5 For it is a day of trouble, and of treading down, and of perplexity by the Lord Jehovah of hosts in the Valley of Visions. They break down the walls, and there is a cry unto the mountains. 6 And Elam beareth the quiver with chariots of men and horsemen, and Kir uncovereth the shield. 7 And it shall come to pass, that thy choicest valleys shall be full of chariots, and the horsemen shall set themselves in array at the city gate. 8 And he shall remove the covering of Judah.

And thou shalt look in that day to the armoury of the House of the Forest. 9 Ye shall see also the breaches of the city of David, that they are many; and ye shall gather up the waters of the Lower Pool. 10 And ye shall number the houses of Jerusalem, and shall break down the houses to fortify the wall. 11 Ye shall make also a Cistern between the two walls for the water of the Old Pool. But ye look not to the Maker thereof, neither have respect to him that fashioned it long ago.

¹² And in that day will the Lord Jehovah of hosts call to weeping, and to mourning, and to baldness, and to girding ¹³ with sackcloth. But behold joy and gladness, slaying oxen, and killing sheep, eating flesh, and drinking wine ; 'let us ¹⁴ 'eat and drink ; for to-morrow we shall die.' And it was revealed in mine ears by Jehovah of hosts, 'Surely this 'iniquity shall not be purged from you till ye die,' said the Lord Jehovah of hosts.

¹⁵ Thus saith the Lord Jehovah of hosts, Go, get thee to this favourite [of Hezekiah], even to Shebna, who is over ¹⁶ the house, [and say,] 'What hast thou here? and whom 'hast thou here, that thou hast hewed for thee a sepulchre 'here? They are hewing his sepulchre on high, and ¹⁷ 'cutting a habitation for him in a rock. Behold, Jeho-'vah will throw thee down with a mighty overthrow, and ¹⁸ 'will surely cover thee. He will surely twist thee about 'like a ball into a country large of space. There shalt thou 'die, and there the chariots of thy glory shall be the shame ¹⁹ 'of thy lord's house. And I will thrust thee off thy stand-'ing-place, and he shall pull thee down from thy station.'

²⁰ And it shall come to pass in that day, that I will call ²¹ my servant Eliakim the son of Hilkiah ; and I will clothe him with thy under coat, and strengthen him with thy girdle, and I will commit thy government into his hand. And he shall be a father to the inhabitants of Jerusalem, ²² and to the house of Judah. And the key of the house of David will I lay upon his shoulder ; so he shall open, and none shall shut ; and he shall shut, and none shall open. ²³ And I will fasten him as a nail in a sure place ; and he ²⁴ shall be for a glorious seat for his father's house. And they shall hang upon him all the glory of his father's house, the offspring both great and small, with all vessels of small quantity, from the vessels of goblets, even to all the vessels of skins.

²⁵ In that day, Jehovah of hosts hath said it, shall the nail that had been fastened in the sure place be removed, and be cut down, and fall ; and the burden that was upon it —shall be cut off ; for Jehovah hath spoken it.

¹ THE BURDEN OF TYRE.

Howl, ye ships of Tarshish [or Tarsus] ; for it is laid waste, so that there is no house, no entering in. From the land of the Chittians [or Cyprians] it was revealed to them. Be silent, ye inhabitants of the isle; thou whom the merchants of Sidon, that pass over the sea, have replenished. And by means of the Great Waters [or Sea] the corn-seed of the Shihor [or Nile], the harvest of the River, is her revenue; and she is a mart of nations.

Be thou ashamed, O Sidon; for the sea hath spoken, even the Fortress of the Sea [or Tyre], saying, 'I travail 'not, nor bring forth children, neither do I nourish up 'young men, nor bring up maidens.' When the report reacheth the Egyptians, they will be sorely pained at the report of Tyre.

Pass ye over to Tarshish; howl, ye inhabitants of the isle. Is this your joyous city, whose antiquity is from ancient days? Her own feet shall carry her afar off to sojourn. Who purposed this against Tyre, the giver of crowns, whose merchants are princes, whose traffickers are the honoured of the earth? Jehovah of hosts hath purposed it, to stain the pride of all glory, and to bring into contempt all the honoured of the earth. Flow over thy land like the River [Nile], O daughter of Tarshish; there is no longer bondage. He hath stretched out his hand over the sea, he hath shaken the kingdoms. Jehovah hath given a command against Canaan, to destroy its strongholds. And he hath said, 'Thou shalt no more rejoice, O thou op'pressed maiden, daughter of Sidon. Arise, pass over to 'the Chittians; there also shalt thou have no rest.'

Behold the land of the Chaldeans; now this people is not. The Assyrians have founded it for the wild beasts of the desert. They have set up their watch-towers, they have laid bare its castles, and have brought it to ruin. Howl, ye ships of Tarshish; for your stronghold is laid waste.

(And it shall come to pass in that day, that Tyre shall be forgotten for seventy years, according to the lifetime of one king. After the end of seventy years it shall be unto Tyre according to the Song of the Harlot;
'Take a harp, go about the city,
'Thou harlot that hast been forgotten;
'Make sweet melody, sing many songs,
'So that thou mayest be remembered.'

And it shall come to pass after the end of seventy years,

that Jehovah will visit Tyre, and she shall return to her hire, and shall commit fornication with all the kingdoms
18 of the world upon the face of the earth. And her merchandise and her hire shall be holiness to Jehovah. It shall not be treasured nor laid up; for her merchandise shall be for them that dwell in the presence of Jehovah, —to eat to their full, and for stately clothing.)

1 BEHOLD, Jehovah emptieth the land [of Judah], and maketh it waste, and turneth it upside down, and scat-
2 tereth abroad its inhabitants. And it shall be, as with the people, so with the priest; as with the servant, so with his master; as with the maid, so with her mistress; as with the buyer, so with the seller; as with the lender, so with the borrower; as with the taker of usury, so with
3 the giver of usury to him. The land shall be utterly emptied, and utterly plundered; for Jehovah hath spoken
4 this word. The land mourneth and fadeth away, the world languisheth and fadeth away, the highest people of the land
5 do languish. The land also is defiled under its inhabitants; because they have transgressed the laws. They have changed the ordinance, they have broken the everlasting
6 covenant. Therefore hath the curse devoured the land, and they that dwell therein are punished. Therefore the in-
7 habitants of the land are burned, and few men are left. The grape juice mourneth, the vine languisheth, all the merry-
8 hearted do sigh. The mirth of timbrels hath ceased, the noise of them that rejoice hath ended, the mirth of the
9 harp hath ceased. They shall not drink wine with a song;
10 strong drink shall be bitter to them that drink it. The city is broken down as a thing of nought; every house is
11 shut up, that no man may come in. There is a crying for wine in the streets; all joy is darkened, the mirth of the
12 land is gone. In the city is left desolation, and the gate is smitten unto ruin.
13 For thus it shall be in the midst of the land among the peoples, as at the shaking of an olive tree, and as at the
14 gleaning of grapes when the vintage is done; they shall lift up their voice, they shall sing for the majesty of Jeho-
15 vah, they shall cry aloud from the West. Therefore glorify ye Jehovah in the East, even the name of Jehovah the God of Israel in the isles of the sea.

¹⁶ From the uttermost part of the earth have we heard the song, 'Glory be to the righteous.' But I said, 'I am 'wretched, I am wretched, woe unto me! The treacherous 'dealers have dealt treacherously; yea, the treacherous 'dealers have dealt very treacherously.' ¹⁷ Fear, and the pit, and the snare, are upon thee, O inhabitant of the land. ¹⁸ And it shall come to pass, that he that fleeth from the noise of the fear shall fall into the pit; and he that cometh up out of the midst of the pit shall be taken in the snare; for the windows from on high are open, and the foundations of the earth do shake. ¹⁹ The earth is utterly broken down, the earth is clean shattered to pieces, the earth is disturbed exceedingly. ²⁰ The earth reeleth to and fro like a drunkard, and is shaken about like a hut; and the transgression thereof shall be heavy upon it; and it shall fall, and not rise again.

²¹ And it shall come to pass in that day, that Jehovah will punish the host of the high ones that are on high, and the ²² kings of the earth upon the earth. And they shall be gathered together, as prisoners are gathered into the pit, and shall be shut up in the prison, and after many days shall they be punished. ²³ Then the pale moon shall blush, and the sun's heat shall be ashamed, when Jehovah of hosts shall reign on mount Zion, and in Jerusalem, and before his elders gloriously.

¹ O Jehovah, thou art my God, I will exalt thee;
I will praise thy name, for thou hast done wonders;
Thy counsels of old are faithfulness and truth.
² For thou hast made of the city [Babylon] a heap of stones;
Of the fenced city a ruin, a citadel of strangers;
Of a city for ever, one not to be built up.
³ Therefore shall the strong people glorify thee,
The city of the nations that terrify shall fear thee.
⁴ For thou hast been a stronghold to the poor,
A stronghold to the needy in his distress,
A refuge from the storm, a shade from the heat,
When the blast of the terrible was as a storm against a wall.
⁵ Thou wilt humble the noise of the strangers,
As heat on a dry place, as heat by the shade of a cloud;
The song of the terrible ones shall be brought low.
⁶ And on this Mountain shall Jehovah of hosts make unto all the peoples a drinking feast of fat things, a drinking feast

of old wines, of fat things full of marrow, of old wines
7 well refined. And he will destroy on this mountain the face of the covering that covereth over all the peoples,
8 and the veil that is spread over all the nations. He will wholly swallow up death; and the Lord Jehovah will wipe away tears from off all faces; and the reproach against his people will he take away from off all the earth; for Jehovah hath spoken it.
9 And it shall be said in that day, 'Lo, this is our God; 'we have waited for him, and he will save us; this is 'Jehovah; we have waited for him, we will be glad and
10 'will rejoice in his salvation.' For on this mountain shall the hand of Jehovah rest, and Moab shall be trodden down under him, even as straw is trodden down for the
11 dunghill. And he will spread forth his hands in the midst of them, as he that swimmeth spreadeth them forth to swim; and he will bring down their pride together
12 with the snares of their hands. And Mibzar [or Petra] the fortress of thy walls will he bring down, lay low, and —strike to the ground, even to the dust.

1 In that day shall this song be sung in the land of Judah;
Our city is strong; salvation maketh walls and ramparts,
2 Open ye the gates, that a nation may enter
Which is righteous and keepeth the truth.
3 A steadfast mind thou wilt keep in peace,
In peace, because it trusteth in thee.
4 Trust ye in Jehovah for ever and ever;
For in Jah-Jehovah is the Rock of ages.
5 For he bringeth down them that dwell on high;
The lofty city he layeth low, he layeth low to the ground;
He striketh it even to the dust.
6 The foot shall tread it down,
Even the feet of the poor, and the steps of the needy.
7 The way of the just is uprightness;
Thou, most upright, makest smooth the path of the just;
8 Yea, in the way of thy judgments, O Jehovah,
We wait for thee; to thy Name,
And to the remembrance of thee, is our soul's desire.
9 With my soul have I desired thee in the night;
Yea, with my spirit within me I seek thee at daybreak;
For when thy judgments are on the earth,
The inhabitants of the world will learn righteousness.

If favour be shewed to the wicked,   10
Yet will he not learn righteousness;
In the land of uprightness will he deal unjustly,
And will not fear the majesty of Jehovah.
O Jehovah, thine uplifted hand they will not see;   11
But they shall see, and be ashamed of envying the people;
Yea, fire upon thine enemies shall devour them.
  O Jehovah, thou wilt ordain peace for us;   12
For thou also hast wrought all our works for us.
O Jehovah our God, other lords beside thee rule over us;   13
But by thee only will we make mention of thy name.
They are dead beings, they shall not live;   14
They are departed spirits, they shall not rise;
Therefore hast thou punished and wilt destroy them,
And thou wilt make all memory of them to perish.
  Thou hast increased the nation, O Jehovah,   15
Thou hast increased the nation; thou art glorified;
Thou hast widened all the ends of the land.
O Jehovah, in trouble have they sought thee,   16
Whispering a prayer when thy chastening was on them.
As a woman with child, that is near to bringing forth,   17
Is in pain, and crieth out in her pangs;
So have we been in thy sight, O Jehovah.
We have been with child, we have been in pain,   18
We have as it were brought forth wind;
So that we have not wrought deliverance to the land,
Neither have the inhabitants of the world fallen.
Thy dead ones shall live, my people's corpses shall arise.   19
Awake and sing, ye that dwell in dust;
For thy dew is as the dew of herbs,
And the earth shall cast forth the departed spirits.

  Come, my people, enter thou into thy chambers, and shut   20
thy doors about thee. Hide thyself as it were for a little
moment, until the indignation be overpast. For, behold,   21
Jehovah cometh out of his place to punish the inhabitants
of the earth for their iniquity. The earth also shall disclose her bloodshed, and shall no more cover her slain. —

  In that day Jehovah with his sore and great and strong   1
sword will punish the crocodile [or Egypt], the cowardly
serpent, even the crocodile that crooked serpent; and he
will slay the dragon that is in the sea.

  In that day sing ye of the Pleasant Vineyard.   2

³ I Jehovah do keep it, I water it every moment;
Lest any hurt it, I will keep it night and day.
⁴ Fury is nothing against me.
Who would set a brier or a thorn against me in battle?
I would rush against it, I would burn them together.
⁵ Or let him hold to my strength, and make peace with me;
Let him make peace with me.
⁶ In days that are to come, Jacob shall take root; Israel shall blossom and bud, and they shall fill the face of the
⁷ world with fruit. Hath He smitten him, according to the smiting of those that smote him? or is he slain according
⁸ to the slaughter of them that slew him? In moderation by casting it forth thou dost chide it. He driveth it
⁹ away by his strong breath in the day of the east wind. By this therefore shall the iniquity of Jacob be purged, and this is all the fruit for taking away his sin; when He maketh all the stones of the altar as broken chalkstones, the groves of Ashera and the Sun-images shall not stand up.
¹⁰ For the fenced city [Babylon] shall be desolate, and the habitation forsaken, and left like the desert; there shall the calf feed, and there shall it lie down, and consume the
¹¹ branches thereof. When its boughs are withered, they are broken off; the women come and set them on fire. For this is a people of no understanding; therefore he that made them will not have mercy on them, and he that formed them will shew them no favour.
¹² And it shall come to pass in that day, that Jehovah will gather his fruit from the channel of the River [Euphrates], unto the valley of Lower Egypt, and ye shall be gathered
¹³ one by one, O ye children of Israel. And it shall come to pass in that day, that he shall blow with a great trumpet, and the wanderers in the land of Assyria, and the outcasts in the land of Egypt, shall come and shall worship Jeho
—vah on the holy mountain at Jerusalem.

¹ WOE TO THE CROWN OF PRIDE, of the drunkards of Ephraim, whose glorious beauty is a fading flower, which is at the head of the fruitful valley of them that are over
² come with wine! Behold, the Lord hath a mighty and strong one [the Assyrian], who as a tempest of hail and a destroying storm, as a flood of mighty waters overflowing,
³ shall cast them down to the earth with his hand. The

crown of pride, of the drunkards of Ephraim, shall be trodden under feet; and the glorious beauty, which is at ⁴ the head of the fruitful valley, shall be a fading flower, and as the early fruit before the summer; which when he that looketh upon it seeth, while it is yet in his hand he devoureth it.

In that day shall Jehovah of hosts be for a crown of ⁵ glory, and for a diadem of beauty, unto the residue of his people, and for a spirit of judgment to him that sitteth in ⁶ judgment, and for strength to them that turn back the battle at the city gate.

But they also have erred through wine, and through ⁷ strong drink they wander about; the priest and the prophet have erred through strong drink, they are swallowed up by wine, they wander about by strong drink; they err in their visions, they stumble in giving judgment. For all ⁸ tables are full of vomit and filthiness, so that there is no place clean.

To whom will he teach knowledge? And whom will ⁹ he make to understand what he heareth? Them that are weaned from the milk, and taken away from the breasts. For precept must be upon precept, precept upon precept; ¹⁰ line upon line, line upon line; here a little, and there a little. Truly by men of stammering lips and by a foreign ¹¹ tongue will he speak to this people. To whom he said, ¹² 'This is the resting-place where ye may cause the weary 'to rest; and this is the refreshing place;' yet they would not hear. But the word of Jehovah was unto them pre- ¹³ cept upon precept, precept upon precept; line upon line, line upon line; here a little, and there a little; so that they might go, and fall backward, and be broken, and ensnared, and taken.

Therefore hear the word of Jehovah, ye scornful men, ¹⁴ that rule this people which is in Jerusalem. Because ye ¹⁵ have said, 'We have made a covenant with Death, and 'with Hell we have made an agreement; when the over- 'flowing scourge shall pass through, it shall not come 'unto us. For we have made lies our refuge, and under 'falsehood have we hidden ourselves.'

Therefore thus said the Lord Jehovah, Behold, I lay in ¹⁶ Zion for a foundation a stone, a tried stone, a precious corner stone, a well-founded foundation; he that believeth shall not be made to flee.

17 Judgment also will I lay down by the line,
And righteousness by the plummet;
And the hail shall sweep away the refuge of lies,
And the waters shall overflow the hiding place.
18 And your covenant with Death shall be annulled,
And your agreement with Hell shall not stand;
When the overflowing scourge shall pass through,
Then ye shall be trodden down by it.
19 As often as it passeth through, it shall take you;
For day after day it shall pass, by day and by night;
And only to understand the report shall be a trouble.
20 For the bed is too short for a man to stretch himself;
And the covering too narrow for him to wrap himself.
21 For Jehovah will rise up as on mount Perazim,
He will be wroth as in the valley of Gibeon,
That he may work his work, his strange work;
And do his doings, his foreign doings.

22 Now therefore be ye not mockers, lest your bonds be made strong; for I have heard from the Lord Jehovah of hosts of destruction being determined even against the whole earth. 23 Give ye ear, and hear my voice; hearken, 24 and hear my speech. Doth the plowman plow to sow, or 25 doth he open and break up his ground every day? When he hath made level the face thereof, doth he not cast abroad the fitches, and scatter the cummin, and cast the wheat in furrows, and the barley in its fit place, and the 26 spelt on its boundary? For his God doth instruct him 27 unto discretion, and doth teach him. For the fitches are not beaten with a threshing instrument, neither is a cart-wheel turned about upon the cummin; but fitches are 28 beaten out with a staff, and cummin with a rod. Bread corn is to be ground; because he will not be continually threshing it, or breaking it with the wheel of his cart; 29 nor will he grind it with his horsemen. This also cometh forth from Jehovah of hosts, who is wonderful in counsel, —and excellent in purpose.

1 WOE TO THE ARIEL-ALTAR, the Ariel-altar [or hearth of God] of the city where David dwelt! Add ye year to year; 2 let the solemn feasts go round. Yet I will distress the Ariel-altar, and there shall be heaviness and sorrow; and 3 it shall be to me as an Ariel [or a hearth of God]. And I will encamp against thee round about, and will lay siege

against thee with a mound, and I will raise forts against thee. And thou shalt be brought down, and shalt speak ⁴ out of the ground, and thy speech shall be low out of the dust, and thy voice shall be as of a speaking bottle [or ventriloquist], out of the ground, and thy speech shall chirp out of the dust. Then the rabble of the strangers among ⁵ thee shall be like small dust, and the rabble of those that terrify shall be as chaff that passeth away; yea, it shall come to pass at an instant suddenly. Thou shalt be visited ⁶ by Jehovah of hosts with thunder, and with earthquake, and great noise, with storm and tempest, and the flame of a devouring fire. And the rabble of all the nations that ⁷ fight against Ariel, even all that fight against her and her fortress, and that distress her, shall be as a dream of a vision in the night. It shall even be as when a hungry man ⁸ dreameth, and, behold, he eateth; but he awaketh, and his soul is empty; or as when a thirsty man dreameth, and, behold, he drinketh; but he awaketh, and, behold, he is faint, and his soul craveth; so shall the rabble of all the nations be, that fight against mount Zion.

Remain idle and wonder; take your pleasure, and be ⁹ blind. They are drunken, but not with wine; they stagger, but not with strong drink. For Jehovah hath poured out ¹⁰ upon you the spirit of deep sleep, and hath closed your eyes, namely the prophets; and your heads, namely the seers of visions, hath he covered. And the whole vision ¹¹ is become unto you as the words of a sealed book, which men deliver to one that understandeth books, saying, 'Read this, I pray thee;' and he saith, 'I cannot; for it 'is sealed.' And the book is delivered to one that under- ¹² standeth not books, saying, 'Read this, I pray thee;' and he saith, 'I understand not books.' Therefore the ¹³ Lord said, Forasmuch as this people draw near me with their mouth, and with their lips they do honour me, but have removed their heart far from me, and their fear toward me is taught by the precept of men; therefore, be- ¹⁴ hold, I will again do a marvellous work among this people, even a marvellous work and a wonder; for the wisdom of their wise men shall perish, and the understanding of their understanding men shall be hidden.

Woe to them that stoop down to hide their counsel from ¹⁵ Jehovah, and their works are in the dark, and they say,

¹⁶ 'Who seeth us? and who knoweth us?' It is your perverseness if the potter is only esteemed as the clay; for shall the work say of him that made it, 'He made me not'? or shall the thing framed say of him that framed it, 'He 'had no understanding'?

¹⁷ Is it not yet less than a little while, and Lebanon shall be turned into Carmel [or a fruitful field], and Carmel shall ¹⁸ be esteemed as the forest [of Lebanon]? And in that day shall the deaf hear the words of the Book, and the eyes of the blind shall see out of obscurity, and out of darkness.

¹⁹ The meek also shall increase their joy in Jehovah, and the poor among men shall rejoice in the Holy One of Israel. ²⁰ For the terrible one is brought to nought, and the scorner is consumed, and all that watch for iniquity are cut off; ²¹ that treat a man as guilty for a word, and lay a snare for him that reproveth at the city gate, and turn aside the righteous for a thing of nought.

²² Therefore thus saith Jehovah, who redeemed Abraham, concerning the house of Jacob; Jacob shall not now be ²³ ashamed, neither shall his face now grow pale. But when he seeth his children, the work of my hands, in the midst of him, they shall sanctify my name, and sanctify the Holy ²⁴ One of Jacob, and shall dread the God of Israel. They also that erred in spirit shall come to understanding, and —they that grumbled shall learn doctrine.

¹ Woe to the rebellious children, Jehovah hath said it, that take counsel, but not of me; and that pour out drink offerings [or make treaties], but not of my spirit, so that ² they may add sin to sin; that walk to go down into Egypt, and have not asked at my mouth; to flee in haste to the strength of Pharaoh, and to seek refuge in the ³ shadow of Egypt! Therefore shall the strength of Pharaoh [Tirhakah] be your shame, and the seeking refuge in the ⁴ shadow of Egypt your confusion. For his princes were at Zoan [or Tanis], and his messengers came to Hanes [or ⁵ Tahpanhes]. They were all ashamed of a people that could not profit them, nor be a help nor profit, but a shame, and also a reproach.

⁶ THE BURDEN OF THE BEASTS OF THE SOUTH COUNTRY [of Judea].

Into a land of trouble and anguish, from whence come the lioness and lion, the viper and fiery serpent with wings, they carry their riches upon the shoulders of young asses, and their treasures upon the bunches of camels, to a people that shall not profit them. For Egypt is vanity, and shall help to no purpose; therefore have I named it, 'The Boaster that sitteth still.'

NOW GO, WRITE IT before them on a tablet; and note it in a book, that it may be for a future day for a testimony for ever; that this is a rebellious people, lying children, children that will not hear the Law of Jehovah; who say to the seers, 'See not;' and to the prophets, 'Prophesy 'not unto us right things, speak to us smooth things, 'prophesy deceits; get you out of the way, turn aside out 'of the path, cause the Holy One of Israel to cease from 'before us.' Therefore thus saith the Holy One of Israel, Because ye have refused this word, and trust in oppression and perverseness, and lean thereon; therefore this iniquity shall be to you as a breach ready to fall, swelling out in a high wall, whose breaking cometh suddenly at an instant. And He will break it as the breaking of the potter's vessel that is crushed in pieces. He will not spare; so that there shall not be found in the crushing of it a sherd to take fire with from the hearth, or to raise up water with out of the cistern.

For thus said the Lord Jehovah, the Holy One of Israel; 'In returning and remaining shall ye be saved; in quiet- 'ness and in confidence shall be your strength.' But ye would not. And ye said, 'No; for we will flee upon horses;' therefore shall ye have to flee; and, 'We will ride upon 'the swift;' therefore shall they that pursue you be swift. One thousand shall flee at the rebuke of one; at the rebuke of five shall ye flee; till ye be left as a post upon the top of a mountain, and as an ensign on a hill.

And therefore will Jehovah wait, that he may be gracious to you, and therefore will he be exalted, that he may have mercy upon you. For Jehovah is a God of justice; blessed are all they that wait for him. For thou, O people that dwellest in Zion in Jerusalem, shalt weep no more. He will be very gracious to thee at the voice of thy cry. When he shall hear it, he will answer thee. And the Lord will give you bread in adversity, and water in affliction, nor shall thy teachers be hidden any more. But thine eyes shall see thy teachers; and thine ears shall hear a

word behind thee, saying, 'This is the way, walk ye in it, 'when ye turn to the right hand, and when ye turn to the
²² 'left.' Ye shall treat as unclean also the silver plating of thy graven images, and the gold coating of thy molten images; thou shalt cast them away as any thing filthy;
²³ thou shalt say unto it, 'Get thee hence.' Then will He give rain for thy seed, wherewith thou sowest the ground; and bread, the increase of the earth; and it shall be fat and plenteous. In that day shall thy cattle feed in large pas-
²⁴ tures. The oxen likewise and the young asses that plow the ground shall eat savoury provender, which hath been
²⁵ winnowed with the fan and with the winnower. And there shall be upon every high mountain, and upon every high hill, rills streaming with waters in the day of the great
²⁶ slaughter, when the towers fall. Moreover the light of the moon shall be as the light of the sunshine, and the light of the sunshine shall be sevenfold, as the light of seven days, in the day that Jehovah bindeth up the breach of his people, and healeth the stroke of their wound.

²⁷ BEHOLD, THE NAME OF JEHOVAH cometh from far, burning with his anger, and its burden is heavy. His lips are full of indignation, and his tongue as a devouring fire.
²⁸ And his breath is as an overflowing stream, which reacheth up to the middle of the neck, to sift the nations with the sieve of vanity. And there shall be a misleading bridle
²⁹ in the jaws of the peoples. Ye shall have a song, as in the night when a holy feast is kept; and gladness of heart, as when one goeth with a pipe to come unto the mountain of
³⁰ Jehovah, to the rock of Israel. And Jehovah will cause the glory of his voice to be heard, and the coming down of his arm to be seen, with burning anger, and with the flame of a devouring fire, with scattering, and tempest, and hail-
³¹ stones. For by the voice of Jehovah shall the Assyrian be
³² terrified. He will smite him with a rod. And every passing by of the appointed staff which Jehovah shall lay upon him, shall be with timbrels and harps; and with the shock
³³ of battles will he fight against him. For Tophet [or the place of burning] was ordained of old; yea, for the king [Sennacherib] it is prepared. He hath made its pile deep and large. There is fire and much wood; the breath of —Jehovah, like a stream of brimstone, will kindle it.

¹ WOE TO THEM that go down to Egypt for help; and rely

on horses, and trust in chariots, because they are many; and in horsemen, because they are very strong; but they look not to the Holy One of Israel, neither seek Jehovah! Yet he also is wise, and will bring evil, and will not call ² back his words; but will arise against the house of the evil-doers, and against the help of them that work iniquity. Now the Egyptians are men, and not gods; and their ³ horses flesh, and not spirit. And Jehovah will stretch out his hand, and he that helpeth shall stumble, and he that is helped shall fall down, and they all shall perish together. For thus hath Jehovah spoken to me, Like as the lion and ⁴ the young lion roaring over its prey, when a multitude of shepherds is called forth against him, he is not afraid of their voice, nor disheartened at their noise; so will Jehovah of hosts come down to fight over mount Zion, and over its hill. As birds hovering about, so will Jehovah of ⁵ hosts be a shield over Jerusalem; shielding also he will deliver it; and passing over he will preserve it.

Return ye to him from whom ye have deeply revolted, ⁶ O children of Israel. For in that day every man shall cast ⁷ away his idols of silver, and his idols of gold, which your own hands have made unto you for a sin. Then shall the ⁸ Assyrian fall by the sword of one not a man; and the sword of one not a son of Adam shall devour him. But he shall flee from the sword, and his young men shall be put to tribute. And he shall pass by his rock for fear, and his ⁹ princes shall be afraid of the ensign; Jehovah hath said it, whose fire is in Zion, and his furnace in Jerusalem.

BEHOLD, A KING shall reign in righteousness, and as for ¹ rulers they shall rule in justice. And each shall be as a ² hiding place from the wind, and a covert from the tempest; as streams of water in a dry place, as the shadow of a great rock in a weary land. And the eyes of them that see shall ³ not be dim, and the ears of them that hear shall hearken. The heart also of the rash shall understand knowledge, ⁴ and the tongue of the stammerers shall be ready to speak plainly. The fool shall be no more called noble, nor the ⁵ cheat be said to be bountiful. For the fool speaketh foolish- ⁶ ness, and his heart worketh iniquity, to work profaneness, and to utter error against Jehovah, to make empty the soul of the hungry, and he causeth the drink of the thirsty to

⁷ fail. The instruments also of the cheat are evil; he counselleth wicked devices to destroy the poor with lying
⁸ words, even when the needy speaketh what is just. But the noble person counselleth noble things; and by noble things shall he stand.
⁹ Rise up, ye women that are at ease, hear my voice; ye
¹⁰ careless daughters, give ear unto my speech. After this year shall ye be troubled, ye careless women; for the vintage shall fail, the after-gathering shall not come.
¹¹ Tremble, ye women that are at ease; be troubled, ye careless ones; strip you, and make yourselves bare, but girded
¹² upon your loins; beating your breasts for the pleasant fields, for the fruitful vine.
¹³ Upon the land of my people shall come up thorns and briers; yea, upon all the houses of pleasure in the joyous
¹⁴ city. For the palaces are forsaken; the rabble of the city is left; the [suburb] Ophel and the watch-tower shall be for dens for ever, a pleasure for wild asses, a pasture for
¹⁵ flocks; until the spirit be poured upon us from on high. Then shall the desert become a fruitful field, and the
¹⁶ fruitful field be counted for a forest. Then justice shall dwell in the desert, and righteousness remain in the fruit-
¹⁷ ful field. And the work of righteousness shall be peace; and the effect of righteousness quietness and security for
¹⁸ ever. And my people shall dwell in a peaceable habitation, and in sure dwellings, and in quiet resting places.
¹⁹ But hail shall hail down on the forest; and the city shall
²⁰ be low in a low place. Blessed are ye that sow beside all —waters, that send forth thither the feet of the ox and the ass.
¹ Woe to thee [Babylon] that oppressest, and thou wast not oppressed; and dealest treacherously, and they dealt not treacherously with thee! When thou shalt cease to oppress thou shalt be oppressed; and when thou shalt make an end of dealing treacherously, they shall deal
² treacherously with thee. ('O Jehovah, be gracious to us; 'we have waited for thee; be thou their arm every
³ 'morning, our salvation also in the time of trouble. At 'the noise of the tumult the peoples fled; at the lifting
⁴ 'up of thyself the nations were scattered.') And your plunder shall be gathered like the clean gathering of the caterpillar; as the running to and fro of locusts shall they run upon it.

Jehovah is exalted; for he dwelleth on high; he hath ⁵ filled Zion with justice and righteousness. And wisdom and ⁶ knowledge shall be the stability of thy times, the strength of salvation; the fear of Jehovah, that is his treasure.

Behold, their valiant ones cry for help without; the ⁷ messengers of peace weep bitterly. The highways lie ⁸ waste, the wayfaring man ceaseth. He [the Babylonian] hath broken the treaty, he hath despised the cities, he regardeth no man. The earth mourneth and languisheth; ⁹ Lebanon is made ashamed and withereth away; Sharon is like the Barren Valley; and Bashan and Carmel are stripped of leaves.

Now will I arise, saith Jehovah; now will I be exalted; ¹⁰ now will I lift up myself. Ye shall conceive chaff, ye shall ¹¹ bring forth stubble; your breath, as fire, shall devour you. And the peoples shall be as the burnings of lime; as ¹² thorns cut up shall they be burned in the fire.

Hear, ye that are far off, what I have done; and, ye that ¹³ are near, acknowledge my might. The sinners in Zion are ¹⁴ afraid; fear hath seized the ungodly. 'Who among us 'shall dwell while the fire devoureth? Who among us shall 'dwell with everlasting burnings?' He that walketh in ¹⁵ righteousness, and speaketh uprightly; he that refuseth the gain of oppressions, that shaketh his hands from taking bribes, that stoppeth his ears from hearing of bloodshed, and shutteth his eyes from looking upon evil; he shall ¹⁶ dwell on high; his place of defence shall be castles upon rocks; bread shall be given him; his waters shall be unfailing. Thine eyes shall see the king in his beauty; they ¹⁷ shall behold the land that is very far off. Thy heart shall ¹⁸ meditate upon the terror. 'Where is the scribe? where is 'the weigher? where is he that counted the towers?' Thou ¹⁹ shalt not see the fierce people, a people of deeper speech than thou canst understand; of a stammering tongue, not to be understood. Look upon Zion, the city of our solemn ²⁰ feasts; thine eyes shall see Jerusalem a quiet habitation, a tent that shall not be taken down; not one of its tent-pins shall ever be pulled up, neither shall any of its cords be broken. For there will Jehovah be mighty unto us, ²¹ as a place of rivers and streams with wide sides; wherein shall go no galleys with oars, neither shall mighty ship pass thereby. For Jehovah is our judge, Jehovah is our ²² lawgiver, Jehovah is our king; he will save us.

23 Thy tacklings [O Babylon] are loosed; they do not hold steady the support of their yard-arm, they do not spread the sail. Then was the prey of a great spoil divided; 24 even the lame seized upon the prey. And the neighbour shall not say, 'I am sick;' the people that dwell therein —shall be forgiven their iniquity.

1 COME NEAR, YE NATIONS, to hear; and hearken, ye peoples; let the earth hear, and the fulness thereof; the 2 world, and all things that come out of it. For the indignation of Jehovah is upon all the Nations, and his wrath upon all their armies; he hath devoted them, he 3 hath delivered them to the slaughter. Their slain also shall be cast out, and their stink shall come up out of their dead bodies, and the mountains shall be watered with 4 their blood. And all the host of heaven shall be dissolved, and the heavens shall be rolled together as a book-roll; and all their host shall wither away, as the leaf withereth from the vine, and as a withered fig from the fig tree. 5 For my sword shall be bathed in heaven; behold, it shall come down upon Edom, and upon the people of my curse unto judgment.
6 The sword of Jehovah is filled with blood, it is made fat with fatness, with the blood of lambs and goats, with fat of the kidneys of rams; for there is a sacrifice to Jehovah in Bozrah, and a great slaughter in the land of Edom. 7 And the buffaloes [or Egyptians] shall be cast down with them, and the bullocks with the bulls [or Syrians]; and their land shall be bathed with blood, and their dust made fat with fatness.
8 For it is the day of Jehovah's vengeance, and the year 9 of recompences for the controversy of Zion. And her [Babylon's] streams shall be turned into pitch, and her dust into brimstone, and the land thereof shall become 10 burning pitch. It shall not be quenched night or day; the smoke thereof shall go up for ever; from generation to generation it shall lie waste; none shall pass through it for ever and ever.
11 But the cormorant and the hedgehog shall possess it; the heron also and the raven shall dwell in it; and he shall stretch out upon it the measuring-line of confusion, 12 and the plummet-stone of emptiness. They shall call the nobles thereof to the kingdom, but none shall be there,

And all her princes shall be nothing. And thorns shall ¹³ come up in her palaces, nettles and brambles in the fortresses thereof; and it shall be a habitation of jackals, and a courtyard for ostriches. The desert-beasts shall ¹⁴ also meet with the howling beasts, and the satyr shall cry to his mate; the night-bird also shall settle there, and find for herself a place of rest. There shall the arrow- ¹⁵ snake make her nest, and lay eggs, and hatch, and cherish them under her shadow; there shall the vultures also be gathered together, every one with her mate. Seek ye out ¹ of the book of Jehovah [Isaiah xiii.], and read. No one of these shall be lacking, no one shall want her mate; for my mouth hath commanded it. And his spirit it hath gathered them; and he hath cast the lot for them, ¹⁷ and his hand hath divided it unto them by measuring-line; they shall possess it for ever, from generation to generation shall they dwell therein. —

The desert and the land of drought shall be glad for ¹ them; and the barren valley shall rejoice, and blossom as the crocus. It shall blossom abundantly, and rejoice even ² with joy and singing. The glory of Lebanon shall be given to it, the excellence of Carmel and Sharon; they shall see the glory of Jehovah, and the excellence of our God.

Strengthen ye the weak hands, and confirm the feeble ³ knees. Say to them that are of a fearful heart, 'Be ⁴ 'strong, fear not; behold, your God.' Vengeance will come, even God's recompence; he will come and save you.

Then the eyes of the blind shall be opened, and the ⁵ ears of the deaf shall be unstopped. Then shall the lame ⁶ man leap as a hart, and the tongue of the dumb sing; for in the desert shall waters break out, and streams in the barren valley. And the heated sands shall become a pool, ⁷ and the thirsty lands shall become springs of water; in the habitation where the jackals lay, shall be a place for the sweet cane and the paper-reed.

And a highway shall be there, and a way, and it shall ⁸ be called 'The way of holiness.' The unclean shall not pass over it; but it shall be for those [the Israelites]. The wayfaring men, though fools, shall not go astray therein. No lion shall be there, nor ravenous beast shall go up ⁹ thereon; none shall be found there; but the redeemed

10 ones shall walk there. And the ransomed of Jehovah shall return, and come to Zion with songs and everlasting joy upon their heads. They shall obtain joy and gladness, —and sorrow and sighing shall flee away.

1 Now IT CAME TO PASS in the fourteenth year of king Hezekiah [B.C. 714], that Sennacherib king of Assyria came up against all the fenced cities of Judah, and took
2 them. And the king of Assyria sent Rab-shakeh [or the chief butler] from Lachish to Jerusalem unto king Hezekiah with a great army. And he stood by the conduit of
3 the Upper Pool in the highway of the fuller's field. Then came forth to him Eliakim, the son of Hilkiah, who was over the House, and Shebna the scribe, and Joah the son
4 of Asaph, the recorder. And Rab-shakeh said to them, 'Say ye now to Hezekiah, Thus saith the Great King, the 'king of Assyria, What trust is this wherein thou trustest?
5 'Thou speakest only words of the lips as counsel and 'strength for war. Now on whom dost thou trust, that
6 'thou hast rebelled against me? Behold, thou trustest on 'the support of this broken reed, even on Egypt; on which 'if a man lean, it will go into his hand, and pierce it. So is
7 'Pharaoh king of Egypt to all that trust on him. But if 'thou say to me, We trust in Jehovah our God; is not that 'he, whose High Places and whose altars Hezekiah hath 'taken away? And he saith to Judah and to Jerusalem,
8 'Ye shall worship him before this altar. Now therefore 'give pledges, I pray thee, to my lord the king of Assyria, 'and I will deliver to thee two thousand horses, if thou be
9 'able on thy part to put chariots to them. How then wilt 'thou turn away the face of one Pasha [or captain] of the 'least of my master's servants, and put thy trust on Egypt
10 'for chariots and for horsemen? And am I now come up 'without Jehovah against this land to destroy it? Jeho-'vah said to me, Go up against this land, and destroy it.'
11 Then said Eliakim and Shebna and Joah to Rab-shakeh, 'Speak, I pray thee, to thy servants in the Syriac lan-'guage; for we understand it. And speak not to us in 'the Jewish language, in the ears of the people that are on
12 'the wall.' But Rab-shakeh said, 'Hath my master sent 'me to thy master and to thee to speak these words? Hath 'he not sent me to the men that sit upon the wall, that

'they may eat their own dung, and drink their own urine 'with you?' Then Rab-shakeh stood, and cried with a ¹³ loud voice in the Jewish language, and said, 'Hear ye the 'words of the Great King, the king of Assyria. Thus ¹⁴ 'saith the king, Let not Hezekiah deceive you; for he will 'not be able to deliver you. Neither let Hezekiah make ¹⁵ 'you trust in Jehovah, saying, Jehovah will surely deliver 'us; this city will not be delivered into the hand of the 'king of Assyria.—Hearken not to Hezekiah. For thus ¹⁶ 'saith the king of Assyria, Make peace with me, and come 'out to me; and eat ye every man of his own vine, and 'every man of his own fig tree, and drink ye every man the 'waters of his own cistern; until I come and take you ¹⁷ 'away to a land like your own land, a land of corn and 'grape juice, a land of bread and vineyards. Let not Heze- ¹⁸ 'kiah persuade you, saying, Jehovah will deliver us.—Hath 'any of the gods of the nations delivered his land out of 'the hand of the king of Assyria? Where are the gods ¹⁹ 'of Hamath and of Arpad? Where are the gods of Se- 'pharvaim? And have they delivered Samaria out of my 'hand? Who are they among all the gods of these coun- ²⁰ 'tries, that have delivered their country out of my hand, 'that Jehovah should deliver Jerusalem out of my hand?' But they held their peace, and answered him not a word; ²¹ for the king's command was, saying, 'Answer him not.'

Then came Eliakim, the son of Hilkiah, who was over ²² the House, and Shebna the scribe, and Joah, the son of Asaph, the recorder, to Hezekiah with their clothes rent,— and told him the words of Rab-shakeh. And it came to ¹ pass, when king Hezekiah heard it, that he rent his clothes, and covered himself with sackcloth, and went into the House of Jehovah. And he sent Eliakim, who was over ² the House, and Shebna the scribe, and the elders of the priests, covered with sackcloth, to Isaiah the prophet, the son of Amoz. And they said to him, 'Thus saith Heze- ³ 'kiah, This day is a day of trouble, and of rebuke, and of 'scoffing; for the children are come to the birth, and there 'is not strength to bring forth. It may be Jehovah thy ⁴ 'God will hear the words of Rab-shakeh, whom the king 'of Assyria his master hath sent to defy the living God, and 'will reprove the words which Jehovah thy God hath heard. 'Therefore lift up thy prayer for the remnant that is left.'

5 So the servants of king Hezekiah came to Isaiah. And
6 Isaiah said to them, 'Thus shall ye say to your master,
'Thus saith Jehovah, Be not afraid of the words that thou
'hast heard, with which the servants of the king of As-
7 'syria have blasphemed me. Behold, I will send a
'breath upon him, and he shall hear a rumour, and shall
'return to his own land; and I will cause him to fall by
'the sword in his own land.'
8 So Rab-shakeh returned, and found the king of Assyria
warring against Libnah; for he had heard that he had
9 moved his camp from Lachish. And he heard say of Tir-
hakah king of Ethiopia, 'He is come out to fight against
'thee.' And when he heard it, he sent messengers to
10 Hezekiah, saying, 'Thus shall ye speak to Hezekiah
'king of Judah, saying, Let not thy God, in whom thou
'trustest, deceive thee, saying, Jerusalem shall not be
11 'given into the hand of the king of Assyria. Behold, thou
'hast heard what the kings of Assyria have done to all
'lands by destroying them utterly; and shalt thou be
12 'delivered? Have the gods of the nations delivered them
'which my fathers have destroyed, as Gozan, and Haran,
'and Rezeph, and the children of Eden who were in Tel-
13 'ashar? Where is the king of Hamath, and the king of
'Arpad, and the king of the city of Sepharvaim, of Hena,
'and of Avah?'
14 And Hezekiah received the letter from the hand of the
messengers, and read it. And Hezekiah went up to the
15 House of Jehovah, and spread it before Jehovah. And
16 Hezekiah prayed unto Jehovah, saying, 'O Jehovah of
'hosts, God of Israel, who dwellest between the cherubs, thou
'art the God, even thou alone, of all the kingdoms of the
17 'earth. Thou hast made the heavens and the earth. Bow
'down thine ear, O Jehovah, and hear. Open thine eyes,
'O Jehovah, and see. And hear all the words of Sennache-
18 'rib, who hath sent to defy the living God. Of a truth, O
'Jehovah, the kings of Assyria have laid waste all the
19 'countries, and their lands, and have cast their gods into
'the fire. For they were no gods, but the work of men's
'hands, wood and stone; therefore they have destroyed
20 'them. Now, therefore, O Jehovah our God, save us out
'of his hand, that all the kingdoms of the earth may know
'that thou art Jehovah, even thou only.'

Then Isaiah the son of Amoz sent to Hezekiah, saying, ²¹
'Thus saith Jehovah the God of Israel, Whereas thou hast
'prayed to me against Sennacherib king of Assyria; this ²²
'is the word that Jehovah hath spoken concerning him;
'The virgin, the daughter of Zion, despiseth thee, she
'laugheth thee to scorn; the daughter of Jerusalem shaketh
'her head after thee. Whom hast thou defied and blas- ²³
'phemed? and against whom hast thou exalted thy voice,
'and lifted up thine eyes on high? even against the Holy
'One of Israel. By the hand of thy servants thou hast de- ²⁴
'fied the Lord, and hast said, With the multitude of my
'chariots I am come up to the height of the mountains, to
'the sides of Lebanon; and I will cut down its tall cedars,
'and its choice fir trees; and I will enter into its remotest
'height, into the thicket of its garden [or Carmel]. I have ²⁵
'digged, and have drunk up the waters; and with the sole
'of my feet have I dried up all the canals of Lower Egypt.—
'Hast thou not heard long ago, how I did it, and of ancient ²⁶
'times, that I purposed it? I have now brought it to pass,
'that it should be for thee to lay waste fenced cities into
'heaps of ruins. But their inhabitants were of small power, ²⁷
'they were dismayed and confounded; they were as the
'grass of the field, and as the green herb, as the grass on the
'housetops, or as corn before it be grown to stalk. But thine ²⁸
'abode, and thy going out, and thy coming in I know, and
'thy rage against me. Because thy rage against me, and ²⁹
'thine insolence, are come up into mine ears, therefore I will
'put my hook in thy nose, and my bridle in thy lips, and I
'will turn thee back by the way by which thou camest. And ³⁰
'this shall be a sign unto thee; in this year shall be eaten
'what groweth of itself; and in the second year that which
'springeth from the same; and in the third year sow ye and
'reap, and plant vineyards, and eat the fruits thereof.
'And the escaped of the house of Judah shall increase, ³¹
'those left shall take root downward, and bear fruit up-
'ward. For out of Jerusalem shall go forth a remnant, ³²
'and they that escape out of mount Zion. The zeal of
'Jehovah of hosts shall do this.

'Therefore thus saith Jehovah concerning the king of ³³
'Assyria, He shall not come into this city, nor shoot an
'arrow there, nor come before it with shields, nor cast up
'a siege-mound against it. By the way that he came, by ³⁴

'the same shall he return; and he shall not come into this
35 'city; Jehovah hath said it. For I will be a shield over
'this city to save it for mine own sake, and for my servant
36 'David's sake.' Then the angel of Jehovah went forth,
and smote in the camp of the Assyrians a hundred and
eighty and five thousand; and when men rose early in the
37 morning, behold, they were all dead corpses. And Sennacherib king of Assyria moved his camp, and went and
returned, and dwelt at Nineveh.
38 (And it came to pass [B.C. 683], as he was worshipping
in the house of Nisroch his god, that Adrammelech and
Sharezer his sons smote him with the sword, and they escaped into the land of Ararat [or Armenia]; and Esar-
—haddon his son reigned in his stead.)

1 In those days [B.C. 713] was Hezekiah sick unto death.
And Isaiah the prophet the son of Amoz came to him,
and said to him, 'Thus saith Jehovah, Set thy house in
2 'order; for thou shalt die, and not live.' Then Hezekiah
turned his face to the wall, and prayed to Jehovah,
3 and said, 'I beseech thee, O Jehovah, remember now how
'I have walked before thee in truth and with a perfect
'heart, and have done what is good in thy sight.' And
Hezekiah wept with a great weeping.
4 Then came the word of Jehovah to Isaiah, saying, Go,
5 and say to Hezekiah, 'Thus saith Jehovah, the God of
'David thy father, I have heard thy prayer, I have seen
'thy tears; behold, I will add unto thy days fifteen years.
6 'And I will deliver thee and this city out of the grasp of
'the king of Assyria; and I will be a shield over this city.
7 'And this shall be a sign unto thee from Jehovah, that
8 'Jehovah will do this thing that he hath spoken; behold,
'I will bring back the shadow of the dial, which is gone
'down on the sun dial of Ahaz, ten degrees backward.' So
the sun returned ten degrees, by which degrees it had gone
down.
9 THE WRITING OF HEZEKIAH king of Judah, when he had
10 been sick, and was recovered of his sickness.—I said,
'In the quiet of my days, I shall go to the gates of hell;
11 'I am deprived of the residue of my years,'—I said,
'I shall not behold Jah-Jah in the land of the living.
'With the dwellers in the grave, I shall see man no more.
12 'My habitation is broken up,

'And is removed from me as a shepherd's tent.
'My life is ended; as a weaver he cutteth me from the loom;
'Between day and night thou wilt make an end of me.'
I meditated until morning, 13
That, as a lion, so will he break all my bones; [saying,]
'Between day and night thou wilt make an end of me.'
Like a crane or a swallow, so did I chatter. 14
I mourned as a dove; my upward eyes failed, [saying,]
'O Jehovah, I am oppressed, deliver me.'—What say I now? 15
'He both promised me, and himself hath done it.
'I will go humbly all my years in bitterness of soul.'
  O Lord, by these things men live, 16
And altogether in them is the life of my spirit;
So wilt thou recover me, and make me to live.
Behold, for peace I had great bitterness, 17
But thou didst draw my soul from the pit of nothingness,
For thou hast cast all my sins behind thy back.
For Hell cannot praise thee, or Death celebrate thee; 18
They that go down into the Pit hope not for thy truth.
The living, the living, shall praise thee, as I do to-day; 19
The father to the children shall make known thy truth.

  Jehovah hath saved me; therefore we will sing my songs 20
to stringed instruments all the days of our life in the House
of Jehovah. (For Isaiah had said, 'Let them take a cake 21
'of figs, and lay it for a plaister upon the boil, and he shall
'recover.' And Hezekiah had said, 'What is the sign that 22
'I shall go up to the House of Jehovah?')

  AT THAT TIME Merodach-baladan, the son of Baladan, 1
king of Babylon, sent letters and a present to Hezekiah;
for he had heard that he had been sick, and was recovered.
And Hezekiah was glad of them, and shewed them the 2
house of his spicery, the silver, and the gold, and the scents,
and the precious ointment, and all the house of his armour,
and all that was found in his treasures. There was nothing
in his house, nor in all his dominion, that Hezekiah shewed
them not.

  Then came Isaiah the prophet to king Hezekiah, and 3
said to him, 'What said these men? And from whence
'came they to thee?' And Hezekiah said, 'They are
'come from a far country to me, even from Babylon.'
Then he said, 'What have they seen in thy house.' And 4
Hezekiah answered, 'All that is in my house have they

'seen. There is nothing among my treasures that I have
5 'not shewed them.' And Isaiah said to Hezekiah, 'Hear
6 'the word of Jehovah of hosts; Behold, days will come,
'when all that is in thy house, and that which thy fathers
'have laid up in store until this day, shall be carried to
7 'Babylon; nothing shall be left, saith Jehovah. And some
'of thy sons that shall issue from thee, which thou shalt
'beget, shall they take away; and they shall be chamber-
8 'lains in the palace of the king of Babylon.' Then said
Hezekiah to Isaiah, 'Good is the word of Jehovah which
'thou hast spoken.' And he said, 'For there shall be peace
—'and certainty in my days.'

---

1 COMFORT YE, COMFORT YE my people, saith your God.
2 Speak ye to the heart of Jerusalem, and cry unto her, that her warfare is accomplished, that her iniquity is pardoned; for she hath received from Jehovah's hand double for all her sins.
3 The voice of one that crieth, 'Prepare ye in the desert 'the way of Jehovah, make straight in the barren valley
4 'a highway for our God.' Every valley shall be exalted, and every mountain and hill shall be made low; and the crooked shall be made straight, and the rough places plain;
5 and the glory of Jehovah shall be revealed, and all flesh shall see it together; for the mouth of Jehovah hath spoken it.
6 A voice said, 'Cry.' And he said, 'What shall I cry?' All flesh is grass, and all the goodness thereof is as the
7 flower of the field. The grass withereth, the flower fadeth, when the breath of Jehovah bloweth upon it.
8 Surely the people are grass; the grass withereth, the flower fadeth, but the word of our God shall stand for ever.
9 Get thee up into the high mountain, O thou that bringest good tidings to Zion; lift up thy voice with strength, O thou that bringest good tidings to Jerusalem; lift it up, be not afraid; say to the cities of Judah, 'Be-
10 'hold your God!' Behold, the Lord Jehovah will come with might, and his arm shall rule for him; behold, his reward is with him, and his recompence for work is be-
11 fore him. He will feed his flock like a shepherd; he will gather the lambs with his arm, and carry them in his bosom, and will gently lead those that have young ones.
12 Who hath measured the waters in the hollow of his

hand, and meted out the heavens with the span, and gathered up the dust of the earth within a measure, and weighed the mountains in a balance, and the hills in a pair of scales? Who hath directed the spirit of Jehovah, [13] or being his counsellor hath taught him? With whom [14] took he counsel, and who instructed him, and taught him in the path of judgment, and taught him knowledge, and shewed to him the way of understanding? Behold, the [15] nations are as a drop of the bucket, and are counted as the dust of the balances. Behold, he taketh up the isles as a very little thing. And Lebanon is not sufficient for [16] fuel, nor the wild beasts thereof sufficient for a burnt offering. All the nations are as nothing before him; and [17] they are counted by him as less than nothing, and vanity. To whom then will ye liken God? or what likeness will [18] ye compare unto him? The workman melteth an image, [19] and the metal-founder spreadeth it over with gold, and casteth silver chains. He that is poor in respect to his [20] heave offering chooseth a tree that will not rot; he seeketh unto him a cunning workman to prepare a graven image, that will not fall down.

Have ye not known? Have ye not heard? Hath it not [21] been told you from the beginning? Have ye not understood from the foundations of the earth? It is He that [22] sitteth upon the earth's arch, and the inhabitants thereof are as grasshoppers; He that stretcheth out the heavens as a curtain, and spreadeth them out as a tent to dwell in; He that bringeth the princes to nothing; He that [23] maketh the judges of the earth as vanity. Yea, they are [24] not planted; yea, they are not sown; yea, their stock hath not taken root in the earth; and he will also blow upon them, and they shall wither, and the whirlwind shall take them away as chaff.

To whom then will ye liken me, or shall I be equal? [25] saith the Holy One. Lift up your eyes on high, and see [26] who hath created these things. When he bringeth out their host by number, he calleth them all by names; by the greatness of his might, and his strong power, not one is lacking.

Why speakest thou, O Jacob, and sayest, O Israel, 'My [27] 'way is hidden from Jehovah, and my rights are passed 'away from my God'? Hast thou not known, hast thou [28]

not heard, that the everlasting God, Jehovah, the Creator of the ends of the earth, fainteth not, neither is weary?
29 There is no searching out his reasons. He giveth power to the faint; and to them that have no might he in-
30 creaseth strength. Even youths may faint and be weary,
31 and young men may utterly fall; but they that wait upon Jehovah shall renew their strength; they shall mount up with wings as eagles; they shall run, and not be weary; —and they shall walk, and not faint.

1 KEEP SILENCE BEFORE ME, O islands; and let the peoples renew their strength; let them come near; then let them speak; let us draw near together to judgment.
2 Who hath raised up the righteous man [Cyrus] from the East, hath called him to be his follower, hath given up the nations before him, and made him rule over kings? He hath given them as the dust to his sword, and as driven
3 chaff to his bow. He pursued them, and passed safely; even by the way that he had not gone with his feet.
4 Who hath worked and done it, calling the generations from the beginning? I Jehovah, who am first, and with
5 the last; I am he. The isles saw it, and were afraid; the ends of the earth trembled; they drew near and came.
6 (Every one helpeth his neighbour, and saith to his brother,
7 'Be of good courage.' So the carpenter encourageth the metal-founder, and he that smootheth with the hammer him that smiteth the anvil, saying, 'It is ready for the 'soldering;' and he fasteneth it with nails, that it should not fall down.)
8 But thou, Israel my servant, Jacob whom I have
9 chosen, the seed of Abraham my friend; thou whom I have taken from the ends of the earth, and called thee from the extremities thereof, and said to thee, ' Thou art 'my servant, I have chosen thee, and not cast thee away;'
10 fear thou not, for I am with thee; look not away, for I am thy God. I will strengthen thee; yea, I will help thee; yea, I will uphold thee with the right hand of my righteousness.
11 Behold, all they that were incensed against thee shall be ashamed and confounded; they shall be as nothing;
12 the men that strive with thee shall perish. Thou shalt seek them, and shalt not find them, even the men that

contended with thee. The men that war against thee shall be as nothing, and as a thing of nought. For I Jehovah thy God will hold thy right hand, saying unto thee, 'Fear not; I will help thee.' [13]

Fear not, thou worm Jacob, ye men of Israel; I will help thee; Jehovah, and thy Redeemer, the Holy One of Israel hath said it. Behold, I will make thee to be a new threshing instrument, cutting and having teeth; thou shalt thresh the mountains, and shalt beat them small, and shalt make the hills as chaff. Thou shalt fan them, and the wind shall carry them away, and the whirlwind shall scatter them; and thou shalt rejoice in Jehovah, and shalt glory in the Holy One of Israel. [14] [15] [16]

The poor and needy are seeking for water, and there is none, and their tongue is parched with thirst; but I Jehovah will answer them, the God of Israel will not forsake them. I will open rivers on the bare heights, and fountains in the midst of the valleys; I will make the desert to be a pool of water, and the dry land to be springs of water. I will plant in the desert the cedar, the acacia tree, and the myrtle, and the olive tree; I will set in the barren valley the fir tree, the pine, and the box tree together; so that men may see, and know, and consider, and understand together, that the hand of Jehovah hath done this; and the Holy One of Israel hath created it. [17] [18] [19] [20]

Bring forward your cause, saith Jehovah; produce your defence, saith the King of Jacob. Let them bring it forth, and shew us what will happen. Let them shew the former things, what they are, that we may consider, and know the latter end of them; or declare to us what is coming. Shew the things that are to come hereafter, that we may know that ye are gods. Yea, make good, or make evil, that we may look about, and behold it together. Behold, ye are of nothing, and your work is of nought; an abomination is he that chooseth you. [21] [22] [23] [24]

I HAVE RAISED UP one [Cyrus] from the north, and he cometh; from the rising of the sun he calleth upon my name, and he shall come upon princes as upon mortar, and as the potter treadeth the clay. [25]

Who declared this from the beginning, that we might know? and beforetime, that we might say, 'It is right'? Yea, there was none that shewed it; yea, there was none [26]

that declared it. Yea, there was none that hearkened to
²⁷ your words, when at first saying to Zion, 'Behold, behold
'them; and I will give to Jerusalem one that bringeth
²⁸ 'good tidings.' For I beheld, and there was no man, even
among them, and there was no counsellor, that, when I
²⁹ asked of them, could answer a word. Behold, they are
all vanity; their works are nothing; their molten images
—are wind and confusion.

¹ Behold my Servant [Zerubbabel], whom I will uphold;
my chosen one in whom my soul delighteth. I have put
my spirit upon him; he shall bring forth judgment upon
² the Nations. He shall not cry, nor lift up, nor cause his
³ voice to be heard abroad. A bruised reed shall he not
break, and the dimly burning flax shall he not quench;
⁴ he shall bring forth judgment unto truth. He shall not
fail nor be discouraged, till he have set up judgment on
the land; and the isles shall wait for his law.
⁵ Thus saith the God Jehovah, he that created the heavens,
and stretched them out; he that spread forth the earth, and
its offspring; he that giveth breath unto the people upon
⁶ it, and spirit to them that walk thereon; I Jehovah have
called thee in righteousness, and I will hold thy hand,
and will guard thee, and give thee for a covenant to the
⁷ People, for a light to the Nations; to open the blind eyes,
to bring out the prisoners from the prison, and them that
⁸ sit in darkness out of the prison house. I am Jehovah;
that is my name; and my glory will I not give to another,
⁹ neither my praise to graven images. Behold, the former
things are come to pass, and new things do I declare;
before they spring forth I tell you of them.
¹⁰ 'Sing ye to Jehovah a new song, and his praise from
'the end of the earth, ye that go down to the sea, and all
'that is therein; the isles and the inhabitants thereof.
¹¹ 'Let the desert and its cities lift up a voice, the villages
'that Kedar doth inhabit; let the inhabitants of Sela [or
'Petra] sing, let them shout from the top of the mountains.
¹² 'Let them give glory unto Jehovah, and declare his praise
¹³ 'in the islands. Jehovah goeth forth as a mighty man, he
'stirreth up jealousy like a man of war; he will cry out, yea,
'he will shout; he will prevail against his enemies.'
¹⁴ I have for a long time held my peace; I have been still,
and restrained myself. Now I cry aloud like a travailing

woman; I will at once both destroy and devour. I will ¹⁵ make waste the mountains and hills, and dry up all their herbs; and I will make the rivers to become islands, and I will dry up the pools. And I will bring the blind by a ¹⁶ way that they know not; in paths that they know not will I lead them; I will make darkness to become light before them, and crooked things to become straight. These things will I do unto them, and I will not forsake them. Those shall be turned back, those shall be greatly ashamed, ¹⁷ that trust in graven images, that say to the molten images, 'Ye are our gods.' Hear, ye deaf; and look, ye blind, that ¹⁸ ye may see.

Who is so blind as my Servant [Zerubbabel]? or so deaf ¹⁹ as my messenger [Jeshua] whom I am sending? Who is so blind as my friend, and so blind as Jehovah's Servant? Thou hast seen many things, but thou observest not; he ²⁰ hath opened the ears, but he heareth not.

Jehovah is well pleased because of his righteousness; he ²¹ magnifieth the Law, and maketh it honourable. But this ²² is a people robbed and plundered; they are all of them ensnared in holes, and they are hidden in prison houses. They are become a prey, and none delivereth; a spoil, and none saith, 'Restore.'

Which among you will give ear to this, and will hearken ²³ and hear for the time to come? Who gave Jacob for a ²⁴ spoil, and Israel to the robbers? Was it not Jehovah, he against whom we have sinned? For they would not walk in his ways, neither were they obedient unto his Law. Therefore he hath poured upon him the wrath of his anger, ²⁵ and the strength of the battle. And it hath set him on fire round about, yet he knew it not; and it burned him, yet he laid it not to heart.

But now thus saith Jehovah that created thee, O Jacob, ¹ and he that formed thee, O Israel. Fear not; for I have redeemed thee, I have called thee by thy name; thou art mine. When thou passest through the waters, I will be ² with thee; and through the rivers, they shall not overflow thee. When thou walkest through the fire, thou shalt not be scorched; neither shall the flame kindle upon thee. For I Jehovah am thy God, the Holy One of Israel, thy ³ Saviour. I have given Egypt for thy ransom, Ethiopia and Seba [or Meroë] in place of thee. Since thou art ⁴ precious in my sight, thou hast been honourable, and I have loved thee. Therefore I will give men for thee, and ⁵ peoples for thy life. Fear not; for I am with thee. I will bring thy seed from the east, and gather thee from ⁶ the west; I will say to the north, 'Give up;' and to the south, 'Keep not back. Bring my sons from far, and my 'daughters from the ends of the earth; even every one ⁷ 'that is called by my name.' For I created him for my glory, I formed him; yea, I made him.

⁸ Bring forth the blind people that have eyes, and the ⁹ deaf that have ears. Let all the Nations be gathered together, and let the peoples be assembled. Who among them did declare this, and did shew us the former things? Let them bring forth their witnesses, that they may be justified; and let men hear, and say, 'It is true.' ¹⁰ Ye are my witnesses, Jehovah hath said it, and my Servant whom I have chosen, that ye may know and believe me, and may understand that I am He. Before me there ¹¹ was no God formed, neither shall there be after me. I, even I, am Jehovah; and beside me there is no saviour. ¹² I have declared it, and have saved, and I have made it known when there was no strange god among you. Therefore ye are my witnesses, Jehovah hath said it, that I am ¹³ God. Yea, before the day was, I was He; and there is none that can deliver out of my hand. I will work, and who shall undo it?

¹⁴ Thus saith Jehovah, your redeemer, the Holy One of Israel; For your sake I have sent to Babylon, and have brought down all the fugitives, and the Chaldeans, ¹⁵ whose shout is in ships. I am Jehovah, your Holy One, the creator of Israel, and your King.

¹⁶ Thus saith Jehovah, he who maketh a way in the sea, ¹⁷ and a path in the mighty waters; who bringeth forth the chariot and horse, the army and the strong ones together; They shall lie down, they shall not rise; they are extinguished, they are quenched as tow.

¹⁸ Remember ye not the former things, neither consider ¹⁹ the things of old. Behold, I will do a new thing; now it shall spring forth; shall ye not know it? I will even make a way in the desert, and rivers in the wilderness. ²⁰ The wild beasts of the field shall honour me, the jackals and the ostriches; because I give waters in the desert,

and rivers in the wilderness, to give drink to my people, my chosen ones. This people have I formed for myself; 21 they shall shew forth my praise.

But thou hast not called upon me, O Jacob; for thou 22 hast been weary of me, O Israel. Thou hast not brought 23 me the lamb or kid of thy burnt offerings; neither hast thou honoured me with thy sacrifices. I have not burdened thee with meal offerings, nor wearied thee with incense. Thou hast bought for me no sweet cane with 24 money, neither hast thou moistened me with the fat of thy sacrifices; but thou hast burdened me with thy sins, thou hast wearied me with thine iniquities. I, even I, am 25 he that blotteth out thy transgressions for mine own sake, and I will not remember thy sins.

Put me in remembrance; let us plead together; declare 26 thou, that thou mayest be justified. Thy first father sinned, 27 and thy teachers have transgressed against me. Therefore 28 I profaned the princes of the Holy Place, and gave up Jacob to the curse, and Israel to reproaches.

Yet now hear, O Jacob my servant, and Israel, whom I 1 have chosen; thus saith Jehovah that made thee, and 2 formed thee from the womb, who will help thee; Fear not, O Jacob, my servant; and thou, Jesurun [or Israel], whom I have chosen. For I will pour water upon the thirsty 3 land, and floods upon the dry ground; I will pour my spirit upon thy seed, and my blessing upon thine offspring. And they shall spring up as among the grass, as willows by 4 the water-courses. One shall say, I am Jehovah's; and 5 he shall call himself by the name of Jacob; and another shall subscribe with his hand unto Jehovah, and surname himself by the name of Israel.

THUS SAITH JEHOVAH the King of Israel, and his re- 6 deemer, Jehovah of hosts; I am the first, and I am the last; and beside me there is no God. And who, as I, 7 will proclaim and will declare it, and will set it in order for me, since I appointed the ancient people? Then let them shew to them the things that are coming, and will come. Fear ye not, neither be afraid; have not I told 8 thee from of old, and have declared it? Ye are even my witnesses. Is there a God beside me? yea, there is no Rock; I know not any.

They that make an image are all of them vanity; and 9

their desirable things shall not profit; and they are their own witnesses; they see not, nor know; so that they are
10 ashamed. Who hath formed a god, or a molten image
11 which is profitable for nothing? Behold, all his fellows shall be ashamed; and the workmen, they are of mankind. Let them all be gathered together, let them stand up; yet they shall fear, and they shall be ashamed to-
12 gether. One forgeth iron into an axe, he worketh in the coals, and fashioneth it with hammers, and worketh it with the strength of his arms; yea, he becometh hungry, and his strength faileth; he drinketh no water, and is faint.
13 The worker in wood stretcheth out his line; he marketh it out with an awl; he shapeth it with planes, and he marketh it out with the compasses, and maketh it after the figure of a man, according to the beauty of men; that it may dwell in a house. [See xli. 6.]
14 One heweth him down cedars, and taketh the ilex and the oak, which he fixeth upon for himself among the trees of the forest. One planteth an ash, and the rain doth
15 nourish it. Then shall it be for a man to burn; for he will take some thereof, and warm himself; yea, he kindleth it, and baketh bread; yea, he maketh a god, and worshippeth it; he maketh it a graven image, and falleth down
16 thereto. He burneth half thereof in the fire; thus with half thereof he eateth flesh; he roasteth roast, and is satisfied; yea, he warmeth himself, and saith, 'Aha! I am warm,
17 'I have seen the flame;' and of what remains of it he maketh a god, even his graven image. He falleth down unto it, and worshippeth it, and prayeth unto it, and saith, 'Deliver me; for thou art my god.'
18 They have not known nor understood; for he hath shut their eyes, that they cannot see; and their hearts, that they
19 cannot understand. And none considereth in his heart, neither is there knowledge or understanding to say, 'I 'have burned half of it in the fire; yea, also I have baked 'bread upon the coals thereof; I have roasted flesh, and 'eaten it; and shall I make the residue thereof an abomi-'nation? shall I fall down before the stock of a tree?'
20 He feedeth on ashes; a deceived heart hath turned him aside; he cannot deliver his soul, nor say, 'Is there not a 'lie in my right hand?'
21 Remember these things, O Jacob and Israel; for thou

art my servant, I have formed thee; thou art my servant, O Israel, thou shalt not be forgotten by me. I have wiped ²² away, as a thick cloud, thy transgressions, and, as a cloud, thy sins. Return unto me; for I have redeemed thee.

'Sing, O ye heavens; for Jehovah hath done it; shout, ²³ 'ye places beneath the earth. Break forth into singing, 'ye mountains, O forest, and every tree therein; for Jeho-'vah hath redeemed Jacob, and he glorifieth himself in 'Israel.'

Thus saith Jehovah, thy redeemer, and he that formed ²⁴ thee from the womb, I am Jehovah that made all things; that alone stretched forth the heavens; that spread abroad the earth by myself; that maketh vain the signs of the ²⁵ liars, and maketh the diviners foolish; that turneth wise men backward, and maketh their knowledge vain; that ²⁶ confirmeth the word of his Servant, and will perform the counsel of his messengers; that saith to Jerusalem, 'Thou 'shalt be inhabited;' and to the cities of Judah, 'Ye shall 'be built up, and I will raise up its decayed places;' that ²⁷ saith to the deep, 'Be dry, and I will dry up thy rivers;' that saith of Cyrus, 'He is my shepherd, and he shall ²⁸ 'perform all my pleasure;' even saying to Jerusalem, 'Thou shalt be built;' and to the temple, 'Thy founda-'tion shall be laid.'

Thus saith Jehovah to his anointed, to Cyrus, whose ¹ right hand I have strengthened, to subdue nations before him; and I will loosen the loins of kings, to open before him the doors; and the gates shall not be shut; I will ² go before thee, and make the rough places level; I will break in pieces the doors of copper, and cut asunder the bars of iron. And I will give thee the treasures of dark- ³ ness, and the hidden riches of secret places, so that thou mayest know that I, Jehovah, who call thee by thy name, am the God of Israel.

For Jacob my servant's sake, and Israel my chosen one, ⁴ I have even called thee by thy name; I have surnamed thee, though thou hast not known me. I am Jehovah, and ⁵ there is none else, there is no God beside me. I girded thee, though thou hast not known me; that they may ⁶ know from the rising of the sun, and from the west, that there is none beside me. I am Jehovah, and there is none else. I form the light, and create darkness; I make safety, ⁷ and I create misfortune; I Jehovah do all these things.

8 Distil down, ye heavens, from above, and let the skies pour down righteousness; let the earth open, and let them bear the fruit of salvation, and let righteousness sprout forth together; I Jehovah have created it.

9 Woe unto him that striveth with his Maker, as a potsherd with the potsherds of the earth! Shall the clay say to him that shapeth it, 'What makest thou?' or thy

10 work say, 'He hath no hands'? Woe unto him that saith to his father, 'What begettest thou?' or to the woman, 'What hast thou brought forth?'

11 Thus saith Jehovah, the Holy One of Israel, and his Maker, Shall the things to come ask of me concerning my sons; and do ye command me concerning the work of my

12 hands? I made the earth, and created man upon it. I, even my hands, stretched out the heavens, and all their

13 host I commanded. I have raised up him [Cyrus] in righteousness, and I will direct all his ways; he shall build up my city, and he shall let go my captives, not for price nor reward, saith Jehovah of hosts.

14 Thus saith Jehovah, The labours of Egypt, and the merchandise of Ethiopia, and the men of Seba [or Meroë], men of stature, shall come over unto thee, and they shall be thine. They shall come after thee; in chains they shall come over, and they shall fall down unto thee, they shall make supplication unto thee, [saying,] 'Surely God is 'with thee; and there is no other God whatever.'

15 'Verily thou art a God that hidest thyself, O God of
16 'Israel, the Saviour. They shall be ashamed, and also 'confounded, all of them together; the makers of idols 'shall go to confusion.'

17 Israel shall be saved by Jehovah with an everlasting salvation; ye shall not be ashamed, ye shall not be confounded

18 for ever and ever. For thus saith Jehovah who created the heavens; God himself that formed the earth and made it; he hath established it, he hath not created it in vain, he formed it to be inhabited; I am Jehovah, and there is

19 none else. I have not spoken in secret, in a dark place of the earth. I said not unto the seed of Jacob, 'Seek ye 'me,' in vain. I Jehovah speak righteousness, I declare the things that are right.

20 Assemble yourselves and come; draw near together, ye that are escaped from the Nations. They have no knowledge

that carry the wood of their graven image, and pray unto a god that cannot save. Tell ye, and bring them near; 21 yea, let them take counsel together; who hath declared this from ancient time? who hath told it from of old? Have not I Jehovah? And there is no God else beside me; a just God and a Saviour; there is none beside me.

Look to me, and be ye saved, all the ends of the earth; 22 for I am God, and there is none else. I have sworn by 23 myself, the truth is gone out of my mouth, the word, and it shall not return, That unto me every knee shall bow, every tongue shall swear. Surely, shall one say, in Jeho- 24 vah have I righteousness and strength; even to him shall men come; and all that are incensed against him shall be ashamed. All the seed of Israel shall be justified, and 25 shall glory in Jehovah.

BEL BOWETH DOWN, Nebo stoopeth, their idols are upon 1 the beasts, and upon the cattle; what were your burdens are loaded as a burden on to the weary beast. They stoop, 2 they bow down together; they cannot rescue the burden, but themselves are gone into captivity.

Hearken to me, O house of Jacob, and all the remnant 3 of the house of Israel, who have been a load upon me from the birth, who have been a burden from the womb. And even to your old age I shall be He; and even to 4 hoary hairs will I carry you; I have made, and I will bear; even I will carry, and will rescue you.

To whom will ye liken me, and make me equal, and 5 compare me, that we may be alike? They lavish gold out 6 of the bag, and weigh silver in the balance; they hire a metal-founder, and he maketh it into a god; they fall down, yea, they worship it. They bear it upon the shoulder, 7 they carry it, and set it in its place, and it standeth; it cannot move from its place. Yea, a man shall cry unto it, yet can it not answer, nor save him out of his trouble.

Remember this, and shew yourselves men; bring it again 8 to mind, O ye transgressors. Remember the former things 9 of old, for I am God, and there is none else; I am God, and there is none like me, declaring the end from the be- 10 ginning, and from ancient times the things that are not yet done; saying, 'My counsel shall stand, and I will do all 'my pleasure;' calling a bird of prey [Cyrus] from the east, 11 the man that executeth my counsel from a far country.

Yea, I have spoken it, I will also bring it to pass; I have purposed it, I will also do it.

12,13 Hearken to me, ye proud of heart, ye that are far from righteousness. I bring near my righteousness; it shall not be far off, and my salvation, it shall not tarry. And I will place salvation in Zion for Israel my glory.

1 Come down, and sit in the dust, O virgin daughter of Babylon; sit on the ground where there is no throne, O daughter of the Chaldeans; for thou shalt no more be 2 called tender and delicate. Take a hand-mill, and grind meal; lift up thy veil, hold up thy skirts, uncover the leg, 3 pass over the rivers. Thy nakedness shall be uncovered, yea, thy shame shall be seen. I will take vengeance, and 4 I will make peace with no man. Our redeemer is Jehovah of hosts; his name is the Holy One of Israel.

5 Sit thou silent, and get thee into darkness, O daughter of the Chaldeans; for thou shalt no more be called, The 6 mistress of kingdoms. I was wroth with my people, I polluted mine inheritance, and gave them into thy hand. Thou didst shew them no mercy; upon the aged hast thou 7 very heavily laid thy yoke. And thou saidst, 'I shall be 'mistress for ever;' thou didst not lay these things to thy heart, neither didst remember the latter end of it.

8 Therefore hear now this, thou that art given to pleasures, thou that dwellest as if in safety, that sayest in thy heart, 'I am she, and there is none else beside me; I shall 'not sit as a widow, neither shall I know the loss of chil-9 'dren.' But these two things shall come to thee in a moment on one day, the loss of children and widowhood. They shall come upon thee in full measure for the multitude of thy sorceries, and for the great abundance of thine 10 enchantments. For thou hast trusted in thy wickedness; thou hast said, 'None seeth me.' Thy wisdom and thy knowledge, it hath perverted thee; and thou hast said in thy heart, 'I am she, and there is none else beside me.' 11 Therefore shall evil come upon thee, thou shalt not know its dawning; and mischief shall fall upon thee, thou shalt not be able to put it off; and desolation shall come upon thee suddenly, which thou shalt not know.

12 Stand up now with thine enchantments, and with the multitude of thy sorceries, wherein thou hast laboured from

thy youth; perhaps thou shalt be able to be of use, perhaps thou mayest terrify. Thou art wearied in the multi- ¹³ tude of thy counsels. Let now those who divide out the heavens, those who gaze on the stars, those who understand the moon's changes, let them stand up, and save thee from the things that are coming upon thee. Behold, they are ¹⁴ as stubble; the fire shall burn them; they shall not deliver themselves from the power of the flame. It shall not be a coal only to warm at, nor a light to sit before it. Thus ¹⁵ shall they be unto thee with whom thou hast laboured, those with whom thou hast traded from thy youth; they shall wander every one to his own quarter; none shall save thee.

HEAR YE THIS, O house of Jacob, ye who are called by ¹ the name of Israel, and are come forth out of the waters of Judah, who swear by the name of Jehovah, and make mention of the God of Israel, but not in truth, nor in righteousness. For they call themselves of the Holy City, ² and lean upon the God of Israel; Jehovah of hosts is his name.

I declared the former things from of old; and they ³ went forth out of my mouth, and I shewed them; I did them suddenly, and they came to pass. Because I knew ⁴ that thou wast stubborn, and thy neck is an iron sinew, and thy forehead is copper. Even from of old I declared ⁵ it to thee; before it came to pass I shewed it thee; lest thou shouldest say, 'Mine idol hath done these things, 'and my graven image, and my molten image, hath com- 'manded them.'

Thou hast heard, thou hast seen all this; and will not, ⁶ ye declare it? I have shewed thee new things from this time, even hidden things, and thou didst not know them. They are created now, and not from of old, or before ⁷ this day; and thou heardest them not, lest thou shouldest say, 'Behold, I knew them.' Yea, thou heardest not; ⁸ yea, thou knewest not; yea, at that time thine ear was not opened; for I knew that thou wouldest deal very treacherously, and thou wast called a transgressor from the womb.

For my name's sake will I delay mine anger, and my ⁹ glory will I keep back for thy sake, that I cut thee not off. Behold, I have refined thee, but not unto being silver; I ¹⁰

¹¹ have proved thee in the furnace of affliction. For mine own sake, for mine own sake, will I do it; for how should [my name] be profaned? and I will not give my glory to another.
¹² Hearken to me, O Jacob and Israel, my called; I am
¹³ He; I am the first, I am also the last. My hand also laid the foundations of the earth, and my right hand spread out the heavens; when I call to them, they stand
¹⁴ up together. All ye, assemble yourselves, and hear; which among them hath declared these things? I Jehovah have loved him [Cyrus]. He shall do his pleasure
¹⁵ on Babylon, and his arm shall be on the Chaldeans. I, even I, have spoken; yea, I have called him; I have brought him, and he shall prosper on his way.
¹⁶ COME YE NEAR to me, hear ye this; I have not spoken in secret from the beginning; from the time that it was, there was I; and now the Lord Jehovah hath sent me,
¹⁷ and his spirit. Thus saith Jehovah, thy redeemer, the Holy One of Israel; I am Jehovah thy God, who teacheth thee to be of use, who leadeth thee by the way that thou
¹⁸ shouldest go. O that thou hadst hearkened to my commandments! then had thy peace been as a river, and thy
¹⁹ righteousness as the waves of the sea. Thy seed also had been as the sand, and the offspring of thy bowels like that of its bowels; his name should not have been cut off nor destroyed from before me.
²⁰ Go ye forth from Babylon, flee ye from the Chaldeans, with a voice of singing declare ye, tell this, utter it to the ends of the earth; say ye, 'Jehovah hath redeemed his
²¹ 'servant Jacob.' And they thirsted not when he led them through the deserts; he poured waters out of the rock for them; he clave the rock also, and the waters gushed out.
²² There is no peace, saith Jehovah, unto the wicked.
— LISTEN TO ME, O ISLES; and hearken, ye peoples, from
¹ far; Jehovah hath called me from the womb; from the bowels of my mother hath he made mention of my name.
² And he hath made my mouth like a sharp sword; in the shadow of his hand hath he hid me, and made me to be a
³ polished arrow; in his quiver hath he hid me. And he said to me, 'Thou art my servant, O Israel, in whom I
⁴ 'will be glorified.' Then I said, 'I have laboured in 'vain, I have spent my strength for nought, and in vain;

'yet surely the judgment on me is with Jehovah, and
'the reward of my work with my God.'

And now, said Jehovah, who formed me from the womb ⁵
to be a servant unto him, to bring back Jacob again to
him, that Israel might be gathered to him, and I might
be glorious in the eyes of Jehovah, and my God might be
my strength; and he said, 'It is a light thing that thou ⁶
'shouldest be a servant unto me to raise up the tribes of
'Jacob, and to bring back the preserved of Israel. I will
'also give thee for a light to the Nations, that thou
'mayest be my salvation unto the ends of the earth.'

Thus saith Jehovah, the Redeemer of Israel, and his ⁷
Holy One, to him whose soul is despised, to him whom a
nation abhorreth, to a servant of rulers, 'Kings shall see
'and rise up, princes also shall worship him, because of
'Jehovah who is faithful, and the Holy One of Israel;
'and he chooseth thee.'

Thus saith Jehovah; In a time of acceptance have I ⁸
answered thee, and in a day of salvation have I helped
thee; and I will guard thee, and give thee for a covenant
of the people, to establish the land, to cause the desolate
heritages to be inherited; that thou mayest say to the ⁹
prisoners, 'Go forth;' to them that are in darkness,
'Shew yourselves.' They shall be fed on the ways, and
shall find pastures on all the bare heights. They shall ¹⁰
not hunger nor thirst; neither shall the heat nor the sun
smite them; for He that hath mercy on them will lead
them, even by the springs of water will he guide them.
And I will make all my mountains to be a path, and my ¹¹
highways shall be exalted. Behold, some shall come ¹²
from far; and, lo, some from the north and from the
west; and some from the land of the Sinites [or Chinese].

'Sing, O heavens, and be joyful, O earth; and break ¹³
'forth into singing, O mountains; for Jehovah hath com-
'forted his people, and will have mercy upon his afflicted
'ones.'

But Zion saith, 'Jehovah hath forsaken me, and my ¹⁴
'Lord hath forgotten me.' Can a woman forget her suck- ¹⁵
ing child, so as not to have compassion on the son of her
womb? Yea, they may forget, yet will I not forget thee.
Behold, I have engraven thee upon the palms of my hands; ¹⁶
thy walls are continually before me. Let thy children ¹⁷

make haste ; thy destroyers and thy desolaters shall go forth from thee.

¹⁸ Lift up thine eyes [O Zion] round about, and behold ; all these gather themselves together, and come to thee. As I live, Jehovah hath said it, thou shalt surely clothe thee with them all, as with an ornament, and bind them ¹⁹ on thee, as a bride doth. For thy waste and thy desolate places, and thy ruined land, shall even now be too narrow for its inhabitants, and they that swallowed thee up shall ²⁰ be far away. The children which thou hadst lost shall say again in thine ears, 'The place is too narrow for me ; ²¹ 'make room for me that I may dwell.' Then shalt thou say in thy heart 'Who hath begotten me these, seeing I 'had lost my children, and I am barren, a captive, and 'exiled? And who hath brought up these? Behold, I 'was left alone ; these, where have they been ?'

²² Thus saith the Lord Jehovah, Behold, I will lift up my hand to the Nations, and set up my standard to the peoples ; and they shall bring thy sons in their bosom, and thy daughters shall be carried upon their shoulders. ²³ And kings shall be thy nursing fathers, and their princesses thy nursing mothers. They shall bow down to thee with their face toward the earth, and lick up the dust of thy feet ; and thou shalt know that I am Jehovah ; for they shall not be ashamed that wait for me.

²⁴ 'Shall the booty be taken from the mighty, or the lawful 'captive be delivered ?'

²⁵ Yea, thus saith Jehovah, Even the captives of the mighty shall be taken away, and the booty of the terrible shall be delivered ; for I will contend with him that contendeth ²⁶ with thee, and I will save thy children. And them that oppress thee I will feed with their own flesh ; and they shall be drunken with their own blood, as with grape juice ; and all flesh shall know that I Jehovah am thy —Saviour and thy Redeemer, the mighty One of Jacob.

¹ Thus saith Jehovah, Where is the bill of your mother's divorcement, with which I have put her away ? Or which of my creditors is it to whom I have sold you ? Behold, for your iniquities have ye been sold, and for your trans- ² gressions is your mother put away. Why, when I came, was there no man ? When I called, was there none to answer ? Is my hand at all shortened, that it cannot re-

deem? Or have I no power to deliver? Behold, at my rebuke I dry up the sea, I make the rivers to be a desert. Their fish stink, because there is no water, and die for thirst. I clothe the heavens with blackness, and I make ³ sackcloth their covering.

THE LORD JEHOVAH HATH GIVEN ME the tongue of a ⁴ scholar, that I should know how to help the weary with a word. He wakeneth me morning by morning, he wakeneth mine ear to hear as a scholar. The Lord Jehovah opened ⁵ mine ear, and I was not rebellious, neither turned away. I gave my back to the smiters, and my cheeks to them ⁶ that plucked off the hair; I have not hidden my face from insult and spitting. For the Lord Jehovah will help me; ⁷ therefore shall I not be insulted; therefore have I set my face like a flint, and I know that I shall not be ashamed. He is near that justifieth me; who will contend with me? ⁸ Let us stand together. Who is mine adversary? let him come near to me. Behold, the Lord Jehovah will help ⁹ me; who is he that shall condemn me? Lo, they all shall wax old as a garment; the moth shall eat them up.

Who is there among you that feareth Jehovah, that ¹⁰ hearkeneth to the voice of his servant? He that yet walketh in darkness, and hath no light, let him trust in the name of Jehovah, and lean upon his God. Behold, ¹¹ all ye that kindle a fire, that gird yourselves with burning darts; walk ye in the light of your fire, and in the burning darts that ye have heated. This shall ye have from my hand, that ye shall lie down in sorrow. ——

HEARKEN TO ME, ye that follow after righteousness, ¹ ye that seek Jehovah. Look to the rock whence ye were hewn, and to the hole of the quarry whence ye were digged. Look to Abraham your father, and to Sarah that ² bare you; for when he was but one I called him, and I blessed him, and made him many. For Jehovah will ³ comfort Zion; he will comfort all her waste places; and he will make her desert like Eden, and her barren valley like the garden of Jehovah; joy and gladness shall be found therein, thanksgiving and the voice of melody.

Attend to me, my people; and give ear to me, O my ⁴ nation; for a law shall proceed from me, and I will establish my judgment as a light of the peoples. My righteousness ⁵

is at hand; my salvation is gone forth, and mine arms shall judge the peoples; the isles shall wait upon me, and for
⁶ mine arm shall they hope. Lift up your eyes to the heavens, and look down upon the earth beneath; for the heavens shall melt away like smoke, and the earth shall wax old like a garment, and they that dwell therein shall die like a gnat; but my salvation shall be for ever, and my righteousness shall not be abolished.

⁷ Hearken to me, ye that know righteousness, the people in whose heart is my law; fear ye not the reproach of
⁸ men, neither be ye afraid of their revilings. For the moth shall eat them up like a garment, and the grub shall eat them like wool; but my righteousness shall be for ever, and my salvation for generations of generations.

⁹ 'Awake, Awake, put on strength, O arm of Jehovah;
'awake, as in the ancient days, in the generations of old.
'Art thou not He that pierced the Boaster [or Egypt],
¹⁰ 'and wounded the dragon [or crocodile]? Art thou not
'He that dried up the sea, the waters of the great deep;
'that made the depths of the sea a way for the ransomed
¹¹ 'to pass over? And the redeemed of Jehovah shall re-
'turn, and shall come with singing unto Zion; and ever-
'lasting joy shall be upon their head. They shall obtain
'gladness and joy; sorrow and sighing shall flee away.'

¹² I, even I, am he that comforteth you; who art thou, that thou shouldest be afraid of a man that shall die, and of a
¹³ son of Adam that shall be made as the grass? And dost thou forget Jehovah, thy maker, who stretched forth the heavens, and laid the foundations of the earth? And dost thou fear continually every day because of the wrath of the oppressor, as if he were ready to destroy? And
¹⁴ where is the wrath of the oppressor? The dejected one hasteneth to be loosed, and that he die not in the dun-
¹⁵ geon-pit, nor that his bread should fail. And I am Jehovah thy God, that stilleth the sea, when its waves roar;
¹⁶ Jehovah of hosts is his name. And I will put my words in thy mouth, and I will cover thee with the shadow of my hand, that I may plant the heavens, and lay the foundations of the earth, and say to Zion, 'Thou art my people.'

¹⁷ Awake, awake, stand up, O Jerusalem, which hast drunk at the hand of Jehovah the cup of his wrath; thou hast drunk to the bottom of the cup of staggering; thou

hast drunk the dregs. She hath no guide among all the ¹⁸ sons whom she hath brought forth; neither is there any that taketh her by the hand of all the sons that she hath brought up. These two things are come unto thee; who ¹⁹ shall be sorry for thee? desolation and destruction, and the famine, and the sword; how shall I comfort thee? Thy sons have fainted, they lie at the head of all the ²⁰ streets, as a deer in a net; they are full of the wrath of Jehovah, of the rebuke of thy God.

Therefore hear now this, thou afflicted one, and drunken, ²¹ but not with wine; thus saith thy Lord Jehovah, and thy ²² God that pleadeth for his people, Behold, I have taken out of thy hand the cup of staggering, the bottom of the cup of my wrath; thou shalt no more drink it again. But ²³ I will put it into the hand of them that afflict thee; who have said to thy soul, 'Bow thyself down, that we may 'go over thee;' and thou hast laid down thy body as the ground, and as the street, to them that went over. —

Awake, awake; put on thy strength, O Zion; put on ¹ thy beautiful garments, O Jerusalem, the holy city; for henceforth there shall no more come into thee the uncircumcised and the unclean. Shake thyself from the dust; ² arise, and sit up, O Jerusalem; loosen thyself from the fetters of thy neck, O captive daughter of Zion. For thus ³ saith Jehovah, Ye were sold for nought; and ye shall be redeemed without money. For thus saith the Lord Jehovah, My people went down at first into Lower Egypt ⁴ to sojourn there; and then the Assyrian oppressed them without cause. Now therefore, what have I here, Jehovah ⁵ hath said it, that my people is taken away for nought? They that rule over them shout aloud, Jehovah hath said it; and my name continually every day is blasphemed. Therefore my people shall know my name; therefore they ⁶ shall know in that day that I am he that doth speak; behold it is I.

How beautiful upon the mountains are the feet of him ⁷ that bringeth good tidings, that publisheth peace; that bringeth good tidings of good, that publisheth salvation; that saith unto Zion, 'Thy God reigneth!' It is the voice ⁸ of thy watchmen; they lift up the voice together; they sing aloud; for they shall see eye to eye, when Jehovah shall return to Zion.

⁹ Break forth into joy, sing together, ye waste places of Jerusalem; for Jehovah hath comforted his people, he hath
¹⁰ redeemed Jerusalem. Jehovah hath made bare his holy arm in the eyes of all the nations; and all the ends of the earth shall see the salvation of our God.
¹¹ Get ye out, get ye out, go ye out from thence [from Babylon], touch no unclean thing; go ye out of the midst of her; be ye clean, ye that carry the vessels of Jehovah.
¹² For ye shall not go out with haste, nor go in flight; for Jehovah will go before you; and the God of Israel will be your rearguard.
¹³ BEHOLD, MY SERVANT [Zerubbabel] dealeth prudently,
¹⁴ he shall be exalted and extolled, and be very high, as that many were astonished at thee. So much as his visage was marred more than any man, and his form more than
¹⁵ the sons of Adam; so much shall he cause many nations to admire. Kings shall shut their mouths before him; for that which had not been told them shall they see; —and that which they had not heard shall they understand.
¹ 'But who believed what we heard? and to whom was
² 'the arm of Jehovah revealed? For he grew up before him 'as a weak plant, and as a root out of a dry soil. He had 'no form nor comeliness, that we should look on him, and
³ 'no beauty that we should desire him. He was despised 'and rejected by men; a man of sorrows, and acquainted 'with grief, and as one from whom men hide their faces;
⁴ 'he was despised, and we esteemed him not. Surely he 'had borne our griefs, and our sorrows he had carried 'them; yet we did esteem him stricken, smitten by God,
⁵ 'and afflicted. But he was wounded for our transgressions, 'he was bruised for our iniquities. The chastisement of 'our welfare was upon him; and with his stripes we were
⁶ 'healed. All we like sheep had gone astray; we had turned 'every one to his own way; and Jehovah laid on him the
⁷ 'iniquity of us all. He was oppressed, and he was afflicted, 'yet he opened not his mouth. He was brought as a lamb 'to the slaughter; and as a sheep before her shearers is
⁸ 'dumb, so he opened not his mouth. Through oppression 'and through judgment he was taken away; and who will 'speak of his generation? For he had been cut off out 'of the land of the living.'

By the transgression of my people violence came upon

him; and he prepared his grave with the wicked, and was ⁹
with the mighty one [of Babylon] among his dead men.
Although he had done no wrong, neither was any deceit
in his mouth; yet it pleased Jehovah to bruise him unto ¹⁰
grief. Although his life was appointed to be a guilt offering, he shall see his seed, he shall prolong his days, and
the pleasure of Jehovah shall prosper in his hand. From ¹¹
the travail of his soul, he shall see and shall be satisfied;
by his knowledge shall my righteous servant justify many;
for he shall carry their iniquities. Therefore will I divide ¹²
to him a portion with the great, and he shall divide the
spoil with the strong; because he laid open his life unto
death; and he was numbered with the transgressors; and
he bare the sins of many, and made intercession for the
transgressors.

SING, O BARREN WOMAN, thou that didst not bear; break ¹
forth into singing, and cry aloud, thou that didst not travail with child; for more are the children of the desolate
woman than the children of the married wife, saith Jehovah. Enlarge the place of thy tent, and let them stretch ²
forth the curtains of thy habitations; spare not, lengthen
thy cords, and make firm thy tent-pins; for thou shalt ³
break forth on the right hand and on the left; and thy
seed shall dispossess the Nations, and make the desolate
cities to be inhabited.

Fear not; for thou shalt not be ashamed; neither be ⁴
thou confounded; for thou shalt not be put to shame. For
thou shalt forget the shame of thy youth, and the reproach
of thy widowhood thou shalt remember no more. For ⁵
thy Maker is thy husband; Jehovah of hosts is his name;
and thy Redeemer is the Holy One of Israel; the God of
the whole earth shall he be called. For Jehovah hath ⁶
called thee as a woman forsaken and grieved in spirit, and
a wife of one's youth, when thou wast refused, saith thy
God. For a small moment had I forsaken thee; but with ⁷
great mercies will I take thee back. In a flood of wrath ⁸
I hid my face from thee for a moment; but with everlasting kindness will I have mercy on thee, saith Jehovah thy
Redeemer.

For this is as the waters of Noah unto me. For as I ⁹
swore that the waters of Noah should no more go over the
earth; so have I sworn that I will not be wroth with thee,

¹⁰ nor rebuke thee. For the mountains shall depart, and the hills be shaken; but my kindness shall not depart from thee, neither shall the covenant of my peace be shaken, saith Jehovah, who hath mercy on thee.

¹¹ O thou afflicted one, tossed with tempest, and not comforted, behold I will lay thy stones with vermilion, and ¹² will make thy foundation with sapphires. And I will make thy battlements of rubies, and thy gates of car-¹³ buncles, and all thy borders of pleasant stones. And all thy children shall be taught by Jehovah; and great shall be ¹⁴ the peace of thy children. In righteousness shalt thou be established. Thou shalt be far from anxiety, for thou shalt not fear; and from terror, for it shall not come near thee.

¹⁵ Behold, they will surely be leagued together, but not by me. Whosoever shall be leagued against thee shall revolt ¹⁶ unto thee. Behold, I create the smith that bloweth the coals in the fire, and that bringeth forth the weapon for ¹⁷ its work; and I create the destroyer to lay waste. No weapon that is formed against thee shall prosper; and every tongue that shall rise against thee in judgment thou shalt punish. This is the heritage of the servants of Jehovah, and their righteousness is from me; Jehovah —hath said it.

¹ Ho, EVERY ONE THAT THIRSTETH, come ye to the waters; and he that hath no money, come ye, buy, and eat; yea, come, buy wine and milk without money and without price.
² Wherefore do ye spend money for that which is not bread? and your labour for that which satisfieth not? Hearken diligently unto me, and eat ye that which is good, and let ³ your soul delight itself in fatness. Incline your ear, and come unto me; hear, and your soul shall live; and I will make an everlasting covenant with you, even the kindness ⁴ assured unto David. Behold, I have given him [Zerubbabel] for a witness to the peoples, a leader and commander ⁵ to the tribes. Behold, thou shalt call to a nation [the Persians] that thou knowest not; and nations that knew not thee shall run unto thee for the sake of Jehovah thy God, and for the Holy One of Israel; for he hath glorified thee.

⁶ Seek ye Jehovah while he may be found, call ye upon ⁷ him while he is near. Let the wicked man forsake his way, and the unrighteous man his thoughts; and let him return

to Jehovah, and he will have mercy upon him, and to our God, for he will abundantly pardon. For my thoughts are ⁸ not your thoughts, neither are your ways my ways; Jehovah hath said it. For as the heavens are higher than the ⁹ earth, so are my ways higher than your ways, and my thoughts than your thoughts. For as the rain cometh ¹⁰ down, and the snow from heaven, and returneth not thither, but watereth the earth, and maketh it bring forth, and maketh it bud, that it may give seed to the sower, and bread to the eater; so shall my word be that goeth ¹¹ forth out of my mouth. It shall not return to me void, but it shall accomplish that which I please, and it shall make that to prosper for which I sent it. For ye shall go ¹² out with joy, and be led forth with peace; the mountains and the hills shall break forth before you into singing, and all the trees of the field shall clap their hands. Instead ¹³ of the thorn bush shall come up the fir tree, and instead of the brier shall come up the myrtle tree; and it shall be to Jehovah for a name, for an everlasting sign that shall not be cut off.

THUS SAITH JEHOVAH, Keep ye justice, and do right- ¹ eousness; for my salvation is near to come, and my righteousness to be revealed. Blessed is the man that ² doeth this, and the son of Adam that layeth hold on it; that keepeth the sabbath from polluting it, and keepeth his hand from doing any evil. Neither let the son of the ³ foreigner, that hath joined himself to Jehovah, speak, saying, 'Jehovah hath utterly separated me from his people;' neither let the eunuch say, 'Behold, I am a dry tree.' For ⁴ thus saith Jehovah to the eunuchs, Those that keep my sabbaths, and choose the things that please me, and take hold of my covenant; even to them will I give in my ⁵ House and within my walls an appointed place and a name better than sons and daughters; I will give them an everlasting name, that shall not be cut off. Also the sons of ⁶ the foreigner, that join themselves to Jehovah, to serve him, and to love the name of Jehovah, to be his servants, every one that keepeth the sabbath from polluting it, and taketh hold of my covenant; even them will I bring to ⁷ my holy mountain, and make them joyful in my House of Prayer. Their burnt offerings and their sacrifices shall be accepted upon mine altar; for my House shall be called

⁸ a house of prayer for all the peoples, the Lord Jehovah hath said it; while gathering in the outcasts of Israel, yet will I gather others to him, beside those that are gathered unto him.

⁹ ALL YE WILD BEASTS OF THE FIELD, come to devour, yea,
¹⁰ all ye wild beasts in the forest. His watchmen are blind; they are all ignorant, they are all dumb dogs, they cannot
¹¹ bark; sleeping, lying down, loving to slumber. Yea, they are greedy dogs which can never have enough, and they are shepherds that cannot understand. They all look to their own way, every one for his own gain, from his own
¹² quarter, [saying,] 'Come ye, I will fetch wine, and we will 'fill ourselves with strong drink; and to-morrow shall be —' as this day, and much more abundant.'

¹ The righteous man perisheth, and no man layeth it to heart; and merciful men are taken away, while none consider that the righteous man is taken away from mis-
² fortune. He entereth into peace; they rest in their beds,
³ each one walking in his uprightness. But do ye draw near hither, ye sons of the sorceress, the seed of the
⁴ adulterer and the harlot. Against whom do ye sport yourselves? Against whom do ye make a wide mouth, and put out the tongue? Are ye not children of transgres-
⁵ sion, the seed of falsehood, inflaming yourselves with idols under every green tree, killing the children in the valleys
⁶ under the clefts of the rocks? Among the smooth stones of the valley is thy portion; these, these are thy lot; even to them hast thou poured a drink offering, thou hast offered up a meal offering. Should I receive comfort in these?

⁷ Upon a lofty and high mountain hast thou set thy bed;
⁸ even thither wentest thou up to sacrifice sacrifices. Behind the doors also and the door-posts hast thou set thy remembrance; for not unto me thou hast uncovered thyself, and art gone up; thou hast enlarged thy bed, and made a covenant with them; thou lovest their bed; thou
⁹ lookest for the appointed place. And thou wentest to the king [of Persia] with ointment, and didst increase thy perfumes, and didst send thy messengers to a distance,
¹⁰ and didst debase thyself even unto hell. Thou art wearied with the length of thy way; yet thou saidst not, 'It is

'to be despaired of.' Thou hast found life in thine own hand; therefore thou wast not grieved.

And of whom hast thou been afraid or dost thou fear, that thou hast lied, and hast not remembered me, nor laid it to thy heart? Have not I held my peace even of old, and so thou fearest me not? It is I who declare thy righteousness, and thy works; and they shall not profit thee. When thou criest, let thy companions [or idols] deliver thee. But the wind shall carry them all away; vanity shall take them. But he that putteth his trust in me shall inherit the land, and shall possess my holy mountain. And he shall say, 'Build ye up the road, build ye up, prepare 'the way, take up the stumbling-block out of the way of 'my people.'

For thus saith the High and Lofty One, he that inhabiteth eternity, whose name is Holy; I dwell in the high and holy place, with him also that is of a contrite and humble spirit, to revive the spirit of the humble, and to revive the heart of the contrite ones. For I will not contend for ever, neither will I be always wroth; for the spirit would fail before me, and the souls which I have made. For the iniquity of his covetousness was I wroth, and I smote him. I hid me, and was wroth, and he walked rebelliously in the way of his heart. I have seen his ways, and will heal him. And I will lead him, and I will restore comforts unto him and to his mourners. I create the fruit of the lips, even peace, peace to him that is far off, and to him that is near, saith Jehovah; and I will heal him. But the wicked are like the sea driven forward, when it cannot rest, and its waters drive forward the mire and dirt. There is no peace, saith my God, for the wicked.

CRY WITH THE THROAT, spare not, lift up thy voice like—a trumpet, and shew to my people their transgression, and to the house of Jacob their sins. For they seek me day by day, and delight to know my ways, as though they were a nation that did righteousness, and forsook not the ordinance of their God. They ask of me the ordinances of justice; they take delight in approaching to God, [saying,] 'Wherefore have we fasted, and thou seest not? We 'have afflicted our soul, and thou takest no knowledge.' Behold in the day of your fast, ye pursue pleasure, and oppress all your labourers. Behold, ye fast for strife and debate, and to smite with the fist of wickedness. Ye should not fast as this day if ye would make your voice to be heard on high.

5 Is this such a fast as I should choose? a day for a man to afflict his soul? Is it to bow down his head as a bulrush, and to make a bed in sackcloth and ashes? Wilt
6 thou call that a fast, and an acceptable day to Jehovah? Is not this the fast that I should choose? to loosen the fetters of injustice, to undo the fastenings of the yoke, and to let
7 the oppressed go free, and that ye break every yoke? Is it not to deal out thy bread to the hungry, and that thou bring the poor that are cast down to thy house? when thou seest the naked, that thou clothe him; and that thou
8 hide not thyself from thine own flesh? Then shall thy light burst forth as the daybreak, and the healing of thy wounds be quickened; and thy righteousness shall go before
9 thee; the glory of Jehovah shall be thy rearguard. Then shalt thou call, and Jehovah will answer; thou shalt cry for help, and he will say, 'Behold it is I.'

If thou take away from the midst of thee the yoke, the
10 pointing of the finger, and speaking vanity; and if thy soul bring forth to the hungry, and thou satisfy the afflicted soul; then shall thy light rise through the obscurity, and
11 thy darkness be as the noon day; and Jehovah will guide thee continually, and satisfy thy soul in time of drought, and strengthen thy bones; and thou shalt be like a watered garden, and like a spring of water, whose waters are not a
12 deception. And some of thee shall build the waste places of the past time. Thou shalt raise up the foundations of many generations; and thou shalt be called, 'The repairer ' of the breach, the restorer of paths to dwell in.'

13 If thou turn away thy foot from the sabbath, from doing thy pleasure on my holy day; and call the sabbath a delight, holy to Jehovah and honourable; and honour it, not doing thine own ways, nor pursuing thine own
14 pleasure, nor talking vain talk; then shalt thou find delight in Jehovah; and I will cause thee to ride upon the high places of the earth, and I will feed thee with the heritage of Jacob thy father; for the mouth of Jehovah —hath spoken it.

1 BEHOLD, JEHOVAH'S HAND is not shortened, that it can-
2 not save; neither his ear heavy, that it cannot hear; but

your iniquities have made a separation between you and your God, and your sins have hid his face from you, that he will not hear. For your hands are defiled with blood, and your fingers with iniquity; your lips have spoken falsehood, your tongue hath muttered perverseness. None summoneth with justice, and none pleadeth with truth; they trust in vanity, and speak falsehood; they conceive mischief, and bring forth iniquity. They hatch vipers' eggs, and weave the spider's web. He that eateth of their eggs dieth, and when one is broken, out breaketh an adder. Their webs will not serve for garments, neither shall they cover themselves with their works; their works are works of iniquity, and the act of violence is in their hands. Their feet run to evil, and they make haste to shed innocent blood; their thoughts are thoughts of iniquity; wasting and destruction are in their highways. The path of peace they know not; and there is no justice in their track. They have made for themselves crooked paths; whosoever goeth therein shall not know peace.

Therefore is justice far from us, neither doth righteousness come near us; we wait for light, but behold obscurity; for brightness, but we walk in darkness. We grope for the wall like the blind, and we grope as if we had no eyes; we stumble at noon day as in the night, in desolate places we are as dead men. We growl all of us like bears, and mourn sore like doves. We wait for justice, but there is none; for salvation, but it is far off from us. For our transgressions are multiplied before thee, and our sins testify against us: for our transgressions are with us; and as for our iniquities, we know them. We have transgressed and lied against Jehovah, and departed away from our God, speaking oppression and revolt, conceiving and uttering from the heart words of falsehood. And justice is turned away backward, and righteousness standeth afar off; for truth stumbleth in the street, and equity cannot enter. And truth is not to be found.

Yea, he that departeth from evil findeth himself plundered. And Jehovah seeth it, and it displeaseth him because there is no justice. And he seeth that there is no man, and wondereth that there is no intercessor. But his own arm worketh salvation to him; and his righteousness it sustaineth him. For he put on righteousness as a breast-

plate, and the helmet of salvation upon his head; and he put on the garments of vengeance for clothing, and was
18 clad with zeal as with a cloak. As were their deeds, so he will repay, wrath to his adversaries, like doings to his enemies; to the [Greek] islands he will repay like doings.
19 And they in the West shall fear the name of Jehovah, and they at the rising of the sun, his glory; when He shall come like a pent-up flood, which the breath of Jeho-
20 vah driveth forward. And the Redeemer shall come to Zion, and to them that turn from transgression in Jacob; Jehovah hath said it.
21 As for me, this is my covenant with them, saith Jehovah; My spirit that is upon thee, and my words, which I have put in thy mouth, shall not depart out of thy mouth, nor out of the mouth of thy seed, nor out of the mouth of thy seed's seed, saith Jehovah, from henceforth —and for ever.

---

1 ARISE [O JERUSALEM], SHINE; for thy light is come,
2 and the glory of Jehovah is risen upon thee. For, behold, the darkness shall cover the earth, and gross darkness the peoples; but Jehovah will arise upon thee, and his glory
3 shall be seen upon thee. And the Nations shall come to
4 thy light, and kings to the brightness of thy rising. Lift up thine eyes round about, and see; they all gather themselves together, they come to thee; thy sons shall come from far, and thy daughters shall nurse [their babes] at thy side.
5 Then thou shalt see, and be gladdened, and thy heart shall throb, and swell; because the riches of the West shall be turned to thee, the wealth of the Nations shall
6 come to thee. The multitude of camels shall cover thee, the dromedaries of Midian and Ephah; all they from Sheba shall come; they shall bring gold and incense; and
7 they shall shew forth the praises of Jehovah. All the flocks of Kedar shall be gathered together to thee, the rams of Nebaioth [or the Nabatæans] shall minister to thee; they shall come up with acceptance on mine altar, and I will glorify the House of my glory.
8 Who are these that fly as a cloud, and as the doves to
9 their windows? Surely the [Greek] isles shall wait for me, and the ships of Tarshish among the first, to bring thy sons from far, their silver and their gold with them, to

the name of Jehovah thy God, and to the Holy One of Israel, because he hath glorified thee. And the sons of ¹⁰ foreigners shall build up thy walls [B.C. 444], and their kings shall minister unto thee ; for in my wrath I smote thee, but in my favour have I had mercy on thee. There- ¹¹ fore thy gates shall be open continually ; they shall not be shut day nor night ; that the wealth of the Nations may be brought to thee, and that their kings may be led captive. For the nation and kingdom that will not serve thee ¹² shall perish ; yea, those nations shall be utterly wasted.

The glory of Lebanon shall come unto thee, the fir tree, ¹³ the pine, and the box tree together, to beautify the place of my Sanctuary ; and I will make the place of my feet glorious. The sons also of them that afflicted thee shall ¹⁴ come bending unto thee ; and all they that despised thee shall bow themselves down at the soles of thy feet ; and they shall call thee, The city of Jehovah, The Zion of the Holy One of Israel. Whereas thou hast been forsaken and ¹⁵ hated, so that no man went through thee, I will make thee an excellence for ever, a joy for generations and generations. Thou shalt also suck the milk of the Nations, ¹⁶ and shalt suck the breast of kings ; and thou shalt know that I Jehovah am thy Saviour and thy Redeemer, the mighty one of Jacob.

Instead of copper I will bring gold, and instead of iron ¹⁷ I will bring silver, and instead of wood copper, and instead of stones iron. I will also make thine overseers peace, and thy tax-gatherers righteousness. Violence shall no ¹⁸ more be heard in thy land, wasting nor destruction within thy borders ; but thou shalt call thy walls Salvation, and thy city gates Praise. The sun shall be no more thy ¹⁹ light by day ; neither for brightness shall the moon give light unto thee ; but Jehovah will be unto thee an everlasting light, and thy God will be thy glory. Thy sun shall ²⁰ no more go down ; neither shall thy moon withdraw itself; for Jehovah will be thine everlasting light, and the days of thy mourning shall be ended. Thy people also shall be ²¹ all righteous ; they shall possess the land for ever, as an off-shoot of my planting, the work of my hands, that I may be glorified. That which was little shall become a ²² thousand, and that which was small, a strong nation ; I Jehovah will hasten it in its time.

¹ The Spirit of the Lord Jehovah is upon me; because Jehovah hath anointed me to preach good tidings to the afflicted; he hath sent me to bind up the broken-hearted, to proclaim liberty to the captives, and the opening of ² the prison to them that are bound; to proclaim the year of acceptance by Jehovah, and the day of vengeance of ³ our God; to comfort all that mourn; to appoint unto them that mourn in Zion, to give to them ornaments in place of ashes, the oil of joy in place of mourning, the garment of praise in place of the spirit of weakness; that they might be called Trees of righteousness, the planting of Jehovah, that he might be glorified.

⁴ And they shall build up the old waste places, they shall raise up the former desolations, and they shall repair the ⁵ waste cities, the desolations of many generations. And strangers shall stand and feed your flocks, and the sons of the foreigner shall be your plowmen and your vine- ⁶ dressers. But ye shall be named the Priests of Jehovah; men shall call you the Ministers of our God. Ye shall eat the riches of the Nations, and in their glory shall ye boast ⁷ yourselves. In place of your shame ye shall have double [reward]; and in place of confusion they shall rejoice in their portion; therefore in their land they shall possess the double; everlasting joy shall be unto them.

⁸ For I Jehovah love justice, I hate plundering with iniquity; and I will reward their work in truth, and I will ⁹ make an everlasting covenant with them. And their seed shall be known among the Nations, and their offspring among the peoples. All that see them shall acknowledge them, that they are the seed blessed by Jehovah.

¹⁰ I WILL GREATLY REJOICE in Jehovah, my soul shall be joyful in my God; for he hath clothed me with the garments of salvation, he hath covered me with the robe of righteousness, as a bridegroom decketh himself with ornaments, and as a bride adorneth herself with her ¹¹ jewels. For as the earth bringeth forth her bud, and as the garden causeth the things that are sown in it to spring forth; so the Lord Jehovah will cause righteous- —ness and praise to spring forth before all the nations.

¹ For Zion's sake I will not keep silence, and for Jerusalem's sake I will not rest, until its righteousness go forth as brightness, and its salvation as a lamp that burneth.

And the Nations shall see thy righteousness, and all ² kings thy glory; and thou shalt be called by a new name, which the mouth of Jehovah shall declare. Thou ³ shalt also be a crown of glory in the hand of Jehovah, and a royal turban in the hand of thy God. Thou shalt ⁴ no more be termed 'Forsaken;' neither shall thy land any more be termed 'Desolate;' but thou shalt be called 'My delight is in her,' and thy land 'The married woman;' for Jehovah delighteth in thee, and thy land shall be married. For as a young man marrieth a maiden, so ⁵ shall thy sons marry thee; and as the bridegroom rejoiceth over the bride, so shall thy God rejoice over thee.

I have set watchmen upon thy walls, O Jerusalem, who ⁶ shall never hold their peace day nor night. Ye that should remind Jehovah, keep not silence, and give him no quiet, ⁷ till he establish, and till he make Jerusalem a praise on the earth. Jehovah hath sworn by his right hand, and ⁸ by the arm of his strength, Surely I will no more give thy corn to be food for thine enemies; and the sons of the foreigner shall not drink thy grape juice, for which thou hast laboured. But they that have reaped it shall ⁹ eat it, and praise Jehovah; and they that have gathered it in shall drink it in the courts of my holiness.

Pass ye on, pass ye on through the city gates; prepare ye ¹⁰ the way of the people; build up, build up the highway; gather out the stones; lift up on high a standard for the peoples. Behold, Jehovah hath proclaimed unto the end ¹¹ of the world, Say ye to the daughter of Zion, 'Behold, thy 'salvation cometh; behold, his reward is with him, and 'his recompense is before him.' And they shall call them, ¹² 'The holy people, The redeemed of Jehovah;' and thou shalt be called, 'Sought out, A city not forsaken.'

'WHO IS THIS that cometh from Edom, with dyed gar- ¹ 'ments from Bozrah? this that is glorious in his apparel, 'bearing himself proudly in the greatness of his strength?'

It is I, I that speak in righteousness, mighty to save.

'Wherefore art thou red in thine apparel, and thy ² 'garments like him that treadeth in the wine-vat?'

I have trodden the winepress alone; and of the peoples ³ there was no man with me; and I will tread them in mine anger, and trample them in my wrath; and their juice shall spurt out upon my garments, and I will stain all my raiment.

⁴ For the day of vengeance is in my heart, and the year of ⁵ my redeemed is come. And I looked, and there was none to help; and I wondered that there was none to uphold; therefore mine own arm wrought salvation for me; and my ⁶ wrath, it upheld me. And I will tread down the peoples in mine anger, and make them drunk in my wrath, and I will pour down their juice to the earth.

⁷ I WILL MENTION THE LOVING-KINDNESSES of Jehovah, and the praises of Jehovah, according to all that Jehovah hath bestowed on us, and the great goodness toward the house of Israel, which he hath bestowed on them according to his mercies, and according to the multitude of his loving- ⁸ kindnesses. For he said, 'Surely they are my people, ⁹ 'children that will not lie;' so he was their Saviour. In all their affliction he was afflicted, and the angel of his presence saved them. In his love and in his pity he redeemed them; and he lifted them up, and carried them all ¹⁰ the days of old. But they rebelled, and vexed his holy spirit; therefore he turned to be their enemy, and he fought against them.
¹¹ But let him remember the days of old, the Moses [or Raiser up] of his people. Where is he that brought them up out of the sea with the shepherd of his flock? Where ¹² is he that put his holy spirit within him? That led them by the right hand of Moses, with his glorious arm dividing the water before them, to make for himself an everlasting ¹³ name? That led them through the deep, as a horse in the ¹⁴ desert, so that they should not stumble? As a beast goeth down into the valley, the spirit of Jehovah causeth him to rest; so didst thou lead thy people, to make for thyself a glorious name.
¹⁵ Look down from heaven, and behold from the habitation of thy holiness and of thy glory. Where is thy jealousy and thy strength, the moving of thy bowels and thy mercies ¹⁶ toward me? Are they restrained? Doubtless thou art our father, though Abraham be ignorant of us, and Israel acknowledge us not. Thou, O Jehovah, art our father, our ¹⁷ redeemer; thy name is from everlasting. Why, O Jehovah, hast thou made us to wander from thy ways, and hardened our heart from fearing thee? Return for the sake of thy servants, who are the tribes of thine inheritance.

The people of thy holiness have possessed it but a little ¹⁸ while; our oppressors have trodden down thy Sanctuary [B.C. 167]. We are from of old; thou barest not rule ¹⁹ over them; they were not called by thy name.

Oh that thou wouldest rend the heavens, that thou ¹ wouldest come down, that the mountains might be shaken at thy presence, (as when fire burneth brushwood, when ² fire causeth the waters to boil,) to make thy name known to thine adversaries, that the nations may tremble at thy presence! When thou didst terrible things which we ³ looked not for, thou camest down, the mountains were shaken at thy presence.

For from of old men have not heard, nor perceived by ⁴ the ear, neither hath the eye seen a God beside thee, who doeth so for him that waiteth for him. Thou meetest him ⁵ that rejoiceth and worketh righteousness, those that remember thee in thy ways. Behold, thou art wroth because we have sinned. We were of old in them, but we shall be saved. And we are all as an unclean thing, and all our ⁶ righteousnesses are as soiled garments; and we all do fade as a leaf; and our iniquities, like the wind, carry us away. And there is no one that calleth upon thy name, that stir- ⁷ reth up himself to take hold of thee; for thou hast hidden thy face from us, and hast consumed us, by reason of our iniquities.

But now, O Jehovah, thou art our father; we are the ⁸ clay, and thou our potter; and we all are the work of thy hand. Be not wroth very sore, O Jehovah, neither re- ⁹ member our iniquity for ever. Behold, see, we beseech thee, we are all thy people. Thy holy cities are a desert, ¹⁰ Zion is a desert, Jerusalem a desolation. Our holy and our ¹¹ beautiful House, where our fathers praised thee, is burned up with fire; and all our pleasant things are laid waste. Wilt thou refrain thyself at these things, O Jehovah? Wilt ¹² thou hold thy peace, and afflict us very sore?

I HAVE BEEN INQUIRED OF by them that asked not; I ¹ have been found by them that sought me not. I said [in ch. lii. 6], '*Behold it is I, behold it is I*,' to a nation that called not upon my name. I spread out my hands all the ² day to a rebellious people, that walketh in a way that is not good, after their own thoughts; a people that provoketh ³ me to anger to my face; that sacrificeth continually in

⁴ gardens, and burneth incense upon altars of brick; who remain among the graves, and lodge in caverns, who eat swine's flesh, and pieces of putrid flesh are in their vessels; ⁵ who say, 'Stand by thyself, come not near to me; for I 'am holier than thou.' These are a smoke in my nose, a ⁶ fire that burneth all the day. Behold, it is written before of me [in ch. lxii. 1], *I will not keep silence.* Nay, I will ⁷ repay, even repay into their bosom, your iniquities, and the iniquities of your fathers together, saith Jehovah, who burned incense upon the mountains, and defied me upon the hills. Therefore will I measure their former work into their bosom.

⁸ Thus saith Jehovah, As grape juice is found in the cluster, and one saith, 'Destroy it not; for a blessing is in it;' so will I do for my servants' sakes, that I may not destroy ⁹ them all. And I will bring forth a seed out of Jacob, and out of Judah an inheritor of my mountain; and my chosen ones shall possess it, and my servants shall dwell ¹⁰ there. And Sharon shall be a fold of flocks, and the valley of Achor a resting place of herds, for my people that have ¹¹ sought me. But ye are they that forsake Jehovah, that forget my holy mountain, that prepare a table unto Good ¹² Fortune, and that fill up a drink offering unto Fate. Therefore will I number you to the sword, and ye shall all bow down to the slaughter. Because when I called, ye did not answer; when I spake, ye did not hear; but did evil before mine eyes, and did choose that wherein I delighted not.

¹³ Therefore thus saith the Lord Jehovah, Behold, my servants shall eat, but ye shall be hungry; behold, my servants shall drink, but ye shall be thirsty; behold, my servants ¹⁴ shall rejoice, but ye shall be ashamed; behold, my servants shall sing for joy of heart, but ye shall cry for sorrow ¹⁵ of heart, and ye shall howl from a broken spirit. And ye shall leave your name for a curse unto my chosen ones. For the Lord Jehovah will slay thee, and he will call his ¹⁶ servants by another name; so that he who blesseth himself on the earth shall bless himself by the God of truth; and he that sweareth on the earth shall swear by the God of truth; because the former troubles are forgotten, and because they are hidden from mine eyes.

¹⁷ For, behold, I will create new heavens and a new earth; and the former shall not be remembered, nor come into

mind. But be ye glad and rejoice for ever in that which ¹⁸ I create; for, behold, I will create Jerusalem a rejoicing, and her people a joy. And I will rejoice in Jerusalem, ¹⁹ and will joy in my people; and the voice of weeping shall be no more heard in her, nor the voice of crying. There ²⁰ shall be no more thenceforth an infant of few days, nor an old man that hath not filled his days. For the young man shall die a hundred years old; but the sinner being a hundred years old shall be accursed. And *they shall build* ²¹ *houses, and inhabit them; and they shall plant vineyards, and eat the fruit thereof.* They shall not build, and another in- ²² habit; they shall not plant, and another eat; for as the days of a tree are the days of my people, and my chosen ones shall use up the work of their own hands. They ²³ shall not labour in vain, nor bear children unto trouble; for *they are the seed of the blessed of Jehovah*, and their offspring with them. And it shall come to pass, that before ²⁴ they call, I will answer; and while they are yet speaking, I will hear. *The wolf and the lamb shall feed together*, and ²⁵ *the lion shall eat straw like the ox;* but dust shall be the serpent's food. They shall not hurt nor destroy in all my holy mountain, saith Jehovah.

Thus saith Jehovah, The heavens are my throne, and ¹ the earth is my footstool; where is the house that ye build unto me? and where is the place of my rest? For ² all those things hath my hand made, and all those things are made already, Jehovah hath said it; but to this man will I look, even to him that is poor and of a contrite spirit, and trembleth at my word. He that killeth an ox also ³ slayeth a man; he that sacrificeth a lamb or kid, also breaketh a dog's neck; he that offereth up a meal-offering doth it with swine's blood; he that maketh a memorial of incense, also blesseth an idol. Yea, they have chosen their own ways, and their soul delighteth in their abominations. I also will choose their calamities, and will bring their ⁴ fears upon them; because when I called, none did answer; when I spake, they did not hear. But they did evil before mine eyes, and chose that in which I delighted not.

Hear the word of Jehovah, ye that tremble at his word. ⁵ Your brethren that hated you, that cast you out for my name's sake, said, 'Let Jehovah be glorified, that we may 'see your joy;' but they shall be ashamed. A voice of noise ⁶

from the city, a voice from the temple, a voice of Jeho-
7 vah rendering recompense to his enemies. Before she
travailed, she brought forth ; before her pain came, she
8 was delivered of a man child. Who hath heard such a
thing? Who hath seen such things? Shall the earth be
made to travail with child in one day? or shall a nation
be brought forth at once? For as soon as Zion travailed,
9 she brought forth her children. Shall I bring to the birth,
and not cause to bring forth? saith Jehovah. Shall I cause
to bring forth, and also shut the womb? saith thy God.
10 Rejoice ye with Jerusalem, and be glad with her, all ye
that love her ; rejoice for joy with her, all ye that mourn
11 for her ; so that ye may suck, and be satisfied with the
breasts of her consolations ; so that ye may milk out, and
be delighted with the abundance of her glory.
12 For thus saith Jehovah, Behold, I will extend peace to
her like a river, and the glory of the Nations like a flowing
stream. Then shall ye suck, ye shall be borne on her side,
13 and be fondled upon her knees. As one whom his mother
comforteth, so will I comfort you ; and ye shall be com-
14 forted in Jerusalem. And when ye see this, your heart
shall rejoice, and your bones shall flourish like an herb ;
and the hand of Jehovah shall be known toward his ser-
15 vants, and his indignation towards his enemies. For, behold, Jehovah will come with fire, and his chariots are like
a whirlwind, to render back his anger with wrath, and his
16 rebuke with flames of fire. For by fire and by his sword
will Jehovah judge all flesh ; and the slain of Jehovah shall
17 be many. They that sanctify themselves, and purify themselves in the gardens behind one [tree] in the midst, eating
swine's flesh, and the abomination, and the mouse, shall
perish together ; Jehovah hath said' it.
18 For I know their works and their thoughts ; it shall
come, that I will gather all nations and tongues ; and they
19 shall come, and see my glory. And I will set a sign among
them, and some of them that escape I will send to the
nations, to Tarshish [or Tarsus], to Pul [or North Africa],
and to Lud [or the Egyptian Arabs], that draw the bow,
to Tubal [or the Tibareni], and to Javan [or the Ionians],
to the isles afar off, that have not heard my fame, neither
have seen my glory ; and they shall declare my glory
20 among the Nations. And they shall bring all your

brethren out of all nations for an offering to Jehovah upon horses, and in chariots, and in litters, and upon mules, and upon dromedaries, to my holy mountain Jerusalem, saith Jehovah, as the children of Israel bring a meal offering in a clean vessel into the House of Jehovah. And I will also 21 take some of them for priests and for Levites, saith Jehovah. For as the new heavens and the new earth, which I 22 will make, shall remain before me, Jehovah hath said it, so shall your seed and your name remain. And it shall 23 come to pass, that from new moon to new moon, and from sabbath to sabbath, shall all flesh come to worship before me, saith Jehovah. And they shall go forth, and look 24 upon the dead bodies of the men that have transgressed against me; for their worm shall not die, neither shall their fire be quenched; and they shall be an abhorring unto all flesh.

JEREMIAH.

THE WORDS OF JEREMIAH the son of Hilkiah, one of 1 the priests that were in Anathoth in the land of Benjamin; to whom the word of Jehovah came in the 2 days of Josiah the son of Amon king of Judah, in the thirteenth year of his reign [B.C. 629]. It came also 3 in the days of Jehoiakim the son of Josiah king of Judah, until the end, in the eleventh year of Zedekiah the son of Josiah king of Judah [B.C. 589], until the carrying away of Jerusalem captive in the fifth month. Then the word of Jehovah came to me, saying, Before I 4 formed thee in the belly I knew thee; and before thou 5 camest forth out of the womb I sanctified thee, and I ordained thee a prophet unto the nations. Then said I, 'Ah, 6 'Lord Jehovah! behold, I know not how to speak; for I am 'a youth.' But Jehovah said to me, Say not, 'I am a 7 'youth;' for thou shalt go to all that I shall send thee, and whatsoever I command thee thou shalt speak. Be not 8 afraid before them; for I am with thee to deliver thee, Jehovah hath said it. Then Jehovah put forth his hand, and 9 touched my mouth. And Jehovah said to me, Behold, I have put my words in thy mouth. See, I have this day set thee 10 over the nations and over the kingdoms, to root out, and to pull down, and to destroy, and to throw down, to build up, and to plant.

11 Moreover the word of Jehovah came to me, saying, Jeremiah, what seest thou? And I said, 'I see the rod 12 'of an almond [or watchful] tree.' Then said Jehovah to me, Thou hast well seen; for I am watching over my word to perform it.

13 And the word of Jehovah came to me the second time, saying, What seest thou? And I said, 'I see a pot which 14 'is boiling; and its face is toward the north.' Then Jehovah said to me, Out of the north an evil shall break 15 forth upon all the inhabitants of the land. For, lo, I will call all the families of the kingdoms of the north, Jehovah hath said it; and they shall come, and they shall set every one his throne at the entering of the gates of Jerusalem, and against all its walls round about, and against all the 16 cities of Judah. And I will utter my judgments touching all their wickedness, against those who have forsaken me, and do burn incense unto other gods, and do worship the 17 works of their own hands. Do thou therefore gird up thy loins, and arise, and speak to them all that I command thee. Be not affrighted at their faces, lest I affright thee 18 before their faces. For, behold, I have made thee this day a fortified city, and a pillar of iron, and walls of copper against the whole land, against the kings of Judah, against its princes, against its priests, and against the 19 people of the land. And they shall fight against thee; but they shall not prevail against thee; for I am with thee, —Jehovah hath said it, to deliver thee.

1 Moreover the word of Jehovah came to me, saying, Go 2 and cry in the ears of Jerusalem, saying, Thus saith Jehovah; I remember thee, the kindness of thy youth, the love of thine espousals, when thou walkedst after me in the 3 desert, in a land that was not sown. Israel is holy unto Jehovah, and the firstfruits of his increase. All that devour him are guilty; evil shall come upon them, Jehovah hath said it.

4 Hear ye the word of Jehovah, O house of Jacob, and all 5 ye families of the house of Israel. Thus saith Jehovah, What injustice have your fathers found in me that they are gone far from me, and have walked after vanity, and

are become vain? Neither said they, 'Where is Jehovah ⁶
'that brought us up out of the land of Lower Egypt, that
'led us through the desert, through a land of barren plains
'and of pitfalls, through a land of drought, and of the
'shadow of death, through a land that no man passed
'through, and where men do not dwell?' And I brought ⁷
you into a land of gardens, to eat its fruit and its goodness. But when ye entered, ye defiled my land, and
made my heritage an abomination. The priests said not, ⁸
'Where is Jehovah?' and they that were skilled in the
Law knew me not. The shepherds also transgressed against
me, and the prophets prophesied by Baal, and walked after
things that do not profit.

Therefore I will yet plead with you, Jehovah hath said ⁹
it, and with your children's children will I plead. For ¹⁰
pass ye over to the isles of Chittim [or the Greeks], and
see; and send unto Kedar [in Arabia], and consider diligently, and see if such a thing hath been. Hath a nation ¹¹
changed their gods, even those which are no gods? But
my people have changed their Glory for that which doth
not profit. Be astonished, O ye heavens, at this, and be ¹²
horribly afraid, be ye very desolate, Jehovah hath said it.
For my people have committed two evils; they have for- ¹³
saken me, the fountain of living waters, in order to hew
out for themselves cisterns, broken cisterns, that can hold
no water.

Is Israel a bond-servant? or is he one born in the ¹⁴
house? Why is he plundered? The young lions [or ¹⁵
Scythians] roar upon him; they raise their cry, and they
make his land a desolation; his cities are burned so as to
be without inhabitant. Also the children of Noph [or ¹⁶
Memphis] and Tahpenes [or Daphnæ] have devoured thee
to the crown of thy head. Hast thou not brought this ¹⁷
upon thyself, in that thou didst forsake Jehovah thy God,
at the time when he led thee by the way? And now what ¹⁸
hast thou to do in the way of Lower Egypt, to drink the
waters of the Shihor [or Nile]? Or what hast thou to do
in the way of Assyria, to drink the waters of the River
[Euphrates]? Thine own wickedness shall correct thee, ¹⁹
and thy backslidings shall reprove thee. Know therefore
and see that it is an evil thing and bitter, that thou hast
forsaken Jehovah thy God, and that the fear of me is not
in thee; the Lord Jehovah of hosts hath said it.

20 For of old time I had broken thy yoke, and burst thy bonds asunder; and thou saidst, 'I will not transgress,' when upon every high hill and under every green tree
21 thou hast lain down, playing the harlot. Yet I had planted thee a noble vine, wholly a right seed. How then art thou changed towards me into the cast off plant of a
22 foreign vine? For though thou wash thyself with nitre, and take to thee much soap, yet thine iniquity is made black before me; the Lord Jehovah hath said it.
23 How canst thou say, 'I am not polluted, I have not 'gone after Baal'? See thy way in the Valley [of Hinnom], know what thou hast done; thou art a swift drome-
24 dary traversing her ways. Thou art a wild ass used to the desert, that snuffeth up the wind in the longing of her soul; in her occasion who can turn her away? All they that seek her need not weary themselves; in her month
25 they shall find her. Withhold thy foot from becoming unshod, and thy throat from thirst. But thou saidst, 'It is in 'vain; no; for I love strangers, and after them will I go.'
26 As the thief is ashamed when he is found out, so is the house of Israel put to shame; they, their kings, their
27 princes, and their priests, and their prophets. They say to a stock of wood, 'Thou art my father;' and to a stone, 'Thou hast brought me forth;' for they have turned their back to me, and not their face; but in the time of their
28 trouble they say, 'Arise and save us.' But where are thy gods that thou hast made for thee? Let them arise, if they can save thee in the time of thy trouble; for according to the number of thy cities are thy gods, O Judah.
29 Wherefore will ye strive with me? Ye have all of you transgressed against me; Jehovah hath said it.
30 In vain have I smitten your children; they did not receive the correction. Your own sword hath devoured
31 your prophets, like a destroying lion. O generation, ye see the word of Jehovah. Have I been a desert unto Israel? or a land of darkness? Wherefore say my people,
32 'We are free; we will come no more unto thee'? Can a maiden forget her ornaments, or a bride her girdle? yet my people have forgotten me days without number.
33 Why trimmest thou thy way to seek love? Therefore
34 hast thou also taught the wicked women thy ways. Also in thy skirts is found the life-blood of the poor and inno-

cent. I did not find them by breaking in, for it is upon all these. Yet thou sayest, 'Because I am innocent, surely ³⁵ 'his anger will turn from me.' Behold, I will have judgment with thee, because thou sayest, 'I have not sinned.' Why gaddest thou about so much to change thy way? ³⁶ Thou also shalt be ashamed of Lower Egypt, as thou wast ashamed of Assyria. Yea, thou shalt go forth from thence, ³⁷ with thy hands upon thy head; for Jehovah hath rejected them in whom thou trustest, and thou shalt not prosper in them. —

It is said, 'If a man put away his wife, and she go from ¹ 'him, and become another man's, shall he return to her 'again?' Will not that land be greatly polluted? But thou hast gone astray after many lovers, and dost thou return again to me? Jehovah hath said it.

Lift up thine eyes to the heights, and see; where hast ² thou not been lain with? In the highways thou hast sat for them, as the Arab woman in the desert; and thou hast polluted the land with thy fornications and with thy wickedness. Therefore the showers have been withheld, ³ and there hath been no latter rain; and thou hadst the forehead of a harlot, thou refusedst to be ashamed. Wilt ⁴ thou not from this time cry to me, 'My father, thou art 'the guide of my youth? Will he retain his anger for ⁵ 'ever? Will he keep it to the end?' Behold, thou hast spoken and done evil things as thou couldest.

AND JEHOVAH SAID TO ME in the days of Josiah the ⁶ king, Hast thou seen that which backsliding Israel hath done? She is gone up upon every high mountain and under every green tree, and there hath played the harlot. And I said, after she had done all these things, 'Return ⁷ 'thou to me.' But she returned not. And her treacherous sister Judah saw it. And I saw, when for all the causes ⁸ whereby backsliding Israel committed adultery I had put her away, and given her a bill of divorce; yet her treacherous sister Judah feared not, but went and played the harlot also. And it came to pass through the vileness ⁹ of her fornication, that she defiled the land, and committed adultery with stones and with stocks of wood. And ¹⁰ yet for all this her treacherous sister Judah hath not returned to me with her whole heart, but feignedly; Jehovah hath said it.

11 And Jehovah said to me, The backsliding Israel hath jus-
12 tified herself more than treacherous Judah. Go and proclaim these words toward the north, and say, Return, thou backsliding Israel, Jehovah hath said it; and I will not cause mine anger to fall upon you. For I am merciful, Jehovah hath said it, and I will not keep anger for ever.
13 Only acknowledge thine iniquity, that thou hast transgressed against Jehovah thy God, and hast scattered thy ways to the strangers under every green tree, and ye have
14 not obeyed my voice, Jehovah hath said it. Return, O backsliding children, Jehovah hath said it; for I am married to you, and I will take you one of a city, and two of a
15 family, and I will bring you to Zion. And I will give you shepherds according to my heart, who shall feed you with knowledge and understanding.
16 And it shall come to pass, when ye be multiplied and have been fruitful in the land, in those days, Jehovah hath said it, they shall say no more, 'The ark of the covenant 'of Jehovah;' neither shall it come to mind; neither shall they remember it; neither shall they visit it; neither
17 shall it be done any more. At that time they shall call Jerusalem the throne of Jehovah; and all the nations shall be gathered to it, to the name of Jehovah, to Jerusalem; neither shall they walk any more after the stub-
18 bornness of their evil heart. In those days the house of Judah shall walk with the house of Israel, and they shall come together out of the land of the North to the land that I gave for an inheritance to your fathers.
19 Then I said, How shall I put thee among the children, and give thee a pleasant land, a glorious heritage of the hosts of nations? And I said, Thou shalt call me, My
20 father; and shalt not turn away from me. Surely as a wife treacherously departeth from her husband, so have ye dealt treacherously with me, O house of Israel; Jehovah hath said it.
21 A voice was heard upon the heights, weeping and supplications of the children of Israel; for they have perverted their way, and they have forgotten Jehovah their
22 God. Return, ye backsliding children, and I will heal your backslidings.

'Behold, we come to thee; for thou art Jehovah our
23 'God. Truly in vain [do we hope] from the hills, and

'from the multitude on the mountains; truly in Jehovah 'our God is the salvation of Israel. For Shame [or 'Baal] hath eaten the produce of our father's labour from 'our youth; their flocks and their herds, their sons and 'their daughters. We lie down in our shame, and our confusion covereth us; for we have sinned against Jehovah 'our God, we and our fathers, from our youth, even to this 'day, and have not obeyed the voice of Jehovah our God.'—

If thou wilt return, O Israel, Jehovah hath said it, wilt return to me; and if thou wilt put away thine abominations out of my sight, then shalt thou not be a wanderer. And thou shalt swear, 'As Jehovah liveth,' in truth, in justice, and in righteousness; and the nations shall bless themselves in Him, and in Him shall they glory.

For thus saith Jehovah to the men of Judah and Jerusalem, Break up your fallow ground, and sow not among thorns. Circumcise yourselves to Jehovah, and take away the foreskins of your heart, ye men of Judah and inhabitants of Jerusalem; lest my fury come forth like fire, and burn so that none can quench it, because of the evil of your doings. Declare ye in Judah, and publish in Jerusalem; and say, 'Blow ye the trumpet in the land.' Cry with a full voice, and say, 'Assemble yourselves, and let 'us go into the fenced cities.' Set up the standard toward Zion; flee in haste, stay not; for I will bring evil from the north, and a great breaking up. The lion [or Scythian] is come up from his thicket, and the destroyer of nations hath moved his camp; he is gone forth from his place to make thy land desolate; and thy cities shall be laid waste, without an inhabitant. Therefore gird you with sackcloth, mourn and howl; for the fierce anger of Jehovah is not turned away from us. And it shall come to pass at that day, Jehovah hath said it, that the heart of the king [of Judah] shall perish, and the heart of the princes; and the priests shall be astonished, and the prophets shall wonder.

Then said I, 'Ah, Lord Jehovah! surely thou hast greatly 'deceived this people and Jerusalem, saying, Ye shall have 'peace; whereas the sword reacheth unto the soul.'

At that time shall it be said to this people and to Jerusalem, A dry wind from the heights in the desert cometh toward the daughter of my people, not to winnow, nor to cleanse. Even a wind stronger than this shall come on my behalf. Now also will I give sentence against them.

¹³ 'Behold, he cometh up as clouds, and his chariots are as 'a whirlwind; his horses are swifter than eagles. Woe 'unto us! for we are spoiled.'

¹⁴ O Jerusalem, wash thy heart from wickedness, that thou ¹⁵ mayest be saved. How long wilt thou lodge within thee thy vain thoughts? For a voice declareth from Dan, and publisheth affliction from the hill country of Ephraim. ¹⁶ Make ye mention to the Nations; behold, publish unto Jerusalem, that the watchmen come in from a far country, and they give out their voice towards the cities of Judah. ¹⁷ As keepers of a field, are they against her round about; because she hath been rebellious against me; Jehovah hath ¹⁸ said it. Thy way and thy doings have procured these things for thee; this is thy wickedness, because it is bitter, because it reacheth unto thy heart.

¹⁹ 'My bowels, my bowels! I am pained at the bottom of 'my heart; my heart maketh a noise within me; I cannot 'hold my peace, because thou hast heard, O my soul, the ²⁰ 'sound of the trumpet, the alarm of war. A breaking up 'upon a breaking up is proclaimed; for the whole land 'is spoiled; suddenly are my tents spoiled, and my tent- ²¹ 'curtains in a moment. How long shall I see the standard, 'and hear the sound of the trumpet?'

²² It is because my people is foolish; they have not known me; they are sottish children, and they have no understanding; they are wise to do evil, but to do good they have no knowledge.

²³ 'I beheld the earth, and, lo, it was without form and ²⁴ 'void; and the heavens, and they had no light. I beheld 'the mountains, and, lo, they were shaken, and all the hills ²⁵ 'trembled. I beheld, and, lo, there was no man, and all ²⁶ 'the birds of the heavens were fled. I beheld, and, lo, 'the fruitful soil was a desert, and all its cities were 'broken down at the presence of Jehovah, and by his 'fierce anger.'

²⁷ For thus hath Jehovah said, The whole land shall be ²⁸ desolate; yet will I not make a full end. For this shall the earth mourn, and the heavens above be darkened; because I have spoken it, I have purposed it, and I have ²⁹ not repented, neither will I turn back from it. The whole city shall flee for the noise of the horsemen and bowmen; they shall go into thick places, and climb up upon

the rocks. Every city shall be forsaken, and not a man shall dwell therein. And when thou art spoiled, what ³⁰ wilt thou do? Though thou clothest thyself with crimson, though thou deckest thee with ornaments of gold, though thou injurest thine eyes with paint, in vain shalt thou make thyself fair; thy lovers will despise thee, they will seek thy life. For I heard a voice as of a woman in ³¹ travail, and the anguish as of her that bringeth forth her first child, the voice of the daughter of Zion. She gaspeth, she spreadeth her hands, [saying,] 'Woe is me now! for 'my soul is wearied because of murderers.'

Run ye to and fro through the streets of Jerusalem, and ¹ see now, and know, and seek in its broad places if ye can find a man, if there be any one that executeth justice, that seeketh the truth; and I will pardon it. And though ² they say, 'As Jehovah liveth,' surely they swear falsely.

'O Jehovah, are not thine eyes upon the truth? Thou ³ 'hast stricken them. But they have not grieved. Thou 'hast consumed them. But they have refused to receive 'correction. They have made their faces harder than a 'rock; they have refused to return. Therefore I said, ⁴ 'Surely these are the poor; they act foolishly; because 'they know not the way of Jehovah, nor the judgment of 'their God.'

I will get me to the great men, and will speak to them; ⁵ for they have known the way of Jehovah, and the judgment of their God; yet they also have altogether broken the yoke, they have burst the bonds asunder. Therefore ⁶ a lion out of the forest shall slay them, a wolf of the barren plains shall spoil them, a leopard shall watch about their cities; every one that goeth out thence shall be torn in pieces; because their transgressions are many, and their backslidings are numerous.

How shall I pardon thee for this? Thy children have ⁷ forsaken me, and sworn by them that are no gods. Though I bound them by an oath, yet they committed adultery, and assembled themselves by troops in the harlots' houses. They were as well fed horses in the morn- ⁸ ing; every one neighed after his neighbour's wife. Shall ⁹ I not punish these things? Jehovah hath said it; and shall not my soul be avenged on such a nation as this?

Go ye up upon her walls, and destroy; but make not a ¹⁰

full end. Take away her branches; for they are not Je-
11 hovah's. For the house of Israel and the house of Judah
have dealt very treacherously against me; Jehovah hath
12 said it. They have lied unto Jehovah, and said, 'It is
'not He; neither shall evil come upon us; neither shall
13 'we see sword nor famine; and the prophets are become
'wind, and the word is not in them; thus shall it be done
'unto them.'
14 Therefore thus saith Jehovah the God of hosts, Because
ye have spoken this word, behold, I will make my words in
thy mouth to be fire, and this people as wood, and it shall
15 devour them. Lo, I will bring a nation [the Scythians]
upon you from far, O house of Israel; Jehovah hath said
it. It is a mighty nation, it is an ancient nation, a nation
whose language thou knowest not, neither understandest
16 thou what they say. Their quiver is as an open sepulchre,
17 they are all warriors, and they shall eat up thy harvest,
and thy bread which thy sons and thy daughters should
eat; they shall eat up thy flocks and thy herds; they
shall eat up thy vines and thy fig trees; they shall break
down thy fenced cities, wherein thou trustedst, with the
18 sword. Nevertheless in those days, Jehovah hath said it,
19 I will not make a full end with you. And it shall come to
pass, when ye shall say, 'Wherefore doeth Jehovah our
'God all these things unto us?' then shalt thou answer
them, 'Like as ye have forsaken me, and served foreign
'gods in your land, so shall ye serve strangers in a land
'that is not yours.'
20 Declare this in the house of Jacob, and publish it in
21 Judah saying, Hear now this, O foolish people, and without heart; who have eyes, and see not; who have ears,
22 and hear not. Do ye not fear me? Jehovah hath said it.
Will ye not tremble at my presence, who placed the sand
for the boundary of the sea by a perpetual decree, that it
cannot pass over it; and though its waves toss themselves,
yet can they not prevail; though they roar, yet can they
23 not pass over it? But this people hath a revolting and a
24 rebellious heart; they are revolted and gone. Neither say
they in their heart, 'Let us now fear Jehovah our God, who
'giveth rain, both the early and the latter, in its season;
'he reserveth unto us the appointed weeks of the harvest.'
25 Your iniquities have turned away these things, and your

11—2

sins have withheld good things from you. For among my ²⁶ people are found wicked men. They lay wait, as he that setteth snares; they set a trap, they catch men. As a ²⁷ cage is full of birds, so are their houses full of deceit; therefore they are become great, and wax rich. They ²⁸ wax fat, they shine; yea, they overpass the deeds of the wicked; they judge not the cause, the cause of the fatherless, yet they prosper; and the right of the needy do they not judge. Shall I not punish these things? Jehovah ²⁹ hath said it. Shall not my soul be avenged on such a nation as this? A dreadful and a horrible thing hath been ³⁰ done in the land; the prophets prophesy falsely, and the ³¹ priests bear rule under their orders; and my people love to have it so; and what will ye do in the end thereof? —

Flee, O ye children of Benjamin, out of the midst of ¹ Jerusalem, and blow the trumpet in Tekoa, and set up a fire-signal in Beth-haccerem; for evil appeareth out of the north, and great destruction. I will destroy the comely ² and delicate daughter of Zion. The shepherds with their ³ flocks shall come upon her; they shall pitch their tents against her round about; they shall feed every one as his hand is able. They consecrate the war against her, [say- ⁴ ing,] 'Arise, and let us go up at noon.' Woe unto us! for the day goeth away, for the shadows of the evening are stretched out. 'Arise, and let us go by night, and let us ⁵ 'destroy her castles.'

For thus saith Jehovah of hosts, Hew ye down her trees, ⁶ and cast a siege mound against Jerusalem. This is the city to be punished; there is wholly oppression in the midst of her. As a fountain casteth forth her waters, so ⁷ she casteth forth her wickedness; violence and spoil is heard in her; before me continually is disease and wounds. Be ⁸ thou instructed, O Jerusalem, lest my soul be separated from thee; lest I make thee desolate, a land not inhabited.

Thus saith Jehovah of hosts, They shall thoroughly glean ⁹ the remnant of Israel as a vine; turn back thy hand as a grape-gatherer to the baskets. To whom shall I speak, ¹⁰ and give warning, that they may hear? Behold, their ear is uncircumcised, and they cannot hearken; behold, the word of Jehovah is unto them a reproach; they have no delight in it. Therefore I am full of the wrath of Jehovah; ¹¹ I am weary with holding in. I will pour it out upon the children abroad, and upon the assembly of young men together; for even the husband with the wife shall be taken, the aged ¹² with him that is full of days. And their houses shall be turned unto others, with their fields and wives together. For I will stretch out my hand upon the inhabitants of the land; ¹³ Jehovah hath said it. For from the least of them even unto the greatest of them every one is greedy of gain; and from the prophet even unto the priest every one ¹⁴ dealeth falsely. They heal also the wound of the daughter of my people slightly, saying, 'Peace, peace;' when ¹⁵ there is no peace. Were they ashamed when they had committed abomination? Nay, they were not at all ashamed, neither knew they how to blush; therefore they shall fall among them that fall. At the time that I visit them they shall be cast down, saith Jehovah.

¹⁶ Thus saith Jehovah, Stand ye in the ways, and see, and ask for the old paths, 'Where is the good way?' and walk therein, and ye shall find rest for your souls. But ¹⁷ they said, 'We will not walk therein.' Also I set watchmen over you, [to say,] 'Hearken to the sound of the 'trumpet.' But they said, 'We will not hearken.'

¹⁸ Therefore hearken, ye nations, and know, O congrega- ¹⁹ tion, what is among them. Hear, O earth; behold, I will bring evil upon this people, even the fruit of their own thoughts, because they have not hearkened to my words, ²⁰ nor to my law, but have rejected it. To what purpose cometh there to me incense from Sheba, and the sweet cane from a far country? Your burnt offerings are not acceptable, and your sacrifices are not sweet unto me. ²¹ Therefore thus saith Jehovah, Behold, I will lay stumbling-blocks before this people, and the fathers and the sons shall stumble over them together; the neighbour and his friend shall perish.

²² Thus saith Jehovah, Behold, a people cometh from the north country, and a great nation shall be raised up from the ²³ end of the earth. They shall lay hold on bow and spear; they are cruel, and have no mercy; their voice roareth like the sea; and they ride upon horses, they are set in array as men for war against thee, O daughter of Zion. ²⁴ 'We have heard the fame thereof; our hands wax 'feeble; anguish hath taken hold of us, and pain, as of a 'woman in travail.'

Go not forth into the field, nor walk in the highway; 25
for the sword of the enemy and terror is on all sides. O 26
daughter of my people, gird thyself with sackcloth, and
roll thyself in ashes; make to thee mourning, as for an
only son, most bitter grieving; for the spoiler will come
upon us suddenly.

I have set thee for a trier among my people, an assayer, 27
that thou mayest know and try their way. They are 28
all grievous revolters, walking with slanders, like copper
and iron; they all act corruptly. The bellows blow hard, 29
the lead is consumed by the fire; the refiner refineth in
vain; for the wicked are not plucked away. Refuse silver 30
shall men call them, because Jehovah hath rejected them.—

THE WORD THAT CAME TO JEREMIAH from Jehovah, say- 1
ing, Stand at the gate of Jehovah's House, and proclaim 2
there this word, and say, Hear the word of Jehovah, all ye
of Judah, that enter in at these gates to worship Jehovah.
Thus saith Jehovah of hosts, the God of Israel, Amend 3
your ways and your doings, and I will cause you to dwell
in this place. Trust ye not in lying words, saying, 'The 4
'temple of Jehovah, The temple of Jehovah, The temple
'of Jehovah, are these.' For if ye thoroughly amend your 5
ways and your doings; if ye thoroughly execute justice
between a man and his neighbour; if ye oppress not the 6
stranger, the fatherless, and the widow, and shed not innocent blood in this place; neither walk after other gods
to your hurt; then will I cause you to dwell in this place, in 7
the land that I gave to your fathers, for ever and for ever.

Behold, ye trust in lying words, that cannot profit. Will 8
ye steal, murder, and commit adultery, and swear falsely, 9
and burn incense unto Baal, and walk after other gods
whom ye know not? And will ye come and stand before 10
me in this House, which is called by my name, and say,
'We have been saved in order to do all these abomina-
'tions?' Is this House, which is called by my name, be- 11
come a den of robbers in your eyes? Behold, even I have
seen it; Jehovah hath said it. But go ye now to my Place 12
which was in Shiloh, where I caused my Name to dwell at
first, and see what I did to it for the wickedness of my
people Israel. And now, because ye have done all these 13
works, Jehovah hath said it, and I spake to you, rising up
early and speaking, but ye heard not; and I called you,

¹⁴ but ye answered not; therefore will I do to this House, which is called by my name, wherein ye trust, and unto the Place which I have given to you and to your fathers, ¹⁵ as I did to Shiloh. And I will cast you out of my presence, as I cast out all your brethren, even the whole seed of Ephraim.

¹⁶ Therefore pray not thou for this people, neither lift up cry nor prayer for them, neither make intercession to me; ¹⁷ for I will not hear thee. Seest thou not what they do in ¹⁸ the cities of Judah and in the streets of Jerusalem? The children gather wood, and the fathers kindle the fire, and the women knead their dough, to make cakes to the Queen of Heaven, and to pour out drink offerings unto other gods, ¹⁹ so that they may provoke me to anger. Do they provoke me to anger? Jehovah hath said it. Do they not provoke ²⁰ themselves to the confusion of their own faces? Therefore thus saith the Lord Jehovah; Behold, mine anger and my wrath shall be poured out upon this place, upon man, and upon beast, and upon the trees of the field, and upon the fruit of the ground; and it shall burn, and shall not be quenched.

²¹ Thus saith Jehovah of hosts, the God of Israel; Put your burnt offerings unto your sacrifices, and eat the ²² flesh. For I spake not to your fathers, nor commanded them in the day that I brought them out of the land of Lower Egypt, concerning burnt offerings or sacrifices. ²³ But this thing commanded I them, saying, 'Obey my voice, 'and I will be your God, and ye shall be my people; and 'walk ye in all the ways that I have commanded you, so ²⁴ 'that it may be well unto you.' But they hearkened not, nor inclined their ear, but walked in the counsels and in the stubbornness of their evil heart, and went backward, ²⁵ and not forward. Since the day that your fathers came forth out of the land of Lower Egypt unto this day I have even sent to you all my servants the prophets, daily rising ²⁶ up early and sending them; yet they hearkened not to me, nor inclined their ear, but hardened their neck. They ²⁷ did worse than their fathers. Therefore thou shalt speak all these words unto them; but they will not hearken to thee; thou shalt also call to them; but they will not ²⁸ answer thee. And thou shalt say to them, 'This is a 'nation that obeyeth not the voice of Jehovah their God,

'nor receiveth correction.' Truth is perished, and is cut off from their mouth.

Cut off thy hair as a Nazarite, [O Jerusalem,] and cast it away, and take up a lamentation on the heights; for Jehovah hath rejected and forsaken the generation of his wrath. For the children of Judah have done evil in my sight; Jehovah hath said it. They have set their abominations in the House which is called by my name, to pollute it. And they have built the High Places [or altars] of Tophet, which is in the Valley of the Son of Hinnom, to burn their sons and their daughters in the fire; which I commanded them not, neither came it into my heart. Therefore, behold the days will come, Jehovah hath said it, that it shall no more be called Tophet, nor the Valley of the Son of Hinnom, but the Valley of Slaughter; for they shall bury in Tophet, for want of space. And the carcases of this people shall be food for the fowls of the heavens, and for the beasts of the earth; and none shall frighten them away. Then will I cause to cease from the cities of Judah, and from the streets of Jerusalem, the voice of mirth, and the voice of gladness, the voice of the bridegroom, and the voice of the bride; for the land shall be desolate.

At that time, Jehovah hath said it, they shall bring out the bones of the kings of Judah, and the bones of its princes, and the bones of the priests, and the bones of the prophets, and the bones of the inhabitants of Jerusalem, out of their graves; and they shall spread them before the sun, and the moon, and all the host of the heavens, which they have loved, and which they have served, and after which they have walked, and which they have inquired of, and which they have worshipped; they shall not be gathered up, nor be buried; they shall be for dung upon the face of the earth. And death shall be chosen rather than life by all the residue of them that remain of this evil family, which remain in all the places whither I have driven them; Jehovah of hosts hath said it.

Moreover thou shalt say to them, Thus saith Jehovah; Shall they fall, and not arise? shall he turn away and not return? Why is this people of Jerusalem slidden back by a complete backsliding? They hold fast deceit, they refuse to return. I hearkened and heard, but they spake not

aright. No man repented him of his wickedness, saying, 'What have I done?' Every one returned to his course,
7 as the horse rusheth into the battle. Yea, the stork in the heavens knoweth her appointed times; and the turtle-dove and the crane and the swallow observe the time of their coming; but my people know not the judgment of Jehovah.
8 How do ye say, 'We are wise, and the Law of Jehovah 'is with us'? Lo, certainly in vain he made it; the pen
9 of the scribes hath been in vain. The wise men are ashamed, they are dismayed and taken; lo, they have rejected the word of Jehovah; and what wisdom is there in
10 them? Therefore will I give their wives to others, and their fields to them that shall seize upon them. For every one from the least even unto the greatest is greedy of gain, from the prophet even unto the priest every one dealeth
11 falsely. For they have healed the wound of the daughter of my people slightly, saying, 'Peace, peace;' and there is no peace.
12 Were they ashamed when they had committed abomination? Nay, they were not at all ashamed, neither knew they how to blush. Therefore shall they fall among them that fall; in the time of their visitation they shall be cast
13 down, saith Jehovah. I will surely pluck them off; Jehovah hath said it. There shall be no grapes on the vine, nor figs on the fig tree, and the leaf shall fade; and I will send to them some that shall pass over them.
14 'Why do we sit still? Assemble yourselves, and let us 'enter into the fenced cities, and let us be silent there; for 'Jehovah our God hath put us to silence, and given us 'water of hemlock to drink, because we have sinned against
15 'Jehovah. We look for peace, but there is no good; and
16 'for a time of health, and behold terror! The snorting 'of his horses is heard from Dan; the whole land trembleth 'at the sound of the shouting of his strong ones; for they 'will come and devour the land and all that is in it; the 'city, and those that dwell therein.'
17 For, behold, I send serpents, vipers, among you, against which there is no charm, and they shall bite you; Jehovah hath said it.
18 OH FOR CONSOLATION in my sorrow! my heart is faint
19 within me. Behold the voice of the cry of the daughter of my people from the land of them that dwell afar off,

[saying,] 'Is not Jehovah in Zion? Is not her king in 'her?'

Why have they provoked me to anger with their graven images, and with foreign vanities?

'The harvest is past, the summer is ended, and we are 20 'not saved.'

By the wound of the daughter of my people am I 21 wounded; I am made to mourn; astonishment hath taken hold on me. Is there no balm in Gilead? is there no phy- 22 sician there? why then is no healing bandage applied to— the daughter of my people? Oh that my head were waters, 1 and mine eyes a fountain of tears, that I might weep day and night for the slain of the daughter of my people!

Oh that I had in the desert a lodging place of wayfaring 2 men; that I might leave my people, and go from them! for they are all adulterers, an assembly of treacherous men. And they aim with their tongues like their bow for lies; 3 but they are not valiant for the truth upon the earth; for they go on from evil to evil, and they know not me; Jehovah hath said it.

Take ye heed every one of his neighbour, and trust ye 4 not in any brother; for every brother will utterly supplant, and every neighbour will walk with slanders. And they 5 will deceive every one his neighbour, and will not speak the truth; they have taught their tongue to speak lies; they weary themselves in doing iniquity. Thy habitation 6 is in the midst of deceit; through deceit they refuse to know me; Jehovah hath said it.

Therefore thus saith Jehovah of hosts, Behold, I will 7 melt them, and try them; for how shall I do for the daughter of my people? Their tongue is a deadly arrow; 8 it speaketh deceit. One speaketh peaceably to his neighbour with his mouth, but in his heart he layeth his snares. Shall I not punish them for these things? Jehovah hath 9 said it. Shall not my soul be avenged on such a nation as this? I will take up a weeping and wailing for the 10 mountains, and for the pastures of the desert a lamentation, because they are burned up, so that none can pass through them; neither can men hear the voice of cattle; from the fowl of the heavens even to the beast they are fled; they are gone. And I will make Jerusalem a heap of ruins, and 11 a den of jackals; and I will make the cities of Judah desolate, without an inhabitant.

12 'Who is the wise man, that may understand this? And 'who is he to whom the mouth of Jehovah hath spoken, 'that he may declare it? For what cause is it that the 'land perisheth and is burned up like the desert, so that
13 'none passeth through?' And Jehovah saith, It is because they have forsaken my Law which I set before them, and
14 have not obeyed my voice, neither walked therein; but have walked after the stubbornness of their own heart, and after
15 Baal, which their fathers taught them. Therefore thus saith Jehovah of hosts, the God of Israel; Behold, I will feed them, even this people, with wormwood, and give them
16 water of hemlock to drink. I will scatter them also among nations, whom neither they nor their fathers have known; and I will send a sword after them, till I have consumed them.
17 Thus saith Jehovah of hosts, Consider ye, and call for women who sing lamentations, that they may come; and
18 send for cunning women, that they may come. And let them make haste, and raise up a wailing for us, that our eyes may run down with tears, and our eyelids gush
19 out with water. For a voice of wailing is heard out of Zion, 'How are we spoiled! We are greatly confounded, 'because we are leaving the land, because our dwellings
20 'have cast us out.' Yet hear the word of Jehovah, O ye women, and let your ear receive the word of his mouth, and teach your daughters wailing, and every woman her
21 neighbour a lamentation. For death is come up into our windows, it is entered into our castles, to cut off the children from the streets, and the young men from the broad
22 places. Say, 'Thus hath Jehovah said. And the carcases 'of men shall fall as dung upon the open field, and as the 'handful after the harvest man, and none shall gather 'them in.'
23 Thus saith Jehovah, Let not the wise man glory in his wisdom, neither let the mighty man glory in his might,
24 let not the rich man glory in his riches; but let him that glorieth glory in this, that he understandeth and knoweth me, that I am Jehovah who exercise loving-kindness, justice, and righteousness, on the earth; for in these things I delight; Jehovah hath said it.

Behold, the days will come, Jehovah hath said it, that 25 I will punish all them that are circumcised with the uncircumcised; Egypt, and Judah, and Edom, and the Children of Ammon, and Moab, and all that are shorn on the cheek, that dwell in the desert; for all these nations are uncircumcised, and all the house of Israel are uncircumcised in the heart. 26

HEAR YE THE WORD which Jehovah speaketh to you, O house of Israel. 1 Thus saith Jehovah, Learn not the way 2 of the Nations, and be not dismayed at the signs of the heavens; for the Nations are dismayed at them. For the 3 customs of the peoples are vain; for they cut a tree out of the forest, the work of the hands of the workman, with the axe. They ornament it with silver and with gold; they 4 fasten it with nails and with hammers, that it tumble not. They are as the palm-tree column of beaten work, and 5 speak not. They must needs be carried, because they cannot walk. Be not afraid of them; for they cannot do evil, neither also is it in them to do good.

'Forasmuch as there is none like unto thee, O Jehovah; 6 'thou art great, and thy name is great in might. Who 7 'would not fear thee, O King of the nations? for to thee 'doth it appertain; forasmuch as among all the wise men 'of the nations, and in all their kingdoms, there is none 'like unto thee. But they are at once both brutish and 8 'foolish. The stock of wood is a doctrine of vanities. 'Silver spread into plates is brought from Tarshish, and 9 'gold from Ophaz, the work of the workman, and of the 'hands of the metal founder; blue and purple is their clothing; they are all the work of cunning men. But Jehovah 10 'is the true God, he is the living God, and a king for ever. 'At his wrath the earth shall tremble, and the nations 'shall not be able to abide his indignation.'

* (Thus shall ye say to them, The gods that have not 11
* made the heavens and the earth, even they shall perish
* from the earth, and from under these heavens.)

He made the earth by his power, he established the 12 world by his wisdom, and stretched out the heavens by his understanding. When he uttereth his voice, there is a 13 tumult of waters in the heavens, and he causeth the clouds to ascend from the ends of the earth; he maketh lightnings for the rain, and bringeth forth the wind out of his trea-

¹⁴ sures. Every man is brutish without knowledge; every metal-founder is put to shame by the graven image; for his molten image is falsehood, and there is no breath in them. ¹⁵ They are vanity, and the work of delusions; in the time ¹⁶ of their visitation they shall perish. The portion of Jacob is not like them. For He is the former of all things; and Israel is the rod of his inheritance; Jehovah of hosts is his name.

¹⁷ GATHER UP THY WARES out of the land, O thou that ¹⁸ dwellest in the besieged place. For thus saith Jehovah, Behold, I will sling out the inhabitants of the land at this once, and will lay siege to them, that they may find it so. ¹⁹ 'Woe is me for my hurt! my wound is grievous. But ²⁰ 'I said, Truly this is a grief, and I must bear it. My tent 'is spoiled, and all my cords are broken. My children are 'gone forth from me, and they are not; there is none to 'stretch forth my tent any more, and to set up my tent- ²¹ 'curtains. For the shepherds are become brutish, and 'have not sought Jehovah. Therefore they have not ²² 'prospered, and all their flocks are scattered. Behold, 'the noise of the tidings is come, and a great commotion 'out of the north country, to make the cities of Judah ²³ 'desolate, and a den of jackals. O Jehovah, I know that 'the way of man is not in himself; it is not in man that ²⁴ 'walketh to direct his own steps. O Jehovah, correct me, 'but with judgment; not in thine anger, lest thou bring ²⁵ 'me to nothing. Pour out thy wrath upon the nations 'that know thee not, and upon the families that call not 'on thy name; for they have eaten up Jacob, both eaten 'him up and consumed him, and have made his habita- —'tion desolate.'

¹ THE WORD THAT CAME TO JEREMIAH from Jehovah, say- ² ing, Hear ye the words of this Covenant, and speak ye to the men of Judah, and to the inhabitants of Jerusalem; ³ and say thou to them, Thus saith Jehovah the God of Israel; Cursed be the man that obeyeth not the words of ⁴ this Covenant, which I commanded your fathers in the day that I brought them forth out of the land of Lower Egypt, from the iron furnace, saying, 'Obey my voice, and do 'these things, according to all which I command you; so ⁵ 'shall ye be my people, and I will be your God; so that 'I may perform the oath which I have sworn unto your

'fathers, to give them a land flowing with milk and honey, 'as it is this day.' Then answered I, and said, 'Amen [or 'So be it], O Jehovah.'

⁵ Then Jehovah said to me, Proclaim all these words in ⁶ the cities of Judah, and in the streets of Jerusalem, saying, 'Hear ye the words of this Covenant, and do them.' For ⁷ I earnestly protested to your fathers in the day that I brought them up out of the land of Lower Egypt, even unto this day, rising up early and protesting, saying, 'Obey 'my voice.' Yet they obeyed not, nor inclined their ear, ⁸ but walked every one in the stubbornness of their evil heart. Therefore I will bring upon them all the words of this Covenant which I commanded them to do; but they did them not.

And Jehovah said to me, A conspiracy is found among ⁹ the men of Judah, and among the inhabitants of Jerusalem. They are turned back to the iniquities of their forefathers, ¹⁰ who refused to hear my words; and they went after other gods to serve them. The house of Israel and the house of Judah have broken my Covenant which I made with their fathers. Therefore thus saith Jehovah, Behold, I will bring ¹¹ evil upon them, which they shall not be able to escape; and though they shall cry to me, I will not hearken to them. Then shall the cities of Judah and inhabitants of ¹² Jerusalem go, and cry unto the gods to whom they offer incense; but they shall not save them at all in the time of their trouble. For according to the number of thy cities ¹³ were thy gods, O Judah; and according to the number of the streets of Jerusalem have ye set up altars to Shame, even altars to burn incense to Baal.—Therefore pray not ¹⁴ thou for this people, neither lift up a cry or prayer for them; for I will not hear them in the time that they cry unto me for their trouble.

What hast thou, my beloved, to do in my House, who ¹⁵ hast wrought wicked devices with many? And the gifts of holy flesh are passed from thee. When thou doest evil, then thou rejoicest. Jehovah called thy name, 'A green ¹⁶ 'olive tree, fair, and of goodly fruit;' with the noise of a great tumult he hath kindled fire upon it, and the branches of it are broken. For Jehovah of hosts, who planted thee, ¹⁷ hath pronounced evil against thee, because of the evil of the house of Israel and of the house of Judah, which they have done against themselves to provoke me to anger in offering incense unto Baal.

18 And Jehovah hath given me knowledge of it, and I know
19 it; and thou shewedst me their doings. But I was like a lamb or an ox that is brought to the slaughter; and I knew not that they had devised devices against me, [saying,] 'Let us destroy the tree with the fruit thereof, and 'let us cut him off from the land of the living, that his
20 'name may be no more remembered.' But, O Jehovah of hosts, that judgest righteously, that triest the reins and the heart, let me see thy vengeance on them; for unto thee have I revealed my cause.
21 Therefore thus saith Jehovah against the men of Anathoth, that seek thy life, saying, 'Prophesy not in the
22 'name of Jehovah, lest thou die by our hand;' therefore thus saith Jehovah of hosts, Behold, I will punish them; the young men shall die by the sword; their sons and
23 their daughters shall die by famine; and there shall be no remnant of them; for I will bring evil upon the men of —Anathoth, even the year of their visitation.

1 'Righteous art thou, O Jehovah, when I plead with 'thee; yet let me talk with thee of thy judgments. Where-'fore doth the way of the wicked prosper? wherefore are
2 'all they happy that deal treacherously? Thou hast planted 'them, yea, they have taken root; they grow, yea, they 'bring forth fruit. Thou art near in their mouth, but far
3 'from their reins. But thou, O Jehovah, knowest me; 'thou hast seen me, and tried my heart toward thee. 'Separate them like sheep for the slaughter, and conse-
4 'crate them for the day of slaying. How long shall the land 'mourn, and the herbs of every field wither, because of the 'wickedness of them that dwell therein? The cattle are 'consumed, and the birds; because they said, He shall 'not see our last end.'
5 If thou hast run with men on foot, and they have wearied thee, then how canst thou rival horses? And if thou trustedst in the land of peace, then how wilt thou do in the
6 pride of the Jordan? For even thy brethren, and the house of thy father, even they have dealt treacherously with thee; yea, they have called a multitude after thee. Believe them not, though they speak fair words unto thee.
7 I have forsaken my house, I have left my heritage; I

have given the love of my soul into the hand of her enemies. My heritage is to me as a lion in the forest; it ⁸ raiseth its voice against me; therefore have I hated it. My heritage is to me as a ravenous hyena; the ravenous ⁹ animals round about are against her. Come ye, assemble all ye wild beasts of the field, make them come to devour. Many shepherds have destroyed my vineyard, they have ¹⁰ trodden my portion under foot, they have made my pleasant portion a desolate desert. They have made it deso- ¹¹ late unto desolation. The whole land mourneth over me, being made desolate, because no man layeth it to heart. The spoilers are come upon all the heights in the desert; ¹² for the sword of Jehovah devoureth from the one end of the land even to the other end of the land; no flesh hath peace. They have sown wheat, but they reap thorns; they ¹³ are grieved, they are not profited; and they are ashamed of your harvest because of the fierce anger of Jehovah.

Thus saith Jehovah against all mine evil neighbours, ¹⁴ that touch the inheritance which I have caused my people Israel to inherit; Behold, I will pluck them out of their land, and pluck out the house of Judah from among them. And it shall come to pass, after that I have plucked them ¹⁵ out I will return, and have compassion on them, and will bring them back again, every man to his heritage, and every man to his land. And it shall come to pass, if they ¹⁶ will diligently learn the ways of my people, to swear by my name, 'As Jehovah liveth;' like as they taught my people to swear by Baal; then shall they be built up in the midst of my people. But if they will not obey, I will utterly ¹⁷ pluck up and destroy that nation; Jehovah hath said it. —

THUS SAITH JEHOVAH to me, ' Go and get thee a linen ¹ ' girdle, and put it upon thy loins; and put it not into ' water.' So I got a girdle according to the word of Je- ² hovah, and put it on my loins. And the word of Jeho- ³ vah came to me the second time, saying, ' Take the girdle ⁴ ' that thou hast got, which is upon thy loins, and arise, go ' to the Euphrates, and hide it there in a hole of the rock.' So I went, and hid it by the Euphrates, as Jehovah com- ⁵ manded me. And it came to pass after many days, that ⁶ Jehovah said to me, ' Arise, go to the Euphrates, and take ' the girdle from thence, which I commanded thee to hide ' there.' Then I went to the Euphrates, and digged, and ⁷

took the girdle from the place where I had hid it; and, behold, the girdle was marred, it was profitable for nothing.
8 Then the word of Jehovah came to me, saying, Thus
9 saith Jehovah, After this manner will I mar the pride of
10 Judah, and the great pride of Jerusalem. This evil people, who refuse to hear my words, who walk in the stubbornness of their heart, and walk after other gods, to serve them, and to worship them, shall even be as this girdle,
11 which is good for nothing. For as the girdle cleaveth to the loins of a man, so I caused to cleave unto me the whole house of Israel and the whole house of Judah, Jehovah hath said it; that they might be unto me for a people, and for a name, and for a praise, and for a glory; but they would not hear.
12 And thou shalt speak to them this word; Thus saith Jehovah the God of Israel, 'Every bottle shall be filled 'with wine.' And they will say to thee, 'Do we not cer- 'tainly know that every bottle shall be filled with wine?'
13 Then shalt thou say to them, Thus saith Jehovah, Behold, I will fill all the inhabitants of this land, even the kings that sit upon David's throne, and the priests, and the prophets, and all the inhabitants of Jerusalem, with drunken-
14 ness. And I will dash them each against his brother, and the fathers and the sons together, Jehovah hath said it. I will not pity, nor spare, nor have mercy, but destroy them.
15 Hear ye, and give ear; be not proud; for Jehovah
16 hath spoken. Give glory to Jehovah your God, before he cause darkness, and before your feet stumble in the twilight upon the mountains, lest while ye look for light, he turn it into the shadow of death, and make it gross dark-
17 ness. But if ye will not hear this, my soul shall weep in secret places for your pride; and mine eye shall weep sore, and run down with tears, because Jehovah's flock is
18 carried away captive. Say to the king [Jehoiakim] and to the queen, 'Humble yourselves, sit down; for from 'your head shall come down the crown of your glory.'
19 The cities of the South Country shall be shut up, and none shall open. Judah shall be carried away captive all of it,
20 it shall be wholly carried away captive. Lift up your eyes, and behold them [the Babylonians] that come from the north. Where is the flock that was given thee, thy beau-
21 tiful flock? What wilt thou say when he shall punish

thee? For thou hast taught them to be captains, and as chief over thee. Shall not pains seize thee, as a woman in travail? And if thou say in thy heart, 'Wherefore come 22 'these things upon me?' for the greatness of thine iniquity are thy skirts uncovered, and thy heels violently seized.

Can the Ethiopian change his skin, or the leopard his 23 spots? then may ye also be able to do good, that are accustomed to do evil. Therefore will I scatter them as the 24 chaff that passeth away by the wind of the desert. This 25 is thy lot, the portion of thy measures from me, Jehovah hath said it; because thou hast forgotten me, and thou trustest in falsehood. Therefore have I lifted up thy skirts 26 upon thy face, that thy shame may appear. I have seen 27 thine adulteries, and thy neighings, the lewdness of thy fornication, thine abominations on the hills in the fields. Alas for thee, O Jerusalem! wilt thou not be made clean? until when shall it be? —

THE WORD OF JEHOVAH that came to Jeremiah on occasion of THE DROUGHT. 1

Judah mourneth, and its city gates languish; they are 2 made to mourn unto the ground; and the cry of Jerusalem is gone up. And their nobles have sent their young men 3 for water; they came to the ditches, and found no water; they returned with their vessels empty; they were ashamed and confounded, and covered their heads; because the 4 ground is broken up; for there was no rain in the earth, the plowmen were ashamed, they covered their heads. Yea, the hind also calved in the field, and forsook its 5 young, because there was no herbage. And the wild asses 6 did stand on the heights, they snuffed up the wind like the jackals; their eyes did fail, because there was no grass.

'O Jehovah, though our iniquities testify against us, do 7 'thou do it for thy name's sake; for our backslidings are 'many; we have sinned against thee. O thou hope of 8 'Israel, the saviour thereof in time of trouble, why should- 'est thou be as a stranger in the land, and as a wayfaring 'man that turneth aside to tarry for a night? Why 9 'shouldest thou be as a man astonished, as a warrior that 'cannot save? Yet thou, O Jehovah, art in the midst of 'us, and we are called by thy name; leave us not.'

Thus saith Jehovah to this people, Thus have they loved 10 to wander, they have not refrained their feet, therefore

Jehovah is not pleased with them; he now remembereth
11 their iniquity, and visiteth their sins. And Jehovah said
12 to me, Pray not for this people for their good. When
they fast, I will not hear their cry; and when they offer
up burnt offering and meal offering, I will not accept
them; but I will consume them by the sword, and by
famine, and by pestilence.
13 Then said I, 'Ah, Lord Jehovah! behold, the prophets
'say to them, Ye shall not see the sword, neither shall ye
'have famine; but I will give you certain peace in this
14 'place.' Then Jehovah said to me, The prophets prophesy
lies in my name. I sent them not, neither have I commanded them, neither spake I to them. They prophesy
to you a false vision and divination, and a thing of nought,
15 and the deceit of their heart. Therefore thus saith Jehovah concerning the prophets that prophesy in my name,
and I sent them not, yet they say, 'Sword and famine
'shall not be in this land;' By sword and famine shall the
16 prophets themselves be consumed. And the people to
whom they prophesy shall be cast out in the streets of
Jerusalem because of the famine and the sword; and they
shall have none to bury them, them, their wives, nor their
sons, nor their daughters; for I will pour their wickedness
upon them.
17 Therefore thou shalt say this word to them; Let mine
eyes run down with tears night and day, and let them
not cease; for the virgin daughter of my people is broken
18 with a great breach, with a very grievous blow. If I go
forth into the field, then behold the slain with the sword!
and if I enter into the city, then behold those that are
sick through famine! yea, both the prophet and the priest
wander forth into a land that they know not.
19 'Hast thou utterly rejected Judah? Hath thy soul
'loathed Zion? Why hast thou smitten us, and there is
'no healing for us? We look for peace, and there is no
20 'good; and for a time of health, and behold terror! We
'acknowledge, O Jehovah, our wickedness, and the ini-
'quity of our fathers; for we have sinned against thee.
21 'Do not abhor us, for thy name's sake do not disgrace the
'throne of thy glory. Remember, break not thy covenant
22 'with us. Are there any among the Vanities of the Nations
'that can cause rain? or can the heavens give showers?

'Art not thou He, O Jehovah our God? Therefore we 'will wait upon thee; for thou hast made all these things.'—

Then said Jehovah to me, Though Moses and Samuel stood before me, yet my soul would not be toward this people. Cast them out of my sight, and let them go forth. And it shall come to pass, if they say to thee, 'Whither 'shall we go forth?' then thou shalt tell them, Thus saith Jehovah; 'Such are as for death, to death; and such as are 'for the sword, to the sword; and such as are for the 'famine, to the famine; and such as are for the captivity, to 'the captivity.' And I will appoint over them four kinds, Jehovah hath said it; the sword to slay, and the dogs to tear, and the fowls of the heaven, and the beasts of the earth, to devour and destroy. And I will give them up to be scattered into all kingdoms of the earth, because of Manasseh the son of Hezekiah king of Judah, for that which he did in Jerusalem. For who will have pity upon thee, O Jerusalem? or who will bemoan thee? or who will go aside to ask health for thee? Thou hast forsaken me, Jehovah hath said it, thou art gone backward; therefore will I stretch out my hand against thee, and destroy thee; I am weary with repenting. And I will winnow them with a fan at the city gates of the land; I will bereave them of children, I will destroy my people, since they return not from their ways. Their widows shall be increased to me above the sand of the ocean. I will bring upon them, even against the mother of the young men, a spoiler at noonday; I will cause anguish and terrors to fall upon her suddenly. She that hath borne seven languisheth; she hath breathed out her soul; her sun is gone down while it was yet day; she hath been ashamed and confounded. And the residue of them will I deliver to the sword before their enemies; Jehovah hath said it.

'Woe is me, my mother, that thou hast borne me to be 'a man of strife and a man of contention to the whole 'earth! I have neither lent on usury, nor have men lent 'to me; yet every one of them doth curse me.'

Jehovah said, Truly I will set thee free unto good; truly I will cause the enemy to be a suppliant to thee in the time of evil and in the time of affliction.

'Shall iron, shall iron from the North and copper be 'broken?'

¹³ Thy substance and thy treasures will I give up to plunder without price, even for all thy sins, even in all thy ¹⁴ borders. And I will make thee to pass with thine enemies into a land which thou knowest not. For a fire is kindled in mine anger, which shall burn upon you.

¹⁵ 'O Jehovah, thou knowest. Remember me, and visit 'me, and revenge me on my persecutors; take me not 'away in the slowness of thine anger. Know that for thy ¹⁶ 'sake I have suffered rebuke. Thy words were found, and 'I did eat them; and thy word was unto me the joy and 'rejoicing of my heart. For I am called by thy name, O ¹⁷ 'Jehovah God of hosts. I sat not in the assembly of the 'mockers, nor rejoiced; I sat apart from them because of ¹⁸ 'thy hand; for thou hast filled me with indignation. Why 'is my pain perpetual, and my wound incurable, which 'refuseth to be healed? Wilt thou surely be unto me as 'a false stream, whose waters are not real?'

¹⁹ Therefore thus saith Jehovah, If thou return, then will I bring thee again, and thou shalt stand before me; and if thou put forth what is precious from what is vile, thou shalt be as my mouth. They shall return unto thee; ²⁰ but return not thou unto them. And I will make thee against this people a fenced wall of copper; and they shall fight against thee, but they shall not prevail against thee; for I am with thee to save thee and to deliver thee; Je- ²¹ hovah hath said it. And I will deliver thee out of the hand of the wicked, and I will redeem thee out of the —grasp of the terrible ones.

¹ THE WORD OF JEHOVAH came also to me, saying, Thou ² shalt not take to thee a wife, neither shalt thou have sons ³ or daughters in this place. For thus saith Jehovah concerning the sons and concerning the daughters that are born in this place, and concerning their mothers that bear them, and concerning their fathers that beget them in this ⁴ land; They shall die of grievous deaths; they shall not be mourned for; neither shall they be buried; they shall be as dung upon the face of the earth. And they shall be consumed by the sword, and by famine; and their carcases shall be food for the fowls of the heavens, and for the beasts of the earth.

⁵ For thus saith Jehovah, Enter not into the house of lamentation, neither go to mourn nor bemoan them; for

I have taken away my peace from this people, Jehovah hath said it, even loving-kindness and mercies. Both the ⁶ great and the small shall die in this land. They shall not be buried, neither shall men mourn for them, nor cut themselves, nor make themselves bald for them. Neither ⁷ shall men break bread with them in mourning, to comfort them for the dead; neither shall men give them the cup of consolation to drink for their father or for their mother. Thou shalt also not go into the house of drinking feasts, ⁸ to sit with them to eat and to drink. For thus saith Je- ⁹ hovah of hosts, the God of Israel; Behold, I will cause to cease out of this place before your eyes, and in your days, the voice of mirth, and the voice of gladness, the voice of the bridegroom, and the voice of the bride.

And it shall come to pass, when thou shalt show this ¹⁰ people all these words, and they shall say to thee, 'Where-'fore hath Jehovah pronounced all this great evil against 'us? or what is our iniquity? or what is our sin that we 'have committed against Jehovah our God?' then shalt ¹¹ thou say to them, It is because your fathers have forsaken me, Jehovah hath said it, and have walked after other gods, and have served them, and have worshipped them, and have forsaken me, and have not kept my law; and ye ¹² have done worse than your fathers; for, behold, ye walk every one after the stubbornness of his evil heart, so as not to hearken unto me. Therefore will I cast you out of this ¹³ land into a land that ye know not, neither ye nor your fathers; and there shall ye serve other gods day and night; where I will not shew you favour.

(Therefore, behold, the days will come, Jehovah hath ¹⁴ said it, that it shall no more be said, 'As Jehovah liveth, 'that brought up the children of Israel out of the land of 'Lower Egypt;' but, 'As Jehovah liveth, that brought up ¹⁵ 'the children of Israel from the land of the North, and 'from all the lands whither he had driven them.' And I will bring them back again into their land that I gave unto their fathers.)

Behold, I will send for many fishers, Jehovah hath said ¹⁶ it, and they shall fish them; and afterwards will I send for many hunters, and they shall hunt them from every mountain, and from every hill, and out of the holes of the rocks. For mine eyes are upon all their ways; they are ¹⁷

not hidden from my face, neither is their iniquity con-
¹⁸ cealed from mine eyes. And first I will repay their
iniquity and their sin to the double; because they have
defiled my land, and with the carcases of their detestable
and abominable things they have filled mine inheritance.
¹⁹ 'O Jehovah, my strength, and my fortress, and my
'refuge in the day of affliction, the Nations shall come
'unto thee from the ends of the earth, and shall say,
'Surely our fathers have inherited lies, vanity, and things
'wherein there is no profit.'
²⁰ Shall a man make gods for himself, and they are no
²¹ gods? Therefore, behold, I will cause them to know this
once, I will cause them to know my hand and my might,
—and they shall know that my name is Jehovah.

¹ The sin of Judah is written with a pen of iron, and with
the point of a diamond; it is engraven on the table of their
² heart, and on the horns of your altars; whilst their children remember their altars and their groves of Ashera by
³ the green trees upon the high hills. O my mountain in
the field, I will give up thy substance and all thy treasures
to plunder, and thy High Places [or altars] for sin,
⁴ throughout all thy borders. And thou, even thyself,
shalt be thrust out from thy heritage that I gave thee; and
I will cause thee to serve thine enemies in the land which
thou knowest not; for ye have kindled a fire in mine
anger, which shall burn for ever.
⁵ THUS SAITH JEHOVAH; Cursed be the man that trusteth
in man, and maketh flesh to be his arm, and whose heart
⁶ departeth from Jehovah. For he shall be like a destitute
man in the barren valley, and shall not see when good
cometh; but shall inhabit the parched places in the desert,
⁷ in a land that is salt and not inhabited. Blessed is the
man that trusteth in Jehovah, and whose hope Jehovah is.
⁸ For he shall be as a tree planted by the waters, and that
spreadeth out its roots by the river, and feareth not when
heat cometh, but its leaf is green; and is not distressed
in the year of drought, neither ceaseth from yielding fruit.
⁹ The heart is deceitful above all things, and cannot be
¹⁰ cured; who can know it? I Jehovah search the heart; I
try the reins, even to give to every man according to his
ways, according to the fruit of his doings.
¹¹ The partridge sitteth on eggs that she hath not laid;

So is he that getteth riches, and not by right.
He shall leave them in the midst of his days,
And at his end he shall be a fool.

'A glorious high throne from the beginning hath been ¹²
'the place of our Sanctuary. O Jehovah, the hope of ¹³
'Israel, all that forsake thee shall be ashamed.'
They that draw back from me shall be written on the earth, because they have forsaken Jehovah, the fountain of living waters.

'Heal me, O Jehovah, and I shall be healed; save me, ¹⁴
'and I shall be saved; for thou art my praise. Behold, ¹⁵
'they say to me, Where is the word of Jehovah? let it
'come now. And, as for me, I have not refused to be a ¹⁶
'shepherd and to follow thee; neither have I desired the
'woful day; thou knowest that what came out of my lips
'was right before thee. Be not a terror to me; thou art ¹⁷
'my refuge in the day of evil. Let them be confounded ¹⁸
'that persecute me, but let not me be confounded; let
'them be dismayed, but let not me be dismayed; bring
'upon them the day of evil, and destroy them with a
'double destruction.'

THUS SAID JEHOVAH to me; Go and stand in the city ¹⁹ gate of the children of the people, by which the kings of Judah come in, and by which they go out, and in all the gates of Jerusalem; and say to them, Hear ye the word of ²⁰ Jehovah, ye kings of Judah, and all Judah, and all the inhabitants of Jerusalem, that enter in by these gates; thus saith Jehovah; Take heed to yourselves, and bear no ²¹ burden on the sabbath day, nor bring it in by the gates of Jerusalem; neither carry forth a burden out of your houses ²² on the sabbath day, neither do ye any work, but keep ye holy the sabbath day, as I commanded your fathers. But ²³ they obeyed not, neither inclined their ear, but made their neck stiff, that they might not hear, nor receive instruction. And it shall come to pass, if ye diligently hearken ²⁴ unto me, Jehovah hath said it, to bring in no burden through the gates of this city on the sabbath day, but keep holy the sabbath day, to do no work therein; then shall ²⁵ there enter into the gates of this city kings and princes sitting upon the throne of David, riding in chariots and on horses, they, and their princes, the men of Judah, and the

inhabitants of Jerusalem; and this city shall remain for
26 ever. And men shall come from the cities of Judah,
and from the places about Jerusalem, and from the land of
Benjamin, and from the Low country, and from the Hill
country, and from the South country, bringing burnt offerings, and sacrifices, and meal offerings, and incense, and
27 bringing thanksgivings, unto the house of Jehovah. But
if ye will not hearken to me to keep holy the sabbath day
and not to bear a burden, even entering in at the gates of
Jerusalem on the sabbath day; then will I kindle a fire in
the gates thereof, and it shall devour the strong towers of
—Jerusalem, and it shall not be quenched.

1   THE WORD WHICH CAME to Jeremiah from Jehovah, say-
2 ing, 'Arise, and go down to the potter's house, and there
3 'I will cause thee to hear my words.' Then I went down
to the potter's house, and, behold, he wrought a work on
4 the wheels. And the vessel that he made was marred in
the hand of the potter, so as to be clay; and he made it
again into another vessel, as it seemed good to the potter
to make it.
5   Then the word of Jehovah came to me, saying, O house
6 of Israel, cannot I do with you as this potter doth? Jehovah hath said it. Behold, as the clay is in the potter's
7 hand, so are ye in my hand, O house of Israel. At whatever instant I shall speak concerning a nation, and concerning a kingdom, to pluck up, and to pull down, and to
8 destroy it; if that nation, against whom I have pronounced,
turn from their evil, I will repent of the evil that I pur-
9 posed to do unto them. And at whatever instant I shall
speak concerning a nation, and concerning a kingdom, to
10 build and to plant it; if it do evil in my sight, that it
obey not my voice, then I will repent of the good, where-
11 with I said I would benefit them. Now therefore go to,
speak to the men of Judah, and to the inhabitants of Jerusalem, saying, Thus saith Jehovah; Behold, I frame
evil against you, and devise a device against you; return
ye now every one from his evil way, and make your ways
and your doings good.
12   Then they said, 'It is in vain; but we walk after our
'own devices, and we do every one after the stubbornness
'of his evil heart.'

Therefore thus saith Jehovah; Ask ye now among the ¹³ Nations, who hath heard such things? The virgin of Israel hath done a very horrible thing. Will the snow of Leba- ¹⁴ non leave the Fortress of the Almighty? or will waters from afar, cold and flowing, be dried up? Because my people hath ¹⁵ forgotten me, they burn incense to Vanities, and these cause them to stumble in their ways, in the ancient paths, to walk in by-paths, in a way not paved; to make their ¹⁶ land desolate, and a perpetual hissing; every one that passeth thereby shall be astonished, and wag his head. I ¹⁷ will scatter them as with an east wind before the enemy; I will shew them my back, and not my face, in the day of their calamity.

Then said they, 'Come, and let us devise devices against ¹⁸ 'Jeremiah; for the law shall not perish from the priest, 'nor counsel from the wise man, nor the word from the 'prophet. Come, and let us smite him on the tongue, 'and let us not give heed to any of his words.'

Do thou give heed to me, O Jehovah, and hearken to ¹⁹ the voice of them that contend with me. Shall evil be ²⁰ repaid for good? For they have digged a pitfall for my soul. Remember that I stood before thee to speak good for them, and to turn away thy wrath from them. Therefore ²¹ deliver thou up their children to the famine, and give them up to the power of the sword; and let their wives be made childless, and be widows; and let their men be slain by pestilence; let their young men be smitten by the sword in battle. Let a cry be heard from their houses, when thou ²² shalt bring a troop suddenly upon them; for they have digged a pitfall to take me, and laid hidden snares for my feet. And, O Jehovah, thou knowest all their counsel ²³ against me to slay me. Forgive not their iniquity, neither blot out their sin from thy sight, but let them be overthrown before thee; deal with them in the time of thine anger.

THUS SAITH JEHOVAH, Go and get a potter's earthen ¹ bottle, and take some of the elders of the people, and of the elders of the priests; and go forth to the Valley of the Son ² of Hinnom, which is by the doorway of the Pottery Gate, and proclaim there the words that I shall tell thee; and ³ say, Hear ye the word of Jehovah, O kings of Judah, and inhabitants of Jerusalem. Thus saith Jehovah of hosts, the

God of Israel; Behold, I will bring evil upon this place,
4 which whosoever heareth, his ears shall tingle. Because they have forsaken me, and have estranged this place, and have burned incense in it to other gods, whom neither they nor their fathers have known, nor the kings of Judah, and
5 have filled this place with the blood of innocents; they have built also the High Places of Baal, to burn their sons with fire for burnt offerings to Baal, which I commanded
6 not, nor spake it, neither came it into my mind. Therefore, behold, the days will come, Jehovah hath said it, that this place shall no more be called Tophet, nor the Valley
7 of the Son of Hinnom, but The valley of slaughter. And I will make void the counsel of Judah and Jerusalem in this place; and I will cause them to fall by the sword before their enemies, and by the hands of them that seek their lives. And their carcases will I give to be food for the fowls of the heavens, and for the beasts of the earth.
8 And I will make this city desolate, and a hissing; every one that passeth thereby shall be astonished and shall hiss
9 because of all the plagues thereof. And I will cause them to eat the flesh of their sons and the flesh of their daughters, and they shall eat every one the flesh of his friend in the siege and the distress, wherewith their enemies, and
10 they that seek their lives, shall distress them. Then shalt thou break the bottle in the sight of the men that go with
11 thee. And thou shalt say to them, Thus saith Jehovah of hosts; Even so will I break this people and this city, as one breaketh a potter's vessel, that cannot be made whole again; and they shall bury them in Tophet, because there
12 is no place to bury. Thus will I do to this place, Jehovah hath said it, and to the inhabitants thereof, and even make
13 this city as Tophet. And the houses of Jerusalem, and the houses of the kings of Judah, shall be defiled as the place of Tophet, even all the houses upon whose roofs they have burned incense unto all the host of the heavens, and have poured out drink offerings to other gods.
14 Then came Jeremiah from Tophet, whither Jehovah had sent him to prophesy. And he stood in the court of Jeho-
15 vah's House; and said to all the people, Thus saith Jehovah of hosts, the God of Israel; Behold, I will bring upon this city and upon all her cities all the evil that I have pronounced against it, because they have hardened their necks, —that they might not hear my words.

Now Pashur the son of Immer the priest, who was also ¹ chief officer in the House of Jehovah, heard that Jeremiah prophesied these things. Then Pashur smote Jeremiah the ² prophet, and put him in the stocks that were in the Upper Gate of Benjamin, which was by the House of Jehovah. And it came to pass on the morrow, that Pashur brought ³ forth Jeremiah out of the stocks. Then said Jeremiah to him, Jehovah hath not called thy name Pashur [or Safety around], but Terror-on-all-sides. For thus saith Jehovah, ⁴ Behold, I will make thee a terror to thyself, and to all thy friends. And they shall fall by the sword of their enemies, and thine eyes shall behold it. And I will give all Judah into the hand of the king of Babylon [Nebuchadnezzar], and he shall carry them captive into Babylon, and shall slay them with the sword. Moreover I will deliver all the ⁵ wealth of this city, and all the fruit of its labours, and all its precious things, and all the treasures of the kings of Judah will I give into the hand of their enemies, who shall plunder them, and take them, and carry them to Babylon. And thou, Pashur, and all that dwell in thy ⁶ house shall go into captivity; and thou shalt come to Babylon, and there thou shalt die, and shalt be buried there, thou, and all thy friends, to whom thou hast prophesied falsely.

O Jehovah, thou didst persuade me, and I was per- ⁷ suaded; thou art stronger than I, and hast prevailed; I am in derision daily, every one mocketh me. For when ⁸ I speak, I cry out, I proclaim violence and plunder; because the word of Jehovah is made a reproach unto me, and a derision daily. And I said, 'I will not make men- ⁹ 'tion of Him, nor speak any more in His name.' But it is in my heart as a burning fire shut up in my bones, and I am weary with forbearing, and I cannot stay.

For I heard the evil report of many, [saying,] 'Terror ¹⁰ 'is on all sides.' 'Tell it, [say they,] and we will tell it.' All my friends who watch by my side, [say,] 'Peradven- 'ture he will be persuaded, and we shall prevail against 'him, and we shall take our revenge on him.' But Jehovah ¹¹ is with me as a terrible warrior; therefore my persecutors shall stumble, and they shall not prevail. They shall be greatly ashamed; for they shall not prosper; their everlasting confusion shall not be forgotten. But, O Jehovah ¹² of hosts, that triest the righteous, and seest the reins and the heart, let me see thy vengeance on them; for unto thee have I opened my cause.

¹³ 'Sing to Jehovah, praise ye Jehovah; for he hath de-'livered the soul of the poor from the hand of evil-doers.'

¹⁴ Cursed be the day wherein I was born; let not the day ¹⁵ wherein my mother bare me be blessed. Cursed be the man who brought tidings to my father, saying, 'A man child ¹⁶ 'is born unto thee;' making him very glad. And let that man be as the cities which Jehovah overthrew, and repented not; and let him hear the cry in the morning, and ¹⁷ the shouting at noontide; because he slew me not from the womb; so that my mother might have been my grave, and ¹⁸ her womb should be always great with me. Wherefore came I forth out of the womb to see labour and sorrow, —that my days should be consumed with shame?

¹ THE WORD WHICH CAME to Jeremiah from Jehovah, when king Zedekiah sent to him Pashur the son of Melchiah, and ² Zephaniah the son of Maaseiah the priest, saying, 'Inquire, 'I pray thee, of Jehovah for us; for Nebuchadrezzar king 'of Babylon maketh war against us; if so be that Jehovah 'will deal with us according to all his wondrous works, ³ 'that he may go up from us.' Then said Jeremiah to them, ⁴ Thus shall ye say to Zedekiah; Thus saith Jehovah the God of Israel; Behold, I will turn back the weapons of war that are in your hands, wherewith ye fight against the king of Babylon, and against the Chaldeans, who besiege you outside the walls, and I will assemble them in the ⁵ midst of this city. And I myself will fight against you with an outstretched hand and with a strong arm, and in ⁶ anger, and in wrath, and in great fury. And I will smite the inhabitants of this city, both man and beast; they shall ⁷ die of a great pestilence. And afterward, Jehovah hath said it, I will give up Zedekiah king of Judah, and his servants, and the people, and such as are left in this city from the pestilence, from the sword, and from the famine, into the hand of Nebuchadrezzar king of Babylon, and into the hand of their enemies, and into the hand of those that seek their life. And he shall smite them with the edge of the sword; he shall not spare them, neither have pity, nor have mercy.

⁸ And to this people thou shalt say, Thus saith Jehovah; Behold, I set before you the way of life, and the way of

death. He that abideth in this city shall die by the sword, ⁹ and by the famine, and by the pestilence; but he that goeth out, and falleth away unto the Chaldeans that besiege you, he shall live, but his life shall be unto him for a prey. For ¹⁰ I have set my face against this city for evil, and not for good, Jehovah hath said it; it shall be given into the hand of the king of Babylon, and he shall burn it with fire.

And touching the house of the king of Judah, hear ye ¹¹ the word of Jehovah; O house of David, thus saith Jeho- ¹² vah; Execute justice in the morning, and deliver him that is plundered out of the hand of the oppressor, lest my wrath go forth like fire, and burn so that none can quench it, because of the evil of your doings.

Behold, I am against thee, O inhabitant of the valley, of ¹³ the rock, and of the table-land, Jehovah hath said it; ye who say, 'Who shall come down against us? or who shall 'enter into our habitations?' But I will punish you ac- ¹⁴ cording to the fruit of your doings, Jehovah hath said it; and I will kindle a fire in the forest, and it shall devour all things round about it.

Thus said Jehovah; Go down to the house of the king ¹ of Judah, and speak there this word, and say, Hear thou ² the word of Jehovah, O king of Judah, that sittest upon the throne of David, thou, and thy servants, and thy people that enter in by these gates. Thus said Jehovah; Execute ³ ye justice and righteousness, and deliver the plundered out of the hand of the oppressor; and do no wrong to the stranger, the fatherless, nor the widow, do no violence, neither shed innocent blood in this place. For if ye do ⁴ indeed according to this word, then shall there enter in by the gates of this House kings sitting upon the throne of David, riding in chariots and on horses, he, and his servants, and his people. But if ye will not hear these words, ⁵ I swear by myself, Jehovah hath said it, that this House shall become a desolation.

For thus said Jehovah concerning the king's house of ⁶ Judah; Thou art Gilead unto me, and the head of Lebanon; yet surely I will make thee a desert, and cities which are not inhabited. And I will consecrate destroyers against ⁷ thee, every one with his weapons; and they shall cut down thy choice cedars, and cast them into the fire. And many ⁸

nations shall pass by this city, and they shall say every man to his neighbour, ' Wherefore hath Jehovah done thus
9 ' unto this great city?' Then they shall answer, 'Because ' they have forsaken the covenant of Jehovah their God, ' and worshipped other gods, and served them.'
10 Weep ye not for the dead [Jehoiakim], neither bemoan him; but weep sore for him that is gone away; for he
11 shall return no more, nor see the land of his birth. For thus said Jehovah touching Shallum [or Jehoahaz] the son of Josiah king of Judah, who reigned instead of Josiah his father, who went forth out of this place; 'He shall
12 'not return thither any more; but he shall die in the ' place whither they have led him captive, and he shall see ' this land no more.'
13 Woe to him that buildeth his house by unrighteousness, and his chambers by injustice; that maketh his neighbour to serve without wages, and payeth him not for his work;
14 that saith, 'I will build me a wide house and airy cham- ' bers,' and that cutteth out for himself windows; and it
15 is panelled with cedar, and painted with vermilion. Shalt thou reign, because thou outrivalest in cedar? Did not thy father eat and drink, and do justice and righteousness?
16 then it was well with him. He judged the cause of the poor and needy; then it was well; was not this to know me?
17 Jehovah hath said it. But thine eyes and thy heart are only upon thine own gain, and upon innocent blood to shed it, and upon oppression, and upon violence, to do it.
18 Therefore thus said Jehovah concerning Jehoiakim the son of Josiah king of Judah; They shall not mourn for him, [saying,] 'Ah my brother!' or, 'Ah sister!' They shall not mourn for him, [saying,] 'Ah lord!' or, 'Ah
19 ' glory!' He shall be buried with the burial of an ass, dragged along and cast forth beyond the gates of Jerusalem.
20 Go up to Lebanon, and cry out; and lift up thy voice in Bashan, and cry out from the Parts Beyond [the Jordan];
21 for all thy lovers are destroyed. I spake unto thee in thy prosperity; but thou saidst, 'I will not hear.' This hath been thy way from thy youth, that thou obeyedst not my
22 voice. Thou shalt feed all thy shepherds on wind, and thy lovers shall go into captivity. Surely then shalt thou
23 be ashamed and confounded for all thy wickedness. O in- habitant of Lebanon, that makest thy nest in the cedars,

how shalt thou be pitied when pangs come upon thee, the pain as of a woman in travail!

As I live, Jehovah hath said it, though Coniah [or Jehoiachin] the son of Jehoiakim king of Judah were the signet-ring upon my right hand, yet would I pluck thee thence; and I will give thee into the hand of them that seek thy life, and into the hand of them whose face thou fearest, even into the hand of Nebuchadrezzar king of Babylon, and into the hand of the Chaldeans. And I will cast thee out, and thy mother that bare thee, into another country, where ye were not born; and there shall ye die. But to the land whither they desire in their soul to return, thither shall they not return. Is this man Coniah a despised broken idol? Is he a vessel wherein men have no pleasure? Wherefore are they cast out, he and his seed, and are cast into a land which they know not?

O earth, earth, earth, hear the word of Jehovah. Thus said Jehovah, Write ye, This man [Zedekiah] shall be childless, as a warrior he shall not prosper in his days; for no man of his seed shall prosper, sitting upon the throne of David, and ruling any more in Judah.

WOE BE TO THE SHEPHERDS that destroy and scatter the sheep of my pasture! Jehovah hath said it. Therefore thus saith Jehovah the God of Israel against the shepherds that feed my people; Ye have scattered my flock, and driven them away, and have not visited them. Behold, I will visit upon you the evil of your doings; Jehovah hath said it. And I will gather up the remnant of my flock out of all countries whither I have driven them, and will bring them again to their folds; and they shall be fruitful and increase. And I will set up shepherds over them which shall feed them; and they shall fear no more, nor be dismayed, neither shall they be lacking; Jehovah hath said it. Behold, the days come, Jehovah hath said it, that I will raise unto David a righteous Branch, and a king shall reign and prosper, and shall execute justice and righteousness in the land. In his days Judah shall be saved, and Israel shall dwell safely. And this is his name whereby he shall be called, Jehovah is our Righteousnes. Therefore, behold, the days come, Jehovah hath said it, when they shall no more say, 'As Jehovah liveth, who brought up

'the children of Israel out of the land of Lower Egypt;'
8 but, 'As Jehovah liveth, who brought up and who led the 'seed of the house of Israel out of the North country, and 'from all countries whither I had driven them;' and they shall dwell in their own land.

9 CONCERNING THE PROPHETS. My heart within me is broken, all my bones shake; I am like a drunken man, and like a man whom wine hath overcome, because of Jeho-
10 vah, and because of the words of his holiness. For the land is full of adulterers; for because of the curse the land mourneth; the pastures of the desert are dried up, and their
11 violence is evil, and their force is not right. Yea, both prophet and priest are profane; yea, in my House have I
12 found their wickedness; Jehovah hath said it. Therefore their way shall be unto them as slippery ways in the dark; they shall be driven on, and fall therein; for I will bring evil upon them, even the year of their visitation; Jehovah
13 hath said it. And I saw folly in the prophets of Samaria; they prophesied by Baal, and caused my people Israel to
14 err. But in the prophets of Jerusalem I have seen a horrible thing; they commit adultery, and walk in lies; they strengthen also the hands of evildoers, so that none doth return from his wickedness; they are all of them unto me
15 as Sodom, and the inhabitants thereof as Gomorrah. Therefore thus saith Jehovah of hosts concerning the prophets; Behold, I will feed them with wormwood, and make them drink the water of hemlock; for from the prophets of Jerusalem is profaneness gone forth into all the land.
16 Thus saith Jehovah of hosts, Hearken not to the words of the prophets that prophesy to you; they lead you astray; they speak a vision of their own heart, and not out of the
17 mouth of Jehovah. They say still to them that despise me, 'Jehovah hath said, Ye shall have peace;' and they say to every one that walketh after the stubbornness of his
18 own heart, 'No evil shall come upon you.' For which of them hath stood in the counsel of Jehovah, and hath perceived and heard his word? Who hath marked his word, and heard it?
19 Behold, the whirlwind of Jehovah, his wrath is gone forth, even a grievous whirlwind; it will fall grievously upon the
20 head of the wicked. The anger of Jehovah will not turn

back, until he have done it, and till he have performed the purposes of his heart ; in the latter days ye shall understand it perfectly. I have not sent the prophets, yet they ²¹ ran ; I have not spoken to them, yet they prophesied. But if they had stood in my counsel, and had caused my ²² people to hear my words, then they would have turned them from their evil way, and from the evil of their doings.

Am I a God when at hand, Jehovah hath said it, and ²³ not a God when afar off? Can any one hide himself in ²⁴ hiding places so that I shall not see him? Jehovah hath said it. Do not I fill the heavens and the earth? Jehovah hath said it.

I have heard what the prophets say, that prophesy lies ²⁵ in my name, saying, 'I have dreamed, I have dreamed.' How long shall this be in the heart of the prophets that ²⁶ prophesy lies? Yea, they are prophets of the deceit of their own heart ; who purpose to cause my people to forget my ²⁷ name by their dreams which they relate every man to his neighbour, as their fathers forgot my name for Baal. The ²⁸ prophet that hath a dream, let him relate the dream ; and he that hath my word, let him speak my word faithfully. What hath the chaff to do with the wheat? Jehovah hath said it. Is not my word like a fire? Jehovah hath said it ; ²⁹ and like a hammer that breaketh the rock in pieces?

Therefore, behold, I am against the prophets, Jehovah ³⁰ hath said it, that steal my words every one from his neighbour. Behold, I am against the prophets, Jehovah hath ³¹ said it, that use their tongues, and utter inspired words. Behold, I am against them that prophesy false dreams, ³² Jehovah hath said it, and do relate them, and cause my people to err by their lies, and by their lightness; yet I sent them not, nor commanded them. Therefore they shall not profit this people at all ; Jehovah hath said it.

And when this people, or the prophet, or a priest, shall ³³ ask thee, saying, 'What is the burden from Jehovah?' thou shalt then tell to them what the burden is, even, 'I 'will forsake you,' is what Jehovah hath said. And as ³⁴ for the prophet, and the priest, and the people, that shall say, 'It is a burden from Jehovah,' I will even punish that man and his house. Thus shall ye say every one to his ³⁵ neighbour, and every one to his brother, 'What hath Je-'hovah answered?' and, 'What hath Jehovah spoken?'

36 And the Burden from Jehovah shall ye mention no more; for every man's word shall be his burden. For ye have perverted the words of the living God, of Jehovah of hosts 37 our God. Thus shalt thou say to the prophet, 'What hath 'Jehovah answered thee?' and, 'What hath Jehovah 38 'spoken?' But since ye say, 'It is a burden from Jeho-'vah;' therefore thus saith Jehovah; Because ye say this word, 'It is a burden from Jehovah,' and I have sent to you, saying, Ye shall not say, 'It is a burden from Jehovah;' 39 therefore, behold, I, even I, will lift you up, and thrust you off, and cast you away, and the city that I gave to you 40 and to your fathers, out of my presence. And I will bring an everlasting reproach upon you, and an everlasting —shame, which shall not be forgotten.

1 JEHOVAH SHEWED ME, and behold, two baskets of figs were set before the Temple of Jehovah, after Nebuchadrezzar king of Babylon had carried away captive Jeconiah [or Jehoiachin] the son of Jehoiakim king of Judah, and the princes of Judah, with the carpenters and smiths, 2 from Jerusalem, and had brought them to Babylon. One basket had very good figs, even like the figs that are first ripe; and the other basket had very bad figs, which could 3 not be eaten, they were so bad. Then said Jehovah to me, 'What seest thou, Jeremiah?' And I said, 'Figs; 'the good figs, very good; and the bad, very bad, that can-'not be eaten, they are so bad.'

4 And the word of Jehovah came to me, saying, thus 5 saith Jehovah, the God of Israel; Like these good figs, so will I acknowledge them of Judah that are carried away captive, whom I have sent out of this place into the land 6 of the Chaldeans, for their good. For I will set mine eyes upon them for good, and I will bring them again to this land; and I will build them up, and not pull them down; 7 and I will plant them, and not pluck them up. And I will give them a heart to know me, that I am Jehovah; and they shall be my people, and I will be their God; for they 8 shall return unto me with their whole heart. And as the bad figs, which cannot be eaten, they are so bad; surely thus saith Jehovah, So will I give up Zedekiah the king of Judah, and his princes, and the residue of Jerusalem, that remain in this land, and them that dwell in the land 9 of Egypt; and I will give them up to be scattered, and to

evil in all the kingdoms of the earth, to be a reproach and a proverb, a taunt and a curse, in all places whither I shall drive them. And I will send on them the sword, the fa- 10 mine, and the pestilence, till they be consumed from off the land that I gave to them and to their fathers. —

(THE WORD THAT CAME TO JEREMIAH concerning all the 1 people of Judah in the fourth year of Jehoiakim the son of Josiah king of Judah [B.C. 607], that was the first year of Nebuchadrezzar king of Babylon; which Jeremiah the 2 prophet spake concerning all the people of Judah, and to all the inhabitants of Jerusalem, saying, From the thir- 3 teenth year of Josiah the son of Amon king of Judah, even until this day, that is the three and twentieth year, the word of Jehovah hath come to me, and I have spoken to you, rising up early and speaking; but ye have not hearkened. And Jehovah hath sent to you all his servants the 4 prophets, rising up early and sending them; but ye have not hearkened, nor inclined your ear to hear. They said, 5 'Turn ye again now every one from his evil way, and from 'the evil of your doings, and dwell in the land that Jeho-'vah hath given to you and to your fathers from everlasting 'to everlasting; and go not after other gods to serve them, 6 'and to worship them, and provoke me not to anger with 'the works of your hands; and I will do you no hurt.' Yet ye have not hearkened unto me, Jehovah hath said it; 7 that ye might provoke me to anger with the works of your hands to your own hurt.

Therefore thus saith Jehovah of hosts: Because ye have 8 not heard my words, behold, I will send and take all the 9 families of the North, Jehovah hath said it, and Nebuchadrezzar the king of Babylon, my servant, and will bring them against this land, and against its inhabitants, and against all these nations round about, and will utterly destroy them, and make them an astonishment, and a hissing, and desolations for ever. Moreover, I will take from 10 them the voice of mirth, and the voice of gladness, the voice of the bridegroom, and the voice of the bride, the sound of the millstones, and the light of the lamp. And 11 this whole land shall be a desolation, and an astonishment; and these nations shall serve the king of Babylon for SEVENTY YEARS.

And it shall come to pass, when seventy years are ac- 12

complished, that I will punish the king of Babylon, and that nation, Jehovah hath said it, for their iniquity, and the land of the Chaldeans, and will make it desolations for
13 ever. And I will bring upon that land all my words which I have pronounced against it, even all that is written in this Book, which Jeremiah hath prophesied against all the
14 Nations. For many nations and great kings shall exact service of them also; and I will recompense them according to their deeds, and according to the work of their own hands.)

15 For thus said Jehovah the God of Israel to me; 'Take this cup of the wine of wrath from my hand, and 'cause all the nations, to whom I send thee, to drink it.
16 'And they shall drink, and be moved, and become mad,
17 'because of the sword that I will send among them.' Then I took the cup from Jehovah's hand, and made all the
18 nations to drink, unto whom Jehovah had sent me; to wit, Jerusalem, and the cities of Judah, and its kings, and its princes, to make them a desolation, an astonish-
19 ment, a hissing, and a curse; as it is this day; Pharaoh king of Egypt, and his servants, and his princes, and all
20 his people; and all the Arabs, and all the kings of the land of Uz, and all the kings of the land of the Philistines, and Askalon, and Gaza, and Ekron, and the remnant of
21 Ashdod, Edom, and Moab, and the Children of Ammon,
22 and all the kings of Tyre, and all the kings of Sidon, and
23 the kings of the Isles which are beyond the sea; Dedan, and Tema, and Buz; and all they that are shorn on the
24 cheek; and all the kings of Arabia; and all the kings of
25 the Arabs that dwell in the desert, and all the kings of the Zimrites, and all the kings of Elam [or Western
26 Persia], and all the kings of the Medes, and all the kings of the North, near and far, one with another, and all the kingdoms of the world, which are upon the face of the earth; and the king of Sheshak [or Babylon] shall drink
27 after them. And thou shalt say to them, Thus saith Jehovah of hosts, the God of Israel; 'Drink ye, and be 'drunken, and vomit, and fall, and rise no more, because
28 'of the sword which I will send among you.' And it shall be, if they refuse to take the cup from thy hand to drink, then shalt thou say to them, Thus saith Jehovah of hosts;

'Ye shall certainly drink. For, lo, I begin to bring evil on ²⁹
'the city which is called by my name; and should ye be
'utterly unpunished? Ye shall not be unpunished; for I
'will call for a sword upon all the inhabitants of the
'earth; Jehovah of hosts hath said it.'

And do thou prophesy against them all these words, and ³⁰
say to them, Jehovah shall roar from on high, and utter
his voice from his holy habitation; he shall mightily roar
against his sheepfold; he shall raise a shout, as of men
marching, against all the inhabitants of the earth. The ³¹
noise shall come even to the ends of the earth; for Jehovah hath a controversy with the nations, he will plead
with all flesh; he will give them that are wicked to the
sword; Jehovah hath said it.

Thus saith Jehovah of hosts, Behold, evil shall go ³²
forth from nation to nation, and a great whirlwind shall
be raised up from the ends of the earth. And the slain ³³
of Jehovah shall be at that day from one end of the earth
even to the other end of the earth; they shall not be
mourned for, neither gathered up, nor buried; they shall
be dung upon the face of the ground.

Howl, ye shepherds, and cry out; and roll yourselves in ³⁴
ashes, ye leaders of the flock; for your days of slaughter
and your dispersions shall be accomplished; and ye shall
fall like a costly vessel. And flight shall be taken away ³⁵
from the shepherds, and escape from the leaders of the
flock. There is a voice of the cry of the shepherds, and a ³⁶
howling of the leaders of the flock, for Jehovah hath spoiled
their pasture. And the peaceable sheepfolds are cut down ³⁷
because of the fierce anger of Jehovah. He hath forsaken ³⁸
his covert, as the lion; for their land is made desolate by
the fierceness of the oppression, and by the fierceness of
his anger.

IN THE BEGINNING OF THE REIGN of Jehoiakim the son ¹
of Josiah king of Judah came this word from Jehovah,
saying, Thus saith Jehovah; Stand in the court of Jeho- ²
vah's House, and speak to all the cities of Judah, which
come to worship in Jehovah's House, all the words that I
command thee to speak to them; diminish not a word.
Perhaps they will hearken, and turn every man from his ³
evil way, that I may repent me of the evil, which I purpose

⁴ to do unto them because of the evil of their doings. And thou shalt say to them, Thus saith Jehovah; 'If ye will 'not hearken to me, to walk in my Law, which I have set ⁵ 'before you, to hearken to the words of my servants the 'prophets, whom I sent to you, both rising up early, and ⁶ 'sending them, (but ye have not hearkened;) then will I 'make this House like Shiloh, and will make this city a 'curse to all the nations of the earth.'

⁷ So the priests and the prophets and all the people heard Jeremiah speaking these words in the House of Jehovah. ⁸ And it came to pass, when Jeremiah had made an end of speaking all that Jehovah had commanded him to speak to all the people, that the priests and the prophets and all ⁹ the people took him, saying, 'Thou shalt surely die. Why 'hast thou prophesied in the name of Jehovah, saying, 'This House shall be like Shiloh, and this city shall be 'desolate without an inhabitant?' And all the people were assembled together against Jeremiah in the House of Jehovah.

¹⁰ When the princes of Judah heard these things, then they came up from the king's house to the House of Jehovah, and sat down in the doorway of the new gate of ¹¹ Jehovah's House. Then spake the priests and the prophets to the princes and to all the people, saying, 'This man 'is worthy to die; for he hath prophesied against this city, ¹² 'as ye have heard with your ears.' Then spake Jeremiah to all the princes and all the people, saying, 'Jehovah sent 'me to prophesy against this House, and against this city, ¹³ 'all the words that ye have heard. Therefore now amend 'your ways and your doings, and obey the voice of Jehovah 'your God; and Jehovah will repent him of the evil that ¹⁴ 'he hath pronounced against you. As for me, behold, I 'I am in your hand. Do with me as is good and right in ¹⁵ 'your eyes. But know ye for certain, that if ye put me to 'death ye will surely bring innocent blood upon yourselves, 'and upon this city, and upon its inhabitants. For of a 'truth Jehovah hath sent me to you to speak all these ¹⁶ 'words in your ears.' Then said the princes and all the people to the priests and to the prophets; 'This man is 'not worthy to die; for he hath spoken to us in the name 'of Jehovah our God.'

¹⁷ Then rose up certain of the elders of the land, and spake

to all the assembly of the people, saying, 'Micaiah [or ¹⁸ 'Micah] the Moresthite prophesied in the days of Hezekiah 'king of Judah, and spake to all the people of Judah, 'saying, *Thus saith Jehovah of hosts; Zion shall be plowed* '*like a field, and Jerusalem shall become heaps of ruins, and* '*the mountain of the House as the High Places* [or altars] *of* '*the forest.* Did Hezekiah king of Judah and all Judah put ¹⁹ 'him at all to death? Did he not fear Jehovah, and be- 'seech the face of Jehovah, and Jehovah repented him of 'the evil which he had pronounced against them? And 'we might procure great evil against our souls.'

And there was also a man that prophesied in the name of ²⁰ Jehovah, Urijah the son of Shemaiah of the city of Jea- rim, who prophesied against this city and against this land according to all the words of Jeremiah. And when Jehoia- ²¹ kim the king, with all his warriors, and all the princes, heard his words, the king sought to put him to death. But when Urijah heard it, he was afraid, and fled, and went into Egypt. And Jehoiakim the king sent men into ²² Egypt, namely, Elnathan the son of Achbor, and certain men with him into Egypt. And they fetched forth Urijah ²³ out of Egypt, and brought him to Jehoiakim the king; who slew him with the sword, and cast his dead body into the graves of the common people. Nevertheless the ²⁴ hand of Ahikam the son of Shaphan was with Jeremiah, that they should not give him into the hand of the people to put him to death.

IN THE BEGINNING OF THE REIGN of Jehoiakim the son ¹ of Josiah king of Judah came this word to Jeremiah from Jehovah, saying, Thus saith Jehovah to me; Make for ² thee bonds and yokes, and put them upon thy neck; and ³ also send them to the king of Edom, and to the king of Moab, and to the king of the Children of Ammon, and to the king of Tyre, and to the king of Sidon, by the hand of the messengers who will come to Jerusalem unto Zedekiah king of Judah; and command them for their masters, ⁴ saying, Thus saith Jehovah of hosts, the God of Israel; Thus shall ye say to your masters; I made the earth, the ⁵ men and the beasts that are upon the face of the ground, by my great power and by my outstretched arm, and I give it to whom it seemeth meet to me. And now have ⁶ I given all these lands into the hand of Nebuchadnezzar the

king of Babylon, my servant; and the wild beasts of the
⁷ field have I given to him also to serve him. (And all nations shall serve him, and his son [Evil-Merodach], and his son's son [Belshazzar], until the very time of his land come; and then many nations and great kings shall exact
⁸ service from him.) And it shall come to pass, that the nation and kingdom which will not serve the same Nebuchadnezzar the king of Babylon, and that will not put their neck under the yoke of the king of Babylon, that nation will I punish with the sword, and with famine, and with pestilence, Jehovah hath said it, until I have con-
⁹ sumed them by his hand. Therefore hearken not ye to your prophets, nor to your diviners, nor to your dreamers, nor to your observers of clouds, nor to your sorcerers, who speak unto you, saying, 'Ye shall not serve the king of
¹⁰ 'Babylon.' For they prophesy falsely unto you, so as to remove you far from your land; and that I should drive
¹¹ you out, and ye should perish. But the nations that bring their neck under the yoke of the king of Babylon, and serve him, those will I let remain still in their own land, Jehovah hath said it; and they shall till it, and dwell therein.
¹² I SPAKE ALSO TO ZEDEKIAH king of Judah according to all these words, saying, Bring your necks under the yoke of the king of Babylon, and serve him and his people,
¹³ and live. Why will ye die, thou and thy people, by the sword, by famine, and by pestilence, as Jehovah hath spoken against the nation that will not serve the king of
¹⁴ Babylon? Therefore hearken not to the words of the prophets that speak to you, saying, 'Ye shall not serve 'the king of Babylon.' For they prophesy falsely to you.
¹⁵ For I did not send them, Jehovah hath said it, yet they prophesy falsely in my name; that I might drive you out, and that ye might perish, ye, and the prophets that prophesy unto you.
¹⁶ Also I spake to the priests and to all this people, saying, Thus saith Jehovah; Hearken not to the words of your prophets that prophesy to you, saying, 'Behold, the vessels 'of the House of Jehovah shall now shortly be brought 'again from Babylon;' for they prophesy falsely unto
¹⁷ you. Hearken not to them; serve the king of Babylon,
¹⁸ and live. Wherefore should this city be laid waste? But if they be prophets, and if the word of Jehovah be with

them, let them now make intercession to Jehovah of hosts, that the vessels which are left in the House of Jehovah, and in the house of the king of Judah, and at Jerusalem, go not to Babylon.

For thus saith Jehovah of hosts concerning the pillars, [19] and concerning the water-cistern, and concerning the basin-stands, and concerning the residue of the vessels that remain in this city, which Nebuchadnezzar king of Babylon [20] took not, when he carried away captive Jeconiah the son of Jehoiakim king of Judah from Jerusalem to Babylon, and all the nobles of Judah and Jerusalem; yea, thus saith [21] Jehovah of hosts, the God of Israel, concerning the vessels that remain in the House of Jehovah, and in the house of the king of Judah and in Jerusalem; they shall be carried [22] to Babylon, and there they shall be until the day that I visit them, Jehovah hath said it; then will I bring them up, and restore them to this place. —

And it came to pass in the same year, in the beginning [1] of the reign of Zedekiah king of Judah, in the fourth year [B.C. 596], and in the fifth month, that Hananiah the son of Azur the prophet, who was of Gibeon, spake to me in the House of Jehovah in the presence of the priests and of all the people, saying, 'Thus speaketh Jehovah of hosts, [2] 'the God of Israel, saying, I have broken the yoke of the 'king of Babylon. Within two years will I bring back [3] 'into this place all the vessels of the House of Jehovah, 'that Nebuchadnezzar king of Babylon took away from 'this place, and carried them to Babylon; and I will bring [4] 'back to this place Jeconiah the son of Jehoiakim king of 'Judah, with all the captives of Judah, that went unto 'Babylon, Jehovah hath said it; for I will break the yoke 'of the king of Babylon.'

Then the prophet Jeremiah said to the prophet Hana- [5] niah in the presence of the priests, and in the presence of all the people that stood in the House of Jehovah, even [6] the prophet Jeremiah, said, 'Amen; may Jehovah do so; 'may Jehovah perform thy words which thou hast pro- 'phesied, to bring back the vessels of the house of Jeho- 'vah, and all that is carried away captive, from Babylon 'into this place. Nevertheless hear thou now this word [7] 'that I speak in thine ears, and in the ears of all the 'people; the prophets that have been before me and before [8]

'thee of old prophesied both against many countries, and
'against great kingdoms, of war, and of evil, and of pesti-
⁹ 'lence. The prophet that prophesieth of peace, when the
'word of the prophet shall come to pass, then shall the
'prophet be known, that Jehovah hath truly sent him.'
¹⁰ Then Hananiah the prophet took the yoke from off the
¹¹ prophet Jeremiah's neck, and brake it. And Hananiah spake
in the presence of all the people, saying, 'Thus saith Jeho-
'vah; Even so will I break the yoke of Nebuchadnezzar
'the king of Babylon from the neck of all nations within
'the space of two years.' And the prophet Jeremiah went
his way.
¹² Then the word of Jehovah came to Jeremiah, after that
Hananiah the prophet had broken the yoke from off the
¹³ neck of the prophet Jeremiah, saying, 'Go and tell Hana-
'niah, saying, Thus saith Jehovah; Thou hast broken the
'yokes of wood; but thou shalt make in place of them
¹⁴ 'yokes of iron. For thus saith Jehovah of hosts, the God
'of Israel; I have put a yoke of iron upon the neck of all
'these nations, that they may serve Nebuchadnezzar king
'of Babylon; and they shall serve him; and I have given
¹⁵ 'to him the wild beasts of the field also.' Moreover the
prophet Jeremiah said to Hananiah the prophet, 'Hear
'now, Hananiah; Jehovah hath not sent thee; but thou
¹⁶ 'makest this people to trust in a falsehood. Therefore thus
'saith Jehovah; Behold, I will cast thee from off the face
'of the earth; this year thou shalt die, because thou hast
¹⁷ 'spoken rebellion against Jehovah.' So Hananiah the
—prophet died the same year in the seventh month.
¹ Now these are the words of THE LETTER that Jeremiah
the prophet sent from Jerusalem to the residue of the elders
who were carried away captives, and to the priests, and
to the prophets, and to all the people whom Nebuchadnezzar had carried away captive from Jerusalem to Baby-
² lon; (after that Jeconiah [or Jehoiachin] the king, and the
queen, and the chamberlains, the princes of Judah and
Jerusalem, and the carpenters, and the smiths, were de-
³ parted from Jerusalem;) by the hand of Elasah the son of
Shaphan, and Gemariah the son of Hilkiah, (whom Zedekiah king of Judah sent unto Babylon to Nebuchadnezzar
king of Babylon,) saying,
⁴ 'Thus saith Jehovah of hosts, the God of Israel, unto

'all that are carried away captives, whom I have caused to
'be carried away from Jerusalem to Babylon; Build ye⁵
'houses, and dwell in them; and plant gardens and eat the
'fruit of them; take ye wives and beget sons and daughters;⁶
'and take wives for your sons, and give your daughters to
'husbands, that they may bear sons and daughters; that
'they may be increased there, and ye be not diminished.
'And seek ye the peace of the city whither I have caused⁷
'you to be carried away captives, and pray unto Jehovah
'for it; for in its peace shall ye have peace. For thus⁸
'saith Jehovah of hosts, the God of Israel; Let not your
'prophets that are in the midst of you, and your diviners,
'deceive you, neither hearken to your dreams which ye
'dream. For they prophesy falsely to you in my name.⁹
'I have not sent them, Jehovah hath said it.

'(For thus saith Jehovah, That after SEVENTY YEARS be ¹⁰
'accomplished at Babylon I will visit you, and perform my
'good word toward you, in causing you to return to this
'place. For I know the thoughts that I think toward you, ¹¹
'Jehovah hath said it, thoughts of peace, and not of evil, to
'give you an hereafter and a hope. Then shall ye call ¹²
'upon me, and ye shall go and pray unto me, and I will
'hearken to you. And ye shall seek me, and find me, ¹³
'when ye shall inquire of me with all your heart. And I ¹⁴
'will be found by you, Jehovah hath said it; and I will
'bring home your captivity, and I will gather you in from
'all the nations, and from all the places whither I have
'driven you, Jehovah hath said it; and I will bring you
'back to the place whence I caused you to be carried away
'captive.)

'Because ye have said, Jehovah hath raised up for us ¹⁵
'prophets in Babylon, therefore thus saith Jehovah con- ¹⁶
'cerning the king that sitteth upon the throne of David,
'and concerning all the people that dwell in this city,
'your brethren that are not gone forth with you into cap-
'tivity; thus saith Jehovah of hosts; Behold, I will send ¹⁷
'upon them the sword, the famine and the pestilence, and
'will make them like vile figs, that cannot be eaten, they
'are so bad. And I will persecute them with the sword, ¹⁸
'with famine, and with pestilence, and will deliver them
'to be scattered into all the kingdoms of the earth, to be
'for a curse, and an astonishment, and a hissing, and a

'reproach, among all the nations whither I have driven
19 'them; because they have not hearkened to my words,
'Jehovah hath said it, when I sent to them my servants
'the prophets, rising up early and sending them; but ye
'would not hear; Jehovah hath said it.
20 'Hear ye therefore the word of Jehovah, all ye of the
'captivity, whom I have sent from Jerusalem to Babylon.
21 'Thus saith Jehovah of hosts, the God of Israel, concern-
'ing Ahab the son of Kolaiah, and concerning Zedekiah
'the son of Maaseiah, who prophesy falsely to you in my
'name; Behold, I will deliver them into the hand of
'Nebuchadrezzar king of Babylon; and he shall slay them
22 'before your eyes; and from them shall be taken up a
'curse by all the captivity of Judah who are in Babylon,
'saying, May Jehovah make thee like Zedekiah, and like
23 'Ahab, whom the king of Babylon roasted in the fire; be-
'cause they have committed villany in Israel, and have
'committed adultery with their neighbours' wives, and
'have spoken words in my name falsely, which I have not
'commanded them; even I know it, and am a witness;
'Jehovah hath said it.'
24 And thou shalt speak to Shemaiah the Nehelamite [or
25 dreamer], saying, Thus speaketh Jehovah of hosts, the God
of Israel, saying, Because thou hast sent letters in thy
name unto all the people that are at Jerusalem, and to
Zephaniah the son of Maaseiah the priest, and to all the
26 priests, saying, 'Jehovah hath made thee to be priest in
'the stead of Jehoiada the priest, that there should be
'officers in the House of Jehovah, over every man that is
'in a frenzy, and maketh himself a prophet, that thou
27 'shouldest put him in the stocks, and in prison. Now
'therefore why hast thou not reproved Jeremiah of Ana-
28 'thoth, who maketh himself a prophet to you? Because
'he sent to us in Babylon, saying, It will be long; build
'ye houses, and dwell in them; and plant gardens, and eat
'the fruit of them.'
29 And Zephaniah the priest read this letter in the ears of
30 Jeremiah the prophet. And the word of Jehovah came
31 to Jeremiah, saying, Send to all them of the captivity,
saying, Thus saith Jehovah concerning Shemaiah the Nehelamite; Because Shemaiah hath prophesied to you, and I
sent him not, and he caused you to trust in a falsehood;

therefore thus saith Jehovah ; Behold, I will punish She- ³² maiah the Nehelamite, and his seed; he shall not have a man to dwell among this people; neither shall he behold the good that I will do for my people, Jehovah hath said it; because he hath spoken rebellion against Jehovah. —

THE WORD THAT CAME TO JEREMIAH from Jehovah, saying, ¹ Thus speaketh Jehovah the God of Israel, saying, Write ² for thyself all the words that I have spoken unto thee in a book. For lo, THE DAYS WILL COME, Jehovah hath said it, ³ that I will bring back the captivity of my people Israel and Judah, saith Jehovah ; and I will cause them to return to the land that I gave to their fathers, and they shall possess it.

And these are the words which Jehovah spake concerning ⁴ Israel and concerning Judah. For thus saith Jehovah ; ⁵ We have heard a voice of trembling, of fear, and not of peace. Ask ye now, and see whether a man doth travail ⁶ with child ? Wherefore do I see every man with his hands on his loins, as a woman in travail, and all faces are turned into paleness ? Alas ! for that will be the great day, so that ⁷ none is like it. It will be even the time of Jacob's trouble ; but he shall be saved out of it. For it shall come to pass ⁸ in that day, Jehovah of hosts hath said it, that I will break his yoke from off thy neck, and I will burst thy bonds asunder, and strangers shall no more exact service of him. But they shall serve Jehovah their God, and a David their ⁹ king, whom I will raise up unto them.

Therefore fear thou not, O my servant Jacob, Jehovah ¹⁰ hath said it ; neither be dismayed, O Israel ; for, lo, I will save thee from afar off ; and thy seed from the land of their captivity ; and Jacob shall return, and shall be at rest ; and he shall be at ease, and none shall make him afraid. For ¹¹ I am with thee, Jehovah hath said it, to save thee. Though I make a full end of all nations whither I have scattered thee, yet will I not make a full end of thee ; I will correct thee, but with judgment, and will not leave thee altogether unpunished.

For thus saith Jehovah, Thy bruise is incurable, and thy ¹² wound is grievous. None pleadeth thy cause, that thou ¹³ mayest be bound up ; thou hast no healing plasters. All ¹⁴ thy lovers have forgotten thee ; they seek thee not ; for I

have wounded thee with the wound of an enemy, with a cruel chastisement, for the greatness of thine iniquity;
15 because thy sins were increased. Why criest thou for thy bruise? Thy sorrow is incurable for the greatness of thine iniquity. Because thy sins were increased, I have done
16 these things unto thee. Therefore all they that devour thee shall be devoured; and all thine oppressors every one of them, shall go into captivity; and they that plunder thee shall be plundered, and all that prey upon thee will
17 I give for a prey. For I will apply a bandage to thee, and I will heal thee of thy wounds, Jehovah hath said it; because they called thee an outcast, [saying,] 'This is Zion 'whom no man seeketh after.'
18 Thus saith Jehovah; Behold, I will bring back the captivity of Jacob's tents, and I will have mercy on his dwelling places; and the city shall be builded up upon her own heap, and the palace shall be inhabited after the manner
19 thereof. And out of them shall proceed thanksgiving and the voice of them that make merry. And I will multiply them, and they shall not be few; I will also glorify them,
20 and they shall not be small. Their children also shall be as aforetime, and their congregation shall be established before
21 me, and I will punish all that oppress them. And their nobles shall be some of themselves, and their governor shall proceed from the midst of them; and I will cause him to draw near, and he shall approach to me. For who is this that pledged his heart to approach to me? Jehovah hath
22 said it. And ye shall be my people, and I will be your God.
23 Behold, the whirlwind of Jehovah; his wrath is gone forth as a cutting whirlwind; it shall rush upon the head
24 of the wicked. The fierce anger of Jehovah shall not return, until he have done it, and until he have performed the purposes of his heart. In the latter days ye shall —understand it.

1 AT THAT TIME, Jehovah hath said it, I will be the God of all the families of Israel, and they shall be my people.
2 Thus saith Jehovah, The people who were left by the sword found grace in the desert, when I went to give rest to Israel.
3 Jehovah appeared from afar unto me, [saying,] Yea, I have loved thee with an everlasting love; therefore I have

prolonged my loving-kindness unto thee. I will yet build 4
thee, and thou shalt be built up, O virgin of Israel; thou
shalt yet be adorned with thy timbrels, and shalt go forth
in the dances of them that make merry. Thou shalt yet 5
plant vineyards upon the mountains of Samaria; the planters
shall plant, and shall enjoy them. For there shall be a day, 6
that the watchmen in the hill country of Ephraim shall
cry, 'Arise ye, and let us go up to Zion unto Jehovah our
'God.'

For thus saith Jehovah; Sing with gladness for Jacob, 7
and shout among the chief of the nations; publish ye,
praise ye, and say, 'O Jehovah, save thy people, the rem-
'nant of Israel.' Behold, I will bring them from the North 8
country, and gather them in from the ends of the earth,
and with them the blind and the lame, the woman with
child and her that travaileth with child together; a great
company shall return thither. They shall come with weep- 9
ing, and with supplications will I lead them. I will cause
them to walk by valleys of waters in a straight path,
wherein they shall not stumble; for I am a father to
Israel, and Ephraim is my firstborn.

Hear the word of Jehovah, O ye nations, and declare it 10
in the isles afar off, and say, 'He that scattered Israel will
'gather him in, and keep him, as a shepherd doth his flock.'
For Jehovah hath redeemed Jacob, and ransomed him 11
from the hand of one stronger than he. Therefore they 12
shall come and sing on the heights of Zion, and shall
stream towards the goodness of Jehovah, for wheat, and
for grape juice, and for oil, and for the young of the flock
and of the herd. And their soul shall be as a watered garden; and they shall not pine away any more at all. Then 13
shall the maiden rejoice in the dance, both young men and
old together; for I will turn their mourning into joy, and
will comfort them, and make them rejoice from their sorrow. And I will water the soul of the priests with fatness, 14
and my people shall be satisfied with my goodness; Jehovah hath said it.

Thus saith Jehovah; A voice was heard in Ramah, la- 15
mentation, and bitter weeping; Rachel weeping for her
children refused to be comforted for her children, because
they were not. Thus saith Jehovah; Refrain thy voice from 16
weeping, and thine eyes from tears; for thy work shall be

rewarded, Jehovah hath said it; and they shall come back
¹⁷ from the land of the enemy. And there is hope for thy
future, Jehovah hath said it, that thy children shall come
back into their own boundary.
¹⁸ I have surely heard Ephraim bemoaning himself, [say-
ing,] 'Thou hast chastised me, and I was chastised, as an
' untrained bullock. Do thou turn me back, and I shall be
¹⁹ ' turned back; for thou art Jehovah my God. Surely after
' that I turned back, I repented; and after that I was in-
' structed, I smote upon my thigh. I was ashamed, yea,
' even confounded, because I did bear the reproach of my
' youth.'
²⁰ Is Ephraim my valued son? is he a beloved child? For
often as I have spoken against him, I will earnestly remember him still; because my bowels were troubled for him, I
will surely have mercy upon him; Jehovah hath said it.
²¹ Set up for thyself waymarks, make for thee high poles;
set thy heart toward the highway, the way which thou
wentest. Return again, O virgin of Israel, return again to
²² these thy cities. How long wilt thou wander about, O thou
backsliding daughter? For Jehovah hath created a new
thing on the earth, A woman shall come round a man.
²³ Thus saith Jehovah of hosts, the God of Israel; They
shall yet use this speech in the land of Judah and in its
cities, when I shall bring home their captivity; ' May Je-
' hovah bless thee, O habitation of justice, and mountain
²⁴ ' of holiness.' And there shall dwell in Judah itself, and
in all its cities together, plowmen, and men that encamp
²⁵ about with flocks. For I have watered the weary soul,
and I have replenished every sorrowful soul.
²⁶ Upon this I awaked, and looked about; and my sleep
had been sweet unto me.

---

²⁷ BEHOLD THE DAYS WILL COME, Jehovah hath said it, that
I will sow the house of Israel and the house of Judah with
²⁸ the seed of man, and with the seed of cattle. And it shall
come to pass, that like as I have watched over them, to
pluck up, and to break down, and to throw down, and to
destroy, and to afflict; so will I watch over them, to build
up, and to plant; Jehovah hath said it.
²⁹ In those days they shall say no more. ' The fathers have
' eaten sour grapes, and the children's teeth are set on

'edge.' But every man shall die for his own iniquity; every son of Adam that eateth the sour grapes, his own teeth shall be set on edge.

Behold, the days will come, Jehovah hath said it, that I will make a new covenant with the house of Israel, and with the house of Judah; not according to the covenant that I made with their fathers in the day that I took them by the hand to bring them out of the land of Lower Egypt; which my covenant they brake, although I was a husband to them; Jehovah hath said it; but this shall be the covenant that I will make with the house of Israel; After those days, Jehovah hath said it, I will put my Law into their inside, and write it on their hearts; and I will be their God, and they shall be my people. And they shall teach no more every man his neighbour, and every man his brother, saying, 'Know Jehovah;' for they shall all know me, from the least of them to the greatest of them; Jehovah hath said it. For I will forgive their iniquity, and I will remember their sin no more.

Thus saith Jehovah, who giveth the sun for a light by day, and the fixed laws of the moon and of the stars for a light by night, who stilleth the sea when its waves roar; Jehovah of hosts is his name; When those fixed laws depart from before me, Jehovah hath said it, then the seed of Israel also shall cease from being a nation before me for ever. Thus saith Jehovah; When the heavens above can be measured, and the foundations of the earth searched out beneath, then I will also cast off all the seed of Israel for all that they have done; Jehovah hath said it.

Behold, the days will come, Jehovah hath said it, that the City shall be built up unto Jehovah from the Tower of Hananeel to the Corner Gate. And the measuring line shall yet go forth over in front of it upon the hill Gareb, and shall encompass about to Goath. And the whole valley of the dead bodies, and of the bone-ashes, and all the fields to the Brook of Kidron, to the corner of the Horse Gate, toward the east, shall be holy unto Jehovah; it shall not be plucked up, nor thrown down any more for ever.

THE WORD THAT CAME TO JEREMIAH from Jehovah in the tenth year of Zedekiah king of Judah [B.C. 590], which was the eighteenth year of Nebuchadrezzar. For at that

time the king of Babylon's army besieged Jerusalem; and Jeremiah the prophet was shut up in the court of the
3 watch-house, which was in the king of Judah's house. For Zedekiah king of Judah had shut him up, saying, 'Wherefore dost thou prophesy, and say, Thus saith Jehovah, 'Behold, I will give this city into the hand of the king of
4 'Babylon, and he shall take it; and Zedekiah king of Judah 'shall not escape out of the hand of the Chaldeans, but 'shall surely be delivered into the hand of the king of 'Babylon, and shall speak with him mouth to mouth, and
5 'his eyes shall behold his eyes; and he shall lead Zedekiah 'to Babylon, and there shall he be until I visit him, Jeho-'vah hath said it. Though ye fight against the Chal-'deans, ye shall not prosper.'
6 And Jeremiah said, The word of Jehovah came to me,
7 saying, 'Behold, Hanameel the son of Shallum thine uncle 'shall come to thee, saying, Buy to thee my field that is 'in Anathoth; for the right of redemption is thine to buy
8 'it.' So Hanameel mine uncle's son came to me in the court of the watch-house, according to the word of Jehovah, and said to me, 'Buy my field, I pray thee, that is 'in Anathoth, which is in the country of Benjamin; for 'the right of inheritance is thine, and the redemption is 'thine; buy it for thyself.' Then I knew that this was
9 the word of Jehovah. And I bought the field from Hanameel mine uncle's son, which was in Anathoth, and I weighed to him the silver, even seven Shekels [half-ounces] and ten
10 pieces of silver. And I wrote it in a deed, and sealed it, and had it witnessed by witnesses, and weighed him the
11 silver in the balances. So I took the writing of the purchase, both that which was sealed according to the law and
12 statutes, and that which was open; and I gave the writing of the purchase to Baruch the son of Neriah, the son of Maaseiah, in the sight of Hanameel mine uncle ['s son], and in the sight of the witnesses that wrote in the deed of the purchase, in the sight of all the Jews that sat in the court
13 of the watch-house. And I charged Baruch in their sight,
14 saying, 'Thus saith Jehovah of hosts, the God of Israel; 'Take these writings, this writing of the purchase, both 'that which is sealed, and this writing which is open; and 'put them in an earthen vessel, so that they may continue
15 'for many days. For thus saith Jehovah of hosts, the

'God of Israel; Houses and fields and vineyards shall be 'again bought in this land.'

Now when I had delivered the writing of the purchase 16 to Baruch the son of Neriah, I prayed to Jehovah, saying, 'Ah Lord Jehovah! behold, thou didst make the heavens 17 'and the earth by thy great power and by thy stretched-'out arm; there is nothing too hard for thee. Thou 18 'shewest loving-kindness to thousands, and repayest the 'iniquity of the fathers into the bosom of their children 'after them; the Great, the Mighty God, Jehovah of hosts, 'is his name, great in counsel, and mighty in doings; for 19 'thine eyes are open on all the ways of the sons of Adam; 'to give to every one according to his ways, and according 'to the fruit of his doings; who didst set signs and wonders 20 'in the land of Lower Egypt, even unto this day, and in 'Israel, and among all men; and hast made to thee a name, 'as at this day; and thou broughtest forth thy people Israel 21 'out of the land of Lower Egypt with signs, and with won-'ders, and with a strong hand, and with a stretched-out 'arm, and with great terror; and hast given them this land, 22 'which thou didst swear to their fathers to give to them, a 'land flowing with milk and honey; and they came in and 23 'possessed it; but they obeyed not thy voice, neither 'walked in thy Law; they have done nothing of all that 'thou commandedst them to do; therefore thou hast called 'down all this evil upon them. Behold the siege-mounds; 24 'they are come unto the city to take it; and the city is 'given into the hand of the Chaldeans, that fight against 'it, because of the sword, and of the famine, and of the 'pestilence. And what thou hast spoken is come to pass; 'and, behold, thou seest it. And thou hast said to me, O 25 'Lord Jehovah, Buy to thee the field for money, and have 'it witnessed by witnesses; and the city is given into the 'hand of the Chaldeans.'

Then came the word of Jehovah to Jeremiah, saying, 26 Behold, I am Jehovah, the God of all flesh; is there any 27 thing too hard for me? Therefore thus saith Jehovah; 28 Behold, I will give this city into the hand of the Chaldeans, and into the hand of Nebuchadrezzar king of Babylon, and he shall take it. And the Chaldeans, that fight against 29 this city, shall come and set this city on fire, and burn it with the houses, on whose roofs they have offered incense '

to Baal, and poured out drink offerings to other gods, so
³⁰ as to provoke me to anger. For the children of Israel and
the children of Judah have done nothing but evil before
mine eyes from their youth; for the children of Israel
have done nothing but provoke me to anger with the
work of their hands; Jehovah hath said it.
³¹ For this city hath been to me as a provocation of mine
anger and of my wrath from the day that they built it even
unto this day; that I should remove it from before my face,
³² because of all the evil of the children of Israel and of the
children of Judah, which they have done to provoke me
to anger, they, their kings, their princes, their priests, and
their prophets, and the men of Judah, and the inhabitants
³³ of Jerusalem. And they have turned to me their back, and
not their face; though I taught them, rising up early and
teaching them, yet they have not hearkened to receive in-
³⁴ struction. But they have set their abominations in the
³⁵ House, which is called by my name, to defile it. And they
have built the High Places of Baal, which are in the Valley
of the Son of Hinnom, to cause their sons and their daughters to pass through [the fire] unto Molech; which I commanded them not, neither came it into my mind, that they
should do this abomination, so as to cause Judah to sin.

---

³⁶ AND NOW THEREFORE THUS SAITH JEHOVAH, the God
of Israel, concerning this city, whereof ye say, It shall be
delivered up into the hand of the king of Babylon by the
³⁷ sword, and by famine, and by pestilence; Behold, I will
gather them out of all countries, whither I have driven
them in mine anger, and in my wrath, and in great fury;
and I will bring them again to this place, and I will cause
³⁸ them to dwell safely. And they shall be my people, and I
³⁹ will be their God. And I will give them one heart, and
one way, that they may fear me for ever, for the good of
⁴⁰ them, and of their children after them. And I will make
an everlasting covenant with them, that I will not turn
away from them, to do them good; and I will put my
fear in their hearts, so that they shall not depart from me.
⁴¹ Yea, I will rejoice over them to do them good, and I will
plant them in this land assuredly with my whole heart
and with my whole soul.
⁴² For thus saith Jehovah; Like as I have brought all this

great evil upon this people, so will I bring upon them all the good that I have promised them. And the fields shall ⁴³ be bought in this land, whereof ye say, 'It is desolate without man or beast; it is given into the hand of the Chaldeans.' Men shall buy fields for money, and shall write ⁴⁴ deeds, and seal them, and have them witnessed by witnesses in the land of Benjamin, and in the places about Jerusalem, and in the cities of Judah, and in the cities of the Hill country, and in the cities of the Low country, and in the cities of the South country; for I will bring home again their captivity; Jehovah hath said it. —

And the word of Jehovah came to Jeremiah the second ¹ time, while he was yet shut up in the court of the watchhouse, saying, Thus saith Jehovah the Maker, Jehovah ² that formed it to establish it; Jehovah is his name; Call ³ to me, and I will answer thee, and I will shew thee great and difficult things, which thou knowest not. For thus ⁴ saith Jehovah the God of Israel, concerning the houses of this city, and concerning the houses of the kings of Judah, which were thrown down by the siege-mounds, and by the sword, when they came to fight against the Chaldeans, and ⁵ to fill them with the dead bodies of men, whom I slew in mine anger and in my wrath, and for all whose wickedness I hid my face from this city; Behold, I will bring on it ⁶ healing and a cure, and I will cure them, and will reveal to them the abundance of peace and truth. And I will ⁷ bring home the captivity of Judah and the captivity of Israel, and will build them up, as at the first. And I will ⁸ cleanse them from all their iniquity, whereby they have sinned against me; and I will pardon all their iniquities, whereby they have sinned, and whereby they have transgressed against me. And it shall be to me a name of joy, ⁹ a praise and an honour before all the nations of the earth, who shall hear of all the good that I do to them; and they shall fear and tremble for all the goodness and for all the prosperity that I bring on it.

Thus saith Jehovah; Again there shall be heard in this ¹⁰ place, which ye say is desolate without man and without beast, even in the cities of Judah, and in the streets of Jerusalem, that are desolate, without man, and without inhabitant, and without beast, the voice of joy, and the ¹¹ voice of gladness, the voice of the bridegroom, and the voice of the bride, the voice of them that shall say, '*Give thanks unto Jehovah of hosts, for Jehovah is good; for his kindness endureth for ever ;*' and of them that shall bring thanksgiving into the House of Jehovah. For I will bring home the captivity of the land, as at the first, saith Jehovah.

12 Thus saith Jehovah of hosts ; Again in this place, which is desolate without man and without beast, and in all its cities, shall be a habitation of shepherds causing their flocks
13 to lie down. In the cities of the Hill country, in the cities of the Low country, and in the cities of the South country, and in the land of Benjamin, and in the places around Jerusalem, and in the cities of Judah, shall the flocks pass again under the hands of him that numbereth them, saith Jehovah.

14 Behold, the days will come, Jehovah hath said it, that I will perform that good thing which I have promised to
15 the house of Israel and to the house of Judah. In those days, and at that time, will I cause a righteous Branch [Zerubbabel] to branch forth unto David ; and he shall
16 execute justice and righteousness in the land. In those days shall Judah be saved, and Jerusalem shall dwell safely ; and this is what she shall be called, 'Jehovah is our
17 'righteousness.' For thus saith Jehovah; David shall never want a man to sit upon the throne of the house of Israel ;
18 neither shall the priests the Levites want a man before me to offer up burnt offerings, and to burn as incense meal offerings, and to make sacrifice continually.

19 And the word of Jehovah came to Jeremiah, saying,
20 Thus saith Jehovah ; When ye can break my covenant of the day, and my covenant of the night, so that there should
21 not be day and night in their season ; then shall also my covenant be broken with David my servant, that he should not have a son to reign upon his throne ; and with the
22 Levites the priests, my ministers. As the host of the heavens cannot be numbered, neither the sand of the sea be measured ; so will I multiply the seed of David my servant, and the Levites that minister to me.

23 Moreover the word of Jehovah came to Jeremiah, saying,
24 Seest thou not what this people have spoken, saying, 'The 'two families which Jehovah had chosen, he hath even cast 'them off'? Thus they have despised my people, that
25 they should be no more a nation before them. Thus saith

Jehovah; If I have not appointed my covenant of day and night, or the fixed laws of heaven and earth; then will I 26 cast away the seed of Jacob, and David my servant, so that I take not any of his seed to be rulers over the seed of Abraham, Isaac, and Jacob; for I will bring home their captivity, and will have mercy on them.

THE WORD WHICH CAME TO JEREMIAH from Jehovah, 1 (when Nebuchadnezzar king of Babylon, and all his army, and all the kingdoms of the land of his hand's dominion, and all the peoples fought against Jerusalem, and against all its cities,) saying, Thus saith Jehovah, the God of Israel; 2 Go and speak to Zedekiah king of Judah, and say to him, Thus saith Jehovah; Behold, I will give this city into the hand of the king of Babylon, and he shall burn it with fire. And thou shalt not escape out of his hand, but shalt surely 3 be taken, and delivered into his hand; and thine eyes shall behold the eyes of the king of Babylon, and his mouth shall speak to thy mouth, and thou shalt go to Babylon. Yet hear thou the word of Jehovah, O Zedekiah king of 4 Judah; Thus saith Jehovah of thee, Thou shalt not die by the sword; thou shalt die in peace; and with the burnings 5 of thy fathers, the former kings which were before thee, so shall they burn [spices] for thee; and they will mourn for thee, [saying,] 'Alas, O lord,' for I have pronounced the word; Jehovah hath said it.

Then Jeremiah the prophet spake all these words to 6 Zedekiah king of Judah in Jerusalem, when the king of 7 Babylon's army fought against Jerusalem, and against all the cities of Judah that were left, against Lachish, and against Azekah; for these fenced cities remained of the cities of Judah.

THE WORD THAT CAME TO JEREMIAH from Jehovah, after 8 that the king Zedekiah had made a covenant with all the people who were at Jerusalem, to proclaim liberty to them; that every man should let his manservant, and every man 9 his handmaid, being a Hebrew man or Hebrew woman, go free; that none should exact service from them, no man from his brother among the Jews. Now when all the princes, 10 and all the people, who had entered into the covenant, heard that every one should let his manservant, and every one his handmaid, go free, that none should exact service

¹¹ of them any more, then they obeyed, and let them go. But afterward they turned, and caused the servants and the handmaids, whom they had let go free, to return, and brought them into subjection for servants and for handmaids.

¹² Therefore the word of Jehovah came to Jeremiah from
¹³ Jehovah, saying, Thus saith Jehovah, the God of Israel; I made a covenant with your fathers in the day that I brought them forth out of the land of Lower Egypt, out of
¹⁴ the house of bondage, saying [Exodus xxi. 2], 'At the 'end of seven years let ye go every man his brother who 'is a Hebrew, who hath been sold to thee; and when he 'hath served thee for six years, thou shalt let him go free 'from thee.' But your fathers hearkened not to me,
¹⁵ neither inclined their ear. And ye were this day turned, and had done right in my sight, in proclaiming liberty every man to his neighbour; and ye had made a covenant
¹⁶ before me in the House which is called by my name. But ye turned again and profaned my name, and caused every man his servant, and every man his handmaid, whom he had set at liberty at their pleasure, to return, and brought them into subjection, to be unto you for servants and for
¹⁷ handmaids. Therefore thus saith Jehovah; Ye have not hearkened unto me, in proclaiming liberty, every one to his brother, and every man to his neighbour. Behold, I proclaim a liberty for you, Jehovah hath said it, to the sword, to the pestilence, and to the famine; and I will make you to be scattered into all the kingdoms of the
¹⁸ earth. And I will give the men that have transgressed my covenant, who have not performed the words of the covenant which they had made before me, when they cut the calf in twain, and passed between its parts [namely],
¹⁹ the princes of Judah, and the princes of Jerusalem, the chamberlains, and the priests, and all the people of the
²⁰ land, who passed between the parts of the calf; I will even give them into the hand of their enemies, and into the hand of them that seek their life. And their dead bodies shall be for food to the fowls of the heavens, and to
²¹ the beasts of the earth. And Zedekiah king of Judah and his princes will I give into the hand of their enemies, and into the hand of them that seek their life, and into the hand of the king of Babylon's army, who are gone up

from you. Behold, I will command, Jehovah hath said it, and will cause them to return to this city; and they shall fight against it, and take it, and burn it with fire. And I will make the cities of Judah a desolation without an inhabitant. ²²

THE WORD WHICH CAME TO JEREMIAH from Jehovah in the days of Jehoiakim the son of Josiah king of Judah, saying, 'Go unto the house of the Rechabites [or chariot- 'drivers], and speak to them, and bring them to the House 'of Jehovah, into one of the chambers, and give them wine 'to drink.' Then I took Jaazaniah the son of Jeremiah, the son of Habaziniah, and his brethren, and all his sons, and the whole house of the Rechabites; and I brought them to the House of Jehovah, into the chamber of Benihannan, the son of Igdaliah, a man of God, which was beside the chamber of the princes, which was above the chamber of Maaseiah the son of Shallum, the keeper of the door. And I set before the sons of the house of the Rechabites pots full of wine, and cups, and I said to them, 'Drink ye the wine.' But they said, 'We will drink no 'wine; for Jonadab the son of Rechab our father com- 'manded us, saying, Ye shall drink no wine, neither ye, 'nor your sons for ever; neither shall ye build a house, 'nor sow seed, nor plant a vineyard, nor have any; but 'all your days ye shall dwell in tents; so that ye may 'live many days on the face of the land where ye sojourn. 'And we have obeyed the voice of Jonadab, the son of 'Rechab [or the chariot-driver], our father in all that he 'hath charged us, to drink no wine all our days, we, our 'wives, our sons, or our daughters; nor to build houses 'for us to dwell in; neither have we vineyard, nor field, 'nor seed. But we dwell in tents, and obey, and do ac- 'cording to all that Jonadab our father commanded us. 'But it came to pass, when Nebuchadrezzar king of Baby- 'lon came up into the land, that we said, Come, and let us 'go to Jerusalem for fear of the army of the Chaldeans, 'and for fear of the army of the Syrians. So we dwell at 'Jerusalem.' 1 2 3 4 5 6 7 8 9 10 11

Then came the word of Jehovah unto Jeremiah, saying, Thus saith Jehovah of hosts, the God of Israel; Go and say to the men of Judah and the inhabitants of Jerusalem, 12 13

Will ye not receive instruction so as to hearken to my
14 words? Jehovah hath said it. The words of Jonadab
the son of Rechab, that he commanded his sons not to
drink wine, are performed; for unto this day they have
drunk none, but have obeyed their father's command. And
I have spoken to you, rising up early and speaking; but ye
15 hearkened not to me. I have also sent to you all my servants
the prophets, rising up early and sending them, saying, 'Re-
' turn ye now every man from his evil way, and amend your
' doings, and go not after other gods to serve them, and ye
' shall dwell in the land which I have given to you and to
' your fathers.' But ye have not inclined your ear, nor
16 hearkened to me. Although the sons of Jonadab the son
of Rechab have performed the command of their father,
which he commanded them, yet this people hath not
17 hearkened to me. Therefore thus saith Jehovah the God
of hosts, the God of Israel; Behold, I will bring upon
Judah and upon all the inhabitants of Jerusalem all the
evil that I have pronounced against them; because I have
spoken to them, but they have not heard, and I have
called to them, but they have not answered.
18 And Jeremiah said to the house of the Rechabites,
' Thus saith Jehovah of hosts, the God of Israel; Because
' ye have obeyed the command of Jonadab your father, and
' ye keep all his commands, and do according to all that
19 ' he commanded you; therefore thus saith Jehovah of
' hosts, the God of Israel; Jonadab the son of Rechab
—' shall not want a man to stand before me for ever.'
1 AND IT CAME TO PASS in the fourth year of Jehoiakim the
son of Josiah king of Judah [B.C. 607], that this word
2 came to Jeremiah from Jehovah, saying, ' Take to thee the
' roll of a book, and write therein all the words that I have
' spoken to thee against Israel, and against Judah, and
' against all the Nations, from the day I spake to thee,
3 ' from the days of Josiah, even unto this day. It may be
' that the house of Judah will hear all the evil which I
' purpose to do to them; so that they may return every
' man from his evil way; that I may forgive their iniquity
4 ' and their sin.' Then Jeremiah called Baruch the son of
Neriah. And Baruch wrote from the mouth of Jeremiah
all the words of Jehovah, which he had spoken to him,
5 upon the roll of a book. And Jeremiah commanded Baruch,

saying, 'I am shut up; I cannot go to the House of Jehovah. Therefore go thou, and read in the roll, which thou hast written from my mouth, the words of Jehovah in the ears of the people in the house of Jehovah on the day of the fast; and also thou shalt read them in the ears of all Judah that come in from their cities. It may be they will lay down their supplication before Jehovah, and will return every one from his evil way; for great is the anger and the wrath that Jehovah hath pronounced against this people.' And Baruch the son of Neriah did according to all that Jeremiah the prophet commanded him, reading in the book the words of Jehovah in the house of Jehovah.

And it came to pass in the fifth year of Jehoiakim the son of Josiah king of Judah [B.C. 606] in the ninth month, that they proclaimed a fast before Jehovah to all the people in Jerusalem, and to all the people that came in from the cities of Judah unto Jerusalem. Then Baruch read in the book the words of Jeremiah in the House of Jehovah, in the chamber of Gemariah the son of Shaphan the scribe, in the Upper Court, at the doorway of the New Gate of the house of Jehovah, in the ears of all the people.

When Michaiah the son of Gemariah, the son of Shaphan, had heard out of the book all the words of Jehovah, then he went down to the king's house, into the scribe's chamber; and, lo, all the princes sat there, even Elishama the scribe, and Delaiah the son of Shemaiah, and Elnathan the son of Achbor, and Gemariah the son of Shaphan, and Zedekiah the son of Hananiah, and all the princes. Then Michaiah declared to them all the words that he had heard, when Baruch read the book in the ears of the people. Therefore all the princes sent Jehudi the son of Nethaniah, the son of Shelemiah, the son of Cushi, to Baruch, saying, 'Take in thy hand the roll wherein thou hast read in the ears of the people, and come.' So Baruch the son of Neriah took the roll in his hand, and came in to them. And they said to him, 'Sit down now, and read it in our ears.' So Baruch read it in their ears. Now it came to pass, when they heard all the words, they looked in fear one to the other, and said to Baruch, 'We will surely tell the king of all these words.' And they asked Baruch, saying, 'Tell us now, How didst thou write all these words at his mouth?' Then Baruch said to them, 'He

'pronounced all these words to me with his mouth, and
19 'I wrote them with ink in the book.' Then said the princes to Baruch, 'Go, hide thyself, thou and Jeremiah; 'and let no man know where ye be.'
20 And they went in to the king into the court, but they laid up the roll in the chamber of Elishama the scribe, and
21 told all the words in the ears of the king. So the king sent Jehudi to fetch the roll; and he took it out of Elishama the scribe's chamber. And Jehudi read it in the ears of the king, and in the ears of all the princes who stood
22 beside the king. Now the king sat in the winter-house in the ninth month; and there was a fire-pot burning before
23 him. And it came to pass, that when Jehudi had read three or four leaves, he cut it with a scribe's knife, and cast it into the fire that was in the fire-pot, until all the
24 roll was consumed in the fire that was in the fire-pot. Yet they were not afraid, nor rent their garments, neither the king, nor any of his servants that heard all these words.
25 Nevertheless Elnathan and Delaiah and Gemariah had made intercession to the king that he would not burn the roll;
26 but he would not hear them. But the king commanded Jerahmeel the king's son, and Seraiah the son of Azriel, and Shelemiah the son of Abdeel, to take Baruch the scribe and Jeremiah the prophet; but Jehovah hid them.
27 THEN THE WORD OF JEHOVAH came to Jeremiah, after that the king had burned the roll and the words which
28 Baruch wrote at the mouth of Jeremiah, saying, 'Take to 'thee again another roll, and write in it all the former 'words that were in the first roll, which Jehoiakim the king
29 'of Judah hath burned. And thou shalt say concerning 'Jehoiakim king of Judah, Thus saith Jehovah; Thou hast 'burned this roll, saying, Why hast thou written therein, 'saying, The king of Babylon shall certainly come and de-
'stroy this land, and shall cause to cease from thence man
30 'and beast? Therefore thus saith Jehovah concerning Je-
'hoiakim king of Judah; He shall have none to sit upon 'the throne of David; and his dead body shall be cast out
31 'to the heat in the day, and to the frost in the night. And 'I will punish him and his seed and his servants for their 'iniquity; and I will bring upon them, and upon the in-
'habitants of Jerusalem, and upon the men of Judah, all 'the evil that I have pronounced against them; but they

'hearkened not.' Then took Jeremiah another roll, and ³² gave it to Baruch the scribe, the son of Neriah; who wrote therein from the mouth of Jeremiah all the words of the book which Jehoiakim king of Judah had burned in the fire. And there were added besides to them many like words. —

AND KING ZEDEKIAH the son of Josiah reigned instead ¹ of Coniah [or Jehoiachin] the son of Jehoiakim, whom Nebuchadrezzar king of Babylon made king in the land of Judah. But neither he, nor his servants, nor the people of ² the land, did hearken to the words of Jehovah, which he spake by the hand of the prophet Jeremiah. And Zede- ³ kiah the king sent Jehucal the son of Shelemiah and Zephaniah the son of Maaseiah the priest to the prophet Jeremiah, saying, 'Pray now to Jehovah our God for us.' Now ⁴ Jeremiah came in and went out among the people; for they had not put him into prison. Then the army of ⁵ Pharaoh [Hophra] was come forth out of Egypt; and when the Chaldeans that besieged Jerusalem heard tidings of them, they departed from Jerusalem.

Then came the word of Jehovah to the prophet Jere- ⁶ miah, saying, 'Thus saith Jehovah, the God of Israel; Thus ⁷ 'shall ye say to the king of Judah, that sent you to me to 'inquire of me; Behold, Pharaoh's army, which is come 'forth to help you, shall return to Egypt, their own land. 'And the Chaldeans shall come again, and fight against ⁸ 'this city, and shall take it, and burn it with fire. Thus ⁹ 'saith Jehovah; Deceive not yourselves, saying, The Chal-'deans will surely depart from us. For they shall not de-'part. For though ye had smitten the whole army of the ¹⁰ 'Chaldeans that fight against you, and there remained but 'wounded men among them, yet would they rise up every 'man in his tent, and burn this city, with fire.'

And it came to pass, that when the army of the Chal- ¹¹ deans was broken up from Jerusalem for fear of Pharaoh's army, then Jeremiah went forth out of Jerusalem to go ¹² into the land of Benjamin, to receive a portion of land there in the midst of the people. And when he was at the ¹³ Gate of Benjamin, a captain of the ward was there, whose name was Irijah, the son of Shelemiah, the son of Hananiah; and he seized Jeremiah the prophet, saying, 'Thou 'revoltest unto the Chaldeans.' Then said Jeremiah, 'It ¹⁴

'is false; I do not revolt to the Chaldeans.' But he hearkened not to him. So Irijah seized on Jeremiah, and
15 brought him to the princes. And the princes were wroth with Jeremiah, and smote him, and put him in a house of fetters in the house of Jonathan the scribe; for they had made that the prison.
16 When Jeremiah was entered into the house with a dungeon-pit, and into the vaults, and Jeremiah had remained
17 there many days; then Zedekiah the king sent, and took him out. And the king asked him secretly in his house, and said, 'Is there any word from Jehovah?' And Jeremiah said, ' There is;' and he said, 'Thou wilt be delivered
18 ' into the hand of the king of Babylon.' Moreover Jeremiah said to king Zedekiah, ' What have I offended against ' thee, or against thy servants, or against this people, that
19 ' ye have put me in prison? Where are now your prophets ' who prophesied to you, saying, The king of Babylon shall
20 ' not come against you, nor against this land? Therefore ' hear now, I pray thee, O my lord the king; let my sup- ' plication, I pray thee, be laid down before thee; and ' cause me not to return to the house of Jonathan the
21 ' scribe, lest I die there.' Then Zedekiah the king commanded that they should commit Jeremiah into the court of the watch-house, and that they should give him daily a circular loaf of bread out of the bakers' street, until all the bread in the city were spent. Thus Jeremiah remained in —the court of the watch-house.
1 Then Shephatiah the son of Mattan, and Gedaliah the son of Pashur, and Jucal the son of Shelemiah, and Pashur the son of Malchiah, heard the words that Jeremiah had
2 spoken to all the people, saying, ' Thus saith Jehovah, He ' that remaineth in this city shall die by the sword, by ' famine, or by pestilence; but he that goeth forth to the ' Chaldeans shall live; for his life shall be for a prey, but
3 ' he shall live. Thus saith Jehovah, This city shall surely ' be given into the hand of the king of Babylon's army,
4 ' which shall take it.' Therefore the princes said to the king, ' We beseech thee, let this man be put to death; ' for thus he weakeneth the hands of the men of war that ' remain in this city, and the hands of all the people, in ' speaking such words unto them. For this man seeketh
5 ' not the welfare of this people, but the hurt.' Then Zede-

kiah the king said, 'Behold, he is in your hand; for the 'king can do nothing against you.' Then took they Jeremiah, and cast him in the pit of Malchiah the king's son, that was in the court of the watch-house; and they let down Jeremiah with cords. And in the pit there was no water, but mire; so Jeremiah sunk into the mire.

Now Ebed-melech the Ethiopian, one of the chamberlains who was in the king's house, heard that they had put Jeremiah into the pit; and the king was sitting at the Gate of Benjamin. And Ebed-melech went forth out of the king's house, and spake to the king, saying, 'My lord 'the king, these men have done evil in all that they have 'done to Jeremiah the prophet, whom they have cast into 'the pit; and he is like to die for hunger in the place 'where he is; for there is no more bread in the city.' Then the king commanded Ebed-melech the Ethiopian, saying, 'Take from hence thirty men with thee, and take 'up Jeremiah the prophet out of the pit, before he die.' So Ebed-melech took the men with him, and went into the house of the king under the treasury, and took thence torn rags and worn-out rags, and let them down by cords into the pit to Jeremiah. And Ebed-melech the Ethiopian said to Jeremiah, 'Put now these torn and worn-out rags 'under thine arm-pits under the cords.' And Jeremiah did so. So they drew up Jeremiah with the cords, and took him up out of the pit. And Jeremiah remained in the court of the watch-house.

Then Zedekiah the king sent, and took Jeremiah the prophet to him into the entrance to [the house of] the chariot-warriors that is in the House of Jehovah; and the king said to Jeremiah, 'I will ask thee a thing; hide 'nothing from me.' Then Jeremiah said to Zedekiah, 'If 'I declare it to thee, wilt thou not surely put me to death? 'And if I give thee counsel, thou wilt not hearken unto 'me.' So Zedekiah the king sware secretly to Jeremiah, saying, 'As Jehovah liveth, that made for us this soul, I 'will not put thee to death, neither will I give thee into 'the hand of these men that seek thy life.' Then said Jeremiah to Zedekiah, 'Thus saith Jehovah, the God of 'hosts, the God of Israel; If thou wilt assuredly go forth 'to the king of Babylon's princes, then thy soul shall live, 'and this city shall not be burned with fire; and thou

18 'shalt live, and thy house. But if thou wilt not go forth to 'the king of Babylon's princes, then shall this city be given 'into the hand of the Chaldeans, and they shall burn it 'with fire, and thou shalt not escape out of their hand.'
19 And Zedekiah the king said to Jeremiah, 'I am afraid of 'the Jews that have revolted to the Chaldeans, lest they 'deliver me up into their hand, and they make sport of
20 'me.' But Jeremiah said, 'They will not deliver thee 'up. Obey, I beseech thee, the voice of Jehovah, which 'I have spoken to thee. So it shall be well unto thee,
21 'and thy soul shall live. But if thou refuse to go forth,
22 'this is the word that Jehovah hath shewed me. And, be-'hold, all the women that are left in the king of Judah's 'house will be brought forth to the king of Babylon's 'princes, and those women will say, Thy friends have 'urged thee on, and have prevailed against thee; thy feet
23 'are sunk in the mire, and they are turned back. So they 'will bring out all thy wives and thy children to the Chal-'deans; and thou wilt not escape out of their hand, but 'wilt be taken by the hand of the king of Babylon; and
24 'this city will be burned with fire.' Then said Zedekiah to Jeremiah, 'Let no man know of these words, and thou
25 'shalt not die. But if the princes hear that I have talked 'with thee, and they come to thee, and say to thee, Declare 'to us now what thou hast said to the king, hide it not 'from us, and we will not put thee to death; also what the
26 'king said to thee; then thou shalt say to them, I laid 'down my supplication before the king, that he would not 'cause me to return to Jonathan's house, to die there.'
27 Then came all the princes to Jeremiah, and asked him. And he told them according to all these words that the king had commanded. So they left off speaking with him; for
28 the matter was not perceived. So Jeremiah abode in the court of the watch-house until the day that Jerusalem was —taken.

1 AND IT CAME TO PASS when Jerusalem was being taken, in the ninth year of Zedekiah king of Judah, in the tenth month, that Nebuchadrezzar king of Babylon and all his
2 army came against Jerusalem, and they besieged it. And in the eleventh year of Zedekiah [B.C. 589], in the fourth month, on the ninth day of the month, the city was broken
3 into. And all the princes of the king of Babylon came in,

and sat in the Middle Gate, even Nergal-sharezer, Samgar-nebo, Sarsechim the chief of the chamberlains, Nergal-sharezer the chief of the Magians, with all the residue of the princes of the king of Babylon.

⁴ And it came to pass, that when Zedekiah the king of Judah saw them, and all the men of war, then they fled, and went forth out of the city by night, by the way of the king's garden, by the gate betwixt the two walls; and he went out by the way of the Barren Valley. ⁵ But the Chaldeans' army pursued after them, and overtook Zedekiah in the barren plains of Jericho. And when they had taken him, they brought him up to Nebuchadnezzar king of Babylon to Riblah in the land of Hamath, where he gave judgment upon him. ⁶ Then the king of Babylon slew the sons of Zedekiah at Riblah before his eyes; also the king of Babylon slew all the nobles of Judah. ⁷ Moreover he put out Zedekiah's eyes, and bound him with copper fetters, to carry him to Babylon.

⁸ And the Chaldeans burned the king's house, and the houses of the people, with fire, and brake down the walls of Jerusalem. ⁹ Then Nebuzar-adan the captain of the guard carried away captive into Babylon the remnant of the people that remained in the city, both those that revolted, that revolted to him, and the rest of the people that remained. ¹⁰ But Nebuzar-adan the captain of the guard left some of the poor of the people, who had nothing, in the land of Judah, and gave them vineyards and plowed lands at the same time.

¹¹ Now Nebuchadrezzar king of Babylon gave charge concerning Jeremiah by the hand of Nebuzar-adan the captain of the guard, saying, ¹² 'Take him, and keep thine eyes on 'him, and do him no harm; but do to him even as he shall 'say to thee.' ¹³ So Nebuzar-adan the captain of the guard sent, and Nebushasban the chief of the chamberlains, and Nergal-sharezer the chief of the Magians, and all the king of Babylon's captains; even they sent, and took Jeremiah ¹⁴ out of the court of the watch-house, and committed him to Gedaliah the son of Ahikam the son of Shaphan, that he should send him home. So he dwelt among the people.

¹⁵ Now the word of Jehovah came to Jeremiah, while he was shut up in the court of the watch-house, saying, ¹⁶ 'Go 'and speak to Ebed-melech the Ethiopian, saying, Thus

'saith Jehovah of hosts, the God of Israel; Behold, I will
'bring my words upon this city for evil, and not for good;
17 'and they shall come to pass before thee in that day. But
'I will save thee in that day, Jehovah hath said it; and
'thou shalt not be given into the hand of the men of whom
18 'thou art afraid. For I will surely deliver thee, and thou
'shalt not fall by the sword, but thy life shall be unto thee
'for a prey; because thóu hast put thy trust in me; Jeho-
—'vah hath said it.'

1 The word that came to Jeremiah from Jehovah, after
that Nebuzar-adan the captain of the guard had let him go
from Ramah, when he had taken him bound in chains
among all that were carried away captive of Jerusalem and
2 Judah, who were carried away captive to Babylon. And
the captain of the guard took Jeremiah, and said to him,
'Jehovah thy God pronounced this evil upon this place.
3 'And Jehovah hath brought it, and hath done according
'as he said; because ye have sinned against Jehovah, and
'have not obeyed his voice, therefore this thing is come
4 'upon you. And now, behold, I loose thee this day from
'the chains which are upon thy hand. If it seem good to
'thee to come with me to Babylon, come; and I will keep
'mine eyes upon thee; but if it seem ill to thee to come
'with me to Babylon, forbear. Behold, all the land is be-
'fore thee; whither it seemeth good and convenient for
5 'thee to go, thither go.' Now while he was not yet gone
back, [he said,] 'Go back also to Gedaliah the son of Ahi-
'kam the son of Shaphan, whom the king of Babylon hath
'made governor over the cities of Judah, and dwell with
'him among the people; or go wheresoever it seemeth con-
'venient to thee to go.' So the captain of the guard gave
6 him victuals and a present, and let him go. Then went
Jeremiah to Gedaliah the son of Ahikam to Mizpah; and
dwelt with him among the people that were left in the land.
7 Now when all the captains of the forces which were in
the fields, even they and their men, heard that the king
of Babylon had made Gedaliah the son of Ahikam governor
in the land, and had committed to him men, and women,
and little children, even of the poor of the land, of them
8 that were not carried away captive to Babylon; then they
came to Gedaliah to Mizpah, even Ishmael the son of Nethaniah, and Johanan and Jonathan the sons of Kareah, and

Seraiah the son of Tanhumeth, and the sons of Ephai the Netophathite, and Jezaniah the son of a Maachathite, they and their men. And Gedaliah the son of Ahikam the son of Shaphan sware to them and to their men, saying, 'Fear not to serve the Chaldeans; dwell in the land, and serve the king of Babylon, and it shall be well with you. As for me, behold, I will dwell at Mizpah, to stand before the Chaldeans, who come unto us; but ye, gather ye wine, and summer fruits, and oil, and put them into your vessels, and dwell in your cities that ye have taken.' Likewise when all the Jews that were in Moab, and among the Children of Ammon, and in Edom, and that were in all the countries, heard that the king of Babylon had left a remnant of Judah, and that he had set over them Gedaliah the son of Ahikam the son of Shaphan; even all the Jews returned out of all places whither they were driven, and came into the land of Judah, unto Gedaliah, at Mizpah, and gathered wine and summer fruits very abundantly. ⁹ ¹⁰ ¹¹ ¹²

Moreover Johanan the son of Kareah, and all the captains of the forces that were in the fields, came to Gedaliah to Mizpah, and said to him, 'Dost thou certainly know that Baalis the king of the Children of Ammon hath sent Ishmael the son of Nethaniah to smite thy life?' But Gedaliah the son of Ahikam believed them not. Then Johanan the son of Kareah spake to Gedaliah in Mizpah secretly, saying, 'Let me go, I pray thee, and I will smite Ishmael the son of Nethaniah, and no man shall know it. Wherefore should he smite thy life, so that all the Jews that are gathered to thee should be scattered, and the remnant in Judah should perish?' But Gedaliah the son of Ahikam said to Johanan the son of Kareah, 'Thou shalt not do this thing; for thou speakest falsely of Ishmael.' ¹³ ¹⁴ ¹⁵ ¹⁶

Now it came to pass in the seventh month, that Ishmael the son of Nethaniah the son of Elishama, of the seed royal, and the princes of the king, even ten men with him, came to Gedaliah the son of Ahikam to Mizpah; and there they did eat bread together in Mizpah. Then arose Ishmael the son of Nethaniah, and the ten men that were with him, and smote Gedaliah the son of Ahikam the son of Shaphan with the sword, and slew him, whom the king of Babylon had made governor over the land. Ishmael also smote all the Jews that were with him, even with Gedaliah, at Miz- ¹ ² ³

pah, and the Chaldeans that were found there, and the
4 men of war. And it came to pass on the second day after
5 he had slain Gedaliah, and no man knew it, that certain men from Shechem, from Shiloh, and from Samaria, even eighty men, having their beards shaven, and their clothes rent, and having cut themselves, came with meal offerings and incense in their hand, to bring them to the House of
6 Jehovah. And Ishmael the son of Nethaniah went forth from Mizpah to meet them, weeping as he went along. And it came to pass, as he met them, he said to them,
7 'Come to Gedaliah the son of Ahikam.' And it was so, when they came into the midst of the city, that Ishmael the son of Nethaniah slew them, and cast them into the
8 midst of the pit, he and the men that were with him. But ten men were found among them that said to Ishmael, 'Slay us not; for we have treasures hidden in the field, of 'wheat, and of barley, and of oil, and of honey.' So he for-
9 bare, and slew them not among their brethren. Now the pit wherein Ishmael had cast all the dead bodies of the men, whom he had slain together with Gedaliah, was that which Asa the king had made for fear of Baasha king of Israel. And Ishmael the son of Nethaniah filled it with them that
10 were slain. Then Ishmael carried away captive all the residue of the people that were in Mizpah, even the king's daughters, and all the people that remained in Mizpah, whom Nebuzar-adan the captain of the guard had committed to Gedaliah the son of Ahikam; and Ishmael the son of Nethaniah carried them away captive, and departed to go over [the Jordan] to the Children of Ammon.
11 But when Johanan the son of Kareah, and all the captains of the forces that were with him, heard of all the evil
12 that Ishmael the son of Nethaniah had done, then they took all the men, and went to fight against Ishmael the son of Nethaniah, and found him by the great waters [or
13 pool] in Gibeon. Now it came to pass, that when all the people that were with Ishmael saw Johanan the son of Kareah, and all the captains of the forces that were with
14 him, then they were glad. So all the people that Ishmael had carried away captive from Mizpah turned about and
15 came back, and went to Johanan the son of Kareah. But Ishmael the son of Nethaniah escaped from Johanan with
16 eight men, and went to the Children of Ammon. Then

Johanan the son of Kareah, and all the captains of the forces that were with him, took all the remnant of the people whom he had brought back from Ishmael the son of Nethaniah, from Mizpah, after that he had smitten Gedaliah the son of Ahikam, even mighty men of war, and the women, and the little children, and the chamberlains, whom he had brought again from Gibeon. And they departed, and ¹⁷ tarried in the halting place of Chimham, which is by Bethlehem, on going to enter into Lower Egypt, because of the ¹⁸ Chaldeans. For they were afraid of them, because Ishmael the son of Nethaniah had smitten Gedaliah the son of Ahikam, whom the king of Babylon made governor in the land.

Then all the captains of the forces, and Johanan the son ¹ of Kareah, and Jezaniah the son of Hoshaiah, and all the people, from the least even unto the greatest, came near; and they said to Jeremiah the prophet, 'Let, we beseech ² 'thee, our supplication be laid down before thee, and pray 'thou for us to Jehovah thy God, on behalf of all this 'remnant; (for we are left but a few out of many, as thine 'eyes do behold us;) that Jehovah thy God may shew ³ 'us the way wherein we should go, and the thing that we 'may do.' Then Jeremiah the prophet said to them, 'I ⁴ 'have heard you. Behold, I will pray to Jehovah your 'God according to your words; and it shall come to pass, 'that whatsoever thing Jehovah shall answer about you, 'I will declare it to you; I will keep nothing back from 'you.' Then they said to Jeremiah, 'May Jehovah be a ⁵ 'true and faithful witness between us, if we do not do even 'according to all things for which Jehovah thy God shall 'send thee to us. Whether it be good, or whether it be ⁶ 'evil, we will obey the voice of Jehovah our God, to whom 'we send thee; so that it may be well with us, when we 'obey the voice of Jehovah our God.'

And it came to pass after ten days, that the word of ⁷ Jehovah came to Jeremiah. Then he called Johanan the ⁸ son of Kareah, and all the captains of the forces who were with him, and all the people from the least even to the greatest, and said to them, 'Thus saith Jehovah, the God of ⁹ 'Israel, to whom ye sent me to lay down your supplication 'before him; If ye will still abide in this land, then will I ¹⁰ 'build you up, and not pull you down, and I will plant you,

'and not pluck you up; for I repent me of the evil that I
11 'have done unto you. Be not afraid of the king of Babylon,
'of whom ye are afraid; be not afraid of him, Jehovah hath
'said it; for I am with you to save you, and to deliver you
12 'from his hand. And I will shew mercies to you, that he
'may have mercy on you, and may cause you to return to
13 'your own land. But if ye say, We will not dwell in this
'land, neither will we obey the voice of Jehovah your God,
14 'saying, No; but we will go into the land of Egypt, where
'we shall see no war, nor hear the sound of the trumpet,
'nor have hunger for bread; and there will we dwell;
15 'even now therefore hear the word of Jehovah, ye remnant
'of Judah; Thus saith Jehovah of hosts, the God of Israel;
'If ye wholly set your faces to enter into Egypt, and go to
16 'sojourn there; then it shall come to pass, that the sword,
'which ye fear, shall overtake you there in the land of
'Egypt, and the famine, whereof ye are afraid, shall follow
17 'close after you there in Egypt; and there ye shall die. So
'shall it be with all the men that set their faces to go into
'Egypt to sojourn there; they shall die by the sword, by
'famine, and by pestilence; and none of them shall remain
18 'or escape from the evil that I will bring upon them. For
'thus saith Jehovah of hosts, the God of Israel; As mine
'anger and my wrath hath been poured forth upon the
'inhabitants of Jerusalem; so shall my wrath be poured
'forth upon you, when ye shall go into Egypt. And ye
'shall be an execration, and an astonishment, and a curse,
'and a reproach; and ye shall see this place no more.
19 'Jehovah hath spoken concerning you, O ye remnant
'of Judah; Go ye not into Egypt; know certainly that I
20 'have protested against you this day. For ye used deceit
'in your hearts, when ye sent me to Jehovah your God,
'saying, Pray for us to Jehovah our God; and according
'to all that Jehovah our God shall say, so declare to us,
21 'and we will do it. And now I have this day declared it
'to you; but ye have not obeyed the voice of Jehovah
'your God, nor anything for which he hath sent me to
22 'you. Now therefore know certainly that ye shall die
'by the sword, by famine, and by pestilence, in the place
—'whither ye desire to go and to sojourn.'
1   And it came to pass, that when Jeremiah had made an
end of speaking to all the people all the words of Jehovah

their God, for which Jehovah their God had sent him to them, even all these words, then spake Azariah the son of ² Hoshaiah, and Johanan the son of Kareah, and all the proud men, saying to Jeremiah, 'Thou speakest falsely. 'Jehovah our God hath not sent thee to say, Go not into 'Egypt to sojourn there. But Baruch the son of Neriah ³ 'setteth thee on against us, to deliver us into the hand of 'the Chaldeans, that they might put us to death, or carry 'us away captives to Babylon.' So Johanan the son of ⁴ Kareah, and all the captains of the forces, and all the people, obeyed not the voice of Jehovah, to dwell in the land of Judah. But Johanan the son of Kareah, and all the ⁵ captains of the forces, took all the remnant of Judah, that were returned from all the nations, whither they had been driven, to sojourn in the land of Judah; even the men, ⁶ and the women, and the little children, and the king's daughters, and every soul that Nebuzar-adan the captain of the guard had left with Gedaliah the son of Ahikam the son of Shaphan, and also Jeremiah the prophet, and Baruch the son of Neriah; and they came into the land of Egypt; ⁷ for they obeyed not the voice of Jehovah. And they came to Tahpanhes.

Then came the word of Jehovah to Jeremiah in Tah- ⁸ panhes, saying, Take great stones in thy hand, and hide ⁹ them in the mortar in the brickwork, which is at the door-way of Pharaoh's house in Tahpanhes, in the sight of the men of Judah; and say to them, Thus saith Jehovah of ¹⁰ hosts, the God of Israel; Behold, I will send and take Nebuchadrezzar the king of Babylon, my servant, and will set his throne upon these stones that I have hidden; and he shall spread his royal canopy over them. And when ¹¹ he cometh, he shall smite the land of Egypt, such as are for death unto death, and such as are for captivity unto captivity, and such as are for the sword unto the sword. And ¹² I will kindle a fire in the houses of the gods of Lower Egypt; and he shall burn them, and carry them away captives. And he shall clothe himself with the land of Egypt, as a shepherd clotheth himself with his garment; and he shall go forth from thence in peace. He shall break also ¹³ the pillars [or obelisks] of Beth-shemesh [or Heliopolis], that is in the land of Lower Egypt; and the houses of the gods of the Egyptians shall he burn with fire. —

1 THE WORD THAT CAME TO JEREMIAH concerning all the Jews that dwell in the land of Lower Egypt, who dwell at Migdol [or Magdolon], and at Tahpanhes, and at Noph [or Memphis], and in the land of Pathros [or Upper Egypt],
2 saying, Thus saith Jehovah of hosts, the God of Israel; Ye have seen all the evil that I have brought upon Jerusalem, and upon all the cities of Judah; and, behold, this day they
3 are a desolation, and no man dwelleth therein, because of their wickedness which they have committed to provoke me to anger, in that they went to burn incense, and to serve other gods, whom they knew not, neither they, nor ye, nor
4 your fathers. Howbeit I sent to you all my servants the prophets, rising up early and sending them, saying, 'Oh, do
5 'not do this abominable thing that I hate.' But they hearkened not, nor inclined their ear to turn from their wicked-
6 ness, so as not to burn incense to other gods. Therefore my wrath and mine anger was poured forth, and was kindled in the cities of Judah and in the streets of Jerusalem; and they are become a waste and a desolation, as at this day.
7 And now thus saith Jehovah, the God of hosts, the God of Israel; Wherefore do ye commit a great evil against your souls, to cut off from you man and woman, babe and suck-
8 ling, out of Judah, so as to leave you none to remain; in that ye provoke me to wrath with the works of your hands, burning incense to other gods in the land of Egypt, whither ye are gone to sojourn, so that ye might cut yourselves off, and so that ye might be a curse and a reproach among all
9 the nations of the earth? Have ye forgotten the wickedness of your fathers, and the wickedness of the kings of Judah, and the wickedness of their wives, and your own wickedness, and the wickedness of your wives, which they have committed in the land of Judah, and in the streets
10 of Jerusalem? They are not humbled even to this day, neither do they fear, nor walk in my Law, nor in my statutes, that I set before you and before your fathers.
11 Therefore thus saith Jehovah of hosts, the God of Israel; Behold, I will set my face against you for evil, and to cut
12 off all Judah. And I will take the remnant of Judah, that have set their faces to go into the land of Egypt to sojourn there, and they shall all be consumed, and fall in the land of Egypt; they shall even be consumed by the sword and by famine. They shall die, from the least even to the

greatest, by the sword and by famine ; and they shall be an execration, and an astonishment, and a curse, and a reproach. For I will punish them that dwell in the land of Egypt, as I have punished Jerusalem, by the sword, by famine, and by pestilence ; and none of the remnant of Judah, who are gone into the land of Egypt to sojourn there, shall escape or remain, so that they should return to the land of Judah, whither they have set their hearts to return to dwell there ; for none shall return but such as shall escape.

Then all the men who knew that their wives had burned incense to other gods, and all the women that stood by, a great assembly, even all the people that dwelt in the land of Lower Egypt, and in Pathros [or Upper Egypt], answered Jeremiah, saying, 'As for the word that thou hast spoken 'to us in the name of Jehovah, we will not hearken to 'thee. But we will certainly do whatsoever word goeth 'forth out of our own mouth, to burn incense to the Queen 'of Heaven, and to pour out drink offerings to her, as we 'have done,we, and our fathers, our kings, and our princes, 'in the cities of Judah, and in the streets of Jerusalem. 'For then had we plenty of bread, and were well, and 'saw no evil. But since we left off burning incense to the 'Queen of Heaven, and pouring out drink offerings to her, 'we have wanted all things, and have been consumed by 'the sword and by famine. And when we burned incense 'to the Queen of Heaven, and poured out drink offerings 'to her, did we make for her cakes to worship her, and 'pour out drink offerings to her, without our husbands ?'

Then Jeremiah said to all the people, about the men, and about the women, and about all the people who had given him that answer, saying, 'The incense that ye burned 'in the cities of Judah, and in the streets of Jerusalem, 'ye, and your fathers, your kings, and your princes, and 'the people of the land, did not Jehovah remember them, 'and came it not into his mind ? So that Jehovah could 'no longer bear, because of the evil of your doings, because 'of the abominations which ye committed ; therefore is your 'land a desolation, and an astonishment, and a curse, 'without an inhabitant, as at this day. Because ye have 'burned incense, and because ye have sinned against Jeho-'vah, and have not obeyed the voice of Jehovah, nor walked 'in his law, nor in his statutes, nor in his testimonies; therefore this evil is happened to you, as at this day.'

24 Moreover Jeremiah said to all the people, and to all the women, 'Hear ye, the word of Jehovah, all Judah that are 25 in the land of Lower Egypt. Thus saith Jehovah of hosts, the God of Israel, saying; Ye and your wives have both spoken with your mouths, and fulfilled with your hand, saying, We will surely perform our vows that we have vowed, to burn incense to the Queen of Heaven, and to pour out drink offerings to her.—Ye will surely accomplish your vows, and surely perform your vows. 26 Therefore hear ye the word of Jehovah, all Judah that dwell in the land of Egypt; Behold, I have sworn by my great name, saith Jehovah, that my name shall no more be named in the mouth of any man of Judah in all the 27 land of Egypt, saying, As the Lord Jehovah liveth. Behold, I will watch over them for evil, and not for good; and all the men of Judah that are in the land of Egypt shall be consumed by the sword and by famine, until 28 there be an end of them. And they that escape the sword shall return out of the land of Egypt into the land of Judah few in number; and all the remnant of Judah, that are gone into the land of Egypt to sojourn there, shall know whose words shall stand, mine, or theirs. 29 'And this shall be a sign to you, Jehovah hath said it, that I will punish you in this place, so that ye may know that my words shall surely stand against you for evil; 30 thus saith Jehovah; Behold, I will give Pharaoh Hophra king of Egypt into the hand of his enemies, and into the hand of them that seek his life; as I gave Zedekiah king of Judah into the hand of Nebuchadrezzar king of Babylon, his enemy, and who sought his life.'

---

1 THE WORD THAT JEREMIAH the prophet spake to Baruch the son of Neriah, when he wrote these words in a book at the mouth of Jeremiah, in the fourth year of Jehoiakim 2 son of Josiah king of Judah [B.C. 607], saying, Thus saith Jehovah, the God of Israel, concerning thee, O Baruch; 3 Thou didst say, 'Woe is me now! for Jehovah addeth grief to my sorrow; I am weary with my sighing, and 4 I find no rest.' Thus shalt thou say to him, Jehovah saith thus; Behold, what I have built up will I break down,

and what I have planted I will pluck up, even this whole land. And seekest thou great things for thyself? Seek them not; for, behold, I will bring evil upon all flesh, Jehovah hath said it; but thy life will I give to thee for a prey in all places whither thou goest.

The word of Jehovah which came to Jeremiah the prophet against the Nations;

AGAINST EGYPT, against the army of Pharaoh Necho king of Egypt, which was by the river Euphrates in Carchemish, whom Nebuchadrezzar king of Babylon smote in the fourth year of Jehoiakim the son of Josiah king of Judah. Set ye in order the buckler and shield, and draw near to battle; harness the horses; and get up, ye horsemen, and stand forth with your helmets; polish the spears, and put on the coats of mail. Wherefore do I see them dismayed and turned away back? and their warriors are beaten down, and are fled apace, and they look not back; for terror is on all sides, Jehovah hath said it. The swift shall not flee away, nor the warrior escape; they shall stumble, and fall toward the north by the banks of the river Euphrates.

Who is this that cometh up as a flood, whose waters are moved as the rivers? Egypt cometh up as a flood, and his waters are moved as the rivers; and he saith, 'I will 'go up, and will cover the land; I will destroy the city 'and its inhabitants.' Come up, ye horses; and rage, ye chariots; and let the warriors come forth; the Ethiopians, and Phut [or the Africans], that handle the shield; and the Lydians [or Egyptian Arabs], that handle and bend the bow. For this is the day of the Lord Jehovah of hosts, a day of vengeance, that he may avenge himself of his adversaries; and the sword shall devour, and it shall be satisfied and shall be soaked with their blood; for the Lord Jehovah of hosts hath a sacrifice in the north country by the river Euphrates.

Go up into Gilead, and take balm, O virgin daughter of Egypt. In vain shalt thou multiply medicines; there shall be no healing plaster for thee. The nations have heard of thy shame, and thy cry hath filled the land; for warrior hath stumbled against warrior, and they are both fallen together.

THE WORD THAT JEHOVAH spake to Jeremiah the prophet, how Nebuchadrezzar king of Babylon should come and smite the land of Egypt.

¹⁴ Declare ye in Egypt, and publish in Migdol [or Magdolon], and publish in Noph [or Memphis], and in Tahpanhes. They said, 'Stand thou fast; and prepare thee, for the ¹⁵ 'sword devoureth round about thee. Why are thy vali- 'ant men swept away?' They stood not, because Jehovah ¹⁶ did drive them away. He made many to stumble, yea, one fell upon another. And they said, 'Arise, and let us 'go again to our own people, and to the land of our ¹⁷ 'birth from the oppressing sword.' They did cry there, 'Pharaoh king of Egypt is but a noise; he hath allowed ¹⁸ 'the appointed time to pass.' As I live, the King hath said it, whose name is Jehovah of hosts, Surely as Tabor is among the mountains, and as Carmel is by the sea, so ¹⁹ surely shall he [Nebuchadnezzar] come. O thou daughter dwelling in Egypt, furnish thyself to go into captivity; for Noph shall be a waste, and burned up without an ²⁰ inhabitant. Egypt is like a very fair heifer, but destruc- ²¹ tion out of the north is coming, is coming. Also her hire- lings [the Greeks] in the midst of her are like stalled bullocks; for they also are turned back, and are fled away together. They did not stand, because the day of their calamity was come upon them, the time of their visitation. ²² Her voice shall go like a serpent; for they [the Babylo- nians] shall march with an army, and shall come against ²³ her with axes, as hewers of wood. They shall cut down her forest, Jehovah hath said it, though it cannot be searched; because they are more than the grasshoppers, ²⁴ and they cannot be counted. The daughter of Egypt shall be confounded; she shall be delivered into the hand of the ²⁵ people of the north. Jehovah of hosts, the God of Israel, saith, Behold, I will punish Amun-Mno [or Thebes], and Pharaoh, and the Egyptians, and their gods, and their ²⁶ kings; even Pharaoh, and them that trust in him. And I will deliver them into the hand of those that seek their lives, and into the hand of Nebuchadrezzar king of Baby- lon, and into the hand of his servants.

But afterward it shall be inhabited, as in the days of ²⁷ old, Jehovah hath said it. And fear not thou, O my ser- vant Jacob, and be not dismayed, O Israel; for, behold, I will save thee from afar off, and thy seed from the land of their captivity; and Jacob shall return, and be in rest, and ²⁸ he shall be at ease, and none shall make him afraid. Fear not thou, O my servant Jacob, Jehovah hath said it, for I am with thee; for I will make a full end of all the nations whither I have driven thee. But I will not make a full end of thee; but with judgment will I correct thee, and I will not leave thee wholly unpunished.

1 The word of Jehovah that came to Jeremiah the prophet AGAINST THE PHILISTINES, before Pharaoh [Necho] smote Gaza.

2 Thus saith Jehovah; Behold, waters rise up out of the North, and they shall be an overflowing flood, and shall overflow the land, and all that is therein; the city, and them that dwell therein. 3 Then the men shall cry, and all the inhabitants of the land shall howl, at the noise of the stamping of the hoofs of his strong horses, at the shaking of his chariots, and at the rumbling of his wheels. The fathers shall not look back to their children for feebleness of hands; 4 because of the day that cometh to destroy all the Philistines, to cut off from Tyre and Sidon every helper that remaineth. For Jehovah will spoil the Philistines, the remnant of the island of Caphtor. 5 Baldness is come upon Gaza; Askalon is cut off with the remnant of their valley.

6 'How long wilt thou be cutting? Alas! O thou sword 'of Jehovah, how long will it be ere thou be quiet? Put 'up thyself into the scabbard; rest, and be still.'

7 How can it be quiet, seeing Jehovah hath given to it a charge against Askalon, and against the sea coast? there hath he appointed it.

1 AGAINST MOAB thus saith Jehovah of hosts, the God of Israel; Woe unto Nebo! for it is destroyed. Kirjathaim is confounded and taken; Misgab is confounded and dismayed. 2 There is no more praise of Moab. In Heshbon they have devised evil against it, [saying,] 'Come, and let 'us cut it off from being a nation.' Also thou shalt be cut down, O Madmenah; the sword shall pursue after thee. 3 There is a voice of crying from Horonaim, spoiling and great destruction. 4 Moab is destroyed; her little ones have caused 5 a cry to be heard. For on the hill-road of Luhith weeping shall go up with weeping; for at the Descent of Horonaim the oppressors have heard a cry of destruction, [saying,] 6 'Flee, save your lives, and be like the heath in the desert.'

7 For because thou hast trusted in thy works and in thy treasures, thou shalt also be seized; and [the god] Chemosh

shall go forth into captivity with his priests and his princes
8 together. And the spoiler shall come upon every city, and
no city shall escape; the valley also shall perish, and the
table-land shall be destroyed, as Jehovah hath spoken.
9 Give wings to Moab, that it may flee and get away; for
its cities shall be desolate, without any to dwell therein.
10 Cursed be he that doeth the work of Jehovah idly, and
cursed be he that keepeth back his sword from blood.
11 Moab hath been at ease from his youth, and he hath
settled [like wine] upon his lees, and hath not been emptied
from vessel to vessel, neither hath he gone into captivity.
Therefore his taste hath remained in him, and his scent is
12 not changed. Therefore, behold, the days will come, Jehovah hath said it, that I will send to him tilters, that shall
tilt him up, and shall empty his vessels, and break their
13 bottles. And Moab shall be ashamed of Chemosh, as the
house of Israel was ashamed of Beth-el their trust.
14 How say ye, 'We are warriors and strong men for the
15 'war?' Moab is spoiled, and her cities with her, and the
chosen of his young men are gone down to the slaughter;
the King, whose name is Jehovah of hosts, hath said it.
16 The calamity of Moab is near to come, and his affliction
17 hasteneth fast. All ye that are about him, bemoan him;
and all ye that know his name; say, 'How is the strong
18 'staff broken, and the beautiful rod!' Thou daughter that
dost inhabit Dibon, come down from thy glory, and sit in
thirst; for the spoiler of Moab is gone up against thee, he
19 will destroy thy strongholds. O inhabitant of Aroer,
stand by the way, and look out; ask him that fleeth, and
her that escapeth; say, 'What is done?'
20 Moab is confounded; for it is broken down. Howl and
21 cry; tell ye it in Arnon, that Moab is spoiled, and judgment is come upon the table-land; upon Holon, and upon
22 Jahazah, and upon Mephaath, and upon Dibon, and upon
23 Nebo, and upon Beth-diblathaim, and upon Kirjathaim,
24 and upon Beth-gamul, and upon Beth-maon, and upon
Kerioth, and upon Bozrah, and upon all the cities of the
25 land of Moab, far or near. The horn of Moab is cut off,
and his arm is broken; Jehovah hath said it.
26 Make ye him drunken; for he magnified himself against
Jehovah. Then Moab shall wallow in his vomit, and he
27 also shall be a derision. For was not Israel a derision unto

thee? Was he found among thieves? For as often as thou spakest of him, thou fleddest away. O ye inhabitants of ²³ Moab, leave the cities, and dwell in Sela [or Petra], and be like the dove that maketh her nest in the parts beyond the mouth of the chasm.

We have heard the pride of Moab, (he is exceeding ²⁹ proud,) his loftiness, and his arrogance, and his pride, and the haughtiness of his heart. I know his wrath, Jehovah ³⁰ hath said it; but it shall not be so; his vain boastings shall not so effect it. Therefore will I howl for Moab, and I will ³¹ cry out for all Moab; there shall be mourning for the men of Kir-haresh. I will weep for thee with the weeping of ³² Jazer; O vine of Sibmah, thy branches are gone over the sea, they reach even to the sea of Jazer. The spoiler is fallen upon thy summer fruits and upon thy vintage. And ³³ joy and gladness are taken away from Carmel, and from the land of Moab; and I have caused wine to fail from the winepresses; none shall tread them with shouting; their shouting shall be no shouting. From the cry of Heshbon even ³⁴ unto Elealeh, even unto Jahaz, they have uttered their voice, from Zoar even unto Horonaim, as a heifer of three years old; for the waters also of Nimrim shall be desolate. Moreover I will cause to cease in Moab, Jehovah hath said ³⁵ it, him that offereth up on the High Places, and him that burneth incense to his gods. Therefore my heart shall ³⁶ sound for Moab like pipes, and my heart shall sound like pipes for the men of Kir-haresh; because the remnant that he hath gotten is perished. For every head shall be ³⁷ bald, and every beard clipped; upon all the hands shall be gashes, and upon the loins sackcloth. There shall be a ³⁸ general mourning upon all the housetops of Moab, and in its broad places; for I have broken Moab like a vessel wherein I have no pleasure; Jehovah hath said it. They ³⁹ shall howl, [saying,] 'How is it broken down! how hath 'Moab turned his back with shame!' So shall Moab be a derision and a dismaying to all them about him.

For thus saith Jehovah; Behold, he [Nebuchadnezzar] ⁴⁰ shall fly as an eagle, and shall spread his wings over Moab. Kerioth is taken, and the strongholds are seized, and the ⁴¹ warrior's hearts in Moab at that day shall be as the heart of a woman in her pangs. And Moab shall be destroyed from ⁴² being a people, because he hath magnified himself against

⁴³ Jehovah. Fear, and the pit, and the snare, shall be upon
⁴⁴ thee, O inhabitant of Moab; Jehovah hath said it. He
that fleeth from the fear shall fall into the pit; and he that
getteth up out of the pit shall be taken in the snare; for
I will bring upon it, even upon Moab, the year of their
⁴⁵ visitation; Jehovah hath said it. Let them that flee
stand under the shadow of Heshbon for want of strength.
For a fire is gone out of Heshbon,
And a flame from the midst of Sihon,
And it shall devour the cheek of Moab,
And the crown of the head of the sons of tumult.
⁴⁶ Alas for thee, O Moab!
The people of [the god] Chemosh is undone.
For thy sons are taken captives,
And thy daughters are in captivity.
⁴⁷ Yet will I bring home again the captivity of Moab in the
latter days; Jehovah hath said it. Thus far is the judg-
—ment of Moab.

¹ AGAINST THE CHILDREN OF AMMON, thus saith Jehovah;
Hath Israel no sons? hath he no heir? Why doth Milcom
[or Molech] inherit Gad, and his people dwell in his cities?
² Therefore, behold, the days come, Jehovah hath said it,
that I will cause an alarm of war to be heard in Rabbah of
the Children of Ammon; and it shall be a desolate heap,
and its suburbs shall be burned with fire. Then shall Israel
dispossess them that dispossessed him, saith Jehovah.
³ Howl, O Heshbon, for Ai is spoiled. Cry, ye daughters
of Rabbah, gird you with sackcloth; mourn, and run to
and fro within the fences; for Milcom shall go into cap-
⁴ tivity, his priests and his princes together. Wherefore
gloriest thou in the valleys, thy flowing valley, O backsliding daughter? that trusted in her treasures, [saying,]
⁵ 'Who shall come unto me?' Behold, I will bring a fear
upon thee, the Lord Jehovah of hosts hath said it, from
all those that are about thee; and ye shall be driven out
every man right forth; and none shall gather up him that
⁶ wandereth. Yet afterwards I will bring home again the
captivity of the Children of Ammon; Jehovah hath said it.
⁷ AGAINST EDOM, thus saith Jehovah of hosts; Is wisdom
no more in Teman? Is counsel perished from the prudent?
⁸ Is their wisdom vanished? Flee ye, turn back, sink down
into your dwellings, O inhabitants of Dedan; for I will

bring the calamity of Esau on him, the time of my visitation on him. If grapegatherers come to thee, will they not ⁹ leave some gleaning grapes? If thieves by night, they will destroy only till they have enough. Although I have made ¹⁰ Esau bare, I have uncovered his hiding places, and he shall not be able to hide himself; his seed is spoiled, and his brethren, and his neighbours; and he is no more. Leave ¹¹ thy fatherless children, I will keep them alive; and let thy widows trust in me.

For thus saith Jehovah; Behold, they who were not con- ¹² demned to drink of the cup have assuredly drunken; and art thou he that shall altogether go unpunished? Thou shalt not go unpunished, but thou shalt surely drink of it. For I have sworn by myself, Jehovah hath said it, that ¹³ Bozrah shall become a desolation, a reproach, a waste, and a curse, and all its cities shall be wastes for ever. I have ¹⁴ heard a rumour from Jehovah, and a messenger is sent to the Nations, [saying,] 'Gather yourselves together, and 'come against her, and rise up for battle.' For, lo, I will ¹⁵ make thee small among the Nations, and despised among men. Thy terribleness hath deceived thee, and the pride ¹⁶ of thy heart, O thou that dwellest in the clefts of Sela [or Petra], that holdest the height of the hill. Though thou shouldest make thy nest as high as the eagle, I will bring thee down from thence; Jehovah hath said it.

Thus Edom shall be a desolation; every one that goeth ¹⁷ by it shall be astonished, and shall hiss at all its calamities. As in the overthrow of Sodom and Gomorrah and their ¹⁸ neighbours, saith Jehovah, no man shall abide there, neither shall a son of Adam sojourn in it. Behold, he ¹⁹ [Nebuchadnezzar] shall come up like a lion from the pride [or headsprings] of the Jordan against the abode of the strong. And I will suddenly make him [Edom] to run away from thence. And who is a chosen man, that I may appoint over her? For who is there like me? And who will meet me in judgment? And who is that shepherd that will stand before me? Therefore hear the counsel of Je- ²⁰ hovah, that he hath taken against Edom; and his purposes, that he hath purposed against the inhabitants of Teman. Surely they will tear them to pieces as little ones of the flock; surely he will make their sheepfolds desolate for them. The earth is moved at the noise of their fall, the ²¹ noise of the cry was heard at the Red sea. Behold, he shall ²²

come up and fly as an eagle, and spread his wings over
Bozrah. And at that day shall the heart of the warriors
of Edom be as the heart of a woman in her pangs.

²³ AGAINST DAMASCUS. Hamath is confounded, and Arpad;
for they have heard evil tidings. They are fainthearted;
²⁴ there is terror on the sea; it cannot be quiet. Damascus
is waxed feeble, she turneth herself to flee, and fear hath
seized on her; anguish and sorrows have taken her, as a
²⁵ woman in travail. 'How is the city of praise not left, the
²⁶ 'city of my joy!' Therefore her young men shall fall in
her broad places, and all the men of war shall be cut off in
²⁷ that day; Jehovah of hosts hath said it. And I will kindle
a fire on the wall of Damascus, and it shall consume the
palace of Ben-hadad.

²⁸ AGAINST KEDAR, and against the kingdoms of Hazor,
which Nebuchadrezzar king of Babylon shall smite, thus
saith Jehovah; Arise ye, go up to Kedar, and spoil the
²⁹ children of the east. Their tents and their flocks shall
they take away; they shall take to themselves their tent-
curtains, and all their vessels, and their camels; and they
shall cry to them, 'Terror is on all sides.'

³⁰ Flee, get you far off, sink down into your dwellings, O
ye inhabitants of Hazor, Jehovah hath said it; for Nebuchadrezzar king of Babylon hath taken counsel against
you, and hath conceived a purpose against you.

³¹ Arise, [O Chaldeans,] get you up to the quiet nation,
that dwelleth as if in safety, Jehovah hath said it, they
³² have neither doors nor cross-bars, they dwell alone. And
their camels shall be a booty, and the multitude of their
cattle a spoil. And I will scatter unto all winds them
that are shorn on the cheek; and I will bring their calamity from all those beyond them; Jehovah hath said it.
³³ And Hazor shall be a dwelling for jackals, a desolation for
ever. There shall no man abide there, nor shall any son
of Adam sojourn in it.

³⁴ The word of Jehovah that came to Jeremiah the prophet
AGAINST ELAM in the beginning of the reign of Zedekiah
³⁵ king of Judah, saying, Thus saith Jehovah of hosts; Behold, I will break the bow of Elam, the chief of their
³⁶ might. And upon Elam will I bring the four winds from
the four quarters of the heavens, and I will scatter them

toward all those winds; and there shall be no nation whither the outcasts of Elam shall not come. For I will ³⁷ cause Elam to be dismayed before their enemies, and before them that seek their life. And I will bring evil upon them, even my fierce anger, Jehovah hath said it; and I will send the sword after them, till I have consumed them. And I will set my throne in Elam, and will destroy from ³⁸ thence the king and the princes; Jehovah hath said it. But ³⁹ it shall come to pass in the latter days, that I will bring home again the captivity of Elam; Jehovah hath said it.—

The word that Jehovah spake AGAINST BABYLON and ¹ against the land of the Chaldeans, by the hand of Jeremiah the prophet. Declare ye among the nations, and publish, ² and lift up a standard; publish, and conceal not. Say, 'Babylon is taken, Bel is confounded. Merodach is broken 'in pieces; her images are confounded, her filthy idols are 'broken in pieces.' For out of the north there is come up ³ a nation [the Medes] against her, who shall make her land desolate; and none shall dwell therein. They have removed, they have departed, both man and beast.

In those days, and in that time, Jehovah hath said it, ⁴ the children of Israel shall come, they and the children of Judah together, going and weeping; they shall go, and seek Jehovah their God. They shall ask the way to ⁵ Zion with their faces thitherward, [saying,] 'Come, and 'let us join ourselves to Jehovah in a perpetual covenant 'that shall not be forgotten.' My people hath been lost ⁶ sheep; their shepherds have caused them to go astray, they have driven them about on the mountains; they have gone from mountain to hill, they have forgotten their resting-place. All that found them have devoured them. And ⁷ their oppressors said, 'We offend not, because they have 'sinned against Jehovah, the habitation of righteousness, 'even Jehovah, the hope of their fathers.'

Remove out of the midst of Babylon, and go forth out ⁸ of the land of the Chaldeans, and be as leader-goats before the flocks. For, lo, I will raise and cause to come up ⁹ against Babylon an assembly of great nations from the north country; and they shall set themselves in array against her; from thence she shall be taken, their arrows shall be as of a skilful warrior. None shall return empty, but Chaldea shall be a spoil; all that spoil her shall be ¹⁰ satisfied; Jehovah hath said it.

11 Because ye were glad, because ye rejoiced, O ye destroyers of my heritage, because ye are grown fat as the
12 heifer at grass, and ye bellow as bulls; your mother shall be sore confounded; she that bare you shall be ashamed. Behold, she shall be the hindermost of nations, a desert, a
13 dry land and a barren plain. Because of the wrath of Jehovah it shall not be inhabited, but it shall be wholly desolate. Every one that goeth by Babylon shall be astonished, and shall hiss at all her calamities.
14 Put yourselves in array against Babylon round about; all ye that bend the bow, shoot at her, spare no arrows;
15 for she hath sinned against Jehovah. Shout ye against her round about; she hath stretched forth her hand; her foundations are fallen, her walls are thrown down; because this is the vengeance of Jehovah. Take ye vengeance upon her;
16 as she hath done, so do ye unto her. Cut off the sower from Babylon, and him that handleth the sickle in the time of harvest. For fear of the oppressing sword they shall turn every one to his own people, and they shall flee every one to his own land.
17 Israel is a sheep driven astray; the lions have driven him away. First the king of Assyria devoured him; and then at last Nebuchadrezzar king of Babylon gnawed his
18 bones. Therefore thus saith Jehovah of hosts, the God of Israel; Behold, I will punish the king of Babylon and his
19 land, as I punished the king of Assyria. And I will bring Israel again to his habitation, and he shall feed on Carmel and Bashan, and his soul shall be satisfied in the hill
20 countries of Ephraim and Gilead. In those days, and in that time, Jehovah hath said it, the iniquity of Israel shall be sought for, and there shall be none; and the sins of Judah, and they shall not be found; for I will pardon them whom I reserve.
21 Go up against the land of Bitterness, even against it, and against the inhabitants of [the land of] Punishment. Waste and utterly destroy the hindermost of them, Jehovah hath said it, and do according to all that I have com-
22 manded thee. A sound of battle is in the land, and of great
23 destruction. How is the hammer of the whole earth cut asunder and broken! How is Babylon become a desolation
24 among the nations! I laid a snare for thee, and thou art taken, O Babylon, and thou wast not aware. Thou art

found, and caught, because thou hast striven against Jehovah. Jehovah hath opened his armoury, and hath brought forth the weapons of his indignation; for this is the work of the Lord Jehovah of hosts in the land of the Chaldeans. Come against her from afar, open her storehouses; cast her up as heaps, and destroy her utterly; let nothing of her be left. Slay all her bullocks; let them go down to the slaughter. Woe unto them! for their day is come, the time of their visitation.

There is the voice of them that flee and escape out of the land of Babylon, declaring in Zion the vengeance of Jehovah our God, the vengeance of his Temple. Shout against Babylon, ye powerful ones; all ye that bend the bow, encamp against it round about; let none thereof escape. Recompense her according to her work; according to all that she hath done, do unto her; for she hath been proud against Jehovah, against the Holy One of Israel. Therefore shall her young men fall in the broad places, and all her men of war shall be cut off in that day; Jehovah hath said it.

Behold, I am against thee, O thou most proud, the Lord Jehovah of hosts hath said it; for thy day is come, the time when I will visit thee. And the most proud shall stumble and fall, and none shall raise him up; and I will kindle a fire in his cities, and it shall devour all round about him.

Thus saith Jehovah of hosts; The children of Israel and the children of Judah were oppressed together; and all that carried them away captive held them fast; they refused to let them go. Their Redeemer is strong; Jehovah of hosts is his name. He will thoroughly plead their cause, so that he may give quiet to the land, and disquiet to the inhabitants of Babylon.

A sword is upon the Chaldeans, Jehovah hath said it, and upon the inhabitants of Babylon, and upon her princes, and upon her wise men. A sword is upon the deceivers; and they shall become foolish; a sword is upon her warriors; and they shall be dismayed. A sword is upon their horses, and upon their chariots, and upon all the mingled people [or Arabs] that are in the midst of her; and they shall become as women. A sword is upon her treasures; and they shall be robbed. A drought is upon her waters; and they shall be dried up; for it is the land of graven images, and

⁳⁹ they boast of their terrifying idols. Therefore the desert-beasts with the howling-beasts shall dwell there, and the ostriches shall dwell therein; and it shall be no more inhabited for ever; neither shall it be dwelt in from genera-
⁴⁰ tion to generation. As God overthrew Sodom and Gomorrah and their neighbours, Jehovah hath said it; so shall no man abide there, neither shall any son of Adam sojourn
⁴¹ therein. Behold, a people shall come from the north, and a great nation [the Medes], and many kings shall be raised
⁴² up from the recesses of the earth. They shall hold the bow and the lance; they are cruel and will not shew mercy; their voice shall roar like the sea, and they shall ride upon horses, every one put in array, like a man for the battle,
⁴³ against thee, O daughter of Babylon. The king of Babylon hath heard the report of them, and his hands waxed feeble; anguish took hold of him, and pangs as of a woman in
⁴⁴ travail. Behold he [Cyrus] shall come up like a lion from the pride [or headsprings] of the Jordan against the abode of the strong. For I will suddenly make them run away from thence. And who is a chosen man, that I may appoint over her? For who is there like me? And who will meet me in judgment? And who is that shepherd that will stand
⁴⁵ before me? Therefore hear ye the counsel of Jehovah, that he hath taken against Babylon; and his purposes, that he hath purposed against the land of the Chaldeans. Surely they shall tear them to pieces as the little ones of the flock; surely he will make their sheepfolds desolate
⁴⁶ for them. At the noise of the taking of Babylon the earth —is moved, and the cry is heard among the nations.

¹ Thus saith Jehovah; Behold, I will raise up against Babylon, and against them that dwell in the midst of them
² that rise up against me, a destroying wind; and I will send to Babylon winnowers that shall winnow her, and shall empty her land; for in the day of trouble they shall be
³ against her round about. Against him that aimeth let the archer aim with his bow, and against him that lifteth himself up in his coat of mail; and spare ye not her young men;
⁴ destroy ye utterly all her host. And the slain shall fall in the land of the Chaldeans, and they that are thrust through
⁵ in her streets. For Israel hath not been forsaken, nor Judah by his God, by Jehovah of hosts; though their land was filled with guilt against the Holy One of Israel.

Flee ye out of the midst of Babylon, and save ye every 6
man his life. Be not cut off in her iniquity ; for this is the
time of Jehovah's vengeance ; he will repay to her a recompence. Babylon hath been a golden cup in the hand of Je- 7
hovah, that made all the earth drunken with her wine.
The nations have drunk ; therefore the nations are mad.
Babylon is suddenly fallen and destroyed. Howl for her ; 8
take balm for her pain, if so be she may be healed.

We would have healed Babylon, but she is not healed. 9
Forsake her, and let us go every one into his own country ;
for her judgment reacheth unto the heavens, and is lifted
up to the skies. Jehovah hath brought forth our righteous- 10
ness. Come, and let us declare in Zion the work of Jehovah our God.

Make bright the arrows ; prepare the shields. Jehovah 11
hath raised up the spirit of the kings of the Medes. For
his purpose is against Babylon, to destroy it ; for this is
the vengeance of Jehovah ; the vengeance of his Temple.
Set up the standard upon the walls of Babylon, make the 12
guard strong, set up the guards, prepare the ambushes ;
for Jehovah hath both devised and hath done what he
spake against the inhabitants of Babylon.

O thou that dwellest upon many waters, abundant in 13
treasures, thine end is come, and the measure of thy covetousness. Jehovah of hosts hath sworn by himself, [saying,] 14
'Surely I will fill thee with men, as with locusts ; and
'they shall utter a shout against thee.'

(He made the earth by his power, he established the 15
world by his wisdom, and stretched out the heavens by his
understanding. When he uttereth his voice, there is a tu- 16
mult of waters in the heavens ; and he causeth the clouds to
ascend from the ends of the earth ; he maketh lightnings for
the rain, and bringeth forth the wind from his treasures.
Every man is brutish without knowledge ; every metal- 17
founder is put to shame by the graven image ; for his molten
image is falsehood, and there is no breath in them. They 18
are vanity, the work of delusions ; in the time of their visitation they shall perish. The Portion of Jacob is not like 19
them. For He is the former of all things ; and [Israel] is
the rod of his inheritance ; Jehovah of hosts is his name.)

Thou art my battle axe, my weapon of war ; for with 20
thee I will break in pieces nations, and with thee will I

²¹ destroy kingdoms; and with thee will I break in pieces the horse and his rider; and with thee will I break in ²² pieces the chariot and its driver; and with thee will I break in pieces man and woman; and with thee will I break in pieces old and young; and with thee will I break in pieces ²³ the young man and the maiden; and with thee will I break in pieces the shepherd and his flock; and with thee will I break in pieces the plowman and his yoke of oxen; and with thee will I break in pieces Pashas [or governors] ²⁴ and rulers. And I will repay to Babylon and to all the inhabitants of Chaldea all their evil that they have done in Zion in your sight; Jehovah hath said it.

²⁵ Behold, I am against thee, O destroying mountain, Jehovah hath said it, that destroyest all the earth. And I will stretch out my hand upon thee, and roll thee down from ²⁶ the rocks, and will make thee a burning mountain. And they shall not take out of thee a stone for a corner, nor a stone for foundations; but thou shalt be desolate for ever; Jehovah hath said it.

²⁷ Set ye up a standard in the land, blow the trumpet among the nations, consecrate the nations against her, call together against her the kingdoms of Ararat, Minni, and Ashkenaz [or Armenia]; appoint a captain against her; cause the ²⁸ horses to come up as the rough locusts. Consecrate against her the nations with the kings of the Medes, his Pashas, ²⁹ and all his rulers, and all the land of his dominion. And the land shall tremble and be in pain; because the purposes of Jehovah shall be performed against Babylon, to make the land of Babylon a desolation without an inha- ³⁰ bitant. The warriors of Babylon have forborne to fight, they remained in their strongholds; their might hath failed; they became as women; her dwelling-places are burned; ³¹ her bars are broken. Runner shall run to meet runner, and messenger to meet messenger, to shew the king of Babylon [Belshazzar] that his city is taken from end to end, and ³² that the fords are seized, and the reed-beds they have burned with fire, and the men of war are affrighted.

³³ For thus saith Jehovah of hosts, the God of Israel; the daughter of Babylon is like a threshing-floor, it is time to trample on her. Yet a little while, and the time of her harvest shall come.

³⁴ 'Nebuchadrezzar the king of Babylon devoured me, he

'crushed me, he made me to be an empty vessel, he 'swallowed me up like a dragon, he filled his belly with 'my delicacies, he cast me out. May my wrongs and my 'flesh be upon Babylon,' saith she that inhabiteth Zion; and 'My blood upon the inhabitants of Chaldea,' saith Jerusalem.

Therefore thus saith Jehovah; Behold, I will plead thy cause, and take vengeance for thee; and I will dry up her sea, and make her springs dry. And Babylon shall become a heap of ruins, a dwelling-place for jackals, an astonishment and a hissing, without an inhabitant. They shall roar together like lions; they shall yell as lions' whelps. In their heat I will prepare their drinking feasts, and I will make them drunken, so that they may rejoice riotously, and sleep a perpetual sleep, and not wake; Jehovah hath said it.

I will bring them down like lambs to the slaughter, like rams with the leader-goats. How is Sheshak [or Babylon] taken! and how is the praise of the whole earth seized! how is Babylon become an astonishment among the nations! The sea is come up upon Babylon; she is covered with the tumult of its waves. Her cities are a desolation, a dry land, and a barren plain, a land wherein no man dwelleth, neither doth any son of Adam pass thereby. And I will punish Bel in Babylon, and I will bring forth out of his mouth what he hath swallowed. And the nations shall not flow together any more unto him; yea, the wall of Babylon shall fall.

My people, go ye out of the midst of her, and save ye every man his life from the fierce anger of Jehovah. And let not your heart faint, nor fear ye for the rumour that shall be heard in the land. And a rumour shall come one year, and after that in another year shall come a rumour, and violence shall be in the land, ruler against ruler. Therefore, behold, the days will come, when I will punish the graven images of Babylon; and her whole land shall be confounded, and all her slain shall fall in the midst of her. Then the heavens and the earth, and all that is therein, shall sing for joy over Babylon; for the spoilers shall come against her from the north; Jehovah hath said it. As Babylon hath caused the slain of Israel to fall, so at Babylon shall fall the slain of all the earth. Ye that have es-

caped the sword, go away, stand not still; remember Jehovah when afar off, and let Jerusalem come into your mind.
⁵¹ 'We are confounded, because we have heard reproach; 'shame hath covered our faces; for strangers are come into 'the sanctuaries of Jehovah's house.'
⁵² Therefore, behold, the days will come, Jehovah hath said it; that I will punish her graven images; and through ⁵³ all her land the wounded shall groan. Though Babylon should mount up to heaven, and though she should fortify the height of her strength, yet from me shall spoilers come on her; Jehovah hath said it.
⁵⁴ The sound of a cry cometh from Babylon, and great de- ⁵⁵ struction from the land of the Chaldeans; because Jehovah hath spoiled Babylon, and destroyed out of her the great sound; when her waves did roar like great waters, the noise ⁵⁶ of their voice was uttered; because the spoiler is come upon her, even upon Babylon, and her warriors are taken, their bows are broken; for Jehovah the God of recompences will ⁵⁷ surely requite. And I will make drunk her princes, and her wise men, her Pashas, and her rulers, and her warriors; and they shall sleep a perpetual sleep, and not wake; the King, whose name is Jehovah of hosts, hath said it.
⁵⁸ Thus saith Jehovah of hosts; The walls of wide Babylon shall be levelled to the ground, and her high gates shall be burned with fire; and the peoples shall labour for nought, and the nations for the sake of the fire, and they shall be weary.
⁵⁹ This is the word which Jeremiah the prophet commanded Seraiah the son of Neriah, the son of Maaseiah, when he went with Zedekiah the king of Judah to Babylon in the fourth year of his reign. And Seraiah was chief chamber- ⁶⁰ lain. So Jeremiah wrote in a book all the evil that should come upon Babylon, even all these words that are written ⁶¹ against Babylon. And Jeremiah said to Seraiah, 'When 'thou comest to Babylon, and shalt see, and shalt read all ⁶² 'these words; then thou shalt say, O Jehovah, thou hast 'spoken against this place, to cut it off, that none shall 'remain in it, neither man nor beast, but that it shall be ⁶³ 'desolate for ever. And it shall be, when thou hast made 'an end of reading this book, that thou shalt bind a stone ⁶⁴ 'to it, and cast it into the midst of the Euphrates. And 'thou shalt say, Thus shall Babylon sink, and shall not rise

'because of the evil that I will bring upon her. And they
'shall be weary.' Thus far are the words of Jeremiah.

ZEDEKIAH was one and twenty years old when he began
to reign, and he reigned eleven years in Jerusalem. And
his mother's name was Hamutal the daughter of Jeremiah
of Libnah. And he did what was evil in the eyes of Jehovah, according to all that Jehoiakim had done. For through
the anger of Jehovah it came to pass in Jerusalem and
Judah, till he had cast them out from his presence, that
Zedekiah rebelled against the king of Babylon.

And it came to pass in the ninth year of his reign, in the
tenth month, on the tenth day of the month, that Nebuchadrezzar king of Babylon came, he and all his army,
against Jerusalem, and encamped against it, and built a
line of forts against it round about. And the city was besieged until the eleventh year of king Zedekiah [B.C. 589].
And in the fourth month, on the ninth day of the month,
the famine prevailed in the city, and there was no bread
for the people of the land. Then the city was broken up,
and all the men of war fled, and went forth out of the city
by night by the way of the gate between the two walls, which
is by the king's garden; (now the Chaldeans were against
the city round about;) and they went by the way of the
Barren Valley. But the army of the Chaldeans pursued
after the king, and overtook Zedekiah in the barren plain
of Jericho; and all his army was scattered from him. Then
they took the king, and brought him up to the king of
Babylon to Riblah in the land of Hamath. And he gave
judgment upon him. And the king of Babylon slew the
sons of Zedekiah before his eyes; he slew also all the
princes of Judah in Riblah. Then he put out the eyes of
Zedekiah; and the king of Babylon bound him in copper
fetters, and carried him to Babylon, and put him in a house
of custody till the day of his death.

Now in the fifth month, on the tenth day of the month,
which was the nineteenth year of Nebuchadrezzar king of
Babylon [B.C. 589], came Nebuzar-adan, captain of the
guard, one who stood in the presence of the king of Babylon, into Jerusalem. And he burned the House of Jehovah,
and the king's house; and all the houses of Jerusalem, and
every great man's house burned he with fire. And all the

army of the Chaldeans, that were with the captain of the guard, brake down all the walls of Jerusalem round about. ¹⁵ Then Nebuzar-adan the captain of the guard carried away captive part of the poor of the people, and the rest of the people that were left in the city, and the deserters that deserted to the king of Babylon, with the rest of the multi- ¹⁶ tude. But Nebuzar-adan the captain of the guard left part of the poor of the land to be vinedressers and husbandmen. ¹⁷ And the pillars of copper that were in the House of Jehovah, and the basin-stands, and the copper water-cistern that was in the House of Jehovah, the Chaldeans brake in pieces, and carried all the copper of them to Babylon. ¹⁸ And the pots, and the shovels, and the snuffers, and the sprinkling buckets, and the [incense] ladles, and all the vessels of copper, wherewith they ministered, took they ¹⁹ away. And of the basins, and the censers, and the sprinkling buckets, and the pots, and the lamp stands, and the [incense] ladles, and the purifying jars; the gold, of those which were of gold, and the silver, of those which were of ²⁰ silver, the captain of the guard took away. Of the two pillars, one water-cistern, and twelve copper bulls that were under the basin-stands, which king Solomon had made for the House of Jehovah, the copper of all these ²¹ vessels was without weight. And of the pillars, the height of one pillar was eighteen cubits; and a line of twelve cubits did encompass it. And its thickness was four fingers; it ²² was hollow. And the capital upon it was of copper; and the height of one capital was five cubits, with trellis-work and pomegranates on the capitals round about, all of copper. The second pillar also and the pomegranates were ²³ like to these. And there were ninety and six pomegranates on a side; and all the pomegranates on the trellis-work were a hundred round about.

²⁴ And the captain of the guard took Seraiah the chief priest, and Zephaniah the second priest, and the three keepers of ²⁵ the door. And out of the city he took a chamberlain, who had the charge of the men of war; and seven men of them that were near the king's person, who were found in the city; and the scribe, the captain of the host, who mustered the people of the land; and sixty men of the people ²⁶ of the land, that were found in the midst of the city. So Nebuzar-adan the captain of the guard took them, and

brought them to the king of Babylon to Riblah. And the 27 king of Babylon smote them, and put them to death at Riblah in the land of Hamath. Thus Judah was carried away captive out of his own land.

THIS IS THE PEOPLE whom Nebuchadrezzar carried away 28 captive; in the seventh year [B.C. 601] three thousand Jews and three and twenty; in the eighteenth year of 29 Nebuchadrezzar [B.C. 590] he carried away captive from Jerusalem eight hundred thirty and two souls; in the three 30 and twentieth year of Nebuchadrezzar [B.C. 585] Nebuzaradan the captain of the guard carried away captive of the Jews seven hundred forty and five souls. All the souls were four thousand and six hundred.

AND IT CAME TO PASS in the seven and thirtieth year of 31 the captivity of Jehoiachin king of Judah, [B.C. 564] in the twelfth month, on the five and twentieth day of the month, that Evil-merodach king of Babylon in the first year of his reign lifted up the head of Jehoiachin king of Judah, and brought him forth out of prison, and spake 32 kindly to him, and set his throne above the throne of the kings that were with him in Babylon, and changed his 33 prison garments. And he did continually eat bread in his presence all the days of his life. And for his diet, there 34 was a continual diet given him from the king of Babylon, every day a portion until the day of his death, all the days of his life.

THE LAMENTATIONS.

LAMENTATION I.

א HOW doth the city sit solitary, that was full of people! 1 she is become as a widow, she that was great among the nations; a princess among the provinces, she is become tributary!

ב She weepeth sore in the night, and her tears are on 2 her cheeks; among all her lovers she hath none to comfort her; all her friends have betrayed her, they are become her enemies.

ג Judah is in captivity through affliction, and through 3 great servitude; she dwelleth among the Nations, she findeth no rest; all her pursuers overtook her between the narrow passes.

ד Zion's paths mourn, because none come to the solemn 4

feasts ; all her gates are desolate, her priests sigh ; her maidens are afflicted, and she is in bitterness.

5 ה Her adversaries are uppermost, her enemies prosper ; for Jehovah afflicteth her for the multitude of her transgressions ; her children are gone into captivity before the enemy.

6 ו And from the daughter of Zion all beauty is departed ; her princes are like harts that find no pasture ; and they are gone without strength before the pursuer.

7 ז Jerusalem in the days of her affliction and of her miseries remembered all her pleasures that she had in the days of old ; when her people fell into the hand of the enemy, and none helped her, the adversaries saw her, they mocked at her calamity.

8 ח Jerusalem hath grievously sinned, therefore she is removed ; all that honoured her despise her, because they have seen her nakedness ; yea, she herself sigheth, and turneth backward.

9 ט Her filthiness is in her skirts, she bore not in mind her future ; therefore she came down wonderfully ; she had no comforter. O Jĕhovah, behold my affliction ; for the enemy hath magnified himself.

10 י The adversary hath spread out his hand upon all her pleasant things ; for she hath seen the Nations enter into her Sanctuary, of whom thou didst command that they should not enter thine assembly.

11 כ All her people sigh, they seek bread ; they have given their pleasant things for food to restore life ; see, O Jehovah, and consider, for I am become vile.

12 ל Is it nothing to you, all ye that pass by the way ? Behold, and see if there be any sorrow like my sorrow, which is brought upon me ; wherewith Jehovah hath afflicted me in the day of his fierce anger.

13 מ From above hath he sent fire into my bones, and it seizeth them ; he hath spread a net for my feet, he hath turned me back ; he hath made me desolate and faint all the day.

14 נ The yoke of my transgressions is fastened by his hand ; they are twisted together, they are come upon my neck ; he hath made my strength to fall ; the Lord hath delivered me into their hands, I cannot rise up.

15 ס The Lord hath made light of all my mighty men in

the midst of me; he hath called an assembly against me to crush my young men; the Lord hath trodden the virgin, the daughter of Judah, as a winepress.

ע 16 For these things I weep with mine eye; mine eye runneth down with water, because the comforter that should restore my life is far from me; my children are desolate, because the enemy prevailed.

פ 17 Zion spreadeth forth her hands, there is none to comfort her; Jehovah hath given charge concerning Jacob that his adversaries be round about him; Jerusalem is an impurity among them.

צ 18 Jehovah is righteous; for I resisted his command; hear, I pray you, all ye peoples, and behold my sorrow; my maidens and my young men are gone into captivity.

ק 19 I called for my lovers [the Egyptians], but they deceived me; my priests and mine elders breathed their last in the city, while they were seeking their food to support their lives.

ר 20 See, O Jehovah, for I am in distress, my bowels are troubled, my heart is turned within me, for I have grievously rebelled; abroad the sword bereaveth, at home there is as death.

ש 21 They have heard that I sigh, there is none to comfort me; all mine enemies heard of my trouble, they rejoiced that thou didst it; O bring the day that thou hast proclaimed, that they may be like me.

ת 22 Let all their wickedness come before thee; and do unto them, as thou hast done to me for all my transgressions; for my sighs are many, and my heart is faint.—

II.

א 1 How hath the Lord cast a cloud over the daughter of Zion in his anger. He hath thrown down from heaven to the earth the beauty of Israel, and remembered not his footstool in the day of his anger!

ב 2 The Lord hath swallowed up without pity all the habitations of Jacob; he hath thrown down in his wrath the strongholds of the daughter of Judah; he hath brought to the ground, he hath polluted the kingdom and its princes.

ג 3 He hath cut off in his fierce anger all the horn of Israel; he hath drawn back his right hand from before the enemy; and he burned up Jacob like a flaming fire, which devoureth around.

4 ד   He bent his bow like an enemy; he placed his right hand as an adversary, and slew all that were pleasant to the eye; in the tent of the daughter of Zion, he poured out his wrath like fire.

5 ה   The Lord was as an enemy; he hath swallowed up Israel; he hath swallowed up all her palaces, he hath destroyed its strongholds, and hath increased in the daughter of Judah mourning and sighing.

6 ו   And he hath broken down its hedge, as of a garden; he hath destroyed its Place of meeting [or Temple]; Jehovah hath caused the solemn assemblies and sabbaths to be forgotten in Zion, and hath despised in the indignation of his anger the king and the priest.

7 ז   The Lord hath cast off his Altar, he abhorreth his Sanctuary; he hath given up into the hand of the enemy the walls of her palaces; they have made a noise in the House of Jehovah, as in the day of a solemn feast.

8 ח   Jehovah purposed to destroy the wall of the daughter of Zion; he stretched out a line, he withdrew not his hand from destroying; therefore he made the rampart and the wall to lament; they languish together.

9 ט   Her gates are sunk into the ground; he hath destroyed and broken her bars; her king and her princes are among the Nations; the Law is no more; her prophets also find no visions from Jehovah.

10 י   The elders of the daughter of Zion sit upon the ground and keep silence; they have cast dust upon their heads; they have girded themselves with sackcloth; the maidens of Jerusalem hang down their heads to the ground.

11 כ   Mine eyes do fail with tears, my bowels are troubled, my liver is poured upon the earth, because of the destruction of the daughter of my people; while the babes and the sucklings swoon in the broad places of the city.

12 ל   They say to their mothers, 'Where is corn and wine?' while they swoon as the wounded in the broad places of the city, while their soul is poured out into their mother's bosom.

13 מ   What shall I urge upon thee? what shall I liken to thee, O daughter of Jerusalem? what shall I equal to thee, that I may comfort thee, O virgin daughter of Zion? for thy breach is great like the sea; who can heal thee?

14 נ   Thy prophets have seen false and foolish visions for

thee; and they have not uncovered thine iniquity, to
bring home thy captivity; but they have seen for thee
false prophecies and misleading visions.

ס   All that pass by the way clap their hands at thee; 15
they hiss and wag their head at the daughter of Jerusalem, [saying,] 'Is this the city that men call The per-
'fection of beauty, The joy of the whole earth?'

פ   All thine enemies open their mouth against thee; 16
they hiss and gnash the teeth; they say, 'We have
'swallowed her up; certainly this is the day that we
'looked for; we have found, we have seen it.'

ע   Jehovah hath done what he devised; he hath fulfilled 17
his word that he commanded in the days of old; he hath
thrown down, and hath not pitied; and he hath caused
the enemy to rejoice over thee, he hath set up the horn
of thine adversaries.

צ   Their heart cried to the Lord; O wall of the daughter 18
of Zion, let tears run down like a river day and night;
give thyself no rest; let not the apple of thine eye cease.

ק   Arise, cry out in the night; in the beginning of the 19
watches, pour out thy heart like water before the face of
the Lord; lift up thy hands towards him for the life of
thy babes, that faint for hunger at the top of every street.

ר   Look, O Jehovah, and consider to whom thou hast 20
done this. Shall the women eat their offspring, babes
that are carried in arms? Shall the priest and the prophet be slain in the Sanctuary of the Lord?

ש   The young and the old lie on the ground in the 21
streets; my maidens and my young men are fallen by
the sword; thou hast slain them in the day of thine
anger; thou hast killed, and hast not pitied.

ת   Thou didst call, as on the day of an assembly, my 22
terrors on all sides, so that in the day of Jehovah's anger
none escaped nor remained; those that I have carried in
arms and brought up hath mine enemy consumed.

III.

א   I am the man that hath seen affliction by the rod of 1
His wrath;

א   He hath led me, and brought me into darkness, but 2
not into light;

א   Surely against me is he turned, he turneth his hand all 3
the day.

4 ב My flesh and my skin hath he made old; he hath broken my bones;
5 ב He hath builded against me, and encompassed me with hemlock and trouble;
6 ב He hath made me to dwell in dark places, as they that died long ago.
7 ג He hath hedged me about, and I cannot get out; he hath made my chain heavy;
8 ג Also when I cry and shout for help, he shutteth out my prayer;
9 ג He hath hedged my ways about with hewn stone, he hath made my paths crooked.
10 ד He was unto me as a bear lying in wait, as a lion in secret places;
11 ד He hath turned aside my ways, and torn me in pieces: he hath made me desolate;
12 ד He hath bent his bow, and set me as a mark for the arrow.
13 ה He hath caused the arrows of his quiver to enter into my reins;
14 ה I have been a derision to all my people; their song all the day;
15 ה He hath filled me with bitterness, he hath bathed me with wormwood.
16 ו And he hath broken my teeth with gravel stones, he hath rolled me in the ashes;
17 ו And thou hast cast my soul far off from peace; I have forgotten prosperity;
18 ו And I said, 'My confidence and my hope is perished 'from Jehovah.'
19 ז To remember mine affliction and my misery, is wormwood and hemlock;
20 ז My soul doth well remember, and is humbled within me;
21 ז This I recall to my mind, therefore have I hope.
22 ח It is the kindness of Jehovah that we are not consumed, because his compassions fail not;
23 ח They are new every morning; great is Thy faithfulness;
24 ח Jehovah is my portion, saith my soul; therefore will I hope in him.
25 ט Good is Jehovah unto them that wait for him, to the soul that seeketh him;

ו Good is it that a man should both hope and quietly 26
wait for the salvation of Jehovah;

ו Good is it for a man that he bear the yoke in his 27
youth;

י That he sit alone and keep silence, because He hath 28
laid it upon him;

י That he put his mouth in the dust; if so be there 29
may be hope;

י That he give his cheek to him that smiteth him; 30
that he be filled full with reproach;

כ For the Lord will not cast off for ever; 31

כ For though he cause grief, yet he hath mercy 32
according to his great kindness;

כ For he doth not willingly afflict or grieve the chil- 33
dren of men.

ל To crush under his feet all the prisoners of the earth; 34

ל To turn aside the right of a man before the face of 35
the Most High;

ל To subvert a man in his cause, the Lord approveth 36
not.

מ Who is he that saith, and it cometh to pass, when 37
the Lord commanded it not?

מ Out of the mouth of the Most High proceedeth not 38
both evil and good?

מ Wherefore doth a living man complain, a man at the 39
punishment of his sins?

נ Let us search and try our ways, and turn again to 40
Jehovah;

נ Let us lift up our heart with our hands unto God in 41
the heavens;

נ We have transgressed and have rebelled; thou hast 42
not pardoned.

ס Thou hast covered with anger, and hast pursued us; 43
thou hast slain; thou hast not pitied;

ס Thou hast covered thyself with a cloud, that our 44
prayer should not pass through;

ס Thou hast made us the offscouring and refuse in the 45
midst of the peoples.

פ All our enemies have opened their mouths against 46
us;

פ Fear and the pit are come upon us, desolation and 47
destruction;

48	פ	Mine eye runneth down with rivers of water for the destruction of the daughter of my people.
49	ע	Mine eye trickleth down, and ceaseth not, without any intermission;
50	ע	Till Jehovah look down, and behold from heaven.
51	ע	Mine eye bringeth grief to my soul because of all the daughters of my city.
52	צ	The enemies chase me sore, like a bird, without cause.
53	צ	They have cut off my life in a pit, and cast a stone upon me.
54	צ	The waters flowed over my head; I said, 'I am cut off.'
55	ק	I called upon thy name, O Jehovah, out of the pit of the parts below.
56	ק	Thou hast heard my voice; hide not thine ear at my breathing, at my cry.
57	ק	Thou drewest near in the day that I called upon thee; thou saidst, 'Fear not.'
58	ר	Thou hast pleaded, O Lord, the cause of my soul; thou hast redeemed my life;
59	ר	Thou hast seen, O Jehovah, my wrong; judge thou my cause.
60	ר	Thou hast seen all their vengeance and all their imaginations against me.
61	ש	Thou hast heard their reproach, O Jehovah, and all their imaginations against me;
62	ש	The lips of those that rose up against me, and their murmuring against me all the day.
63	ש	Consider their sitting down, and their rising up; I am their song.
64	ת	Do thou render to them a recompence, O Jehovah, according to the work of their hands.
65	ת	Do thou give to them stubbornness of heart, as thy curse on them.
66	ת	Do thou pursue them in anger and destroy them from under the heavens, O Jehovah.

IV.

1	א	How is the gold become dim! the most fine gold is changed, the stones of the Holy Place are poured out at the top of every street.
2	ב	The precious sons of Zion, who may be weighed against fine gold, how are they esteemed as earthen pitchers, the work of the potter's hands!

ב   Even the dragons draw out the breast, they give suck 3
to their young; but the daughter of my people is become cruel, like the ostriches in the desert.

ד   The tongue of the sucking child cleaveth to the roof 4
of his mouth for thirst; the babes ask for bread, and
no man breaketh it to them.

ה   They that did feed on delicacies are desolate in the 5
streets; they that were brought up in scarlet embrace
dunghills.

ו   For the iniquity of the daughter of my people is 6
greater than the sin of Sodom, that was overthrown as
in a moment, when no hands fell upon her.

ז   Her Nazarites were purer than snow, they were whiter 7
than milk, they were more ruddy in body than rubies,
their polishing was of the sapphire;

ח   Their visage is become blacker than darkness; they 8
are not known in the streets; their skin cleaveth to
their bones; it is withered, it is like a stick.

ט   They that are slain with the sword are better than 9
they that are slain with hunger; for these pine away,
stricken for want of the fruits of the field.

י   Hands of pitying women have boiled their own chil- 10
dren; they were their food at the destruction of the
daughter of my people.

כ   Jehovah hath accomplished his fury; he hath poured 11
out his fierce anger, and hath kindled a fire in Zion,
and it hath devoured its foundations.

ל   The kings of the earth, and all the inhabitants of the 12
world, did not believe that the adversary and the enemy
could have entered the gates of Jerusalem.

מ   It was through the sins of her prophets, and the ini- 13
quities of her priests, who have shed the blood of the
righteous ones in the midst of her.

נ   These wandered as blind men in the streets, they 14
were polluted with blood, so that men could not touch
their garments.

ס   Men cried to them, 'Depart ye; it is unclean; de- 15
'part, depart, touch not;' when they fled away and
wandered, men said among the Nations, 'They shall no
'more sojourn there.'

פ   The frown of Jehovah hath scattered them; he will 16
no more regard them; they respected not the persons
of the priests, they favoured not the elders.

17 ע   While we were yet in being our eyes failed in our watching for our help in vain; we watched for a nation [the Egyptians] that could not save us.
18 צ   They hunt our steps, so that we cannot walk in our broad places; our end is near, our days are fulfilled; for our end is come.
19 ק   Our pursuers were swifter than eagles in the heavens; they followed us on the mountains, they laid wait for us in the desert.
20 ר   The Breath of our nostrils [Jehoiachin], the anointed of Jehovah, was taken in their pit-falls, of whom we said, 'Under his shadow we shall live among the Nations.'
21 ש   Rejoice and be glad [O Zion]. O daughter of Edom, that dwellest in the land of Uz, the cup also shall pass over unto thee; thou shalt be drunken, and shalt make thyself naked.
22 ת   Thy punishment is accomplished, O daughter of Zion; he will no more carry thee away into captivity. He will visit thine iniquity, O daughter of Edom; he will uncover thy sins.

v.

1 Remember, O Jehovah, what is come upon us;
Consider, and behold our reproach.
2 Our inheritance is turned to strangers,
Our houses to foreigners.
3 We are orphans without a father,
Our mothers are as widows.
4 We have drunken our water for money;
Our wood is sold unto us for a price.
5 We are driven with a yoke upon our necks;
We are weary, and have no rest.
6 We had given the hand to the Egyptians,
And to the Assyrians, to be satisfied with bread.
7 Our fathers sinned, and they are not;
And we have borne their iniquities.
8 Servants have ruled over us;
There is none that doth deliver us out of their hand.
9 We get our bread with the peril of our lives,
Because of the drought in the desert.
10 Our skin is burnt as in an oven,
Because of the violence of the famine.
11 They ravished the women in Zion,

And the maidens in the cities of Judah.
Princes were hanged up by their hands ; 12
The faces of the elders were not honoured.
The young men carry the mill-stones, 13
And the youths stagger under the wood.
The elders have ceased from the city gate, 14
The young men from their singing.
The joy of our heart is ceased ; 15
Our dancing is turned into mourning.
The crown is fallen from our head ; 16
Woe unto us, that we have sinned !
Because of this our heart is faint ; 17
Because of these things our eyes are dim ;
Because of the mountain of Zion, 18
That it is desolate, that the foxes walk on it.
Thou, O Jehovah, remainest for ever ; 19
Thy throne from generation to generation.
Wherefore dost thou wholly forget us, 20
And forsake us for so long a time ?
Turn thou us unto thee, O Jehovah, 21
And we shall be turned ; renew our days as of old.
But thou hast utterly rejected us, 22
Thou art very wroth against us.

EZEKIEL.

NOW IT CAME TO PASS in the thirtieth year [of Nabo- 1
pulassar, B.C. 596] in the fourth month, on the fifth
day of the month, as I was among the captives by the river
Chebar [or Chaboras], that the heavens were opened, and I
saw visions of God. On the fifth day of the month, which 2
was in the fifth year of king Jehoiachin's captivity, it came 3
to pass that the word of Jehovah came unto Ezekiel the
priest, the son of Buzi, in the land of the Chaldeans by
the river Chebar ; and the hand of Jehovah was there
upon him.

And I looked, and, behold, a stormy wind came out of 4
the north, a great cloud, and a fire curling itself ; and a
brightness was about it, and out of the midst thereof as the
colour of brass, out of the midst of the fire. Also out of 5
the midst thereof came the likeness of four living creatures.
And this was their appearance ; they had the likeness of a
man. And every one of them had four faces, and every 6

7 one had four wings. And their feet were upright feet; the sole of their feet was like the sole of a calf's foot; and they
8 sparkled like the colour of burnished copper. And they had the hands of a man under their wings on their four
9 sides; and they four had their faces and their wings. Their wings were joined one to another; they turned not themselves when they went; they went every one in the direc-
10 tion of its face. As for the likeness of their faces, they had the face of a man; and they four had the face of a lion on the right side; and they four had the face of an ox on the
11 left side; they four also had the face of an eagle. Thus were their faces. And of their wings two of every one were stretched upward, joined one to another; and two
12 covered their bodies. And they went every one in the direction of its face. Whither the spirit was to go, they went; and they turned not themselves when they went.
13 As for the likeness of the living creatures, their appearance was like coals of fire, burning like the appearance of lamps. It went up and down among the living creatures; and the fire was bright; and out of the fire went forth
14 lightning. And the living creatures ran and returned as the appearance of a flash of lightning.
15 Now as I beheld the living creatures, behold, one wheel upon the earth joined to the living creatures, for each of its
16 four faces. The appearance of the wheels and their work was like unto the colour of a chrysolite. And they four had one likeness; and their appearance and their work was
17 as it were a wheel in the middle of a wheel. When they went, they went towards their four sides; they turned
18 themselves not when they went. As for the rings of their wheels, they were so high that they were dreadful; and
19 their rings were full of eyes round about them four. And when the living creatures went, the wheels went together with them; and when the living creatures were lifted up
20 from the earth, the wheels were lifted up. Whithersoever the spirit was to go, they went, thither was their spirit to go; and the wheels were lifted up with them; for the
21 spirit of the living creature was in the wheels. When those went, these went; and when those stood, these stood; and when those were lifted up from the earth, the wheels were lifted up with them; for the spirit of the living creature was in the wheels.

And the likeness of a firmament was upon the heads of ²² the living creatures as the colour of a brilliant crystal, stretched forth upon their heads above. And under the ²³ firmament were their wings straight, the one toward the other; every one had two, which covered on this side, and every one had two, which covered on that side, their bodies. And when they went, I heard the noise of their wings, ²⁴ like the noise of great waters, as the voice of the Almighty, the voice of speech, as the noise of a camp; when they stood, they let down their wings. And there was a voice ²⁵ above the firmament that was upon their heads, when they stood, and had let down their wings.

And above the firmament that was upon their heads was ²⁶ the likeness of a throne, as the appearance of a sapphire stone. And upon the likeness of the throne was the likeness as the appearance of a man above upon it. And I ²⁷ saw as the colour of brass, as the appearance of fire round about within it, from the appearance of his loins even upward; and from the appearance of his loins even downward, I saw as it were the appearance of fire, and it had brightness round about. As the appearance of the bow that is ²⁸ in the cloud in a day of rain, so was the appearance of the brightness round about. This was the appearance of the likeness of the Glory of Jehovah. And when I saw it, I fell upon my face, and I heard a voice of one that spake. —

And he said to me, 'Son of Adam, stand upon thy feet, ¹ 'and I will speak to thee.' And the spirit entered into me ² when he spake to me, and set me on my feet, so that I heard him that spake to me. And he said to me, 'Son of ³ 'Adam, I send thee to the children of Israel, to rebellious 'nations, that have rebelled against me. They and their 'fathers have transgressed against me, even unto this 'very day. For they are children hard of face and stiff of ⁴ 'heart. I send thee to them; and thou shalt say to them, 'Thus saith the Lord Jehovah. And they, whether they ⁵ 'hear, or whether they forbear to hear, (for they are a re- 'bellious house,) yet shall they know that there hath been 'a prophet among them. And thou, son of Adam, be not ⁶ 'afraid of them, neither be afraid of their words, though 'briars and thorns be with thee, and thou dost dwell among 'scorpions. Be not afraid of their words, nor be dismayed 'at their looks, though they be a rebellious house. And ⁷

'thou shalt speak my words to them, whether they hear,
'or whether they forbear to hear; for they are rebellious.
8 'But thou, son of Adam, hear what I say to thee; Be not
'thou rebellious like that rebellious house; open thy mouth,
9 'and eat what I give thee.' And when I looked, behold, a
hand was put forth to me; and, lo, in it was the roll of a
10 book; and he spread it open before me. And it was
written on the front and on the back; and therein were
—written lamentations, and mourning, and woe.

1 And he said to me, 'Son of Adam, eat what thou findest;
'eat this book-roll, and go speak unto the house of Israel.'
2 So I opened my mouth, and he caused me to eat that book-
3 roll. And he said to me, 'Son of Adam, cause thy belly
'to eat, and fill thy bowels with this book-roll that I give
'thee.' Then did I eat it; and it was in my mouth as
honey for sweetness.
4 And he said to me, 'Son of Adam, go, get thee to the
5 'house of Israel, and speak with my words to them. For
'thou art not sent to a people thick of lips and slow of
6 'tongue, but to the house of Israel; not to many peoples
'thick of lips and slow of tongue, whose words thou canst
'not understand. If I had sent thee to them, would they
7 'not have hearkened to thee? But the house of Israel
'will not hearken to thee; for they will not hearken to
'me; for all the house of Israel are bold of forehead and
8 'hard of heart. Behold, I have made thy face strong
'against their faces, and thy forehead strong against their
9 'foreheads. As an adamant harder than flint have I made
'thy forehead. Fear them not, neither be dismayed at
'their looks, though they be a rebellious house.'
10 And he said to me, 'Son of Adam, all my words that I
'shall speak to thee receive in thy heart, and hear with
11 'thine ears. And go, get thee to them of the captivity, to
'the children of thy people, and speak to them, and say to
'them, Thus saith the Lord Jehovah; whether they hear,
12 'or whether they forbear to hear.' Then the spirit took
me up, and I heard behind me the voice of a great rushing,
[saying,] 'Blessed be the glory of Jehovah from his place.'
13 I heard also the noise of the wings of the living creatures
that touched one another, and the noise of the wheels over
14 against them, and the noise of a great rushing. So the
spirit lifted me up and took me away, and I went in bitter-

ness, in the wrath of my spirit; and the hand of Jehovah was strong upon me.

15 Then I came to them of the captivity at Tel-abib, that dwelt by the river Chebar, and where they sat, there I also sat, astonished among them for seven days. 16 And it came to pass at the end of seven days, that the word of Jehovah came to me, saying, 17 'Son of Adam, I have made thee 'a watchman to the house of Israel; therefore hear the 'word at my mouth, and give them warning from me. 18 'When I say to the wicked man, Thou shalt surely die; 'and thou givest him not warning, nor speakest to warn 'the wicked from his wicked way, to save his life; the 'same wicked man shall die in his iniquity; but his blood 'will I require at thy hand. 19 Yet if thou warn the wicked 'man, and he turn not from his wickedness, nor from his 'wicked way, he shall die in his iniquity; but thou hast 'saved thy soul. 20 Again, When a righteous man doth turn 'from his righteousness, and commit injustice, and I lay a 'stumbling-block before him, he shall die; because thou 'didst not give him warning, he shall die in his sin, and 'his righteousness which he had done shall not be remem-'bered; but his blood will I require at thy hand. 21 Never-'theless if thou warn the righteous man, so that the 'righteous sin not, and he doth not sin, he shall surely 'live, because he is warned; also thou hast saved thy soul.'

22 And the hand of Jehovah was upon me there; and he said to me, 'Arise, go forth into the valley, and I will there 'talk with thee.' 23 Then I arose and went forth into the valley, and, behold, the Glory of Jehovah stood there, as the Glory which I saw by the river Chebar. And I fell on my face. 24 Then the spirit entered into me, and set me on my feet. And he spake with me, and said to me, 'Go 'in, shut thyself within thy house. 25 But thou, O son of 'Adam, behold, they shall put cords upon thee, and shall 'bind thee therewith, and thou shalt not go out among them. 26 'And I will make thy tongue to cleave to the roof of thy 'mouth, and thou shalt be dumb, and shalt not be to them 'a reprover; for they are a rebellious house. 27 But when 'I speak with thee, I will open thy mouth, and thou shalt 'say to them, Thus saith the Lord Jehovah; He that 'heareth, let him hear; and he that forbeareth to hear, 'let him forbear; for they are a rebellious house.

1 'Thou also, son of Adam, take to thee a white tile, and lay it before thee, and engrave upon it a city, even Jeru-
2 salem. And lay siege against it, and build a line of forts against it, and cast a siege-mound against it; set a camp also against it, and set battering-rams against it round
3 about. And take thou to thee an iron pan, and set it for a wall of iron between thee and the city; and set thy face against it, and it shall be besieged, and thou shalt lay siege
4 against it. This shall be a sign to the house of Israel. Lie thou also on thy left side, and lay the iniquity of the house of Israel upon it; according to the number of the days that
5 thou shalt lie on it thou shalt bear their iniquity. For I have laid upon thee the years of their iniquity, according to the number of the days, three hundred and ninety days;
6 so shalt thou bear the iniquity of the house of Israel. And when thou hast accomplished them, lie again on thy right side, and thou shalt bear the iniquity of the house of Judah for forty days. I have appointed to thee one day
7 for each year. Then thou shalt set thy face toward the siege of Jerusalem, and thine arm shall be uncovered, and
8 thou shalt prophesy against it. And, behold, I will put cords upon thee, and thou shalt not turn thee from one side to another, till thou hast ended the days of thy siege.
9 'Take thou also to thee wheat, and barley, and beans, and lentils and millet, and spelt, and put them into one vessel, and make to thee bread thereof, according to the number of the days that thou shalt lie upon thy side, three
10 hundred and ninety days shalt thou eat thereof. And thy food which thou shalt eat shall be by weight, twenty Shekels [or ten ounces] a day; from time to time shalt
11 thou eat it. Thou shalt drink also water by measure, the sixth part of a Hin [or one pint]; from time to time shalt
12 thou drink. And thou shalt eat it as barley cakes, and thou shalt bake it with dung that cometh out of man, in their sight.'
13 And Jehovah said, 'Even thus shall the children of Israel eat their defiled bread among the nations, whither I shall
14 drive them.' Then said I, 'Ah Lord Jehovah! behold, my soul hath not been polluted. For from my youth up even till now have I not eaten of that which dieth of itself, or is torn in pieces; neither came there putrid flesh
15 into my mouth.' Then he said to me, 'Lo, for thyself I

'have given cow's dung instead of man's dung, and thou
'shalt prepare thy bread therewith.' And he said to me, 16
'Son of Adam, behold, I will break the staff of bread in
'Jerusalem; and they shall eat bread by weight, and with
'care; and they shall drink water by measure, and in de-
'spair; so that they may want bread and water, and be in 17
'despair one with another, and pine away for their iniquity.—

'And thou, son of Adam, take to thee a sharp knife, a 1
'barber's razor shalt thou take to thee, and cause it to pass
'upon thy head and upon thy beard. Then take to thee
'balances to weigh and divide the [hair]. Thou shalt burn 2
'in the flame a third part in the midst of the city, when
'the days of the siege are fulfilled; and thou shalt take a
'third part, and smite round about it with a knife; and a
'third part thou shalt scatter in the wind; and I will draw
'out a sword after them. Thou shalt also take thereof a 3
'few in number, and bind them in thy skirts. Then take 4
'some of them again, and cast them into the midst of the
'fire, and burn them in the fire; for therefrom shall a fire
'come forth unto all the house of Israel.'

Thus saith the Lord Jehovah; This is Jerusalem. I 5
have set her in the midst of the nations and the countries
that are round about her. And she hath rebelled against 6
my judgments unto wickedness more than the nations, and
against my statutes more than the countries that are round
about her; for they have refused my judgments and my
statutes, they have not walked in them. Therefore thus 7
saith the Lord Jehovah; Because ye railed against me more
than the nations that are round about you, and ye have not
walked in my statutes, neither have kept my judgments,
neither have done according to the judgments of the nations
that are round about you; therefore thus saith the Lord 8
Jehovah; Behold, I, even I, am against thee, and will
execute judgments in the midst of thee in the sight of the
nations. And I will do in thee what I have not done, and 9
whereunto I will not do any more the like, because of all
thine abominations. Therefore the fathers shall eat their 10
sons in the midst of thee, and the sons shall eat their fathers;
and I will execute judgments on thee, and the whole remnant of thee will I scatter to all the winds. Therefore, as 11
I live, the Lord Jehovah hath said it, surely, because thou
hast defiled my Sanctuary with all thy detestable things,

and with all thine abominations, therefore will I also diminish thee; neither shall mine eye pity, neither will I ¹² spare. A third part of thee shall die by pestilence, and by famine shall they be consumed in the midst of thee; and a third part shall fall by the sword round about thee; and I will scatter a third part to all the winds, and I will draw ¹³ out a sword after them. And when mine anger is accomplished, and I have caused my wrath to rest upon them, and I have been comforted; then they shall know that I Jehovah have spoken it in my zeal, when I have accom- ¹⁴ plished my wrath against them. Moreover, I will make thee a waste, and a reproach among the nations that are ¹⁵ round about thee, in the sight of all that pass by. So it shall be a reproach and a taunt, an instruction and an astonishment to the nations that are round about thee, when I have executed judgments on thee in anger and in wrath ¹⁶ and in furious rebukes. I Jehovah have spoken it. When I shall send upon them the evil arrows of famine, which shall be for their destruction, and which I will send to destroy you; then I will increase the famine upon you. ¹⁷ And I will break your staff of bread, and will send upon you famine and evil beasts; and they shall bereave thee; then pestilence and blood shall pass though thee; and I —will bring the sword upon thee; I Jehovah have spoken it.

¹ And the word of Jehovah came to me, saying, Son of ² Adam, set thy face toward the MOUNTAINS OF ISRAEL, and ³ prophesy against them, and say, Ye mountains of Israel, hear the word of the Lord Jehovah; Thus saith the Lord Jehovah to the mountains, and to the hills, to the streams, and to the valleys; Behold, I, even I, will bring a sword upon you, and I will destroy your High Places [or Altars]. ⁴ And your altars shall be desolate, and your sun-images shall be broken; and I will cast down your slain men before ⁵ your filthy idols. And I will lay the carcases of the children of Israel before their filthy idols; and I will scatter ⁶ your bones round about your altars. In all your dwelling-places the cities shall be laid waste, and the High Places shall be desolate; so that your altars may be laid waste and made desolate, and your filthy idols may be broken and may cease, and your sun-images may be cut down, and ⁷ your works may be abolished. And the slain shall fall in the midst of you, and ye shall know that I am Jehovah.

⁸ Yet will I leave a remnant, when ye shall have some that escape the sword among the nations, when ye shall be scattered through the countries. ⁹ And they that escape of you shall remember me among the nations whither they shall be carried captives, because I will break their straying heart, which hath departed from me, and their eyes, which go astray after their filthy idols. And they shall loathe themselves for the evils which they have committed in all their abominations. ¹⁰ And they shall know that I am Jehovah, and that I have not said in vain that I would do this evil to them.

¹¹ Thus saith the Lord Jehovah; Smite with thy hand, and stamp with thy foot, and say, 'Alas for all the evil abomin-'ations of the house of Israel!' for they shall fall by the sword, by famine, and by pestilence. ¹² He that is far off shall die by pestilence; and he that is near shall fall by the sword; and he that remaineth and is besieged shall die by famine; and thus will I accomplish my wrath upon them. ¹³ Then shall ye know that I am Jehovah, when their slain men shall be among their filthy idols round about their altars, upon every high hill, on all the tops of the mountains, and under every green tree, and under every thick oak, the places where they did offer sweet savour to all their filthy idols. ¹⁴ So will I stretch out my hand upon them, and I will make the land desolate, yea, desolate from the [southern] desert unto Diblah, [or Riblah,] in all their habitations; and then they shall know that I am Jehovah.—

¹ And the word of Jehovah came to me, saying, Also, thou son of Adam, ² thus saith the Lord Jehovah to the land of Israel; The end, the end is come upon the four corners of the land. ³ Now is the end come upon thee, and I will send mine anger upon thee, and will judge thee according to thy ways, and will recompense upon thee all thine abominations. ⁴ And mine eye shall not pity thee, neither will I spare; but I will recompense thy ways upon thee, and thine abominations shall be in the midst of thee; and ye shall know that I am Jehovah.

⁵ Thus saith the Lord Jehovah; An evil, an only evil, behold, is come. ⁶ The end is come, the end is come; it waketh up for thee; behold, it is come. ⁷ The circle of events is come round to thee, O thou that dwellest in the land. The time is come, the day of trouble is near, and not the

8 shout of joy on the mountains. Now will I shortly pour out my wrath upon thee, and accomplish mine anger upon thee. And I will judge thee according to thy ways, and
9 will recompense upon thee all thine abominations. And mine eye shall not pity, neither will I spare. I will recompense thee according to thy ways, and thine abominations shall be in the midst of thee; and ye shall know that I am Jehovah that smiteth.
10 Behold the day, behold, it is come. The circle of events is gone forth; the rod hath blossomed, pride hath budded.
11 Violence is risen up into a rod of wickedness; none of them shall remain, and none of their rabble, nor of any of their
12 tumult. Neither shall there be wailing for them. The time is come, the day draweth near. Let not the buyer rejoice, nor the seller mourn, when wrath is upon all its
13 rabble, when the seller shall not return for the produce of the sale, although they are both yet alive, for the vision is touching all its rabble. He shall not return; neither shall any one strengthen himself in the iniquity of his life.
14 They have blown the trumpet, even to make all ready; but none goeth to the battle; for my wrath is upon all its
15 rabble. The sword is without, and pestilence and famine within. He that is in the field shall die by the sword; and he that is in the city, famine and pestilence shall de-
16 vour him. And they that escape of them shall escape, and shall be on the mountains like doves of the valleys, all of
17 them moaning, every one for his iniquity. All hands shall
18 be feeble, and all knees shall be weak as water. They shall also gird themselves with sackcloth, and horror shall cover them; and shame shall be on all faces, and baldness on all
19 their heads. They shall cast their silver into the streets, and their gold shall be as impurity. Their silver and their gold shall not be able to deliver them in the day of Jehovah's wrath. They shall not satisfy their souls, neither fill their bowels; because it is the stumbling-block
20 of their iniquity. As for the beauty of his ornament, they turned it into pride; and they made the images of their abominations and of their detestable things therewith.
21 Therefore have I made it impurity unto them. And I will give it into the hands of the strangers for a prey, and to the wicked of the earth for a spoil; and they shall pollute
22 it. My face will I turn also from them, and they shall

pollute my secret place; for robbers shall enter into it, and pollute it.

Make the chain; for the land is full of bloody crimes, 23 and the city is full of violence. Therefore I will bring in 24 the worst of the Nations, and they shall possess their houses. I will also make the pride of the strong to cease; and their holy places shall be defiled. Destruction cometh; and they 25 shall seek for peace, and there shall be none. Woe shall 26 come upon woe, and rumour shall be upon rumour; then shall they seek for a vision from the prophet. But the Law shall perish from the priest, and counsel from the elders. The king [Jehoiachin] shall mourn, and the prince 27 [Zedekiah] shall be clothed with desolation, and the hands of the people of the land shall tremble. I will do to them after their own way, and according to their own judgments will I judge them; and they shall know that I am Jehovah.—

AND IT CAME TO PASS in the sixth year [of the Captivity, 1 B.C. 595], in the sixth month, on the fifth day of the month, as I sat in my house, and the elders of Judah sat before me, that the hand of the Lord Jehovah fell upon me there. Then I beheld, and lo, a likeness as the appear- 2 ance of fire; from the appearance of his loins and downward, fire; and from his loins and upward, as the appearance of brightness, as the colour of brass. And he put 3 forth the form of a hand, and took me by a lock of my head; and the spirit lifted me up between the earth and the heavens, and brought me in the visions of God to Jerusalem, to the doorway of the Inner Gate that looketh toward the north; where was the seat of the Image of Jealousy, which provoketh to jealousy. And behold, the Glory 4 of the God of Israel was there, according to the appearance that I saw in the valley. Then said he to me, 'Son of 5 'Adam, lift up thine eyes now the way toward the north.' So I lifted up mine eyes the way toward the north, and behold, northward at the gate of [the court of] the Altar was this Image of Jealousy in the entrance. He said fur- 6 thermore to me, 'Son of Adam, seest thou what they do? ' even the great abominations that the house of Israel com- ' mitteth here, to drive me far off from my Sanctuary? ' But turn thee yet again, and thou shalt see greater abom- ' inations.'

And he brought me to the doorway of the Court; and 7

⁸ when I looked, behold, a hole in the wall. Then said he to me, 'Son of Adam, dig now into the wall.' And when ⁹ I had digged into the wall, behold, a doorway. And he said to me, 'Go in, and look at the wicked abominations ¹⁰ 'that they do here.' So I went in and saw; and behold every form of creeping things, and abominable beasts, and all the filthy idols of the house of Israel, engraved upon ¹¹ the wall round about. And there stood before them seventy men of the elders of the house of Israel, and in the midst of them stood Jaazaniah the son of Shaphan, with every man his censer in his hand; and a thick cloud of incense ² went up. Then said he to me, 'Son of Adam, hast thou 'seen what the elders of the house of Israel do in the 'dark, every man in the chambers of his idols? For they 'say, Jehovah seeth us not; Jehovah hath forsaken the ³ 'earth.' He said also to me, 'Turn thee yet again, and 'thou shalt see greater abominations that they do.'
⁴ Then he brought me to the doorway of the gate of the House of Jehovah which was toward the north; and, behold, there sat women weeping for Tammuz [or Adonis]. ⁵ And said he to me, 'Hast thou seen this, O son of Adam? 'Turn thee yet again, and thou shalt see greater abomina- 'tions than these.'
⁶ Then he brought me into the Inner Court of the House of Jehovah, and behold, at the doorway of the Great Hall of Jehovah, between the porch and the Altar, were about five and twenty men, with their backs toward the Great Hall of Jehovah, and their faces toward the east; and ⁷ they worshipped the sun toward the east. And he said to me, 'Hast thou seen this, O son of Adam? Is it a light 'thing to the House of Judah that they commit the 'abominations which they commit here? For they have 'filled the land with violence, and have returned to pro- 'voke me to anger; and lo, they put the twig to their ⁸ 'nose. Therefore will I also deal in wrath. Mine eye 'shall not have pity, neither will I spare. And though 'they cry in mine ears with a loud voice, yet will I not —'hear them.'

He cried also in mine ears with a loud voice, saying 'Draw near, ye that have charge over the city, even every 'man with his destroying weapon in his hand.' And behold, six men came from the way of the Upper Gate, which faceth the north, and every man a drawn weapon in his hand; and one man among them was clothed with linen, with a writer's inkhorn at his waist; and they went in, and stood beside the copper altar. And the glory of ³ the God of Israel was gone up from off the cherub, whereupon it was, to the threshold of the House. And he called to the man clothed with linen, who had the writer's inkhorn at his waist; and Jehovah said to him, 'Go through ⁴ 'the midst of the city, through the midst of Jerusalem, 'and set a mark upon the foreheads of the men that sigh 'and that groan for all the abominations that are done in 'the midst thereof.'

And to the others he said in my hearing, 'Go ye after ⁵ 'him through the city, and smite. Let not your eye have 'pity, neither spare ye. Slay utterly old and young, both ⁶ 'maidens, and little children, and women; but come not 'near any man upon whom is the mark. And begin at my 'Sanctuary.' Then they began with the elders who were before the House. And he said to them, 'Defile the House, ⁷ 'and fill the courts with the slain. Go ye forth.' And they went forth, and smote in the city.

And it came to pass, while they were smiting them, and ⁸ I was left, that I fell on my face, and cried, and said, 'Ah 'Lord Jehovah! wilt thou destroy all the residue of Israel 'in thy pouring out of thy wrath upon Jerusalem?' And ⁹ he said to me, 'The iniquity of the house of Israel and 'Judah is exceeding great, and the land is full of blood-'shed, and the city full of perverseness. For they say, 'Jehovah hath forsaken the earth, and Jehovah seeth not. 'And as for me also, mine eye shall not have pity, neither ¹⁰ 'will I spare; I will recompense their way upon their 'head. And behold, the man clothed with linen, who ¹¹ had the inkhorn at his waist, brought back word, saying, 'I have done as thou hast commanded me.'

Then I looked, and behold, on the firmament that was ¹ upon the heads of the cherubs there appeared over them as it were a sapphire stone, as the appearance of the likeness of a throne. And He spake to the man clothed with linen, ² and said, 'Go in between the wheelwork, under the 'cherub, and fill thy two hands with coals of fire from be-'tween the cherubs, and scatter them over the city.' And he went in in my sight. Now the cherubs stood on the ³

right side of the House, when the man went in; and the
⁴ cloud filled the Inner Court. Then the Glory of Jehovah
went up from off the cherub, over the threshold of the
House; and the House was filled with the cloud, and the
court was full of the brightness of the Glory of Jehovah.
⁵ And the sound of the cherubs' wings was heard even to
the Outer Court, as the voice of God Almighty when he
⁶ speaketh. And it came to pass, that when he had commanded the man clothed with linen, saying, 'Take fire
'from between the wheelwork, from between the cherubs;'
⁷ then he went in, and stood beside the wheels. And the
cherub stretched forth his hand from between the cherubs
unto the fire that was between the cherubs, and took thereof, and put it into the two hands of him that was clothed
⁸ with linen; who took it and went out. And there appeared
on the cherubs the form of a man's hand under their wings.
⁹ And when I looked, behold, the four wheels by the
cherubs, one wheel by one cherub, and another wheel by
another cherub; and the appearance of the wheels was as
¹⁰ the colour of a chrysolite stone. And as for their appearances, they four had one likeness, as if a wheel had been
¹¹ in the midst of a wheel. When they went, they went
toward their four sides. They turned not as they went.
But to the place whither the head looked they followed it;
¹² they turned not as they went. And their whole body,
and their backs, and their hands, and their wings, and the
wheels, were full of eyes round about, even the wheels that
¹³ they four had. As for the wheels, they were called in my
¹⁴ hearing, Wheelwork. And every one had four faces. The
first face was the face of a cherub, and the second face was
the face of a man, and the third the face of a lion, and the
¹⁵ fourth the face of an eagle. And the cherubs were lifted
up. This is the living creature that I saw by the river
Chebar.
¹⁶ And when the cherubs went, the wheels went fixed to
them. And when the cherubs lifted up their wings to
mount up from the earth, the same wheels also turned not
¹⁷ from beside them. When they stood, these stood; and
when they were lifted up, these lifted up themselves also;
¹⁸ for the spirit of the living creature was in them. Then the
Glory of Jehovah departed from off the threshold of the
¹⁹ House, and stood over the cherubs. And the cherubs

lifted up their wings, and mounted up from the earth in my sight. When they went out, the wheels also were beside them, and every one stood at the doorway of the east gate of the House of Jehovah; and the Glory of the God of Israel was over them above. This is the living 20 creature that I had seen under the God of Israel by the river Chebar; and I knew that they were cherubs. Every 21 one had four faces apiece, and every one four wings; and the likeness of the hands of a man was under their wings. And the likeness of their faces was the same faces which I 22 saw by the river Chebar, their appearances and themselves. They went every one in the direction of its face. —

MOREOVER THE SPIRIT lifted me up, and brought me unto 1 the east gate of the House of Jehovah, which looketh eastward. And behold, at the doorway of the gate five and twenty men; among whom I saw Jaazaniah the son of Azur, and Pelatiah the son of Benaiah, princes of the people. Then said He to me, 'Son of Adam, these are the men 2 'that devise mischief, and give wicked counsel in this city; 'who say, It is not near; let us build houses; this [city] 3 'is the caldron, and we are the flesh. Therefore prophesy 4 'against them, prophesy, O son of Adam.'

And the spirit of Jehovah fell upon me, and said to me, 5 Say; Thus saith Jehovah; Thus have ye said, O house of Israel; for I know the things that arise in your mind, every one of them. Ye have multiplied your slain in this 6 city, and ye have filled its streets with the slain. There- 7 fore thus saith the Lord Jehovah; Your slain whom ye have laid in the midst of it, they are the flesh, and this [city] is the caldron. But I will bring you forth out of the midst of it. Ye have feared the sword; and I will bring 8 a sword upon you; the Lord Jehovah hath said it. And 9 I will bring you out of the midst of it, and deliver you into the hands of strangers, and I will execute judgments among you. Ye shall fall by the sword. I will judge you at the 10 boundary of Israel; and ye shall know that I am Jehovah. This [city] shall not be your caldron, neither shall ye be 11 the flesh in the midst of it; but I will judge you at the boundary of Israel. And ye shall know that I am Jeho- 12 vah. For ye have not walked in my statutes, neither executed my judgments, but have done after the manners of the nations that are round about you.

¹³ And it came to pass, when I prophesied, that Pelatiah the son of Benaiah died. Then fell I down upon my face, and cried with a loud voice, and said, 'Ah Lord Jehovah! 'wilt thou make a full end of the remnant of Israel?'
¹⁴ Again the word of Jehovah came to me, saying, Son of
¹⁵ Adam, thy brethren, even thy brethren, the men of thy kindred, and all the house of Israel the whole of it, are those unto whom the inhabitants of Jerusalem have said, 'Get you far from Jehovah [or Jerusalem]; unto us is this
¹⁶ 'land given for a possession.' Therefore say, Thus saith the Lord Jehovah; although I have cast them far off among the Nations, and although I have scattered them among the countries, yet will I be to them as a Sanctuary for a
¹⁷ short time in the countries where they shall come. Therefore say, Thus saith the Lord Jehovah, When I gather you in from the peoples, and assemble you out of the countries where ye have been scattered, then I will give to you the
¹⁸ land of Israel; and they shall come thither, and they shall put away all its detestable things, and all its abominations
¹⁹ from thence; and I will give them one heart, and I will put a new spirit within you; and I will put the stony heart
²⁰ out of their flesh, and will give them a heart of flesh; so that they may walk in my statutes, and keep my ordinances, and do them. And they shall be my people, and I will be
²¹ their God. But as for those whose heart walketh after the heart of their detestable things and their abominations, I will recompense their way upon their own heads; the Lord Jehovah hath said it.
²² Then did the cherubs lift up their wings, and the wheels, beside them; and the Glory of the God of Israel was over
²³ them above. And the Glory of Jehovah went up from the midst of the city, and stood upon the mountain which is on the east side of the city.
²⁴ Afterwards the spirit took me up, and brought me in a vision by the spirit of God into Chaldea, to them of the captivity. Then the vision that I had seen went up from
²⁵ me. And I spake to them of the captivity of all the things —of Jehovah that he had shewed me.
¹ AND THE WORD OF JEHOVAH came to me, saying, Son
² of Adam, thou dwellest in the midst of a rebellious house; they have eyes to see, and see not; they have ears to hear,
³ and hear not; for they are a rebellious house. Therefore,

thou son of Adam, prepare for thee baggage for REMOVING INTO CAPTIVITY, and remove by day before their eyes; and thou shalt remove from thy place to another place before their eyes. It may be they will see, though they are a rebellious house. And thou shalt bring forth thy baggage by day before their eyes, as baggage for removing. And thou shalt go forth at evening before their eyes, as they that go forth into captivity. Dig thou through the wall before their eyes, and bring forth thereby. Before their eyes shalt thou bear it upon thy shoulders, and carry it forth in the dark. Thou shalt cover thy face, that thou see not the ground; for I have set thee for a sign unto the house of Israel.

And I did as I was commanded. I brought forth my baggage by day, as baggage for captivity, and in the evening I digged through the wall with my hand; I brought it forth in the dark, and I bare it upon my shoulder before their eyes.

And in the morning came the word of Jehovah to me, saying, Son of Adam, hath not the house of Israel, the rebellious house, said to thee, 'What doest thou?' Say thou to them, Thus saith the Lord Jehovah; This burden [or prophecy] concerneth the prince [Zedekiah] in Jerusalem, and all the house of Israel that are among them. Say thou, I am your sign. Like as I have done, so shall it be done to them. They shall remove and go into captivity. And the prince that is among them shall bear upon his shoulder in the dark, and shall go forth. They shall dig through the wall to carry out thereby. He shall cover his face, that he see not the ground with his eyes. My net also will I spread upon him, and he shall be taken in my snare. And I will bring him to Babylon to the land of the Chaldeans; yet shall he not see it, though he shall die there. And I will scatter toward every wind all that are about him to help him, and all his troops; and I will draw out the sword after them. And they shall know that I am Jehovah, when I shall scatter them among the Nations, and disperse them in the countries. But I will leave a few men of them from the sword, from famine, and from pestilence; so that they may relate all their abominations among the nations whither they come; and they shall know that I am Jehovah.

ⁱ⁷ AND THE WORD OF JEHOVAH came to me, saying, Son of ¹⁸ Adam, eat thy bread with quaking, and drink thy water ¹⁹ with trembling and with carefulness; and say to the people of the land, Thus saith the Lord Jehovah against the inhabitants of Jerusalem, and against the land of Israel; They shall eat their bread with carefulness, and drink their water in despair, because her land is desolate from its fulness, because of the violence of all them that dwell ²⁰ therein. And the cities that are inhabited shall be laid waste, and the land shall be desolate; and ye shall know that I am Jehovah.

²¹ AND THE WORD OF JEHOVAH came to me, saying, Son of ²² Adam, what is that proverb that ye have in the land of Israel, ²³ saying, 'The days are delayed, and every vision faileth'? Tell them therefore, Thus saith the Lord Jehovah; I will make this proverb to cease, and they shall no more use it as a proverb in Israel. But say thou to them, 'The days ²⁴ 'are at hand, and the doing of every vision.' For there shall be no more any false vision nor flattering divination ²⁵ within the house of Israel. For I am Jehovah. I will speak, and the word that I shall speak shall come to pass; it shall be no more delayed. For in your days, O rebellious house, will I speak the word, and I will perform it; the Lord Jehovah hath said it.

²⁶ And the word of Jehovah came to me, saying, Son of ²⁷ Adam, behold, they of the house of Israel say, 'The vision 'that he seeth is for distant days, and he prophesieth of the ²⁸ 'times that are far off.' Therefore say to them, Thus saith the Lord Jehovah; There shall none of my words be delayed any more, but the word which I shall speak shall be —done; the Lord Jehovah hath said it.

¹ AND THE WORD OF JEHOVAH came to me, saying, Son of ² Adam, prophesy AGAINST THE PROPHETS of Israel that prophesy, and say thou to them that prophesy out of their own ³ hearts, Hear ye the word of Jehovah; Thus saith the Lord Jehovah; Woe to the foolish prophets, that follow their ⁴ own spirit, and have seen nothing! O Israel, thy prophets ⁵ are like the foxes in desolate places. Ye did not go up into the breaches, neither did ye make up the wall for the house of Israel to stand in the battle in the day of ⁶ Jehovah. They have had false visions and lying divination, saying, 'Jehovah hath said it;' but Jehovah did not

send them. And they failed to confirm the word. Have ⁷ ye not seen a false vision, and spoken a lying divination, whereas ye say, 'Jehovah hath said it,' even when I have not spoken? Therefore thus saith the Lord Jehovah; Be- ⁸ cause ye have spoken falsely, and had lying visions, therefore, behold, I am against you; the Lord Jehovah hath said it. And my hand shall be upon the prophets that have false ⁹ visions, and lying divinations. They shall not be in the council of my people, neither shall they be written in the writing of the house of Israel, neither shall they enter into the land of Israel; and ye shall know that I am the Lord Jehovah. Because and whereas they have misled my ¹⁰ people, saying, 'Peace;' and there was no peace; and one buildeth up a wall, and lo, others daub it with mortar; say to them that daub it with mortar, that it shall fall, ¹¹ there will be an overflowing shower; and ye, O great hailstones, will fall; and a stormy wind will rend it. And lo, ¹² when the wall is fallen, shall it not be said to you, 'Where 'is the daubing wherewith ye have daubed it?' Therefore ¹³ thus saith the Lord Jehovah; I will even rend it with a stormy wind in my wrath; and there shall be an overflowing shower in mine anger, and great hailstones in my wrath to consume it. And I will break down the wall that ye ¹⁴ have daubed with mortar, and bring it down to the ground, so that its foundation shall be laid bare, and it shall fall, and ye yourselves shall be consumed in the midst thereof; and ye shall know that I am Jehovah. And thus will I ¹⁵ accomplish my wrath upon the wall, and upon them that have daubed it with mortar, and I will say to you, The wall is no more, and they that daubed it are no more; to ¹⁶ wit, the prophets of Israel who prophesy concerning Jerusalem, and who see visions of peace for her, when there is no peace; the Lord Jehovah hath said it.

Likewise, thou son of Adam, set thy face AGAINST THE ¹⁷ DAUGHTERS of thy people, who prophesy out of their own heart; and prophesy thou against them. And say, thus ¹⁸ saith the Lord Jehovah; Woe to the women that sew ruffles to all wrists, and make kerchiefs upon heads of every height to hunt souls! Ye hunt the souls of my people, and will ye save your own souls alive? And ye ¹⁹ pollute me among my people for handfuls of barley and for pieces of bread, to slay the souls that should not die, and

to save souls alive that should not live, by your lying
²⁰ to my people that hear your lies. Therefore thus saith the Lord Jehovah; Behold I am against your ruffles, wherewith ye there hunt the souls as they fly away, and I will tear them from your arms, and will let the souls go, even the
²¹ souls that ye hunt as they fly. Your kerchiefs also will I tear, and will deliver my people out of your hand, and then they shall be no more in your hand to be hunted;
²² and ye shall know that I am Jehovah. Because with lies ye have made the heart of the righteous sad, whom I have not made sad; and strengthened the hands of the wicked man, so that he should not turn from his wicked way, so
²³ as to save his life. Therefore ye shall have no more false visions, nor shall ye divine divinations; for I will deliver my people out of your hand; and ye shall know that I —am Jehovah.

¹ Then came certain of THE ELDERS OF ISRAEL to me, and
² sat down before me. And the word of Jehovah came to
³ me, saying, Son of Adam, these men have set up their filthy idols in their heart, and have put the stumbling-block of their iniquity before their face. Should I be inquired of at
⁴ all by them? Therefore speak to them, and say to them, Thus saith the Lord Jehovah; Every man of the house of Israel that setteth up his filthy idols in his heart, and placeth the stumbling-block of his iniquity before his face, and cometh to the prophet, I Jehovah will answer him that cometh according to the multitude of his filthy idols;
⁵ so that I may take the house of Israel through their own heart, because they are all estranged from me through their filthy idols.
⁶ Therefore say to the house of Israel, Thus saith the Lord Jehovah; Return, and turn away from your filthy idols;
⁷ and turn away your faces from all your abominations. For every one of the house of Israel, or of the strangers that sojourn in Israel, who separateth himself from me, and setteth up his filthy idols in his heart, and putteth the stumbling-block of his iniquity before his face, and cometh to a prophet to inquire of him concerning me, I Jehovah
⁸ will answer him of myself. And I will set my face against that man, and will make him a sign and a proverb, and I will cut him off from the midst of my people; and ye
⁹ shall know that I am Jehovah. And if the prophet be

deceived and should solemnly say that I Jehovah had deceived that prophet, then I will stretch out my hand upon him, and will destroy him from the midst of my people Israel. And they shall bear their iniquity; the iniquity of the prophet shall be even as the iniquity of him that inquireth of him; so that the house of Israel may go no more astray from me, neither be polluted any more with all their transgressions; but that they may be my people, and then I will be their God; the Lord Jehovah hath said it.

AND THE WORD OF JEHOVAH came to me, saying, Son of Adam, when the land sinneth against me by trespassing grievously, then will I stretch out my hand upon it, and will break the staff of its bread, and will send famine upon it, and will cut off man and beast from it; though these three men, Noah, Daniel, and Job, were in it, they should save only their own souls by their righteousness; the Lord Jehovah hath said it.

If I cause noisome beasts to pass through the land, and they spoil it, so that it be desolate, that no man pass through it because of the beasts; though these three men were in it, as I live, the Lord Jehovah hath said it, they should save neither sons nor daughters; they only should be saved, but the land should be desolate.

Or if I bring a sword upon that land, and say, 'Sword, 'go through the land;' so that I cut off man and beast from it; though these three men were in it, as I live, the Lord Jehovah hath said it, they should save neither sons nor daughters; but they themselves only should be saved.

Or if I send a pestilence into that land, and pour out my wrath upon it in blood, to cut off from it man and beast; though Noah, Daniel, and Job, were in it, as I live, the Lord Jehovah hath said it, they should save neither son nor daughter; they should save only their own souls by their righteousness.

For thus saith the Lord Jehovah; How much more when I send my four sore judgments upon Jerusalem, sword, and famine, and noisome beast, and pestilence, to cut off from it man and beast! Yet, behold, therein shall be left an escaped few that shall be brought forth, both sons and daughters. Behold, they shall come forth to you, and ye shall see their way and their doings; and ye shall be comforted

concerning the evil that I have brought upon Jerusalem,
²³ even concerning all that I have brought upon it. And
they shall comfort you, when ye see their ways and their
doings; and ye shall know that I have not done without
cause all that I have done in it; the Lord Jehovah hath
—said it.

¹ AND THE WORD of Jehovah came to me, saying, Son of
² Adam, What is the wood of the vine more than any tree of
³ branches, which is among the trees of the forest? Shall
wood be taken therefrom to do any work? Or will men take
⁴ a peg therefrom to hang any vessel thereon? Behold, it is
cast into the fire for fuel. The fire devoureth both the ends
of it, and the midst of it is burned. Is it meet for any
⁵ work? Behold, when it was whole, it was used for no
work. How much less shall it be used for work, when the
⁶ fire hath devoured it, and it is burned. Therefore thus
saith the Lord Jehovah; As the wood of the vine among
the trees of the forest, which I have given up to the fire for
⁷ fuel, so have I given up the inhabitants of Jerusalem. And
I have set my face against them; they shall go out from one
fire, and another fire shall devour them; and ye shall know
that I am Jehovah, when I set my face against them.
⁸ And I have made the land desolate, because they have
—committed a trespass; the Lord Jehovah hath said it.

¹ AND THE WORD OF JEHOVAH came to me, saying, Son of
² Adam, cause JERUSALEM to know her abominations, and
³ say, Thus saith the Lord Jehovah unto Jerusalem; Thy
bringing forth and thy birth was of the land of Canaan;
⁴ thy father was an Amorite, and thy mother a Hittite. And
as for thy birth, in the day thou wast born thy navel-string
was not cut, neither wast thou washed in water for cleans-
⁵ ing; thou wast not salted at all, nor swaddled at all. No
eye pitied thee, to do any of these to thee, to have compassion on thee; but thou wast cast out in the open field,
in the loathing of thy person, in the day that thou wast
⁶ born. And when I passed by thee, and saw thee trampled
on in thine own blood, I said to thee when thou wast in
thy blood, 'Live;' yea, I said to thee when thou wast in thy
⁷ blood, 'Live.' I caused thee to grow bigger as the herb of
the field, and thou didst grow bigger and wax great, and
thou camest to be an ornament of ornaments. Thy breasts
were fashioned, and thy hair grew, but thou wast naked

and bare. And when I passed by thee, and saw thee, behold, thy time was the time of love. And I spread my skirt over thee, and covered thy nakedness. Yea, I sware unto thee, and entered into a covenant with thee, the Lord Jehovah hath said it, and thou becamest mine. Then washed I thee with water; yea, I thoroughly washed away thy blood from thee, and I anointed thee with oil. I clothed thee also with embroidered work, and shod thee with seal's skin, and I girded thee about with fine linen, and I covered thee with silk. I decked thee also with ornaments, and I put bracelets upon thy hands, and a chain on thy neck. And I put a ring on thy nose, and earrings in thine ears, and a beautiful crown upon thy head. Thus wast thou decked with gold and silver; and thy raiment was of fine linen, and silk, and embroidered work; thou didst eat fine flour, and honey, and oil; and thou wast exceeding beautiful, and thou didst prosper into a kingdom. And thy name went forth among the Nations for thy beauty; for it was made perfect through my ornaments, which I had put upon thee; the Lord Jehovah hath said it.

But thou didst trust in thine own beauty, and playedst the harlot because of thy name, and pouredst out thy fornications on every one that passed by; it was his. And thou didst take some of thy garments, and didst make for thyself High Places [or altars] with divers colours, and playedst the harlot thereupon. The like never did come, neither shall it be so. Thou hast also taken thy fair jewels of my gold and of my silver, which I had given thee, and madest to thyself male images, and didst commit fornication with them, and tookest thy embroidered garments, and clothedst them. And thou hast set mine oil and mine incense before them. My bread also which I gave thee, fine flour, and oil, and honey, wherewith I fed thee, thou hast even set it before them for a sweet savour. And thus it was; the Lord Jehovah hath said it. Moreover thou hast taken thy sons and thy daughters, whom thou hast borne unto me, and these hast thou sacrificed to them to be devoured. Is this of thy fornications a small matter, that thou hast slain my children, and given them up to cause them to pass through [the fire] for them? And in all thine abominations and thy fornications thou hast not remembered the days of thy youth, when thou wast naked and

23 bare, and wast trampled upon in thy blood. And it came pass after all thy wickedness, (Woe, woe unto thee! the
24 Lord Jehovah hath said it,) that thou hast also built unto thee a den, and hast made thee a raised place in every
25 street. Thou hast built thy raised place at every head of the way, and hast made thy beauty to be abhorred, and hast opened thy feet to every one that passed by, and
26 multiplied thy fornications. Thou didst also commit fornication with the sons of Egypt, thy neighbours, great of flesh; and didst increase thy fornications, to provoke me to anger.
27 Behold, therefore I stretched out my hand over thee, and diminished thine allowance, and delivered thee to the will of them that hate thee, the daughters of the Philis-
28 tines, who were ashamed of thy lewd way. Thou didst also play the harlot with the sons of Assyria, because thou wast not satisfied; yea, thou didst play the harlot with
29 them, and yet couldest not be satisfied. Thou didst moreover multiply thy fornication in the land of Canaan unto
30 Chaldea; and yet thou wast not satisfied herewith. How weak is thy heart, the Lord Jehovah hath said it, seeing thou doest all these things, the work of an imperious har-
31 lot; in that thou buildest thy den in the head of every way, and makest thy raised place in every street. And yet thou hast not been as an harlot; in that thou scornest
32 hire; but as a wife that committeth adultery, who taketh
33 strangers instead of her husband. Men give gifts to all harlots; but thou givest thy gifts to all thy lovers, and thou hirest them, that they may come to thee on every
34 side for thy fornication. And the contrary is in thee from other women in thy fornications, whereas none followeth thee to commit fornication; and in that thou givest hire, and no hire is given to thee, therefore thou art contrary.
35 Therefore, O harlot, hear the word of Jehovah. Thus
36 saith the Lord Jehovah; Because thy copper money hath been poured out, and thy nakedness discovered in thy fornications with thy lovers, and with all the filthy idols of thy abominations, and by the blood of thy children, which
37 thou didst give to them; behold, therefore I will gather in all thy lovers, with whom thou hast taken pleasure, and all them that thou hast loved, with all them that thou hast hated; I will even gather them round about

against thee, and will uncover thy nakedness to them, that they may see all thy nakedness. And I will judge thee, ³⁸ as women that break wedlock and shed blood are judged; and I will give to thee the blood of wrath and jealousy. And I will also give thee into their hand, and they shall ³⁹ throw down thy den, and shall break down thy raised places; they shall strip thee also of thy clothes, and shall take thy fair jewels, and leave thee naked and bare. They ⁴⁰ shall also bring up an assembly [of witnesses] against thee, and they shall stone thee with stones, and thrust thee through with their swords. And they shall burn thy ⁴¹ houses with fire, and execute judgments upon thee in the sight of many women; and I will cause thee to cease from playing the harlot, and thou also shalt give no hire any more. So will I make my wrath toward thee to rest, and ⁴² my jealousy shall depart from thee, and I will be quiet, and will be angry no more.

Because thou hast not remembered the days of thy ⁴³ youth, but hast fretted me in all these things; behold, therefore I also will recompense thy way upon thy head, the Lord Jehovah hath said it; and thou shalt not commit this lewdness above all thine abominations. Behold, ⁴⁴ every one that useth proverbs shall use this proverb against thee, saying, 'As was the mother, so is her daughter.' Thou ⁴⁵ art thy mother's daughter, that loathed her husband and her children; and thou art the sister of thy sisters, who loathed their husbands and their children. Your mother was a Hittite, and your father an Amorite. And thine ⁴⁶ elder sister is Samaria, she and her daughters that dwell at thy left hand [or northward]; and thy younger sister, that dwelleth at thy right hand, is Sodom and her daughters. Yet hast thou not walked after their ways, nor done ⁴⁷ after their abominations. This was disdained as a very little thing, and thou wast corrupted more than they in all thy ways.

As I live, the Lord Jehovah hath said it, Sodom thy ⁴⁸ sister hath not done, she nor her daughters, as thou hast done, thou and thy daughters. Behold, this was the iniquity ⁴⁹ of thy sister Sodom; pride, fulness of bread, and slothful idleness was in her and in her daughters, neither did she strengthen the hand of the poor and needy. And ⁵⁰ they were haughty, and committed abomination before

⁵¹ me. Therefore I took them away when I saw it. Neither hath Samaria committed half of thy sins; but thou hast multiplied thine abominations more than they, and hast justified thy sisters by all thine abominations which thou ⁵² hast done. Bear thou also thine own shame, who hast taken the blame off thy sisters, by thy sins that thou hast done more abominable than they. They are more righteous than thou. Yea, be thou confounded also, and bear thou thine own shame, in that thou hast justified thy sisters. ⁵³ When I shall bring home their captivity, the captivity of Sodom and her daughters, and the captivity of Samaria and her daughters, then will I bring home thy captivity ⁵⁴ in the midst of them; so that thou mayest bear thine own shame, and mayest be ashamed of all that thou hast done, ⁵⁵ in that thou art a comfort unto them. When thy sisters, Sodom and her daughters, shall return to their former estate, and Samaria and her daughters shall return to their former estate, then thou and thy daughters shall return to ⁵⁶ your former estate. Should not thy sister Sodom have been ⁵⁷ a warning in thy mouth in the day of thy pride, before thy wickedness was laid bare, as at the time of the reproach of the daughters of Syria, and all that are round about her, the daughters of the Philistines, who despise thee ⁵⁸ round about? Thou hast borne thy lewdness and thine abominations; Jehovah hath said it.
⁵⁹ For thus saith the Lord Jehovah; I have even done with thee as thou hast done, who hast despised the oath in ⁶⁰ breaking the covenant. Nevertheless I remember my covenant with thee in the days of thy youth, and I will estab- ⁶¹ lish unto thee an everlasting covenant. Then thou shalt remember thy ways, and be ashamed, when thou shalt receive thy sisters, thine elder with thy younger; and I will give them to thee for daughters, but not by thy cove- ⁶² nant. And I will establish my covenant with thee; and ⁶³ thou shalt know that I am Jehovah; so that thou mayest remember, and be confounded, and never open thy mouth any more because of thy shame, when I am pacified toward thee for all that thou hast done; the Lord Jehovah —hath said it.

¹ AND THE WORD OF JEHOVAH came to me, saying, Son ² of Adam, put forth A RIDDLE, and speak a parable to the ³ house of Israel; and say, Thus saith the Lord Jehovah;

A great eagle with great wings, long-winged, full of feathers, which had divers colours, came to Lebanon, and took the highest branch of the cedar. He cropped off the top of its young twigs, and carried it into a land of traffic; he set it in a city of merchants. He took also some of the seed of the land, and sowed it in a field; he placed it by great waters, and set it as a willow tree. And it branched forth, and became a spreading vine of low stature, whose twigs turned toward him, and its roots were under him. So it became a vine, and brought forth branches, and shot forth sprigs. There was also another great eagle with great wings and many feathers. And behold, this vine did bend its roots in thirst toward him, and shot forth its twigs toward him, that he might water it through the furrows of its plantation. It was planted in a good soil by great waters, that it might bring forth branches, and that it might bear fruit, that it might be a goodly vine. Say thou, Thus saith the Lord Jehovah; Shall it prosper? Shall he not pull up its roots, and cut off its fruit, that it may wither? It shall wither in all the leaves of its branches, even without a great arm or many people to pluck it up by its roots. Yea, behold, when it is planted, shall it prosper? Shall it not utterly wither, when the east wind toucheth it? It shall wither in the furrows where it grew.

Moreover the word of Jehovah came to me, saying, Say now to the rebellious house, Know ye not what these things mean? Behold, the king of Babylon [Nebuchadnezzar] is come to Jerusalem, and hath taken its king [Jehoiachin], and its princes, and led them with him to Babylon; and hath taken one of the king's seed [Zedekiah], and made a covenant with him, and hath brought him under an oath. He hath also taken the mighty of the land; that the kingdom might be low, that it might not lift itself up, but that it might keep his covenant and might stand. But he rebelled against him in sending his messengers into Egypt, that they might give him horses and much people. Shall he prosper? Shall he escape that doeth such things? And shall he break the covenant, and escape? As I live, the Lord Jehovah hath said it, surely in the place belonging to the king that made him king, whose oath he despised, and whose covenant he brake, even with him in the midst of Babylon he shall die. Neither shall Pharaoh [Hophra] with his mighty army and great company help him in the war, by casting up a siege-mound, and building a line of forts, ¹⁸ so as to cut off many persons; since he despised the oath by breaking the covenant, when, lo, he had given his hand [in promise], and hath done all these things, he shall not ¹⁹ escape. Therefore thus saith the Lord Jehovah; As I live, surely mine oath that he [Zedekiah] hath despised, and my covenant that he hath broken, even it will I ²⁰ recompense upon his own head. And I will spread my net on him, and he shall be taken in my snare, and I will bring him to Babylon, and will have judgment against him there for his trespass that he hath trespassed against me. ²¹ And all his fugitives in all his troops shall fall by the sword, and they that remain shall be scattered toward all winds; and ye shall know that I Jehovah have spoken it. ²² Thus saith the Lord Jehovah; I will also take part of the highest branch of the high cedar, and will set it; I will crop off from the top of its young twigs a tender one, ²³ and will plant it on a mountain high and built up; on the mountain of the height of Israel will I plant it. And it shall bring forth boughs, and bear fruit, and be a goodly cedar. And under it shall dwell all fowl of every wing; ²⁴ in the shadow of its branches shall they dwell. And all the trees of the field shall know that I Jehovah have brought down the high tree, I have exalted the low tree, I have dried up the green tree, and I have made the dry —tree to flourish. I Jehovah have spoken and have done it.

¹ AND THE WORD OF JEHOVAH came to me, saying, What ² mean ye, that ye use THIS PROVERB concerning the land of Israel, saying, 'The fathers have eaten sour grapes, and the ³ 'children's teeth are set on edge'? As I live, the Lord Jehovah hath said it, ye shall not have any more to use ⁴ this proverb in Israel. Behold, all souls are mine; as the soul of the father, so also the soul of the son is mine; the soul that sinneth, it shall die.

⁵ But if a man be righteous, and do that which is lawful ⁶ and right, and hath not eaten upon the mountains, neither hath lifted up his eyes to the filthy idols of the house of Israel, neither hath defiled his neighbour's wife, neither ⁷ hath come near to a woman during her impurity, and hath not oppressed any, but hath restored to the debtor his pledge, hath spoiled none by violence, hath given his

bread to the hungry, and hath covered the naked with a garment; he that hath not lent upon usury, neither hath taken any increase, that hath withdrawn his hand from dishonesty, hath executed true judgment between man and man, hath walked in my statutes, and hath kept my judgments, to deal truly; he is righteous, he shall surely live; the Lord Jehovah hath said it.

If a man that is a housebreaker, a shedder of blood, and that doeth to his brother any one of these things, beget a son; and that [son] doeth not any of these things; yet if he hath eaten upon the mountains, and defiled his neighbour's wife, hath oppressed the poor and needy, hath plundered by violence, hath not restored the pledge, and hath lifted up his eyes to the filthy idols, hath committed abomination, hath lent upon usury, and hath taken increase; shall he then live? He shall not live. He hath done all these abominations; he shall surely die. His blood shall be upon him.

Now, lo, if he beget a son, that seeth all his father's sins which he hath done, and considereth, and doeth not such like, that hath not eaten upon the mountains, neither hath lifted up his eyes to the filthy idols of the house of Israel, hath not defiled his neighbour's wife, neither hath oppressed any, hath not taken a pledge, neither hath spoiled by violence, but hath given his bread to the hungry, and hath covered the naked with a garment, that hath taken off his hand from the poor, that hath not received usury nor increase, hath executed my judgments, hath walked in my statutes; he shall not die for the iniquity of his father, he shall surely live. As for his father, because he cruelly oppressed, spoiled his brother by violence, and did what is not good among his people, lo, even he shall die in his iniquity.

Yet say ye, 'Why? Doth not the son bear the iniquity 'of the father?' When the son hath done what is lawful and right, and hath kept all my statutes, and hath done them, he shall surely live. The soul that sinneth, it shall die. The son shall not bear the iniquity of the father, neither shall the father bear the iniquity of the son. The righteousness of the righteous shall be upon him, and the wickedness of the wicked shall be upon him.

But if the wicked will turn from all his sins that he hath

committed, and keep all my statutes, and do what is lawful
²² and right, he shall surely live, he shall not die. All his
transgressions that he hath committed, they shall not be
remembered against him; in his righteousness that he hath
²³ done he shall live. Have I any pleasure at all that the
wicked should die? the Lord Jehovah hath said it; and
not that he should return from his ways, and live?
²⁴ But when the righteous turneth away from his righteousness, and committeth iniquity, and doeth according to all
the abominations that the wicked man doeth, shall he live?
All his righteousness that he hath done shall not be remembered; in his trespass that he hath trespassed, and in
his sin that he hath sinned, in them shall he die.
²⁵ Yet ye say, 'The way of the Lord is not equal.' Hear
now, O house of Israel; Is not my way equal? Are not
²⁶ your ways unequal? When a righteous man turneth away
from his righteousness, and committeth iniquity, and
dieth because of those things; for his iniquity that he
²⁷ hath done he dieth. Again, when the wicked man turneth
away from his wickedness that he hath committed, and
doeth what is lawful and right, he shall save his soul alive.
²⁸ Because he considereth, and turneth away from all his
transgressions that he hath committed, he shall surely live,
²⁹ he shall not die. Yet saith the house of Israel, 'The way
'of the Lord is not equal.' O house of Israel, are not my
³⁰ ways equal? Are not your ways unequal? Therefore I
will judge you, O house of Israel, every one according to
his ways, the Lord Jehovah hath said it.
Repent, and turn away from all your transgressions;
³¹ so iniquity shall not be a stumbling-block to you. Cast
away from you all your transgressions, whereby ye have
transgressed; and make for you a new heart and a new
³² spirit; for why will ye die, O house of Israel? For I have
no pleasure in the death of him that dieth, the Lord Jehovah hath said it; therefore turn yourselves, and live ye.
¹ MOREOVER take thou up a lamentation for the PRINCES
² OF ISRAEL, and say, What is thy mother? She lay down a
lioness among lions, she nourished her whelps among young
³ lions. And she brought up one of her whelps [Jehoahaz];
it became a young lion, and it learned to tear in pieces the
⁴ prey; it devoured men. The nations also heard of him;
he was taken in their pit, and they brought him with chains

to the land of Egypt. Now when she saw that after she had waited her hope was lost, then she took another of her whelps [Jehoachin], and made him a young lion. And he went up and down among the lions, he became a young lion, and learned to tear in pieces the prey, and he devoured men. And he knew their desolations, and he laid waste their cities; and the land was desolate, and its fulness, by the noise of his roaring. Then the nations set against him on every side from the provinces, and spread their net over him; he was taken in their pit; and they put him in a cage with chains, and brought him to the king of Babylon [Nebuchadnezzar]. They brought him into strongholds, so that his voice should no more be heard upon the mountains of Israel.

Thy mother was like a vine in thy likeness, planted by the waters; she was fruitful and branching by reason of many waters. And she had strong rods for the sceptres of the rulers, and her stature was exalted among the thick branches, and she was seen in her height by the multitude of her branches. But she was plucked up in wrath, she was cast down to the ground, and the east wind dried up her fruit; her strong rods were broken and withered; the fire consumed them. And now she is planted in the desert, in a dry and thirsty ground. And fire is gone out of a rod of her branches, it hath devoured her fruit, so that she hath no strong rod to be a sceptre to rule.

This is a lamentation, and shall be for a lamentation. —

AND IT CAME TO PASS in the seventh year [B.C. 594], in the fifth month, on the tenth day of the month, that certain of the elders of Israel came to inquire of Jehovah, and they sat before me. Then came the word of Jehovah to me, saying, Son of Adam, speak to THE ELDERS OF ISRAEL, and say to them, Thus saith the Lord Jehovah; Are ye come to inquire of me? As I live, the Lord Jehovah hath said it, I will not be inquired of by you. Wilt thou plead for them, son of Adam, wilt thou plead? Cause them to know the abominations of their fathers. And say to them, Thus saith the Lord Jehovah; In the day when I chose Israel, and lifted up my hand [in oath] unto the seed of the house of Jacob, and made myself known to them in the land of Egypt, when I lifted up my hand to them, saying, 'I am Jehovah your God;' in the day that I lifted up my hand [in oath] unto them, that I would bring them forth out of the land of Egypt into a land which I had spied out for them, flowing with milk and honey, which ⁷ is the beauty of all lands; then said I to them, 'Cast ye 'away every man the abominations of his eyes, and defile 'not yourselves with the filthy idols of Egypt; I am Je- ⁸ 'hovah your God.' But they rebelled against me, and would not hearken unto me. They did not every man cast away the abominations of their eyes, neither did they forsake the filthy idols of Egypt. Then I said I would pour out my wrath upon them, to accomplish my anger ⁹ against them in the midst of the land of Egypt. But I wrought for my name's sake, that it should not be polluted in the eyes of the nations, among whom they were, in whose sight I made myself known to them, in bringing them forth ¹⁰ out of the land of Egypt. And I caused them to go forth out of the land of Egypt, and brought them into the de- ¹¹ sert. And I gave them my statutes, and shewed them my judgments, which if a man do, he shall even live in them. ¹² Moreover also I gave them my sabbaths, to be a sign be- tween me and them, that they might know that I am Je- hovah that sanctify them.

¹³ But the house of Israel rebelled against me in the desert. They walked not in my statutes, and they despised my judgments, which if a man do, he shall even live in them; and my sabbaths they greatly polluted. Then I said, I would pour out my wrath upon them in the desert, to con- ¹⁴ sume them. But I wrought for my name's sake, that it should not be polluted in the eyes of the nations, in whose sight I brought them out.

¹⁵ Yet also I lifted up my hand [in oath] to them in the desert, that I would not bring them into the land which I had given them, flowing with milk and honey, which is ¹⁶ the beauty of all lands; because they despised my judg- ments, and walked not in my statutes, but polluted my sabbaths; for their heart went after their filthy idols. ¹⁷ Nevertheless mine eye spared them from destroying them, ¹⁸ neither did I make an end of them in the desert. But I said to their children in the desert, 'Walk ye not in the 'statutes of your fathers, neither keep their judgments, ¹⁹ 'nor defile yourselves with their filthy idols. I am Jehovah 'your God; walk in my statutes, and keep my judgments,

'and do them; and keep holy my sabbaths; and they ²⁰ 'shall be a sign between me and you, that ye may know that 'I am Jehovah your God.' Notwithstanding the children ²¹ rebelled against me. They walked not in my statutes, neither kept my judgments to do them, which if a man do, he shall even live in them; they polluted my sabbaths. Then I said, I would pour out my wrath upon them, to accomplish my anger against them in the desert. Never- ²² theless I withdrew my hand, and wrought for my name's sake, that it should not be polluted in the eyes of the nations, in whose sight I brought them forth.

I also lifted up my hand [in oath] to them in the desert, ²³ that I would scatter them among the nations, and disperse them through the countries; because they had not exe- ²⁴ cuted my judgments, but had despised my statutes, and had polluted my sabbaths, and their eyes were after their fathers' filthy idols. Therefore I gave them also statutes ²⁵ that were not good, and judgments whereby they should not live; and I polluted them in their own gifts, in that ²⁶ they caused to pass through [the fire] all that openeth the womb, so that I might make them desolate, to the end that they might know that I am Jehovah.

Therefore, son of Adam, speak to the house of Israel, ²⁷ and say to them, Thus saith the Lord Jehovah; Yet in this your fathers have blasphemed me, in that they have committed a trespass against me. For when I had brought ²⁸ them into the land, for which I lifted up my hand [in oath] that I would give it to them, then they saw every high hill, and all the thick trees, and they sacrificed there their sacrifices, and there they presented the provocation of their gifts. There also they made their sweet savour, and poured out there their drink offerings. Then I said to them, ²⁹ 'What is the High Place [or Altar] whereunto ye go?' And the name thereof is called Bamah [or High Place] unto this day.

Therefore say to the house of Israel, Thus saith the Lord ³⁰ Jehovah; Are ye polluted after the manner of your fathers? and do ye go astray after their abominations? For when ye ³¹ bring your gifts, when ye make your sons to pass through the fire, ye pollute yourselves with all your filthy idols, even unto this day. And shall I be inquired of by you, O house of Israel? As I live, the Lord Jehovah hath said

³² it, I will not be inquired of by you. And that which cometh into your mind shall by no means come to pass, when ye say, 'We will be as the nations, as the families of the coun- 'tries, to serve wood and stone.'

³³ As I live, the Lord Jehovah hath said it, surely with a mighty hand, and with a stretched-out arm, and with wrath ³⁴ poured out, will I rule over you. And I will bring you out from the peoples, and will gather you in from the countries wherein ye are scattered, with a mighty hand, and ³⁵ with a stretched-out arm, and with wrath poured out. And I will bring you into the desert of the peoples, and there ³⁶ will I plead with you face to face. Like as I pleaded with your fathers in the desert of the land of Egypt, so will I ³⁷ plead with you; the Lord Jehovah hath said it. And I will cause you to pass under the rod, and I will bring ³⁸ you into the bond of the covenant. And I will purge out from among you the rebels, and them that transgress against me. I will bring them forth out of the country of their pilgrimage, and they shall not enter into the land of Israel; ³⁹ and ye shall know that I am Jehovah. As for you, O house of Israel, thus saith the Lord Jehovah; Go ye, serve ye every one his filthy idols, and hereafter also, if ye will not hearken unto me; but pollute ye my holy name no more ⁴⁰ with your gifts, and with your filthy idols. For on my holy mountain, on the mountain of the height of Israel, the Lord Jehovah hath said it, there shall all the house of Israel, all of them in the land, serve me; there will I accept them, and there will I require your heave offerings, and the best ⁴¹ of your gifts, with all your holy things. I will accept you with your sweet savour, when I bring you out from the peoples, and gather you out of the countries wherein ye have been scattered; and I will be sanctified in you in the ⁴² eyes of the Nations. And ye shall know that I am Jehovah, when I shall bring you into the land of Israel, into the country for which I lifted up my hand [in oath] to ⁴³ give it to your fathers. And there shall ye remember your ways, and all your doings, wherein ye have been defiled; and ye shall loathe yourselves in your own sight for all your ⁴⁴ evils that ye have committed. And ye shall know that I am Jehovah, when I have wrought with you for my name's sake, not according to your wicked ways, nor according to your corrupt doings, O ye house of Israel; the Lord Jehovah hath said it.

Moreover the word of Jehovah came to me, saying, Son ⁴⁵ of Adam, set thy face toward the right hand, and speak ⁴⁶ toward the south, and prophesy against the forest of the SOUTH COUNTRY [of Judea]; and say to the forest of the ⁴⁷ South Country, Hear the word of Jehovah; Thus saith the Lord Jehovah; Behold, I will kindle a fire in thee, and it shall devour every green tree in thee, and every dry tree. The flame of the lightning shall not be quenched, and all faces from the south to the north shall be scorched thereby. And all flesh shall see that I Jehovah have kindled it. It ⁴⁸ shall not be quenched. Then said I, 'Ah Lord Jehovah! ⁴⁹ 'they say of me, Doth he not speak parables?'

And the word of Jehovah came to me, saying, Son of ¹ Adam, set thy face toward Jerusalem, and speak toward ² the holy places, and prophesy AGAINST THE LAND OF ISRAEL, and say to the land of Israel, Thus saith Jehovah; Behold, ³ I am against thee, and will draw forth my sword out of its sheath, and will cut off from thee the righteous and the wicked. Seeing then that I will cut off from thee the ⁴ righteous and the wicked, therefore shall my sword go forth out of its sheath against all flesh from the south to the north; that all flesh may know that I Jehovah have drawn ⁵ forth my sword out of its sheath; it shall not return any more. Sigh therefore, thou son of Adam, with the breaking ⁶ of thy loins; and with bitterness sigh before their eyes. And it shall be, when they say to thee, 'Wherefore sighest ⁷ 'thou?' that thou shalt say, 'For the tidings; because it 'cometh.' And every heart shall melt, and all hands shall be feeble, and every spirit shall faint, and all knees shall be weak as water. Behold, it cometh, and it shall be brought to pass; the Lord Jehovah hath said it.

And the word of Jehovah came to me, saying, Son of ⁸ Adam, prophesy, and say, Thus saith Jehovah; Say, A ⁹ SWORD, A SWORD is sharpened, and is also polished. It is ¹⁰ sharpened to make a sore slaughter; it is polished that there may be a glitter on it. Should we then make mirth? The rod of my son despiseth every other wood. And he ¹¹ hath given it to be polished, that it may be held in the hand. This sword is sharpened, and it is polished, to give it into the hand of the slayer. Cry and howl, thou son ¹² of Adam; for it shall be upon my people, it shall be upon all the princes of Israel. Terrors by reason of the sword

shall be upon my people. Smite therefore upon thy thigh.
13 Because it is a trial; and what if even the rod which despiseth shall be no more? the Lord Jehovah hath said it.
14 Thou therefore, son of Adam, prophesy, and smite thy hands together, and let the sword be brought again the third time. It is the sword of the slain, the sword of the
15 great slaughter, which besetteth them. I have set the destruction of the sword against all their city gates, so that their heart may faint, and their stumbling-blocks be multiplied. Alas! it is made to glitter, it is sharpened
16 for the slaughter. Form close ranks, turn to the right, set yourselves straight, turn to the left, whithersoever thy face
17 is set. Then I will smite my hands together, and I will cause my wrath to rest; I Jehovah have spoken.
18 And the word of Jehovah came to me, saying, Also, thou
19 son of Adam, mark out to thee TWO WAYS, by which the sword of the king of Babylon [Nebuchadnezzar] may come. Both twain shall come forth out of one land. And set thou up a finger-post, set it up at the head of the way to
20 the city. Mark out the way, that the sword may come to Rabbah of the Children of Ammon, or to Judah in Jeru-
21 salem the fortified. For the king of Babylon stood at the parting of the way, at the head of the two ways, to use divination. He made his arrows shake together, he consulted with Teraphs [or images], he looked into the liver.
22 At his right hand was the divination for Jerusalem, to place battering-rams, to open the mouth with the war-cry, to lift up the voice with shouting, to place battering-rams against the city gates, to cast a siege-mound, and to build a
23 line of forts. And it shall be to them a divination false in their sight, as when they swore oaths to them. And He will call to remembrance the iniquity, that they may be
24 taken captives. Therefore thus saith the Lord Jehovah; Because ye have made your iniquity to be remembered, in that your transgressions are uncovered, so that in all your doings your sins do appear,—because that ye are come to remembrance, ye shall be taken captive by the hand.
25 And as for thee, thou profane wicked prince of Israel [Zedekiah], whose day is come, when iniquity shall have
26 an end, thus saith the Lord Jehovah; Remove the diadem, and take off the crown; this is not he. Exalt him
27 that is low, and abase him that is high. A ruin, a ruin,

a ruin will I make it; and it shall be no more, until he come whose right it is; and I will give it to him.

And thou, son of Adam, prophesy and say, Thus saith [28] the Lord Jehovah concerning the Children of Ammon, and concerning their reproach; even say thou, The sword, the sword is drawn for the slaughter; it is polished to endure so that it may glitter; while they see false visions about [29] thee, while they divine a lie about thee, to bring thee upon the necks of them that are slain, of the wicked, whose day is come, when their iniquity shall have an end. Shall I cause it to return into its sheath? I will judge [30] thee in the place where thou wast created, in the land of thy nativity. And I will pour out mine indignation upon [31] thee, I will blow against thee in the fire of my wrath, and deliver thee into the hand of men who burn and are skilful to destroy. Thou shalt be for fuel to the fire; thy blood [32] shall be in the midst of the land; thou shalt be no more remembered; for I Jehovah have spoken.

And the word of Jehovah came to me, saying, Now, thou [1] son of Adam, wilt thou plead, wilt thou plead for THE CITY [2] OF BLOODSHED? or wilt thou shew her all her abominations? Then say thou, Thus saith the Lord Jehovah; The [3] city sheddeth blood in the midst of her, that her time may come, and she maketh filthy idols for herself to defile herself. Thou art become guilty by thy blood that thou hast [4] shed; and thou hast defiled thyself by thy filthy idols which thou hast made; and thou hast caused thy days to draw near, and art come even unto thy years. Therefore have I made thee a reproach unto the Nations, and a mocking to all countries. Those near, and those far from thee, [5] shall mock thee. Thou art defiled in name and much disturbed. Behold, the princes of Israel, every one was in [6] thee with his arm, to shed blood. In thee men have neg- [7] lected father and mother; in the midst of thee have they dealt by oppression with the stranger; in thee have they vexed the fatherless and the widow. Thou hast despised [8] my holy things, and hast profaned my sabbaths. In thee [9] men are tale-bearers in order to shed blood; and in thee they eat upon the mountains; in the midst of thee they commit lewdness. In thee have they uncovered their [10] fathers' nakedness; in thee have they humbled her that was set apart in her impurity. And one hath committed [11] abomination with his neighbour's wife; and another hath lewdly defiled his daughter in law; and another in thee ¹² hath humbled his sister, his father's daughter. In thee have they taken bribes to shed blood; thou hast taken usury and increase, and thou hast plundered thy neighbours by extortion; and me thou hast forgotten; the Lord Jehovah hath said it.

¹³ Behold, therefore I have clapped my hands at thy dishonest gain which thou hast made, and at thy blood which ¹⁴ hath been in the midst of thee. Can thy heart endure, or can thy hands be strong, in the days when I shall deal with thee? I Jehovah have spoken it, and I will do it. ¹⁵ And I will scatter thee among the Nations, and disperse thee in the countries, and will consume thy filthiness out ¹⁶ of thee. And thou shalt be defiled in thyself in the sight of the Nations, and thou shalt know that I am Jehovah.

¹⁷ AND THE WORD OF JEHOVAH came to me, saying, Son ¹⁸ of Adam, the house of Israel is become dross to me. All they are copper, and mixed metal, and iron, and lead, in the midst of the furnace; they are even the dross of silver. ¹⁹ Therefore thus saith the Lord Jehovah; Because ye are all become dross, behold, therefore I will gather you into ²⁰ the midst of Jerusalem; as a gathering of silver, and copper, and iron, and lead, and mixed metal, into the midst of the furnace, to blow the fire upon it, to melt it, so will I gather you in mine anger and in my wrath, and I will ²¹ leave you there, and melt you. Yea, I will heap you together, and blow upon you in the fire of my wrath, and ²² ye shall be melted in the midst thereof. As silver is melted in the midst of the furnace, so shall ye be melted in the midst thereof; and ye shall know that I Jehovah have poured out my wrath upon you.

²³ AND THE WORD OF JEHOVAH came to me, saying, Son ²⁴ of Adam, say to her, Thou art a land that is not cleansed; she shall not be rained upon in the day of indignation. ²⁵ There is a conspiracy of her prophets in the midst of her, like a roaring lion tearing in pieces the prey. They have devoured souls; they have taken the treasure and the precious things; they have made her widows many in the ²⁶ midst of her. Her priests have done violence to my Law, and they profane my holy things. They have put no separation between the holy and unholy, neither have they

shewed difference between the unclean and the clean, and have hidden their eyes from my sabbaths, and I am profaned among them. Her princes in the midst of her are 27 like wolves tearing in pieces the prey, to shed blood, and to destroy souls, in order to get dishonest gain. And her 28 prophets have daubed themselves with mortar, seeing false visions, and divining lies to them, saying, 'Thus saith the 'Lord Jehovah,' when Jehovah hath not spoken. The 29 people of the land have used oppression, and exercised robbery, and have vexed the poor and needy; yea, they have oppressed the stranger wrongfully. And I am in 30 search for a man among them, that should make up the hedge, and stand in the gap before me on behalf of the land, that I should not destroy it; but I have found none. Therefore will I pour out mine indignation on them; I 31 will consume them with the fire of my wrath. Their own way will I recompense upon their heads; the Lord Jehovah hath said it. —

And the word of Jehovah came to me, saying, Son of 1 Adam, there were TWO WOMEN, the daughters of one 2 mother. And they committed fornication in Egypt; they 3 committed fornication in their youth. There were their breasts pressed, and there men handled the teats of their virginity. And the names of them were Aholah [or Her own 4 Tent] the elder, and Aholibah [or My Tent is in her] her sister. And they were mine, and they bare sons and daughters. Thus were their names; Samaria is Aholah, and Jerusalem Aholibah. And Aholah played the harlot when 5 she was mine; and she doted on her lovers, on the Assyrians her neighbours, who were clothed with blue, Pashas 6 [or governors] and rulers, all of them desirable young men, horsemen riding upon horses. Thus she bestowed her 7 fornications on them, all them that were the chosen sons of Assyria; and with all on whom she doted, with all their filthy idols she defiled herself. Neither left she her 8 fornications brought from Egypt; for in her youth they had lain with her, and they had handled the breasts of her virginity, and poured their fornication on her. Therefore I delivered her into the hand of her lovers, into the 9 hand of the sons of Assyria, on whom she doted. These 10 uncovered her nakedness. They took her sons and her daughters, and slew her with the sword. And she became famous among women; for they had executed judgment on her.

¹¹ And when her sister Aholibah saw this, she was more corrupt in her inordinate love than she, and in her forni- ¹² cations more than her sister in her fornications. She doted upon the sons of Assyria her neighbours, Pashas and rulers clothed most gorgeously, horsemen riding upon horses, all ¹³ of them desirable young men. Then I saw that she also ¹⁴ was defiled. Both women took one way, and she increased her fornications. For when she saw men portrayed upon the wall, the images of the Chaldeans portrayed with ¹⁵ vermilion, girded with girdles upon their loins, overflowing with dyed attire upon their heads, all of them Chiefs-of-three [or chariot warriors] to look at, after the manner of the Chaldeans, the sons of Babylon the land of their ¹⁶ birth; and as soon as she saw them with her eyes, she doted upon them, and sent messengers to them into Chaldea. ¹⁷ And the sons of Babylon came to her into the bed of love, and they defiled her with their fornication, and she was defiled with them. And her mind was alienated because ¹⁸ of them. And she uncovered her fornications, and uncovered her nakedness. Then my mind was alienated from ¹⁹ her, like as my mind was alienated from her sister. Yet she multiplied her fornications, in calling to remembrance the days of her youth, wherein she had played the harlot ²⁰ in the land of Egypt. For she doted upon their paramours, whose flesh is as the flesh of asses, and whose issue is like the issue of horses.

²¹ Thus thou callest to remembrance the lewdness of thy youth, in the bruising of thy teats by the Egyptians for ²² the paps of thy youth. Therefore, O Aholibah, thus saith the Lord Jehovah; Behold, I will raise up thy lovers against thee, from whom thy mind is alienated, and I ²³ will bring them against thee on every side; the sons of Babylon, and all the Chaldeans, prefect and rich man and noble, and all the sons of Assyria with them, all of them desirable young men, Pashas and rulers, all of them Chiefs- ²⁴ of-three and renowned, riding upon horses. And they shall come against thee with arms, chariots, and wheels, and with an assembly of peoples, who shall set against thee buckler and shield and helmet round about. And I will set judgment before them, and they shall judge thee according to

their own judgments. And I will set my jealousy against ²⁵
thee, and they shall deal with thee in wrath. They shall
take away thy nose and thine ears; and thy remnant'shall
fall by the sword. They shall take thy sons and thy
daughters; and thy remnant shall be devoured by the fire.
They shall also strip thee out of thy clothes, and take ²⁶
away thy fair jewels. Thus will I make thy lewdness to ²⁷
cease from thee, and thy fornication brought from the
land of Egypt; so that thou shalt not lift up thine eyes
to them, nor remember Egypt any more.

For thus saith the Lord Jehovah; Behold, I have de- ²⁸
livered thee into the hand of them whom thou hatest, into
the hand of them from whom thy mind is alienated. And ²⁹
they shall deal with thee in hatred, and shall take away
all the fruit of thy labour, and shall leave thee naked and
bare. And the nakedness of thy fornications shall be uncovered, both thy lewdness and thy fornications. I will ³⁰
do these things to thee, because thou hast gone astray
after the Nations, and because thou art polluted with their
filthy idols. Thou hast walked in the way of thy sister; ³¹
therefore have I given her cup into thy hand.

Thus saith the Lord Jehovah; Thou shalt drink of thy ³²
sister's cup deep and large. Thou shalt be a scorn and a
derision; it containeth much. Thou shalt be filled with ³³
drunkenness and sorrow, with the cup of despair and desolation, with the cup of thy sister Samaria. Thou shalt ³⁴
even drink it and suck it out, and thou shalt lick its sherds;
and thou shalt pluck off thine own breasts; for I have
spoken it; the Lord Jehovah hath said it.

Therefore thus saith the Lord Jehovah; Because thou ³⁵
hast forgotten me, and cast me behind thy back, therefore
bear thou also thy lewdness and thy fornications.

And Jehovah said to me; Son of Adam, wilt thou plead ³⁶
for Aholah and Aholibah? Yea, declare to them their
abominations; that they have committed adultery, and ³⁷
blood is in their hands, and with their filthy idols have
they committed adultery, and have also caused their sons,
whom they bare unto me, to pass for them through [the fire]
to be devoured. Moreover this they have done unto me. ³⁸
They have defiled my Sanctuary in the same day, and have
polluted my sabbaths. For when they had slain their ³⁹
children to their filthy idols, then they came the same day

into my Sanctuary to pollute it; and lo, thus have they
40 done in the midst of my House. And furthermore, that
ye have sent for men to come from far, unto whom a messenger was sent. And lo, they came, for whom thou didst wash thyself, didst paint thine eyes with black, and didst
41 deck thyself with ornaments, and satest upon a stately bed, and a table was prepared before it, whereupon thou
42 hast set mine incense and mine oil. And the voice of an idle rabble was with her. And with the men of the common sort there were brought drunkards from the desert, who put bracelets on the women's hands, and beautiful
43 crowns on their heads. Then said I of her that was worn out with adulteries, 'Will they now commit fornications
44 'with her, and she with them?' Yet they went in unto her, as they go in unto a woman that playeth the harlot; so went they in unto Aholah and unto Aholibah, the lewd women.
45 And the righteous men, they shall judge them after the manner of adulteresses, and after the manner of women that shed blood; because they are adulteresses, and blood
46 is in their hands. For thus saith the Lord Jehovah; I will bring up an Assembly [of witnesses] against them,
47 and will give them up to be scattered and plundered. And the Assembly shall stone them with stones, and cut them down with their swords; they shall slay their sons and their daughters, and shall burn up their houses with fire.
48 Thus will I cause lewdness to cease out of the land, that all
49 women may be taught not to do after your lewdness. And they shall recompense your lewdness upon you, and ye shall bear the sins of your filthy idols; and ye shall know
—that I am the Lord Jehovah.
1 AND IN THE NINTH YEAR [B.C. 592], in the tenth month, on the tenth day of the month, the word of Jeho-
2 vah came unto me, saying, Son of Adam, write unto thee the name of the day, even of this same day; the king of Babylon [Nebuchadnezzar] hath set himself against Jeru-
3 salem on this same day. And utter A PARABLE unto the rebellious house, and say to them, Thus saith the Lord Jehovah; Set on a pot, set it on, and also pour water into
4 it. Gather its pieces into it, even every good piece, the thigh, and the shoulder; fill it with the choice bones,
5 taking the choicest of the flock. And also set a pile of

bones under it, and make it boil well, and let them boil the bones of it therein.

⁶ Therefore thus saith the Lord Jehovah; Woe to the city of bloodshed, to the pot whose rust is in it, and whose rust is not gone out of it! Bring it out piece by piece; let no lot be cast upon it. ⁷ For her blood is in the midst of her; she set it upon the sun-burnt top of a rock; she poured it not upon the ground, to cover it with dust; ⁸ so that she caused Wrath to come up to take vengeance. I have set her blood upon the sun-burnt top of a rock, that it should not be covered.

⁹ Therefore thus saith the Lord Jehovah; Woe to the city of bloodshed! I will even make the pile of fire great. ¹⁰ Heap on wood, kindle the fire, consume the flesh, and spice it with spices, and let the bones be burned. ¹¹ Then set [the pot] when empty upon the coals thereof, that the copper of it may be hot, and may burn, and that the filthiness of it may be melted in it, that the rust of it may be consumed. ¹² She hath wearied herself with toil, and her great rust went not forth out of her; her rust shall be in the fire. ¹³ In thy filthiness is lewdness. Because I have purged thee, and thou wast not purged, thou shalt not be purged from thy filthiness any more, till I have caused my wrath to rest upon thee. ¹⁴ I Jehovah have spoken it; it shall come to pass, and I will do it; I will not go back, neither will I spare, neither will I repent; according to thy ways, and according to thy doings, shall they judge thee; the Lord Jehovah hath said it.

¹⁵ ALSO THE WORD OF JEHOVAH came unto me, saying, ¹⁶ Son of Adam, behold, I take away from thee the desire of thine eyes by a stroke; yet neither shalt thou mourn nor weep, neither shall thy tears run down. ¹⁷ Groan in silence for the dead, make no mourning, bind thy head-dress upon thee, and put on thy shoes upon thy feet, and cover not thy beard; but eat not the bread of men.

¹⁸ So I spake to the people in the morning; and at evening my wife died; and I did in the morning as I was commanded. ¹⁹ And the people said to me, 'Wilt thou not tell 'us what these things are to us, that thou doest so?'

²⁰ Then I said to them, The word of Jehovah came to me, saying, ²¹ Say to the house of Israel, Thus saith the Lord Jehovah; Behold, I will profane my Sanctuary, the excel-

lence of your strength, the desire of your eyes, and the longing of your soul; and your sons and your daughters
²² whom ye have forsaken shall fall by the sword. And ye shall do as I have done; ye shall not cover your beard,
²³ nor eat the bread of men. And your head-dress shall be on your heads, and your shoes upon your feet. Ye shall not mourn nor weep; but ye shall pine away for your
²⁴ iniquities, and groan one toward another. Thus Ezekiel is to you a sign. According to all that he hath done shall ye do; and when this cometh, ye shall know that I am the Lord Jehovah.
²⁵ Also, thou son of Adam, shall it not be in the day when I take from them their strength, the joy of their glory, the desire of their eyes, and the burden of their minds, their
²⁶ sons and their daughters; that he that escapeth in that day shall come to thee, to cause thee to hear it with thine
²⁷ ears? In that day shall thy mouth be opened to him which is escaped, and thou shalt speak, and be no more dumb. And thou shalt be a sign to them; and they shall know that I am Jehovah.

¹ And the word of Jehovah came to me, saying, Son of
² Adam, set thy face against THE CHILDREN OF AMMON, and
³ prophesy against them; and say to the Children of Ammon, Hear the word of the Lord Jehovah; Thus saith the Lord Jehovah; Because thou saidst, 'Aha,' against my Sanctuary, when it was profaned; and against the land of Israel, when it was made desolate; and against the house
⁴ of Judah, when they went into captivity; behold, therefore I will give thee to the Children of the East for a possession, and they shall set their strongholds in thee, and make their dwellings in thee. They shall eat thy fruit, and they
⁵ shall drink thy milk. And I will make Rabbah to be a stable for camels, and the Children of Ammon a couching-place for flocks; and ye shall know that I am Jehovah.
⁶ For thus saith the Lord Jehovah; Because thou hast clapped thy hands, and stamped with the feet, and rejoiced
⁷ in heart with all thy spite against the land of Israel; behold, therefore I will stretch out my hand upon thee, and will deliver thee for a spoil to the Nations; and I will cut thee off from the peoples, and I will cause thee to perish out of the countries; I will destroy thee; and thou shalt know that I am Jehovah.

Thus saith the Lord Jehovah ; Because that MOAB AND ⁸
SEIR do say, 'Behold the house of Judah is like all the
'Nations;' therefore, behold, I will lay open to the Children ⁹
of the East the side of Moab from the cities, even from its
cities which are on its frontier, the beauty of the country,
Beth-jeshimoth, Baal-maon, and Kirjathaim, with the ¹⁰
Children of Ammon ; and I will give them also in possession, so that the Children of Ammon may not be remembered among nations. And I will execute judgments ¹¹
upon Moab ; and they shall know that I am Jehovah.

Thus saith the Lord Jehovah ; Because EDOM hath dealt ¹²
against the house of Judah by taking vengeance, and is
very guilty, and hath revenged himself on them ; therefore thus saith the Lord Jehovah ; I will also stretch out ¹³
my hand upon Edom, and will cut off man and beast from
it, and will make it desolate ; from Teman even to Dedan
they shall fall by the sword. And I will lay my vengeance ¹⁴
upon Edom by the hand of my people Israel ; and they
shall do in Edom according to mine anger and according
to my wrath ; and they shall know my vengeance ; the
Lord Jehovah hath said it.

Thus saith the Lord Jehovah ; 'Because the PHILISTINES ¹⁵
have dealt by revenge, and have taken vengeance with a
spiteful heart, to destroy it for old hatred ; therefore thus ¹⁶
saith the Lord Jehovah ; Behold, I will stretch out my
hand upon the Philistines, and I will cut off the Cherethites, and destroy the remnant of the sea coasts. And I ¹⁷
will execute great vengeance upon them with wrathful
rebukes ; and they shall know that I am Jehovah, when
I shall lay my vengeance upon them. —

And it came to pass in the eleventh year [B.C. 590], ¹
on the first day of the month, that the word of Jehovah
came to me, saying, Son of Adam, because Tyre hath said ²
against Jerusalem, ' Aha, she is broken down ; the door of
' the peoples is turned to me ; I shall be replenished, now
' that she is laid waste ;' therefore thus saith the Lord ³
Jehovah ; Behold, I am AGAINST THEE, O TYRE, and will
cause many nations to come up against thee, as the sea
causeth its waves to come up. And they shall destroy the ⁴
walls of Tyre, and break down her towers ; I will also scrape
her earth from her, and make her like the sun-burnt top of a
rock. It shall be a place to spread nets upon in the midst ⁵

of the sea. For I have spoken it, the Lord Jehovah hath
6 said it; and it shall become a spoil to the nations. And
its suburbs which are on the land shall be slain by the
sword; and they shall know that I am Jehovah.

7 For thus saith the Lord Jehovah; Behold, I will bring
upon Tyre Nebuchadrezzar king of Babylon, a king of kings,
from the north, with horses, and with chariots, and with
8 horsemen, and companies, and much people. He shall slay
with the sword thy suburbs on the land. And he shall
make a line of forts against thee, and cast a siege-mound
9 against thee, and lift up the buckler against thee. And
he shall set his battering-ram against thy walls, and with
10 his axes he shall break down thy towers. By reason of
the abundance of his horses their dust shall cover thee;
thy walls shall shake at the noise of the horsemen, and of
the wheels, and of the chariots, when he shall enter into
11 thy gates, as men enter into a city by a breach. With
the hoofs of his horses shall he tread down all thy streets;
he shall slay thy people by the sword, and the pillars of
12 thy strength shall go down to the ground. And they shall
plunder thy riches, and make a prey of thy merchandise;
and they shall break down thy walls, and destroy thy
pleasant houses; and they shall cast thy stones, and thy
13 timber, and thine earth, into the midst of the water. And
I will cause the noise of thy songs to cease; and the sound
14 of thy harps shall be no more heard. And I will make thee
like the sun-burnt top of a rock. Thou shalt be a place to
spread nets upon; thou shalt be built up no more; for I
Jehovah have spoken it, the Lord Jehovah hath said it.

15 Thus saith the Lord Jehovah to Tyre; Shall not the isles
shake at the sound of thy fall, when the wounded groan,
16 when the slaughter is made in the midst of thee? Then all
the princes of the sea shall come down from their thrones,
and lay aside their robes, and put off their embroidered
garments; they shall clothe themselves with trembling;
they shall sit upon the ground, and shall tremble at every
17 moment, and be astonished at thee. And they shall take
up a lamentation for thee, and say to thee, ' How art thou
' destroyed, that wast inhabited in the ocean, the renowned
' city, which wast strong in the sea, she and her inhabitants,
18 ' who sent their terror on all that inhabit it! Now shall
' the isles tremble in the day of thy fall; yea, the isles in

'the sea shall be troubled at thy departure.' For thus saith [19] the Lord Jehovah; When I shall make thee a desolate city, like the cities that are not inhabited; when I shall bring up the deep over thee, and the great waters shall cover thee; when I shall bring thee down with them that [20] descend into the Pit, unto the people of old time, and shall make thee to dwell in the world below, in places desolate of old, with them that go down to the Pit, so that thou be not inhabited; then I will set Beauty [or Jerusalem] in the land of the living. I will destroy thee, and thou shalt be [21] no more. Though thou be sought for, yet shalt thou never be found again; the Lord Jehovah hath said it. —

And the word of Jehovah came to me, saying, Now, thou [1] son of Adam, take up A LAMENTATION FOR TYRE; and say [2] to Tyre, O thou that art situate at the entrance of the sea, [3] who art the merchant of the peoples unto many isles, Thus saith the Lord Jehovah; O Tyre, thou hast said, 'I am of 'perfect beauty.' Thy boundaries are in the heart of the [4] ocean, thy builders have perfected thy beauty. They have [5] made all thy ship timbers of fir trees from Senir; they have taken cedars from Lebanon to make masts for thee. Of [6] the oaks from Bashan have they made thine oars; they have made thy benches of ivory, inlaid in cedar from the isles of the Chittians [or Cyprus]. Fine linen with embroid- [7] ered work from Egypt was that which thou spreadest forth to be thy sail; blue and purple from the isles of Elishah [or Greece] was thine awning. The inhabitants of Sidon [8] and Arvad were thy rowers; thy skilful men, O Tyre, that were in thee, were thy sailors. The elders of Gebal [or [9] Byblus] and its skilful men were in thee to stop thy chinks; all the ships of the sea with their mariners were in thee to attend to thy cargoes. They of Persia and of Lud [or the [10] Egyptian Arabs] and of Phut [or the Africans] were in thine army, thy men of war; they hanged up the shield and helmet in thee; they set forth thy comeliness. The [11] Children of Arvad with thine army were upon thy walls round about, even as warriors on thy towers; they hanged their shields upon thy walls round about; they have made thy beauty perfect. Tarshish [or Tarsus] was thy place of [12] trade by reason of the multitude of all kind of riches in silver; iron, mixed metal, and lead, they brought for thy commerce. Javan [or Ionia], Tubal [or the Tibareni], [13] and Meshech [or the Muscovites], they were thy merchants for the persons of men [or slaves]; and they brought ¹⁴ vessels of copper as thy merchandise. They of the house of Togarmah [or Armenia] brought for thy commerce horses ¹⁵ and saddle-horses and mules. The children of Dedan were thy merchants; many isles were the places of trade at thy hand; they sent back to thee in payment ivory tusks and ¹⁶ ebony. Syria was thy place of trade by reason of the multitude of the wares of thy making; they sent for thy commerce emeralds, purple, and embroidered work, and fine ¹⁷ linen, and coral, and rubies. Judah, and the land of Israel, they were thy merchants; they brought for thy merchandise wheat of Minnith, and cakes, and sweetmeats, and oil, ¹⁸ and balm. Damascus was thy place of trade in the multitude of the wares of thy making, for the multitude of all riches; in the wine of Helbon [or Aleppo], and white ¹⁹ wool. Vedan and Javan [in Arabia] brought thread for thy commerce; wrought iron, cassia, and the sweet cane, ²⁰ were among thy merchandise. Dedan was thy merchant ²¹ in precious cloths for riding. Arabia, and all the princes of Kedar, were merchants at thy hand in lambs, and rams, ²² and goats; in these were they thy merchants. The merchants of Sheba and Raamah, they were thy merchants; they brought for thy commerce the chief of all spices, ²³ and all precious stones, and gold. Haran, and Canneh, and Aden, the merchants of Sheba, Assyria, and Chilmad, ²⁴ were thy merchants. These were thy merchants in things of excellence, in mantles of blue cloth, and embroidered work, and in chests of rich apparel, bound with cords, and made ²⁵ of cedar, among thy merchandise. The ships of Tarshish were thy caravans for thy merchandise; and thou wast filled, and made very glorious in the heart of the ocean.

²⁶ Thy rowers have brought thee into great waters; the east wind hath broken thee to pieces in the heart of the ²⁷ ocean. Thy riches, and thy commerce, thy merchandise, thy mariners, and thy sailors, those who stop thy chinks, and those who attend to thy cargoes, and all thy men of war, that are in thee, and in all thy company which is in the midst of thee, shall fall into the heart of the ocean in ²⁸ the day of thy ruin. The district around shall shake at the ²⁹ sound of the cry of thy sailors. And all that handle the oar, the mariners, and all the sailors of the sea, shall come down from their ships, they shall stand upon the land;

and shall cause their voice to be heard against thee, and ³⁰
shall cry bitterly, and shall cast up dust upon their heads,
they shall roll themselves in the ashes ; and they shall ³¹
make themselves utterly bald for thee, and gird them with
sackcloth, and they shall weep for thee with bitterness of
heart, mourning bitterly. And their sons shall take up a ³²
lamentation for thee, and lament over thee, [saying,]
' Who is like Tyre, like the ruin in the midst of the sea ?
' When thy wares went forth upon the ocean, ³³
' Thou filledst many people with thy great riches ;
' And didst enrich kings of the earth with thy cargoes.
' Now thou art broken upon the ocean ; ³⁴
' Thy cargoes, and all thy company in the midst of thee,
' Are fallen into the depths of the waters.
' All who dwell in the isles are amazed at thee, ³⁵
' And their kings are sore afraid.
' They are troubled in their countenance.
' The merchants among the peoples hiss at thee ; ³⁶
' Thou shalt be destroyed, and never shalt be any more.' —

And the word of Jehovah came to me, saying, Son of ¹
Adam, say to the prince of Tyre, Thus saith the Lord Jeho- ²
vah ; Because thy heart is lifted up, and thou sayest, ' I
' am a God, I sit in the seat of God, in the heart of the
' ocean ;' yet thou art a man, and not a God, though thou
shouldst set thy heart as the heart of a God. Behold, thou ³
art wiser than Daniel ; there is no secret that they can hide
from thee ; with thy wisdom and with thine understanding ⁴
thou hast gotten to thee riches, and gettest gold and silver
into thy treasures. By thy great wisdom and by thy ⁵
traffic thou hast increased thy riches, and thy heart is
lifted up because of thy riches. Therefore thus saith the ⁶
Lord Jehovah ; Because thou settest thy heart as the heart
of God ; behold, therefore I will bring strangers upon ⁷
thee, the terrible of the nations. And they shall draw their
swords against the beauty of thy wisdom, and they shall
defile thy brightness. They shall bring thee down to the ⁸
Pit, and thou shalt die the death of them that are slain in
the heart of the ocean. Wilt thou yet say before him that ⁹
slayeth thee, ' I am God ' ? But thou shalt be a man, and
no God, in the hand of him that slayeth thee. Thou shalt ¹⁰
die the death of the uncircumcised by the hand of strangers ;
for I have spoken it, the Lord Jehovah hath said it.

¹¹ Moreover the word of Jehovah came to me, saying, Son ¹² of Adam, take up a lamentation upon the king of Tyre, and say to him, Thus saith the Lord Jehovah ; Thou wast a beautiful signet ring, full of wisdom, and perfect in beauty. ¹³ Thou wast in Eden the garden of God. Every precious stone was thy covering, the ruby, the topaz, and the diamond, the chrysolite, the onyx, and the jasper, the sapphire, the emerald, and the carbuncle, and gold ; the workmanship of thy settings and of thy jewel-holes was prepared ¹⁴ in thee in the day that thou wast created. Thou wast an out-stretched cherub that coveredst [the Ark]; and I did set thee so. Thou wast upon the holy mountain of God ; thou hast walked up and down in the midst of the stones of fire. ¹⁵ Thou wast perfect in thy ways from the day that thou wast ¹⁶ created, till iniquity was found in thee. By the multitude of thy merchandise they have filled the midst of thee with violence, and thou hast sinned. Therefore I will cast thee as profane out of the mountain of God ; and I will destroy thee, O cherub that coveredst, from the midst of the stones ¹⁷ of fire. Thy heart was lifted up because of thy beauty, thou hast corrupted thy wisdom by reason of thy brightness ; I will cast thee to the ground, I will lay thee before ¹⁸ kings, that they may behold thee. Thou hast defiled thy sanctuaries by the multitude of thine iniquities, by the dishonesty of thy traffic ; therefore will I bring forth a fire from the midst of thee, it shall devour thee ; and I will bring thee to ashes upon the earth in the sight of all them ¹⁹ that behold thee. All they that know thee among the peoples shall be astonished at thee. Thou shalt be destroyed, and never shalt thou be any more.

²⁰ . And the word of Jehovah came to me, saying, Son of ²¹ Adam, set thy face AGAINST SIDON, and prophesy against ²² it, and say, Thus saith the Lord Jehovah ; Behold, I am against thee, O Sidon ; and I will be glorified in the midst of thee. And they shall know that I am Jehovah, when I shall have executed judgments in her, and shall be sanc- ²³ tified in her. For I will send into her pestilence, and blood into her streets ; and the wounded shall fall in the midst of her by the sword that is upon her on every side ; ²⁴ and they shall know that I am Jehovah. And she shall be no more a pricking brier unto the house of Israel, nor any painful thorn of all those round about them, that de-

spise them; and they shall know that I am the Lord Jehovah. Thus saith the Lord Jehovah; when I shall 25 have gathered the house of Israel from the peoples among whom they are scattered, and I shall be sanctified in them in the sight of the Nations, then shall they dwell in their land that I gave to my servant Jacob. And they shall 26 dwell safely therein, and shall build houses, and plant vineyards; yea, they shall dwell with confidence, when I have executed judgments upon all those that despise them round about them. And they shall know that I am Jehovah their God.

In the tenth year, in the tenth month [B.C. 591], on the 1 twelfth day of the month, the word of Jehovah came to me, saying, Son of Adam, set thy face AGAINST PHARAOH 2 king of Egypt, and prophesy against him, and against all Egypt; speak, and say, Thus saith the Lord Jehovah; Be- 3 hold, I am against thee, Pharaoh [Hophra] king of Egypt, thou great dragon that lieth in the midst of his rivers, who hath said, 'My river is mine own, and I made it for 'myself.' But I will put hooks into thy jaws, and I will 4 cause the fish of thy rivers to stick to thy scales, and I will bring thee up out of the midst of thy rivers, and all the fish of thy rivers shall stick to thy scales. And I will 5 throw thee into the desert, thee and all the fish of thy rivers. Thou shalt fall upon the face of the field; thou shalt not be brought together, nor gathered up. I have given thee for food to the wild beasts of the earth and to the fowls of the heavens. And all the inhabitants of Egypt 6 shall know that I am Jehovah, because they have been a staff of reed to the house of Israel. When they took hold 7 of thee by thy hand, thou didst crack, and didst rend all their shoulder; and when they leaned upon thee, thou brakest, and madest all their loins to be at a stand.

Therefore thus saith the Lord Jehovah; Behold, I will 8 bring a sword upon thee, and cut off man and beast out of thee. And the land of Egypt shall be desolate and waste; 9 and they shall know that I am Jehovah; because he said, 'The river is mine and I made it.' Behold, therefore I 10 am against thee, and against thy rivers, and I will make the land of Egypt utterly waste and desolate, from Magdolon to Syene, even to the boundary of Ethiopia. No foot of 11 man shall pass through it, nor foot of cattle shall pass

through it, neither shall it be inhabited for forty years.
¹² And I will make the land of Egypt desolate in the midst of the countries that are desolate, and her cities among the cities that are laid waste; they shall be desolate for forty years. And I will scatter the Egyptians among the nations, and will disperse them through the countries.
¹³ Yet thus saith the Lord Jehovah; At the end of forty years will I gather the Egyptians from the peoples whither
¹⁴ they were scattered. And I will bring home again the captivity of Egypt, and will cause them to return into the land of Pathros [or the Thebaid], into the land of their
¹⁵ birth; and they shall be there a base kingdom. It shall be the basest of kingdoms; neither shall it exalt itself any more above the nations. For I will diminish them, that
¹⁶ they shall no more rule over the nations. And it shall be no more a cause of trust to the house of Israel. It shall bring their iniquity to remembrance, when they look after them [the Egyptians]; and they shall know that I am the Lord Jehovah.
¹⁷ (AND IT CAME TO PASS in the seven and twentieth year [B.C. 574], in the first month, on the first day of the
¹⁸ month, the word of Jehovah came to me, saying, Son of Adam, Nebuchadrezzar king of Babylon hath caused his army to serve a great service against Tyre. Every head was made bald, and every shoulder was peeled; yet had he no wages, nor his army, for Tyre, for the service that he
¹⁹ had served against it. Therefore thus saith the Lord Jehovah; Behold, I will give the land of Egypt to Nebuchadrezzar king of Babylon; and he shall carry away her rabble, and take her plunder, and take her prey; and it shall be
²⁰ the wages for his army. I have given him the land of Egypt as wages for his labour wherewith he served against it, because they worked for me; the Lord Jehovah hath said
²¹ it. In that day will I cause the horn of the house of Israel to branch forth, and I will give thee to open thy mouth in the midst of them; and they shall know that I am Je—hovah.
¹ And the word of Jehovah came to me, saying, Son of
² Adam, prophesy and say, Thus saith the Lord Jehovah;
³ Howl ye, 'Woe to the day!' For the day is near, even the day of Jehovah is near, a cloudy day; it shall be the time
⁴ of the Nations. And the sword shall come upon Egypt,

and great pain shall be in Ethiopia, when the slain shall fall in Egypt, and they shall take away her rabble, and her foundations shall be broken down. Ethiopia and Phut [or the Africans], and Lud [or the Egyptian Arabs], and all the Arabs, and Cub [or Nubia], and the children of the land that is in league with them, shall fall by the sword. Thus saith Jehovah; They also that uphold Egypt shall fall; and the pride of her power shall come down; from Magdolon to Syene shall they fall in it by the sword; the Lord Jehovah hath said it. And they shall be desolate in the midst of the countries that are desolate, and her cities shall be in midst of the cities that are wasted. And they shall know that I am Jehovah, when I have set a fire in Egypt, and when all her helpers shall be destroyed. In that day shall the messengers go forth from me in ships to make the careless Ethiopians afraid, and great pain shall come upon them, as in the day of Egypt; for, lo, it cometh.

Thus saith the Lord Jehovah; I will also make the rabble of Egypt to cease by the hand of Nebuchadrezzar king of Babylon. He and his people with him, the terrible of the nations, shall be brought to destroy the land. And they shall draw their swords against Egypt, and fill the land with the slain. And I will make the rivers dry, and sell the land into the hand of the wicked. And I will make the land desolate, and all that is therein, by the hand of strangers; I Jehovah have spoken it.

Thus saith the Lord Jehovah; I will also destroy the filthy idols, and I will cause their vain images to cease out of Noph [or Memphis]; and there shall be no more a prince of the land of Egypt. And I will put a fear into the land of Egypt. And I will make Pathros [or the Thebaid] desolate, and will set a fire in Zoan [or Tanis], and will execute judgments in No [or Thebes]. And I will pour my fury upon Sin [or Sais], the strength of Egypt; and I will cut off the rabble of No. And I will set a fire in Egypt; Sin shall have great pain, and No shall be rent asunder, and Noph shall have distresses daily. The young men of Aven [or the City of Vanity] and of Pibeseth [or Bubastis] shall fall by the sword; and these cities shall go into captivity. At Tahpenes [or Daphnæ] also the day shall be darkened, when I shall break there the sceptres of Egypt; and the pomp of her strength shall cease in her.

As for her, a cloud shall cover her, and her daughters shall
¹⁹ go into captivity. Thus will I execute judgments in Egypt ;
and they shall know that I am Jehovah.)
²⁰ AND IT CAME TO PASS in the eleventh year [B.C. 590],
in the first month, on the seventh day of the month, that
²¹ the word of Jehovah came to me, saying, Son of Adam, I
have broken the arm of Pharaoh [Hophra] king of Egypt ;
and, lo, it shall not be bound up to be healed, to put a
bandage to bind it up, to make it strong to hold the sword.
²² Therefore thus saith the Lord Jehovah ; Behold, I am
against Pharaoh king of Egypt, and will break his arms,
both the strong one, and that which was broken ; and I
²³ will cause the sword to fall out of his hand. And I will
scatter the Egyptians among the nations, and will disperse
²⁴ them through the countries. And I will strengthen the
arms of the king of Babylon, and put my sword into his
hand. But I will break Pharaoh's arms, and he shall
groan before him with the groanings of a deadly wounded
²⁵ man. But I will strengthen the arms of the king of Babylon, and the arms of Pharaoh shall fall down ; and they
shall know that I am Jehovah, when I shall put my sword
into the hand of the king of Babylon, and he shall stretch
²⁶ it out upon the land of Egypt. And I will scatter the
Egyptians among the Nations, and disperse them among
—the countries ; and they shall know that I am Jehovah.
¹ AND IT CAME TO PASS in the eleventh year, in the third
month, on the first day of the month, that the word of
² Jehovah came to me, saying, Son of Adam, say to Pharaoh
king of Egypt, and to his rabble ; Whom art thou like in
³ thy greatness ? Behold, the Assyrian was a cedar in Lebanon with fair branches, and with a shadowing thicket,
and of a high stature ; and his top twig was among thick
⁴ boughs. The waters made him great, the deep set him up
on high with its rivers running round about his plants, and
sent forth its little streams unto all the trees of the field.
⁵ Therefore his height was exalted above all the trees of the
field, and his boughs were multiplied, and his branches
became long because of the multitude of waters, when they
⁶ were sent forth. All the fowls of the heavens made their
nests in his boughs, and under his branches did all the wild
beasts of the field bring forth their young, and under his
⁷ shade dwelt all great nations. Thus was he fair in his

greatness, in the length of his branches; for his root was by great waters. The cedars in the garden of God could ⁸ not overtop him. The fir trees were not like his boughs, and the plane trees were not like his branches; nor any tree in the garden of God was like to him in his beauty. I made him fair by the multitude of his branches, so that ⁹ all the trees of Eden, that were in the garden of God, envied him.

Therefore thus said the Lord Jehovah; Because thou ¹⁰ hast lifted up thyself in height, and he hath shot up his top twig among the thick boughs, and his heart is lifted up in his height; I will therefore deliver him into the hand of ¹¹ the God of the Nâtions; he shall surely deal with him. I will drive him out for his wickedness. And strangers, the ¹² terrible of the nations, will cut him off, and will forsake him upon the mountains; and in all the valleys his branches will fall, and his boughs be broken by all the rivers of the land; and all the peoples of the earth will go down from his shade, and will forsake him. Upon his ruin will ¹³ all the fowls of the heavens dwell, and all the wild beasts of the field will be upon his branches; to the end that ¹⁴ none of all the trees by the waters shall lift themselves up in their height, neither shoot up their top twig among the thick boughs. Neither shall any that drink water stand up against them in their height. For they are all delivered up unto death, to the world below, in the midst of the children of Adam, with them that are gone down to the Pit.

Thus saith the Lord Jehovah; In the day when he [the ¹⁵ Assyrian] went down to hell I caused a mourning. I covered the deep for him, and I restrained its floods, and the great waters were stayed. And I clothed Lebanon in black for him, and all the trees of the field were veiled for him. I made nations to shake at the sound of his fall, ¹⁶ when I cast him down to hell with them that are gone down into the Pit. And all the trees of Eden, the choicest and the best of Lebanon, all that drink water, shall be comforted in the world below. They also went down into ¹⁷ hell with him unto them that were slain with the sword; and they that were his arm, that had dwelt under his shade in the midst of the Nations.

To whom art thou [Pharaoh] thus like in glory and in ¹⁸ greatness among the trees of Eden? And thou also shalt be brought down with the trees of Eden unto the world below. Thou shalt lie in the midst of the uncircumcised with them that were slain by the sword. This is Pharaoh —and all his rabble; the Lord Jehovah hath said it.

1 AND IT CAME TO PASS in the twelfth year, in the twelfth month [B.C. 589], on the first day of the month, that the
2 word of Jehovah came to me, saying, Son of Adam take up a lamentation for Pharaoh king of Egypt, and say to him, Thou art like a young lion of the Nations, and thou art as a dragon in the ocean. And thou rushedst forth in thy rivers, and muddiedst the waters with thy feet, and
3 fouledst their rivers. Thus saith the Lord Jehovah; I will therefore spread out my net over thee with a company of many peoples; and they shall bring thee up in
4 my net. Then will I leave thee upon the land, I will cast thee forth upon the open field, and will cause all the fowls of the heavens to dwell upon thee, and I will satisfy the
5 wild beasts of the whole earth with thee. And I will lay thy flesh upon the mountains, and fill the valleys with thy
6 height. I will also water the land with the flood from thy blood, even to the mountains; and the pools shall be
7 full of thee. And in quenching thee [as a flame], I will cover the heavens, and make the stars thereof dark; I will cover the sun with a cloud, and the moon shall not
8 give her light. All the bright lights of the heavens will I make dark over thee, and set darkness upon thy land; the Lord Jehovah hath said it.
9 I will also vex the hearts of many peoples, when I shall bring thy broken limbs among the Nations, into the coun-
10 tries which thou hast not known. Yea, I will make many peoples amazed at thee, and their kings shall be horribly afraid at thee, when I shall brandish my sword before their faces; and they shall tremble at every moment every man for his own life, in the day of thy fall.
11 For thus saith the Lord Jehovah; The sword of the
12 king of Babylon shall come on thee. By swords of warriors will I cause thy rabble to fall, the terrible of the Nations, all of them; and they shall plunder the pomp of Egypt,
13 and all its rabble shall be destroyed. And I will destroy all its cattle from the great waters; and the foot of man shall muddy them no more, nor the hoofs of cattle muddy
14 them. Then I will make their waters shallow, and cause

their rivers to trickle like oil ; the Lord Jehovah hath said it. When I shall make the land of Egypt desolate, and ¹⁵ the country shall be destitute of its fulness ; when I shall smite all them that dwell therein, then shall they know that I am Jehovah. This is the Lamentation wherewith ¹⁶ they shall lament her. The daughters of the Nations shall lament over her ; they shall lament for her, even for Egypt, and for all her rabble ; the Lord Jehovah hath said it.

AND IT CAME TO PASS in the twelfth year [B.C. 589], on ¹⁷ the fifteenth day of the month, that the word of Jehovah came to me, saying, Son of Adam, wail for the rabble of ¹⁸ Egypt, and cast them down, even her, and the daughters of the mighty nations, to the world below, with them that go down into the Pit. Whom dost thou surpass in ¹⁹ beauty ? Go down, and be thou laid with the uncircumcised. They shall fall in the midst of them that are slain ²⁰ by the sword. The sword is sent forth. Draw her away and all her rabble. The warrior gods shall speak to him ²¹ out of the midst of hell with them that help him. They are gone down, they lie uncircumcised, slain by the sword. Assyria is there and all her company ; his ²² graves are about him ; all of them slain, fallen by the sword ; whose graves are set in the back of the Pit, and ²³ her company is round about her grave ; all of them slain, fallen by the sword, they who caused terror in the land of the living. There is Elam [or Western Persia] ²⁴ and all her rabble round about her grave, all of them slain, fallen by the sword ; they are gone down uncircumcised into the world below, they who caused a terror of themselves in the land of the living. And they bear their shame with them that are gone down into the Pit. They have set for her a bed in the midst of the slain ²⁵ with all her rabble. Her graves are round about him ; all of them uncircumcised, slain by the sword. Though the terror of them was caused in the land of the living, yet they bear their shame with those that are gone down into the Pit ; she is put in the midst of them that are slain. There are Meshech [or the Muscovites], Tubal [or the Tiba- ²⁶ reni], and all their rabble. Their graves are round about him ; all of them uncircumcised, slain by the sword, though they caused a terror of themselves in the land of the living. But they shall not lie with the warriors that are fallen of the ²⁷ uncircumcised, who are gone down to hell with their weapons of war, and have laid their swords under their heads; but their iniquities shall be upon their bones, though they were the terror of the warriors in the land of ²⁸ the living. Yea, thou shalt be broken in the midst of the uncircumcised, and shalt lie with them that are slain by ²⁹ the sword. There is Edom, her kings, and all her princes, who with their might are added to them that were slain by the sword. They lie with the uncircumcised, and with ³⁰ them that are gone down into the Pit. There are the anointed princes of the north, all of them, and all the Sidonians, who are gone down with the slain; in the midst of those terrified by them they are put to shame, away from their might; and they lie uncircumcised with them that were slain by the sword, and they bear their shame with them ³¹ that are gone down into the Pit. Pharaoh shall see them, and will be comforted over all his rabble, even Pharaoh and all his army slain by the sword; the Lord Jehovah hath ³² said it. For I spread terror of him in the land of the living; and he shall be laid in the midst of the uncircumcised with them that were slain with the sword, even Pharaoh —and all his rabble; the Lord Jehovah hath said it.

¹ And the word of Jehovah came to me, saying, Son of ² Adam, speak to THE CHILDREN OF THY PEOPLE, and say to them, When I bring the sword upon a land, if the people of the land take a man of their borders, and set him for ³ their watchman; if when he seeth the sword coming upon ⁴ the land, he blow the trumpet, and warn the people; then whosoever heareth the sound of the trumpet, and taketh not warning; if the sword come, and take him away, his ⁵ blood will be upon his own head. He heard the sound of the trumpet, and took not warning; his blood shall be upon himself. But he that taketh warning will save his ⁶ life. But if the watchman see the sword come, and blow not the trumpet, and the people be not warned; if the sword come, and take any life from among them, he is taken away in his iniquity; but his blood will I require ⁷ at the watchman's hand. So thou, O Son of Adam, I have set thee a watchman to the house of Israel; therefore thou shalt hear the word at my mouth, and warn them from me. ⁸ When I say to the wicked, 'O wicked man, thou shalt 'surely die;' then if thou dost not speak to warn the wicked

from his way, that wicked man shall die in his iniquity; but his blood will I require at thy hand. Again, if thou warn the wicked of his way to turn from it; if he do not turn from his way, he shall die in his iniquity; but thou hast saved thy soul. Therefore, O thou son of Adam, say to the house of Israel; Ye speak thus, saying, 'If our 'transgressions and our sins be upon us, and we pine away 'in them, how should we then live?' Say to them, As I live, the Lord Jehovah hath said it, I have no pleasure in the death of the wicked; but that the wicked man turn from his way and live. Turn ye, turn ye from your evil ways; for why will ye die, O house of Israel?

Therefore, thou son of Adam, say to the children of thy People, The righteousness of the righteous man shall not deliver him in the day of his transgression. And as for the wickedness of the wicked man, he shall not fall thereby in the day that he turneth from his wickedness; neither shall the righteous man be able to live for his righteousness in the day that he sinneth. When I shall say to the righteous man, that he shall surely live; yet if he trust to his righteousness, and commit iniquity, all his righteousnesses will not be remembered; but for his iniquity that he hath committed, he shall die for it. Again, when I say to the wicked man, 'Thou shalt surely die;' then if he turn from his sin, and do what is lawful and right; if the wicked man restore the pledge, and give back what he had robbed, and walk in the statutes of life, without committing iniquity; he shall surely live, he shall not die. None of his sins that he hath committed shall be remembered against him; he hath done what is lawful and right; he shall surely live.

Yet the Children of thy People say, 'The way of the Lord 'is not equal.' But as for them, their way is not equal. When the righteous man turneth from his righteousness, and committeth iniquity, then he shall die thereby. But when the wicked man turneth from his wickedness, and doth that which is lawful and right, he shall live thereby. Yet ye say, 'The way of the Lord is not equal.' O ye house of Israel, I will judge you every one after his own ways.

AND IT CAME TO PASS in the twelfth year of our captivity [B.C. 589], in the tenth month, on the fifth day of the month, that one that had escaped out of Jerusalem

²² came to me, saying, 'The city is smitten.' Now the hand of Jehovah had been upon me in the evening, before he that was escaped came. But He had opened my mouth before he came to me in the morning; and my mouth was opened, and I was no more dumb.

²³ And the word of Jehovah came to me, saying, Son of ²⁴ Adam, they that inhabit those wastes of the land of Israel speak, saying, 'Abraham was one, and he gained posses-'sion of the land. And we are many; the land was given ²⁵ 'to us for a possession.' Therefore say thou to them, Thus saith the Lord Jehovah; Ye eat meat with the blood, and lift up your eyes toward your filthy idols, and ²⁶ shed blood; and shall ye possess the land? Ye stand upon your sword, ye work abomination, and ye defile every one his neighbour's wife; and shall ye possess the ²⁷ land? Say thou thus to them, Thus saith the Lord Jehovah; As I live, surely they that are in the wastes shall fall by the sword, and him that is in the open field will I give to the wild beasts to be devoured, and they that are in the strongholds and in the caves shall die of the pesti- ²⁸ lence. For I will lay the land desolate and waste, and the pomp of her strength shall cease; and the mountains of Israel shall be desolate, so that none shall pass through. ²⁹ Then shall they know that I am Jehovah, when I have laid the land desolate and waste, because of all their abominations which they have committed.

³⁰ Also, thou son of Adam, the Children of thy People are still talking about thee by the walls and in the doorways of the houses, and they speak one to another, every one to his brother, saying, 'Come, I pray you, and hear ³¹ 'what is the word that goeth forth from Jehovah.' And they will come to thee as a people cometh, and they will sit before thee as my people, and hear thy words, but they will not do them; for with their mouth they shew much love, but their heart goeth after their covetousness. ³² And lo, thou art to them as the song of loves of one that hath a pleasant voice, and can play well on an instrument; and they will hear thy words, but they will not ³³ do them. But when this cometh to pass, (lo, it will come,) —then will they know that a prophet hath been among them.

¹ And the word of Jehovah came to me, saying, Son of ² Adam, prophesy AGAINST THE SHEPHERDS of Israel, pro-

phesy, and say to them, Thus saith the Lord Jehovah to the shepherds ; Woe to the shepherds of Israel that feed themselves! should not the shepherds feed the flocks? Ye eat the fat, and ye clothe yourselves with the wool, ³ ye kill them that have been fattened ; but ye feed not the flock. The weak ye have not strengthened, neither ⁴ have ye healed the sick, neither have ye bound up the wounded, neither have ye brought back that which was driven away, neither have ye sought that which was lost ; but with force have ye ruled them, and with cruelty. And they were scattered, because there was no shepherd ; ⁵ and they became food to all the wild beasts of the field, when they were scattered. My sheep wandered through ⁶ all the mountains, and upon every high hill. Yea, my flock was scattered upon all the face of the earth, and none did search or seek after them.

Therefore, ye Shepherds, hear the word of Jehovah ; As ⁷ I live, the Lord Jehovah hath said it, surely because my ⁸ flock became a prey, and my flock became food to every wild beast of the field, because there was no shepherd, neither did my shepherds search for my flock ; but the shepherds fed themselves, and fed not my flock ; there- ⁹ fore, O ye Shepherds, hear the word of Jehovah ; thus ¹⁰ saith the Lord Jehovah ; Behold, I am against the Shepherds ; and I will require my flock at their hand, and will cause them to cease from being shepherds of the flock. Neither shall the shepherds feed themselves any more ; for I will deliver my flock from their mouth, that they may not be food for them.

For thus saith the Lord Jehovah ; Behold, I, even I, ¹¹ will both search for my flock, and I will seek them out. As a shepherd seeketh out his flock in the day that he is ¹² among his flock that are scattered ; so will I seek out my flock, and will deliver them out of all places where they were scattered in the cloudy and dark day. And I will ¹³ bring them out from the peoples, and gather them in from the countries, and will bring them to their own land, and feed them upon the mountains of Israel by the pools, and in all the inhabited places of the land. I will feed them ¹⁴ in a good pasture, and on the high mountains of Israel shall their fold be. There shall they lie in a good fold, and in a fat pasture shall they feed upon the mountains of Israel.

¹⁵ I will feed my flock, and I will cause them to lie down; ¹⁶ the Lord Jehovah hath said it. I will seek the lost, and bring back that which was driven away, and will bind up the wounded, and will strengthen the sick; but I will destroy the fat and the strong; I will feed them with judg- ¹⁷ ment. And as for you, O my flock, thus saith the Lord Jehovah; Behold, I will judge between small cattle and ¹⁸ small cattle, between the rams and the he goats. Is it a small thing for you to feed upon the good pasture, but ye must tread down with your feet the residue of your pastures'; and to drink of the shallow waters, but ye must ¹⁹ foul the residue with your feet? And as for my flock, shall they feed upon what ye have trodden with your feet; and shall they drink what ye have fouled with your feet?

²⁰ Therefore thus saith the Lord Jehovah to them; Behold, I, even I, will judge between the fat cattle and the lean ²¹ cattle. Because ye have thrust with side and with shoulder, and have pushed all the weak with your horns, till ²² ye have scattered them abroad; therefore will I save my flock, and they shall no more be a prey; and I will judge ²³ between cattle and cattle. And I will set up one shepherd over them, and he shall feed them, even my servant David; ²⁴ he shall feed them, and he shall be their shepherd. And I Jehovah will be their God, and my servant David a ²⁵ prince among them; I Jehovah have spoken it. And I will make with them a covenant of peace, and will cause the evil beasts to cease out of the land. And they shall dwell safely in the desert, and shall sleep in the forests. ²⁶ And I will make them and the places round about my Hill a blessing; and I will cause the shower to come down in ²⁷ its season; the showers shall be a blessing. And the tree of the field shall yield its fruit, and the earth shall yield its increase, and they shall be safe in their land; and they shall know that I am Jehovah, when I have broken the rods of their yoke, and delivered them out of the hand of ²⁸ those that made servants of them. And they shall no more be a prey to the Nations, neither shall the wild beast of the land devour them; but they shall dwell ²⁹ safely, and none shall make them afraid. And I will raise up for them a Plant of renown, and they shall be no more taken off by famine in the land, neither shall they

bear the reproach of the Nations any more. Thus they ³⁰ shall know that I Jehovah their God am with them, and that they, even the house of Israel, are my people; the Lord Jehovah hath said it. And ye my flock, the flock ³¹ of my pasture, are men, and I am your God; the Lord Jehovah hath said it.

And the word of Jehovah came to me, saying, Son of ¹ man, set thy face AGAINST MOUNT SEIR, and prophesy ² against it, and say to it, Thus saith the Lord Jehovah; Be- ³ hold, O mount Seir, I am against thee, and I will stretch out my hand against thee, and I will make thee desolate and waste. I will lay thy cities waste, and thou shalt be ⁴ desolate, and thou shalt know that I am Jehovah. Be- ⁵ cause thou hast had a hatred of old, and hast given up the children of Israel to the power of the sword in the time of their calamity, in the time that their iniquity cut them off; therefore, as I live, the Lord Jehovah hath said it, I will ⁶ prepare thee for blood, and blood shall pursue thee; since thou hast not hated blood, even blood shall pursue thee. Thus will I make mount Seir wholly desolate, and will ⁷ cut off from it him that passeth through and him that returneth. And I will fill its mountains with its slain men. ⁸ In thy hills, and in thy valleys, and in all thy pools, shall they fall down slain by the sword. I will make thee ⁹ perpetual desolations, and thy cities shall not be inhabited; and ye shall know that I am Jehovah. Because thou hast ¹⁰ said, 'These two nations [Judah and Israel] and these two 'countries shall be mine, and we will possess them;' whereas Jehovah was there; therefore, as I live, the Lord Jehovah ¹¹ hath said it, I will even do according to thine anger, and according to thine envy which thou hast used out of thy hatred against them; and I will make myself known among them, when I have judged thee. And thou shalt ¹² know that I am Jehovah. I have heard all thy blasphemies which thou hast spoken against the mountains of Israel, saying, 'They are laid desolate, they are given to us 'to consume.' Thus with your mouth ye have boasted ¹³ against me, and have multiplied your words against me; I have heard them. Thus saith the Lord Jehovah; When ¹⁴ the whole earth rejoiceth, I will make thee desolate. As ¹⁵ thou didst rejoice at the inheritance of the house of Israel, because it was desolate, so will I do to thee. Thou shalt

be desolate, O mount Seir, and all Edom, even all of it;
—and they shall know that I am Jehovah.

1 Also, thou son of Adam, prophesy to THE MOUNTAINS OF
ISRAEL, and say, Ye mountains of Israel, hear the word of
2 Jehovah. Thus saith the Lord Jehovah; Because the
enemy hath said against you, 'Aha, even the ancient high
3 'places are ours for a possession;' therefore prophesy, and
say, Thus saith the Lord Jehovah; Whereas and because
they have made you desolate, and swallowed you up on
every side, that ye might be a possession unto the residue
of the Nations, and ye are taken up on the lips of talkers,
4 and are the scoff of the people; therefore, ye Mountains of
Israel, hear the word of the Lord Jehovah; Thus saith the
Lord Jehovah to the mountains, and to the hills, to the
pools, and to the valleys, to the desolate wastes, and to the
cities that are forsaken, which became a prey and a derision
5 to the residue of the nations that are round about; therefore thus saith the Lord Jehovah; Surely in the fire of my
jealousy have I spoken against the residue of the Nations,
and against all Edom, who had appointed my land unto
themselves for a possession with the joy of all their heart,
with spite of soul, so as to drive it away as a prey.
6 Prophesy therefore concerning the land of Israel, and
say to the mountains, and to the hills, to the pools, and to
the valleys, Thus saith the Lord Jehovah; Behold, I have
spoken in my jealousy and in my wrath, because ye have
7 borne the reproach of the Nations. Therefore thus saith
the Lord Jehovah; I have lifted up my hand [in oath],
Surely the Nations that are about you, they shall bear their
8 own shame. But ye, O Mountains of Israel, ye shall shoot
forth your branches, and yield your fruit to my people
9 Israel; for they are at hand to come. For, behold, I am
for you, and I will turn to you, and ye shall be tilled and
10 sown. And I will multiply men upon you, all the house
of Israel, even all of it; and the cities shall be inhabited,
11 and the wastes shall be builded up. And I will multiply
upon you man and cattle; and they shall increase and bring
fruit; and I will make you to be inhabited after your old
state, and will do better unto you than at your beginnings;
12 and ye shall know that I am Jehovah. Yea, I will cause
men to walk upon you, even my people Israel; and
they shall possess thee, and thou shalt be their inherit-

ance, and thou shalt no more henceforth leave them childless.

Thus saith the Lord Jehovah; Because they say to you, ⁱ³ 'Thou [O land] devourest men, and hast left thy nations 'childless;' therefore thou shalt devour men no more, ¹⁴ neither shalt thou leave thy nations childless any more; the Lord Jehovah hath said it. Neither will I cause men ¹⁵ to hear in thee the reproach of the Nations any more, neither shalt thou bear the rebuke of the peoples any more, neither shalt thou cause thy nations to fall any more; the Lord Jehovah hath said it.

AND THE WORD OF JEHOVAH came to me, saying, Son of ¹⁶ Adam, when the house of Israel dwelt in their own land, ¹⁷ they defiled it in their way and in their doings; their way was before me as the uncleanness of a removed woman. Therefore I poured my wrath upon them for the blood that ¹⁸ they had poured out upon the land, and for their filthy idols wherewith they had polluted it. And I scattered ¹⁹ them among the Nations, and they were dispersed through the countries; according to their way, and according to their doings I judged them. And when they entered ²⁰ unto the nations, whither they went, they profaned my holy name, when they said of them, ' These are the people ' of Jehovah, and they are gone forth out of his land.'

But I have pity upon my holy name, which the house of ²¹ Israel have profaned among the nations, whither they went. Therefore say to the house of Israel, Thus saith the Lord ²² Jehovah; I do this not for your sakes, O house of Israel, but for my holy name's sake, which ye have profaned among the nations, whither ye went. And I will sanctify my great ²³ name, which was profaned among the Nations, which ye have profaned in the midst of them; and the Nations shall know that I am Jehovah, (the Lord Jehovah hath said it,) when I shall be sanctified in you before their eyes. For ²⁴ I will take you from among the Nations, and gather you in from all the countries, and will bring you into your own land. And I will sprinkle clean water upon you, and ye ²⁵ shall be clean; from all your filthiness, and from all your filthy idols, will I cleanse you. A new heart also will I ²⁶ give you, and a new spirit will I put within you. And I will take away the stony heart out of your flesh, and I will give you a heart of flesh. And I will put my spirit ²⁷

within you, and cause you to walk in my statutes, and ye
²⁸ shall keep my judgments, and do them. And ye shall
dwell in the land that I gave to your fathers; and ye shall
²⁹ be my people, and I will be your God. I will also save
you from all your uncleannesses. And I will call for the
corn, and will increase it, and will lay no famine upon you.
³⁰ And I will multiply the fruit of the tree, and the increase
of the field, so that ye shall receive no more reproach of
³¹ famine among the Nations. Then shall ye remember your
own evil ways, and your doings that were not good, and
shall loathe yourselves in your own sight for your iniquities
³² and for your abominations. Not for your sakes do I this,
(the Lord Jehovah hath said it,) be it known to you. Be
ye ashamed and confounded for your own ways, O house
of Israel.

³³ Thus saith the Lord Jehovah; In the day that I cleanse
you from all your iniquities I will also cause your cities to
³⁴ be inhabited, and the wastes shall be builded up. And
the desolate land shall be tilled, whereas it lay desolate in
³⁵ the sight of all that passed by. And they shall say, 'This
'land that was desolate is become like the garden of Eden;
'and the waste and desolate and ruined cities are become
³⁶ 'fenced, and are inhabited.' Then the Nations that are left
round about you shall know that I Jehovah build up the
ruined places, and I plant what was desolate. I Jehovah
have spoken it, and I will do it.

³⁷ Thus saith the Lord Jehovah; I will yet for this time
be inquired of by the house of Israel, to do it for them. I
³⁸ will increase them with men like a flock. As the flock of
holy animals, as the flock of Jerusalem in its solemn feasts;
so that the waste cities be filled with flocks of men; and
—they shall know that I am Jehovah.

¹ The hand of Jehovah was upon me, and carried me out
in the spirit of Jehovah, and set me down in the middle
² of the valley; and it was full of bones. And he caused
me to pass among them round about. And behold, there
were very many on the face of the valley; and, lo, they
³ were very dry. And he said to me, 'Son of Adam, can
'these bones live?' And I said, 'O Lord Jehovah, thou
⁴ 'knowest.' Again he said to me, 'Prophesy upon these
'bones, and say to them, O YE DRY BONES, hear the word
⁵ 'of Jehovah. Thus saith the Lord Jehovah to these bones;

'Behold, I will cause breath to enter into you, and ye shall live. And I will lay sinews upon you, and will bring up flesh upon you, and cover you with skin, and put breath into you, and ye shall live; and ye shall know that I am Jehovah.' So I prophesied as I was commanded; and as I prophesied, there was a noise, and behold a shaking, and the bones came together, bone to its bone. And when I looked, lo, the sinews and the flesh came up upon them, and the skin covered them above; but there was no breath in them. Then he said to me, 'Prophesy to the wind, prophesy, son of Adam, and say to the wind, Thus saith the Lord Jehovah; Come from the four winds, O wind, and blow upon these slain, that they may live.' So I prophesied as he commanded me, and the wind [or breath] came into them, and they lived, and stood up upon their feet, an exceeding great army.

Then he said to me, Son of Adam, these bones are the whole house of Israel; behold, they say, 'Our bones are dried, and our hope is lost. As for us, we are cut off.' Therefore prophesy thou, and say to them, Thus saith the Lord Jehovah; Behold, I will open your graves, and cause you, O my people, to come up out of your graves, and I will bring you into the land of Israel. And ye shall know that I am Jehovah, when I have opened your graves, O my people, and brought you up out of your graves, and I have put my breath into you, and ye live, and I have placed you in your own land. Then shall ye know that I Jehovah have spoken it, and have performed it; Jehovah hath said it.

THE WORD OF JEHOVAH came again to me, saying, Moreover, thou son of Adam, take thee one stick, and write upon it, 'For Judah, and for the children of Israel his companions.' Then take another stick, and write upon it, 'For Joseph, the stick of Ephraim, and for all the house of Israel his companions.' And join them one to another into one stick; and they shall become one in thy hand. And when the children of thy people shall speak to thee, saying, 'Wilt thou not shew us what thou meanest by these?' say to them, Thus saith the Lord Jehovah; Behold, I will take the stick of Joseph, which is in the hand of Ephraim, and the sceptres of Israel his companions, and will put them to it, with the stick of Judah, and make them to be

²⁰ one stick, and they shall be one in my hand. And the sticks whereon thou writest shall be in thy hand before their eyes.

²¹ And say to them, Thus saith the Lord Jehovah; Behold, I will take the children of Israel from among the Nations, whither they are gone, and will gather them together from ²² every side, and bring them into their own land. And I will make them to be one nation in the land upon the mountains of Israel; and one king shall be king of them all. And they shall be no more two nations, neither shall ²³ they be divided into two kingdoms any more at all. Neither shall they defile themselves any more with their filthy idols, nor with their detestable things, nor with any of their transgressions. But I will save them out of all their dwelling-places, wherein they have sinned, and will cleanse them; so shall they be my people, and I will be their God. ²⁴ And David my servant shall be king over them; and they shall all have one shepherd. They shall also walk in my judgments, and shall observe my statutes, and do them. ²⁵ And they shall dwell in the land that I gave to Jacob my servant, wherein your fathers have dwelt; and they shall dwell therein, even they, and their children, and their children's children for ever; and my servant David shall be ²⁶ their prince for ever. Moreover I will make a covenant of peace with them; it shall be an everlasting covenant with them. And I will place them, and multiply them, and will ²⁷ set my Sanctuary in the midst of them for evermore. My Tabernacle also shall be with them; yea, I will be their ²⁸ God, and they shall be my people. And the Nations shall know that I Jehovah do sanctify Israel, when my Sanctuary —shall be in the midst of them for evermore.

¹ And the word of Jehovah came to me, saying, Son of ² Adam, set thy face AGAINST GOG of the land of Magog [or Scythia], the prince of Rosh [or the Russians], of Meshech [or the Muscovites], and of Tubal [or the Tibareni], and ³ prophesy against him, and say, Thus saith the Lord Jehovah; Behold, I am against thee, O Gog, prince of Rosh of ⁴ Meshech, and of Tubal. And I will bring thee again, and put hooks into thy jaws, and I will bring thee forth, and all thine army, horses and horsemen, all of them clothed most gorgeously, even a great company with bucklers and ⁵ shields, all of them handling swords; Persia, Ethiopia, and

Phut [or Africa] with them; all of them with shield and helmet; Gomer [or the Cimmerians], and all his hordes; ⁶ the house of Togarmah [or Armenia] of the back part of the north, and all his hordes of many peoples with thee. Be thou prepared, and prepare thyself, thou, and all thy ⁷ company that are assembled unto thee, and be thou a guard to them. After many days thou shalt be visited; in the ⁸ latter years thou shalt come into the land that is brought back from the sword, and is gathered out of many peoples, against the mountains of Israel, which have been a long time waste. But it hath been brought forth out of the peoples, and they shall dwell as if in safety all of them. Thou shalt go up and come like a storm, thou shalt be ⁹ like a cloud to cover the land, thou, and all thy hordes, and many peoples with thee.

Thus saith the Lord Jehovah; It shall also come to pass ¹⁰ in that day, that things shall come into thy mind, [O Gog,] and thou shalt purpose an evil purpose; and thou ¹¹ shalt say, 'I will go up to the land of villages; I will go to 'them that are at rest, that dwell as if in safety, all of them 'dwelling without walls, and having neither bars nor doors, 'to seize plunder, and to take prey;' to turn thy hand upon ¹² the desolate places that are now inhabited, and upon the people that have been gathered out of the Nations, who have got cattle and goods, who dwell in the very middle spot of the earth [or Jerusalem]. Sheba, and Dedan, ¹³ and the merchants of Tarshish, with all their young lions, shall say to thee, 'Art thou come to seize plunder? Hast 'thou gathered together thy company to take prey? to 'carry away silver and gold, to take away cattle and goods, 'to seize great plunder?'

Therefore, son of Adam, prophesy and say to Gog, Thus ¹⁴ saith the Lord Jehovah; In that day when my people of Israel dwelleth as if in safety, shalt thou not know it? And thou shalt come from thy place out of the back parts ¹⁵ of the north, thou, and many peoples with thee, all of them riding on horses, a great company, and a mighty army; and thou shalt come against my people of Israel, ¹⁶ as a cloud to cover the land; it shall be in the latter days, and I will bring thee against my land, so that the Nations may know me, when I shall be sanctified by means of thee, O Gog, before their eyes.

17 (Thus saith the Lord Jehovah; Art thou he [Nebuchadnezzar] of whom I have spoken in old time by the hand of my servants the prophets of Israel, who prophesied in those days, for many years, that I would bring thee against them?)
18 And it shall come to pass in that day, in the day when Gog shall come against the land of Israel, the Lord Jehovah hath said it, that my wrath shall come up in my face.
19 For in my jealousy and in the fire of my wrath have I spoken, Surely in that day there shall be a great shaking
20 in the land of Israel; so that the fishes of the sea, and the fowls of the heavens, and the wild beasts of the field, and all creeping things that creep upon the earth, and all the men that are upon the face of the earth, shall shake at my presence; and the mountains shall be thrown down, and the steep places shall fall, and every wall shall fall to
21 the ground. And I will call for a sword against him throughout all my mountains, the Lord Jehovah hath said
22 it; every man's sword shall be against his brother. And I will plead against him with pestilence and with blood; and I will rain upon him, and upon his hordes, and upon the many peoples that are with him, an overflowing rain,
23 and great hailstones, fire, and brimstone. Thus will I magnify myself, and sanctify myself; and I will be known in the eyes of many nations, and they shall know that I —am Jehovah.
1 Therefore, thou son of Adam, prophesy against Gog, and say, Thus saith the Lord Jehovah; Behold, I am against thee, O Gog, prince of Rosh, of Meshech, and of
2 Tubal; and I will bring thee again, and lead thee about, and will cause thee to come up from the back parts of the north, and will bring thee upon the mountains of Israel.
3 Then I will smite thy bow out of thy left hand, and I
4 will cause thine arrows to fall out of thy right hand. Thou shalt fall upon the mountains of Israel, thou, and all thy hordes, and the peoples that are with thee. I will give thee to the ravenous birds of every sort, and to the wild
5 beasts of the field to be devoured. Thou shalt fall upon the face of the field; for I have spoken, the Lord Jeho-
6 vah hath said it. And I will send a fire on Magog, and on them that dwell as if in safety in the isles; and they shall
7 know that I am Jehovah. So will I make my holy name

to be known in the midst of my people Israel; and I will not let them pollute my holy name any more. And the Nations shall know that I am Jehovah, the Holy One in Israel.

Behold, it is come, and it is past, the Lord Jehovah hath said it; this is the day whereof I have spoken. And they that dwell in the cities of Israel shall go forth, and shall burn and make fires of the weapons, both the shields and the bucklers, the bows and the arrows, and the handstaves, and the spears, and they shall make fires of them for seven years; so that they shall take no wood out of the field, neither shall they cut down any out of the forests; for of the weapons they shall make their fires; and they shall plunder those that plundered them, and make a prey of those that made a prey of them; the Lord Jehovah hath said it. ^{8 9 10}

And it shall come to pass in that day, that I will give to Gog a burial-place there in Israel, the Valley of the Passengers on the east of the [Great] Sea; and it shall stop the [noses of] the passengers. And there shall they bury Gog and all his rabble. And they shall call it The Valley of Hamon-gog [or Gog's rabble]. And seven months shall the house of Israel be burying of them, that they may cleanse the land. Yea, all the people of the land shall bury them; and it shall be to them a renown on the day that I shall be glorified; the Lord Jehovah hath said it. And they shall set apart men of continual employment, who shall pass through the land to bury with the passengers those that remain upon the face of the land, to cleanse it. After the end of seven months shall they be yet searching. And the passengers that pass through the land, when any one seeth a man's bone, then shall he set up a way-mark [or burial-stone] by it, till the buriers have buried it in the valley of Hamon-gog. And also the name of the city shall be Hamonah [or Rabble]. Thus shall they cleanse the land. ^{11 12 13 14 15 16}

And, thou son of Adam, thus saith the Lord Jehovah; Say to the fowl of every kind, and to every wild beast of the field, Assemble yourselves, and come; gather yourselves on every side to my sacrifice that I do sacrifice for you, even a great sacrifice upon the mountains of Israel, that ye may eat flesh, and drink blood. Ye shall eat the flesh of the warriors, and drink the blood of the princes ^{17 18}

of the earth, of rams, of lambs, and of goats, of bullocks,
19 all of them fatlings of Bashan. And ye shall eat fat till
ye be full, and drink blood till ye be drunken, of my sacri-
20 fice which I have sacrificed for you. Thus ye shall be
filled at my table with horses and chariots, with mighty
men, and with all men of war; the Lord Jehovah hath said it.
21 And I will set my glory among the Nations, and all the
Nations shall see my judgment that I have executed, and
22 my hand that I have laid upon them. So the house of
Israel shall know that I am Jehovah their God from that
23 day and forward. And the Nations shall know that the
house of Israel went into captivity for their iniquity; because they trespassed against me, therefore hid I my face
from them, and gave them into the hand of their enemies;
24 so they all fell by the sword. According to their uncleanness and according to their transgressions have I done to
them, and have hidden my face from them.
25 Therefore thus saith the Lord Jehovah. Now will I
bring home the captivity of Jacob, and have mercy on
the whole house of Israel, and I will be jealous for my
26 holy name. And they shall forget their shame, and all
their trespasses wherein they have trespassed against me,
when they dwelt safely in their land; and none shall
27 make them afraid. When I have brought them again from
the peoples, and gathered them out of their enemies' lands,
and when I am sanctified among them in the sight of
28 many nations; then shall they know that I am Jehovah
their God, in that I caused them to be led into captivity
among the Nations; but I have gathered them unto their
own land, and have left none of them any more there.
29 Neither will I hide my face any more from them. For I
have poured out my spirit upon the house of Israel; the
—Lord Jehovah hath said it.

---

1 IN THE FIVE AND TWENTIETH YEAR of our captivity
[B.C. 576], in the beginning of the year, on the tenth day
of the month, in the fourteenth year after that the city
was smitten, in the selfsame day the hand of Jehovah was
2 upon me, and he brought me thither. In the visions of
God he brought me into the land of Israel, and set me
upon a very high mountain, upon which was as the frame
3 of a city toward the south. And he brought me thither,
and behold, there was a man, whose appearance was like

the appearance of copper, with a thread of flax in his hand, and a measuring reed; and he stood in the city gate. And the man said to me, 'Son of Adam, behold ⁴ 'with thine eyes, and hear with thine ears, and set thy 'heart on all that I shall shew thee; for to the intent 'that thou mightest see them art thou brought hither. 'Declare thou all that thou seest to the house of Israel.' And behold a wall on the outside of the House [or ⁵ Temple] round about, and in the man's hand a measuring reed of six cubits long [or ten feet] by the cubit and a hand breadth. So he measured the breadth of the building, one reed [or ten feet]; and the height, one reed.

Then came he to the gate which looketh TOWARD THE ⁶ EAST, and went up its stairs, and measured the threshold of the gate, which was one reed broad; and the other threshold [or the lintel], which was one reed broad. And ⁷ every little chamber was one reed long, and one reed broad; and between the little chambers were five cubits; and the threshold of the gate by the side of the porch of the gate inward was one reed. He measured also the ⁸ porch of the gate inward, one reed. Then measured he ⁹ the porch of the gate, eight cubits; and its pilasters, two cubits. And the porch of the gate was inward. And the ¹⁰ little chambers of the eastern gate were three on this side, and three on that side. The three were of one measure; and the pilasters had one measure on this side and on that side. And he measured the breadth of the entrance of ¹¹ the gate, ten cubits; and the depth of the gate, thirteen cubits. The space also before the little chambers was one ¹² cubit on this side, and the space was one cubit on that side. And each little chamber was six cubits on this side, and six cubits on that side. He measured then the gate ¹³ from the roof of one little chamber to the roof of another; the breadth was five and twenty cubits, doorway against doorway. (He made also pilasters of threescore cubits, ¹⁴ even to the pilaster of the court, round about the gate.) And from the face of the Gate of the Entrance to the face ¹⁵ of the porch of the Inner Gate were fifty cubits. And there ¹⁶ were barred windows to the little chambers, both at their pilasters within the gate round about, and likewise at the cornices; and the windows were round about inward. And upon each pilaster were palm leaves.

17 Then brought he me into the OUTER COURT, and, lo, there were chambers, and a pavement made for the court round about. Thirty chambers were upon the pavement.
18 And the pavement by the side of the gates over against
19 the depth of the gates was the Lower Pavement. Then he measured the breadth from the front of the Lower Gate to the front of the Inner Court without, a hundred cubits eastward and northward.
20 And the gate of the Outer Court that looked toward the
21 north, he measured its depth, and its breadth. And its little chambers were three on this side and three on that side; and its pilasters and its cornices were after the measure of the first gate. Its depth was fifty cubits, and its
22 breadth five and twenty cubits. And their windows, and their cornices, and their palm leaves, were after the measure of the gate that looketh toward the east. And they went up into it by seven steps; and its cornices were before
23 them. And there was a gate to the Inner Court over against the gate toward the north, and toward the east. And he measured from gate to gate a hundred cubits.
24 After that he brought me toward the south, and behold, a gate toward the south; and he measured its pilasters and
25 its cornices according to the same measures. And there were windows in it and at its cornices round about, like those windows. The depth was fifty cubits, and the
26 breadth five and twenty cubits. And there were seven steps to go up to it, and its cornices were before them. And it had palm leaves, one on this side, and another on that side, upon its pilasters.
27 And there was a gate in the INNER COURT toward the south. And he measured from gate to gate toward the
28 south a hundred cubits. And he brought me to the Inner Court by the south gate; and he measured the south gate
29 according to the same measures. And its little chambers, and its pilasters, and its cornices, were according to the same measures. And there were windows in it and at its cornices round about. It was fifty cubits deep, and five
30 and twenty cubits broad. And the cornices round about were five and twenty cubits long, and five cubits broad.
31 And its cornices were toward the Outer Court; and palm leaves were upon its pilasters. And the going up to it had eight steps.

And he brought me into the Inner Court toward the ³² east; and he measured the gate according to the same measures. And its little chambers, and its pilasters, and ³³ its cornices, were according to the same measures; and there were windows to it and at its cornices round about. It was fifty cubits long, and five and twenty cubits broad. And its cornices were toward the Outer Court; and palm ³⁴ leaves were upon its pilasters, on this side, and on that side. And the going up to it had eight steps.

And he brought me to the NORTH GATE, and mea- ³⁵ sured it according to the same measures; its little cham- ³⁶ bers, its pilasters, and its cornices, and the windows to it round about. The depth was fifty cubits, and the breadth five and twenty cubits. And its pilasters were toward ³⁷ the Outer Court; and palm leaves were upon its pilasters, on this side, and that side. And the going up to it had eight steps. And there was a chamber; and its entrance ³⁸ was by the pilasters of the gates, where they washed the burnt offering. And in the Porch of the Gate were two ³⁹ tables on this side, and two tables on that side, to slay thereon the burnt offering and the sin offering and the guilt offering. And without, at the side, as one goeth up ⁴⁰ to the entrance of the North Gate, were two tables; and on the other side, which was at the porch of the gate, were two tables. Four tables were on this side, and four tables ⁴¹ on that side, by the side of the gate; eight tables, whereupon they slew [the sacrifices]. And the four tables for the ⁴² burnt offering, were of hewn stone, each of a cubit and a half long, and a cubit and a half broad, and one cubit high; whereupon also they laid the instruments wherewith they slew the burnt offering and the sacrifice. And within ⁴³ were cattle-fastenings, a hand-breadth broad, fixed round about; and upon the tables was the flesh of the offering.

And on the outside of the Inner Gate were the chambers ⁴⁴ of the singers in the Inner Court; one of which was at the side of the north gate, and their prospect was toward the south; one at the side of the east gate having the prospect toward the north. And he said to me, 'This chamber, ⁴⁵ ' whose prospect is toward the south, is for the priests, the ' keepers of the charge of the House. And the chamber ⁴⁶ ' whose prospect is toward the north is for the priests, the ' keepers of the charge of the Altar. These are the sons ' of Zadok among the sons of Levi, who come near to Je-

⁴⁷ 'hovah to minister to him.' So he measured the court, a hundred cubits long, and a hundred cubits broad, four-square; and the Altar was in front of the House.

⁴⁸ Then he brought me to the PORCH OF THE HOUSE, and measured each pilaster of the Porch, five cubits on this side, and five cubits on that side, and the breadth of the gate was three cubits on this side, and three cubits on that ⁴⁹ side. The depth of the porch was twenty cubits, and the breadth eleven cubits, even at the steps whereby men go up to it. And there were pillars by the pilasters, one on —this side, and another on that side.

¹ And he brought me to the GREAT HALL, and measured the pilasters, six cubits broad on the one side, and six cubits broad on the other side, which was the breadth of ² the Tent. And the breadth of the doorway was ten cubits; and on the sides of the doorway were five cubits on the one side, and five cubits on the other side. And he measured its length, forty cubits; and the breadth, twenty cubits.

³ Then went he into the INNER ROOM, and measured the pilaster of the doorway, two cubits; and the doorway, six cubits; and the breadth of the doorway, seven cubits.
⁴ Then he measured the length [of the Inner Room], twenty cubits; and the breadth, twenty cubits, on the face of the Great Hall. And he said to me, 'This is the Holy of 'Holies.'

⁵ Afterward he measured the wall of the House, six cubits; and the breadth of the ROWS OF CHAMBERS, four cubits, ⁶ round about the House on every side. And the Rows of Chambers were three, one over another, and there were thirty in each; and they entered into a wall which was against the House for the Rows of Chambers round about, that they might have hold, but they had not hold in the ⁷ wall of the House. The Rows of Chambers were broader and were changed from story to story; according to the circuit of the House, from story to story round about the House; so was the breadth of the House on each story, and thus they increased from the lowest row to the highest ⁸ towards the middle [of the House]. I saw also the height of the House round about; the foundations of the Rows of ⁹ Chambers were a full reed of six great cubits. Five cubits was the thickness of the wall, which was for the Rows of

22—2

Chambers outside, and that of the space left between the House and the Rows of Chambers which were towards the House. And the size of the Chambers was a breadth of ¹⁰ twenty cubits round about the House on every side. And ¹¹ the entrance to the Rows of Chambers was by the space that was left, one entrance toward the north, and another entrance toward the south. And the breadth of the place that was left was five cubits round about.

Now the BUILDING that was before the Separate Place ¹² at the side toward the west was seventy cubits broad; and the wall of the Building was five cubits thick round about, and the length thereof ninety cubits.

So he measured the House, a hundred cubits long; and ¹³ the Separate Place, and the Building, with its walls, each a hundred cubits long; also the breadth of the face of the ¹⁴ House, and of the Separate Place toward the east, a hundred cubits. And he measured the length of the BUILD- ¹⁵ ING over against the Separate Place which was behind it, and its Galleries on the one side and on the other side, each a hundred cubits.

And the Great Hall, the Inner Room, and the porches of the court, the lintels, and the barred windows, and the ¹⁶ Galleries round about on their three stories, over against the lintel, were panelled with wood round about, and from the ground up to the windows; and the windows ¹⁷ were covered, on the part above the doorway, and unto the Inner Room, and the Outer; and on all the wall round about in the Inner Room and the Outer were hangings. And it was made with cherubs and palm trees, so that a ¹⁸ palm tree was between a cherub and a cherub; and every cherub had two faces; so that the face of a man was to- ¹⁹ ward the palm tree on the one side, and the face of a young lion toward the palm tree on the other side; thus it was made through all the House round about. From the ²⁰ ground unto above the doorway were the cherubs and palm trees made, and they were on the wall of the Great Hall. The door-posts of the Great Hall were squared, as ²¹ were those of the face of the Sanctuary; the appearance of the one as the appearance of the other.

The altar of wood was three cubits high, and its length, ²² two cubits; and it had corners; and its length, and its walls, were of wood; and he said to me, 'This is THE 'TABLE that is in the presence of Jehovah.'

²³ And the Great Hall and the Sanctuary had two doors.
²⁴ And the doors had two leaves each, two turning leaves; two leaves for the one door, and two leaves for the other.
²⁵ And there were made on them, on the doors of the Great Hall, cherubs and palm trees, like as were made upon the walls; and there was a thick beam of wood over the face
²⁶ of the Porch without. And there were barred windows and palm trees on the one side and on the other side, on the sides of the Porch, and on the Rows of Chambers of —the House, and thick beams.

¹ Then he brought me forth into the Outer Court, by the way toward the north; and he brought me into the chamber that was over against the Separate Place, and which was
² before the BUILDING TOWARD THE NORTH. In front of the length of a hundred cubits was the north doorway, and
³ the breadth was fifty cubits. Over against the twenty cubits which were for the Inner Court, and over against the pavement which was for the Outer Court, was gallery
⁴ facing gallery in three stories. And before the chambers was a walk of ten cubits breadth toward the Inner [Court], a foot-way of one cubit; and their doorways were toward
⁵ the north. Now the upper chambers were shorter (for the galleries took space from them) than the lower, and
⁶ than the middlemost of the Building. For they were in three stories, but had not pillars as the pillars of the courts. Therefore they were narrowed more than the
⁷ lowest and the middlemost from the ground. And the fence-wall that was on the outside over against the chambers, toward the Outer Court in front of the chambers,
⁸ its length was fifty cubits. For the length of the chambers that were in the Outer Court was fifty cubits; but
⁹ those before the Great Hall were a hundred cubits. And from under these chambers was the entrance on the east side, as one goeth into them from the Outer Court.
¹⁰ There were chambers in the thickness of the fence-wall of the Court toward the east, over against the Separate
¹¹ Place, and over against the Building; and a way was before them. They were like the appearance of the chambers which were toward the north, as long as they, and as broad as they; and all their goings out were both according to the fashions of those, and according to their door-
¹² ways. And according to the doorways of the chambers

that were toward the south was a doorway at the head of the way, even the way before the fence-wall directly toward the east, as one entereth into them.

Then said he to me, 'The north chambers and the south ¹³ 'chambers, which are before the Separate Place, they are 'holy chambers, where the priests that approach unto Jeho-'vah shall eat the most holy things; there shall they lay 'the most holy things, and the meal offering, and the sin 'offering, and the guilt offering; for the place is holy. 'When the priests enter in, then shall they not go out of ¹⁴ 'the Holy Place into the Outer Court, but there shall they 'lay their garments wherein they minister; for they are 'holy; and they shall put on other garments, when they 'approach to those places which are for the people.'

Now when he had made an end of measuring the inner ¹⁵ house, he brought me out by the way of the gate whose prospect is toward the east, and measured A SPACE ROUND ABOUT IT. He measured the east side with the measuring ¹⁶ reed, five hundred reeds, with the measuring reed round about. He measured the north side, five hundred reeds, ¹⁷ with the measuring reed round about. He measured the ¹⁸ south side, five hundred reeds, with the measuring reed. He turned about to the west side, and measured five hun- ¹⁹ dred reeds with the measuring reed. He measured it on ²⁰ the four sides. It had a wall round about, on its length five hundred, and on its breadth five hundred, to make a separation between the holy and the unholy. —

Then he brought me to the gate, even the gate that ¹ looketh toward the east; and, behold, the glory of the God ² of Israel came from the way of the east; and his voice was like a noise of many waters; and the earth shined with his glory. And the appearance of the vision which I saw was ³ according to the vision that I saw when I came about the destruction of the city; and the visions were like the vision that I saw by the river Chebar. And I fell upon my face. And the glory of Jehovah came into the House by the way ⁴ of the gate whose prospect is toward the east.

So the spirit took me up, and brought me into the Inner ⁵ Court; and, behold, the glory of Jehovah filled the House. And I heard one speaking to me out of the House; and ⁶ the man stood near to me. And he said unto me, 'Son of ⁷ 'Adam, the place of my throne, and the place of the soles

'of my feet, where I will dwell in the midst of the chil-
'dren of Israel for ever, and my holy name, shall the house
'of Israel no more defile, neither they, nor their kings, by
'their fornication, nor by the carcases of their kings at
8 'their death. By their setting of their threshold near my
'thresholds, and their door-post by the side of my door-
'posts, (and there is a wall between me and them,) they
'even defiled my holy Name by their abominations that
'they have committed. Therefore I consumed them in
9 'mine anger. Now let them put away their fornication,
'and the carcases of their kings, far from me, and I will
'dwell in the midst of them for ever.
10   'Thou Son of Adam, shew the House to the house of
'Israel, that they may be ashamed of their iniquities; and
11 'let them measure the pattern. And if they be ashamed
'of all that they have done, shew them the form of the
'House, and its pattern, and its goings out, and its
'comings in, and all its forms, and all its ordinances, and
'all its forms, and all its laws; and write it in their sight,
'that they may keep its whole form, and all its ordinances,
'and do them.
12   'This is the LAW OF THE HOUSE; Upon the top of the
'mountain the whole limit thereof round about shall be
'most holy. Behold, this is the Law of the House.
13   'And these are the MEASURES OF THE ALTAR after the
'cubits; (the cubit is a cubit and a hand breadth;) and
'the Hollow [or trench] shall be a cubit [deep], and a
'cubit broad, and the border thereof by its edge round
'about shall be a span. And this shall be the ditch of
14 'the altar. And from the Hollow upon the ground, to
'the lower platform shall be two cubits. And the breadth
'shall be one cubit. And from the lesser platform to the
'greater platform shall be four cubits, and the breadth
15 'one cubit; and from the Harel-platform [or Mount of
'God] shall be four cubits. And from the Ariel-altar [or
16 'Hearth of God] and upward shall be four horns. And
'the Ariel-altar shall be twelve cubits long, twelve broad,
17 'square in its four sides. And the [Harel-] platform shall
'be fourteen cubits long and fourteen broad in its four
'sides; and the border round about it shall be half
'a cubit; and its Hollow shall be a cubit round about;
'and its steps shall look toward the east.'

And he said to me, 'Son of Adam, thus saith the Lord ¹⁸
'Jehovah; These are the ORDINANCES OF THE ALTAR in
'the day when they shall make it, to offer up burnt offer-
'ings thereon, and to sprinkle blood thereon. And thou ¹⁹
'shalt give to the priests, the Levites that are of the seed
'of Zadok, who approach to me, to minister to me, (the
'Lord Jehovah hath said it,) a young bullock for a sin
'offering. And thou shalt take some of its blood, and put ²⁰
'it on the four horns of it, and on the four corners of the
'platform, and upon the border round about; thus shalt
'thou cleanse it from sin, and shalt make atonement for
'it. Thou shalt take the bullock also of the sin offering, ²¹
'and he shall burn it in the appointed place of the House,
'outside the Sanctuary. And on the second day thou ²²
'shalt bring a kid of the goats without blemish for a sin
'offering; and they shall cleanse the altar from sin, as
'they did cleanse it with the bullock. When thou hast ²³
'made an end of cleansing it from sin, thou shalt bring a
'young bullock without blemish, and a ram out of the
'flock without blemish. And thou shalt bring them be- ²⁴
'fore Jehovah, and the priests shall cast salt upon them,
'and they shall offer them for a burnt offering to Jehovah.
'Seven days shalt thou offer every day a goat for a sin ²⁵
'offering; they shall also offer a young bullock, and a ram
'out of the flock, without blemish. During seven days ²⁶
'shall they make atonement for the Altar and purify it,
'and fill their hands [with offerings]. And when these ²⁷
days are expired, it shall be, that upon the eighth day,
'and so forward, the priests shall make your burnt offer-
'ings upon the altar, and your peace offerings; and I will
'accept you; the Lord Jehovah hath said it.'

Then he brought me back the way of the outer gate of ¹
the Sanctuary which looketh toward the east; and it was
shut. Then said Jehovah to me; 'This gate shall be ²
'shut, it shall not be opened, and no man shall enter in
'by it; because Jehovah, the God of Israel, hath entered
'in by it, therefore it shall be shut. It is for the Prince; ³
'the Prince [Zerubbabel], he shall return through it to
'eat bread before Jehovah. He shall enter by the way
'of the porch of that gate, and shall go out by the way
'of the same.'

Then he brought me the way of the north gate in front ⁴

of the House. And I looked, and behold, the glory of Jehovah filled the House of Jehovah; and I fell upon my ⁵ face. And Jehovah said to me, 'Son of Adam, mark well, 'and behold with thine eyes, and hear with thine ears all 'that I say to thee concerning all the ordinances of the 'House of Jehovah, and all its laws; and mark well the 'entrance of the House, with all who go forth from the ⁶ 'Sanctuary. And thou shalt say to the rebellious people, 'even to the house of Israel, Thus saith the Lord Jehovah; 'O ye house of Israel, let it suffice you of all your abomin- ⁷ 'ations, in that ye have brought sons of foreigners, uncir- 'cumcised in heart, and uncircumcised in flesh, to be in my 'Sanctuary, to pollute it, even my House, when ye bring 'my bread, the fat and the blood, and they have broken ⁸ 'my covenant because of all your abominations. And ye 'have not kept the charge of my holy things; but ye have 'set keepers of my charge in my Sanctuary for yourselves.'

⁹ Thus saith the Lord Jehovah; 'No son of a foreigner, 'uncircumcised in heart, nor uncircumcised in flesh, shall 'enter into my Sanctuary, of any son of a foreigner that is ¹⁰ 'among the children of Israel. And the LEVITES WHO 'WENT AWAY far from me, when Israel went astray, who 'went astray from me after their filthy idols; even they ¹¹ 'shall bear their iniquity. Yet they shall be ministers in 'my Sanctuary, having charge at the gates of the House, 'and ministering to the House. They shall slay the burnt 'offering and the sacrifice for the people, and they shall ¹² 'stand before them to minister for them. Because they 'ministered for them before their filthy idols, and were a 'stumbling-block to the house of Israel unto iniquity; 'therefore have I lifted up my hand [in oath] against them, 'the Lord Jehovah hath said it, and they shall bear their ¹³ 'iniquity; and they shall not come near to me, to do the 'office of a priest to me, nor to come near to any of my 'holy things, in the Holy of Holies; but they shall bear 'their shame, and their abominations which they have ¹⁴ 'committed. But I will make them keepers of the 'charge of the House, for all the service thereof, and for 'all that shall be done therein.

¹⁵ 'But THE PRIESTS, the Levites the sons of Zadok, that 'kept the charge of my Sanctuary when the children of 'Israel went astray from me, they shall come near to me

'to minister to me, and they shall stand in my presence to
'bring to me the fat and the blood; the Lord Jehovah
'hath said it. They shall enter into my Sanctuary, and
'they shall come near to my Table, to minister to me, and
'they shall keep my charge. And it shall come to pass,
'that when they enter in at the gates of the Inner Court,
'they shall be clothed with linen garments; and no wool
'shall be upon them, while they minister at the gates of
'the Inner Court, and within. They shall have linen
'head-dresses upon their heads, and shall have linen
'breeches upon their loins; they shall not gird themselves
'with any thing that causeth sweat. And when they go
'forth into the Outer Court, even into the Outer Court
'to the people, they shall put off their garments wherein
'they ministered, and lay them in the holy chambers, and
'they shall put on other garments; and they shall not
'sanctify the people with their garments.

'And they shall not shave their heads, nor suffer their
'locks to grow long; they shall only poll their heads.
'Neither shall any priest drink wine, when they enter into
'the Inner Court. Neither shall they take for their wives
'a widow, nor her that is put away; but they shall take
'maidens of the seed of the house of Israel, or a widow that
'was the widow of a priest. And they shall teach my
'people the difference between the holy and the unholy,
'and cause them to discern between the unclean and the
'clean. And in controversy they shall stand to judge; and
'they shall judge it according to my judgments; and they
'shall keep my laws and my statutes in all my solemn
'feasts, and they shall keep holy my sabbaths. And they
'shall come near no dead person to defile themselves; but
'for father, or for mother, or for son, or for daughter, for
'brother, or for sister that hath had no husband, they may
'defile themselves. And after he is cleansed, they shall
'reckon unto him seven days. And in the day that he
'goeth into the Holy Place, unto the Inner Court, to
'minister in holy things, he shall bring his sin offering; the
'Lord Jehovah hath said it. And it shall be to them for
'an inheritance; I am their inheritance. And ye shall give
'them no possession in Israel; I am their possession. They
'shall eat the meal offering, and the sin offering, and the
'guilt offering; and every devoted thing in Israel shall be

³⁰ 'theirs. And all the first of all the firstfruits, and of every
'heave offering, all out of every sort of your heave offer-
'ings, shall be for the priests. Ye shall also give to the
'priest the first of your dough, that he may cause a
³¹ 'blessing to rest on thy house. The priests shall not eat
'of anything that hath died of itself, or been torn in
—'pieces, whether it be fowl or beast.
¹ 'And when ye shall divide by lot the Land for inherit-
'ance, ye shall offer as a Heave Offering to Jehovah, a
'HOLY PORTION OF LAND. The length shall be the length
'of five and twenty thousand [reeds, or 37 miles], and the
'breadth shall be ten thousand. This shall be holy in all
² 'its borders round about. Of this there shall be for the
'Holy Place five hundred by five hundred, square round
'about; and fifty cubits of waste space round about it.
³ 'And by this measure shalt thou measure the length of
'the five and twenty thousand, and the breadth of the
'ten thousand; and in it shall be the Sanctuary, the Holy
⁴ 'of Holies. This holy portion of the land shall be for THE
'PRIESTS, the ministers of the Sanctuary, who come near
'to minister to Jehovah; and it shall be a place for their
'houses, and a holy place for the Sanctuary.
⁵ 'And five and twenty thousand of length, and ten
'thousand of breadth, shall also THE LEVITES, the min-
'isters of the House, have for themselves for a possession,
'for twenty chambers.
⁶ 'And ye shall appoint a possession for THE CITY five
'thousand broad, and five and twenty thousand long, over
'against the holy Heave Offering. It shall be for the
'whole house of Israel.
⁷ 'And a portion shall be for THE PRINCE on the one
'side and on the other side of the holy Heave Offering,
'and of the possession for the city, in front of the holy
'Heave Offering, and in front of the possession for the city,
'from the west side westward, and from the east side
'eastward; and the length shall be over against one of
'the portions, from the west boundary unto the east
⁸ 'boundary. In the land shall be his possession in Israel.
'And my princes shall no more oppress my people; and
'[the rest of] the land shall they give to the house of
'Israel according to their tribes.'
⁹ Thus saith the Lord Jehovah; 'Let this suffice you, O

'princes of Israel. Remove violence and robbery, and
'execute justice and righteousness, take away your expul-
'sions from my people; the Lord Jehovah hath said it.
'Ye shall have just balances, and a just Ephah, and a just ¹⁰
'Bath. The Ephah and the Bath shall be of one measure, ¹¹
'so that the Bath may contain the tenth part of a Homer,
'and the Ephah the tenth part of a Homer. The measure
'thereof shall be after the Homer [of 75 gallons]. And ¹²
'the Shekel shall be twenty Gerahs. Twenty Shekels, five
'and twenty Shekels, fifteen Shekels [or 60 Shekels], shall
'be your Minah [of 30 ounces].

'This is the heave offering that ye shall offer; the sixth ¹³
'part of an Ephah out of every Homer of wheat, and ye
'shall give the sixth part of an Ephah out of every Homer
'of barley; concerning the ordinance of oil, the Bath of ¹⁴
'oil, ye shall offer the tenth part of a Bath out of every
'Cor of ten Baths, which is a Homer; for ten Baths are
'a Homer; and one lamb or kid out of the flock, out of ¹⁵
'every two hundred, out of the meadow land of Israel;
'for a meal offering, and for a burnt offering, and for
'peace offerings, to make atonement for them; the Lord
'Jehovah hath said it. All the people of the land shall ¹⁶
'give this heave offering for the Prince in Israel. And it ¹⁷
'shall be the Prince's part to give burnt offerings, and meal
'offerings, and drink offerings, in the feasts, and in the
'new moons, and in the sabbaths, in all appointed times
'of the house of Israel. He shall give the sin offering, and
'the meal offering, and the burnt offering, and the peace
'offerings, to make atonement for the house of Israel.'

Thus saith the Lord Jehovah; 'In the first month, on ¹⁸
'the first day of the month, thou shalt take a young bul-
'lock without blemish, in order to cleanse the Sanctuary
'from sin; and the priest shall take some of the blood of ¹⁹
'the sin offering, and put it upon the door-posts of the
'House, and upon the four corners of the platform of the
'Altar, and upon the door-posts of the gate of the Inner
'Court. And so thou shalt do on the seventh day of the ²⁰
'month for every one that sinneth in ignorance, and for
'him that hath been enticed. So shall ye make atone-
'ment for the House. In the first month, on the fourteenth ²¹
'day of the month, ye shall have THE PASSOVER, a feast of
'seven days; unleavened bread shall be eaten. And upon ²²

'that day shall the Prince give for himself and for all the
23 'people of the land a bullock for a sin offering. And
'during seven days of the feast he shall give a burnt
'offering to Jehovah, seven bullocks and seven rams with-
'out blemish daily the seven days; and a kid of the goats
24 'daily for a sin offering. And he shall give a meal offer-
'ing of an Ephah [or bushel] for each bullock, and an
'Ephah for each ram, and a Hin [or ten pints] of oil for
'each Ephah.
25 'In the seventh month, on the fifteenth day of the
'month, at THE FEAST [of Tabernacles] shall he do the
'like for seven days, as to the sin offering, as to the burnt
—'offering, as to the meal offering, and as to the oil.'

1 Thus saith the Lord Jehovah; 'The gate of the Inner
'Court that looketh toward the east shall be shut during
'the six working days; but on the day of the sabbath it
'shall be opened, and on the day of the new moon it shall
2 'be opened. And the Prince shall enter by the way of the
'porch of that gate from without, and shall stand by the
'door-post of the gate, and the priests shall offer his burnt
'offering and his peace offerings, and he shall worship at
'the threshold of the gate. Then he shall go out; but the
3 'gate shall not be shut until the evening. Likewise the
'people of the land shall worship at the entrance of this
'gate before Jehovah on the sabbaths and on the new
4 'moons. And the burnt offering that the Prince shall
'bring to Jehovah on the sabbath day shall be six lambs
5 'without blemish, and a ram without blemish. And the
'meal offering shall be an Ephah for each ram, and the
'meal offering for the lambs as his hand can give, and a
6 'Hin of oil to each Ephah. And on the day of the new
'moon it shall be a young bullock without blemish, and six
7 'lambs, and a ram; they shall be without blemish. And
'he shall give as a meal offering, an Ephah for the bullock,
'and an Ephah for the ram, and for the lambs according
'as his hand shall attain to, and a Hin of oil to each Ephah.
8 'And when the Prince shall enter, he shall go in by the
'way of the porch of that gate, and he shall go forth by
'the way thereof.
9 'And when the people of the land shall come before
'Jehovah on the solemn days, he that entereth in by the
'way of a north gate to worship shall go out by the way

'of a south gate; and he that entereth in by the way of
'a south gate shall go out by the way of a north gate.
'He shall not return by the way of the gate whereby he
'came in, but shall go forth the opposite way. And the 10
'Prince shall be in the midst of them. When they go in,
'he shall go in; and when they go forth, he shall go forth.
'And in the feasts and on the solemn days the meal 11
'offering shall be an Ephah to each bullock, and an Ephah
'to each ram, and to the lambs as his hand can give, and
'a Hin of oil to each Ephah. Now when the Prince shall 12
'bring a freewill burnt offering or freewill peace offerings
'to Jehovah, some one shall then open to him the gate
'that looketh toward the east, and he shall bring his burnt
'offering and his peace offerings, as he did on the sabbath
'day. Then he shall go forth, and after his going forth
'some one shall shut the gate.

'Thou shalt daily prepare a burnt offering unto Jehovah 13
'of a lamb of the first year without blemish; thou shalt
'prepare it every morning. And thou shalt prepare a meal 14
'offering for it every morning, the sixth part of an Ephah,
'and the third part of a Hin of oil, to moisten the fine
'flour; a meal offering unto Jehovah continually by a
'perpetual ordinance. Thus shall they prepare the lamb, 15
'and the meal offering, and the oil, every morning for a
'continual burnt offering.'

Thus saith the Lord Jehovah; 'If the Prince give a gift 16
'to any of his sons, the inheritance thereof shall be his
'sons'; it shall be their possession by inheritance. But if 17
'he give a gift out of his inheritance to one of his ser-
'vants, then it shall be his until the year of liberty; after-
'wards it shall return to the Prince; his inheritance shall
'certainly be his sons' for them. Moreover the Prince 18
'shall not take any of the people's inheritance, to thrust
'them out of their possession; but he shall give his sons
'inheritance out of his own possession so that my people
'be not scattered every man from his possession.'

And he brought me through the entrance, which was at 19
the side of the gate, into the holy chambers of the priests
which looked toward the north; and behold, there was a
place at the back westward. Then said he to me, 'This is 20
'the place where the priests shall boil the guilt offering
'and the sin offering, where they shall bake the meal

'offering; that they bring them not out into the Outer
21 'Court, to sanctify the people.' Then he brought me forth
into the Outer Court, and caused me to pass by the four
corners of the court; and, behold, in every corner of the
22 court there was a court. In the four corners of the court
there were roofed courts of forty [cubits] long and thirty
23 broad. These four corner-courts were of one measure. And
there was a [cooking] range round about in them, round
about them on their four sides; and it was made with
24 boiling places under the ranges round about. Then said
he unto me, 'These are the places of them that boil, where
'the ministers of the House shall boil the sacrifice of the
—'people.'

1 Afterward he brought me back to the doorway of the
House; and behold, waters issued out from under the
threshold of the House eastward; for the face of the House
stood toward the east, and the waters came down from
below, from the right front corner of the House, at the
2 south side of the Altar. Then he brought me out by the
way of the gate northward, and led me round by the way
on the outside to the outer gate on the way that looketh
eastward; and, behold, there ran out waters from the right
3 front corner. And when the man that had the line in his
hand went forth eastward, he measured a thousand cubits,
and he brought me through the waters; the waters were
4 to the ankles. Again he measured a thousand, and brought
me through the waters; the waters were to the knees.
Again he measured a thousand, and brought me through
5 the waters, which were to the loins. Afterward he measured a thousand; and it was a river that I could not pass
over. For the waters were risen, waters to swim in, a river
6 that could not be passed over. And he said unto me, 'Son
'of Adam, hast thou seen this?' Then he brought me,
7 and caused me to return to the bank of the river. Now
when I had returned, behold, at the bank of the river
were very many trees on the one side and on the other.
8 Then said he unto me, 'These waters go forth toward the
'Eastern Circle [of the Jordan], and they go down into
'the Barren Valley, and come into the [Dead] Sea, into
'the sea of the drainage, and the waters will be healed.
9 'And it shall come to pass, that everything that liveth,
'which moveth, whithersoever the rivers shall come, shall

'live. And there shall be a very great multitude of fish, 'because these waters shall come thither; for they shall 'be healed; and everything shall live whither the river 'cometh. And it shall come to pass, that the fishermen 10 'shall stand upon it [the Dead Sea] from Ain-gedi even 'unto Ain-eglaim. These shall be places to spread nets. 'Their fish shall be according to their kinds, as the fish of 'the Great Sea [or the Mediterranean], exceeding many. 'But its miry places and its marshes shall not be healed; 11 'they shall be given up to the salt. And by the river 12 'shall come up upon its bank on this side and on that side, 'all trees for food. Their leaf shall not fade, neither shall 'their fruit be consumed; each shall bring forth new fruit 'according to its months, because their waters issued out 'of the Sanctuary. And its fruit shall be for food, and its 'leaf for medicine.'

Thus saith the Lord Jehovah; This shall be THE BOUN- 13 DARY, whereby ye shall inherit the land according to the twelve tribes of Israel. (Joseph shall have two portions.) And ye shall inherit it, one as well as another; concern- 14 ing which I lifted up my hand [in oath] to give it to your fathers; and this land shall be divided by lot unto you for an inheritance. And this shall be the boundary of the land 15 toward the north side, from the Great Sea, the way of Hethlon, as men go to Zedad, Hamath, Berothah [or Bey- 16 rout], Sibraim, which is between the boundary of [the land of] Damascus and the boundary of [the land of] Hamath; the Village of Hatticon, which is by the boundary of [the land of] Hauran. And the boundary from the Sea shall 17 be the Village of Ainen, the boundary of Damascus, and the north northward, and the boundary of Hamath. And this is the north side. And the east side ye shall measure 18 between Hauran and Damascus, and between Gilead and the land of Israel by the Jordan, as a boundary unto the East [or Dead] Sea. And this is the east side. And the 19 south or right hand side, from Tamar even to the Waters of Meribah at Kadesh, to the Valley at the Great Sea. And this is the right hand or south side. The west side also 20 shall be the Great Sea as a boundary, until over against the way to Hamath. This is the west side. And ye shall 21 divide this land to you according to the tribes of Israel.

And it shall come to pass, that ye shall divide it by lot 22

for an inheritance to you, and to the strangers that sojourn among you, who have begotten children among you. And they shall be to you as born in the country among the children of Israel; they shall have inheritance divided unto
23 them by lot with you among the tribes of Israel. And it shall come to pass, that in what tribe the stranger sojourneth, there shall ye give him his inheritance; the Lord —Jehovah hath said it.

1 NOW THESE ARE THE NAMES of the tribes. From the north end at the finger-post on the way of Hethlon, as one goeth to Hamath, the Village of Ainen, the boundary of Damascus northward, to the finger-post of Hamath; for these are its sides east and west; one portion for Dan.

2 And by the boundary of Dan, from the east side to the west side, one portion for Asher.

3 And by the boundary of Asher, from the east side even to the west side, one portion for Naphtali.

4 And by the boundary of Naphtali, from the east side to the west side, one portion for Manasseh.

5 And by the boundary of Manasseh, from the east side to the west side, one portion for Ephraim.

6 And by the boundary of Ephraim, from the east side even to the west side, one portion for Reuben.

7 And by the boundary of Reuben, from the east side to the west side, one portion for Judah.

8 And by the boundary of Judah, from the east side to the west side, shall be the HEAVE OFFERING [of land] which ye shall offer of five and twenty thousand [reeds, or 37 miles] in breadth, and in length as one of the other portions, from the east side to the west side; and the Sanctuary shall be in the midst of it.

9 The Heave Offering that ye shall offer to Jehovah shall be of five and twenty thousand in length, and of ten thou-
10 sand in breadth. Even for them, even for THE PRIESTS, shall be this holy Heave Offering; on the north five and twenty thousand, and on the west ten thousand in breadth, and on the east ten thousand in breadth, and on the south five and twenty thousand in length; and the Sanctuary of
11 Jehovah shall be in the midst of it. This shall be for the Priests that are sanctified of the sons of Zadok; who have kept my charge, who went not astray when the children
12 of Israel went astray, as the Levites went astray. And

this Heave offering of land that is offered shall be to them a thing most holy; it shall be by the boundary of the Levites.

¹³ And over against the boundary of the Priests, THE LEVITES shall have five and twenty thousand in length, and ten thousand in breadth; all the length shall be five and twenty thousand, and the breadth ten thousand. ¹⁴ And they shall not sell any part of it, neither exchange, nor alienate the firstfruits of the land; for it is holy to Jehovah.

¹⁵ And the five thousand, that are left in the breadth over against the five and twenty thousand, shall be as not holy for THE CITY, for dwelling, and for its waste space; and the city shall be in the midst thereof. ¹⁶ And these shall be the measures thereof; the north side four thousand and five hundred, and the south side four thousand and five hundred, and on the east side four thousand and five hundred, and the west side four thousand and five hundred. ¹⁷ And the waste space of the city shall be toward the north two hundred and fifty, and toward the south two hundred and fifty, and toward the east two hundred and fifty, and toward the west two hundred and fifty. ¹⁸ And the residue in length over against the holy Heave Offering shall be ten thousand eastward, and ten thousand westward; and it shall be over against the holy Heave Offering; and the increase thereof shall be for food for them that serve the city. ¹⁹ And they that serve the city shall serve it out of all the tribes of Israel.

²⁰ The whole Heave Offering shall be five and twenty thousand by five and twenty thousand; ye shall offer the holy Heave Offering foursquare, with the City's possession.

²¹ And the residue shall be for THE PRINCE, on the one side and on the other of the holy Heave Offering, and of the City's possession, over against the five and twenty thousand of the Heave Offering toward the east boundary, and westward over against the five and twenty thousand toward the west boundary. And over against the portions for the Prince shall be the holy Heave Offering; and the Sanctuary of the House shall be in the midst thereof. ²² Thus from out of the possession of the Levites, and from out of the possession for the City, (which are in the midst of that which is the Prince's,) between the boundary of Judah and the boundary of Benjamin, shall be that for the Prince.

23 As for the rest of the tribes, from the east side to the west side, one portion for Benjamin.
24 And by the boundary of Benjamin, from the east side to the west side, one portion for Simeon.
25 And by the boundary of Simeon, from the east side to the west side, one portion for Issachar.
26 And by the boundary of Issachar, from the east side to the west side, one portion for Zebulun.
27 And by the boundary of Zebulun, from the east side to the west side, one portion for Gad.
28 And by the boundary of Gad, at the south or right hand side, the boundary shall be even from Tamar to the Waters of Meribah at Kadesh, and to the Valley toward the Great Sea.
29 This is the land which ye shall divide by lot to the tribes of Israel for inheritance, and these are their portions; the Lord Jehovah hath said it.
30 And these are the goings out of THE CITY; on the north side, four thousand and five hundred measures.
31 And the gates of the city shall be after the names of the tribes of Israel; three gates northward; one gate of Reuben, one gate of Judah, one gate of Levi.
32 And at the east side four thousand and five hundred; and three gates; even one gate of Joseph, one gate of Benjamin, one gate of Dan.
33 And the south side four thousand and five hundred measures; and three gates; one gate of Simeon, one gate of Issachar, one gate of Zebulun.
34 The west side four thousand and five hundred, with their three gates; one gate of Gad, one gate of Asher, one gate of Naphtali.
35 It was eighteen thousand measures round about. And the name of the city from that day shall be, 'Jehovah is there.'

DANIEL.

1 IN THE THIRD YEAR of the reign of Jehoiakim king of Judah [B.C. 608] came Nebuchadnezzar king of Babylon
2 to Jerusalem, and besieged it. And the Lord gave Jehoiakim king of Judah into his hand, with a part of the vessels of the House of God, which he carried into the land of Shinar to the house of his own god; and he brought the vessels into the treasure house of his own god.
3 And the king spake to Ashpenaz the chief of his cham-

berlains, that he should bring some of the children of Israel, and of the king's seed, and of the princes; children 4 in whom was no blemish, but of good countenance, and skilful in all wisdom, and cunning in knowledge, and understanding science, and such as had ability in them to stand in the king's palace, and that he should teach them the writing and the tongue of the Chaldeans. And the king 5 appointed to them a daily provision of the king's delicacies, and of the wine which he drank; so nourishing them for three years, that at the end thereof they might stand before the king. Now among these were some of the children of 6 Judah, Daniel, Hananiah, Mishael, and Azariah. And the 7 prince of the chamberlains gave names to them; for he gave to Daniel the name of Belteshazzar; and to Hananiah, of Shadrach; and to Mishael, of Meshach; and to Azariah, of Abed-nego.

But Daniel purposed in his heart that he would not 8 defile himself with the king's delicacies, nor with the wine which he drank; therefore he requested of the prince of the chamberlains that he might not defile himself. Now 9 God had brought Daniel into favour and tender love with the prince of the chamberlains. And the prince of the 10 chamberlains said to Daniel, 'I fear my lord the king, who 'hath appointed your food and your drink; for why should 'he see your faces worse looking than the children which 'are of your age? then shall ye endanger my head to the 'king.' Then said Daniel to the steward, whom the prince 11 of the chamberlains had set over Daniel, Hananiah, Mishael, and Azariah, 'Prove thy servants, I beseech thee, 12 'for ten days; and let them give us some pulse to eat, and 'water to drink. Then let our countenances be looked 13 'upon before thee, and the countenance of the children 'that eat of the king's delicacies; and as thou seest, deal 'with thy servants.' So he hearkened to them in this 14 matter, and proved them for ten days. And at the end of 15 ten days their countenances appeared fairer and fatter in flesh than all the children that did eat the king's delicacies. Thus the steward took away their delicacies, and the wine 16 that they should drink; and gave them pulse.

As for these four children, God gave them knowledge 17 and skill in all writing and wisdom; and Daniel had understanding in all visions and dreams. And at the end of 18

the days that the king had said he should bring them in, then the prince of the chamberlains brought them in before
19 Nebuchadnezzar. And the king talked with them; and among them all was found none like Daniel, Hananiah, Mishael, and Azariah; therefore stood they before the king.
20 And in all matters of wisdom and understanding, that the king inquired of them, he found them ten times better than all the magicians and soothsayers that were in all his
21 kingdom. And Daniel continued even unto the first year —of king Cyrus [B.C. 538].

1   AND IN THE SECOND YEAR of the reign of Nebuchadnezzar [B.C.606], Nebuchadnezzar dreamed dreams, and his spirit was troubled, and his sleep was no longer upon him.
2 Then the king commanded to call the magicians, and the soothsayers, and the sorcerers, and the Chaldeans, to shew to the king his dreams. So they came and stood before the
3 king. And the king said to them, 'I have dreamed a dream,
4 'and my spirit is troubled to know the dream.' Then spake the Chaldeans to the king in Syriac, 'O king, * 'live for ever; tell thy servants the dream, and we will *
5 'shew the interpretation.' The king answered and said * to the Chaldeans, 'The thing is gone from me; if ye make * 'not known to me the dream, with the interpretation * 'thereof, ye shall be cut in pieces, and your houses shall *
6 'be made dunghills. But if ye shew the dream, and the * 'interpretation thereof, ye shall receive of me gifts and * 'rewards and great honour; therefore shew me the *
7 'dream, and the interpretation thereof.' They answered * again and said, 'Let the king tell his servants the dream, *
8 'and we will shew the interpretation of it.' The king * answered and said, 'I know of certainty that ye would * 'gain the time, because ye see that the thing is gone from *
9 'me. But if ye make not known to me the dream, this * 'alone is your purpose; for ye have prepared lying and * 'corrupt words to speak before me, till the time be * 'changed; therefore tell me the dream, and I shall know *
10 'that ye can shew me the interpretation thereof.' The * Chaldeans answered before the king and said, 'There is * 'not a man upon the earth that is able to shew the king's * 'matter; for this cause no king, lord, nor ruler hath * 'asked such things of any magician, or soothsayer, or Chal- *
11 'dean. And it is a rare thing that the king requireth, *

* ' and there is none other that can shew it before the king,
* ' except the gods, whose dwelling is not with flesh.'
*   For this cause the king was angry and very furious, 12
* and commanded to destroy all the wise men of Babylon.
* And the decree went forth that the wise men should be 13
* slain; and they sought Daniel and his fellows that they
* might be slain.
*   Then Daniel answered with counsel and wisdom to 14
* Arioch the chief of the king's guard, who was gone forth
* to slay the wise men of Babylon; he answered and said 15
* to Arioch the king's captain, ' Why is the decree so hasty
* ' from the king?' Then Arioch made the thing known
* to Daniel. Then Daniel went in, and desired of the 16
* king that he would appoint him a time, and that he
* would shew the king the interpretation. Then Daniel 17
* went to his house, and made the thing known to Hana-
* niah, Mishael, and Azariah, his companions; that they 18
* would desire mercies from the God of heaven concern-
* ing this secret; that Daniel and his companions should
* not perish with the rest of the wise men of Babylon.
*   Then was the secret revealed to Daniel in a vision of 19
* the night. Then Daniel blessed the God of heaven. 20
* Daniel answered and said,
* ' Blessed be the name of God for ever and ever
* ' For wisdom and might are his;
* ' And he changeth the times and the seasons;   21
* ' He removeth kings, and he setteth up kings;
* ' He giveth wisdom to the wise,
* ' And knowledge to them that know understanding;
* ' He revealeth the deep and secret things;   22
* ' He knoweth what is in the darkness,
* ' And the light dwelleth with him.
*   ' I thank thee, and praise thee, O God of my fathers, 23
* ' because thou hast given me wisdom and might, and
* ' hast made known to me now what we asked of thee;
* ' for thou hast made known to us the king's matter.'
*   Thereupon Daniel went in unto Arioch, whom the king 24
* had ordained to destroy the wise men of Babylon; he
* went and said thus to him; ' Destroy not the wise men
* ' of Babylon; bring me in before the king, and I will
* ' shew to the king the interpretation.' Then Arioch 25
* brought in Daniel before the king in haste, and said

thus to him, 'I have found a man of the children of the 'captivity of Judah, that will make known to the king ²⁶ 'the interpretation.' The king answered and said to Daniel, whose name was Belteshazzar, 'Art thou able to 'make known to me the dream which I have seen, and ²⁷ 'the interpretation thereof?' Daniel answered in the presence of the king, and said, 'The secret which the king 'hath demanded, the wise men, the soothsayers, the ma-²⁸ 'gicians, the astrologers, cannot shew to the king; but 'there is a God in heaven that revealeth secrets, and 'maketh known to the king Nebuchadnezzar what shall 'be in the latter days. Thy dream, and the visions of ²⁹ 'thy head upon thy bed, are these; as for thee, O king, 'thy thoughts came up upon thy bed, what should come 'to pass hereafter; and He that revealeth secrets will ³⁰ 'make known to thee what shall come to pass. But as 'for me, this secret is not revealed to me for any wisdom 'that I have more than any one living, but for their 'sakes that shall make known the interpretation to the 'king, and that thou mightest know the thoughts of thy 'heart.

³¹ 'Thou, O king, sawest, and behold a great image. 'This great image, whose brightness was excellent, stood ³² 'before thee; and his appearance was terrible. This 'image's head was of fine gold, his breast and his arms of ³³ 'silver, his belly and his thighs of copper, his legs of ³⁴ 'iron, his feet part of iron and part of pottery. Thou 'lookedst till a stone was cut out without hands, which 'smote the image upon his feet that were of iron and ³⁵ 'pottery, and brake them to pieces. Then was the iron, 'the pottery, the copper, the silver, and the gold, broken 'to pieces together, and became like the chaff of the 'summer threshing-floors; and the wind carried them 'away, so that no trace of them was found; and the 'stone that smote the image became a great rock, and ³⁶ 'it filled the whole earth. This is the dream; and we 'will tell the interpretation thereof before the king.

³⁷ 'Thou, O king [of Babylon], art a king of kings; for 'the God of heaven hath given thee a kingdom, riches, ³⁸ 'and strength, and glory. And wheresoever the sons of 'men dwell, the beasts of the field and the fowls of the 'heavens hath he given into thy hand, and hath made

'thee ruler over them all. Thou art this head of gold. And after thee shall arise another kingdom [the Medes] inferior to thee, and another third kingdom of copper [the Persians], which shall bear rule over all the earth. And the fourth kingdom [the Greeks] shall be strong as iron; forasmuch as iron breaketh in pieces and subdueth all things; and as iron that bruiseth all these, shall it break in pieces and bruise. And whereas thou sawest the feet and toes, part of potters' work, and part of iron, the kingdom shall be divided; but there shall be in it some of the strength of the iron, forasmuch as thou sawest the iron mixed with earthen pottery. And as the toes of the feet were part of iron, and part of pottery, so part of the kingdom shall be strong, and part brittle. And whereas thou sawest the iron mixed with earthen pottery, they [the kings] shall be united by marriages; but they shall not cleave one to another, even as iron cannot be mixed with pottery. And in the days of these kings shall the God of heaven set up a kingdom, which shall never be destroyed; and the kingdom shall not be left to other people, but it shall break in pieces and consume all these kingdoms, and it shall stand for ever. Forasmuch as thou sawest that the stone was cut out of the rock without hands, and that it brake in pieces the iron, the copper, the pottery, the silver, and the gold; the great God hath made known to the king what shall come to pass hereafter; and the dream is certain, and the interpretation thereof sure.'

Then the king Nebuchadnezzar fell upon his face, and worshipped Daniel, and commanded that they should offer a meal offering and sweet odours to him. The king answered to Daniel, and said, 'Of a truth it is, that your God is a God of gods, and a Lord of kings, and a revealer of secrets, seeing that thou couldest reveal this secret.' Then the king made Daniel a great man, and gave him many great gifts, and made him ruler over the whole province of Babylon, and chief of the governors over all the wise men of Babylon. Then Daniel requested of the king, and he set Shadrach, Meshach, and Abednego, over the affairs of the province of Babylon; but Daniel sat in the gate of the king.

1 Nebuchadnezzar the king made an image of gold, whose height was sixty cubits, and its breadth six cubits; he set it up in the plain of Dura, in the province
2 of Babylon. Then Nebuchadnezzar the king sent to gather together the Satraps [or princes], the governors, and the Pashas [or captains], the chief judges, the treasurers, the counsellors, the lawyers, and all the Sultans [or rulers] of the provinces, to come to the dedication of the image which Nebuchadnezzar the king had set up.
3 Then the Satraps, the governors, and Pashas, the chief judges, the treasurers, the counsellors, the lawyers, and all the Sultans of the provinces, were gathered together to the dedication of the image that Nebuchadnezzar the king had set up; and they stood before the image that
4 Nebuchadnezzar had set up. Then a herald cried aloud,
5 'To you it is commanded, O peoples, nations, and lan-
' guages, that at what time ye hear the sound of the cornet,
' pipe, harp, sackbut, psaltery, symphony, and all kinds of
' music, ye fall down and worship the golden image that
6 ' Nebuchadnezzar the king hath set up; and whoso
' falleth not down and worshippeth shall at the same
' moment be cast into the midst of a burning fiery fur-
7 ' nace.' Thereupon at that time, when all the peoples heard the sound of the cornet, pipe, harp, sackbut, psaltery, and all kinds of music, all the peoples, the nations, and the languages, fell down and worshipped the golden image that Nebuchadnezzar the king had set up.
8 Whereupon at that time certain Chaldeans came near,
9 and accused the Jews. They spake and said to the king
10 Nebuchadnezzar, ' O king, live for ever. Thou, O king,
' hast made a decree, that every man that shall hear the
' sound of the cornet, pipe, harp, sackbut, psaltery, and
' symphony, and all kinds of music, shall fall down and
11 ' worship the golden image; and whoso falleth not down
' and worshippeth, that he should be cast into the midst
12 ' of a burning fiery furnace. There are certain Jews
' whom thou hast set over the affairs of the province of
' Babylon, Shadrach, Meshach, and Abed-nego; these
' men, O king, have not regarded thee; they serve not
' thy gods, nor worship the golden image which thou
' hast set up.'
13 Then Nebuchadnezzar in rage and fury commanded to

bring Shadrach, Meshach, and Abed-nego. Then they brought these men before the king. Nebuchadnezzar 14 spake, and said to them, 'Is it on purpose, O Shadrach, 'Meshach, and Abed-nego, that ye do not serve my gods, 'nor worship the golden image which I have set up? 'Now, behold, be ye ready at what time ye hear the 15 'sound of the cornet, pipe, harp, sackbut, psaltery, and 'symphony, and all kinds of music, and fall down and 'worship the image which I have made. But if ye wor-'ship not, ye shall be cast at the same moment into the 'midst of a burning fiery furnace; and who is that God 'that shall deliver you out of my hands?' Shadrach, 16 Meshach, and Abed-nego, answered and said to the king, 'O Nebuchadnezzar, we have no need to answer thee in 'this matter. If it be so, our God whom we serve is 17 ' able to deliver us from the burning fiery furnace, and he ' will deliver us out of thy hand, O king. But if not, 18 ' be it known to thee, O king, that we will not serve thy ' gods, nor worship the golden image which thou hast ' set up.'

Then was Nebuchadnezzar full of fury, and the form 19 of his countenance was changed against Shadrach, Meshach, and Abed-nego. He spake, and commanded that they should heat the furnace seven times more than it was wont to be heated. And he commanded 20 the most mighty men that were in his army to bind Shadrach, Meshach, and Abednego, and to cast them into the burning fiery furnace. Then these men were 21 bound in their loose trowsers, their coats, and their tur-bans, and their robes, and were cast into the midst of the burning fiery furnace. Thereupon because the king's 22 command was strict, and the furnace exceeding hot, the flame of the fire slew those men that took up Shadrach, Meshach, and Abed-nego. And these three men, Sha- 23 drach, Meshach, and Abed-nego, fell down bound into the midst of the burning fiery furnace.

Then Nebuchadnezzar the king was astonished, and 24 rose up in haste, and spake, and said to his counsellors, ' Did not we cast three men bound into the midst of ' the fire?' They answered and said to the king, 'True, ' O king.' He answered and said, 'Lo, I see four men 25 ' loose, walking in the midst of the fire, and they have

'no hurt; and the form of the fourth is like a son of
'God.'

²⁶ Then Nebuchadnezzar came near to the mouth of the burning fiery furnace, and spake, and said, 'Shadrach, 'Meshach, and Abed-nego, ye servants of the most high 'God, come forth, and come.' Then Shadrach, Meshach, and Abed-nego, came forth from the midst of the fire.
²⁷ And the Satraps, governors, and Pashas, and counsellors of the king being gathered together, saw these men, upon whose bodies the fire had no power, nor was a hair of their head singed, neither were their loose trowsers changed, nor had the smell of fire passed on them.
²⁸ Then Nebuchadnezzar spake, and said, 'Blessed be the 'God of Shadrach, Meshach, and Abed-nego, who hath 'sent his angel, and delivered his servants that trusted 'in him, and broke the king's command, and yielded 'their bodies, that they might not serve nor worship any
²⁹ 'god, except their own God. Therefore of myself I 'make a decree, That every people, nation, and language, 'who speak wrongfully against the God of Shadrach, 'Meshach, and Abed-nego, shall be cut in pieces, and 'their houses shall be made dunghills; because there is
³⁰ 'no other god that can deliver after this manner.' Then the king promoted Shadrach, Meshach, and Abed-nego, —in the province of Babylon.

¹ NEBUCHADNEZZAR THE KING, unto all peoples, nations, and languages, that dwell in all the land; Peace be multiplied unto you.
² I thought it good to shew the signs and wonders that
³ the high God hath wrought toward me. How great are his signs! and how mighty are his wonders! his kingdom is an everlasting kingdom, and his dominion is from generation to generation.
⁴ I Nebuchadnezzar was at rest in my house, and flour-
⁵ ishing in my palace; I saw a dream which made me afraid, and the thoughts upon my bed and the visions
⁶ of my head troubled me. Therefore, of myself, I made a decree to bring in all the wise men of Babylon before me, that they might make known to me the interpreta-
⁷ tion of the dream. Then came in the magicians, the soothsayers, the Chaldeans, and the astrologers; and I told the dream before them; but they did not make

known to me the interpretation thereof. But at last 8
Daniel came in before me, whose name was Belteshazzar,
according to the name of my god [Baal], and in whom
is the spirit of the holy gods; and before him I told the
dream, [saying,] O Belteshazzar, chief of the magicians, 9
because I know that the spirit of the holy gods is in thee,
and no secret is hard for thee, tell me the visions of my
dream that I have seen, and the interpretation thereof.
Thus were the visions of my head on my bed; I saw, and 10
behold a tree in the midst of the earth, and its height
was great. The tree grew, and became strong, and its 11
height reached to the heavens, and the sight thereof to
the end of all the earth. Its leaves were fair, and its 12
fruit large, and in it was food for all; the beasts of the
field had shade under it, and the fowls of the heavens
dwelt in its branches, and all flesh was fed from it. I saw 13
in the visions of my head upon my bed, and, behold, a
guardian angel and a holy one came down from heaven;
he cried aloud, and said thus, 'Hew down the tree, and 14
'cut off its branches, shake off its leaves, and scatter its
'fruit; let the beasts get away from under it, and the
'fowls from its branches; nevertheless leave the stump 15
'of its roots in the earth, even with a band of iron and
'copper, in the tender grass of the field; and let it be
'wet with the dew of heaven, and let its portion be with
'the beasts in the grass of the earth; let his heart be 16
'changed from man's, and let a beast's heart be given to
'him; and let seven times [or years] pass over him. This 17
'command is by the decree of the guardian angels, and
'the demand by the word of the holy ones; to the in-
'tent that the living may know that the Most High ruleth
'in the kingdom of men, and giveth it to whomsoever he
'will, and setteth up over it the basest of men.' This 18
dream I king Nebuchadnezzar have seen. Now thou, O
Belteshazzar, declare the interpretation thereof, forasmuch as all the wise men of my kingdom are not able
to make known to me the interpretation; but thou art
able; for the spirit of the holy gods is in thee.

Then Daniel, whose name was Belteshazzar, was asto- 19
nished for a moment, and his thoughts troubled him.
The king spake, and said, 'Belteshazzar, let not the
'dream, or the interpretation thereof, trouble thee.' Bel-

teshazzar answered and said, 'My lord, may the dream be
' to them that hate thee, and the interpretation thereof to
20 ' thine enemies. The tree that thou sawest, which grew,
' and was strong, whose height reached to the heavens,
21 ' and the sight thereof to all the earth; whose leaves were
' fair, and its fruit large, and in it was food for all; under
' which the beasts of the field dwelt, and upon whose
' branches the fowls of the heavens had their habitation;
22 ' it is thou, O king, who art grown and become strong;
' for thy greatness is grown, and reacheth to the heavens,
23 ' and thy dominion to the end of the earth. And whereas
' the king saw a guardian angel and a holy one coming
' down from heaven, and saying, Hew the tree down, and
' destroy it; yet leave the stump of its roots in the earth,
' even with a band of iron and copper, in the tender grass
' of the field; and let it be wet with the dew of heaven,
' and let his portion be with the beasts of the field, till
24 ' seven times [or years] pass over him; this is the inter-
' pretation, O king, and this is the decree of the Most
25 ' High, which is come upon my lord the king; that they
' shall drive thee from men, and thy dwelling shall be
' with the beasts of the field, and they shall make thee
' to eat grass as oxen, and they shall wet thee with the
' dew of heaven, and seven times [or years] shall pass over
' thee, till thou know that the Most High ruleth in the
' kingdom of men, and giveth it to whomsoever he will.
26 ' And whereas they commanded to leave the stump of the
' roots of the tree; thy kingdom shall be made sure to
' thee, after that thou shalt have known that the heavens
27 ' do rule. Therefore, O king, let my counsel be accept-
' able to thee; and break off thy sins by righteousness,
' and thine iniquities by shewing mercy to the poor; oh
' may it be a lengthening of thy tranquillity.'
28 All this came upon the king Nebuchadnezzar. At the
29 end of twelve months he walked in the palace of the
30 kingdom of Babylon. The king spake, and said, 'Is not
' this great Babylon, that I have built for the house of
' the kingdom by the might of my power, and for the
31 ' honour of my majesty?' While the word was in the
king's mouth, there fell a voice from heaven, saying, 'O
' king Nebuchadnezzar, to thee it is spoken; The king-
32 ' dom is departed from thee. And they shall drive thee

'from men, and thy dwelling shall be with the beasts of
'the field; they shall make thee to eat grass as oxen,
'and seven times [or years] shall pass over thee, until
'thou know that the Most High ruleth in the kingdom
'of men, and giveth it to whomsoever he will.' At the ³³
same moment was the thing fulfilled upon Nebuchadnezzar; and he was driven from men, and did eat grass as
oxen, and his body was wet with the dew of heaven,
till his hairs were grown like the eagles, and his nails
like the birds.

And at the end of the days I Nebuchadnezzar lifted up ³⁴
mine eyes to heaven and mine understanding returned to
me, and I blessed the Most High, and I praised and
honoured him that liveth for ever, whose dominion
is an everlasting dominion, and his kingdom is from
generation to generation; and all the inhabitants of the ³⁵
earth are reputed as nothing; and he doeth according to
his will in the army of heaven, and among the inhabitants of the earth; and none can stay his hand, or say to
him, 'What doest thou?' At the same time my reason ³⁶
returned to me; and for the glory of my kingdom, my
honour and brightness returned to me; and my counsellors and my lords sought unto me; and I was established in my kingdom, and excellent majesty was added
to me. Now I Nebuchadnezzar praise and extol and ³⁷
honour the King of Heaven, all whose works are truth,
and his ways justice; and those that walk in pride he is
able to abase.

BELSHAZZAR THE KING made a great feast to a thou- ¹
sand of his lords, and drank wine before the thousand.
Belshazzar, while he tasted the wine, commanded to ²
bring the golden and silver vessels which his father
Nebuchadnezzar had taken out of the Temple which was
in Jerusalem; that the king, and his lords, his wives, and
his concubines, might drink therein. Then they brought ³
the golden vessels that were taken out of the temple [or
great hall] of the House of God which was at Jerusalem;
and the king, and his lords, his wives, and his concubines,
drank in them. They drank wine, and praised the gods ⁴
of gold, and of silver, of copper, of iron, of wood, and
of stone. At the same moment came forth the fingers ⁵
of a man's hand, and wrote over against the lampstand

upon the plaster of the wall of the king's palace; and
⁶ the king saw the part of the hand that wrote. Then the king's countenance was changed, and his thoughts troubled him, so that the joints of his loins were weakened,
⁷ and his knees smote one against another. The king cried aloud to bring in the soothsayers, the Chaldeans, and the astrologers. And the king spake, and said to the men of Babylon, 'Whosoever shall read this writing, 'and shew me the interpretation thereof, shall be clothed 'in purple, and have a chain of gold about his neck, and
⁸ 'shall be the third ruler in the kingdom.' Then came in all the king's wise men; but they could not read the writing, nor make known to the king the interpretation
⁹ thereof. Then was king Belshazzar greatly troubled, and his countenance was changed in him, and his lords were astonished.
¹⁰ Now the queen by reason of the words of the king and his lords came into the banquet house; and the queen spake and said, 'O king, live for ever; let not thy 'thoughts trouble thee, nor let thy countenance be
¹¹ 'changed. There is a man in thy kingdom, in whom is 'the spirit of the holy gods; and in the days of thy father 'light and understanding and wisdom, like the wisdom of 'the gods, was found in him; whom the king Nebuchad- 'nezzar thy father, thy royal father, made chief of the
¹² 'magicians, soothsayers, Chaldeans, and astrologers; for- 'asmuch as an excellent spirit, and knowledge, and 'understanding, interpreting of dreams, and shewing of 'hard sentences, and solving of doubts, were found in 'the same Daniel, to whom the king gave the name of 'Belteshazzar; now let Daniel be called, and he will shew
¹³ 'the interpretation.' Then was Daniel brought in before the king. And the king spake and said to Daniel, 'Art 'thou that Daniel, who is one of the children of the cap- 'tivity of Judah, whom the king my father brought out
¹⁴ 'of Judea? I have even heard of thee, that the spirit of 'the gods is in thee, and that light and understanding
¹⁵ 'and excellent wisdom is found in thee. And now the 'wise men, the soothsayers, have been brought in before 'me, that they should read this writing, and make known 'to me the interpretation thereof; but they could not
¹⁶ 'shew the interpretation of the thing. And I have heard

‘ of thee, that thou canst make interpretations, and solve
‘ doubts; now if thou canst read the writing, and make
‘ known to me the interpretation thereof, thou shalt be
‘ clothed in purple, and have a chain of gold about thy
‘ neck, and shalt be the third ruler in the kingdom.’

Then Daniel answered and said before the king, ‘Let 17
‘ thy gifts be to thyself, and give thy rewards to another;
‘ yet I will read the writing to the king, and make known
‘ to him the interpretation. O thou king, the most high 18
‘ God gave to Nebuchadnezzar thy father a kingdom, and
‘ majesty, and glory, and honour; and for the majesty 19
‘ that he gave him, all peoples, nations, and languages,
‘ trembled and feared before him; whom he would he
‘ slew; and whom he would he kept alive; and whom
‘ he would he set up; and whom he would he put
‘ down. But when his heart was lifted up, and his mind 20
‘ hardened in pride, he was deposed from his kingly
‘ throne, and they took his glory from him; and he was 21
‘ driven from the sons of men; and his heart was made
‘ like the beasts, and his dwelling was with the wild
‘ asses; they fed him with grass like oxen, and his body
‘ was wet with the dew of heaven; till he knew that the
‘ most high God ruled in the kingdom of men, and that
‘ he appointeth over it whomsoever he will. And thou 22
‘ his son, O Belshazzar, hast not humbled thy heart,
‘ though thou knewest all this; but hast lifted up thy- 23
‘ self against the Lord of Heaven; and they have brought
‘ the vessels of His House before thee, and thou, and thy
‘ lords, thy wives, and thy concubines, have drunk wine
‘ in them; and thou hast praised the gods of silver, and
‘ gold, of copper, iron, wood, and stone, which see not,
‘ nor hear, nor know; and the God in whose hand thy
‘ breath is, and whose are all thy ways, hast thou not
‘ glorified; then was the part of the hand sent from him; 24
‘ and this writing was written. (And this is the writing 25
‘ that was written, MENE, MENE [or Numbered], TEKEL
‘ [or Weighed], U-PERESIN [or And Divided].) This is 26
‘ the interpretation of the thing; MENE; God hath
‘ numbered thy kingdom, and finished it. TEKEL; Thou 27
‘ art weighed in the balances, and art found wanting.
‘ PERES; Thy kingdom is divided, and given to the Medes 28
‘ and Persians.’ Then commanded Belshazzar, and they 29

clothed Daniel in purple, and put a chain of gold about
his neck, and made a proclamation concerning him, that
he should be the third ruler in the kingdom.

30 In that night [B.C. 539] was Belshazzar the king of
31 the Chaldeans slain. And DARIUS THE MEDE [or Cyaxares II.] took the kingdom, being about sixty and two
—years old.

1 It pleased Darius to set over the kingdom a hundred
and twenty Satraps, who should be over the whole king-
2 dom; and over these, three presidents, of whom Daniel
was first; that the Satraps might give accounts to them,
3 and the king should have no damage. Then this Daniel
was preferred above the presidents and Satraps, because
an excellent spirit was in him; and the king purposed to
4 set him over the whole kingdom. Then the presidents
and Satraps sought to find occasion against Daniel concerning the kingdom; but they could find none occasion
nor fault; forasmuch as he was faithful, neither was
5 there any error or fault found in him. Then said these
men, 'We cannot find any occasion against this Daniel,
'except we find it against him concerning the law of his
6 'God.' Then these presidents and Satraps pressed
upon the king, and said thus to him, 'King Darius,
7 'live for ever. All the presidents of the kingdom, the
'governors, and the Satraps, the counsellors, and the
'Pashas, have consulted together to establish a royal
'statute, and to make a firm decree, that whosoever shall
'ask a petition of any God or man for thirty days, save
'of thee, O king, he shall be cast into the den of lions.
8 'Now, O king, establish the decree, and sign the writing,
'that it be not changed, according to the law of the
9 'Medes and Persians, which altereth not.' Whereupon
king Darius signed the writing and the decree.
10 Now when Daniel knew that the writing was signed,
he went into his house; and his windows being open in
his chamber toward Jerusalem, he kneeled upon his
knees three times a day, and prayed, and gave thanks
11 before his God, as he did aforetime. Then these men
pressed in, and found Daniel praying and making supplication before his God.
12 Then they came near, and spake before the king concerning the king's decree; 'Hast thou not signed a

'decree, that every man that shall ask a petition of any 'God or man within thirty days, save of thee, O king, 'shall be cast into the den of lions?' The king answered and said, 'The thing is true, according to the law of the 'Medes and Persians, which altereth not.' Then answered they and said before the king, 'That Daniel, 'who is one of the children of the captivity of Judah, 'regardeth not thee, O king, nor the decree that thou 'hast signed, but maketh his petition three times a day.' Then the king, when he heard these words, was sore displeased with himself, and set his heart on Daniel to deliver him; and he laboured till the going down of the sun to deliver him. Then these men pressed upon the king, and said to the king, 'Know, O king, that the 'law of the Medes and Persians is, That no decree nor 'statute which the king establisheth may be changed.' Then the king commanded, and they brought Daniel, and cast him into the den of lions. Now the king spake and said to Daniel, 'Thy God whom thou servest con- 'tinually, he will deliver thee.' And a stone was brought, and laid upon the mouth of the den; and the king sealed it with his own signet, and with the signet of his lords; that the purpose might not be changed concerning Daniel.

Then the king went to his palace, and passed the night fasting; neither did he cause any concubines to be brought before him; and his sleep went from him. Then the king arose at daybreak in the morning, and went in haste to the den of lions. And when he came to the den, he cried with a sorrowful voice unto Daniel; and the king spake and said to Daniel, 'O Daniel, servant of the 'living God, is thy God, whom thou servest continually, 'able to deliver thee from the lions?' Then said Daniel to the king, 'O king, live for ever. My God hath sent 'his angel, and hath shut the lions' mouths, that they 'have not hurt me; forasmuch as before him innocence 'was found in me; and also before thee, O king, have I 'done no hurt.' Then was the king exceeding glad for him, and commanded that they should take Daniel up out of the den. So Daniel was taken up out of the den, and no manner of hurt was found upon him, because he believed in his God. And the king commanded, and they brought those men which had accused Daniel, and they cast them into the den of lions, them, their children, and their wives; and the lions had the mastery of them, and brake all their bones in pieces before ever they came to the bottom of the den.

25 Then king Darius wrote to all peoples, nations, and languages, that dwelt in all the land; 'Peace be multi-
26 'plied unto you. Of myself I make a decree, That in every 'dominion of my kingdom men tremble and fear before 'the God of Daniel; for he is the living God, and stead-'fast for ever, and his kingdom is that which shall not 'be destroyed, and his dominion shall be even unto the
27 'end. He delivereth and rescueth, and he worketh signs 'and wonders in the heavens and on earth. It is he who 'hath delivered Daniel from the power of the lions.'
28 So this Daniel prospered in the reign of Darius, and —in the reign of Cyrus the Persian.

---

1 IN THE FIRST YEAR OF BELSHAZZAR king of Babylon [B.C. 555], Daniel saw a dream and visions of his head upon his bed. Then he wrote the dream, and told the
2 sum of the matters. Daniel spake and said, I saw in my vision by night, and behold, the four winds of
3 the heavens rushed forth upon the Great Sea. And FOUR GREAT BEASTS came up from the sea, diverse one
4 from another. THE FIRST [the Assyrians] was like a lion, and had eagle's wings; I looked till its wings were plucked, and it was lifted up from the earth, and made to stand upon its feet as a man, and a man's heart was
5 given to it. And behold another Beast, THE SECOND [the Babylonians], like to a bear, and it raised up itself on one side, and it had three ribs in its mouth between its teeth; and they said thus to it, 'Arise, devour much
6 'flesh.' After this, I looked, and lo, ANOTHER [the Persians], like a leopard, which had upon its back the four wings of a fowl; the beast had also four heads [Assyria, Babylonia, Media and Persia]; and dominion was given
7 to it. After this I saw in visions of the night, and behold THE FOURTH BEAST [the Greeks], dreadful and mighty, and strong exceedingly; and it had great iron teeth; it devoured and brake in pieces, and stamped the residue with its feet; and it was diverse from all the beasts that

* were before it; and it had ten Horns [or kings]. I con- 8
* sidered the horns, and, behold, there came up among
* them another, a mean Horn [Antiochus Epiphanes], before
* whom there were three of the first horns plucked up;
* and behold, in this horn were eyes like the eyes of a
* man, and a mouth speaking great things.

* I looked till the thrones were placed, and the Ancient 9
* of days did sit, whose garment was white as snow, and
* the hair of his head like pure wool; his throne was a
* fiery flame, and his wheels a burning fire. A fiery stream 10
* issued and came forth from before him; a thousand
* times a thousand ministered to him, and ten thousand
* times ten thousand stood before him; the judges were
* seated, and the books were opened. I looked then be- 11
* cause of the voice of the great words which the Horn
* spake; I looked even till the Beast was slain, and its
* body destroyed, and given to the burning flame. As con- 12
* cerning the rest of the Beasts, they had their dominion
* taken away; yet a lengthening of their lives was granted
* to them for a season and a time.

* I saw in visions of the night, and, behold, ONE LIKE A 13
* SON OF MAN came with the clouds of heaven, and came
* to the Ancient of days, and they brought him near be-
* fore him. And there was given to him dominion, and 14
* glory, and a kingdom, that all peoples, nations, and lan-
* guages, should serve him; his dominion is an everlasting
* dominion, which shall not pass away, and his kingdom
* that which shall not be destroyed.

* I Daniel was grieved in my spirit in the midst of my 15
* body, and the visions of my head troubled me. I came 16
* near to one of them that stood by, and asked him the
* truth of all this. So he told me, and made me know the
* interpretation of the things. ' These great Beasts, which 17
* ' are four, are four kings, who shall arise out of the earth.
* ' But the Holy People of the Most High shall take the 18
* ' kingdom, and possess the kingdom for ever, even for
* ' ever and ever.' Then I wished to know the truth of 19
* the Fourth Beast, which was diverse from all the others,
* exceeding dreadful, whose teeth were of iron, and its claws
* of copper; who devoured, brake in pieces, and stamped
* the residue with its feet; and of the ten Horns that were 20
* on its head, and of the other which came up, and before

whom the three fell; even of that Horn that had eyes, and a mouth that spake very great things, whose look was ²¹ more stout than its fellows. I looked, and the same Horn made war against the Holy People, and prevailed ²² against them; until the Ancient of days came, and judgment was given to the Holy People of the Most High; and the time came that the Holy People possessed the ²³ kingdom. Thus he said, 'The Fourth Beast shall be the 'fourth kingdom upon earth, which shall be diverse from 'all kingdoms, and shall devour the whole earth, and shall ²⁴ 'tread it down, and break it in pieces. And the ten 'Horns of this kingdom are ten kings that shall arise; 'and another shall rise after them; and he shall be 'diverse from those who were before, and he shall subdue ²⁵ 'three kings. And he shall speak words against the Most 'High, and shall wear out the Holy People of the Most 'High; and shall think to change the appointed times and 'the laws; and they shall be given into his hands until 'a time and times and the half of a time [or three years ²⁶ 'and a half.] But the judges shall be seated, and they 'shall take away his dominion, to consume and to de- ²⁷ 'stroy it unto the end. And the kingdom and dominion, 'and the greatness of the kingdom under the whole 'heavens, shall be given to the people of the Holy Ones 'of the Most High, whose kingdom is an everlasting 'kingdom, and all dominions shall serve and obey it.' ²⁸ Thus far is the end of the matter. As for me Daniel, my thoughts troubled me much, and my countenance —changed in me; but I kept the matter in my heart.

---

¹ IN THE THIRD YEAR of the reign of king Belshazzar [B.C. 553] a vision appeared to me, to me Daniel, after that which ² had appeared to me at the first. And I saw in a vision; and it came to pass, when I saw, that I was at Susa, the royal city, which is in the province of Elam [or Western Persia]; and I saw in a vision, and I was by the river Eu- ³ laeus. Then I lifted up mine eyes, and looked, and, behold, there stood before the river a RAM which had two Horns. And the two Horns were high; but one was higher than ⁴ the other, and the higher came up last. I saw the Ram pushing westward, and northward, and southward; so that no beasts might stand before him, neither was there any

that could deliver out of his hand; but he did according to his will, and became great. And as I was considering, behold, a HE GOAT came from the west against the face of the whole earth, and no one came near to him on the earth; and the goat had a notable HORN between his eyes. And he came to the Ram that had two Horns, which I had seen standing before the river, and ran at him in the fury of his power. And I saw him come close to the Ram, and he was moved with anger against him, and smote the Ram, and brake his two Horns; and there was no power in the Ram to stand before him, but he cast him down to the ground, and stamped upon him; and there was no one that could deliver the Ram out of his hand. And the He Goat waxed very great; and when he was strong, the Great Horn was broken; and instead of it came up four notable ones toward the four winds of heaven. And out of one of them came forth a MEAN HORN, which waxed exceeding great, against the south, and against the east, and against Beauty [or Jerusalem]. And it waxed great, even up to the host of heaven; and it cast down some of the host and of the stars to the ground, and stamped upon them. Yea, he magnified himself even up to the Prince of the host; and by him the daily sacrifice was taken away, and the place of his Sanctuary was cast down. And an army was sent against the daily sacrifice in rebellion; and it cast down the truth to the ground, and it practised, and prospered.

Then I heard a holy one speaking, and another holy one said to that certain one that spake, 'How long shall be the 'vision concerning the daily sacrifice, and the rebellion 'which desolateth, and giveth both the Holy Place and the 'host [or temple-servants] to be trodden under foot?' And he said to me, 'Until two thousand and three hundred 'evenings and mornings; then shall the Holy Place be jus-'tified.' And it came to pass, when I, even I Daniel, had seen the vision, and sought for the meaning, then, behold, there stood before me as the appearance of a man. And I heard a man's voice between the banks of the Eulaeus, who called, and said, 'Gabriel, make this man to understand the 'appearance.' So he came near where I stood; and when he came, I was afraid, and fell upon my face. But he said to me, 'Understand, O son of Adam; for unto the time of 'the end belongeth the vision.' Now as he was speaking

with me, I was in a deep sleep on my face toward the ground; but he touched me, and made me stand upright.
19 And he said, 'Behold, I will make thee know what shall be 'in the last end of the indignation; for at the time appointed
20 'the end shall be. The Ram which thou sawest hath two
21 'Horns, which are the kings of Media and Persia. And the 'rough Goat is the king of Greece; and the great Horn that 'is between his eyes is the first king [Alexander the Great].
22 'Now that being broken, whereas four stood up instead of 'it, four kingdoms [Macedonia, Asia Minor, Syria and 'Egypt] shall stand up out of the nation, but not in his
23 'power. And in the latter time of their kingdom, when 'the transgressions are come to the full, a king [Antiochus 'Epiphanes] of fierce countenance, and understanding dark
24 'sentences, shall stand up. And his power shall be mighty, 'but not by his own power. And he shall destroy won-'derfully, and shall prosper, and shall practise, and shall 'destroy mighty ones and the nation of the Holy People.
25 'And through his policy also he shall cause craft to prosper 'in his hand; and he shall magnify himself in his heart, 'and while in peace he shall destroy many. He shall also 'stand up against the Prince of princes; but he shall be
26 'broken, but not by any hand. And the appearance of the 'evening and the morning which hath been told is true; 'therefore do thou keep the vision secret; for it shall be
27 'after many days.' And I Daniel fainted; and I was sick for some days; afterward I rose up, and did the king's business; and I was astonished at the appearance, but in —no wise understood it.

---

1 IN THE FIRST YEAR OF DARIUS [or Cyaxares II.] the son of Ahasuerus, of the seed of the Medes, who [B.C. 538]
2 was made king over the kingdom of the Chaldeans; in the first year of his reign I Daniel understood by books the number of the years, about which the word of Jehovah came to Jeremiah the prophet, that he would accomplish seventy
3 years in the desolations of Jerusalem. And I set my face unto the Lord God, to seek him by prayer and supplica-
4 tions, with fasting, and sackcloth, and ashes. And I prayed to Jehovah my God, and made my confession, and said, 'O 'Lord, O great and dreadful God, keeping the covenant 'and kindness to them that love him, and to them that

'keep his commandments; we have sinned, and have com- 5
'mitted iniquity, and have done wickedly, and have rebelled,
'even by departing from thy commandments and from thy
'judgments; neither have we hearkened to thy servants 6
'the prophets, who spake in thy name to our kings, our
'princes, and our fathers, and to all the people of the land.
'O Lord, righteousness belongeth to thee, but to us con- 7
'fusion of face, as at this day; to the men of Judah, and
'to the inhabitants of Jerusalem, and to all Israel, that are
'near, and that are far off, through all the countries whither
'thou hast driven them, because of their trespass that they
'have trespassed against thee. O Lord, to us belongeth 8
'confusion of face, to our kings, to our princes, and to our
'fathers, because we have sinned against thee. To the 9
'Lord our God belong mercies and forgivenesses, though
'we have rebelled against him, and have not hearkened to 10
'the voice of Jehovah our God, to walk in his laws, which
'he set before us by the hand of his servants the prophets.
'Yea, all Israel have transgressed thy Law, even by de- 11
'parting, that they might not hearken to thy voice; there-
'fore the curse is poured upon us, and the oath that is
'written in the Law of Moses the servant of God [Deut.
'xxvii. 15], because we have sinned against him. And 12
'he hath confirmed his words, which he spake against us,
'and against our judges that judged us, by bringing upon
'us a great evil; for under the whole heavens hath not
'been done as hath been done upon Jerusalem. As it is 13
'written in the Law of Moses [Deut. xxviii. 15.], all this
'evil is come upon us; yet we entreated not the face of
'Jehovah our God, that we might turn from our iniquities,
'and understand thy truth. Therefore hath Jehovah 14
'watched over the evil, and brought it upon us; for (Je-
'hovah our God is righteous in all his works which he
'doeth;) for we hearkened not to his voice.

 'And now, O Lord our God, that didst bring thy people 15
'forth out of the land of Egypt with a mighty hand, and
'hast made for thyself a name, as at this day; we have sinned,
'we have done wickedly. O Lord, according to all thy 16
'righteousness, I beseech thee, let thine anger and thy wrath
'be turned away from thy city Jerusalem, thy holy moun-
'tain; because for our sins, and for the iniquities of our
'fathers, Jerusalem and thy people are become a reproach

17 'among all that are about us. Now therefore, O our God, 'hearken to the prayer of thy servant, and to his supplica-'tions, and cause thy face to shine upon thy Sanctuary
18 'that is desolate, for the Lord's sake. O my God, incline 'thine ear, and hear; open thine eyes, and behold our 'desolations, and the city which is called by thy Name; 'for we do not lay down our supplications before thee for
19 'our righteousnesses, but for thy great mercies. O Lord, 'hear; O Lord, forgive; O Lord, give heed and do; delay 'not, for thine own sake, O my God; for thy city and thy 'people are called by thy Name.'
20 And while I was speaking, and praying, and confessing my sin and the sin of my people Israel, and laying down my supplication before Jehovah my God for the holy
21 mountain of my God; yea, while I was speaking in prayer, even the man Gabriel, whom I had seen in the vision at the beginning, wearied with flying, came up to me about
22 the time of the evening meal offering. And he explained, and talked with me, and said, 'O Daniel, I am now come
23 'forth to teach thee understanding. At the beginning of 'thy supplications the command went forth, and I am 'come to shew thee; for thou art greatly beloved; there-'fore understand the matter, and consider the appearance.
24 'Seventy weeks [or 490 years] are determined for thy 'people and for thy holy city, to finish the transgression, 'and to make an end of sins, and to make atonement for 'iniquity, and to bring in everlasting righteousness, and to 'put the seal upon the vision and the prophet, and to
25 'anoint the Holy of Holies. Know therefore and under-'stand, that from the going forth of the command [to 'Zerubbabel, B.C. 538] to lead back home, and to build 'up Jerusalem, unto an Anointed Ruler [Ezra], shall be 'seven weeks [or 49 years]. Then in sixty and two weeks, '[or 434 years] the Broad Place [of the Temple] shall 'be built again [B.C. 55] and the ditch, even amid the
26 'distress of the times. And after the sixty and two weeks 'shall an Anointed One [king Aristobulus] be cut off, and 'nothing shall remain to him. And the people of the 'ruler [or Roman general] that shall come will destroy the 'city and the Holy Place; and the end thereof will be 'with a flood; and until the end of the war desolations
27 'are determined. And he will confirm a treaty with Many

'[or the Aristocracy] for one week. And in the middle of
'the week [B.C. 51] he will cause the sacrifice and the
'meal offering to cease, and upon the battlements shall be
'the abominations [or idolatrous ensigns] of desolation;
'even until the consummation, and that which has been
'determined, shall be poured out upon the desolator.' —

IN THE THIRD YEAR OF CYRUS king of Persia [B.C. 536] ¹
a word was revealed to Daniel whose name was called Belteshazzar; and the word was true, but the warfare was long. And he understood the word, and had understanding of the vision.

In those days I Daniel was mourning three weeks of ²
days. I ate no pleasant bread, neither came flesh nor wine ³
in my mouth, neither did I anoint myself at all, till three
weeks of days were fulfilled. And on the four and twen- ⁴
tieth day of the first month, as I was by the side of the
great river, which is the Hiddekel [or Tigris]; then I lifted ⁵
up mine eyes, and looked, and behold a certain man clothed
in linen, whose loins were girded with fine gold of Ophiz
[or Ophir]. His body also was like the chrysolite, and his ⁶
face as the appearance of lightning, and his eyes as lamps
of fire, and his arms and his feet like in colour to polished
copper, and the voice of his words like the voice of a multitude. And I Daniel alone saw the vision; for the men ⁷
that were with me saw not the vision; but a great quaking
fell upon them, so that they fled to hide themselves. There- ⁸
fore I was left alone, and saw this great vision, and there
remained no strength in me; for my comeliness was turned
in me into corruption, and I retained no strength. Yet ⁹
heard I the voice of his words. And when I heard the
voice of his words, then was I in a deep sleep on my face,
and my face toward the ground.

And behold, a hand touched me, which roused me on ¹⁰
to my knees and the palms of my hands. And he said to ¹¹
me, 'O Daniel, O man greatly beloved, understand the
'words that I speak to thee, and stand upright; for to thee
'am I now sent.' And whilst he spoke this word to me,
I stood up trembling. Then said he to me, 'Fear not, ¹²
'Daniel; for from the first day that thou didst set thy
'heart to understand, and to afflict thyself before thy
'God, thy words were heard, and I am come because of

13 'thy words. But the prince of the kingdom of Persia with-
'stood me for one and twenty days; but lo, Michael, one
'of the chief princes, came to help me; and I remained
14 'there with the kings of Persia. Now I am come to make
'thee understand what shall befall thy people in the
15 'latter days; for the vision is for yet many days.' And
whilst he spoke such words to me, I set my face toward
the ground, and I became dumb.
16 And behold, one like the similitude of the sons of Adam
touched my lips. Then I opened my mouth, and spake,
and said to him that stood before me, 'O my lord, because
'of the vision my sorrows are turned upon me, and I
17 'have retained no strength. For how can the servant of
'this my lord talk with my lord himself? For as for
'me, there now remaineth no strength in me, neither is
'there breath left in me.'
18 Then there came again and touched me one like the
19 appearance of a man, and he strengthened me, and said,
'O man greatly beloved, fear not; peace be unto thee, be
'strong, yea, be strong.' And whilst he spoke to me, I
was strengthened, and I said, 'Let my lord speak; for
20 'thou hast strengthened me.' Then said he, 'Knowest
'thou wherefore I come to thee? And now will I return
'to fight against the prince of Persia; and when I am
21 'gone, lo, the prince of Greece will come. And I will
'shew thee what is noted in the Writings of Truth; and
—'there is none that holdeth fast with me in these things,
1 'but Michael your prince. Also I in the first year of
'Darius the Mede I stood to confirm and to strengthen him.
2 'And now will I shew thee the truth. Behold, there
'shall stand up yet three kings in Persia; and the fourth
'[Xerxes I.] shall be far more powerful than they all; and
'according to his strength through his power he shall stir
3 'up all against the kingdom of Greece. And a mighty
'king [Alexander the Great] shall stand up, who shall
'rule with great dominion, and do according to his own
4 'will. And when he shall stand up, his kingdom shall be
'broken, and shall be divided toward the four winds of
'heaven [Macedonia, Asia Minor, Syria and Egypt]; and
'not to his posterity, nor according to his dominion with
'which he ruled; for his kingdom shall be plucked up,
'even for others beside those.

' 'And the king of the South [Ptolemy I.] shall be ⁵
' strong ; and one of his generals, even he shall be strong
' above him, and shall have dominion ; his dominion [Syria]
' shall be a great dominion. And at the end of years they ⁶
' shall make an alliance together ; for the king's daughter
' of the South [Berenice] shall come to the king of the North
' [or Syria] to make an agreement [of marriage] ; but the
' arm shall not retain power ; neither shall he stand, nor
' his arm ; and she shall be given up, and they that
' brought her, and her offspring, and whoever strengthened
' her in those times. But out of an off-shoot from her roots ⁷
' shall one [Ptolemy Energetes] stand up in his stead, who
' shall come to the army, and shall enter into the fortress
' of the king of the North, and shall deal against them,
' and shall prevail ; and shall also carry into captivity in ⁸
' Egypt their gods, with their molten images, and with
' their precious vessels of silver and of gold ; and he shall
' continue more years than the king of the North. So the ⁹
' king of the South shall come into his kingdom [Syria],
' and then he shall return into his own land.
 'But his sons shall carry on the war, and shall assemble ¹⁰
' a multitude of great forces; and one [Antiochus the Great]
' shall certainly come, and overwhelm, and pass through.
' Then shall he return, and they shall carry on the war,
' even to his fortress. And the king of the South [Ptolemy ¹¹
' Philopator] shall be moved with anger, and shall go forth
' and fight with him, even with the king of the North.
' And he shall set forth a great multitude ; and the multi-
' tude shall be given into his hand. And when he hath ¹²
' taken away the multitude, his heart shall be lifted up ;
' and he shall cast down tens of thousands ; but he shall
' not be strengthened. And the king of the North shall ¹³
' return, and shall set forth a multitude greater than the
' former, and shall certainly come at the end of the times
' of years with a great army and with much riches.
 'And in those times there shall many stand up against ¹⁴
' the king of the South. Also children of robbers of thy
' people [Israel] shall exalt themselves to establish the
' vision ; but they shall stumble. So the king of the North ¹⁵
' [Antiochus] shall come, and cast up a siege-mound, and
' shall take a city of fortresses [Sidon]. And the arms of
' the South shall not withstand, neither shall His chosen

'people; neither shall there be any strength to with-
16 'stand. But he that cometh against him shall do accord-
'ing to his own will, and none shall stand before him;
'and he shall stand in the Land of Beauty [or Palestine],
'which by his hand shall be consumed.
17 'And he shall set his face to enter [Egypt] with the
'strength of his own kingdom, and Upright ones [or Jews]
'with him; thus shall he do. And he shall give to him
'[Ptolemy Epiphanes] a daughter of women, corrupting
'her. But she shall not stand, or be for him.
18 'Then shall he turn his face to the isles [or Greece],
'and shall take many; but a commander [Scipio] shall
'cause his reproach of him to cease; without his own re-
19 'proach he shall cause it to turn upon him. Then he
'shall turn his face toward the fortresses of his own land
'[Syria]; but he shall stumble and fall, and shall not be
'found.
20 'Then shall stand up in his stead one [Seleucus Philo-
'pator] who sends a tribute collector [Heliodorus] unto
'the Glory of the Kingdom [or Jerusalem]. But within
'a few days he shall be destroyed, neither in anger, nor
'in battle.
21 'And in his stead shall stand up a vile person [Anti-
'ochus Epiphanes], to whom they shall not give the honour
'of the kingdom [of Syria]. But he shall come in peace-
22 'ably, and obtain the kingdom by flatteries. And with the
'arms of a flood shall they be overwhelmed before him,
'and shall be broken; yea, also the ruler of the Covenant
23 '[Onias III.]. And after the league made with him he
'shall work deceit; for he shall come up, and shall be-
24 'come strong with a small people. He shall enter peace-
'ably even upon the fattest places of the Province [or
'Judea]; and he shall do that which his fathers have not
'done, nor his fathers' fathers; he shall scatter among them
'the prey, and the spoil, and riches; yea, and he shall de-
'vise his devices against the strongholds, even for a time.
25 'Then he shall stir up his power and his courage against
'the king of the South with a great army. And the king
'of the South shall carry on the war to battle with a very
'great and mighty army; but he shall not stand; for
26 'they shall devise devices against him. Yea, they that
'feed on his delicacies shall destroy him, and his army

'shall be overwhelmed; and many shall fall down slain.
'And both these kings' hearts shall be set to do mischief, 27
'and they shall speak lies at one table; but it shall not
'prosper; for yet the end shall be at the time appointed.

'Then shall he [Antiochus] return into his land with 28
'great riches; and his heart shall be against the Holy
'Covenant [in Jerusalem]; and so he shall do; and he
'shall return to his own land.

'At the time appointed he shall return, and come to- 29
'ward the South; but it shall not be as the first time, or
'as the after time. For the ships of Chittim [or the 30
'Romans] shall come against him; and he shall be grieved,
'and shall return, and have indignation against the Holy
'Covenant; so shall he do. Then he shall return, and
'have intelligence with them that forsake the Holy Cove-
'nant. And men's arms shall stand up on his behalf, and 31
'they shall pollute the Sanctuary of the fortress, and shall
'put away the daily sacrifice, and they shall place there the
'Abomination [or idolatrous ensigns] of Desolation. And 32
'the evil-doers of the Covenant shall he corrupt by flat-
'teries; but the people that know their God shall be
'strong, and shall do so. And they that understand among 33
'the people shall instruct the many; yet they shall fall
'by the sword, and by flame, by captivity, and by spoil,
'during many days. Now when they shall fall, they shall 34
'be helped with a little help; but many shall cleave to
'them with flatteries. And some of them that understand 35
'shall fall, in order to make trial of them, and to purge,
'and to make them white, even to the time of the end;
'because it is yet for a time appointed.

'And the king [Antiochus] shall do according to his will; 36
'and he shall exalt himself, and magnify himself above
'every god, and shall speak marvellous things against the
'God of gods, and shall prosper till the indignation shall
'be accomplished; for that which is decreed shall be done.
'Neither shall he regard the Gods of his fathers, nor the 37
'Delight of Women, nor regard any god; for he shall
'magnify himself above all. But instead shall he 38
'honour the god of the Fortress of the Sea [or Tyre]; and
'a god whom his fathers knew not shall he honour with
'gold, and silver, and with precious stones, and pleasant
'things. Thus shall he do in the citadels of the Fortress 39

'of the Sea. The people of a foreign god, whom he shall
'acknowledge, he will increase with glory; and he will
'cause them to rule over many, and will divide the land
'for a reward.

40 'And at the time of the end shall the king of the South
'push at him. But the king of the North shall come against
'him like a whirlwind, with chariots, and with horsemen,
'and with many ships; and he shall enter into the coun-
41 'tries, and shall overwhelm and pass over. He shall enter
'also into the land of Beauty, and many countries shall
'be overthrown; but these shall escape out of his hand,
'even Edom, and Moab, and the chief city of the Children
42 'of Ammon. He shall stretch forth his hand also upon the
43 'countries; and the land of Egypt shall not escape; but
'he shall have power over the treasures of gold and of
'silver, and over all the precious things of Egypt; and the
44 'Libyans and the Ethiopians shall be at his steps. But
'tidings out of the east [from Parthia] and out of the north
'[from Armenia] shall trouble him. Therefore he shall
'go forth with great fury to destroy, and utterly to make
45 'away with many. And he shall plant the tents of his
'palace between the two seas, on the holy mountain of
'Beauty [or Zion]; yet he shall come to his end, and none
—'shall help him.

1 'And at that time shall Michael stand up, the great
'prince who standeth up for the children of thy people.
'And there shall be a time of trouble, such as never was
'since it was a nation to that same time; and at that time
'thy people shall be delivered, every one that shall be found
2 'written in the Book. And many of them that sleep in
'the dust of the earth shall awake, some to everlasting life,
3 'and some to shame and everlasting contempt. And they
'that be wise shall shine as the brightness of the firma-
'ment; and they that turn many to righteousness shall
4 'be as the stars for ever and ever. But thou, O Daniel,
'keep the words secret, and seal the Book, until the time
'of the end, when many shall search into it, and know-
'ledge shall be increased.'

5 Then I Daniel looked, and, behold, there stood two
others, the one on this side of the bank of the river, and
6 the other on that side of the bank of the river. And one
said to the man clothed in linen, who was above the

waters of the river, 'How long shall it be to the end of
'these wonders?' And I heard the man clothed in linen, 7
who was above the waters of the river, when he held up
his right hand and his left hand to heaven, and sware by
Him that liveth for ever, that it shall be for a time, times,
and a half; and when he shall have finished scattering the
power of the Holy People, all these things shall be finished.
And I heard, but I understood not; then said I, 'O my 8
'Lord, what will be after these things?' And he said, 9
'Go thy way, Daniel; for the words are kept secret and
'sealed to the time of the end. Many shall be purified, 10
'and made white, and tried; but the wicked shall do
'wickedly; and none of the wicked shall understand;
'but the wise shall understand. And from the time that 11
'the daily sacrifice shall be put away, and the Abomination
'of Desolation shall be set up, there shall be a thousand
'two hundred and ninety days. Blessed is he that waiteth, 12
'and cometh to the thousand three hundred and five and
'thirty days. But go thou thy way till the end be; for thou 13
'shalt rest, and stand in thy lot at the end of the days.'

HOSEA.

THE WORD OF JEHOVAH that came to Hosea, the son 1
of Beeri, in the days of Uzziah, Jotham, Ahaz, and
Hezekiah, kings of Judah, and in the days of Jeroboam
the son of Joash, king of Israel.

The beginning of the word of Jehovah by Hosea. And 2
Jehovah said to Hosea, 'Go, take unto thee a wife of lewd-
'ness, and children of lewdness; for the land committeth
'great lewdness, departing from Jehovah.' So he went 3
and took Gomer the daughter of Diblaim; who conceived
and bare to him a son. And Jehovah said to him, 'Call 4
'his name Jezreel; for yet a little while, and I will avenge
'the blood of Jezreel upon the house of Jehu, and will
'cause the kingdom of the house of Israel to cease. And 5
'it shall come to pass at that day, that I will break the
'bow of Israel in the valley of Jezreel.'

And she conceived again and bare a daughter. And 6
[God] said to him, 'Call her name Not-pitied; for I will
'no more have pity upon the house of Israel, that I should

⁷ 'wholly pardon them. But I will have pity upon the 'house of Judah, and will save them by Jehovah their 'God. And I will not save them by bow, nor by sword, 'nor by battle, by horses, nor by horsemen.'

⁸ Now when she had weaned Not-pitied, she conceived, ⁹ and bare a son. Then said [God], Call his name Not-my-people; for ye are not my people, and I will not be your ¹⁰ [God]. Yet the number of the children of Israel shall be as the sand of the sea, which cannot be measured nor numbered; and it shall come to pass, that in the place where it was said to them, 'Ye are not my people,' there it shall ¹¹ be said to them, 'Ye are the sons of the living God.' And the children of Judah and the children of Israel shall be gathered together, and appoint to themselves one head, —and they shall come up out of the land [of Assyria]; for ¹ great shall be the day of Jezreel. Say ye to your brethren, 'Ye are my people;' and to your sisters, 'Ye are Pitied.'

² Plead against your mother, plead ye; for she is not my wife, neither am I her husband. Let her therefore put away her lewdness out of her sight, and her adulteries from ³ between her breasts; lest I strip her naked, and set her as in the day that she was born, and make her as the desert, ⁴ and set her like a dry land, and slay her with thirst. And I will not have mercy on her children; for they are the ⁵ children of lewdness. For their mother hath gone astray; she that conceived them hath done shamefully. For she said, 'I will go after my lovers, that give me my bread and 'my water, my wool and my flax, mine oil and my strong ⁶ 'drinks.' Therefore, behold, I will hedge up thy way with thorns, and make a wall, that she shall not find her paths. ⁷ And she shall follow after her lovers, but she shall not overtake them; and she shall seek them, but shall not find them. Then shall she say, 'I will go and return to my 'first husband; for then was it better with me than now.' ⁸ For she doth not know that I gave her the corn, and the grape juice, and the oil, and multiplied her silver and gold, ⁹ which they have prepared for Baal. Therefore will I return, and take away my corn in its time, and my grape juice in its season, and will recover my wool and my flax ¹⁰ from covering her nakedness. And now will I uncover her shamefulness in the sight of her lovers, and none shall de- ¹¹ liver her out of my hand. I will also cause all her mirth to

cease, her feast days, her new moons, and her sabbaths, and all her solemn feasts. And I will make desolate her ¹² vines and her fig trees, whereof she hath said, 'These are 'my rewards that my lovers have given me.' And I will make them a forest, and the wild beasts of the field shall eat them; and I will punish her for the days of Baal, where- ¹³ in she burned incense to them, and she decked herself with her rings and her jewels, and she went after her lovers, and forgot me; Jehovah hath said it.

Therefore, behold, I will allure her, and bring her into ¹⁴ the desert, and speak to her heart. And I will give her her ¹⁵ vineyards from thence, and the valley of Achor [or afflic- tion] for a doorway of hope. And she shall sing there, as in the days of her youth, and as in the day when she came up out of the land of Lower Egypt. And it shall come to ¹⁶ pass at that day, Jehovah hath said it, that thou shalt call me My Husband; and shalt call me no more My Master [or My Baal]. For I will take away the names of Baal out ¹⁷ of her mouth, and they shall no more be remembered by their name.

And in that day will I make a covenant for their sakes ¹⁸ with the wild beasts of the field, and with the fowls of the heavens, and with the creeping things of the ground; and I will break the bow and the sword and the battle out of the earth; and I will make them to lie down in safety. And I will betroth thee to me for ever; yea, I will betroth ¹⁹ thee to me in righteousness, and in judgment, and in loving- kindness, and in mercies. I will even betroth thee to me ²⁰ in faithfulness; and thou shalt know Jehovah.

And it shall come to pass in that day, that I will give ²¹ answer, Jehovah hath said it, I will give answer to the heavens; and they shall give answer to the earth; and the ²² earth shall give answer to the corn, and the grape juice, and the oil; and they shall give answer to Jezreel. And ²³ I will sow her to me in the earth; and I will have pity upon her that was Not-pitied; and I will say to them that were Not-my-people, 'Thou art my people;' and they shall say, 'Thou art my God.'

Then said Jehovah to me, 'Go yet, love a woman that ¹ 'loveth a neighbour, and is an adulteress; according to the 'love of Jehovah toward the children of Israel, who look 'to other gods, and love cakes of raisins.' So I bought ² her to me for fifteen pieces of silver, and for a Homer [or

nine bushels] of barley, and a Lethach [or half Homer] of
3 barley. And I said to her, 'Thou shalt abide for me many
'days; thou shalt not go astray, and thou shalt not be for
4 'another man; so will I also be for thee.' For the children
of Israel shall abide many days without a king, and without a prince, and without a sacrifice, and without a pillar,
and without an Ephod [or priestly robe], and without Te-
5 raphs [or images]. Afterward shall the children of Israel
return, and seek Jehovah their God, and David their king;
—and shall fear Jehovah and his goodness in the latter days.

1 HEAR THE WORD OF JEHOVAH, ye children of Israel; for
Jehovah hath a controversy with the inhabitants of the
land, because there is no truth, nor kindness, nor know-
2 ledge of God in the land. Swearing, and lying, and
killing, and stealing, and adultery break forth, and blood-
3 shed toucheth upon bloodshed. Therefore shall the land
mourn, and every one that dwelleth therein shall languish, with the wild beasts of the field, and with the
fowls of the heavens; yea, the fishes of the sea also shall
4 be taken away. Yet let no man strive, nor reprove another; for thy people are as they that strive against the
5 priest. Therefore shalt thou stumble in the day, and
the prophet also shall stumble with thee in the night, and
I will destroy thy mother.
6 My people are destroyed for lack of knowledge. Because
thou hast rejected knowledge, I will also reject thee, so
that thou shalt be no priest to me; seeing thou hast forgotten the Law of thy God, I will also forget thy children.
7 As they were increased, so they sinned against me; there-
8 fore will I change their glory into shame. They [the priests]
eat up the sin offerings of my people, and they lift up their
9 heart to their iniquity. And it hath come to pass, 'Like
'people, like priest.' And I will punish them for their
10 ways, and reward them for their doings. For they shall
eat, and not be satisfied; they shall commit fornications,
and shall not increase; because they have ceased to take
11 heed to Jehovah. Lewdness and wine and grape juice
take away the heart.
12 My people ask counsel of their blocks of wood, and their
staff declareth it to them. For the spirit of lewdness hath
caused them to err, and they have gone astray from under
13 their God. They sacrifice on the tops of the mountains,

and burn incense on the hills, under oaks and poplars and elms, because the shade thereof is good; therefore your daughters shall commit fornication, and your daughters-in-law shall commit adultery. I will not punish your daughters when they commit fornication, nor your daughters-in-law when they commit adultery; for the men themselves go aside with harlots, and they sacrifice with fornicators. Therefore the people that doth not understand shall perish.

Though thou, Israel, go astray, yet let not Judah be guilty; and come not ye [Judah] unto Gilgal, neither go ye up to Beth-aven, nor swear, 'As Jehovah liveth.' While Israel rebelleth as a rebellious heifer; now Jehovah feedeth them [of Judah] as a lamb in a large place. Ephraim is joined to idols; do ye [Judah] let him alone. When their strong drink is removed, they commit fornication continually; her defenders love shame. The wind hath bound her up in her wings, and they shall be ashamed because of their sacrifices.

HEAR YE THIS, O PRIESTS; and hearken, ye house of Israel; and give ye ear, O house of the king; for judgment is against you, because ye were a snare at Mizpeh, and a net spread upon Tabor [1 Sam. x. 3, 17]. And the rebels have deepened their slaughter, though I have been a rebuker of them all. I know Ephraim, and Israel is not hid from me; for now, O Ephraim, thou committest fornication, and Israel is defiled. They will not frame their doings to turn to their God; for the spirit of fornication is in the midst of them and they have not known Jehovah. And the pride of Israel doth testify to his face. Therefore shall Israel and Ephraim stumble in their iniquity; Judah also shall stumble with them. They shall go with their flocks and with their herds to seek Jehovah; but they shall not find him; he hath withdrawn himself from them. They have dealt treacherously against Jehovah; for they have begotten strange children. Now shall the new moon day [by usury] devour them with their portions.

Blow ye the cornet in Gibeah, and the trumpet in Ramah; they cry aloud at Beth-aven after thee, O Benjamin. Ephraim shall be desolate in the day of rebuke; among the tribes of Israel have I made known what is certain. The

princes of Judah were like them that remove a boundary;
therefore I will pour out my wrath upon them like water.
¹¹ Ephraim is oppressed and broken in judgment, because
¹² he willingly walked after the Decree [of Jeroboam]. Therefore will I be unto Ephraim as a moth, and to the house
¹³ of Judah as rottenness. When Ephraim saw his sickness,
and Judah saw his wound, then went Ephraim to the
Assyrian, and he [Judah] sent to king Jareb [or Sennacherib]. Yet could he not heal you, nor cure you of
¹⁴ your wound. For I will be unto Ephraim as a roaring lion,
and as a young lion to the house of Judah; I, even I, will
tear and go away; I will take away, and none shall rescue.
¹⁵ I will go and return to my place, till they own themselves
—guilty, and seek my face. In their affliction they will seek
¹ me early, [saying,] 'Come, and let us return to Jehovah;
'for he hath torn, and he will heal us; he hath smitten,
² 'and he will bind us up. After two days will he revive
'us; on the third day he will raise us up, and we shall
³ 'live in his sight. Then shall we know, we shall follow
'on to know Jehovah. His going forth is prepared as the
'daybreak; and he will come to us as the rain, as the
'latter rain which watereth the earth.'
⁴ O Ephraim, what shall I do to thee? O Judah, what shall
I do to thee? for your good will is as a morning cloud,
⁵ and as the early dew it passeth away. Therefore have I
hewed them down by the prophets; I have slain them
by the words of my mouth; and my judgments are as the
⁶ light that goeth forth. For I delight in kindness, and not
in sacrifice; and the knowledge of God is more than burnt
⁷ offerings. But they like Adam have transgressed the covenant; there have they dealt treacherously against me.
⁸ Gilead is a city of them that work iniquity, and is slippery
⁹ with blood. And as troops of robbers wait for a man,
so the company of priests murder on the way to Shechem;
¹⁰ for they commit lewdness. I have seen a horrible thing
in the house of Israel; there is the fornication of Ephraim,
¹¹ Israel is defiled. Also for thee, O Judah, a harvest is appointed.
— When I was bringing home the captivity of my people,
¹ when I would have healed Israel, then the iniquity of
Ephraim was discovered, and the wickedness of Samaria.
For they commit falsehood; and the thief cometh in, and

the troop of robbers spoileth outside. And they consider ² not in their hearts that I remember all their wickedness. Now their own doings have beset them about; they are before my face. They make the king glad with their ³ wickedness, and the princes with their lies. They are all ⁴ adulterers, as an oven heated by the baker, who ceaseth from stirring after he hath kneaded the dough, until it be leavened. On the [birth] day of our king the princes were ⁵ sick with the heat of wine; he stretched out his hand with scorners. For they have made ready their heart like an ⁶ oven, while they lie in wait; their baker sleepeth all the night; in the morning it burneth as a flaming fire. They ⁷ are all hot as an oven, and have devoured their judges; all their kings are fallen; no one among them calleth to me. Ephraim, he hath mixed himself among the peoples. ⁸ Ephraim is a cake not turned. Strangers have devoured ⁹ his strength, and he knoweth it not; yea, gray hairs are sprinkled upon him, yet he knoweth not. And the pride ¹⁰ of Israel testifieth to his face; and they return not to Jehovah their God, nor seek him for all this.

Ephraim also is like an enticed dove without sense; they ¹¹ call to Egypt, they go to Assyria. When they shall go, I ¹² will spread my net over them; I will bring them down as the fowls of the heavens; I will chastise them, as hath been made known to their congregation.

Woe unto them! for they have fled from me. Destruc- ¹³ tion is upon them! because they have transgressed against me. Though I redeemed them, yet they have spoken lies against me. And they cried not to me with their heart, ¹⁴ when they howled upon their beds. They assemble themselves for corn and grape juice; they rebel against me. Though I have instructed and strengthened their arms, yet ¹⁵ do they imagine mischief against me. They return not to ¹⁶ the Most High. They are like a deceitful bow. Their princes shall fall by the sword for the rage of their tongue. This shall be their derision in the land of Egypt.

Set the trumpet to thy mouth. [Assyria is] as an eagle ¹ against the House of Jehovah, because they have transgressed my covenant, and have trespassed against my law. Israel will cry to me, 'My God, we know thee.' Israel hath ² cast off what is good; the enemy shall pursue him. They ³ have set up kings, but not by me; they have made princes, ⁴ and I knew them not. Of their silver and their gold have they made for themselves idols, so that they may be cut off.

5 Thy calf, O Samaria, hath cast thee off; mine anger is kindled against them; how long will it be ere they attain
6 to innocence? For of Israel is this also. The workman made it; and it is not a god; but the calf of Samaria shall
7 be broken in pieces. For they sow the wind, and they shall reap the whirlwind. It hath no stalk; the bud shall yield no meal; if so be that it yield, strangers shall swallow it up.

8 Israel is swallowed up; now shall they be among the
9 Nations as a vessel wherein man hath no pleasure. For they are gone up to Assyria, as a wild ass alone by himself;
10 Ephraim hath hired lovers. Yea, though they have hired among the Nations, now will I gather them, and they shall be free for a little while from the tribute of the king of
11 princes [or Sennacherib]. Because Ephraim hath made many altars unto Sin, the altars shall be unto him for a sin.
12 I have written to him many things of my Law, but they
13 were counted as a strange thing. The sacrifices of mine offerings they sacrifice as flesh, and eat it; but Jehovah accepteth them not. Now will he remember their iniquity,
14 and visit their sins; they shall return into Egypt. For Israel hath forgotten his Maker, and buildeth temples; and Judah hath multiplied fenced cities. But I will send a fire —upon his cities, and it shall devour the palaces thereof.

1 REJOICE NOT, O ISRAEL, joy not, as the peoples; for thou hast gone astray from thy God, thou hast loved hire upon
2 every threshing-floor of the corn. The threshing-floor and the winepress shall not feed them, and the grape juice shall
3 fail in her. They shall not dwell in Jehovah's land; but Ephraim shall return to Egypt, and they shall eat unclean
4 things in Assyria. They shall not pour out wine offerings to Jehovah, neither shall their sacrifices be pleasing to him; they shall be to them as the bread of mourners; all that eat thereof shall be polluted. For their bread for their
5 appetite shall not come into the House of Jehovah. What will ye do in the solemn day, and in the day of the
6 feast of Jehovah? For, lo, they are gone because of destruction. Egypt shall gather them up, Memphis shall bury them. The pleasant places for their silver, nettles shall

possess; thorns shall be in their tents. The days of visi- ⁷
tation are come, the days of recompence are come; Israel
shall know it. The prophet is a fool, the spiritual man is
in a frenzy, for the multitude of thine iniquity, and the
great hatred. The watchman of Ephraim was with my God; ⁸
but the prophet is a fowler's snare in all his ways; hatred
is in the house of his God. They have deeply corrupted ⁹
themselves, as in the days of Gibeah [Judg. xx.]; therefore
He will remember their iniquity, he will visit their sins.

I found Israel like grapes in the desert. I saw your ¹⁰
fathers as the first-ripe on the fig tree at her first time. But
they went to Baal-peor, and separated themselves unto
Shame; and their abominations were according as they
loved. As for Ephraim, their glory shall fly away like a ¹¹
bird, from the birth, and from the womb, and from the
conception. If they bring up their sons, yet will I bereave ¹²
them of men; yea, woe also to them when I depart from
them! Ephraim, as I saw, was on a rock, planted in a quiet ¹³
place; but Ephraim shall bring forth his children to the
murderer.

'Give to them, O Jehovah; what wilt thou give? Give ¹⁴
'to them a miscarrying womb and dry breasts.'

All their wickedness is in Gilgal; for there I hated them. ¹⁵
For the wickedness of their doings I will drive them out
of my House, I will love them no more; all their princes
are rebels. Ephraim is smitten, their root is dried up, they ¹⁶
shall bear no fruit. Yea, though they bring forth, yet will
I slay even the desire of their womb.

'My God will cast them away, because they did not hearken ¹⁷
'to him; and they shall be wanderers among the Nations.'—

Israel is a flourishing vine, he bringeth forth his fruit. ¹
According to the multitude of his fruit he hath increased
the altars; according to the goodness of his land they have
made their images goodly. Their heart is slippery; now ²
shall they be found guilty. He shall break down their altars,
he shall destroy their images. For now they say, 'We have ³
'no king, because we feared not Jehovah; and what should
'a king do for us?' They have spoken mere words, swear- ⁴
ing falsely in making a covenant; thus judgment springeth
up as hemlock in the furrows of the field. The neighbour- ⁵
ing Samaria shall fear for the calf of Beth-aven. For its
people shall mourn over it, and its idolatrous priests

that rejoiced on it, for its glory, because it is departed from
6 it. It shall be also carried to Assyria as a present to king
Jareb [or Sennacherib]. Ephraim shall receive shame,
7 and Israel shall be ashamed of his own counsel. Samaria
is cut off, her king is as the foam upon the face of the
8 water. The High Places also of Aven [or Beth-el], the
sin of Israel, shall be destroyed; the thorn and the thistle
shall come up on their altars. And they shall say to the
mountains, 'Cover us;' and to the hills, 'Fall on us.'
9 O Israel, thou hast been sinning from the days of Gibeah;
there they stood. The battle in Gibeah against the chil-
10 dren of iniquity did not overtake them. It is in my desire
that I should chastise them; and the peoples shall be gathered against them, when I shall chastise them for their
11 two iniquities. And Ephraim is as a heifer that is taught.
I wished her to tread out the corn; and I passed a yoke
upon her fair neck. I will make Ephraim to carry a rider;
Judah shall plow, and Jacob shall break the clods for him.
12 Sow to yourselves in righteousness, reap kindness accord-
ingly. Break up your fallow ground; for it is time to seek
Jehovah, till he come and rain down righteousness upon
13 you. Ye have plowed wickedness, ye have reaped iniquity;
ye have eaten the fruit of falsehood; because thou didst
trust in thine own way, in the multitude of thy warriors.
14 Therefore shall a tumult arise among thy people, and all
thy fortresses shall be spoiled, as Shalman [or Shalman-
ezer] spoiled Beth-arbel in the day of battle. The mother
15 was dashed in pieces upon her children. So shall Beth-el
do to you because of your wicked wickedness; at daybreak
--shall the king of Israel be utterly cut off.
1 When Israel was a child, then I loved him; and I called
2 my son out of Egypt. But when they called them, so they
went from them; they sacrificed to Baal, and burned in-
3 cense to graven images. I taught Ephraim also to walk,
taking them by their arms; but they knew not that I
4 healed them. I drew them with the cords of a man, with
the bands of love; and I was to them as they that take
the yoke off their jaws, and I laid food before them.
5 He shall not return into the land of Egypt, but the Assyrian [Sennacherib] shall be his king, because they refused
6 to return. And the sword shall go about in his cities, and
shall consume his crossbars, and devour them, because of

their counsels. And my people are bent on backsliding 7 from me; though they are called to the Most High, none at all will exalt him.

How shall I do with thee, O Ephraim? Shall I deliver 8 thee up, O Israel? How shall I make thee as Admah? Shall I set thee as Zeboim? My heart is turned within me, my repentings are kindled together. I will not exe- 9 cute the fierceness of mine anger. I will not return to destroy Ephraim. For I am God, and not man, the Holy One in the midst of thee; and I will not come in anger. They shall walk after Jehovah. He will roar like a lion. 10 When he shall roar, then the children shall hasten from the west. They shall hasten as a bird out of Egypt, and 11 as a dove out of the land of Assyria; and I will place them in their houses; Jehovah hath said it.

Ephraim encompasseth me with falsehood, and the house 12 of Israel with deceit; and Judah yet acteth disobediently toward God, even toward the Most Holy and faithful One.— Ephraim feedeth on wind, and followeth after the east 1 wind. He daily increaseth lies and desolation; and they make a covenant with the Assyrians, and oil is carried into Egypt. Jehovah hath a controversy also with Judah, and 2 will punish Jacob according to his ways; according to his doings will he recompense him. He took his brother by 3. the heel in the womb, and in his manhood he wrestled with God. Yea, he wrestled with the angel, and prevailed. 4 He wept, and made supplication unto him. He found him in Beth-el, and there he spake with him; even Jehovah the 5 God of hosts, Jehovah is his memorial. Therefore return 6 thou to thy God; keep kindness and judgment, and wait on thy God continually.

Ephraim is a merchant, deceitful balances are in his 7 hand; he loveth to oppress, and he saith, 'Yet I am become 8 'rich, I have found for myself substance; in all my labours 'they shall find no iniquity in me that were sin.' And I 9 Jehovah that have been thy God from the land of Egypt will yet make thee to dwell in tents, as in the days of the solemn feast. I have also spoken by the prophets, and I 10 have multiplied visions, and used parables, by the hand of the prophets. Is there iniquity in Gilead? Surely they 11 are vanity; they sacrifice bullocks in Gilgal; yea, their altars are as heaps of stones by the furrows of the

¹² fields. And Jacob fled into the Fields of Syria, and Israel served for a wife, and for a wife he watched over [sheep].
¹³ And by a prophet Jehovah brought up Israel out of
¹⁴ Egypt, and by a prophet was he watched over. Ephraim provoked him to anger most bitterly; therefore his bloodshed shall be left upon him, and his reproach will his —Lord return unto him.

¹ When Ephraim spake with trembling, he was exalted in Israel; but when he was guilty in the matter of Baal,
² he died. And now they sin more and more, and have made to them molten images of their silver, idols according to their own understanding, all of it the work of the craftsmen. They say of them, 'Let them that sacrifice men
³ 'kiss the calves.' Therefore they shall be as the morning cloud, and as the early dew that passeth away, as the chaff that is driven by the whirlwind off the threshing-floor, and as the smoke out of the window.
⁴ Yet I Jehovah have been thy God from the land of Egypt, and thou shalt know no god but me; for there is
⁵ no saviour beside me. I did know thee in the desert, in
⁶ the land of drought. According to their feeding, so were they filled; they were filled, and their heart was exalted;
⁷ therefore they forgot me. And I will be to them as a roaring lion; as a leopard by the way will I lie on the
⁸ watch. I will meet them as a bear that is bereaved of her whelps, and will rend the coating of their heart, and there will I devour them like a lioness; the wild beasts of the field shall tear them.
⁹ O Israel, thou hast destroyed thyself; for thou art
¹⁰ against me, against thy help. Where is now thy king [B.C. 720], that he may save thee in all thy cities? and thy Judges to whom thou saidst, 'Give me a king and
¹¹ 'princes'? I gave thee a king in mine anger, and I took him away in my wrath.
¹² The iniquity of Ephraim is stored up; his sin is trea-
¹³ sured up. The pains of a travailing woman shall come upon him. He is an unwise son; for he did not stay his
¹⁴ time at the childbirth. I will ransom them from the hand of Hell; I will redeem them from death. O Death, where will be thy plagues? O Hell, where will be thy destruction? Repentance is hidden from mine eyes.
¹⁵ Though he be fruitful among his brethren, an east wind

shall come, the wind of Jehovah shall come up from the desert; and his spring shall become dry, and his fountain shall be dried up. It shall spoil the treasure of all pleasant vessels. Samaria is guilty; for she hath rebelled against 16 her God. They shall fall by the sword; their babes shall be dashed in pieces, and their women with child shall be ripped up.

O Israel, return to Jehovah thy God; for thou hast 1 stumbled by thine iniquity. Take with you words, and 2 turn to Jehovah. Say to him, 'Take away all iniquity, ' and bring the good; so will we give in return the fruit ' of our lips. The Assyrian shall not save us; we will not 3 ' ride upon horses. Neither will we say any more to the ' work of our hands, Ye are our gods. For in Thee the ' fatherless findeth mercy.'

I will heal their backsliding, I will love them of my free- 4 will; for mine anger is turned away from him. I will be as 5 the dew unto Israel. He shall flourish as the lily, and strike forth his roots as Lebanon. His branches shall spread, 6 and his beauty shall be as the olive tree, and his scent as Lebanon. They that dwell under his shade shall return; 7 they shall revive as the corn, and flourish as the vine. The memory thereof shall be as the wine of Lebanon. Ephraim 8 [shall say], 'What have I to do any more with idols?' I have afflicted him, and I will observe him; I am like a green fir tree. From me is thy fruit found.

'Who is wise, and he shall understand these things? 9 ' prudent, and he shall know them? For the ways of ' Jehovah are right, and the righteous walk in them. ' But the transgressors shall stumble therein.'

JOEL.

THE WORD OF JEHOVAH that came to Joel the son of 1 Pethuel.

Hear this, ye old men, and give ear, all ye inhabitants 2 of the land. Hath this been in your days, or even in the days of your fathers? Tell ye your children of it, and 3 let your children tell their children, and their children another generation. That which the grasshopper hath left 4 hath the cricket eaten; and that which the cricket hath left hath the locust eaten; and that which the locust hath left hath the great locust eaten.

⁵ Awake, ye drunkards, and weep; and howl, all ye drinkers of wine, because of the grape juice; for it is cut ⁶ off from your mouth. For a nation [Assyria] is come up upon my land, strong, and without number, whose teeth are the teeth of a lion, and he hath the cheek teeth of a ⁷ lioness. He hath laid my vine waste, and barked my fig tree; he hath made it clean bare, and cast it away; its ⁸ branches are made white. Lament like a maiden girded ⁹ with sackcloth for the husband of her youth. The meal offering and the drink offering are cut off from the House ¹⁰ of Jehovah; the priests, Jehovah's ministers, mourn. The field is wasted, the land mourneth; for the corn is wasted, the grape juice is dried up, the oil languisheth.

¹¹ Be ye ashamed, O ye husbandmen; howl, O ye vine-dressers, because of the wheat and because of the barley; ¹² for the harvest of the field is perished. The vine is dried up, and the fig tree languisheth; the pomegranate tree, the palm tree also, and the apple tree, even all the trees of the field, are withered; because joy is withered away from the sons of Adam.

¹³ Gird yourselves, and lament, ye priests; howl, ye ministers of the altar; come, lie all night in sackcloth, ye ministers of my God; for the meal offering and the drink offering ¹⁴ are withheld from the House of your God. Sanctify ye a fast, proclaim a day of restraint [from work], gather the elders of all the inhabitants of the land into the House of ¹⁵ Jehovah your God, and cry to Jehovah, 'Alas for the day!' For the day of Jehovah is at hand, and as a destruction ¹⁶ from the Almighty it cometh. Is not the food cut off before our eyes, yea, joy and gladness from the House of our God?

¹⁷ The seed is rotten under their clods, the garners are laid desolate, the barns are broken down; for the corn is withered. ¹⁸ How do the beasts groan! The herds of cattle are perplexed, because they have no pasture; yea, the flocks of ¹⁹ sheep perish. O Jehovah, to thee will I cry; for the fire hath devoured the pastures of the desert, and the flame ²⁰ hath burned all the trees of the field. The cattle of the field cry also to thee; for the pools of water are dried up, —and the fire hath devoured the pastures of the desert.

Blow ye the trumpet in Zion, and sound an alarm on my ¹
holy mountain; let all the inhabitants of the land tremble.
For the day of Jehovah cometh, for it is nigh at hand; a ²
day of darkness and of gloom, a day of clouds and of
thick darkness. There is a people great and strong [the
Assyrians], spread like the daybreak upon the mountains;
there hath not been ever the like, neither shall there be any
more after it, even to the years of generations and generations. A fire devoureth before them; and behind them a ³
flame burneth. The land is as the garden of Eden before
them, and behind them a wasted desert; yea, and nothing
escapeth them. The appearance of them is as the appear- ⁴
ance of horses; and as horsemen, so do they run. Like the ⁵
noise of chariots on the tops of mountains they leap, like the
noise of a flame of fire that devoureth the stubble, like a
strong people set in battle array. Before their face the ⁶
peoples are much pained; all faces lose their colour. They ⁷
run like warriors; they climb the wall like men of war;
and they march every one on his ways, and they vary not
from their paths; neither doth one thrust another; they ⁸
walk every warrior in his own path; and when they fall
upon the sword, they are not wounded. They run to and ⁹
fro in the city; they run upon the wall, they climb up
upon the houses; they enter in by the windows like a
thief. The earth quaketh before them; the heavens ¹⁰
tremble; the sun and moon are dark, and the stars withdraw their shining. And Jehovah uttereth his voice ¹¹
before his army; for his camp is very great. For he is
strong that executeth His word; for the day of Jehovah
is great and very terrible; and who can abide it?

Therefore also now, Jehovah hath said it, turn ye to me ¹²
with all your heart, and with fasting, and with weeping,
and with mourning. And rend your heart, and not your ¹³
garments, and turn to Jehovah your God; for he is gracious
and merciful, slow to anger, and of great kindness, and re-
penteth him of the evil. Who knoweth but he [Tiglath- ¹⁴
pilezer] will turn back and repent, and will leave a blessing behind him, even a meal offering and a drink offering
unto Jehovah your God?

Blow the trumpet in Zion, sanctify a fast, proclaim a day ¹⁵
of restraint [from work]. Gather the people, sanctify the ¹⁶
assembly, bring together the elders, gather the little child-

ren, and those that suck the breasts; let the bridegroom go forth out of his chamber, and the bride out of her closet. ¹⁷ Let the priests, the ministers of Jehovah, weep between the porch and the Altar, and let them say, 'Have pity on 'thy people, O Jehovah, and give not thy heritage to re-'proach, that the Nations should rule over them. Why 'should they say among the peoples, Where is their God?' ¹⁸ Then will Jehovah be jealous for his land, and pity his ¹⁹ people. Yea, Jehovah will answer and say to his people, 'Behold, I will send you corn, and grape juice, and oil, 'and ye shall be satisfied therewith; and I will no more ²⁰ 'make you a reproach among the Nations. But I will re-'move far off from you the northern people, and will drive 'him into a land barren and desolate, with his face to-'ward the East Sea, and his rear toward the Western 'Sea, and his stink shall come up, and his ill savour shall 'come up, because he hath done great things.'

²¹ Fear not, O land; be glad and rejoice; for Jehovah will ²² do great things. Be not afraid, ye cattle of the field; for the pastures of the desert do spring up, for the tree beareth its fruit, the fig tree and the vine do yield their strength. ²³ Be glad then, ye children of Zion, and rejoice in Jehovah your God. For he giveth you the early rain in just measure, and he causeth to come down for you the showers of ²⁴ the early rain, and the latter rain as formerly. And the threshing-floors shall be full of wheat, and the vats shall ²⁵ overflow with grape juice and oil. And I will repay you for the years that the grasshopper hath eaten, the locust, and the great locust, and the caterpillar, my great army ²⁶ which I sent among you. And ye shall eat in plenty, and be satisfied, and praise the name of Jehovah your God, who hath dealt wondrously with you; and my people shall ²⁷ never be ashamed. And ye shall know that I am in the midst of Israel, and that I am Jehovah your God, and none else. And my people shall never be ashamed.

²⁸ (AND IT SHALL COME TO PASS AFTERWARD, that I will pour out my spirit upon all flesh; and your sons and your daughters shall prophesy, your old men shall dream dreams, ²⁹ your young men shall see visions. And also upon the menservants and upon the handmaids in those days will I ³⁰ pour out my spirit. And I will shew wonders in the heavens and on the earth, blood, and fire, and pillars of

smoke. The sun shall be turned into darkness, and the ³¹ moon into blood, before the great and the terrible day of Jehovah come. And it shall come to pass, that whosoever ³² shall call on the name of Jehovah shall escape; for on mount Zion and in Jerusalem shall be deliverance, as Jehovah hath said, and among the remnant whom Jehovah shall call.

For, behold, in those days, and at that time, when I ¹ shall bring back home the captivity of Judah and Jerusalem, I will also gather all the Nations, and will bring them ² down into the valley of Jehoshaphat [or Jehovah judgeth], and I will have judgment against them there on account of my people and of my heritage Israel, whom they have scattered among the Nations. And they parted my land, ³ and they cast lots for my people; and have given a boy for a harlot, and sold a girl for wine, that they might drink.

Yea, and what have ye to do with me, O Tyre, and Sidon, ⁴ and all the Circle of the Philistines? Will ye repay to me a recompence? And if ye do recompense me, swiftly and speedily will I return your recompence upon your own head; because ye have taken my silver and my gold, and have ⁵ carried into your own temples my goodly pleasant things. The children also of Judah and the children of Jerusalem ⁶ have ye sold to the children of the Greeks, that ye might remove them far from their boundary. Behold, I will raise ⁷ them out of the place whither ye have sold them, and I will return your recompence upon your own head. And I ⁸ will sell your sons and your daughters into the hand of the children of Judah, and they shall sell them to the men of Sheba, to a nation far off; for Jehovah hath spoken it.)

Proclaim ye this among the Nations; Consecrate the war, ⁹ wake up the warriors, let all the men of war draw near, let them come up. Beat your plowshares into swords, and ¹⁰ your pruninghooks into spears; let the weak man say, 'I 'am strong.' Hasten, and come, all ye Nations round about, ¹¹ and gather yourselves together; thither wilt thou cause thy warriors to come down, O Jehovah. Let the Nations ¹² be awakened, and come up to the valley of Jehoshaphat; for there will I sit to judge all the nations round about.

Put ye in the sickle, for the harvest is ripe. Come, get ¹³ you down; for the winepress is full, the vats overflow; for

¹⁴ their wickedness is great. Multitudes, multitudes are in the valley of Decision; for the day of Jehovah is near in ¹⁵ the valley of Decision. The sun and the moon shall be ¹⁶ darkened, and the stars shall withdraw their shining. Jehovah also will roar out of Zion, and will utter his voice from Jerusalem; and the heavens and the earth shall shake. But Jehovah will be the refuge of his people, and ¹⁷ the strength of the children of Israel. So shall ye know that I am Jehovah your God, dwelling on Zion my holy mountain; then shall Jerusalem be holy, and there shall no strangers pass through her any more.

¹⁸ And it shall come to pass in that day, that the mountains shall drop down grape juice, and the hills shall flow with milk, and all the pools of Judah shall flow with waters, and a fountain shall come forth out of the House of Jeho- ¹⁹ vah, and shall water the valley of Shittim. Egypt shall be a desolation, and Edom shall be a wasted desert, for the violence against the children of Judah, because they have ²⁰ shed innocent blood in their land. But Judah shall dwell for ever, and Jerusalem from generation to generation. ²¹ For I will cleanse them of the bloodshed that I have not cleansed; for Jehovah dwelleth in Zion.

AMOS.

¹ THE WORDS OF AMOS, who was among the sheep-masters of Tekoa, of which he had a vision concerning Israel in the days of Uzziah king of Judah, and in the days of Jeroboam the son of Joash king of Israel, two years before the earthquake.

² And he said, Jehovah will roar from Zion, and utter his voice from Jerusalem; and the pastures of the shepherds shall mourn, and the top of Carmel shall wither.

³ Thus said Jehovah; Because of three transgressions of Damascus, and because of four, I will not restore it; because they have threshed Gilead with threshing instru- ⁴ ments of iron. But I will send a fire into the house of ⁵ Hazael, which shall devour the palaces of Ben-hadad. I will break also the cross-bars of Damascus, and cut off the inhabitant from the valley of Aven, and him that holdeth

the sceptre from Beth-Eden ; and the people of Syria shall go into captivity to Kir, said Jehovah.

Thus said Jehovah; Because of three transgressions of Gaza, and because of four, I will not restore it; because they carried away captive the whole body of captives, to deliver them up to Edom. But I will send a fire on the wall of Gaza, which shall devour its palaces. And I will cut off the inhabitant from Ashdod, and him that holdeth the sceptre from Askalon, and I will turn my hand against Ekron. And the remnant of the Philistines shall perish, said the Lord Jehovah.

Thus said Jehovah ; Because of three transgressions of Tyre, and because of four, I will not restore it; because they delivered up the whole body of captives to Edom, and remembered not the covenant of brethren. But I will send a fire on the wall of Tyre, which shall devour its palaces.

Thus said Jehovah ; Because of three transgressions of Edom, and because of four, I will not restore it ; because he did pursue his brother with the sword, and did cast off his pity, and his anger teareth perpetually, and he keepeth his wrath for ever. But I will send a fire upon Teman, which shall devour the palaces of Bozrah.

Thus said Jehovah ; Because of three transgressions of the Children of Ammon, and because of four, I will not restore them ; because they have ripped up the women with child of Gilead, in order that they might enlarge their boundary. But I will kindle a fire in the wall of Rabbah, and it shall devour its palaces, with a shout in the day of battle, with a tempest in the day of the whirlwind. And their king shall go into captivity, he and his princes together, said Jehovah.

Thus said Jehovah ; Because of three transgressions of Moab, and because of four, I will not restore it ; because he burned the bones of the king of Edom into lime. But I will send a fire upon Moab, and it shall devour the palaces of Kerioth ; and Moab shall die with a noise, with a shout, and with the sound of the trumpet. And I will cut off the judge from the midst thereof, and will slay all its princes with him, said Jehovah.

Thus said Jehovah ; Because of three transgressions of Judah, and because of four, I will not restore them ; because they have despised the Law of Jehovah, and have not kept his statutes; and their deceivers, after whom their fathers

⁵ walked, have caused them to err. But I will send a fire upon Judah, and it shall devour the palaces of Jerusalem.
⁶ Thus said Jehovah; Because of three transgressions of Israel, and because of four, I will not restore them; because they sold the righteous for silver, and the poor in
⁷ exchange for a pair of shoes. They wish for the dust of the earth on the head of the poor, and turn aside the way of the meek; and a man and his father will go in unto the same young woman, to profane my holy name.
⁸ And they lay themselves down upon clothes taken in pledge near every altar, and the wine of those condemned in fines they drink in the house of their god.
⁹ Yet I destroyed the Amorite before them, whose height was like the height of the cedars, and he was strong as the oaks; yet I destroyed his fruit from above, and his roots
¹⁰ from beneath. Also I brought you up from the land of Egypt, and led you for forty years through the desert, to
¹¹ possess the land of the Amorites. And I raised up some of your sons for prophets, and some of your young men for Nazarites. Is it not even thus, O ye children of Israel?
¹² Jehovah hath said it. But ye gave to the Nazarites wine to drink; and commanded the prophets, saying, 'Prophesy
¹³ not.' Behold, I am pressed under you, as a cart is pressed
¹⁴ that is full of sheaves. Therefore flight shall perish from the swift, and the strong man shall not strengthen his force,
¹⁵ neither shall the warrior save his life. Neither shall he stand that handleth the bow; and the swift of foot shall not escape. Neither shall he that rideth the horse save
¹⁶ his life. And he that is strong of heart among the warriors shall flee away naked in that day; Jehovah hath said it.

¹ HEAR YE THIS WORD that Jehovah hath spoken against you, O children of Israel, against the whole family which
² I brought up from the land of Egypt, saying, 'You only have I known of all the families of the earth;' therefore I
³ will punish you for all your iniquities. Can two walk to-
⁴ gether, except they be agreed? Will a lion roar in the forest, when it hath no prey? Will a young lion give forth its voice
⁵ out of its den, if it have taken nothing? Can a bird fall into a snare upon the earth, when there is no trap for it? Shall one lift up a snare from the ground, when it hath taken
⁶ nothing at all? Shall a trumpet be blown in the city, and the people not be afraid? Shall there be evil in a city, and

Jehovah hath not done it? Surely the Lord Jehovah doeth 7 nothing without revealing his secret counsel to his servants the prophets. The lion hath roared, who will not fear? 8 The Lord Jehovah hath spoken, who will not prophesy?

Publish ye in the palaces at Ashdod, and in the palaces 9 in the land of Egypt, and say, 'Assemble yourselves upon the mountains of Samaria, and behold the great tumults in the midst thereof, and the oppressed in the midst thereof.' For they know not how to do right, Jehovah 10 hath said it, who store up violence and robbery in their palaces. Therefore thus saith the Lord Jehovah; An adver- 11 sary there shall be even round about the land; and he shall bring down thy strength from thee, and thy palaces shall be plundered.

Thus said Jehovah; As the shepherd delivereth out of 12 the mouth of the lion two legs, or a piece of an ear; so shall the children of Israel be delivered that sit in Samaria on the corner of a bed, and on a Damascus couch.

Hear ye, and bear witness in the house of Jacob, the 13 Lord Jehovah, the God of hosts, hath said it, that in the 14 day that I shall visit the transgressions of Israel upon him, I will also visit the altars of Beth-el; and the horns of the altar shall be cut off, and fall to the ground. And I will 15 smite the winter house with the summer house; and the houses of ivory shall perish, and the great houses shall have an end; Jehovah hath said it.

HEAR YE THIS WORD, ye cows of Bashan [or Syrians], 1 that are in the hill country of Samaria, who oppress the poor, who crush the needy, who say to their masters, 'Bring, and let us drink.' The Lord Jehovah hath sworn 2 by his holiness, that, lo, the days shall come upon you, that he will take you away with hooks, and your posterity with fishhooks. And ye shall go out at the breaches, every 3 woman straight before her; and ye shall be cast into the palace-tower; Jehovah hath said it.

Come to Beth-el, and transgress; at Gilgal multiply 4 transgression; and bring your sacrifices every morning, and your tithes on the third year; and burn incense of 5 thanksgiving with leaven, and proclaim and publish the freewill offerings; for this pleaseth you, O ye children of Israel; the Lord Jehovah hath said it.

And I also have given you cleanness of teeth in all your 6

cities, and want of bread in all your places; yet ye have not returned to me; Jehovah hath said it.

7 And also I have withheld the showers from you, when there were but three months to the harvest. And I caused it to rain upon one city, and caused it not to rain upon another city. One piece of ground was rained upon, and 8 the piece whereupon it rained not, withered. So two or three cities wandered unto one city, to drink water; but they were not satisfied; yet ye have not returned to me; Jehovah hath said it.

9 I have smitten you with blight and mildew; the increase of your gardens and of your vineyards and of your fig trees and of your olive trees hath the caterpillar devoured; yet ye have not returned to me; Jehovah hath said it.

10 I have sent among you the pestilence after the manner of Egypt; your young men have I slain with the sword, when I took your horses into captivity; and I have made the stink of your camps to come up into your nostrils; yet ye have not returned to me; Jehovah hath said it.

11 I have overthrown some among you, as God overthrew Sodom and Gomorrah, and ye were as a firebrand plucked out of the burning; yet ye have not returned to me; Jehovah hath said it.

12 Therefore thus will I do to thee, O Israel; and because I will do this to thee, prepare to meet thy God, O Israel.

13 For, lo, He that formed the mountains, and created the wind, and declareth to man what is his thought, he that maketh the daybreak out of darkness, and treadeth upon the high places of the earth, Jehovah, the God of hosts, is —his name.

1 HEAR YE THIS WORD which I take up against you as a lamentation, O house of Israel;

2 'The virgin of Israel is fallen; she shall no more rise; 'She is forsaken upon her land; no one raiseth her up.'

3 For thus said the Lord Jehovah; The city that went forth a thousand shall leave a hundred, and that which went forth a hundred shall leave ten, to the house of Israel.

4 For thus said Jehovah to the house of Israel, Seek ye 5 me, and ye shall live; but seek not Beth-el, nor enter into Gilgal, and pass not to Beer-sheba. For Gilgal shall surely go into captivity, and Beth-el shall become nought [or 6 Beth-aven]. Seek Jehovah, and ye shall live; lest he

break out like fire on the house of Joseph, and devour it, and there be none to quench it in Beth-el. Ye who turn ⁷ judgment to wormwood, and cast righteousness on to the earth, [seek] him that made the Cluster [or the Pleiades] ⁸ and Orion, and turneth the shadow of death into the morning, and maketh the day dark with night; that calleth for the waters of the sea, and poureth them out upon the face of the earth; Jehovah is his name; who maketh destruc- ⁹ tion burst upon the strong, so that destruction cometh upon the fortress.

They hate him that rebuketh at the city gate, and they ¹⁰ abhor him that speaketh uprightly. Forasmuch therefore ¹¹ as ye trample upon the poor, and ye take from him burdens of wheat; ye have built houses of hewn stone, but ye shall not dwell in them; ye have planted pleasant vineyards, but ye shall not drink wine of them. For I know your many ¹² transgressions and your mighty sins; ye who afflict the righteous, who take a bribe, and who turn aside the poor at the city gate. Therefore the prudent shall keep silence ¹³ in that time; for it is an evil time.

Seek good, and not evil, so that ye may live; and thus ¹⁴ Jehovah the God of hosts, will be with you, as ye have said. Hate evil, and love good, and establish justice at the ¹⁵ city gate; it may be that Jehovah the God of hosts will be gracious to the remnant of Joseph.

Therefore Jehovah, the God of hosts, the Lord, said ¹⁶ thus; Mourning shall be in all broad places; and they shall say in all the streets, 'Alas! alas!' and they shall call the plowman to wailing, and there shall be mourning among such as are skilful in lamentation. And in all vineyards ¹⁷ shall be mourning; for I will pass through the midst of thee, said Jehovah.

Alas for you that desire the day of Jehovah! What is ¹⁸ the day of Jehovah to you? It will be darkness, and not light. As if a man did flee from a lion, and a bear met him; ¹⁹ or went into the house, and placed his hand on the wall, and a serpent bit him. Shall not the day of Jehovah be ²⁰ darkness, and not light? even thick darkness, and no brightness in it?

I hate, I despise your feast days, and I will not smell on ²¹ your days of restraint [from work]. Though ye offer up ²² unto me burnt offerings and your meal offerings, I will

not accept them; neither will I regard the peace offerings
23 of your fat beasts. Take thou away from me the noise of
thy songs; for I will not hear the melody of thy psal-
24 teries. But let judgment roll down as waters, and righteousness as an unfailing stream.
25 Did ye bring to me sacrifices and meal offerings in the
26 desert for forty years, O house of Israel? Yet ye have
carried the tabernacle of your Moloch and Chiun your
images, the star of your god, which ye made to yourselves.
27 Therefore will I cause you to go into captivity beyond Da-
—mascus, saith Jehovah, whose name is the God of hosts.
1 Alas for them that are at ease in Zion, and who feel safe
in the hill country of Samaria, who are nobles of the chief
2 of nations, to whom the house of Israel came! Pass ye
over to Calneh, and see; and from thence go ye to Great
Hamath; then go down to Gath of the Philistines; are
they better than these kingdoms? or is their border greater
3 than your border? [Alas for] them that put far away the
4 evil day, and cause the seat of violence to come near; that
lie upon beds of ivory, and stretch themselves upon their
couches, and eat lambs out of the flock, and calves out of
5 the midst of the stall; that chant to the sound of the
psaltery like David, and invent to themselves instruments
6 of music, that drink wine in sprinkling buckets, and anoint
themselves with the chief ointments; but they are not
7 grieved for the affliction of Joseph. Therefore now shall
they go captive with the first that go captive, and the cheerful noise of them that stretched themselves on couches shall
be removed.
8 The Lord Jehovah hath sworn by himself, Jehovah the
God of hosts hath said it, I abhor the excellence of Jacob,
and hate his palaces; therefore will I deliver up the city
9 with all that is therein. And it shall come to pass, if there
10 remain ten men in one house, that they shall die. And a
man's uncle, or he that burneth him, shall take him up,
to bring out the bones out of the house, and shall say to
him that is in the inside of the house, 'Is there yet any
'with thee?' And he shall say, 'No.' Then shall he say,
'Hold thy tongue; for we may not make mention of the
11 'name of Jehovah.' For, behold, Jehovah commandeth,
and he will smite the great house with ruins, and the little
house with clefts.

Shall horses run upon the rock? Will a man plow there ¹²
with oxen?-that ye should have turned judgment into
hemlock; and the fruit of righteousness into wormwood;
ye who rejoice in a thing of nought, who say, 'Have we not ¹³
'taken to us horns by our own strength?' But, behold, I ¹⁴
will raise up against you a nation [the Assyrians], O house
of Israel, Jehovah the God of hosts hath said it; and they
shall afflict you from the Pass of Hamath unto the Valley
of Arabah.

THUS HATH THE LORD JEHOVAH shewed to me. And, ¹
behold, he formed locusts in the beginning of the shooting
up of the latter growth; and, lo, it was the latter growth
after the king's mowings. And it came to pass that when ²
they had made an end of eating the grass of the land, then
I said, 'O Lord Jehovah, forgive, I beseech thee. By
'whom shall Jacob arise? for he is small.' Jehovah re- ³
pented for this; 'It shall not be,' said Jehovah.

Thus hath the Lord Jehovah shewed unto me. And, ⁴
behold, the Lord Jehovah called for a contention by fire,
and it devoured the great deep, and did eat up the fields.
Then said I, 'O Lord Jehovah, cease, I beseech thee. By ⁵
'whom shall Jacob arise? for he is small.' Jehovah re- ⁶
pented for this; 'This also shall not be,' said the Lord
Jehovah.

Thus hath he shewed me. And, behold, the Lord stood ⁷
near a wall, made by a plumbline, with a plumbline in his
hand. And Jehovah said to me, 'Amos, what seest thou?' ⁸
And I said, 'A plumbline.' Then said the Lord, 'Behold,
'I will set a plumbline in the midst of my people Israel;
'I will not again pass by [or spare] them any more. And ⁹
'the High Places [or Altars] of Isaac shall be desolate, and
'the Sanctuaries of Israel shall be laid waste; and I will
'rise against the house of Jeroboam with the sword.'

Then Amaziah the priest of Beth-el sent to Jeroboam ¹⁰
king of Israel, saying, 'Amos hath conspired against thee
'in the midst of the house of Israel; the land is not able to
'bear all his words. For thus Amos hath said, Jeroboam ¹¹
'shall die by the sword, and Israel shall surely be led away
'captive out of their own land.' And Amaziah said to Amos, ¹²
'O thou seer, go, flee thee away into the land of Judah,
'and there eat bread, and prophesy there. But prophesy ¹³
'not again any more at Beth-el. For it is the king's Sanc-

¹⁴ 'tuary, and it is the royal house.' Then answered Amos, and said to Amaziah, 'I was no prophet, neither was I a 'prophet's son; but I was a herdsman, and a gatherer of ¹⁵ 'sycamore fruit. And Jehovah took me from following 'the flock, and Jehovah said to me, Go, prophesy to my ¹⁶ 'people Israel. Now therefore hear thou the word of 'Jehovah. Thou sayest, Prophesy not against Israel, 'and drop not thy word against the house of Isaac. ¹⁷ 'Therefore thus saith Jehovah; Thy wife shall be a har-'lot in the city, and thy sons and thy daughters shall fall 'by the sword, and thy land shall be divided by line; 'and thou shalt die in a polluted land; and Israel shall —'surely go forth into captivity out of his land.'

¹ Thus hath the Lord Jehovah shewed to me. And be-² hold there was a basket of summer fruit. And he said, 'Amos, what seest thou?' And I said, 'A basket of sum-'mer fruit.' Then said Jehovah to me, 'The end is come 'upon my people of Israel; I will not again pass by them ³ 'any more. And the songs of the temple shall be howl-'ings in that day, the Lord Jehovah hath said it. There 'shall be many dead bodies in every place; they shall 'cast them forth in silence.'

⁴ Hear this, O ye that would swallow up the needy, even ⁵ to make the poor of the land to fail, saying, 'When will 'the new-moon day be gone, that we may sell corn? and 'the sabbath, that we may set forth wheat?' making the Ephah [or measure] small, and making the Shekel [or ⁶ money] great, and bending the balances in deceit; buying the poor with silver, and the needy in exchange for a pair of shoes; yea, and the refuse of the wheat ye sell for ⁷ food. Jehovah hath sworn by the excellence of Jacob, ⁸ 'Surely I will never forget any of their works.' Shall not the land tremble for this, and every one mourn that dwelleth therein? and it shall rise up wholly as a river; and it shall be cast out and sink down as the river of Egypt. ⁹ And it shall come to pass in that day, the Lord Jehovah hath said it, that I will cause the sun to go down at noon, ¹⁰ and I will darken the earth in clear day. And I will turn your feast days into mourning, and all your songs into lamentation; and I will bring up sackcloth upon all loins, and baldness upon every head; and I will make it as the mourning for an only son, and its end as a bitter day.

Behold, the days will come, the Lord Jehovah hath ¹¹ said it, that I will send a famine into the land, not a famine of bread, nor a thirst for water, but of hearing the words of Jehovah. And they shall wander from Sea ¹² to Sea, and from the north even to the east, they shall run to and fro to seek the word of Jehovah, and shall not find it. In that day shall the fair maidens and young ¹³ men faint for thirst. They that swear by the Guilt [or ¹⁴ idol] of Samaria, and say, 'As thy god, O Dan, liveth;' and, 'As the manner of Beer-sheba liveth;' even they shall fall, and never rise up again. —

I SAW THE LORD STANDING beside the altar. And he ¹ said, Smite the head of the column [or the king], that the door-posts [or nobles] may shake; and cut them on the head, all of them; and I will slay the last of them with the sword; he that fleeth of them shall not flee away, and he that escapeth of them shall not be saved. Though they ² dig down to hell, thence shall my hand take them; though they climb up to the heavens, thence will I bring them down. And though they hide themselves on the top of ³ Carmel, I will search and take them out thence; and though they be hid from my sight at the bottom of the sea, thence will I command the serpent, and he shall bite them. And though they go into captivity before their ⁴ enemies, thence will I command the sword, and it shall slay them; and I will set mine eyes upon them for evil, and not for good.

And the Lord Jehovah of hosts is he that toucheth the ⁵ land, and it melteth, and all that dwell therein mourn; and it riseth up wholly as a river; and sinketh down as the river of Egypt. It is He that buildeth his upper ⁶ chambers in the heavens, and hath founded his arched vault on the earth; he that calleth for the waters of the sea, and poureth them out upon the face of the earth; Jehovah is his name.

Are ye not as the children of the Ethiopians to me, O ⁷ ye children of Israel? Jehovah hath said it. Have not I brought up Israel out of the land of Lower Egypt? and the Philistines from Caphtor, and the Syrians from Kir? Behold, the eyes of the Lord Jehovah are upon the sinful ⁸ kingdom, and I will destroy it from off the face of the earth; saving that I will not utterly destroy the house of

⁹ Jacob; Jehovah hath said it. For, lo, I will command, and I will shake the house of Israel among all nations, like as one shaketh in a sieve, yet shall not a grain fall ¹⁰ upon the earth. All the sinners of my people shall die by the sword, who say, 'The evil shall not overtake nor 'meet us.'

¹¹ In that day will I raise up the tabernacle of David that is fallen, and close up its breaches; and I will raise up its ruins, and I will build it up as in the days of old; ¹² so that they may possess the remnant of Edom, and of all the Nations, who are called by my name; Jehovah that doeth this hath said it.
¹³ Behold, the days are coming, Jehovah hath said it, that the plowman shall overtake the reaper, and the treader of grapes him that soweth the seed; and the mountains shall ¹⁴ drop grape juice, and all the hills shall melt. And I will bring home again the captivity of my people of Israel, and they shall build up the desolate cities, and inhabit them; and they shall plant vineyards, and drink the wine thereof; they shall also make gardens, and eat the fruit of them. ¹⁵ And I will plant them upon their land, and they shall no more be plucked up out of their land which I have given them, saith Jehovah thy God.

OBADIAH.

¹ THE VISION OF OBADIAH.
Thus saith the Lord Jehovah against Edom. We heard a rumour from Jehovah, and an ambassador was sent among the Nations [saying], 'Arise ye, and let us rise up ² 'against her in battle.' Behold, I have made thee small ³ among the nations; thou art greatly despised. The pride of thy heart hath deceived thee, thou that dwellest in the clefts of the Rock [or of Petra], whose habitation is high; that saith in his heart, 'Who shall bring me down to the ⁴ 'ground?' Though thou exalt thyself as the eagle, and though thou set thy nest among the stars, thence will I bring thee down; Jehovah hath said it.
⁵ If thieves came to thee, if robbers by night, (how art thou cut off!) would they not steal only till they had

enough? if the grapegatherers came to thee, would they not leave a gleaning of grapes? How is Esau searched ⁶ through! his hidden places sought out to the very boundary! All the men of thy confederacy have sent thee ⁷ away; the men that were at peace with thee have deceived thee, and prevailed against thee; they that eat thy bread have laid a snare before thee; there is no understanding in him.

Shall I not in that day, Jehovah hath said it, even de- ⁸ stroy the wise men out of Edom, and understanding out of the hill country of Esau? And thy warriors, O Teman, ⁹ shall be dismayed, to the end that every one of the hill country of Esau may be cut off because of thy slaughter. Because of thy violence against thy brother Jacob, shame ¹⁰ shall cover thee, and thou shalt be cut off for ever. In ¹¹ the day that thou stoodest at a distance, in the day that the strangers carried away captive his forces, and foreigners entered into his city gates, and cast lots upon Jerusalem, even thou wast as one of them. But thou shalt not again ¹² look on the day of thy brother, on the day of his misfortune; neither shalt thou rejoice over the children of Judah in the day of their destruction; neither shalt thou speak proudly in the day of distress. Thou shalt not enter into ¹³ the city gate of my people in the day of their calamity; yea, thou shalt not look on their affliction in the day of their calamity, nor lay hands on their substance in the day of their calamity. Neither shalt thou stand in the ¹⁴ crossway, to cut off those of his that escape; neither shalt thou deliver up those of his that remain in the day of distress.

For the day of Jehovah is near upon all the Nations. ¹⁵ As thou hast done, it shall be done unto thee; thy like doings shall return upon thine own head. For as ye have ¹⁶ drunk upon my holy mountain, so shall all the Nations drink continually; yea, they shall drink, and they shall swallow down, and they shall be as though they had not been.

But upon mount Zion shall be a deliverance, and it ¹⁷ shall be holy; and the house of Jacob shall possess their own possessions. And the house of Jacob shall be a fire, ¹⁸ and the house of Joseph a flame, and the house of Esau for stubble; and they shall kindle against them and devour them; and there shall not be any remaining of the house of Esau; for Jehovah hath spoken it. ¹⁹ And they of the South country shall possess the mountains of Esau; and they of the Low country shall possess the Philistines; and they [Judah] shall possess the fields of Ephraim, and the fields of Samaria; and ²⁰ Benjamin shall possess Gilead. And the captives of this host of the children of Israel shall possess those of the Canaanites, even unto Zarephath [or Sarepta]; and the captives of Jerusalem, who are in Sepharad, shall ²¹ possess the cities of the South country. And saviours shall come up on mount Zion to judge the mountains of Esau; and the kingdom shall be Jehovah's.

JONAH.

¹ NOW THE WORD OF JEHOVAH came to Jonah the son of ² Amittai, saying, 'Arise, go to Nineveh, that great city, 'and cry against it; for their wickedness is come up before ³ 'me.' And Jonah rose up to flee to Tarshish [or Tarsus] from the presence of Jehovah [or from Jerusalem], and he went down to Joppa. And he found a ship going to Tarshish; so he paid the fare thereof, and went down into it, to go with them to Tarshish from the presence of Jehovah.

⁴ And Jehovah sent out a great wind into the sea, and there was a great tempest in the sea, so that the ship was ⁵ like to be broken. Then the sailors were afraid, and cried every man unto his god, and cast forth the wares that were in the ship into the sea, to lighten it of them. But Jonah was gone down into the hollow of the cabin; and ⁶ he lay, and was fast asleep. So the shipmaster came to him, and said to him, 'What meanest thou, O sleeper? 'Arise, call upon thy God, if so be that God will think ⁷ 'upon us, that we perish not.' And they said every one to his fellow, 'Come, and let us cast lots, that we may 'know for whose cause this evil is upon us.' So they cast ⁸ lots, and the lot fell upon Jonah. Then said they to him, 'Tell us, we pray thee, For whose cause this evil is upon 'us? What is thine occupation? and whence comest 'thou? What is thy country? and of what people art thou?'

And he said to them, 'I am a Hebrew; and I fear Jehovah, ⁹
'the God of heaven, who made the sea and the dry land.'
Then the men feared with a great fear, and said to him, ¹⁰
'Why hast thou done this?' For the men knew that he
had fled from the presence of Jehovah, because he had told
them.

Then said they to him, 'What shall we do to thee, that ¹¹
'the sea may be calm unto us?' For the sea grew more
and more tempestuous. And he said to them, 'Take me ¹²
'up, and cast me forth into the sea; so shall the sea be
'calm unto you. For I know that because of me this great
'tempest is upon you.' Nevertheless the men rowed hard ¹³
to bring it to the land; but they could not; for the sea
grew more and more tempestuous against them. Therefore ¹⁴
they cried to Jehovah, and said, 'We beseech thee, O Jeho-
'vah, we beseech thee, let us not perish for this man's life;
'and lay not upon us innocent blood; for thou, O Jehovah,
'hast done as it pleased thee.' So they took up Jonah, ¹⁵
and cast him forth into the sea. And the sea ceased from
its raging. Then the men feared Jehovah with a great fear, ¹⁶
and sacrificed a sacrifice to Jehovah, and vowed vows.

Then Jehovah prepared a great fish to swallow up Jonah. ¹⁷
And Jonah was in the belly of the fish three days and three
nights. And Jonah prayed to Jehovah his God out of the ¹
fish's belly, and said, ²
'In my distress I cried to Jehovah, and he answered me;
'From the belly of hell I called; thou heardest my voice.
'Yea, thou hast cast me to the deep, in the heart of the ³
   ocean;
'And the floods compassed me about;
'All thy waves and thy billows are gone over me.
'Then I said, I am driven away from before thine eyes; ⁴
'Yet I will look again toward thy holy temple.
'The waters have encompassed me, even to the soul; ⁵
'The depth hath closed round me,
'The weeds are wrapped about my head.
'I have gone down to the roots of the mountains; ⁶
'The earth with her bars is about me for ever;
'Yet wilt thou bring up my life from the pit, O Jehovah
   my God.
'While my soul fainteth within me I remember Jehovah; ⁷
'And my prayer shall come to thee, to thy holy temple.

⁸ 'They that regard lying vanities forsake their own good.
⁹ 'But I will sacrifice to thee with the voice of praise;
'I will pay what I have vowed. Salvation is of Jehovah.'
¹⁰ And Jehovah spake to the fish, and it vomited out Jonah —upon the dry land.

¹ AND THE WORD OF JEHOVAH came to Jonah a second time,
² saying, 'Arise, go to Nineveh, that great city, and preach
³ 'to it the preaching that I bid thee.' So Jonah arose, and went to Nineveh, according to the word of Jehovah. Now Nineveh was a city great before God, of three days' journey.
⁴ And Jonah began to enter into the city a day's journey, and he cried out, and said, 'Yet forty days, and Nineveh 'shall be overthrown.'
⁵ So the people of Nineveh believed God, and proclaimed a fast, and put on sackcloth, from the greatest of them even
⁶ to the least of them. And word came to the king of Nineveh, and he arose from his throne, and he laid his robe from him, and covered himself with sackcloth, and sat in the
⁷ ashes. And it was proclaimed and published through Nineveh by the decree of the king and his great men, saying, 'Let neither man nor beast, herd nor flock, taste any-
⁸ 'thing; let them not feed, nor drink water; but let man 'and beast be covered with sackcloth, and cry mightily 'unto God. Yea, let them turn every one from his evil
⁹ 'way, and from the violence that is in their hands. Who 'knoweth if God will turn and repent, and turn away from
¹⁰ 'his fierce anger, that we perish not ?' And God saw their works, that they turned from their evil way; and God repented of the evil that he had said that he would do unto —them; and he did it not.

¹ But it displeased Jonah exceedingly, and he was very
² angry. And he prayed to Jehovah, and said, 'I pray thee, 'O Jehovah, was not this my saying, when I was yet in my 'country? Therefore I made haste to flee to Tarshish; for 'I knew that thou art a *gracious God, and merciful, slow* '*to anger, and abundant in kindness, and repentest thee of the*
³ '*evil.* Therefore now, O Jehovah, take, I beseech thee, my 'life from me; for it is better for me to die than to live.'
⁴ And Jehovah said, 'Doest thou well to be angry?'
⁵ So Jonah went out of the city, and sat on the east side of the city, and there made him a booth, and sat under it in the shade, till he might see what would become of the

city. And Jehovah God prepared a gourd, and made it to come up over Jonah, that it might be a shade over his head, to deliver him from his grief. So Jonah rejoiced because of the gourd with great joy. But God prepared a worm when the daybreak rose on the next day, and it smote the gourd that it withered. And it came to pass, when the sun did arise, that God prepared a cutting east wind; and the sun beat upon the head of Jonah, that he fainted, and wished in himself to die, and said, 'It is better 'for me to die than to live.' And God said to Jonah, 'Doest thou well to be angry for the gourd?' And he said, 'I do well to be angry, even unto death.' Then said Jehovah, 'Thou hast had pity on the gourd, for the which thou 'didst not labour, neither madest it grow; which was the 'child of a night, and perished in a night; and should not 'I have pity on Nineveh, that great city, wherein are more 'than twelve times ten thousand persons that cannot dis-'cern between their right hand and their left hand; and 'also much cattle?'

MICAH.

THE WORD OF JEHOVAH that came to Micah the Moresthite in the days of Jotham, Ahaz, and Hezekiah, kings of Judah, which he saw concerning Samaria and Jerusalem. Hear, all ye peoples; hearken, O earth, and all that therein is; and let the Lord Jehovah be witness against you, the Lord from his holy temple. For, behold, Jehovah goeth forth out of his place, and cometh down; and he will tread upon the high places of the earth. And the mountains shall be melted under him, and the valleys shall be cleft, as wax before the fire, and as the waters that are poured down a steep place. All this is for the transgression of Jacob, and for the sins of the House of Israel. What is the transgression of Jacob? is it not Samaria? And what are the High Places of Judah? are they not Jerusalem? Therefore I will make Samaria as a heap in the field, for the plantings of a vineyard; and I will pour down its stones into the valley, and I will uncover its foundations. And all her graven images shall be beaten to pieces, and all her wages shall be burnt with the fire, and all her idols will I lay desolate; for she gathered it from the wages of a harlot, and they shall return to the wages of a harlot.

8 'Therefore I will wail and howl, I will go stripped and 'naked; I will make a wailing like the jackals, and mourn-
9 'ing as the ostriches. For she is sick of her wounds; for 'he [Sennacherib] is come unto Judah; he is come unto 'the gate of my people, even to Jerusalem.'

10 Declare ye it not in Gath; weep ye not in Cho [or Accho]; in the house of Ophrah roll thyself in the dust.
11 Pass ye away, thou inhabitant of Saphir having thy shame naked. The inhabitant of Zaanan came not forth in the wailing of Beth-ezel; he shall receive from you his abiding
12 place. For the inhabitant of Maroth hoped for good, when evil came down from Jehovah upon the gate of Jerusalem.
13 The inhabitant of Lachish bound the chariot to the swift beast; that was the beginning of the sin to the daughter of Zion; for the transgressions of Israel were found in
14 thee. Therefore shalt thou give parting-presents to Moreshah near Gath. The houses of Achzib shall be false to
15 the kings of Israel. Yet will I bring a dispossessor against thee, O inhabitant of Moreshah; the glory of Israel shall
16 go to [the cave of] Adullam. Make thee bald, and poll thee for the children of thy delight; enlarge thy baldness —as the eagle; for they are gone into captivity from thee.

1 Alas for them that devise iniquity, and work evil upon their beds! When the morning is light, they practise it,
2 because it is in the power of their hand. And they covet fields, and seize them; and houses, and take them away; so they oppress a chief and his house, even a man and his heritage.
3 Therefore thus saith Jehovah; Behold, against this family do I purpose an evil, from which ye shall not remove your necks; neither shall ye go haughtily; for this
4 time is evil. In that day shall one take up a parable against you, and wail with a woeful wailing, and say, 'We are 'utterly laid waste; He hath changed the portion of my 'people. How hath he removed it from me! He hath
5 'divided our fields to the backslider.' Therefore thou shalt have none that shall cast a line by lot in the assembly of Jehovah.
6 Prophesy not. They that prophesy shall not prophesy

concerning these things. Shame shall not depart. Doth 7
the house of Jacob say, 'Is the spirit of Jehovah im-
'patient? Are these his doings?'—Do not my words do
good to him that walketh uprightly? But of late my people 8
is risen up as an enemy. Ye pull the robe from off the
cloak from them that pass by securely, returning from war.
The women of my people have ye cast out from their pleas- 9
ant houses; from their little children have ye taken away
my glory for ever. Arise ye, and depart; for this is not 10
a resting-place; because it is polluted, it shall be destroyed,
even with a sore destruction. If a man go about lying 11
in spirit and in falsehood, [saying,] 'I will prophesy unto
'thee of wine and of strong drink;' even he will be the
prophet of this people.

I will surely assemble, O Jacob, all of thee; I will surely 12
gather the remnant of Israel; I will put them together as
the sheep of Bozrah; as a flock in the midst of their pasture, they shall make great noise by reason of the men.
The breaker down [the Assyrian] is come up before them. 13
They have broken down; and they pass through the city
gate, and go out by it; and their king [Hezekiah] passeth
before them, and Jehovah at the head of them. —

And I said, Hear, I pray you, O heads of Jacob, and ye 1
princes of the house of Israel; Is it not for you to know
judgment? Ye hate the good, and love the evil; ye pluck 2
off their skin from off them, and their flesh from off their
bones; who also eat the flesh of my people, and flay their 3
skin from off them. And they break their bones, and chop
them in pieces, as for the pot, and as flesh within the caldron. Then they will cry to Jehovah, but he will not 4
answer them. He will even hide his face from them at
that time, because they have behaved themselves ill in
their doings.

Thus saith Jehovah concerning the prophets that make 5
my people to err, that bite with their teeth, and cry, 'Peace;'
and whoever putteth not into their mouths, they even consecrate war against him. Therefore night shall be on you, 6
that ye shall have no vision; and it shall be dark unto
you, that ye shall not divine; and the sun shall go down
over the prophets, and the day shall be dark over them.
Then shall the seers be ashamed, and the diviners con- 7
founded; yea, they shall all cover their beard; for there

⁸ is no answer from God. But truly I am full of power by the spirit of Jehovah, and of judgment, and of might, to declare to Jacob his transgression, and to Israel his sin.

⁹ Hear this, I pray you, ye heads of the house of Jacob, and princes of the house of Israel, that abhor judgment, ⁰ and pervert all equity, that build up Zion with bloodshed, ¹ and Jerusalem with iniquity. Her heads judge for bribes, and her priests teach for hire, and her prophets divine for money ; yet they lean upon Jehovah, and say ' Is not Je- ² ' hovah among us ? No evil can come upon us.' Therefore shall Zion for your sake be plowed as a field, and Jerusalem shall become heaps of ruins, and the mountain of the House —as the High Places [or altars] in the forest.

¹ (BUT IN THE LAST DAYS it shall come to pass, that the mountain of the House of Jehovah shall be established on the top of the mountains, and it shall be exalted above ² the hills ; and peoples shall flow unto it. And many nations shall come, and say, 'Come, and let us go up to the mountain ' of Jehovah, and to the House of the God of Jacob; and ' he will teach us his ways, and we will walk in his paths.' For the Law shall go forth out of Zion, and the word of ³ Jehovah from Jerusalem. And he will judge among many peoples, and rebuke strong nations afar off; and they shall beat their swords into plowshares, and their spears into pruninghooks. Nation shall not lift up sword against na- ⁴ tion, neither shall they learn war any more. But they shall sit every man under his vine and under his fig tree ; and none shall make them afraid ; for the mouth of Jehovah ⁵ of hosts hath spoken it. For all the peoples walk every one in the name of his own god, but we will walk in the name of Jehovah our God for ever and ever.

⁶ In that day, Jehovah hath said it, I will assemble those that halt, and I will gather in those that are driven out, ⁷ and those that I have afflicted ; and I will make those that halt a remnant, and those that were removed far off a strong nation ; and Jehovah shall reign over them on ⁸ mount Zion from henceforth, and for ever. And thou, O Tower of Edar, the stronghold of the daughter of Zion, to thee shall it come, even the former dominion ; the kingdom shall come to the daughter of Jerusalem.

⁹ Why dost thou now cry out aloud ? Is there no king in thee ? Is thy counsellor perished ? For pangs have

taken thee as a woman in travail. Be in pain, and labour ¹⁰ to bring forth, O daughter of Zion, like a woman in travail; for now [B.C. 600] shalt thou go forth out of the city, and thou shalt dwell in the field, and thou shalt go even to Babylon. There [B.C. 538] shalt thou be set free; there Jehovah will redeem thee from the hand of thine enemies. But now many nations are gathered against ¹¹ thee, that say, 'Let her be defiled, and let our eye look 'upon Zion.' But they know not the thoughts of Jeho- ¹² vah, neither understand they his counsel; for he shall gather them as the sheaves on to the threshing-floor. Arise and tread them out, O daughter of Zion; for I will ¹³ make thy horn iron, and I will make thy hoofs copper. And thou shalt beat in pieces many peoples; and I will devote their booty to Jehovah, and their substance to the— Lord of the whole earth. Now gather thyself in troops, ¹ O daughter of troops. He hath laid siege against us; they smite the judge of Israel with a rod upon the cheek.

But thou, Beth-lehem Ephratah, though thou be little ² to be among the thousands of Judah, yet out of thee goeth forth for me he [Zerubbabel] that is to be ruler in Israel; whose goings forth are from former times, from days of old. Therefore will he give them up, until the ³ time that she that travaileth hath brought forth. Then the remnant of his brethren shall return to the children of Israel. And he shall stand and feed his flock in the ⁴ strength of Jehovah, in the majesty of the name of Jehovah his God; and they shall abide; for now shall he be great unto the ends of the land. And this man shall be prosperous. If the Assyrian shall come into our land, ⁵ and if he shall tread in our palaces, then will we raise against him seven shepherds, and eight princes of men. And they shall waste the land of Assyria with the sword, ⁶ and the land of Nimrod in the entrances thereof. Thus shall he deliver us from the Assyrian, if he cometh into our land, and if he treadeth within our boundaries.

And the remnant of Jacob shall be in the midst of many ⁷ peoples as dew from Jehovah, as the showers upon the grass, that tarrieth not for man, nor waiteth for the sons of Adam. And the remnant of Jacob shall be among the ⁸ Nations in the midst of many peoples as a lion among the cattle of the forest, as a young lion among the flocks of

sheep; who, if he go through, both treadeth down, and
⁹ teareth in pieces, and none can deliver. Thy hand shall
be lifted up upon thine oppressors, and all thine enemies
shall be cut off.
¹⁰ And it shall come to pass in that day, Jehovah hath said
it, that I will cut off thy horses out of the midst of thee,
¹¹ and I will destroy thy chariots. And I will cut off the
cities of thy land, and throw down all thy strongholds.
¹² And I will cut off witchcrafts out of thy hand; and thou
¹³ shalt have no more observers of clouds. Thy graven images
also will I cut off, and thy standing images out of the midst
of thee; and thou shalt no more bow down to the work
¹⁴ of thine own hands. And I will pluck up thy groves of
Ashera out of the midst of thee. And I will destroy thy
¹⁵ cities; and I will execute vengeance in anger and wrath
—upon the Nations, such as they have not heard.)

¹ HEAR YE NOW what Jehovah saith. Arise, contend
thou before the mountains, and let the hills hear thy
² voice. Hear, O ye mountains, Jehovah's controversy,
and ye unfailing foundations of the earth. For Jehovah
hath a controversy against his people, and he will contend with Israel.
³ O my people, what have I done to thee? and wherein
⁴ have I wearied thee? Answer me. For I brought thee
up out of the land of Egypt, and redeemed thee out of the
house of bondage; and I sent before thee Moses, Aaron,
⁵ and Miriam. O my people, remember now what Balak
king of Moab consulted, and what Balaam the son of Beor
answered him, from Shittim to Gilgal, so that the righteousness of Jehovah may be known.
⁶ 'Wherewith shall I come before Jehovah, and bow myself before the high God? Shall I come before him
⁷ 'with burnt offerings, with calves of the first year? Will
'Jehovah be pleased with thousands of rams, or with ten
'thousands of rivers of oil? Shall I give my firstborn for
'my transgression, the fruit of my body for the sin of my
'soul?'
⁸ He hath shewed thee, O man, what is good; and what
doth Jehovah require of thee, but to do justly, and to love
kindness, and to walk humbly with thy God?
⁹ The voice of Jehovah crieth unto the city, and the man
of prudence shall fear thy name. Hear ye the rod, and

Him who hath appointed it. Are there yet treasures of ¹⁰ wickedness in the house of the wicked, and the scanty Ephah [or measure] that is abominable? Shall I count ¹¹ them pure with the wicked balances, and with the bag of deceitful weights? For her rich men are full of violence, ¹² and her inhabitants have spoken lies, and their tongue is deceitful in their mouth. Therefore also will I make thee ¹³ sick in smiting thee, in making thee desolate because of thy sins. Thou shalt eat, but not be satisfied; and thine ¹⁴ emptiness shall be in the midst of thee; and thou shalt carry off, but shalt not save; and that which thou savest will I give up to the sword. Thou shalt sow, but thou shalt ¹⁵ not reap. Thou shalt tread the olives, but thou shalt not anoint thee with oil; and grape juice, but shalt not drink the wine. For the decrees of Omri are kept, and all the ¹⁶ works of the house of Ahab, and ye walk in their counsels; so that I should make thee a desolation, and the inhabitants thereof a hissing. Therefore ye shall bear the reproach of my people. —

'Woe is me! for I am as the after gatherings of the ¹ 'summer fruits, as the grape-gleanings of the vintage. 'There is no cluster to eat; my soul desired the first-ripe 'fruit. The good man is perished out of the land; and ² 'there is none upright among men. They all lie in wait 'for bloodshed; they hunt every man his brother with a 'net. Their hands are towards wickedness to make it ³ 'good. The prince asketh, and the judge, for a reward; 'and the great man, he uttereth his soul's mischief; so they 'entangle matters. The best of them is as a brier, more ⁴ 'pointed than a thorn hedge. The day of thy watchmen and 'thy visitation cometh; now shall be their perplexity.

'Trust ye not in a friend, put ye not confidence in a ⁵ 'guide; keep the doors of thy mouth from her that lieth 'in thy bosom. For son dishonoureth father, daughter ⁶ 'riseth up against her mother, daughter-in-law against her 'mother-in-law; a man's enemies are the men of his own 'house. But as for me I will look to Jehovah; I will ⁷ 'wait for the God of my salvation; my God will hear me.

'Rejoice not against me, O mine enemy. When I fall, ⁸ 'I shall arise; when I sit in darkness, Jehovah will be a 'light to me. I will bear the indignation of Jehovah, be- ⁹ 'cause I have sinned against him, until he plead my cause,

'and execute judgment for me. He will bring me forth
¹⁰ 'to the light, I shall behold his righteousness. Then mine
'enemy shall see it, and shame shall cover her. She said
'to me, Where is Jehovah thy God? Mine eyes shall
'look upon her; now shall she be trodden down as the
'mire of the streets.'
¹¹ (In the day that THY WALLS ARE TO BE BUILT UP [O
Jerusalem], in that day shall the decree [of Omri] be far
¹² removed. In that day also man shall come even to thee
from Assyria, and from the cities of Egypt; even from
Egypt to the River [Euphrates], and from sea to sea, and
¹³ from mountain to mountain; when the land hath been
desolate because of them that dwell therein, for the fruit
of their doings.)
¹⁴ 'Feed thy people with thy rod, the flock of thy heritage,
'who dwell solitarily in the forest. In the midst of Carmel
'let them feed, in Bashan and Gilead, as in the days of old.'
¹⁵ As in the days of thy coming out of the land of Egypt
¹⁶ will I shew to him marvellous things. The Nations shall
see and be confounded at all their might; they shall lay
their hand upon their mouth, their ears shall be deaf.
¹⁷ They shall lick the dust like a serpent, they shall move
out of their holes like creeping things of the earth.

'They will be afraid of Jehovah our God, and will fear,
¹⁸ 'because of thee. Who is a God like thee, that pardoneth
'iniquity, and passeth by the transgression of the rem-
'nant of his heritage? He retaineth not his anger for
¹⁹ 'ever, because he delighteth in kindness. He will turn
'again, he will have compassion on us; he will subdue
'our iniquities; and thou wilt cast all their sins into the
²⁰ 'depths of the sea. Thou wilt perform the truth to Jacob,
'and the kindness to Abraham, which thou hast sworn
'unto our fathers from the days of old.'

NAHUM.

¹ THE BURDEN OF NINEVEH. The book of the vision of Nahum the Elkoshite.
² Jehovah is a God jealous and vengeful; Jehovah is vengeful and full of wrath; Jehovah will take vengeance on his
³ adversaries, and he reserveth wrath for his enemies. Jeho-

vah is slow to anger, and great in power, and he will not wholly acquit. Jehovah hath his way in the whirlwind and in the storm, and the clouds are the dust of his feet. He rebuketh the sea, and maketh it dry, and he drieth up 4 all the rivers. Bashan languisheth, and Carmel, and the flower of Lebanon languisheth. The mountains quake at 5 him, and the hills melt, and the earth is lifted up at his presence, yea, the world, and all that dwell therein. Who 6 can abide before his indignation? and who can stand up in the fierceness of his anger? His wrath is poured out like fire, and the rocks are thrown down by him.

Jehovah is good, a stronghold in the day of trouble; and 7 he knoweth them that trust in him. But with an over- 8 flowing torrent he will make an utter end of the place thereof, and darkness shall pursue his enemies. What do 9 ye devise against Jehovah? He will make an utter end; affliction will not rise up a second time. For while they 10 are entangled as thorns, and while they are drunken as drunkards, they shall be devoured as stubble fully dry. There went forth out of thee [O Nineveh], one that de- 11 vised evil against Jehovah; a counsellor of wickedness.

Thus saith Jehovah; 'Though they be prosperous, and 12 'likewise many, yet thus shall they be carried off and pass 'away. Though I have afflicted thee [O Judah], I will 'afflict thee no more. For now will I break his yoke 13 'from off thee, and will burst thy bonds asunder.'

And Jehovah hath given a commandment concerning 14 thee [O Nineveh], that no more of thy name be sown. Out of the house of thy gods will I cut off the graven image and the molten image; I will make thy grave; for thou art vile.

Behold upon the mountains the feet of him that bringeth 15 good tidings, that publisheth peace! O Judah, keep thy solemn feasts, perform thy vows; for the wicked one shall no more pass through thee; he is utterly cut off.

The destroyer [the Babylonian] is come up against thee, 1 [O Nineveh]. Guard the fortress, watch the road, make thy loins strong, fortify thy power mightily. For Jehovah 2 hath restored the excellence of Jacob, as the excellence of Israel. For the wasters have wasted themselves, and destroyed their own vine branches. The shield of his 3 warriors is made red, the valiant men are dyed in scarlet;

the steel of the chariots shineth with fire in the day of his making ready, and the spear-shafts are terribly shaken.
4 The chariots rage in the streets, they run to and fro in the broad ways; they seem like torches, they run like the
5 lightnings. He recounteth his mighty men; they stumble in their march; they make haste to the wall thereof, and
6 the covering is prepared. The gates of the rivers are opened, and the palace melts in fear.
7 And [Queen] Huzzab shall be taken captive, she shall be led away, and her maids shall sigh as with the voice of
8 doves, beating upon their breasts. Though Nineveh hath been all its days like a pool of water, yet they shall flee away. 'Stand, stand,' [they cry]; but none looketh back.
9 Take ye the spoil of silver, take the spoil of gold; for there is no end of the store of glory out of all the desirable jewels.
10 She is empty, and emptiness, and a waste; and the heart melteth, and the knees smite together, and much pain is in all loins, and the faces of them all lose their colour.
11 Where is the dwelling of the Lions, and that feeding-place of the young Lions, where the Lion and the Lioness walked,
12 and the Lion's whelp, and none made them afraid? The Lion did tear in pieces enough for his whelps, and strangled for his Lionesses, and filled his holes with prey, and his
13 dens with what he had torn. Behold, I am against thee, Jehovah of hosts hath said it, and I will burn her chariots in the smoke, and the sword shall devour thy young Lions; and I will cut off thy prey from the earth, and the voice —of thy messengers shall no more be heard.
1 WOE TO THE CITY of bloodshed! it is wholly false and
2 full of robbery; it letteth not the prey escape. There is the noise of a whip, and the noise of the rattling of wheels,
3 and of prancing horses, and of jolting chariots. The horseman lifteth up both the bright sword and the glittering spear; and there is a multitude of slain, and a great number of carcases, and no end of corpses; they stumble over their corpses.
4 Because of the multitude of the fornications of the well-favoured harlot, the mistress of witchcrafts, that selleth nations by her fornications, and families by her witch-
5 crafts; behold, I am against thee, Jehovah of hosts hath said it; and I will uncover thy skirts over thy face, and I

will shew nations thy nakedness, and kingdoms thy shame. And I will cast abominable filth upon thee, and I will make thee vile, and will set thee up as a gazingstock. And it shall come to pass, that all that look upon thee shall flee from thee, and shall say, 'Nineveh is laid waste; who will 'bemoan her?'

Whence shall I seek comforters for thee? Art thou better than No-Amun [or Thebes], that was situate on the river [Nile], with the waters round about her, whose rampart was a sea, and the waters her wall? Ethiopia and Lower Egypt were her strength, and it was boundless; Phut [or Africa] and the Lubites [or Libyans] were thy helpers. Yet was she carried away, she went into captivity; her babes were also dashed in pieces at the top of all the streets; and they cast lots for her honourable men, and all her great men were bound in chains. Thou also shalt be made drunk; thou shalt be hidden; thou also shalt seek help against the enemy. All thy strongholds shall be like fig-trees with the first-ripe figs; if they be shaken, they shall even fall into the mouth of the eater. Behold, thy people in the midst of thee are as women; the gates of thy land shall be set wide open unto thine enemies; the fire shall devour thy cross-bars. Draw for thee water for the siege, fortify thy strongholds. Go to the clay, and tread mortar, make strong the brickwork. There shall the fire devour thee; the sword shall cut thee off, it shall eat thee up like the locust. Make thyself many as the locust, make thyself many as the grasshoppers. Thou hast multiplied thy merchants above the stars of the heavens; the locust spreadeth itself, and then fleeth away.

Thy crowned ones are as the grasshoppers, and thy captains as swarms of locusts, which encamp in the hedges in the cool of the day, but when the sun ariseth they flee away, and their place is not known where they are. Thy shepherds slumber, O king of Assyria; thy nobles take their rest; thy people is scattered upon the mountains, and no man gathereth them together. There is no ease for thy bruise; thy wound is grievous. All that hear the report of thee will clap hands over thee; for upon whom hath not thy wickedness passed continually?

HABAKKUK.

¹ THE BURDEN WHICH HABAKKUK the prophet did see.
² ' O Jehovah, how long shall I cry for help, and thou wilt
'not hear? I cry out to thee of violence, and thou dost
³ 'not save! Why dost thou shew me iniquity, and cause
'me to behold trouble? For spoiling and violence are
'before me; and there are some that raise up strife and
⁴ 'contention; therefore the law is slack, and judgment doth
'not go forth in truth. For the wicked man doth compass
'the righteous; therefore wrong judgment goeth forth.'
⁵ Look ye among the Nations, and regard, and wonder
greatly; for I will work a work in your days, which ye
⁶ will not believe, though it be recounted to you. For, lo, I
will raise up the Chaldeans, that bitter and hasty nation,
who shall march through the breadth of the land, to possess
⁷ dwelling-places that are not their own. They are terrible
and dreadful; their judgment and their might proceed from
⁸ themselves. Their horses also are swifter than leopards,
and are more fierce than evening wolves; and their horsemen shall spread themselves. And their horsemen shall
come from afar; they shall fly as the eagle that hasteneth
⁹ to eat. They shall come all for violence. The crowd of
their faces is forward, and they shall gather up captives as
¹⁰ the sand. And they shall scoff at kings, and princes shall
be a derision unto them. They shall deride every strong-
¹¹ hold; for they shall heap up earth, and take it. Then
shall their spirit be changed, and they shall transgress;
and this is their guilt, that their own strength is their god.
¹² ' Art thou not from everlasting, O Jehovah my God? My
'Holy One, let us not die. O Jehovah, thou hast ordained
'them for judgment; and, O my Rock, thou hast estab-
¹³ 'lished them for correction. Thou art of purer eyes than
'to behold evil, and thou canst not look upon iniquity.
'Wherefore lookest thou upon them that deal treacher-
'ously, and art silent when the wicked man devoureth one
¹⁴ 'more righteous than himself; and makest thou men as
'the fishes of the sea, as the creeping things, that have no
¹⁵ 'ruler over them? They take up all of them with a hook,
'they draw them out with their net, and gather them in
¹⁶ 'their drag-net. Therefore they rejoice and are glad.

'Therefore they sacrifice to their net, and burn incense unto their drag-net; because by them their portion is fat, and their food plenteous. Shall they therefore empty their net 17 and shall they not spare to slay the Nations continually?'—

I will stand upon my watch tower, and set me upon the 1 stronghold, and will look out to see what he will say to me, and what I shall answer when I am reproved. And 2 Jehovah answered me, and said, Write the vision, and make it plain upon the tablets, so that he may run that readeth it. For the vision is yet for an appointed time, 3 but it hasteneth to the end, and will not deceive. Though it tarry, wait for it; for it will surely come, it will not be behind. Behold, his soul which is puffed up is not upright 4 in him; but he that is righteous, in his faithfulness shall he live.

Yea also, because wine deceiveth the proud man, neither 5 is he quiet, who enlargeth his desire like Hell, and is like Death, and cannot be satisfied; but he gathereth unto himself all nations, and heapeth unto himself all the peoples. Shall not all these take up a parable against him, and a taunt- 6 ing proverb against him, and say, 'Woe to him that increaseth what is not his!' How long shall he lade himself with debts? Shall not thy usurers rise up suddenly, and 7 they awake that shall vex thee, and thou be for booty unto them? Because thou hast plundered many nations, all the 8 remnant of the peoples shall plunder thee; because of men's blood, and for the violence against the land, against the city, and against all that dwell therein.

Woe to him that gaineth a gain that is evil to his own 9 house, that he may set his nest on high, that he may be delivered from the grasp of adversity! Thou hast coun- 10 selled shame to thy house by cutting off many peoples, and hast sinned against thine own soul. For the stone crieth 11 out of the wall, and the beam out of the timbers answereth it.

Woe to him that buildeth a town with bloodshed, and 12 establisheth a city by iniquity! Behold, is it not of Jeho- 13 vah of hosts that the peoples shall labour for the sake of the fire, and nations shall weary themselves for nought? For the earth shall be filled with the knowledge of the 14 glory of Jehovah, as the waters cover the sea.

Woe to him that giveth his neighbour drink, pouring 15

out thy poison and drunkenness also, so that thou mayest
16 look on their nakedness! Thou art filled with shame rather than glory. Drink thou also, and thou shalt be unclean; the cup of Jehovah's right hand shall be turned unto thee,
17 and shameful vomiting shall be on thy glory. For the violence against Lebanon shall cover thee, and the plunder of the cattle shall terrify; because of men's blood, and for the violence against the land, against the city, and against all that dwell therein.
18 What profiteth the graven image that its maker hath graven it; the molten image, and the teacher of lies, that the maker of his work trusteth therein, so as to make dumb
19 idols? Woe to him that saith to the wood, 'Awake;' to the dumb stone, 'Arise'! Can it teach? Behold, it is laid over with gold and silver, and there is no breath at
20 all within it. But Jehovah is in his holy temple; let all —the earth keep silence before him.

1 A PRAYER OF HABAKKUK the prophet, for a hymn.
2 O Jehovah, I heard a report of thee, and was afraid;
O Jehovah, revive thy work within these years,
Within these years make it known;
In thy wrath remember mercy.
3 God came from Teman [or the south],
And the Holy One from the mountain of Paran.
(A pause.) His glory covered the heavens,
And the earth was full of his praise;
4 And his brightness was as the sun-light;
He had horns [or rays] coming out of his hand;
And the veil over his power was there.
5 Before him went pestilence,
And burning fevers followed in his footsteps.
6 He stood, and measured the earth;
He beheld, and made the Nations to tremble;
And the ancient mountains were scattered,
The everlasting hills did bow; His ways are everlasting.
7 I saw the tents of Cushan under affliction;
The tent-curtains of the land of Midian did tremble.
8 Was Jehovah displeased against the rivers?
Was thine anger against the rivers?
Was thy wrath against the sea,
That thou didst ride upon thy horses,
And thy chariots of victory?

Thy bow was made quite naked,   9
As sworn unto the tribes by thy word. (A pause.)
    Thou didst cleave the earth with the rivers.
The mountains saw thee, and they trembled;   10
The overflowing of the water passed by;
The deep uttered his voice, lifting up his hands on high.
The sun and moon stood still in their dwelling;   11
By the light of thine arrows they moved on,
By the shining of thy glittering spear.
Thou didst march through the land in indignation,   12
Thou didst trample on the Nations [of Assyria] in anger.
Thou wentest forth for the salvation of thy people,   13
For the salvation of thine anointed one;
Thou didst wound the head of the house of the wicked,
Laying bare the foundation to the neck. (A pause.)
    Thou didst pierce his head with his own arrows;   14
His village-rulers rushed out to scatter me;
They rejoiced as if to devour the poor in secret.
Thou didst walk through the sea with thy horses,   15
Through the heap of great waters.
    I have heard; my bowels tremble,   16
My lips quiver at the sound [of the Chaldeans];
Rottenness entereth my bones, and my knees tremble,
Whether I may have rest in the day of trouble,
At the coming up of the invader against the people.
    Although the fig tree shall not blossom,   17
Neither shall fruit be on the vines;
Though the labour of the olive tree shall fail,
And the fields shall yield no food;
Though the flock shall be cut off from the fold,
And there shall be no herd in the stalls;
Yet I will rejoice in Jehovah,   18
I will joy in the God of my salvation.
Jehovah my Lord is my strength,   19
And he will make my feet like hinds' feet,
And he will make me to walk upon my high places.
    For the chief Musician on the stringed instruments.

ZEPHANIAH.

¹ THE WORD OF JEHOVAH which came to Zephaniah the son of Cushi, the son of Gedaliah, the son of Amariah, the son of Hezekiah, in the days of Josiah the son of Amon, king of Judah.
² I will utterly take away all things from off the face of the
³ land; Jehovah hath said it. I will take away both man and beast; I will take away the fowls of the heavens, and the fishes of the sea, and the stumbling-blocks [or idols] together with the wicked; and I will cut off man from off
⁴ the face of the land; Jehovah hath said it. I will also stretch out my hand upon Judah, and upon all the inhabitants of Jerusalem; and I will cut off the remnant of Baal from this place, and the name of the idolaters with the
⁵ priests; and them that worship the host of the heavens upon the housetops; and them that worship and that swear
⁶ by Jehovah, and them that swear by their Molech; and them that are turned back from following Jehovah; and them that have not sought Jehovah, nor inquired of him.
⁷ Hold thy peace at the presence of the Lord Jehovah; for the day of Jehovah is at hand; for Jehovah hath pre-
⁸ pared a sacrifice, he hath sanctified his guests. And it shall come to pass on the day of Jehovah's sacrifice that I will punish the princes, and the king's children, and all
⁹ such as are clothed with apparel of foreigners. And on that day will I punish all those that leap over the threshold,
¹⁰ who fill their masters' houses with violence and deceit. And it shall come to pass on that day, Jehovah hath said it, that there shall be the noise of a cry from the Fish Gate and a howling from the Second [or lower city], and a great crashing from the hills.
¹¹ Howl, ye inhabitants of Maktesh, for all the merchant people are cut down; all they that are laden with silver are cut off.
¹² And it shall come to pass at that time that I will search Jerusalem with lamps, and I will punish the men that are settled on their lees; that say in their heart, 'Jehovah will
¹³ 'not do good, neither will he do evil.' Therefore their goods shall become a booty, and their houses a desolation;

they shall also build houses, but not inhabit them; and they shall plant vineyards, but not drink the wine thereof.

14 The great day of Jehovah is near, it is near, and hasteneth greatly, even the voice of the day of Jehovah; the warrior shall raise therein a bitter cry. 15 That day is a day of wrath, a day of trouble and distress, a day of wasteness and desolation, a day of darkness and gloominess, a day of clouds and thick darkness, 16 a day of the trumpet and of shouting against the fenced cities, and against the high corner-towers. 17 And I will bring distress upon men, and they shall walk like blind men, because they have sinned against Jehovah. And their blood shall be poured out as dust, and their flesh as dung. 18 Neither their silver nor their gold shall be able to deliver them in the day of Jehovah's wrath; but the whole land shall be devoured by the fire of his jealousy; for he shall make even a terrible riddance of all them that dwell in the land.

1 Gather yourselves together, yea, gather together, O nation without shame; 2 before the decree give birth, and the day pass away as chaff; before the fierce anger of Jehovah come upon you, before the day of Jehovah's anger come upon you. 3 Seek ye Jehovah, all ye meek of the earth, ye who have executed his judgments; seek righteousness, seek meekness; it may be ye shall be hidden in the day of Jehovah's anger.

4 For Gaza shall be forsaken, and Askalon a desolation. They shall drive out Ashdod at the noon day, and Ekron shall be rooted up. 5 Woe to the inhabitants of the sea coasts, the nation of the Cherethites [or Philistines]! The word of Jehovah is against you; O Canaan, land of the Philistines, I will even destroy thee, so that there shall be no inhabitant. 6 And the sea coast shall be pastures, with tanks for shepherds, and folds for flocks. 7 And the coast shall be for the remnant of the house of Judah; they shall feed thereupon. In the houses of Askalon shall they lie down in the evening; for Jehovah their God will visit them, and bring home their captivity.

8 I have heard the reproach of Moab, and the revilings of the Children of Ammon, whereby they have reproached my people, and have magnified themselves against their boundary. 9 Therefore as I live, Jehovah of hosts, the God of Israel, hath said it, surely Moab shall be as Sodom, and

the Children of Ammon as Gomorrah, a possession for nettles, and saltpits, and a perpetual desolation. The residue of my people shall plunder them, and the remnant of
10 my nation shall inherit them. This shall they have for their pride, because they have reproached and magnified
11 themselves against the people of Jehovah of hosts. Jehovah will be terrible unto them ; for he will famish all the gods of the earth ; and men shall worship him, every one from his place, even all the isles of the Nations.
12 Ye Ethiopians also, ye shall be slain by my sword.
13 And he will stretch out his hand against the North, and destroy Assyria ; and will make Nineveh a desolation, and
14 dry like the desert. And flocks shall lie down in the midst of her, all the wild beasts of the nations. Both the pelican and the hedgehog shall lodge in the capitals of its columns; their voice shall sing in the windows ; desolation shall be within the thresholds ; for he will lay bare the
15 cedar work. This is the rejoicing city that dwelt without care, that said in her heart, ' I am she, and there is none ' beside me.' How is she become a desolation, a place for wild beasts to lie down in ! every one that passeth by her —shall hiss, and shake his hand.

1 WOE TO HER THAT IS REBELLIOUS and polluted, to the
2 oppressing city [Jerusalem] ! She obeyed not the voice ; she received not instruction ; she trusted not in Jehovah ;
3 she drew not near to her God. Her princes within her are roaring lions ; her judges are evening wolves ; they leave
4 not the bones to gnaw in the morning. Her prophets are boasters and treacherous men ; her priests have polluted
5 the Holy Place, they have done violence to the Law. The righteous Jehovah is in the midst thereof ; he will not do iniquity. Every morning doth he bring his judgment to
6 light, he faileth not ; but the unjust knoweth no shame. I cut off the nations ; their corner-towers were made desolate ; I made their streets waste, so that none passed by. Their cities were taken by snares, so that there was
7 no man, there was no inhabitant. I said, 'Surely thou ' wilt fear me, thou wilt receive instruction;' so that her dwelling should not be cut off, howsoever I punished her. Nevertheless they rose up early, and corrupted all their doings.

8 Therefore wait ye upon me, Jehovah hath said it, until the day that I rise up to the prey. For my determination is to gather nations, that I may assemble kingdoms, to pour upon them mine indignation, even all my fierce anger; for all the land shall be devoured with the fire of my jealousy. 9 For then will I again give to the peoples a pure lip, that they may all call upon the name of Jehovah, to serve him with one consent. 10 From beyond the rivers of Ethiopia my suppliants, even the daughter of my dispersed ones, shall bring mine offering. 11 In that day shalt thou not be ashamed for all thy doings, wherein thou hast transgressed against me. For then I will take away out of the midst of thee them that rejoice in thy pride, and thou shalt no more be haughty upon my holy mountain. 12 And I will leave in the midst of thee an afflicted and poor people, and they shall put their trust in the name of Jehovah. 13 The remnant of Israel shall not do iniquity, nor speak lies; neither shall a deceitful tongue be found in their mouth; for they shall feed and lie down, and none shall make them afraid.

14 Sing, O daughter of Zion; shout, O Israel; be glad and rejoice with all thy heart, O daughter of Jerusalem. 15 Jehovah hath taken away the judgments against thee, he hath turned aside thine enemy. The King of Israel, even Jehovah, is in the midst of thee; thou shalt not see evil any more. 16 In that day it shall be said to Jerusalem, 'Fear 'thou not, O Zion; let not thy hands be feeble. 17 Jehovah 'thy God in the midst of thee is mighty. He will save, he 'will rejoice over thee with joy; he will pardon in his 'love, he will joy over thee with singing.' 18 Those that are grieving far from the place of meeting [or Temple] I will gather together. They are far from thee; the reproach was a burden to her. 19 Behold, at that time I will deal with all that afflict thee; and I will save her that halteth, and gather in her that was driven out; and I will make them to be a praise and a name in every land of their shame. 20 At that time will I bring you back, even at the time that I gather you up. For I will make you to be a name and a praise among all the peoples of the earth, when I bring home your captivity before your eyes, saith Jehovah.

HAGGAI.

¹ IN THE SECOND YEAR of Darius the king [B.C. 520], in the sixth month, on the first day of the month, came the word of Jehovah by the hand of Haggai the prophet to Zerubbabel the son of Shealtiel, the Pasha [or governor] of Judah, and to Joshua the son of Josedech, the high ² priest, saying, Thus speaketh Jehovah of hosts, saying, This people say, ' The time is not come, the time that the House ³ ' of Jehovah should be built.' Then came the word of ⁴ Jehovah by the hand of Haggai the prophet, saying, Is it a time for you, O ye, to dwell in your panelled houses, ⁵ and this House lieth waste? Now therefore, thus saith ⁶ Jehovah of hosts; Consider your ways. Ye have sown much, but have brought in little; ye eat, but ye are not satisfied; ye drink, but ye are not filled with drink; ye clothe yourselves, but not unto warmth; and he that earneth wages earneth for a purse with holes.

⁷ Thus saith Jehovah of hosts; Consider your ways. Go ⁸ up to the hill country, and bring wood, and build the House; and I will take pleasure in it, and I will be glorified, saith ⁹ Jehovah. Ye looked for much, and, lo, it came to little; and when ye brought it home, I did blow upon it. Why? Jehovah of hosts hath said it; because of my House that ¹⁰ is waste, and ye run every man to his own house. Therefore the heavens over you are stayed from dew, and the ¹¹ earth is stayed from its increase. And I called for a drought upon the land, and upon the mountains, and upon the corn, and upon the grape juice, and upon the oil, and upon that which the ground bringeth forth, and upon men, and upon cattle, and upon all the labours of the hands.

¹² Then Zerubbabel the son of Shealtiel, and Joshua the son of Josedech, the high priest, with all the remnant of the people, obeyed the voice of Jehovah their God, and the words of Haggai the prophet, because Jehovah their God had sent him, and the people did fear before Jeho- ¹³ vah. Then spake Haggai Jehovah's messenger in Jehovah's message to the people, saying, ' I am with you, Je- ' hovah hath said it.'

¹⁴ And Jehovah stirred up the spirit of Zerubbabel the son of Shealtiel, the Pasha of Judah, and the spirit of Joshua

the son of Josedech, the high priest, and the spirit of all the remnant of the people; and they came and did the work in the House of Jehovah of hosts, their God, on the four and twentieth day of the sixth month, in the second year of Darius the king.

IN THE SEVENTH MONTH, on the one and twentieth day of the month, came the word of Jehovah by the hand of the prophet Haggai, saying, Speak now to Zerubbabel the son of Shealtiel, the Pasha of Judah, and to Joshua the son of Josedech, the high priest, and to the remnant of the people, saying, Who is left among you that saw this House in its first glory? And how do ye see it now? Is it not in your eyes in comparison of it as nothing? Yet now be strong, O Zerubbabel, Jehovah hath said it; and be strong, O Joshua, son of Josedech, the high priest; and be strong, all ye people of the land, Jehovah hath said it, and work; for I am with you, Jehovah of hosts hath said it. According to the word that I covenanted with you when ye came out of Lower Egypt, so my spirit shall remain among you. Fear ye not.

For thus saith Jehovah of hosts; Yet once, it is a little while, and I will shake the heavens, and the earth, and the sea, and the dry land; and I will shake all the nations; and the treasures of all the nations shall come; and I will fill this House with glory, saith Jehovah of hosts. The silver is mine, and the gold is mine, Jehovah of hosts hath said it. The glory of this latter House shall be greater than of the former, saith Jehovah of hosts; and in this place will I give peace, Jehovah of hosts hath said it.

ON THE FOUR AND TWENTIETH DAY of the ninth month, in the second year of Darius, came the word of Jehovah by the hand of Haggai the prophet, saying, Thus saith Jehovah of hosts; Ask now the priests concerning the Law, saying, 'If one carry holy flesh in the skirt of his garment, 'and with his skirt do touch bread, or pottage, or wine, 'or oil, or any food, shall it be holy?' And the priests answered and said, 'No.' Then said Haggai, 'If one that 'is unclean by a dead body touch any of these, shall it be 'unclean?' And the priests answered and said, 'It shall 'be unclean.' Then answered Haggai, and said, So is this people, and so is this nation before me, Jehovah hath said it. And so is every work of their hands; and what

¹⁵ they bring as a gift there is unclean. And now, I pray you, consider from this day and upward, from before a stone ¹⁶ was laid upon a stone in the Temple of Jehovah; since those days were, one came to a heap of corn of twenty sheaves, and there were but ten; one came to the wine-vat to draw out fifty measures out of the press, and there were ¹⁷ but twenty. I smote you with blasting and with mildew and with hail in all the labours of your hands; yet none of ¹⁸ you turned to me; Jehovah hath said it. Consider now from this day and upward, from the four and twentieth day of the ninth month, even from the day that the foundation of the Temple of Jehovah hath been laid, consider; ¹⁹ is the seed yet in the barn? Yea, as yet the vine, and the fig tree, and the pomegranate, and the olive tree, have not brought forth; but from this day will I bless you.

²⁰ AND AGAIN THE WORD of Jehovah came unto Haggai on ²¹ the four and twentieth day of the month, saying, Speak to Zerubbabel, the Pasha of Judah, saying, I will shake the ²² heavens and the earth; and I will overthrow the throne of the kingdoms, and I will destroy the strength of the kingdoms of the nations; and I will overthrow the chariots, and those that ride in them; and the horses and their riders shall come down, every one by the sword of his brother. ²³ In that day, Jehovah of hosts hath said it, I will take thee, O Zerubbabel, my servant, the son of Shealtiel, Jehovah hath said it, and will make thee as a signet ring; for I have chosen thee; Jehovah of hosts hath said it.

ZECHARIAH.

¹ IN THE EIGHTH MONTH, in the second year of Darius [B.C. 520], came the word of Jehovah unto Zechariah the son of ² Berechiah the son of Iddo, the prophet, saying, 'Jehovah ³ 'hath been sore displeased with your fathers. Therefore 'say thou to them, Thus saith Jehovah of hosts; Turn ye 'to me, Jehovah of hosts hath said it, and I will turn to ⁴ 'you, saith Jehovah of hosts. Be ye not as your fathers, 'to whom the former prophets did call, saying, Thus saith 'Jehovah of hosts; Turn ye now from your evil ways, and 'from your evil doings; but they did not hear, nor hearken ⁵ 'to me, Jehovah hath said it. Your fathers, where are

'they? and the prophets, do they live for ever? But my ⁶ 'words and my statutes, which I commanded my servants 'the prophets, did they not overtake your fathers?' And they returned and said, 'Like as Jehovah of hosts thought 'to do to us, according to our ways, and according to our 'doings, so hath he dealt with us.'

UPON THE FOUR AND TWENTIETH day of the eleventh ⁷ month, which is the month Sebat, in the second year of Darius, came the word of Jehovah to Zechariah the son of Berechiah the son of Iddo, the prophet, saying, 'I looked ⁸ 'by night, and behold a man riding upon a red horse, and 'he stood among the myrtle trees that were in the shady 'bottom; and behind him were horses, red, brown, and 'white.' Then said I, 'O my lord, what are these?' And ⁹ the angel that talked with me said to me, 'I will shew thee 'what these are.' And the man that stood among the ¹⁰ myrtle trees answered and said, 'These are they whom Je-'hovah hath sent to walk to and fro upon the earth.' And ¹¹ they answered the angel of Jehovah that stood among the myrtle trees, and said, 'We have walked to and fro upon 'the earth, and, behold, all the earth sitteth still, and is at 'rest.' Then the angel of Jehovah answered and said, 'O ¹² 'Jehovah of hosts, how long wilt thou not have mercy on 'Jerusalem and on the cities of Judah, against which thou 'hast had indignation these seventy years?' And Jeho- ¹³ vah answered the angel that talked with me with good words and comfortable words. So the angel that talked ¹⁴ with me said to me, 'Call thou, saying, Thus saith Jehovah 'of hosts; I am jealous for Jerusalem and for Zion with a 'great jealousy. And I am very sore displeased with the ¹⁵ 'Nations that are at ease. For when I was but a little dis-'pleased, then they helped forward the affliction. There- ¹⁶ 'fore thus saith Jehovah; I am returned to Jerusalem with 'mercies; my House shall be built in it, Jehovah of hosts 'hath said it, and a line shall be stretched forth upon 'Jerusalem. Call thou yet, saying, Thus saith Jehovah ¹⁷ 'of hosts; My cities shall yet overflow with prosperity; 'and Jehovah will yet comfort Zion, and will yet choose 'Jerusalem.'

Then I lifted up mine eyes, and looked, and behold, four ¹⁸ horns. And I said to the angel that talked with me, ¹⁹ 'What are these?' And he said to me, 'These are the

'horns which have scattered Judah, Israel, and Jerusalem.'
20 And Jehovah shewed me four instruments. Then said I,
21 'What come these to do?' And he spake, saying, 'Those
'were the horns which scattered Judah, so that no man
'lifted up his head; but these are come to frighten them,
'to cast out the horns of the Nations, who lifted up their
—'horn against the land of Judah to scatter it.'

1   I lifted up mine eyes again, and looked, and behold a
2 man with a measuring line in his hand. Then said I,
'Whither goest thou?' And he said to me, 'To measure
'Jerusalem, to see what is its breadth, and what is its
3 'length.' And, behold, the angel that talked with me went
4 forth, and another angel went forth to meet him, and said
to him, 'Run, speak to this young man, saying, Jerusalem
'shall be inhabited like the villages for the multitude of
5 'men and cattle therein; for I will be unto her, Jehovah
'hath said it, a wall of fire round about, and I will be the
'Glory in the midst of her.
6   'Ho, ho; yea, flee from the land of the north, Jehovah
'hath said it. For I have spread you abroad as the four
7 'winds of the heavens, Jehovah hath said it. Ho, Zion,
'deliver thyself, thou that dwellest with the daughter of
8 'Babylon. For thus saith Jehovah of hosts; After glory
'hath he sent me to the nations who spoiled you. For
9 'he that toucheth you toucheth the apple of his eye. For,
'behold, I will shake my fist at them, and they shall be a
'spoil to their servants; and ye shall know that Jehovah
'of hosts hath sent me.
10   'Sing, and rejoice, O daughter of Zion; for, lo, I come,
'and I will dwell in the midst of thee, Jehovah hath said
11 'it. And many nations shall be joined to Jehovah in that
'day, and shall be my people. And I will dwell in the
'midst of thee, and thou shalt know that Jehovah of
12 'hosts hath sent me to thee. And Jehovah will inherit
'Judah as his portion in the Holy Land, and will choose
13 'Jerusalem again. O be silent, all flesh, before Jehovah;
—'for he is risen up out of his holy habitation.'

1   And he shewed me Joshua the high priest standing before the angel of Jehovah, and Satan [or the Accuser] stand-
2 ing at his right hand to accuse him. And Jehovah said
to Satan, 'Jehovah rebuketh thee, O Satan; even Jehovah
'who hath chosen Jerusalem rebuketh thee. Is not this

'man a brand plucked out of the fire?' Now Joshua was ³ clothed with filthy garments, and stood before the angel. And he answered and spake to those that stood before him, ⁴ saying, 'Take away the filthy garments from him.' And to him he said, 'Behold, I have caused thine iniquity to 'pass from thee, and I will clothe thee with holiday rai-'ment.' And I said, 'Let them set a clean turban upon ⁵ 'his head.' So they set a clean turban upon his head, and clothed him with garments. And the angel of Jehovah stood by. And the angel of Jehovah protested unto Joshua, ⁶ saying, Thus saith Jehovah of hosts; 'If thou wilt walk ⁷ 'in my ways, and if thou wilt keep my charge, then thou 'shalt also judge my House, and shalt also keep my Courts, 'and I will give thee companions among these that stand 'by. Hear now, O Joshua, high priest, thou, and thy ⁸ 'fellows that sit before thee; for they are men to be 'wondered at; for, behold, I will bring forth my servant '[Zerubbabel] the Branch. For behold the stone that I ⁹ 'have laid before Joshua; upon one stone shall be seven 'eyes; behold, I will engrave the graving thereof, Jehovah 'of hosts hath said it; and I will remove the iniquity of 'that land in one day. In that day, Jehovah of hosts hath ¹⁰ 'said it; shall ye call every man to his neighbour under 'the vine and under the fig tree.' —

And the angel that talked with me came again, and ¹ waked me, as a man that is awakened out of his sleep, and ² said to me, 'What seest thou?' And I said, 'I have looked, 'and behold a lamp-stand of solid gold, with a bowl upon 'the top of it, and its seven lamps thereon, and seven pipes 'to the seven lamps which are upon the top thereof; and ³ 'two olive trees by it, one upon the right side of the bowl, 'and the other upon its left side.' And I answered and ⁴ spake to the angel that talked with me, saying, 'What are 'these, my lord?' Then the angel that talked with me, an- ⁵ swered and said to me, 'Knowest thou not what these 'are?' And I said, 'No, my lord.' Then he answered and ⁶ spake to me, saying, 'This is the word of Jehovah unto 'Zerubbabel, saying, Not by might, nor by power [shall it 'be], but by my spirit, saith Jehovah of hosts. Who art ⁷ 'thou, O great mountain? Before Zerubbabel thou shalt 'become a table-land. And he shall bring forth the head-'stone with the shouts of, Mercy, mercy on it.'

⁸ MOREOVER THE WORD of Jehovah came to me, saying,
⁹ 'The hands of Zerubbabel have laid the foundation of this
'House; his hands shall also finish it; and thou shalt know
¹⁰ 'that Jehovah of hosts hath sent me to you. For who
'hath despised the day of small things? They shall even
'rejoice, and shall see the plummet in the hand of Zerub-
'babel. These seven are the eyes of Jehovah, which
¹¹ 'run to and fro upon the whole earth.' Then answered I,
and said to him, 'What are these two olive trees upon the
¹² 'right side of the lamp-stand and upon its left side?' And
I answered again, and said to him, 'What are these two
'olive branches which through the two golden pipes empty
¹³ 'the golden [oil] out of themselves?' And he spake to me,
saying, 'Knowest thou not what these are?' And I said,
¹⁴ 'No, my lord.' Then said he, 'These are the two anointed
'ones [Zerubbabel and Joshua], that stand by the Lord
—'of the whole earth.'

¹ Then I turned, and lifted up my eyes, and looked, and
² behold a book-roll flying. And he said to me, 'What seest
'thou?' And I said, 'I see a book-roll flying; its length
³ 'is twenty cubits, and its breadth ten cubits.' Then said
he to me, 'This is the curse that goeth forth over the face
'of the whole earth. For every one that stealeth, from
'this and in this wise must clear himself; and every one
'that sweareth, from this and in this wise must clear him-
⁴ 'self. I will bring it forth, Jehovah of hosts hath said it;
'and it shall enter into the house of the thief, and into
'the house of him that sweareth falsely by my name;
'and it shall remain in the midst of his house, and shall
'consume it with its timber and its stones.'

⁵ Then the angel that talked with me went forth, and said
to me, 'Lift up now thine eyes, and see what is this that
⁶ 'goeth forth.' And I said, 'What is it?' And he said,
'This is an Ephah [or Bushel measure] that goeth forth.'
He said moreover, 'This is their resemblance upon all the
⁷ 'earth.' And, behold, there was lifted up a Kikar [or
Hundred-weight] of lead, and this woman was sitting in the
⁸ midst of the Ephah. And he said, 'This is wickedness.'
And he cast her into the midst of the Ephah; and he cast
⁹ the weight of lead upon its mouth. Then I lifted up mine
eyes, and looked, and behold, there came forth two women,
and the wind was in their wings; for they had wings like

the wings of a stork; and they lifted up the Ephah between the earth and the heavens. Then said I to the angel that ¹⁰ talked with me, 'Whither do these bear the Ephah?' And ¹¹ he said to me, 'To build for it a house in the land of 'Shinar [or Babylonia]; and it shall be established, and 'set there upon its own base.'

And I turned, and lifted up mine eyes, and looked, and ¹ behold, there came four chariots out from between two mountains; and the mountains were mountains of copper. In the first chariot were red horses; and in the second ² chariot black horses; and in the third chariot white horses; ³ and in the fourth chariot strong spotted horses. Then I ⁴ answered and said to the angel that talked with me, 'What 'are these, my lord?' And the angel answered and said to ⁵ me, 'These are the four spirits of the heavens, which go 'forth from standing before the Lord of all the earth. The ⁶ 'black horses which are in the one go forth into the north 'country; and the white go forth after them; and the 'spotted go forth toward the south country.' And the ⁷ strong ones went forth, and sought to go that they might go and walk to and fro upon the earth. And he said, 'Get you hence, walk to and fro upon the earth.' So they walked to and fro upon the earth. Then cried he ⁸ upon me, and spake to me, saying, 'Behold, these that go 'toward the north country have quieted my spirit in the 'north country.'

AND THE WORD of Jehovah came to me, saying, Take ⁹ some of them of the captivity, even Heldai, Tobijah, and ¹⁰ Jedaiah, and come thou the same day, and go into the house of Josiah the son of Zephaniah. These are come from Babylon. And take silver and gold, and make ¹¹ crowns, and set one upon the head of Joshua the son of Josedech, the high priest; and speak to him, saying, Thus ¹² saith Jehovah of hosts, saying, 'Behold, there is a man '[Zerubbabel] whose name is The Branch; and he shall 'branch forth from his place, and shall build the temple of 'Jehovah.' Even this one shall build the temple of Jeho- ¹³ vah; and that one [Joshua] shall raise up the Glory, and shall sit and rule upon his throne, and shall be a priest upon his throne. And the counsel of peace shall be between the two. And the other crowns shall be for Helem, ¹⁴ and for Tobijah, and for Jedaiah, and for Hen [or Kind-

ness] the son of Zephaniah, for a memorial in the temple
15 of Jehovah. And they that are far off shall come and build in the temple of Jehovah, and ye shall know that Jehovah of hosts hath sent me unto you. And this shall come to pass, if ye will diligently obey the voice of Jeho-
—vah your God.

1 AND IT CAME TO PASS in the fourth year of king Darius [B.C. 518], that the word of Jehovah came to Zechariah on the fourth day of the ninth month, even in the month
2 Chisleu; when he had sent to the house of God Sherezer and Regem-melech, and their men, to entreat the presence
3 of Jehovah, and to speak to the priests that were in the House of Jehovah of hosts, and to the prophets, saying, 'Should I weep in the fifth month, separating myself [as 'a Nazarite], as I have done these so many years?'
4 Then came the word of Jehovah of hosts to me, saying,
5 Speak to all the people of the land, and to the priests, saying, 'When ye fasted and mourned in the fifth and in 'the seventh month, even those seventy years, did ye when
6 'fasting fast unto me, even to me? And when ye did eat, ' and when ye did drink, did not ye eat for yourselves, and
7 'drink for yourselves? Should ye not hear the words 'which Jehovah hath cried by the hand of the former 'prophets, when Jerusalem was inhabited and in pros-'perity, and men inhabited her cities round about her, 'and the South country and the Low country?'
8 AND THE WORD OF JEHOVAH came to Zechariah, saying,
9 Thus speaketh Jehovah of hosts, saying, 'Execute true 'judgment, and shew kindness and compassion every man
10 ' to his brother; and oppress not the widow, nor the father-'less, the stranger, nor the poor; and let none of you devise
11 'evil against his brother in your heart.' But they refused to hearken, and turned a stubborn shoulder, and made
12 their ears dull, that they should not hear. Yea, they made their hearts as an adamant stone, lest they should hear the Law, and the words which Jehovah of hosts hath sent by his spirit by the hands of the former prophets.
13 Therefore came a great wrath from Jehovah of hosts; and it came to pass, that as He cried, and they would not hear; 'so they will cry, and I will not hear,' said Jehovah of
14 hosts; 'but I will scatter them with a whirlwind among 'all the nations whom they know not.' Thus the land

was made desolate after them, that no man passed through nor returned. For they made the Pleasant Land [or Judea] a desolation.

¹ AGAIN THE WORD of Jehovah of hosts came, saying, ² Thus saith Jehovah of hosts; I was jealous for Zion with great jealousy, and I was jealous for her with great wrath.

³ Thus saith Jehovah; I am returned to Zion, and will dwell in the midst of Jerusalem; and Jerusalem shall be called a city of truth; and the mountain of Jehovah of hosts the holy mountain.

⁴ Thus saith Jehovah of hosts; There shall yet old men and old women dwell in the broad places of Jerusalem, and every man with his staff in his hand because of the number of his days. ⁵ And the broad places of the city shall be full of boys and girls playing in its broad places.

⁶ Thus saith Jehovah of hosts; If it shall be marvellous in the eyes of the remnant of this people in those days, should it also be marvellous in mine eyes? Jehovah of hosts hath said it.

⁷ Thus saith Jehovah of hosts; Behold, I will save my people from the east country, and from the west country; ⁸ and I will bring them, and they shall dwell in the midst of Jerusalem. And they shall be my people, and I will be their God, in truth and in righteousness.

⁹ Thus saith Jehovah of hosts; Let your hands be strong, ye that hear in these days these words by the mouth of the prophets that were in the day that the foundation of the House of Jehovah of hosts was laid, that the temple may be built. ¹⁰ For before those days there was no hire for man, nor any hire for beast; neither to him that went out or came in was there any peace from the oppression. For I set all men every one against his neighbour. ¹¹ But now I will not be unto the residue of this people as in the former days, Jehovah of hosts hath said it. ¹² For the seed shall be prosperous, the vine shall give her fruit, and the ground shall give her increase, and the heavens shall give their dew; and I will cause the remnant of this people to possess all these things. ¹³ And it shall come to pass, that as ye were a curse among the Nations, O house of Judah, and house of Israel; so will I save you, and ye shall be a blessing. Fear not, but let your hands be strong.

¹⁴ For thus saith Jehovah of hosts; As I thought to bring

evil upon you, when your fathers provoked me to wrath,
15 saith Jehovah of hosts, and I repented not; so again have
I thought in these days to bring good upon Jerusalem and
16 upon the house of Judah. Fear ye not. These are the
things that ye shall do; Speak ye every man the truth to
his neighbour; judge in truth and in the judgment of peace
17 at your city gates; and let none of you devise evil in your
hearts against his neighbour; and love no false oath; for
all these are things that I hate; Jehovah hath said it.
18 AND THE WORD OF JEHOVAH of hosts came to me, say-
19 ing, Thus saith Jehovah of hosts; The fast of the fourth
month, and the fast of the fifth, and the fast of the seventh,
and the fast of the tenth, shall be to the house of Judah
for joy and for gladness, and for solemn feasts of cheerful-
ness. Therefore love truth and peace.
20 Thus saith Jehovah of hosts; It shall yet be, that there
21 shall come peoples, and the inhabitants of many cities;
and the inhabitants of one city shall go to another, saying,
'Let us go speedily to entreat the presence of Jehovah,
22 'and to seek Jehovah of hosts; I will go also.' Yea, many
peoples and strong nations shall come to seek Jehovah of
hosts in Jerusalem, and to entreat the presence of Jehovah.
23 Thus saith Jehovah of hosts; In those days it shall be,
that ten men out of all the languages of the Nations shall
take hold, even shall take hold of the skirt of him that is
a Jew, saying, 'We will go with you; for we have heard
—'that God is with you.'

---

1 THE BURDEN OF THE WORD of Jehovah against the
land of Hadrach, and Damascus its resting-place, when
the eyes of men, as of all the tribes of Israel, shall be
2 toward Jehovah; and also against Hamath which bor-
dereth thereto; against Tyre, and Sidon, though it be
very wise.
3 And Tyre buildeth for herself a stronghold, and heapeth
up silver as dust, and fine gold as the mire of the streets.
4 Behold, the Lord will cast her out, and he will smite her
power in the sea; and she shall be devoured with fire.
5 Askalon shall see it, and shall fear; Gaza also, and shall
be very sorrowful; and Ekron, for her expectation shall
be ashamed. And the king shall perish from Gaza, and
6 Askalon shall not be inhabited. And he that is base-born

shall dwell in Ashdod, and I will cut off the pride of the Philistines. And I will take away his bloodshed out of his ⁷ mouth, and his abominations from between his teeth. But he that remaineth, even he, shall be for our God, and he shall be as a governor in Judah, and Ekron shall be as a Jebusite. And I will encamp about my House, against the ⁸ army [of Assyria], against it when it passeth by, and against it when it returneth. And no tribute-gatherer shall pass through them any more; for now have I seen with mine eyes.

Rejoice greatly, O daughter of Zion; shout, O daughter ⁹ of Jerusalem. Behold, thy king [Hezekiah] cometh to thee; he is just, and hath been saved; lowly, and riding upon an ass, even upon a colt, the foal of a she-ass. And ¹⁰ I will cut off the [enemy's] chariot from Ephraim, and the horse from Jerusalem, and the battle bow shall be cut off. And he shall speak peace unto the Nations; and his dominion shall be from Sea to Sea, and from the River [Euphrates] even to the ends of the land.

(As for thee also, by the blood of thy covenant I have ¹¹ sent forth thy prisoners out of the dungeon-pit wherein is no water. Turn you to the stronghold, ye prisoners of ¹² hope; even to-day do I declare that I will repay double to thee. For I have guided the aim of Judah for me, I have ¹³ prepared the bow of Ephraim, and have raised up thy sons, O Zion, against thy sons, O Greece, and made thee as the sword of a warrior. And Jehovah shall be seen over them, ¹⁴ and his arrows shall go forth as the lightning; and the Lord Jehovah will blow the trumpet, and will go with whirlwinds of the south. Jehovah of hosts will be a shield ¹⁵ to them; and they shall devour, and subdue with stones from the sling; and they shall drink, and make a noise as through wine; and they shall be filled like the sprinkling buckets, as the corners of the Altar. And Jehovah their ¹⁶ God will save them in that day as the flock of his people. For they shall be as the stones of a crown, lifted up as an ensign upon his land. For how great is his goodness, and ¹⁷ how great is his beauty! Corn shall make the young men flourish, and grape juice the maids.) —

Ask ye from Jehovah rain in the time of the latter rain, ¹ from Jehovah who maketh the lightning-storms; and he will give to them showers of rain, to every one grass in the field. For the Teraphs [or idols] have spoken vanity, and ² the diviners have seen false visions, and have told vain dreams; they comfort in vain. Therefore they went their way as a flock, they were troubled, because there was no shepherd.

³ Mine anger is kindled against the shepherds, and I will punish the leader-goats. For Jehovah of hosts hath visited his flock the house of Judah, and hath made them as his ⁴ goodly horse in the battle. Out of it is departed the corner-turret, out of it the tent-pin, out of it the battle bow, ⁵ out of it every tribute-gatherer together. And they shall be as warriors, who trample down in battle, as in the mire of the streets; and they shall fight, because Jehovah is with them, and the riders on horses shall be confounded. ⁶ And I will strengthen the house of Judah, and I will save the house of Joseph, and I will place them at home again; for I have pity upon them. And they shall be as though I had not cast them off; for I am Jehovah their God, and ⁷ will answer them. And Ephraim shall be like a warrior, and their heart shall rejoice as through wine; yea, their children shall see it, and rejoice; their heart shall be glad ⁸ in Jehovah. I will whistle for them, and gather them in; for I have redeemed them; and they shall increase as they ⁹ have increased. And I will sow them among the peoples. And they shall remember me in far countries; and they ¹⁰ shall live with their children, and return home. I will bring them home also out of the land of Egypt, and gather them out of Assyria; and I will bring them into the land of Gilead and Lebanon; and room shall not be found for ¹¹ them. And he shall pass through the narrow [or Red] sea, and he shall smite the waves in the sea, and all the deeps of the river [Nile] shall dry up; and the pride of Assyria shall be brought down, and the sceptre of Egypt ¹² shall depart away. And I will strengthen them in Jehovah; and they shall walk up and down in his name, Jehovah hath said it.

---

¹ OPEN THY DOORS, O Lebanon, that the fire may devour ² thy cedars. Howl, thou fir tree; for the cedar is fallen; because the mighty ones are plundered. Howl, O ye oaks ³ of Bashan; for the fenced forest is come down. There is a sound of the howling of the shepherds; for their glory is spoiled; a sound of the roaring of young lions [or Assyrians]; for the pride of the Jordan is laid waste.

Thus saith Jehovah my God ; 'Feed the flock of the ⁴ 'slaughter ; whose possessors slay them, and hold them- ⁵ 'selves not guilty. And they that sell them say, Blessed 'be Jehovah ; for I am rich. And their own shepherds 'pity them not. For I will no more pity the inhabitants ⁶ 'of the land, Jehovah hath said it. But lo, I will deliver 'the men every one into his neighbour's hand, and into the 'hand of his king. And they shall smite the land, and 'out of their hand I will not deliver them.' And I fed ⁷ the flock of the slaughter, even you, O poor of the flock. And I took to me two staves ; the one I called Beauty, and the other I called Bands ; and I fed the flock. Three ⁸ shepherds also I cut off in one month [Jeroboam II., Zachariah and Shallum] ; and my soul was weary of them, and their soul also abhorred me.

Then said I, 'I will not feed you. That which dieth, ⁹ 'let it die ; and that which is to be cut off, let it be cut 'off ; and let the rest eat each the flesh of his neighbour.' ¹⁰ And I took my staff, even Beauty, and cut it asunder, that I might break my covenant which I had made with all the peoples. And it was broken in that day ; and so the poor ¹¹ of the flock that waited upon me knew that it was the word of Jehovah. And I said to them, 'If ye think good, give ¹² 'me my hire ; and if not, forbear.' So they weighed for my hire thirty pieces of silver. And Jehovah said to me, ¹³ 'Cast it into the treasury ;' a goodly price that I was prized at by them. And I took the thirty pieces of silver, and cast them into the treasury in the House of Jehovah. Then ¹⁴ I cut asunder mine other staff, even Bands, that I might break the brotherhood between Judah and Israel.

And Jehovah said to me, 'Take to thee yet again the ¹⁵ 'instruments of a foolish shepherd. For, lo, I have raised ¹⁶ 'up a shepherd [Menahem] in the land, who shall not visit 'those that are cut off, nor shall he look after the young, 'nor heal that which is broken, nor support that which 'standeth still ; but he shall eat the flesh of the fattened 'ones, and tear off their hoofs. Woe to the worthless ¹⁷ 'shepherd that leaveth the flock ! the sword shall be upon 'his arm, and upon his right eye. His arm shall be clean 'dried up, and his right eye shall be utterly darkened.' —

THE BURDEN OF THE WORD of Jehovah against Israel ; ¹

Jehovah hath said it, who stretched forth the heavens, and laid the foundation of the earth, and formed the spirit of man within him.

2 Behold, I will make Jerusalem a cup of reeling unto all the peoples round about; and against Judah also it shall
3 be, in the siege against Jerusalem. And in that day will I make Jerusalem a burdensome stone for all the peoples. All that burden themselves with it shall be cut in pieces, though all the people of the earth be gathered together
4 against it. In that day, Jehovah hath said it, I will smite every horse with astonishment, and his rider with madness; and I will open mine eyes upon the house of Judah, and will smite every horse of the peoples with blindness.
5 And the governors of Judah shall say in their heart, 'The 'inhabitants of Jerusalem shall be my strength in Jeho-'vah of hosts their God.'
6 In that day will I make the governors of Judah like a pan of fire among the wood, and like a torch of fire in a sheaf; and they shall devour all the peoples round about, on the right hand and on the left; and Jerusalem shall be
7 inhabited again in her own place, even in Jerusalem. Jehovah also shall save the tents of Judah first, so that the glory of the house of David and the glory of the inhabitants of Jerusalem shall not magnify themselves against
8 Judah. In that day shall Jehovah defend the inhabitants of Jerusalem. And he that is feeble among them at that day shall be as David; and the house of David shall be as God, as the angel of Jehovah before them.
9 And it shall come to pass in that day, that I will seek to destroy all the nations that come against Jerusalem.
10 And I will pour upon the house of David, and upon the inhabitants of Jerusalem, the spirit of grace and of supplications. And they shall look upon him whom they have pierced [Jehoiakim]; and they shall mourn for him, as one mourneth for his only son, and shall be in bitterness for him, as one that is in bitterness for his firstborn.
11 In that day shall there be a great mourning in Jerusalem, as the mourning of Hadadrimmon [for Josiah] in the
12 valley of Megiddon. And the land shall mourn, family and family apart; the family of the house of David apart, and their wives apart; the family of the house of Nathan [or Nethaniah, Jer. xli. 1,] apart, and their wives apart;

the family of the house of Levi apart, and their wives ¹³ apart; the family of Shimei [or Shemaiah, Jer. xxxvi. 12,] apart, and their wives apart; all the families that remain, ¹⁴ family and family apart, and their wives apart. —

In that day there shall be a fountain opened to the ¹ house of David and to the inhabitants of Jerusalem for sin and for uncleanness. And it shall come to pass in that ² day, Jehovah of hosts hath said it, that I will cut off the names of the idols out of the land, and they shall no more be remembered. And also I will cause the prophets and the spirit of uncleanness to pass out of the land. And it ³ shall come to pass, that when any one shall yet prophesy, then his father and his mother that begat him shall say to him, 'Thou shalt not live; for thou speakest false-'hoods in the name of Jehovah.' And his father and his mother that begat him shall thrust him through when he prophesieth. And it shall come to pass in that day, that ⁴ the prophets shall be ashamed every one of his vision, when he hath prophesied; neither shall they wear a garment of hair in order to deceive. But he shall say, 'I am ⁵ 'no prophet, I am a tiller of the ground; for a man pur-·chased me from my youth.' And one shall say to him, ⁶ 'What are these wounds in thy hands?' Then he shall answer, 'Those with which I was wounded in the house 'of my friends.'

AWAKE, O SWORD, against my shepherd [Jehoiachin], ⁷ and against the man of my friendship, Jehovah of hosts hath said it. Smite the shepherd, and the sheep shall be scattered; and I will turn my hand against the vile ones. And it shall come to pass, that in all the land, Jehovah ⁸ hath said it, two parts therein shall be cut off and die; but the third shall be left therein. And I will bring the ⁹ third part through the fire, and will refine them as silver is refined, and will try them as gold is tried. They shall call on my name, and I will answer them; I will say, 'It 'is my people;' and they shall say, 'Jehovah is my God.'—

Behold, the day of Jehovah cometh, and thy spoil shall ¹ be divided in the midst of thee. For I will gather all the ² Nations against Jerusalem to battle; and the city shall be taken, and the houses rifled, and the women ravished; and half of the city shall go forth into captivity [B.C. 600], but the residue of the people shall not be cut off from the city.

³ Then shall Jehovah go forth, and fight against those nations, as in the day of battle, in the day when he fought.
⁴ And his feet shall stand in that day upon the mount of Olives, which is before Jerusalem on the east; and the mount of Olives shall be cleft in the midst thereof toward the east and toward the west, and there shall be a very great valley; and half of the mountain shall be removed
⁵ toward the north, and half of it toward the south. And ye shall flee by the valley of the mountains; for the valley of the mountains shall reach to Ezel; yea, ye shall flee, like as ye fled from before the earthquake in the days of Uzziah king of Judah. And Jehovah my God shall come,
⁶ and all the Holy Ones with him. And it shall come to pass in that day, that there shall be no light, but cold and
⁷ frost. But it shall be a day which shall be known to Jehovah, which shall be neither day nor night; but it shall come to pass, that at evening time it shall be light.
⁸ And it shall be on that day, that living waters shall go out from Jerusalem; half of them toward the Eastern [or Dead] Sea, and half of them toward the Western [or Mediterranean] Sea. Both in summer and in winter
⁹ shall it be. And Jehovah shall be king over all the earth; and in that day Jehovah shall be one, and his
¹⁰ name shall be One. All the land shall be turned round as the Barren Plain from Geba to Rimmon on the south of Jerusalem. And it shall be lifted up, and then shall abide in its own place, from the Gate of Benjamin to the place of the First Gate, to the Corner Gate, and from the
¹¹ tower of Hananeel to the King's Winepresses. And men shall dwell in it, and there shall be no more utter destruction; but Jerusalem shall be safely inhabited.
¹² And this shall be the plague wherewith Jehovah will smite all the peoples that have fought against Jerusalem; it shall cause their flesh to consume away while they stand upon their feet, and their eyes shall consume away in their holes, and their tongue shall consume away in
¹³ their mouth. And it shall come to pass in that day, that a great tumult from Jehovah shall be among them; and they shall lay hold every one on the hand of his neighbour, and his hand shall rise up against the hand of his
¹⁴ neighbour. And Judah also shall fight at Jerusalem. And the wealth of all the Nations round about shall be

gathered together, gold, and silver, and apparel, in great abundance. And thus shall be the plague of the horse, of the mule, of the camel, and of the ass, and of all the cattle that shall be in those camps, as this plague.

And it shall come to pass, that every one that is left of all the nations which came against Jerusalem shall even go up from year to year to worship the King, Jehovah of hosts, and to keep the Feast of Tabernacles. And it shall be, that whoso will not come up of all the families of the earth to Jerusalem to worship the King, Jehovah of hosts, even upon them shall be no rain. And if the family of Egypt go not up, and come not, even upon them there shall be none ; there shall be the plague, wherewith Jehovah will smite the Nations that come not up to keep the Feast of Tabernacles. This shall be for the sins of Egypt, and for the sins of all nations that come not up to keep the Feast of Tabernacles.

In that day shall there be upon the bells of the horses, 'Holy to Jehovah ;' and the pots in the House of Jehovah shall be like the sprinkling buckets before the altar. Yea, every pot in Jerusalem and in Judah shall be holy to Jehovah of hosts. And all they that sacrifice shall come and take some of them, and cook therein. And in that day there shall be no more a dealer in the House of Jehovah of hosts.

MALACHI.

THE BURDEN OF THE WORD of Jehovah to Israel by the hand of Malachi.
I have loved you, saith Jehovah. Yet ye say, 'Wherein 'hast thou loved us ?'—Was not Esau Jacob's brother ? Jehovah hath said it ; yet I loved Jacob, and I hated Esau ; and I have made his mountains a waste, and have given his heritage to the jackals of the desert [B.C. 410]. Whereas Edom saith, 'We are impoverished, but we will 'return and build up the desolate places ;' thus saith Jehovah of hosts, They shall build, but I will throw down ; and they shall call them, 'The boundary of wickedness,' and 'The people against whom Jehovah hath indignation 'for ever.' And your eyes shall see, and ye shall say,

'Jehovah will be magnified beyond the boundary of 'Israel.'

6 A son honoureth his father, and a servant his master. But if I am a father, where is my honour? and if I am a master, where is the fear of me? saith Jehovah of hosts to you, O priests, that despise my name. And ye say, 'Where-
7 'in have we despised thy name?'—Ye bring polluted bread to mine altar. And ye say, 'Wherein have we polluted 'thee?'—In that ye say, 'The table of Jehovah is to be
8 'despised.' And when ye bring the blind for sacrifice, is it not evil? And when ye bring the lame and sick, is it not evil? Offer it now to thy Pasha [or governor]; will he be pleased with thee, or accept thy person? saith Jehovah of hosts.
9 And now, I pray you, entreat the face of God that he may be gracious to us. This hath been done by your hands; will he regard your persons? saith Jehovah of hosts.
10 Who is there even among you that would shut the [temple] doors? neither do ye kindle fire on mine altar, without pay. I have no pleasure in you, saith Jehovah of hosts, neither
11 will I be pleased with a meal offering at your hand. For from the rising of the sun even unto the going down of the same my name is great among the Nations; and in every place incense is offered to my name, and a pure meal offering; for my name is great among the Nations,
12 saith Jehovah of hosts. But ye have profaned it, in that ye say, 'The table of Jehovah is polluted; and the fruit
13 'thereof, even its food, is to be despised.' Ye said also, 'Behold, What a weariness it is!' And ye have snuffed at it, saith Jehovah of hosts; and ye brought the torn, and the lame, and the sick. And thus ye brought the meal offering. Could I be pleased with this at your hand?
14 saith Jehovah. But cursed be the deceiver, who hath in his flock a male, and who voweth it, and then sacrificeth to the Lord a corrupt thing. For I am a great King, saith Jehovah of hosts; and my name is dreaded among —the Nations.

1 And now, O ye priests, this command is for you. If ye
2 will not hear, and if ye will not lay it to heart, to give glory to my name, saith Jehovah of hosts, I will even send the curse upon you, and I will curse your blessings; yea, I have
3 cursed them already, because ye do not lay it to heart. Be-

hold, I will order away your seed, and spread dung upon your faces, the dung of your solemn feasts; and one shall carry you unto it. And ye shall know that I have sent ⁴ this command to you, that my covenant might be with Levi, saith Jehovah of hosts. My covenant of life and ⁵ peace was with him; and I gave them to him because of the fear wherewith he feared me, and was afraid before my name. The law of truth was in his mouth, and ⁶ iniquity was not found in his lips; he walked with me in peace and equity, and he did turn many away from iniquity. For the priest's lips should keep knowledge, ⁷ and men should seek the Law at his mouth; for he is the messenger of Jehovah of hosts.

But ye are departed out of the way; ye have caused many ⁸ to stumble at the Law; ye have corrupted the covenant of Levi, saith Jehovah of hosts. Therefore have I also made ⁹ you despised and base before all the people, according as ye have not kept my ways, but have accepted men's persons in the Law.

Have we not all one father? Hath not one God created ¹⁰ us? Why deal we treacherously each against his brother, by profaning the covenant of our fathers? Judah hath ¹¹ dealt treacherously, and an abomination is committed in Israel and in Jerusalem; for Judah hath profaned the Holy Place of Jehovah which he loveth, and hath married the daughter of a foreign god. Jehovah will cut off the man ¹² that doeth this, him that watcheth and him that answereth, out of the tents of Jacob, and him that bringeth a meal offering unto Jehovah of hosts.

And this have ye done again, covering the Altar of Je- ¹³ hovah with tears, with weeping, and with groans, so that he regardeth not the meal offering any more, or receiveth it with good will at your hand. Yet ye say, 'Wherefore?' ¹⁴ —Because Jehovah hath been witness between thee and the wife of thy youth, against whom thou hast dealt treacherously. Yet is she thy partner, and the wife of thy covenant. And did not He make [the two] one? though ¹⁵ the residue of the spirit belonged to him. And wherefore one?—That he might seek a seed unto God. Therefore take heed to your spirit, and let no one deal treacherously against the wife of his youth. For the putter away is ¹⁶ hateful, saith Jehovah the God of Israel; and he hideth the violence against his companion, saith Jehovah of hosts. Therefore take heed to your spirit, that ye deal not treacherously.

7 Ye have wearied Jehovah with your words. Yet ye say, 'Wherein have we wearied him?'—In that ye say, 'Every one that doeth evil is good in the sight of Jehovah, 'and he delighteth in them;' or, 'Where is the God of —'judgment?'

1 Behold, I will send my messenger, and he shall prepare the way before me; and the Lord, whom ye seek, shall suddenly come to his temple, and the messenger of the covenant, which ye delight in. Behold, he shall come, 2 saith Jehovah of hosts. But who may abide the day of his coming? and who shall stand when he appeareth? For he 3 is like a refiner's fire, and like the washers' soap. And he shall sit as a refiner and purifier of silver; and he shall purify the sons of Levi, and purge them as gold and as silver, that they may bring to Jehovah a meal offering 4 in righteousness. Then shall the meal offering of Judah and Jerusalem be pleasant to Jehovah, as in the days of 5 old, and as in former years. And I will come near to you to judgment; and I will be a swift witness against the sorcerers, and against the adulterers, and against false swearers, and against those that oppress the hireling in his wages, the widow, and the fatherless, and that turn away the stranger, and fear not me, saith Jehovah of hosts. 6 For I am Jehovah, I change not; therefore ye sons of Jacob are not consumed.

7 Even from the days of your fathers ye are gone away from mine ordinances, and have not kept them. Return to me, and I will return to you, saith Jehovah of hosts. But ye say, 'Wherein shall we return?'

8 Shall a man cheat God? Yet ye have cheated me. But ye say, 'Wherein have we cheated thee?'—In tithes and in 9 heave offerings. Ye are cursed with a curse; for ye have 10 cheated me, even this whole nation. Bring ye all the tithes into the storehouse, that there may be meat in my House. And prove me now in this, saith Jehovah of hosts, if I will not open to you the windows of the heavens, and pour out to you a blessing, until there shall not be room enough for 11 it. And I will rebuke the devourer for your sakes, and he shall not destroy the fruits of your ground; neither shall

your vine be barren in the field, saith Jehovah of hosts. And all the Nations shall call you blessed; for ye shall be a delightful land, saith Jehovah of hosts.

Your words have been stout against me, saith Jehovah. Yet ye say, 'What have we spoken against thee?'—Ye have said, 'It is vain to serve God; and what profit is it 'that we have kept his charge, and that we have walked 'mournfully before Jehovah of hosts? And now we call 'the proud happy. Yea, they that work wickedness are 'built up. Yea, they that tempt God are even delivered.'

Then they that feared Jehovah spake one to another. And Jehovah hearkened, and heard it, and a book of remembrance was written before him for them that feared Jehovah, and that thought upon his name. And they shall be mine, saith Jehovah of hosts, in that day when I make up my peculiar treasure; and I will be tender to them, as a man is tender to his own son that serveth him. Then shall ye return, and discern between the righteous and the wicked, between him that serveth God and him that serveth him not.—

For, behold, the day cometh, that shall burn as an oven; and all the proud, yea, and all that do wickedly, shall be stubble. And the day that cometh shall burn them up, saith Jehovah of hosts, so that it shall leave to them neither root nor branch. But unto you that fear my name shall the sun of righteousness arise with healing on its wings; and ye shall go forth, and grow fat as calves of the stall. And ye shall tread down the wicked; for they shall be ashes under the soles of your feet in the day that I shall do this, saith Jehovah of hosts.

Remember ye the Law of Moses my servant, which I commanded to him in Horeb for all Israel, with the statutes and judgments.

Behold, I will send to you Elijah the prophet before the coming of the great and dreadful day of Jehovah. And he shall bring back the heart of the fathers to the children, and the heart of the children to their fathers, lest I come and smite the earth with a curse.

THE END.

BILLING, PRINTER, GUILDFORD.

www.ingramcontent.com/pod-product-compliance
Lightning Source LLC
Chambersburg PA
CBHW032003300426
44117CB00008B/877